Clause 8 Publishing

Intellectual Property in the New Technological Age: 2016

Volume I: Perspectives, Trade Secrets and Patents

Mark A. Lemley

William H. Neukom
Professor of Law

Director, Stanford
Program in Law, Science
& Technology

Stanford Law School

Peter S. Menell

Koret Professor of Law

Director, Berkeley Center
for Law & Technology

University of California
at Berkeley School of Law

Robert P. Merges

Wilson, Sonsini, Goodrich
& Rosati Professor of Law

Director, Berkeley Center
for Law & Technology

University of California
at Berkeley School of Law

ISBN-13: 978-1945555008 (Clause 8 Publishing)
ISBN-10: 1945555009

For Rose, as always

M.A.L.

For Claire, Dylan, and Noah

P.S.M.

For my brothers, Bruce, Paul, and Matt

R.P.M

PREFACE

When we embarked on this project more than two decades ago, we envisioned many things, but not that it would lead to self-publishing a casebook.

A lot has changed since we began collaborating. At the time that we launched this project, most intellectual property courses were taught along particular mode of protection lines: patent law, copyright law, trademark law, and trade secret law. From our research and real world experience, we recognized that digital technology blurred the traditional doctrinal lines. We set out to design a book for the emerging technological age. We built the book around core philosophical frameworks, broad integrated coverage, and a pedagogical model that emphasizes problem-solving.

Over the ensuing years, our insight and framing proved enduring. Nearly all manner of enterprise and organization—from high technology start-ups to traditional manufacturing and media companies, government agencies, and even educational institutions—came to confront a broad range of intellectual property issues spanning the full spectrum of protection modes. The survey intellectual property course became a core subject at our law schools and many others across the United States and around the world. That much we had at least dreamed of.

But we did not foresee entering the publishing business. During the formative stage of our careers, we were thrilled to gain the interest of established publishers. Our book hit the market just as the Internet was gaining traction. The IP field expanded rapidly and we found ourselves churning out new editions every two or three years to keep pace with the increasing velocity of IP law. Little, Brown's law book division was acquired by Aspen, which was then acquired by Wolters Kluwer. The market for our book continued to grow.

Yet as advances in digital technology reshaped the world around us—from Internet search to online publishing—we, and our adopters and students, saw relatively little change in our publishing market. Prices continued to rise each year. Publishing schedules remained rigid. The publishing of our book seemed suspended in time. Most frustratingly, our students were paying well over $200 for a book that generated just $15 in total royalties. This pattern conflicted with the thrust of our book and scholarship. Advances in digital technology and competition should have been driving prices down, not up. Our frustration grew.

These issues came to a head in September 2014. When our publisher indicated that we missed the deadline for getting our book into the summer 2015 catalog, we dusted off our original publishing contract from December 1993. In checking the revision clause, we recognized that we held the copyright in the work *and* retained the right to prepare derivative works.

Once we realized that we had the right to shift to self-publishing, we faced a choice: stay with a leading publisher or take on the start-up costs and day-to-day operations of self-publishing. Peter had been writing about disintermediation in the media industries and strongly believed the time was ripe to branch out on our own. He posed a simple question: how would we view this choice ten years down the road? A quick review of self-publishing options indicated that we could substantially reduce the cost of our book while providing students with more convenient access—both digital versions and print-on-demand. We could also move to annual editions and take control over the production pipeline. This would ensure that our book was always current. Although striking out on our own involved some risk and additional tasks, failing to take this path would perpetuate an obsolete and unjustifiably costly burden on students at a time when they can ill afford it. We decided to take the plunge.

After reviewing options, we decided to begin our self-publishing experiment with Amazon. (We retain copyright ownership and hence flexibility to try other platforms as the marketplace evolves, an important lesson from various media markets.) Amazon's publishing platform imposes size limits that required us to divide our book into two volumes: Volume I covering Philosophical Perspectives, Trade Secrets, and Patent Law (we also included the patent preemption cases from Chapter VI for those interested in studying those materials in conjunction with the trade secret and patent law chapters); Volume II covering Copyright Law, Trademark Law, and State Law IP Protections (including the preemption materials). The volumes will be available as eBooks and through Amazon's on-demand publishing platform. This has the virtues of reducing the weight of what students need to carry around on a daily basis and creating more modular teaching options. We also plan to distribute Chapters I and II on SSRN so that students can sample the book before committing to the class.

Which brings us to what we hope is a New Publishing Age for all manner of academic publishing. In addition to releasing IPNTA2016 (we plan to designate new editions by publication year rather than volume number), we are launching Clause 8 Publishing, a new publishing venture to "promote Progress" in intellectual property education (and possibly more). We plan to introduce a series of complementary products, enhancements, supplementary texts, multimedia, and other resources for adopters and students—at low cost and with easy accessibility. You will be able to learn about these resources at IPNTA.com and Clause8Publishing.com over the coming year.

While we are exploring new paths in many respects with this book, in one respect we decided on a traditional approach: as is customary in legal academic writing, the authors are listed alphabetically. You shouldn't read anything into that other than an effort to follow the norm. Rob and Mark want to express our appreciation to Peter for the extraordinary work he has put in this year making this project a reality. Peter has managed the transition of our book to a self-publishing model and will be taking the lead on establishing this platform. Those interested in adopting our book (or anything else about the project) should contact him at pmenell@law.berkeley.edu. (Please include "IPNTA" or "Clause 8" in the subject line.)

In retrospect, the subject matter covered by our original edition—philosophical perspectives on intangible resources, promoting progress in technology and creative expression, and competition policy—set us on the path to DIY/New Age publishing. Copyright law seeks to harness market forces to encourage creative expression and widespread dissemination. It builds bridges between creators and those who value their work. Digital technology and the Internet enhance these powerful forces by lowering the costs of creation and providing the virtual dissemination bridges. We feel fortunate to have liberated our book and very much look forward to working with law professors and students in building a more productive marketplace and community for IP teaching materials.

Mark A. Lemley   Peter S. Menell   Robert P. Merges

June 2016

NEW FEATURES

Rapid advances in digital and life sciences technology continue to spur the evolution of intellectual property law. As professors and practitioners in this field know all too well, Congress and the courts continue to develop intellectual property law and jurisprudence at a rapid pace. For that reason, we have significantly augmented and revised our text.

The 2016 Edition reflects the following principal developments:

- **Trade Secrets**: Congress passed the Defend Trade Secrets Act of 2016, one of the most momentous changes in the history of trade secret protection. The new law opens up the federal courts to trade secret cases, provides for ex parte seizures of misappropriated trade secrets in "extraordinary circumstances," and establishes immunity for whistleblowers.

- **Patent Law**: The past several years have witnessed some of the most significant developments in U.S. patent history—from the establishment of the new administrative review proceedings at the Patent Office to important shifts in patent-eligibility, claim indefiniteness, and enhanced damages at the Supreme Court and means-plus-function claim interpretation and infringement doctrine at the Federal Circuit. We have restructured the patent chapter to illuminate these areas. We have also significantly expanded coverage of design patents in response to the growing importance of this form of protection.

- **Copyright Law**: The Supreme Court issued important decisions addressing the public performance right and the first sale doctrine. The past few years also witnessed important developments in the Online Service Provider safe harbor, fair use, and state protection for pre-1972 sound recordings. We have also integrated the digital copyright materials into a unified treatment of copyright law and substantially revamped the fair use section to reflect the broadening landscape of this important doctrine.

- **Trademark Law**: We have integrated important cases on federal registrability of disparaging marks, merchandising rights, likelihood of confusion on the Internet, and remedies.

- **Other State IP Protections**: We have updated material on the right of publicity, an active and growing area. We have also reorganized the chapter and focused it on IP regimes.

ABOUT  Clause 8 Publishing

Clause 8 Publishing is a digital publishing venture founded and managed by Peter Menell. Mark Lemley and Robert Merges serve on the Editorial Board. Inspired by Article I, Section 8, Clause 8 of the U.S. CONSTITUTION, Clause 8 Publishing seeks to promote production and dissemination of the highest quality and most up-to-date educational resources at fair prices and in a way that ensures that much of the revenue flows to authors. It aims to streamline the publishing process, take full advantage of evolving digital platforms and print-on-demand functionality, and develop innovative educational resources.

Clause 8 Publishing plans to produce annual editions of INTELLECTUAL PROPERTY IN THE NEW TECHNOLOGICAL AGE.

Over the coming years, Clause 8 Publishing aims to support a series of complementary products (statutory supplement, primers, problem sets, multi-media presentations) and resources for intellectual property professors, students, judges, and policy makers. It aspires to lead the academy toward more productive and just publishing models. More information will be available at Clause8Publishing.com and IPNTA.com.

ACKNOWLEDGMENTS

We are indebted to a great many people who have helped us since this project began in 1991. We would like to thank our many colleagues who reviewed earlier drafts of the book and provided helpful guidance. While many of these reviews were anonymous, we have also benefitted from the advice of Lynn Baker, Paul Heald, Tom Jorde, and Pam Samuelson, each of whom read several different drafts of the book as it made its way through the editorial process. We gratefully acknowledge the research assistance of Evelyn Findeis, Edwin Flores, Ryan Garcia, Shari Heino, Toni Moore Knudson, Christopher Leslie, and Barbara Parvis. We would also like to thank Michele Co for exceptional secretarial and administrative assistance in completing the original text.

We are grateful to many colleagues for providing suggestions for improving this book over the years. In particular, we would like to thank Fred Abbott, Amit Agarwal, John Allison, Ann Bartow, Julie Cohen, Ken Dam, Robin Feldman, Terry Fisher, Marshall Leaffer, Glynn Lunney, Ron Mann, David McGowan, Chuck McManis, Roberta Morris, David Nimmer, Ruth Okediji, Malla Pollack, Peggy Radin, Lisa Ramsey, Jerry Reichmann, Sharon Sandeen, Paul Schwartz, Lon Sobel, Mark Thurmon, and several anonymous reviewers for their comments and suggestions in preparing the second, third, fourth, fifth, and sixth editions. We have also benefitted greatly from the research assistance and proofreading of Adam Blankenheimer, Will Buckingham, Amber Burroff, Brian Carver, Colleen Chien, Sarah Craven, Will Devries, Tom Fletcher, Ryan Garcia, Ines Gonzalez, David Grady, Jade Jurdi, Robert Damion Jurrens, Victoria H. Kane, Jeffrey Kuhn, Michelle A. Marzahn, Selena R. Medlen, David Moore, Roberta Morris, Pilar Ossorio, Ryan Owens, Stephanie N.-P. Pham-Quang, Laura Quilter, John Sasson, Michael Sawyer, Helaine Schweitzer, Shannon Scott, Michael Liu Su, Laurence Trask, Allison Watkins, Joel Wallace, Reid Whitaker, Emily Wohl, and Tarra Zynda.

We thank Andrea Hall for exceptional efforts in formatting, design, and editorial assistance in the transition to this self-published edition. We also thank Israel Vela for design and website development assistance.

SUMMARY OF CONTENTS

 # TABLE OF CONTENTS

Chapter III: Patent Law

A. Introduction
1. Historical Background
2. An Overview of the Patent System
   - i. Requirements for Patentability
   - ii. Rights Conferred by a Patent
   - iii. Patent Prosecution
3. Theories of Patent Law

B. The Elements of Patentability
1. Novelty
   - i. The 1952 Regime
   - ii. The Nature of Novelty
     Rosaire v. National Lead Co., 218 F.2d 72 (5th Cir. 1955)
   - iii. Statutory Bars
     In re Hall, 781 F.2d 897 (Fed. Cir. 1986)
   - iv. Statutory Bars: Public Use and On Sale
     Egbert v. Lippmann, 104 U.S. 333 (1881)
   - v. Statutory Bars: The Experimental Use Exception
     City of Elizabeth v. Pavement Company, 97 U.S. 126 (1877)
   - vi. Priority Rules and First-to-Invent
     Griffith v. Kanamaru, 816 F.2d 624 (Fed. Cir. 1987)
   - vii. The America Invents Act Regime
     - a. The AIA: A Simpler Structure
     - b. No Geographic Restrictions on Prior Art
     - c. Novelty vs. Priority
     - d. The AIA Grace Period
     - e. Scope of Prior Art: Public Use
2. Nonobviousness
   Graham v. John Deere Co., 383 U.S. 1 (1966)
   - i. Combining References
     KSR International Co. v. Teleflex Inc., 550 U.S. 398 (2007)
     In re Kubin, 561 F.3d 1351 (Fed. Cir. 2009)
   - ii. "Secondary" Considerations
   - iii. The AIA
3. Utility
   Brenner v. Manson, 383 U.S. 519 (1966)
   In re Fisher, 421 F.3d 1365 (2005)
4. Disclosure
   O'Reilly v. Morse, 56 U.S. 62 (1853)
   - i. Enablement
     The Incandescent Lamp Patent, 159 U.S. 465 (1895)

H.R. REP. No. 94-1476, 94th Cong., 2d Sess. 52-53 (1976)
  3. Formalities
     i.   Notice
     ii. Publication
          a. 1909 Act
          b. 1976 Act/Pre-Ratification of Berne Convention
          c. Post-Ratification of the Berne Convention
     iii. Registration
          a. 1909 Act
          b. 1976 Act/Pre-Ratification of Berne Convention
          c. Post-Ratification of the Berne Convention
     iv. Deposit
  4. Note on the Restoration of Foreign Copyrighted Works

C. Copyrightable Subject Matter
  1. The Domain and Scope of Copyright Protection
     H.R. REP. No. 94-1476, 94th Cong., 2d Sess. (1976)
     i.   Literary Works
     ii.   Pictorial, Graphic, and Sculptural Works
     iii. Architectural Works
     iv.   Musical Works and Sound Recordings
     v.   Dramatic, Pantomime, and Choreographic Works
     vi.   Motion Pictures and Other Audiovisual Works
     vii. Semiconductor Chips Designs (Mask Works)
     viii. Vessel Hull Designs
     ix.   Derivative Works and Compilations
  2. Limitations on Copyrightability: Distinguishing Function and
     Expression
     i.   The Idea-Expression Dichotomy
          Baker v. Selden, 101 U.S. 99 (1879)
          Lotus Development Corp. v. Borland International, 49 F.3d 807
          (1st Cir. 1995), *aff'd by equally divided court*, 526 U.S. 233 (1996)
          Morrissey v. Procter & Gamble, 379 F.2d 675 (1st Cir. 1967)
     ii. The Useful Article Doctrine
          H.R. REP. No. 94-1476, 94th Cong., 2d Sess., 47, 54-55 (1976)
          Brandir International, Inc. v. Cascade Pacific Lumber Co., 834
          F.2d 1142 (2d Cir. 1987)
     iii. Government Works

D. Ownership and Duration
  1. Initial Ownership of Copyrights
     i.   Works Made for Hire

White v. Samsung Electronics America, Inc, 989 F.2d 1512 (9th Cir. 1993)
Comedy III Productions, Inc. v. Gary Saderup, Inc., 25 Cal. 4th 387, 21 P.3d 797, 106 Cal. Rptr. 2d 126 (2001)

EDITORIAL NOTE

We have selectively omitted citations and footnotes from cases without the uses of ellipses or other indications. All footnotes are numbered consecutively within each chapter, except that footnotes in cases and other excerpts correspond to the actual footnote numbers in the published reports. Many of the problems in this text are taken from actual cases. In many instances, have altered the facts and the names of the parties for pedagogical purposes. In a few cases, however, particularly in the trademark chapter, we felt that it was important to the problem to use the name of a product or company with which the reader would be familiar. Readers should understand that the problems are hypothetical in nature and that we do not intend them to represent the actual facts of any case or situation.

CHAPTER I: INTRODUCTION

The concept of property is well understood in Western society. It is among the oldest institutions of human civilization. It is widely recognized that people may own real property and tangible objects. The common law and the criminal law protect private property from interference by others. The Fifth Amendment to the U.S. Constitution protects private property against takings by the government without just compensation. The philosophical bases for protection of private property are well entrenched in our culture: Private property results when labor is applied to nature, as an incentive for discovery, as an essential part of personhood, and as a foundation for an ordered economic system.

Ideas, by definition, are less tangible. They exist in the mind and work of humans. Legal protection for intellectual work evolved much later in the development of human society than did protection for tangible property. The protection of such "intellectual property" raises complex philosophical questions. Should the first person to discover a way of performing an important task—for example, a procedure for closing a wound—be entitled to prevent others from using this procedure? Should the first person to pen a phrase or hum a melody be entitled to prevent others from copying such words or singing the song? Should such "intellectual property rights" be more limited than traditional property rights (i.e., the fee simple)? This book explores the legal institutions and rules that have developed to protect intellectual property.

This chapter has two principal purposes. It first explores the principal philosophical foundations for the protection of intellectual property. Understanding the reasons why we protect intellectual property—and how those reasons differ from the justifications for real property—will help the reader grasp the details of the many legal rules that will follow in this book. The second section provides a comparative overview of the principal modes of intellectual property protection: patent, copyright, trademark/trade dress, and trade secret. Understanding the intellectual property landscape requires thinking about each form of intellectual property not just in isolation but as it interacts with all the others. The remainder of this book will explore these areas in detail, highlighting their logic and interplay in promoting progress in technology and the arts.

A. PHILOSOPHICAL PERSPECTIVES

All justifications for intellectual property protection, whether economic or moral, must contend with a fundamental difference between ideas and tangible property. Tangible property, whether land or chattels, is composed of atoms, physical things that can occupy only one place at any given time. This means that possession of a physical thing is necessarily "exclusive"—if I have it, you don't. Indeed, the core of the Western concept of property lies in the right granted to the "owner" of a thing or a piece of land to exclude others from certain uses of it. Settled ownership rights in land and goods are thought to prevent both disputes over who can use the property for what purpose, and the overuse of property that would result if everyone had common access to it.

Ideas, though, do not have this characteristic of excludability. If I know a particular piece of information, and I tell it to you, you have not deprived me of it. Rather, we both possess it. The fact that the possession and use of ideas is largely "nonrivalrous" is critical to intellectual property theory because it means that the traditional economic justification for tangible property does not fit intellectual property. In the state of nature, there is no danger of overusing or overdistributing an idea, and no danger of fighting over who gets to use it. Everyone can use the idea without diminishing its value. *See generally* Peter S. Menell & Suzanne Scotchmer, *Intellectual Property Law*, in 2 HANDBOOK OF LAW AND ECONOMICS 1474 (A. Mitchell Polinsky & Steven Shavell eds., 2007).

Theorists have therefore turned elsewhere to justify exclusive rights in ideas. Over the course of human history, numerous theories have been put forth to explain intellectual property protection. The principal basis for such protection in the United States is the utilitarian or economic incentive framework. Nonetheless, other theories— most notably the natural rights and personhood justifications—have been important in understanding the development and scope of intellectual property law, both here and abroad. The two excerpts that follow justify tangible property. Consider how well they apply to intangible ideas.

1. The Natural Rights Perspective

JOHN LOCKE
TWO TREATISES ON GOVERNMENT
Third Edition, 1698

Though the earth and all inferior creatures be common to all men, yet every man has a "property" in his own "person." This nobody has any right to but himself. The "labour" of his body and the "work" of his hands, we may say, are properly his. Whatsoever, then, he removes out of the state that Nature hath provided and left it in, he hath mixed his labor with it, and joined to it something that is his own, and thereby makes it his property. It being by him removed from the common state Nature placed it in, it hath by this labour something annexed to it that excludes the common right of other men. For this "labour" being the unquestionable property of the labourer, no man but he can have a right to what that is once joined to, at least where there is enough, and as good left in common for others. → Lockean proviso

He that is nourished by the acorns he picked up under an oak, or the apples he gathered from the trees in the wood, has certainly appropriated them to himself. . . . . That labour put a distinction between them and common. . . . And will any one say he had no right to those acorns or apples he thus appropriated because he had not the consent of all mankind to make them his? Was it a robbery thus to assume to himself what belonged to all in common? If such a consent as that was necessary, man had starved, notwithstanding the plenty God had given him. We see in commons, which remain so by compact, that it is the taking any part of what is common, and removing it out of the state Nature leaves it in, which begins the property, without which the common is of no use. And the taking of this or that part does not depend on the express consent of all the commoners. . . .

It will, perhaps, be objected to this, that if gathering the acorns or other fruits, of the earth, etc., makes a right to them, then any one may engross as much as he will. To which I answer, Not so. The same law of Nature that does by this means give us property, does also bound that property too. . . . As much as any one can make use of to any advantage of life before it spoils, so much he may by his labor fix his property in. Whatever is beyond this is more than his share, and belongs to others. . . .

As much land as a man tills, plants, improves, cultivates, and can use the product of, so much is his property. He by his labor does, as it were, enclose it from the common. . . . Nor was this appropriation of any parcel of land, by improving it, any prejudice to any other man, since there was still enough and as good left, and more than the yet unprovided could use. So that, in effect, there was never the less left for others because of his enclosure for himself. For he that leaves as much as another can make use of does as good as take nothing at all.

Lockean proviso

COMMENTS AND QUESTIONS

1. How do Locke's theories of real property apply to intellectual property? Should we treat the two as the same for ownership purposes? What would Locke say about the exclusive rights granted by the patent laws, to prevent others from using the claimed invention for up to 20 years, whether or not they discovered the invention on their own? Surely if Locke considered the working of land and raw materials to be ''labor'' that justified ownership of the resulting product, he would have considered labor toward the creation of a new *idea*—the ''sweat of the brow''—to be equally deserving of protection. Or do the differences between real and intellectual property mean that Locke's arguments shouldn't apply to intellectual property?

For illumination on these and related points, *see* Edwin C. Hettinger, *Justifying Intellectual Property*, 18 PHIL. & PUB. AFF. 31 (1989). Hettinger critiques the major theories of intellectual property rights. As to Lockean labor theory, Hettinger makes these useful observations:

- [A]ssuming that labor's fruits are valuable, and that laboring gives the laborer a property right in this value, this would entitle the laborer only to the value she added, and not to the *total* value of the resulting product. Though exceedingly difficult to measure, these two components of value (that attributable to the object labored on and that attributable to the labor) need to be distinguished. [p. 37]

- Property rights in the thing produced are…not a fitting reward if the value of these rights is disproportional to the effort expended by the laborer. ''Effort'' includes (1) how hard someone tries to achieve a result, (2) the amount of risk voluntarily incurred in seeking this result, and (3) the degree to which moral considerations played a role in choosing the result intended. The harder one tries, the more one is willing to sacrifice, and the worthier the goal, the greater are one's deserts. [pp. 41-42]

The philosopher Robert Nozick made the first point by means of *reductio ad absurdum:* he asks whether the owner of a can of tomato juice who dumps it into the ocean can thereafter claim ownership of all the high seas. *See* ROBERT NOZICK, ANARCHY, STATE AND UTOPIA 175 (1984).

2. An application of the Lockean approach with an especially detailed consideration of the Lockean "proviso" (i.e., that "as much and as good" be left for others after appropriation) can be found in Wendy J. Gordon, *A Property Right in Self-Expression: Equality and Individualism in the Natural Law of Intellectual Property*, 102 YALE L.J. 1533 (1993). The proviso poses a problem we will see throughout the course: how to delimit the rights of a creator in the face of claims by consumers and other members of the public at large.

More particularly, Gordon challenges the extreme view taken by some commentators that a creator's rights should be absolute. The absolutist view proceeds from the idea that since the creator is solely responsible for the creation, no one is harmed if the creation is withheld from the public entirely. And since the creator can withhold it entirely, he or she can naturally restrict its availability in any manner, including a high price or conditions on its purchase. *See, e.g.*, JOHN STUART MILL, PRINCIPLES OF POLITICAL ECONOMY 142 (1872); Steven N.S. Cheung, *Property Rights and Invention*, in 8 RESEARCH IN LAW AND ECONOMICS: THE ECONOMICS OF PATENTS AND COPYRIGHTS 5, 6 (John Palmer & Richard O. Zerbe, Jr. eds., 1986). Through the examination of various examples—such as the Church of Scientology's efforts to restrain books critical of its teachings, West Publishing's suit to enjoin Lexis from offering page numbers corresponding to West's case reports, and Disney's efforts to prevent bawdy parodies of its images that ridicule sanitized popular culture—Gordon suggests that, sometimes at least, the public can be worse off if a creation is offered and then limited in its use than it would have been had the creation never been made.

Should it matter whether Locke's hypothetical creator was the only one likely to come up with his particular invention or discovery? If others would have discovered the same phenomenon a few years (or a few weeks) later, does Locke's argument for property rights lose its force? We might distinguish between a Lockean theory of copyright, which prevents copying, and an effort to justify patent law, which precludes even independent invention and therefore restricts the labor of others.

For detailed discussions of the "Lockean proviso," *see* Jeremy Waldron, *Enough and as Good Left for Others*, 29 PHIL. Q. 319 (1979); ROBERT NOZICK, ANARCHY, STATE AND UTOPIA 175-82 (1984); DAVID GAUTHIER, MORALS BY AGREEMENT 190-232 (1986). For more detailed treatment of another problem addressed by Gordon—the follow-on creator who builds on a preexisting work—*see* Lawrence C. Becker, *Deserving to Own Intellectual Property*, 68 CHI.-KENT L. REV. 609 (1993). For insightful historical analysis of Locke's theory and its application to intellectual property, *see* Justin Hughes, *Copyright and Incomplete Historiographies: Of Piracy, Propertization, and Thomas Jefferson*, 79 S. CAL. L. REV. 993 (2006). If labor or effort is the key to property claims under Locke, how should we handle situations where numerous dispersed people accumulate their labor to produce something useful? *See* Robert P. Merges, *Locke for the Masses*, 36 HOFSTRA L. REV. 1179 (2008).

3. Nozick's ANARCHY, STATE AND UTOPIA offers a different philosophical perspective on intellectual property, one rooted in the libertarian tradition. It is not clear how libertarians should think of intellectual property rights. On the one hand, ownership of property seems necessary to the market exchange that is at the heart of the libertarian model of society. On the other hand, one might view the free flow of information unfettered by property rights as the norm, and view government-enforced intellectual property rights as an unnecessary aberration. For a libertarian approach that is decidedly hostile to intellectual property, *see* John Perry Barlow, *The Economy of Ideas*, 2.03 WIRED 84 (Mar. 1994).

4. Natural rights are strongly emphasized in the continental European justifications for intellectual property. Those justifications to some extent parallel Locke's arguments, but there are important differences. Continental scholars emphasize the importance of reputation and noneconomic aspects of intellectual property, factors that lead them to support moral rights in copyright law. Professor Alfred Yen presents a thorough account of the role of natural rights in American copyright law. *See* Alfred Yen, *Restoring the Natural Law: Copyright as Labor and Possession*, 51 OHIO ST. L.J. 517 (1990). For a detailed comparison of efficiency, natural rights, and other foundational theories of intellectual property law, *see* ROBERT P. MERGES, JUSTIFYING INTELLECTUAL PROPERTY (2011).

PROBLEM

Problem 1-1. You are a botanist exploring a remote region of a small tropical country. You stumble across a field of strange flowers that you have never encountered before. The tribespeople tell you that they use the flower to heal various ailments by rubbing its petals on the skin and chanting a healing prayer. You pluck one of the flowers and when you return to your campsite that night, you show it to a fellow explorer who is an expert in biochemistry. The biochemist smells the flower and says that it is vaguely reminiscent of Substance P. Substance P is a medicine widely used to treat a variety of serious diseases. She tells you that Substance P is easy to detect: It turns bright yellow when exposed to intense heat. That evening, you put the flower over the campfire and, sure enough, it turns bright yellow. When you return home, you work for months to isolate the active ingredient in the flower. It is not Substance P, but a close structural analog. In chemical experiments, the extract shows great promise for fighting many of the diseases that Substance P can treat without Substance P's dreaded side effects.

What rights, if any, should you have in this discovery and research? Should those rights prevent anyone else from going back to the tropical country, finding the flower, and isolating the chemical you have discovered?

You make a profit selling your medicine throughout the world, including to the native tribespeople of the tropical country. John, a chemist in your company, is angered by this policy. Your formula is a carefully guarded secret, but John publishes it in THE NEW ENGLAND JOURNAL OF MEDICINE. A nonprofit organization begins producing the medicine and selling your product to the native tribespeople at a discount. The organization advertises that it is selling your medicine for pennies a year. Should you be able to stop them from selling your medicine? Should you be able to stop them from using the name of your medicine in their ads?

You have named your medicine "Tropicurical." To advertise the product, one of the employees in your advertising department writes a song based on the very distinctive sounds of the wind in the inland coves of the country mixed with the native birds' calls. The tribespeople of the tropical country have a song that sounds remarkably similar to your advertising tune. The song is important to their tribal identity, and they argue that it is inappropriate to use their distinctive tribal song to commercialize your product. They ask you to stop using it. Should they be able to stop you from using the name or song?

When you refuse to stop using the Tropicurical song to advertise your product, the tribespeople write a new version of their song entitled "Tropicursical" with angry lyrics claiming that your product destroys culture. Should you be able to stop them from singing the song? National Geographic records the tribespeople singing "Tropicursical." The recording plays as part of the news report on their television show. It is also available for download on NATIONAL GEOGRAPHIC's website. Individuals download copies of the song and e-mail it to their friends. It spreads like wildfire over the Internet, and eventually popular radio stations play it over the air. Should you be able to stop these copies and performances?

2. The Personhood Perspective

Margaret Jane Radin
Property and Personhood
34 Stanford Law Review 957 (1982)

This article explores the relationship between property and personhood, a relationship that has commonly been both ignored and taken for granted in legal thought. The premise underlying the personhood perspective is that to achieve proper self-development—to be *a person*—an individual needs some control over resources in the external environment. The necessary assurances of control take the form of property rights. Although explicit elaboration of this perspective is wanting in modern writing on property, the personhood perspective is often implicit in the connections that courts and commentators find between property and privacy or between property and liberty. In addition to its power to explain certain aspects of existing schemes of property entitlement, the personhood perspective can also serve as an explicit source of values for making moral distinctions in property disputes and hence for either justifying or criticizing current law....

In what follows I shall discuss the personhood perspective as Hegel developed it in *Philosophy of Right*, trace some of its later permutations and entanglements with other perspectives on property, and try to develop a contemporary view useful in the context of the American legal system. . . .

I. Property for Personhood: An Intuitive View

Most people possess certain objects they feel are almost part of themselves. These objects are closely bound up with personhood because they are part of the way we constitute ourselves as continuing personal entities in the world. They may be as different as people are different, but some common examples might be a wedding ring, a portrait, an heirloom, or a house.

One may gauge the strength or significance of someone's relationship with an object by the kind of pain that would be occasioned by its loss. On this view, an object is closely related to one's personhood if its loss causes pain that cannot be relieved by the object's replacement. If so, that particular object is bound up with the holder. For instance, if a wedding ring is stolen from a jeweler, insurance proceeds can reimburse the jeweler, but if a wedding ring is stolen from a loving wearer, the price of a replacement will not restore the status quo—perhaps no amount of money can do so.

The opposite of holding an object that has become a part of oneself is holding an object that is perfectly replaceable with other goods of equal market value. One holds such an object for purely instrumental reasons. The archetype of such a good is, of course, money, which is almost always held only to buy other things. A dollar is worth no more than what one chooses to buy with it, and one dollar bill is as good as another. Other examples are the wedding ring in the hands of the jeweler, the automobile in the hands of the dealer, the land in the hands of the developer, or the apartment in the hands of the commercial landlord. I shall call these theoretical opposites—property that is bound up with a person and property that is held purely instrumentally—personal property and fungible property respectively....

III. Hegel, Property, and Personhood

A.   Hegel's Philosophy of Right

. . . Because the person in Hegel's conception is merely an abstract unit of free will or autonomy, it has no concrete existence until that will acts on the external world....

Hegel concludes that the person becomes a real self only by engaging in a property relationship with something external. Such a relationship is the goal of the person. In perhaps the best-known passage from this book, Hegel says:

> The person has for its substantive end the right of placing its will in any and every thing, which thing is thereby mine; [and] because that thing has no such end in itself, its destiny and soul take on my will. [This constitutes] mankind's absolute right of appropriation over all things.

Hence, "property is the first embodiment of freedom and so is in itself a substantive end." . . .

Hegel seems to make property "private" on the same level as the unit of autonomy that is embodying its will by holding it. He argues that property is private to individuals when discussing it in the context of the autonomous individual will and that it is essentially common within a family, when discussing it in the context of the autonomous family unit. He does not make the leap to state property, however, even though his theory of the state might suggest it. For Hegel, the properly developed state (in contrast to civil society) is an organic moral entity. . . . and individuals within the state are subsumed into its community morality. . . .

B.   Hegel and Property for Personhood

[A] theory of personal property can build upon some of Hegel's insights. First, the notion that the will is embodied in things suggests that the entity we know as a person cannot come to exist without both differentiating itself from the physical environment and yet maintaining relationships with portions of that environment. The idea of embodied will, cut loose from Hegel's grand scheme of absolute mind, reminds us that people and things have ongoing relationships which have their own ebb and flow, and that these relationships can be very close to a person's center and sanity. If these relationships justify ownership, or at least contribute to its justification, Hegel's notion that ownership requires continuous embodiment of the will is appealing.

Second, Hegel's incompletely developed notion that property is held by the unit to which one attributes autonomy has powerful implications for the concept of group development and group rights. Hegel thought that freedom (rational self-determination) was only possible in the context of a group (the properly organized and fully developed state). Without accepting this role for the state, one may still conclude that in a given social context certain groups are likely to be constitutive of their members in the sense that the members find self-determination only within the groups. This might have political consequences for claims of the group on certain resources of the external world (i.e., property).

Third, there may be an echo of Hegel's notion of an objective community morality in the intuition that certain kinds of property relationships can be presumed to bear close bonds to personhood. If property in one's body is not too close to personhood to be considered property at all, then it is the clearest case of property for personhood. The property/privacy nexus of the home is also a relatively clear case in our particular history and culture. . . .

[T]he personhood theory helps us understand the nature of the right dictating that discrete units [i.e., an undivided, individual asset] ought to be protected.

An argument that discrete units are more important than total assets takes the following form. A person cannot be fully a person without a sense of continuity of self over time. To maintain that sense of continuity over time and to exercise one's liberty or autonomy, one must have an ongoing relationship with the external environment, consisting of both "things" and other people. One perceives the ongoing relationship to the environment as a set of individual relationships, corresponding to the way our perception separates the world into distinct "things." Some things must remain stationary if anything is to move; some points of reference must be constant or thought and action is not possible. In order to lead a normal life, there must be some continuity in relating to "things." One's expectations crystallize around certain "things," the loss of which causes more disruption and disorientation than does a simple decrease in aggregate wealth. For example, if someone returns home to find her sofa has disappeared, that is more disorienting than to discover that her house has decreased in market value by 5%. If, by magic, her white sofa were instantly replaced by a blue one of equal market value, it would cause no loss in net worth but would still cause some disruption in her life.

This argument assumes that all discrete units one owns and perceives as part of her continuing environment are to some degree personal. If the white sofa were totally fungible, then magically replacing it with a blue one would cause no disruption. In fact, neither would replacing it with money. . . .

But the theory of personal property suggests that not all object-loss is equally important. Some objects may approach the fungible end of the continuum so that the justification for protecting them as specially related to persons disappears. They might just as well be treated by whatever general moral rules govern wealth-loss at the hands of the government. If the moral rules governing wealth-loss correspond to Michelman's utilitarian suggestion—government may take whatever wealth is necessary to generate higher welfare in which the individual can confidently expect to share—then the government could take some fungible items without compensation. In general, the moral inquiry for whether fungible property could be taken would be the same as the moral inquiry for whether it is fair to impose a tax on this particular person.

On the other hand, a few objects may be so close to the personal end of the continuum that no compensation could be "just." That is, hypothetically, if some object were so bound up with me that I would cease to be ''myself'' if it were taken, then a government that must respect persons ought not to take it. If my kidney may be called my property, it is not property subject to condemnation for the general public welfare. Hence, in the context of a legal system, one might expect to find the characteristic use of standards of review and burdens of proof designed to shift risk of error away from protected interests in personal property. For instance, if there were reason to suspect that some object were close to the personal end of the continuum, there might be a prima facie case against taking it. That prima facie case might be rebutted if the government could show that the object is not personal, or perhaps that the object is not "too" personal compared with the importance to the government of acquiring that particular object for social purposes.

COMMENTS AND QUESTIONS

1. How well does Professor Radin's theory of real property apply to intellectual property? Can an individual be so "bound up" in their inventions or works of authorship that their loss would occasion more than economic damage? Does it affect your answer that intellectual property can be used simultaneously by many people without depleting its functional value to anyone—so that an author's "loss" is not the physical deprivation of stolen chattels, but the less personal fact that someone else has copied her work?

It may be that the investment of "personhood" in intellectual property varies greatly, both with the type of intellectual property at issue and with the time and effort the owner put into developing it. For example, a novel on which one has worked for several years may have more personal value than a massive software program for navigating a jumbo jet or a company's customer list. Should the law take account of these differences, giving greater protection to more personal works?

For applications of Radin's "personhood" ideas in the context of intellectual property, *see* Neil W. Netanel, *Copyright Alienability Restrictions and the Enhancement of Author Autonomy: A Normative Evaluation*, 24 RUTGERS L.J. 347 (1993); Steven Cherensky, Comment, *A Penny for Their Thoughts: Employee-Inventors, Preinvention Assignment Agreements, Property, and Personhood*, 81 CAL. L. REV. 595, 641 (1993). Cherensky argues, using personhood theory and the related idea of market-inalienability, that employee-inventors should retain greater property interests in their inventions than they typically do under conventional employee assignment contracts. On market-inalienability, i.e., things which should not be subject to market exchange at all, *see* Margaret Jane Radin, *Market-Inalienability*, 100 HARV. L. REV. 1849 (1987). *Cf.* Justin Hughes, *The Philosophy of Intellectual Property*, 77 GEO. L.J. 287, 350-53 (1988) (suggesting various strains of the personhood justification in American copyright law). Professor Roberta Kwall offers a related "moral" basis for legal protection emphasizing the dignity, honor, self-worth, and autonomy of the author. *See* ROBERTA KWALL, THE SOUL OF CREATIVITY: FORGING A MORAL RIGHTS LAW FOR THE UNITED STATES 37 (2009). For more on control over one's economic situation—i.e., economic autonomy—and its role in contemporary intellectual property debates, *see* Robert P. Merges, *The Concept of Property in the Digital Era*, 45 HOUS. L. REV. 1239 (2008). For a detailed explication of Hegel's approach to property, *see* JEREMY WALDRON, THE RIGHT TO PRIVATE PROPERTY (1988).

2. For a critique of Radin's broader personhood perspective, *see* Stephen J. Schnably, *Property and Pragmatism: A Critique of Radin's Theory of Property and Personhood*, 45 STAN. L. REV. 347 (1993) (challenging Radin's appeal to consensus and arguing that this focus obscures issues of power and the like). For further elaboration and defense of the personhood perspective, *see* MARGARET JANE RADIN, REINTERPRETING PROPERTY (1993) (a collection of related essays); A. JOHN SIMMONS, THE LOCKEAN THEORY OF RIGHTS (1992); JEREMY WALDRON, THE RIGHT TO PRIVATE PROPERTY (1991) (comparing Lockean and Hegelian property rights theories); Symposium, *Property Rights*, 11 SOC. PHIL. & POL'Y 1-286 (1994).

3. Personhood theories of IP rights tend to focus on the connection between the creator's identity and the thing created. But consumers too may identify with creative works; indeed, Radin's example of the couch suggests that buyers too have an identity interest bound up with the things they own (or, perhaps, read). How should the law take that interest into account? Does it suggest that we need to give broader scope for user-generated content like fan fiction and videos that incorporate literary characters or songs? Or might it suggest the opposite – that consumers have an interest in the purity of their iconic works, free from the unauthorized modification of those works by others? *See* Justin Hughes, *"Recoding" Intellectual Property and Overlooked Audience Interests*, 77 TEX. L. REV. 923 (1999). More recent work has suggested that creators

are often motivated as much if not more by attribution and fairness than by the prospect of money. *See* JESSICA SILBEY, THE EUREKA MYTH: CREATORS, INVENTORS, AND EVERYDAY INTELLECTUAL PROPERTY (2014); Jeanne Fromer, *Expressive Incentives in Intellectual Property*, 98 VA. L. REV. 1745 (2012).

4. A radical critique of some bedrock notions implicit in intellectual property—most notably, the concept of "*the* author" herself—has grown up in recent years, fueled by a general deconstructive trend in literary criticism. While not aimed directly at Radin's personhood approach to certain forms of property, these ideas do pose a challenge to the application of Radin's approach in the intellectual property context. They suggest that the concept of authorship is so malleable, contingent, and "socially constructed" that we should be wary about identifying a creative work too closely with a particular author, let alone her personality. In this view, all creations are largely a product of communal forces. Dividing the stream of intellectual discourse into discrete units—each owned by and closely associated with a particular author—is therefore a logically incoherent exercise subject more to the political force of asserted authors' groups than to recognition of inherent claims of "personhood." *See, e.g.*, MARTHA WOODMANSEE & PETER JASZI EDS., THE CONSTRUCTION OF AUTHORSHIP: TEXTUAL APPROPRIATION IN LAW AND LITERATURE (1994); Peter Jaszi, *Toward a Theory of Copyright: The Metamorphoses of "Authorship,"* 1991 DUKE L.J. 455; James Boyle, *A Theory of Law and Information: Copyright, Spleens, Blackmail and Insider Trading*, 80 CAL. L. REV. 1413 (1992).

If authorship is an incoherent concept, is there any role at all for copyright law? How can one protect the rights (natural, moral, or economic) of the author, if there is, in fact, no author? Does the literary critique answer the charge that authors will not create in the absence of economic reward? Or is it directed only at personality-based theories of intellectual property?

5. Consider the observations of philosopher Lawrence Becker:

So if property-as-personality [à la Hegel] again turns out to be a dead end, perhaps we should dispense with the search for a deep justification for property rights (from metaphysics, moral psychology, sociobiology, or whatever) and focus on the behavioral surface: the observed, persistent, robust behavioral connections between various property arrangements and human well-being, broadly conceived. This may provide a foundation for egalitarian arguments that is more secure than speculative metaphysics, and a foundation for private property that is more stable than a pluralistic account of the standard array of bedrock justifications for it.

Lawrence Becker, *Too Much Property*, 21 PHIL. & PUB. AFF. 196, 206 (1992).

3. The Utilitarian/Economic Incentive Perspective

Utilitarian theory and the economic framework built upon it have long provided the dominant paradigm for analyzing and justifying the various forms of intellectual property protection. *See generally* Peter S. Menell & Suzanne Scotchmer, *Intellectual Property Law*, in 2 HANDBOOK OF LAW AND ECONOMICS 1474, 1525 (A. Mitchell Polinsky & Steven Shavell eds., 2007); WILLIAM M. LANDES & RICHARD A. POSNER, THE ECONOMIC STRUCTURE OF INTELLECTUAL PROPERTY LAW (2003). For purposes of exploring the economic dimensions of the intellectual property field, it is important to distinguish between two quite distinct functions. The principal objective of much of intellectual property law is the promotion of new and improved works—whether technological or expressive. This purpose encompasses patent, copyright, and trade secret law, as well as several more specialized protection systems (for mask works (semiconductor chip layouts), databases, and designs). Trademark and related bodies of unfair competition law focus primarily on a very different economic problem—ensuring the integrity of the marketplace.

i. *Promoting Innovation and Creativity*

Both the United States Constitution and judicial decisions emphasize incentive theory in justifying intellectual property. The Constitution expressly conditions the grant of power in the patent and copyright clause on a particular end, namely "to Promote the Progress of Science and useful Arts." U.S. CONST., ART. I, CL. 8. As the Supreme Court explained in *Mazer v. Stein*, 347 U.S. 201 (1954): The copyright law, like the patent statutes, makes reward to the owner a "secondary consideration." *United States v. Paramount Pictures*, 334 U.S. 131, 158. However, it is "intended definitely to grant valuable, enforceable rights to authors, publishers, etc., without burdensome requirements: 'to afford greater encouragement to the production of literary [or artistic] works of lasting benefit to the world.'" *Washington Pub. Co. v. Pearson*, 306 U.S. 30. The economic philosophy behind the clause empowering Congress to grant patents and copyrights is the conviction that it is the best way to advance public welfare through the talents of authors and inventors in "Science and useful Arts." Sacrificial days devoted to such creative activities deserve rewards commensurate with the services rendered.

To understand why the Framers thought exclusive rights in inventions and creations would promote the public welfare, consider what would happen absent any intellectual property protection. Invention and creation require the investment of resources—the time of an author or inventor, and often expenditures on facilities, prototypes, supplies, etc. In a private market economy, individuals will not invest in invention or creation unless the expected return from doing so exceeds the cost of doing so—that is, unless they can reasonably expect to make a profit from the endeavor. To profit from a new idea or work of authorship, the creator must be able either to sell it to others or to put it to some use that provides her with a comparative advantage in a market, such as by reducing the cost of producing goods.

But ideas (and writings, for that matter) are notoriously hard to control. Even if the idea is one that the creator can use herself, for example, to boost productivity in her business, she will reap a reward from that idea only to the extent that her competitors don't find out about it. A creator who depends on secrecy for value, therefore, lives in constant peril of discovery and disclosure. Competitors may steal the idea or learn of it from an ex-employee. They may be able to figure it out by watching the creator's production process or by examining the products she sells. Finally, they may come upon the idea on their own or discover it in the published literature. In all of these cases, the secrecy value of the idea will be irretrievably lost.

The creator who wants to sell her idea is in an even more difficult position. Selling information requires disclosing it to others. Once the information has been disclosed outside a small group, however, it is extremely difficult to control. Information has the characteristics of what economists call a "public good"—it may be "consumed" by many people without depletion, and it is difficult to identify those who will not pay and prevent them from using the information. *See* Kenneth J. Arrow, *Economic Welfare and the Allocation of Resources for Invention*, in THE RATE AND DIRECTION OF INVENTIVE ACTIVITY: ECONOMIC AND SOCIAL FACTORS 609, 614-16 (Nat'l Bureau of Economic Research ed., 1962). Once the idea of the intermittent windshield wiper is disclosed, others can imitate its design relatively easily. Once a book is published, others can copy it at low cost. It is difficult to exclude nonpurchasers from sharing in the benefits of the idea. Ideas and information can also be used by many without depleting the enjoyment of others. Unlike an ice cream cone, a good story or the concept of intermittent windshield wipers can be enjoyed by many without diminishing enjoyment of these creations by others.[1] If we assume that it is nearly costless to distribute information to others—an assumption that was once unrealistic, but now has become much more reasonable with advances in digital technology (including the Internet)—it will prove virtually impossible to charge for information over the medium run in the absence of effective intellectual property or some other means of protection (such as technological protection measures). If the author of a book charges more than the cost of distribution, hoping to recover some of her expenditures in writing the work, competitors will quickly jump in to offer the book at a lower price. Competition will drive the price of the book toward its marginal cost—in this case, the cost of producing and distributing one additional copy. In such a competitive market, the author will be unable to recoup the fixed cost of writing the book. More to the point, if this holds true generally, authors may be expected to leave the profession in droves, since they cannot

---

[1] To some extent this statement oversimplifies the problem by ignoring possible second-order distorting effects. In practice, if you taught several hundred million people to fish, the result might be depletion of a physical resource (fish) that would otherwise not have occurred. Similarly, wide dissemination of some information may have particular effects on secondary markets.

make any money at it. The result, according to economic theory, would be an underproduction of books and other works of invention and creation with similar public goods characteristics.

Information is not the only example of a public good. Economists generally offer lighthouses and national defense as examples of public goods, since it is virtually impossible to provide the benefits of either one only to paying clients. It is impossible, for example, to exclude some ships and not others from the benefits of a lighthouse. Furthermore, the use of the lighthouse by one ship does not deplete the value of its hazard warning to others. As a result, it would be inefficient to exclude nonpayers from using the lighthouse's warning system even if we could, since consumption of this good is "nonrivalrous" (meaning that everyone can benefit from it once it is produced). For these reasons, the market will in theory undersupply such goods because producers cannot reap the marginal (incremental) value of their investment in providing them.[2]

Can you see why broadcast television signals, beautiful gardens on a public street, and national defense are also public goods? Nope - Nat'l defense benefits ppl on coasts more.

By contrast, markets for pure private goods, such as ice cream cones, feature exclusivity and rivalrous competition—the ice cream vendor provides the good only to those who pay the price, and the consumer certainly depletes the amount of the good available to others. Thus, the market system provides adequate incentives for the creation of ice cream cones: sellers can exact their cost of production, and the value of the product is fully enjoyed by the purchaser.

In the case of national defense (and most lighthouses), we avoid the underproduction that would result from leaving it to the market by having the government step in and pay for the public good. For a variety of good reasons, we have not gone that route with many forms of information. Instead, the government has created intellectual property rights to give authors and inventors control over the use and distribution of their ideas, thereby encouraging them to invest in the production of new ideas and works of authorship. Thus, the economic justification for intellectual property lies not in rewarding creators for their labor but in ensuring that they (and other creators) have appropriate incentives to engage in creative activities.

Unfortunately, this approach comes at a cost. Granting authors and inventors the right to exclude others from using their ideas necessarily limits the diffusion of those ideas and so prevents many people from benefiting from them. In economic terms, intellectual property rights prevent competition in the sale of the particular work or invention covered by those rights, and therefore may allow the intellectual property owner to raise the price of that work above the marginal cost of reproducing it. This means that in many cases fewer people will buy the work than if it were distributed on

---

[2] Ronald Coase has offered evidence casting doubt on the economic assumption that lighthouses must be publicly provided. *See* Ronald H. Coase, *The Lighthouse in Economics*, in THE FIRM, THE MARKET, AND THE LAW (1988).

a competitive basis, and they will pay more for the privilege. A fundamental principle of our economic system is the proposition that free market competition will ensure an efficient allocation of resources, absent market failures. In fact, the principal thrust of the antitrust laws serves precisely this goal. In this limited sense, then, intellectual property rights appear to run counter to free market competition: they limit the ability of competitors to copy or otherwise imitate the intellectual efforts of the first person to develop an idea. These rights enable those possessing intellectual property rights to charge monopoly prices or to otherwise limit competition, such as by controlling the use of the intellectual work in subsequent products.

Because intellectual property rights impose social costs on the public, the intellectual property laws can be justified by the public goods argument only to the extent that they do on balance encourage enough creation and dissemination of new works to offset those costs. One of the reasons that intellectual property rights are limited in scope, duration, and effect is to balance these costs and benefits. For example, the limited term of intellectual property rights ensures that inventions will be freely available after that fixed term. The key to economic efficiency lies in balancing the social benefit of providing economic incentives for creation and the social costs of limiting the diffusion of knowledge. We will encounter this critical trade-off throughout our study of intellectual property. The two examples below highlight some of the major issues.

a. *Economic Incentive Benefit*

Intellectual property protection is necessary to encourage inventors, authors, and artists to invest in the process of creation. Without such protection, others could copy or otherwise imitate the intellectual work without incurring the costs and effort of creation, thereby inhibiting the original creators from reaping a reasonable return on their investment. Consider the following example: After years of effort and substantial expense, Earnest Inventor develops the Mousomatic, a significantly better mousetrap. Not only does it catch mice better than the competition's trap, but it also neatly packages the dead mice in disposable sanitary bags. Consumers are willing to pay substantially more for this product than for its competitors. The Mousomatic catches the attention of Gizmo Gadget Incorporated. Gizmo copies the basic design of the Mousomatic and offers its version of the Mousomatic at a substantial discount. (Gizmo can still earn a profit at this lower price because it had minimal research and development expense.) To stay in business, Earnest is forced to lower his price. Market competition pushes the price down to the cost of production and distribution. In the end, Earnest is unable to recover his cost of research and development and suffers a loss. Although he has numerous other interesting ideas, he decides that they are not worth pursuing because Gizmo, or some other company, will simply copy them if they turn out well.

The existence of intellectual property rights encourages Earnest and other inventors to pursue their creative efforts. If Earnest can obtain the right to prevent others from copying his inventions, then he stands a much better chance to reap a profit. Hence, he will be much more inclined to make the initial investment in research and development. In the end, not only will Earnest be wealthier, but the public will be enriched by the new and better products brought forth by intellectual property protection.

b.   Costs of Limiting Diffusion

Legal protection for ideas and their expression prevents others from using those works to develop similar works that build upon them. Knowledge in society is cumulative. In the words of Sir Isaac Newton, "If I have seen further [than others], it is by standing on the shoulders of giants." Hence, society at large can be harmed by intellectual property protection to the extent that it unnecessarily raises the cost of acquiring a product (through monopoly pricing by the right holder) and limits others from making further advances. Consider the following scenario: Professor Lee conducts research on drug treatments at University College. Grants from the federal government generously fund her laboratory. For the past decade, Professor Lee has competed with colleagues at other laboratories to discover the cure for a prevalent form of cancer. It is likely that the first person to discover the cure will win a Nobel prize, as well as numerous other financial and professional rewards. In early 1995, Professor Lee hits upon the Alpha drug, which cures the disease. She files for and receives a patent. Professor Hu, a researcher at another research institution, independently discovers the identical cure a few months later. With patent in hand, Professor Lee starts a company to sell Alpha and charges a price 100 times the cost of production. Because Alpha is a life-saving cure, those stricken with the disease who can afford the treatment are more than willing to pay the price. Then, to relieve the suffering of millions, Professor Hu begins selling Alpha at the cost of production. Moreover, she has developed an improvement on the Alpha drug, Alpha+, that reduces the side effects of the treatment. Professor Lee quickly obtains an injunction preventing Hu from selling either version of Alpha for the life of the patent.

This example raises serious questions about whether intellectual property protection is desirable, at least for this class of invention. Professor Lee does not bear significant risk in pursuing the invention because the government and university generously fund her research. Furthermore, the potential for a Nobel prize, expanded research funding, and professional recognition provide substantial encouragement for Professor Lee to pursue a cure whether or not she gains financially from sales of Alpha. Moreover, other researchers were poised to make the same discovery at about the time that Professor Lee made her discovery. Yet she has the right not only to block sales of Alpha by competitors, but also to block sales of improvements such as Alpha+. Does such a system benefit society? One must also consider that without the financial incentive of a patent, there would perhaps have been less competition to discover and market any cure for cancer. Problems such as this one have led some scholars to question the economic efficiency of the patent system in particular circumstances. *See* F. M. SCHERER, INDUSTRIAL MARKET STRUCTURE AND ECONOMIC PERFORMANCE 445-55 (2d ed. 1980).

Similar problems can arise in the copyright domain. In 1936, Margaret Mitchell published her epic novel GONE WITH THE WIND. The plot revolves around Scarlett O'Hara, a hard-working and ambitious Southern woman who lives through the American Civil War and Reconstruction. GONE WITH THE WIND quickly became one of the most popular books ever written, eventually selling more than 28 million copies throughout the world. Ms. Mitchell would receive a Pulitzer Prize, and the novel would become the basis for one of the most successful movies ever.

Sixty-five years later, Alice Randall, an African-American historian, set out to tell the history of the Civil War–era South from another viewpoint. She invented the character of Cynara, a mulatto slave on Scarlett's plantation who also happened to be Scarlett's half-sister. Although Mitchell's novel did not depict a character named Cynara, many other characters in Randall's novel mimic characters in the original. Randall's THE WIND DONE GONE depicts the mistreatment and suffering of slaves in their vernacular dialect. Randall believed that GONE WITH THE WIND, as the lens through which millions viewed the deep South during the Civil War era, provided a unique vehicle for communicating the racial injustice of American history. Margaret Mitchell's estate sued Randall for copying GONE WITH THE WIND without authorization, obtaining a preliminary injunction. Although Randall eventually prevailed on appeal under the fair use doctrine, *Suntrust Bank v. Houghton Mifflin Co.*, 268 F.3d 1257 (11th Cir. 2001), this controversy illustrates how strong copyright protection can potentially inhibit cumulative creativity.

In applying a utilitarian framework, the economic incentive benefits of intellectual property rights must be balanced against the costs of limiting diffusion of knowledge. A critical issue in assessing the need for intellectual property protection is whether innovators have sufficient means to appropriate an adequate return on investment in research and development. In this regard, the market itself often provides means by which inventors can realize sufficient rewards to pursue innovation without formal intellectual property rights beyond contract law. The first to introduce a product can in many contexts earn substantial and long-lived advantages in the market. In many markets, the costs or time required to imitate a product (for example, to reverse engineer a complex machine) are so great that the first to market a product has substantial opportunity for profit. Moreover, as we will see in Chapter II, inventors can often prevent imitation through contractual means, such as trade secrecy and licensing agreements with customers. Where the invention relates to a manufacturing process, the innovator may be able to maintain protection through secrecy even after the product is on the market. Alternatively, a producer may be able to bundle products with essential services and contracts for updates of the product. In addition, the producer may be able to spread the costs of research and development among a group of firms through research joint ventures.

In those areas in which economic incentives for innovation are inadequate, and the creation of intellectual property rights is the most efficacious way of encouraging progress, society must determine the appropriate requirements for, duration and scope of, and set of rights afforded intellectual property. Over the past several decades, economists have developed and refined models to assess the appropriate trade-off between the social benefits of providing economic incentives for innovation through intellectual property rights and the social costs of limiting diffusion of knowledge. Professor William Nordhaus developed the first formal model analyzing the optimal duration of intellectual property. His model of the innovative process assumed that investments in research produced a single independent innovation. WILLIAM NORDHAUS, INVENTION, GROWTH, AND WELFARE: A THEORETICAL TREATMENT OF TECHNOLOGICAL CHANGE 3-7 (1969). The principal policy implication of this model is that the term of intellectual property protection should be calibrated to balance the incentive benefits of protection against the deadweight loss of monopoly pricing and the resulting limitations on dissemination.

Since Nordhaus's important early work, economic historians and economic theorists have greatly enriched our understanding of the innovative process and the implications for public policy. Historical and industry studies of the innovation process find that inventions are highly interdependent: "Technologies . . . undergo a gradual, evolutionary development which is intimately bound up with the course of their diffusion." Paul David, *New Technology, Diffusion, Public Policy, and Industrial Competitiveness* 20 (Center for Economic Policy Research, Pub. No. 46, Apr. 1985). In fact, "secondary inventions"—including essential design improvements, refinements, and adaptations to a variety of uses—are often as crucial to the generation of social benefits as the initial discovery. *See, e.g.*, J.L. Enos, *A Measure of the Rate of Technological Progress in the Petroleum Refining Industry*, 6 J. INDUS. ECON. 180, 189 (1958); James Mak & Gary Walton, *Steamboats and the Great Productivity Surge in River Transportation*, 32 J. ECON. HIST. 619, 625 (1972). Economic theorists have more recently developed models of the innovative process incorporating concepts of rivalrous and cumulative innovation, *see* Suzanne Scotchmer, *Standing on the Shoulders of Giants: Cumulative Research and the Patent Law*, 5 J. ECON. PERSPECTIVES 29 (1991); Robert P. Merges & Richard Nelson, *On the Complex Economics of Patent Scope*, 90 COLUM. L. REV. 839 (1990); Peter S. Menell, *Tailoring Legal Protection for Computer Software*, 39 STAN. L. REV. 1329 (1987), uncovering a range of important effects. Most notably, excessive protection for first-generation innovation can impede later innovations if licensing is costly. More generally, these models cast doubt on the notion that society can perfectly calibrate intellectual property rewards for each innovation.

As is increasingly evident, the range of innovative activity and creative expression in our society is vast and ever changing. As the materials in this book will highlight, the intellectual property institutions and rules that have evolved to promote technology and the arts are intricate. It will be the challenge of future generations of policymakers, judges, and lawyers to refine the ability of the intellectual property system to enhance the public welfare.

COMMENTS AND QUESTIONS

1. One significant difference between the natural rights perspective and the utilitarian perspective relates to who is entitled to the fruits of productive labor. In the natural rights framework, the inventor or author is entitled to all the social benefits produced by his or her efforts. In the utilitarian framework, reward to the inventor or author is a secondary consideration; the principal objective is to enrich the public at large. Which view is more compelling? Consider in this regard the optimal division of benefits from the invention of Alpha among Professor Lee, Professor Hu, and the public at large. Is Professor Lee entitled to all or even a lion's share of the benefits?

2. In 1966, the REPORT OF THE PRESIDENT'S COMMISSION ON THE PATENT SYSTEM identified four major economic justifications for the patent laws. First, a patent system provides an incentive to invent by offering the possibility of reward to the inventor and to those who support him. This prospect encourages the expenditure of time and private risk capital in research and development efforts. Second, and complementary to the first, a patent system stimulates the investment of additional capital needed for the further development and marketing of the invention. In return, the patent owner is given the right, for a limited period, to exclude others from making, using, or selling the invented product or process. Third, by affording protection, a patent system encourages early public disclosure of technological information, some of which might otherwise be kept secret. Early disclosure reduces the likelihood of duplication of effort by others and provides a basis for further advances in the technology involved. Fourth, a patent system promotes the beneficial exchange of products, services, and technological information across national boundaries by providing protection for industrial property of foreign nationals.

While directed specifically at the patent system, many of these arguments have application to all forms of intellectual property.

Are these incentives necessary to invention and creation? Using cost and other data from publishing companies, Professor (now Justice) Stephen Breyer contended that lead time advantages and the threat of retaliation reduce the cost advantages of copiers, thus obviating if not eliminating the need for copyright protection for books. *See* Stephen Breyer, *The Uneasy Case for Copyright: A Study in Copyright of Books, Photocopies and Computer Programs*, 84 HARV. L. REV. 281 (1970). *Cf.* Barry W.

Tyerman, *The Economic Rationale for Copyright Protection for Published Books: A Reply to Professor Breyer*, 18 UCLA L. REV. 1100 (1971); Stephen Breyer, *Copyright: A Rejoinder*, 20 UCLA L. REV. 75 (1972). This debate took place decades ago. Have advances in technology strengthened or weakened Breyer's argument?

3. *Intellectual Property as Property*. It is tempting to view intellectual property through a tangible property lens. *See* Richard Epstein, *The Disintegration of Intellectual Property? A Classical Liberal Response to a Premature Obituary*, 62 STAN. L. REV. 455 (2010). After all, intellectual property draws on tangible property concepts of first-in-time, exclusivity, and transferability, and scholars have explored the philosophy of tangible property rules and institutions for centuries. However, simplistic Blackstonian conceptions of land and other tangible resources miss a lot of the most important economic and social concerns relating to protecting intangible resources. *See* Peter S. Menell, *Governance of Intellectual Resources and Disintegration of Intellectual Property in the Digital Age*, 26 BERKELEY TECH. L.J. 1523 (2011); Mark A. Lemley, *Property, Intellectual Property, and Free Riding*, 83 TEX. L. REV. 1031 (2005). Nonetheless, tangible property law and institutions dealing with more complex resources (such as water, wild animals, oil and natural gas) and circumstances (control of the dead hand, shared use of resources) offer valuable insights into the design of intellectual property rules and institutions. *Cf.* Molly Van Houweling, *Intellectual Property as Property*, in RESEARCH HANDBOOK ON THE ECONOMICS OF INTELLECTUAL PROPERTY LAW (Peter S. Menell & Ben Depoorter eds., forthcoming 2016)

4. *Comparative Institutional Analysis*. Numerous institutional mechanisms exist for addressing the public goods problem inherent in the production of ideas and information—direct government funding of research, government research subsidies, promotion of joint ventures, and prizes. The case for intellectual property rights ideally compares all of these options. Intellectual property rights have the advantage of limiting the government's role in allocating resources to a finite set of decentralized decisions: whether particular inventions are worthy of a fixed period of protection. The market then serves as the principal engine of progress. Decentralized consumers generate demand for products and competing decentralized sellers produce them. By contrast, most other incentive systems, especially large-scale research funding, require central planning on a mass scale. Most economists place more confidence in the former means of allocating resources. The case for intellectual property rights, then, is based more on a generalized perception of institutional choice than on strong direct evidence of the superiority of intellectual property rights relative to the alternatives. *basic research*

5. *The Open Source Movement*. The emergence of cooperative working environments for the development of software has raised questions about the core precept underlying the utilitarian/economic perspective: that exclusive property rights represent the most effective means for promoting creative enterprise. *See generally* STEVEN WEBER, THE SUCCESS OF OPEN SOURCE (2004); Yochai Benkler, *Coase's*

Penguin, or Linux and the Nature of the Firm, 112 YALE L.J. 369 (2002); David McGowan, *The Legal Implications of Open Source Software*, 2001 U. ILL. L. REV. 241. Open source software traces its origins to the early 1970s and the culture of collaborative research on computer software that existed in many software research environments. To perpetuate that model in the face of increasingly proprietary software, Richard Stallman, a former researcher in MIT's Artificial Intelligence Laboratory, established the Free Software Foundation (FSF) to promote users' rights to use, study, copy, modify, and redistribute computer programs. Such rights obviously conflict with the default bundle of rights of copyright law. For that reason, FSF developed the GNU General Public License (GPL), a complex licensing agreement designed to prevent programmers from building proprietary limitations into "free" software. Stallman set forth a task list for the development of a viable UNIX-compatible open source operating system. Many programmers from throughout the world contributed to this effort on a voluntary basis, and by the late 1980s most of the components had been assembled. The project gained substantial momentum in 1991 when Linus Torvalds developed a UNIX-compatible kernel, which he called "Linux." Torvalds structured the evolution of his component on the GNU GPL "open source" model. The integration of the GNU and Linux components resulted in a UNIX-compatible open source program (referred to as GNU/Linux) and has since become widely used throughout the computing world. In the process, it has spawned a large community of computer programmers and service organizations committed to the principles of open source development. The growth and success of Linux has brought the open source movement into the mainstream computer software industry. Today, a variety of vendors, such as Red Hat, Caldera, and Ubuntu, distribute open source software, and it has tens of millions of users worldwide. Does this experience refute the logic underlying the property rights paradigm or merely broaden the range of viable governance structures?

6. Drawing upon Thomas Jefferson's natural rights insight that "ideas should freely spread from one to another over the globe, for the moral and mutual instruction of man, and improvement of his condition, seems to have been peculiarly and benevolently designed by nature," ANDREW A. LIPSCOMB & ALBERT ELLERY BERGH EDS., THE WRITINGS OF THOMAS JEFFERSON, vol. 13: 333-35 (Writings (document 12): letter from Thomas Jefferson to Isaac McPherson, 13 Aug. 1813) (1905), John Perry Barlow's essay "The Economy of Ideas" has emerged as a manifesto for a new libertarianism that resists intellectual property protection in cyberspace. John Perry Barlow, *The Economy of Ideas*, 2.03 WIRED 84 (Mar. 1994). Barlow questions whether a right of property can or should exist in a medium (digital networks) lacking physical structure or any significant cost of distribution. This approach resonates with many in the computer hacker community who believe that "information wants to be free." Professor Lawrence Lessig explores and expands upon this perspective in his books FREE CULTURE: HOW BIG MEDIA USES TECHNOLOGY AND THE LAW TO LOCK DOWN

CULTURE AND CONTROL CREATIVITY (2004) and THE FUTURE OF IDEAS: THE FATE OF THE COMMONS IN A CONNECTED WORLD (2001), although his focus is not on eliminating intellectual property but on preserving spaces free of such property. For historical analysis of Jefferson's thinking and its application to intellectual property, *see* Adam Mossoff, *Who Cares What Thomas Jefferson Thought About Patents? Reevaluating the Patent Privilege in Historical Context*, 92 CORNELL L. REV. 953 (2007); Justin Hughes, *Copyright and Incomplete Historiographies—of Piracy, Propertization, and Thomas Jefferson*, 79 S. CAL. L. REV. 993 (2006).

What is likely to happen if we abolish the concept of ownership of information on the Internet? In general? Consider the implications for particular works of authorship: musical compositions, sound recordings, software, movies, databases. Will people stop producing these works? Or will other types of incentives and appropriation mechanisms (e.g., encryption, secrecy) continue to encourage invention and creativity? What are the advantages and disadvantages of these alternative mechanisms? For a controversial argument that we don't need IP at all, *see* MICHELE BOLDRIN & DAVID LEVINE, AGAINST INTELLECTUAL MONOPOLY (2007).

ii. Ensuring Integrity of the Marketplace

Unlike patent and copyright, trademark law does not protect innovation or creativity directly. Rather, it aims to protect the integrity of the marketplace by prohibiting the use of marks associated with particular manufacturers in ways that would cause confusion as to the sources of the goods. In so doing, trademark law reduces consumer confusion and enhances incentives for firms to invest in activities (including R&D) that improve brand reputation. This function, however, is part of a larger framework of laws and institutions that regulate the quality of information in the marketplace. *See generally* Peter S. Menell & Suzanne Scotchmer, *Intellectual Property Law*, in 2 HANDBOOK OF LAW AND ECONOMICS 1474, 1536-56 (A. Mitchell Polinsky & Steven Shavell eds., 2007)

The efficiency of the marketplace depends critically upon the quality of information available to consumers. In markets in which the quality of goods is uniform or easily inspected at the time of purchase, consumers can determine the attributes themselves and no information problem arises. In many markets, however—such as used automobiles, computers, watches, as well as designer handbags—an information asymmetry exists: sellers typically have better information about their products or services than buyers can uncover without buying the product. *See* George A. Ackerlof, *The Market for "Lemons": Quality Uncertainty and the Market Mechanism*, 84 Q.J. ECON. 488 (1970). Unscrupulous sellers will be tempted to make false or misleading product claims or copy the trademark of a rival producer known for superior quality. It is often easier to copy a trademark than to duplicate production techniques, quality assurance programs, and the like. For example, two watches that look the same on the outside may have very different mechanical features, manufacturing quality, and composition of materials used.

Proliferation of unreliable information in the marketplace increases consumers' costs of search and distorts the provision of goods. Consumers will have to spend more time and effort inspecting goods, researching the product market, and testing products. Manufacturers will have less incentive to produce quality goods as others will be able to free-ride on such reputations. In markets for products where quality is costly to observe, high-quality manufacturers might not be able to survive without effective mechanisms for policing the source of products and the accuracy of claims relating to unobservable product characteristics.

Trademarks, as concise and unequivocal indicators of the source (e.g., Intel) and nature (e.g., Pentium) of particular goods, counteract the "market for lemons" problem by communicating to consumers the enterprise responsible for the goods and, in some cases, the specifications of the goods. The brand name Coca-Cola, for example, informs the consumer of the maker of the soft drink beverage as well as the taste that they can expect. If the product meets or exceeds expectations, then the trademark owner gains a loyal customer who will be willing to pay a premium in future transactions; if the product disappoints, then the trademark owner will have more difficulty making future sales to that consumer (or will have to offer a discount to attract their business). In this way, trademarks implicitly communicate unobservable characteristics about the quality of branded products, thereby fostering incentives for firms to invest in product quality, even when such attributes are not directly observable prior to a purchasing decision. Sellers who enter the high-quality segment of the market must initially invest in building a strong reputation. Only after consumers become acquainted with the attributes of their brand can they recoup these costs. As this process unfolds, high-quality items can sell for a premium above their costs of production, since consumers will expect them to be of high quality. Trademarks also facilitate efficient new business models, such as franchising, which generate economies of scale and scope in marketing and facilitate rapid business diffusion across vast geographic areas.

The marking of products also creates incentives for disreputable sellers to pass off their own wares as the goods of better-respected manufacturers. Trademark law (as well as false advertising and unfair competition laws more generally) harnesses the incentives of sellers in the marketplace to police the use of marks and advertising claims of competitors. Sellers often have the best information about the quality of products in the marketplace; they also have a direct stake in preventing competitors from free-riding on their brand, reputation, and consumer loyalty. By creating private causes of action, trademark and false advertising law take advantage of this informational base and incentive structure as well as the vast, decentralized enforcement resources of trademark owners to regulate the informational marketplace, effectively in the name of consumers.

As with patent and copyright law, the creation of intellectual property rights in words, phrases, logos, and other identifying product features can entail several types of costs. Protection of descriptive terms as trademarks can increase search costs and impair competition by raising the marketing costs of competitors. For example, if a cookie manufacturer were to obtain a trademark on the word "cookie," then other companies interested in selling cookies would have a much more difficult time communicating the nature of their goods to consumers. If, however, the trademark was to "Mrs. Fields Cookies" and any protection for "cookies" was disclaimed, then potential competitors would be able to describe their products in the most easily recognized manner and would be able to develop their own marks—such as "ACME Cookies." At a minimum, trademark protection for descriptive terms significantly reduces the effective range of terms that others can use commercially.

More generally, trademark protection for descriptive terms can impede competition. Gaining control over the most effective term for describing a product raises the costs of potential competitors seeking to sell in that marketplace. By not being able to use a term or means of communication most easily understood by the consuming public, the entrant must bear higher marketing costs. Limitations on the use of trademarked terms for purposes of comparative advertising would also impede vigorous competition.

Trademark protection can also interfere with both communicative and creative expression. Broad exclusive trademark rights would limit the ability of others (including non-competitors) to comment on and poke fun at trademarks and their owners. As we will see, various doctrines limit such adverse effects. But as trademark protection has expanded beyond the traditional core—for example, to encompass a broad conception of connection to, sponsorship of, and affiliation with a trademark owner—it becomes more difficult to assess the boundaries, leading film and television production companies, for example, to tread carefully (and increasingly incur the costs of licensing transactions) in the use of trademarks in their works.

COMMENTS AND QUESTIONS

1. *Comparative Institutional Analysis.* In addition to private rights of action for trademark infringement and false advertising, several other mechanisms are available to provide and regulate market information, such as deceit and fraud common law causes of action and privately enforced consumer protection statutes, public regulation and public enforcement of unfair competition laws, and industry self-regulation and certification organizations. How do these institutions compare with trademark protection? Should they supplement or substitute for trademark protection? *See* Dan L. Burk & Brett McDonnell, *Trademarks and the Theory of the Firm*, 51 WM. & MARY L. REV. 345 (2009).

2. *Status Goods.* Some trademarks also serve a more ambiguous function: signaling status or identity for some consumers. Some have referred to such commodities as

"Veblen" goods, reflecting Thorstein Veblen's theory of conspicuous consumption. *See* THORSTEIN VEBLEN, THE THEORY OF THE LEISURE CLASS: AN ECONOMIC STUDY OF INSTITUTIONS (1899). This theory posits that unlike normal goods, demand for status goods increases with their price. Purchasers of such goods may be interested in being associated with a particular brand—such as a Rolex watch, a t-shirt with the name and colors of a particular university, or a corporate brand—possibly apart from whether it is authentic or the quality associated with the authentic good. Some purchasers of such goods may well prefer a less expensive, counterfeit version. They presumably would not be confused when purchasing such goods (e.g., a Rolex watch sold on a street corner for $10). Of course, where both buyers and sellers are aware of the difference between cheap imitations of a luxury good and the genuine article, things might be different. It could be that cheap imitations in some ways promote sales of the luxury good. *See* Jonathan Barnett, *Shopping for Gucci on Canal Street: Status Consumption, Intellectual Property and the Incentive Thesis*, 91 VA. L. REV. 1381 (2005).

The marketing of less expensive, lower quality imitations of status goods creates the possibility of separate harm to the sellers and purchasers of authentic goods. The availability of counterfeit articles could well divert some consumers who would otherwise purchase the authentic article, although this effect is likely to be relatively small due to the large price differential and the availability of the authentic goods for those who are interested. The lower quality of the counterfeit goods could, however, erode the goodwill associated with the authentic manufacturer through post-sale confusion—on-lookers who mistake the shoddier counterfeit good for the authentic good and are thereby less inclined to purchase the authentic version, thereby reducing sales by the trademark owner. In addition, due to the proliferation of non-easily recognized "fakes," prior and potential purchasers of the authentic "status" goods may be less interested in owning a much less rare commodity. The value of ownership may be sullied. In essence, status goods exhibit a negative network externality, whereby proliferation of such goods erodes the value to prior purchasers. Should trademark law be concerned with this effect?

3. *Protection Against Dilution.* In 1996, Congress expanded trademark protection beyond the prevention of consumer confusion to safeguard famous marks—such as Coca-Cola, Nike, Rolls Royce, Disney, and Tiffany's—against blurring (loss of distinctiveness) and tarnishment of brand identity. As consumers develop their mental lexicon of brands, they associate both specific products and general attributes with particular trademarks. For example, Rolls Royce connotes both the source of a luxury automobile as well as a brand of uncompromising quality and ornate styling (as well as high cost). If another company were to introduce Rolls Royce candy bars, it is unlikely that many (if any) consumers would believe that the automobile manufacturer was the source. Whether intended or not, the candy company might benefit from the particular general attributes that the consuming public associates with the Rolls Royce brand. They might also gain some "status" equity to the extent that consumers value

the signal associated with a mark. Thus, adopting the Rolls Royce name enables the newcomer some ability to free-ride on the general brand reputation of the famous trademark owner.

Such use, however, might impose some costs on consumers and the owner of the famous trademark. As this new use of the Rolls Royce term gained popularity, the association between the mark and a particular source would become blurred. Furthermore, as more companies in unrelated markets adopt this moniker—Rolls Royce tennis racquets, Rolls Royce landscaping, Rolls Royce tacos—the distinctive quality of the mark would become further eroded. Over time, consumers would lose the non-product specific identity (i.e., Rolls Royce as a brand of uncompromising quality and ornate styling) that the original Rolls Royce mark once evoked. Arguably this raises consumers' search costs: consumers' mental lexicon has become more difficult to parse. *See* Stacey L. Dogan & Mark A. Lemley, *The Merchandising Right: Fragile Theory or Fait Accompli?*, 54 EMORY L.J. 461 (2005).

As another example, Disney has developed a strong reputation for wholesome, family entertainment. If a pornographic filmmaker were to brand its films Disney Smut Productions, it is unlikely that many consumers would be confused as to the source of such films. Nonetheless, consumers' shopping lexicon would arguably be distorted because the Disney name would trigger associations with both family-oriented content and pornography. Such a negative association could well injure the Disney Corporation's brand equity.

Anti-dilution protection prevents this erosion of the distinctive quality of a mark by prohibiting famous marks from being used by others—even in unrelated product markets and in non-confusing ways. This preserves distinctive brands and affords the owners exclusive rights to carry their brand names into wholly new markets (or not). We see examples of such brand migration in many markets. Sony Corporation which honed its reputation in the consumer electronics marketplace, has now developed products in the sound recording and motion picture marketplaces. Cross-branding, such as the marketing of a Barbie doll adorned with Coca-Cola's logo and a distinctive red ensemble, is also increasingly common.

What are the costs of anti-dilution protection? Is the harm to consumers of non-confusing, diluting uses of famous marks likely to be significant? Would scaling back or eliminating anti-dilution protection significantly weaken the incentives of firms to invest in and maintain their brand equity?

4. Distributive and Social Justice

In A THEORY OF JUSTICE (1971)—probably the most influential work of political philosophy written in the past century—John Rawls offers an "ideal contractarian" theory of distributive shares. To determine the just allocation of the benefits and burdens of social life, he asks what distributive principles would suitably disinterested persons choose. To ask what selfish people would want, or what social contract would actually result from a convocation of all members of society, Rawls argues, would ensure that the naturally smart or strong, or people who shared a particular race, nationality, religion, or ideology, dominated the rest, if any agreement could be reached at all. Rawls rejects this construction of the "original position" for choosing social rules—which more libertarian philosophers, such as David Gauthier, come closer to favoring—because he finds this consequence intuitively unacceptable. He assumes instead that the resources and opportunities a person should have available should not depend primarily on how fortunate he or she was in the natural lottery of talents and parents, or in what group that person happens to be born.

Rawls, therefore, tries to determine principles that rational people behind a "veil of ignorance" would choose. Rawls contends that the veil must be quite opaque. It must, for example, exclude from the minds of those choosing principles of justice all knowledge of their own abilities, desires, parentage, and social stratum.

Rawls concludes that people behind the veil of ignorance would adopt what he calls the "difference principle." They would agree, he says, that the fundamental institutions of society should be arranged so that the distribution of "primary goods"—not only wealth, income, and opportunities for work or leisure, but also what Rawls terms the "bases of self-respect"—is to the maximal advantage of a representative member of the least advantaged social class. Defining the least advantaged class and the proper set of primary goods is difficult and contentious. In POLITICAL LIBERALISM (1993), Rawls refines his theory of distributive justice in the following passage:

> [M]easures are required to assure that the basic needs of all citizens can be met so that they can take part in political and social life.

> About this last point, the idea is not that of satisfying needs as opposed to mere desires and wants; nor is it that of redistribution in favor of greater equality. The constitutional essential here is rather that below a certain level of material and social well-being, and of training and education, people simply cannot take part in society as citizens, much less equal citizens.

Id. at 166.

COMMENTS AND QUESTIONS

1. Do you agree with Rawls that people behind the veil of ignorance would agree that the fundamental institutions of society should be arranged so that the distribution of "primary goods"—including property—is to the maximal advantage of a representative member of the least advantaged social class? Would you agree to this principle if you were behind a veil of ignorance?

Consider political scientist James Q. Wilson's critique:

> [E]verybody in Rawls's universe is averse to risk; each wants to make certain that, if he winds up on the bottom of the heap, the bottom is as attractive as possible.

loss aversion > appetite for gain

But many people are in fact not averse to risk, they are risk takers; to them, a just society would be one in which inequalities in wealth were acceptable provided that the people at the top of the heap got there as a result of effort and skill. And even people who are not risk takers may endorse this position because they think it fair that rewards should be proportional to effort, even if some people lose out entirely. (These same people might also expect their church or government to take care of those who lost out.) They have this view of fairness because they recognize that people differ in talent, energy, temperament, and interests; that conflicts among such people are inevitable; and that matching, as best one can, rewards to contributions is the best way of handling that conflict. . . .

Equality is a special and, as it turns out, rare and precarious case of equity. Settled living, and in particular the accumulation of private property, makes equality of outcomes impossible because inequality of contributions become manifest. The task of settled societies is to devise ways of assuring that outcomes are proportional to worth, reasonably defined.

JAMES Q. WILSON, THE MORAL SENSE 73-76 (1993); *see also* ERIC RAKOWKSI, EQUAL JUSTICE (1991) (advocating a more meritocratic "equality of fortune" that affords all members of society a just initial distribution of resources but tolerates inequalities resulting from exercise of free will—notably, occupational preferences, wise business decisions, and diligence in school, training, and work).

2. What do Rawls' principles of distributive justice imply for the rights in intellectual property? Doesn't the essential mechanism of intellectual property protection—rewarding time-limited monopoly power in exchange for advancing society's knowledge base—inexorably produce inequality?

3. *Justifying Intellectual Property?* At a basic level, technological advance produces higher standards of living. It enables society to accomplish more with fewer resources and therefore increases productivity. Furthermore, no one is required to purchase IP-protected goods. Therefore, in an exchange economy, only those who value such goods more than their cost will purchase the goods. Moreover, patent and copyright protection eventually expire. At a coarse level of granularity, modern societies have the benefit of all manner of innovation and creativity—from sanitation technologies that support safe drinking water to telecommunications and modern medicines. As such, innovation tends to reduce poverty and raise standards of living in an absolute sense over the long run (but as John Maynard Keynes famously observed, "In the long run we are all dead"). *See* Peter S. Menell, *Property, Intellectual Property, and Social Justice: Mapping the Next Frontier*, 5 BRIGHAM-KANNER PROPERTY CONFERENCE JOURNAL (forthcoming 2016); *cf.* ROBERT P. MERGES, JUSTIFYING INTELLECTUAL PROPERTY (2011).

4. *Access to Medicine.* The argument that intellectual property protection increases productivity and eventually becomes available to all affords little solace to those who

cannot afford to purchase patented, life-saving medicines. Should the patent rights give way for life-saving medicines and treatments? To what extent would such a rule undermine the race to discover cures for disease? Is unequal access to medicine best addressed through social insurance institutions? *Cf.* Amy Kapczynski, *Access to Knowledge Mobilization and the New Politics of Intellectual Property*, 117 YALE L.J. 804 (2008); William W. Fisher & Talha Syed, *Global Justice in Healthcare: Developing Drugs for the Developing World*, 40 U.C. DAVIS L. REV. 581 (2007).

5. *Access to Culture and Cumulative Creativity*. We can also see distributive values in the broadening of expressive opportunities for authors and artists. Since expression often builds on and reacts to prior expressive works, such distributive values can run counter to the provision of exclusive rights. Limiting doctrines and the fair use privilege implicitly cross-subsidizes cumulative creators. Such freedom to build on the work of others can, however, adversely affect authors' moral and dignitary interests. *See* Molly Shaffer Van Houweling, *Distributive Values in Copyright*, 83 TEX. L. REV. 1535 (2005); *see also* Peter S. Menell, *Adapting Copyright for the Mashup Generation*, 164 U. PA. L. REV. 441 (2016).

6. *IP and Inequality*. While the digital revolution has provided especially rapid technological advance, it has also contributed to skewing of wealth distribution. Like the technological advances of the Industrial Revolution, the Digital Revolution of the past several decades—characterized by scalability of information technologies, network effects, and displacement of labor by smart machines—has produced a new Gilded Age. *See* Menell, *Property, Intellectual Property, and Social Justice, supra*; ERIK BRYNJOLFSSON & ANDREW MCAFEE, RACE AGAINST THE MACHINE: HOW THE DIGITAL REVOLUTION IS ACCELERATING INNOVATION, DRIVING PRODUCTIVITY, AND IRREVERSIBLY TRANSFORMING EMPLOYMENT AND THE ECONOMY (2011). Many of the wealthiest people in the world are technology entrepreneurs. The sports and entertainment professions, which depend critically upon copyright, trademark, and publicity right protections, also contribute to high wealth for a relatively small "superstar" class.

7. *Gender and Racial Equality*. The concentration of wealth and economic leverage that intellectual property produces places vast power in the hands of a relatively small group of entrepreneurs and their representatives. The class of venture capitalists, corporate titans, Hollywood moguls, and technology and entertainment lawyers reflect historical gender and race biases. *See* Menell, *Property, Intellectual Property, and Social Justice, supra*; K.J. Greene, *Intellectual Property at the Intersection of Race and Gender: Lady Sings the Blues*, 16 AM. U. J. GENDER, SOC. POL'Y & L. 365 (2008). Yet copyright protection has been especially effective in providing whatever limited "equality of opportunity" African-Americans have enjoyed in the United States. Indeed, for the wealthiest African-Americans, copyright has been the most important form of property for social and economic advancement. *See* Justin Hughes & Robert P.

Merges, *Copyright and Distributive Justice*, 92 NOTRE DAME L. REV. (forthcoming 2016).

Moreover, adequately funded and well-produced film, art, music, and literature play an inestimable role in promoting social and cultural understanding and tolerance. As much as lawyers emphasize the role of legal advocacy in shifting the law, the television series *Will and Grace* likely had more influence in shifting the nation's and Supreme Court's views on gay marriage than anything that lawyers argued. Similarly, works such as TO KILL A MOCKINGBIRD and THE HELP powerfully communicated the indignity of the Jim Crow South. The public's gradual embrace of R&B, jazz, and gospel—what was once referred to as "race music"—played a critical role in building a more cohesive and inclusive nation. *See* Menell, *Property, Intellectual Property, and Social Justice, supra.*

8. *IP and the Environment.* While motivating the development of better environmental technologies, the patent system potentially constrains the diffusion of technological advances that seek to ameliorate environmental harms. Even if advances in wind turbine and solar technologies dramatically lowered the cost of producing electricity, distributing that energy to consumers depends critically upon a grid infrastructure that can move decentralized sources of electricity to market. Moreover, such energy must compete with harmful alternatives. Without fees to internalize those harmful effects, renewable sources of energy face a competitive disadvantage. Thus, intellectual property cannot be the sole policy to address problems like pollution and climate change. Prizes, subsidies, and externality-internalizing fees on fossil fuels offer complementary tools for balancing the R&D appropriability problem, the environmental externalities of fossil fuel consumption, and the geopolitical distortions of reliance on oil. *See generally* PETER S. MENELL & SARAH M. TRAN, INTELLECTUAL PROPERTY, INNOVATION AND THE ENVIRONMENT (2014).

PROBLEM

Problem I-2. Building on your lifelong interest in music and computers, you have just spent ten years creating a computer-based encyclopedia of music called Musipedia. The encyclopedia includes text, snippets of recorded music (no longer than 60 seconds each), pictures, and other graphics, all of which can be called up by the user.

Like many other multimedia products, your encyclopedia allows the user to select a topic of interest and see (or hear) more about it. For example, from the opening menu, a user can select classical composers, then select Mozart, and then choose from a biographical sketch, with text, pictures, video clips, and samples of sheet music and audio recordings.

To make it easier for computer users to access all the information in your encyclopedia, you have used an "access interface" similar to the widely used "MediaMate" interface written and made popular by billionaire computer impresario

Gil Bates. (Bates adapted the "MediaMate" interface from a publicly available interface designed by the U.S. Army to teach electronics and other technical subjects to recruits.) Although MediaMate has now become the standard interface program, Bates, because of his prodigious programming talent, wrote the program in his spare time over several weeks while watching soap operas. According to his autobiography, he "never broke a sweat" while writing it.

Since Bates's company, MacroLoft, also owns many of the legal rights needed to play music from such musicians as Jimi Hendrix and Aretha Franklin, you have decided it is time to negotiate directly with Bates prior to placing your encyclopedia on the market. Note that although Bates has received *licenses* in the relevant copyrights, it is widely known that some of the musicians, notably Neil Young, who created the songs are not pleased with the use of short snippets on low fidelity computer sound systems, some of which sound "tinny."

You are aware that negotiating with Bates is far different from standard business practice. He is known to do all negotiating standing up in an unheated room in a mountain cabin with no lawyers or assistants of any kind. Most unusually, he is not interested at all in formal legal rights. Reflecting his photographic memory of all of the great works of philosophy, he insists on negotiating from what he calls "first principles." This usually involves long discussions of who should have which rights in which situations, and why.

You would like to convince Bates to let you market your encyclopedia without paying him any royalties for songs, the access interface, or anything else. Failing this, you would like to keep these royalties to a minimum. What are your strongest arguments? What are Bates's best counter-arguments and how would you counter them?

B.   OVERVIEW OF INTELLECTUAL PROPERTY

Intellectual property law has traditionally been taught along doctrinal lines. Separate courses have covered patent, copyright, and trademarks, with trade secrets often lost between the gaps. Yet the practice of intellectual property law increasingly cuts across these lines. Computer technology companies, for example, frequently require lawyers to address trade secret, copyright, patent, trademark, and antitrust issues simultaneously. Moreover, from a purely practical standpoint, clients are ultimately interested in appropriating a return from their investments, not in how many patents, copyrights, trademarks, or trade secrets their lawyers can obtain. Thus, intellectual property lawyers must possess an integrated understanding of these various fields to provide sound advice.

With this objective in mind, our book integrates the various modes of intellectual property in a functional manner. Nonetheless, it is still necessary to devote significant time to mastering each of the distinct fields. Therefore, the next five chapters survey the principal modes of intellectual property—trade secret, patent, copyright, trademark/trade dress, and related state law doctrines—while emphasizing the overlaps and interactions of the various bodies of law. Later chapters integrate this material and explore advanced topics.

Before we begin this more detailed study, however, a brief survey of the overall landscape of intellectual property is in order. The following section sketches the elements of each of the principal modes of intellectual property protection in a comparative framework. These elements are summarized in Table 1-1. As an initial exploration, we conclude the chapter with a problem highlighting the integrated nature of intellectual property law and the challenges of applying its many branches to a real-world problem.

TABLE 1-1
Principal Modes of Legal Protection for Intellectual Work

	Trade secret	*Patent*	*Copyright*	*Trademark/dress*
Underlying Theory	Freedom of contract; protection against unfair means of competition	Limited monopoly to encourage production of utilitarian works in exchange for immediate disclosure and ultimate enrichment of the public domain	Limited (although relatively long-lived) monopoly to encourage the authorship of expressive works; developed initially as a means of promoting publishing	Perpetual protection for distinctive nonfunctional names and dress to improve the quality of information in the marketplace
Source of Law	State statute (Uniform Trade Secrets Act); common law	Patent Act (federal)	Copyright Act (federal); common law (limited)	Lanham Act (federal); common law (unfair competition)
Subject Matter	Formula, pattern, compilation, program, device, method, technique, process	Process, machine, manufacture, or composition of matter; plants (asexually reproducing); designs—*excluding:* laws of nature, natural substances, printed matter (forms), mental steps	Literary, musical, choreographic, dramatic and artistic works as well as computer software and aesthetic elements of useful articles *limited by* idea/expression dichotomy (no protection for ideas, systems, methods, procedures); no	Trademarks; service marks; certification marks (e.g., Good Housekeeping); collective marks (e.g., American Automobile Association); trade dress (§43(a)); *no protection for* functional features, descriptive terms, geographic names, misleading aspects, or "generic" terms (e.g., thermos)

TABLE 1-1
Principal Modes of Legal Protection for Intellectual Work

	Trade secret	*Patent*	*Copyright*	*Trademark/dress*
Standard for Protection	Information not generally known or available; reasonable efforts to maintain secrecy; commercial value	Novelty; non-obviousness; and utility (distinctiveness for plant patents; ornamentality for design patents)	Originality; authorship; fixation in a tangible medium protection for facts/research	Distinctiveness; secondary meaning (for descriptive and geographic marks); use in commerce (minimal); famous mark (for dilution protection)
Scope of Protection	Protection against misappropriation—acquisition by improper means or unauthorized disclosure	Exclusive rights to make, use, sell, offer to sell, or import innovation as Limited by contribution to art; extends to "equivalents"	Rights of performance, display, distribution, reproduction, derivative works; limited protection for attribution and integrity afforded some works of visual art; protection against circumvention of technical protection measures	Exclusive rights in U.S.; likelihood of confusion; false designation of origin (§43(a)); dilution (for famous marks)
Period of Protection	Until becomes public knowledge	20 years from filing (utility); extensions up to 5 years for drugs, medical devices and additives;	Life of author + 70 years; "works for hire": minimum of 95 years after publication or 120 years after creation	Perpetual, subject to abandonment

TABLE 1-1
Principal Modes of Legal Protection for Intellectual Work

	Trade secret	Patent	Copyright	Trademark/dress
		15 years from issuance (design)		
Disclosure	Loss of protection (unless sub rosa)	Right to patent lost if inventor delays too long after publishing before filing application; full disclosure is required as part of application; notice of patent required for damages in some cases	© notice and publication no longer required, but confer certain benefits	® notice optional; establishes prima facie evidence of validity. constructive knowledge of registration. confers federal jurisdiction. becomes incontestable after 5 years of continuous use, authorizes treble damages and attorney fees, and right to bar imports bearing infringing mark
Rights of Others	Independent discovery; reverse engineering	Only if licensed; can request reexamination of patent by Patent Office	Fair use; compulsory licensing for musical compositions, cable TV, et al.; independent creation	Truthful reflection of source of product; fair and collateral use (e.g., comment)
Costs of Protection	Security expenses; personnel dissatisfaction; litigation costs	Filing, issue, and maintenance fees; litigation costs	None (protection attaches upon fixation); publication requires notice; suit requires	Registration search; marking product (optional—see above); litigation costs

TABLE 1-1
Principal Modes of Legal Protection for Intellectual Work

	Trade secret	*Patent*	*Copyright*	*Trademark/dress*
			registration; litigation costs	
Licensing and Assignment	Complicated by inherent nature of bargaining (seller wants guarantee before disclosure; buyer wants to know what is offered)	Encouraged by completeness of property rights, subject to antitrust constraints	Assignor has termination right between 36th and 41st years following transfer	No naked licenses (owner must monitor licensee); no sales of trademark "in gross"
Remedies	Civil suit for misappropriation; conversion, unjust enrichment, breach of contract; damages (potentially treble) and injunctive relief; criminal prosecution for theft	Injunctive relief and damages (potentially treble); attorney fees (in exceptional cases)	Injunction against further infringement; destruction of infringing articles; damages (actual or profits); statutory ($200–$150,000 damages within court's discretion); attorney fees (within court's discretion); criminal prosecution	Injunction; accounting for profits; damages (potentially treble); attorney fees (in exceptional cases); seizure and destruction of infringing goods; criminal prosecution for trafficking in counterfeit goods or services

1.   Trade Secret

Trade secret protection arises from state law statutes and common law doctrines that protect against the misappropriation of confidential information that is the subject of reasonable efforts to maintain secrecy. As such, they are more akin to traditional tort and contract law than to patent or copyright law. While protection for trade secrets has long been a part of the common law, most states today protect trade secrets by statute. The federal government has taken a growing interest in protecting trade secrets as concerns about international espionage and hacking have grown. The purpose of protecting trade secrets is to prevent "theft" of information by unfair or commercially unreasonable means. In essence, trade secret law is a form of *private* intellectual property law under which creators establish contractual limitations or build legal "fences" that afford protection from misappropriation.

The definition of subject matter eligible for protection is quite broad: business or technical information of any sort. To be protected by trade secret laws, the information must be a secret. However, only relative and not absolute secrecy is required. In addition, the owner of a trade secret must take reasonable steps to maintain its secrecy. Trade secrets have no definite term of protection but may be protected only as long as they are secret. Once a trade secret is disclosed, protection is lost.

There is no state agency that "issues" (or even registers) trade secrets. Rather, any information that meets the above criteria can be protected. Courts will find misappropriation of trade secrets in two circumstances: (1) where the secrets were obtained by theft or other improper means, or where they were used; or (2) disclosed in violation of a confidential relationship agreement. However, trade secret laws do not protect against independent discovery or invention. Nor do they prevent competitors from "reverse engineering" a legally obtained product to determine the secrets contained inside. Violations of trade secret law entitle the owner to damages and in some cases injunctions against use or further disclosure.

2.   Patent

Patent law is the classic example of an intellectual property regime modeled on the utilitarian framework. Following the constitutional authorization to promote progress in the "useful Arts," what we would today call technology and scientific discovery, patent law offers the possibility of a limited period of exclusive rights to encourage research and development aimed at discovering new processes, machines, articles of manufacture, and compositions of matter, and improvements thereof. The public benefits directly through the spur to innovation and disclosure of new technology. After the term of the patent expires, the innovation becomes part of the public domain, freely available to all.

To obtain a utility patent, an inventor must submit an application to the Patent and Trademark Office (PTO) that meets five requirements: patentable subject matter, usefulness, novelty, nonobviousness, and disclosure sufficient to enable others skilled in the art to make and use the invention. While the threshold for usefulness is low, the novelty and non-obviousness standards are substantial, and the PTO conducts an independent review of the application to ensure that it meets these requirements. If the PTO grants the patent, the inventor obtains exclusive rights to make, use, and sell the innovation for a term of up to 20 years (from the application filing date). The patent grant is nearly absolute, barring even those who independently develop the invention from practicing its art. Infringement will be found where the accused device, composition, or process embodies all of the elements of a valid patent claim (or accomplishes substantially the same function in substantially the same way to achieve the same result).

The PTO also issues plant patents for distinctive plants and design patents for ornamental designs for articles of manufacture. Design patents have a term of 15 years (from issuance).

3. Copyright

Although the copyright and patent laws flow from the same constitutional basis and share the same general approach—statutorily created monopolies to foster progress—they feature different elements and rights, reflecting the very different fields of human ingenuity that they seek to encourage. In general, copyrights are easier to secure and last substantially longer than patents, although the scope of protection afforded copyrights is narrower and less absolute than that given to patents.

Copyright law covers the broad range of literary and artistic expression—including books, poetry, song, dance, dramatic works, computer programs, movies, sculpture, and paintings. Ideas themselves are not copyrightable, but the author's particular expression of an idea is protectable. A work must exhibit a modicum of originality and be fixed in a "tangible medium of expression" to receive protection. Copyright protection attaches as soon as a work is fixed. There is no examination by a governmental authority, although the Copyright Office registers copyrightable works. Such registration is no longer required for validity, but U.S. authors must register their works prior to filing an infringement suit. A copyright lasts for the life of the author plus 70 years or a total of 95 years in the case of entity authors.

The breadth and ease of acquisition of copyright protection are balanced by the more limited rights that copyright law confers. Ownership of a valid copyright protects a copyright holder from unauthorized copying, public performance, and display, and it entitles the holder to make derivative works and to control sale and distribution of the work. These rights, however, are limited in a number of ways. Others may make "fair use" of the material in certain circumstances. The Copyright Act also establishes compulsory licensing for musical compositions and cable television. A limited set of moral rights protects against misattribution or destruction of a narrow class of works of visual art.

Copyright law protects only against *copying* of protected expression. Independent creation of a copyrighted work does not violate the Copyright Act, nor does copying the unprotected elements of a work. Therefore, copyright law must have some mechanism for determining when a work has been copied illegally. While in rare cases direct proof of copying may be available, usually it is not. In its place, courts infer copying from proof that the defendant has had *access* to the plaintiff's work combined with evidence that the two works are *similar.* Even if copying is established, it must be further shown that the defendant's work is *substantially similar* to protected elements (e.g., excluding ideas) of the plaintiff's work.

With the proliferation of digital technology, Congress has augmented traditional copyright protection by prohibiting the circumvention of technical protection measures intended to prevent unauthorized use and distribution of copyrighted works and alteration of copyright management information. These new rights are subject to various exceptions and limitations.

4. Trademark/Trade Dress

Trademarks are also protected by state statute and common law as well as federal statute, although the source of constitutional authority is different from that of the Patent and Copyright Acts. Rather than deriving from a specific grant of constitutional power, federal power to regulate trademarks and unfair competition is based on the Commerce Clause, which authorizes Congress to regulate foreign and interstate commerce. Unlike patent and copyright protection, trademark law did not evolve from a desire to stimulate particular types of economic activity. Rather, its original purpose was to protect consumers from unscrupulous sellers attempting to fly under the banner of someone else's logo or identifying symbol. Trademark law has more recently embraced incentive and natural rights rationales. The Lanham Act (the federal trademark statute) protects words, symbols, and other attributes that serve to identify the nature and source of goods or services. Examples of marks protectable under the Lanham Act include corporate and product names, symbols, logos, slogans, pictures and designs, product configurations, colors, and even smells. Not all such marks are protectable, however. To receive trademark protection, a mark need not be new or previously unused, but it must represent to consumers the source of the good or service identified. It cannot be merely a description of the good itself or a generic term for the class of goods or services offered. Further, the identifying mark may not be a functional element of the product itself but must serve a purely identifying purpose. Since 1996, famous marks also receive federal protection against "dilution" by blurring or tarnishment. Finally, trademark protection is directly tied to the use of the mark to identify goods in commerce. Trademarks do not expire on any particular date but continue in force until they are "abandoned" by their owner or become unprotectable.

The PTO examines trademark applications and issues trademark registrations that confer significant benefits upon the registrants, including prima facie evidence of validity; constructive notice to others of the claim of ownership; federal subject matter jurisdiction; incontestability after five years, which confers exclusive right to use the mark; authorization to seek treble damages and attorney fees; and the right to bar importation of goods bearing the infringing mark. Federal trademark registration, however, is not necessary to obtain trademark protection. A trademark owner who believes that another is using the same or a similar mark to identify competing goods can bring suit for trademark infringement. Infringement turns on whether consumers are likely to be confused as to the origin of the goods or services. If so, the trademark owner is entitled to an injunction against the confusing use, damages for past infringement, and in some cases the seizure and destruction of infringing goods.

PROBLEM

Problem I-3

MEMORANDUM
To: Associate
From: Senior Partner
Re: HEALTHWARE Inc.

Janet Peterson called me yesterday about a new venture that she plans to try to get off the ground. As you may know, Janet is a computer programmer and a registered nurse. She has an interesting idea for a new venture and would like our advice on how she might structure the business to have the best potential for success.

She would like to call the venture Healthware. Janet believes that she can tap into the diet/health/environmental/mobile device craze by developing a user-friendly app that would monitor the user's diet and fitness activity. The user would input information on his or her health (e.g., age, weight, medical history, dietary restrictions). Each day, the program would collect information on the user's diet and physical exercise. An accelerometer built into the user's smartphone would collect exercise information. The user could manually enter their food consumption, or could use a Quick Response Code (a matrix barcode) reader to scan dietary information on a growing array of packaged and restaurant foods. The software would periodically provide an analysis of the user's health, as well as suggestions for achieving the user's goals, whether weight reduction, better fitness, or general health. In addition, the program would compile a record of the user's activities which they could bring to annual physicals. Other subroutines would be available for pregnant and lactating women, children, the elderly, diabetics, vegetarians, triathletes, etc.

Janet thinks that she could put together the diverse people necessary to pull this project off: programmers, a nutritionist, a physician, a fitness consultant. She is concerned, however, that one of these people could, after they are familiar with the product, develop a competing program.

What are the options for structuring Healthware? What problems do you foresee in structuring this venture? Assuming that the product is popular, what are the major risks to Healthware's success? How can we structure Healthware so as to overcome these problems?

CHAPTER II:
TRADE SECRET LAW

A. INTRODUCTION

1. Historical Background

The idea that information should be protected against "theft" (which may include the physical taking of tangible goods containing information or simply the copying or memorization of data) is a venerable one in the law. One scholar traces the earliest legal protection against "misappropriation of trade secrets" to the Roman empire. *See* A. Arthur Schiller, *Trade Secrets and the Roman Law: The* Actio Servi Corrupti, 30 COLUM. L. REV. 837 (1930).[1] The Roman courts created a cause of action called "actio servi corrupti" — literally, an action for corrupting a slave. According to Schiller, the actio servi corrupti was used to protect slave owners from third parties who would "corrupt" slaves (by bribery or intimidation) into disclosing their owners' confidential business information. The law made such third parties liable to the slave owner for twice the damages he suffered as a result of the disclosure.

While scholarship has cast some doubt on the enforcement of trade secret protection in the Roman empire, *see* Alan Watson, *Trade Secrets and Roman Law: The Myth Exploded*, 11 TUL. EUR. & CIV. L.F. 19 (1996), the concept that so-called business or "trade secrets" were entitled to legal protection spread rapidly throughout the world. As early as the Renaissance, most European nation-states had laws that protected businesses (notably, the guild cartels) from those who used their secret processes and ideas without permission. During the Industrial Revolution, courts and legislatures translated these early laws into statutes that protected "industrial secrets." Many of these statutes are still in force today, albeit in modified form.

The modern trade secret regime traces most clearly and directly to the Industrial Revolution. In preindustrial economies, craftsmen passed along their knowledge of the trade to their apprentice with the understanding that the know-how would be kept secret during the apprenticeship period. *See* Catherine L. Fisk, *Working Knowledge: Trade Secrets, Restrictive Covenants in Employment, and the Rise of Corporate Intellectual Property*, 1800–1920, 52 HASTINGS L.J. 441, 450-51 (2001). After this train-

---

[1] Arguably, trade secrets existed before this time, albeit in unusual forms. Consider Mark C. Suchman, *Invention and Ritual: Notes on the Interrelation of Magic and Intellectual Property in Preliterate Societies*, 89 COLUM. L. REV. 1264, 1274 (1989):

> [L]et us imagine a hypothetical preliterate inventor who, through diligence or good fortune, discovers that her maize crop is larger when she plants a small fish next to each kernel of corn. . . . Clearly, this technique has economic value and could garner its creator material and social rewards if she could monopolize it and license it for a fee. Unfortunately, the odds of keeping such a discovery secret are slight. . . . [T]he procedure is so simple that even a casual observer could replicate the process. . . . Magic, however, provides a way out of the dilemma. By claiming, for example, that the power of the fish is activated by a talisman that she alone possesses, the inventor can remove her idea from the public domain. . . . [T]he magicked process is far easier to monopolize than the simple technology alone.

ing, the apprentice was free to practice the trade. These protections were reinforced by custom, trade guilds, and close-knit communities. *See* Carlo M. Cipolla, Before the Industrial Revolution: European Economy and Society 1000-1700 (2d ed. 1980).

This informal system, governed principally through social norms and restrictions on apprentice mobility through mandatory periods of service, eroded as industrialization shifted production to factories and labor mobility increased. Factories operated on a far larger scale than traditional craft enterprises and without the social and guild constraints on the dissemination of proprietary techniques and know-how. While patents afforded protection for larger, discrete advances, smaller-bore, incremental know-how was more vulnerable to misappropriation in the impersonal, specialized factory setting. By the early nineteenth century, factory owners in England pressed for a broader form of protection for workplace trade secrets. The know-how behind industrial processes gradually gained recognition and enforcement by common law courts. *See Newbery v. James*, 35 Eng. Rep. 1011, 1011-12 (Ch.) (1817); Fisk, *supra*, at 450-88. The practice spread to the United States by the mid-nineteenth century and developed rapidly. *See Vickery v. Welch*, 36 Mass. (19 Pick.) 523, 525–27 (1837).

Trade secret protection could encompass information that was not generally known to the public so long as the employer undertook reasonable precautions to preserve secrecy. This latter requirement brought non-disclosure agreements ("NDAs") into common practice. Failure to guard against disclosure of trade secrets by employees and contractors would jeopardize trade secret protection.

The emerging law of trade secrets was thus collected in the Restatement of Torts, published in 1939. The Restatement protected as a trade secret any information "used in one's business" that gives its owner "an opportunity to obtain an advantage over competitors who do not know or use it," so long as the information was in fact a secret. When the Restatement (Second) of Torts was published in 1979, the authors omitted sections 757 and 758 on the grounds that the law of trade secrets had developed into an independent body of law that no longer relied on general principles of tort law. Nonetheless, the original Restatement has remained influential because so many judicial decisions have relied on it, and statutes and other key sources have integrated its tenets.

By the mid-twentieth century, "the body of state and federal law that ha[d] traditionally coped with [industrial espionage] languish[ed] in a deepening maze of conflict and confusion." *See* Note, *Theft of Trade Secrets: The Need for a Statutory Solution*, 120 U. Pa. L. Rev. 378 (1971). Recognizing this doctrinal muddle and the growing economic importance of trade secret protection, the American Bar Association established a special committee to investigate the drafting of a uniform trade secret act to harmonize protection among the states in 1968. Over the course of the next decade, that committee drafted and refined the Uniform State Trade Secrets Act

(UTSA), which the National Commission on Uniform State Laws promulgated in 1979. The UTSA has since been adopted by 47 states and the District of Columbia. In the 1990s, the American Law Institute integrated trade secret law into the RESTATE-MENT (THIRD) OF UNFAIR COMPETITION. In 2016, Congress enacted the Defend Trade Secrets Act, which brought uniformity of federal law without significantly changing the rules that have developed in state law. Before turning to these modern sources of trade secret protection, it will useful to examine the principles undergirding trade secret protection.

2. Theoretical Justifications for Trade Secrets

Trade secret law has long been justified on one of two competing grounds. Some treat trade secrets as a form of property, while others view it as a law grounded in unfair competition.

i. *Property Rights*

Some jurists have conceptualized "intellectual property" as a species of the broader concept of "property." In addressing whether government disclosure of proprietary information constituted a taking under the Fifth Amendment to the U.S. Constitution, the Supreme Court held that trade secrets constituted a form of property. *Ruckelshaus v. Monsanto Co.*, 467 U.S. 986, 1001-04 (1984). In finding that trade secrets were "property," the court reasoned in part that "[t]rade secrets have many of the characteristics of more tangible forms of property. A trade secret is assignable. A trade secret can form the res of a trust, and it passes to a trustee in bankruptcy." *Id.* at 1002-04.

Courts routinely characterized trade secrets as "property"[2] and granted injunctive relief to prevent their disclosure. The nature of the "property" interest was, however, limited by the relational character of trade secrets. *See* Robert G. Bone, *A New Look at Trade Secret Law: Doctrine in Search of Justification*, 86 CAL. L. REV. 241, 251-60 (1998). As the court in *Peabody v. Norfolk*, 98 Mass. 452, 458 (1868), noted, if a party "invents or discovers and keeps secret a process of manufacture, whether a proper subject for a patent or not, he has not indeed an exclusive right to it as against the public, or against those who in good faith acquire knowledge of it, but he has property in it which a court of chancery will protect against one who, in violation of contract and breach of confidence, undertakes to apply it to his own use, or to disclose it to third persons." The court explained that courts of equity would intervene to "prevent such a breach of trust, when the injury would be irreparable and the remedy

---

[2] *See, e.g., Tabor v. Hoffman*, 118 N.Y. 30, 23 N.E. 12 (1889) (holding that "independent of copyright or letters patent, an inventor or author has, by the common law, an exclusive property in his invention or composition, until by publication it becomes the property of the general public").

at law inadequate, is well established by authority." Thus, injunctions were available for breaches of trust "in the course of confidential employment."

Treatment of trade secrets as property rights vested in the trade secret "owner" is consistent with a view of trade secrets law as providing an additional incentive to innovate, beyond those provided in patent law. The Supreme Court has offered some support for this incentive view:

> Certainly the patent policy of encouraging invention is not disturbed by the existence of another form of incentive to invention. In this respect the two systems are not and never would be in conflict. . . .

> Trade secret law will encourage invention in areas where patent law does not reach, and will prompt the independent innovator to proceed with the discovery and exploitation of his invention. Competition is fostered and the public is not deprived of the use of valuable, if not quite patentable, invention.

Kewanee Oil Co. v. Bicron Corp., 416 U.S. 470, 481-85 (1974).

ii. *Tort Law*

An alternate explanation for much of trade secrets law is what might be described as a "duty-based" theory, or what Melvin Jager calls "the maintenance of commercial morality." 1 MELVIN JAGER, TRADE SECRETS LAW §1.03, at 1-4. As noted above, Justice Oliver Wendell Holmes questioned the "property" view of trade secrets in *E.I. du Pont & Co. v. Masland*, 244 U.S. 100, 102 (1917), preferring to characterize these rights in relational terms. As Justice Holmes explained,

> the word 'property' as applied to . . . trade secrets is an unanalyzed expression of certain secondary consequences of the primary fact that the law makes some rudimentary requirements of good faith. Whether the plaintiffs have any valuable secret or not, the defendant knows the facts, whatever they are, through a special confidence that he accepted. The property may be denied, but the confidence cannot be. Therefore, the starting point for the present matter is not property or due process of law, but that the defendant stood in confidential relations with the plaintiffs.

E.I. duPont de Nemours Powder Co. v. Masland, 244 U.S. 100, 102 (1917).[3] Closely related to *Masland*'s theory of "breach of confidence" is the contract basis for trade secret law. While not always applicable, many trade secret cases arise out of a "duty" explicitly stated in a contract, such as a technology license or an employment agreement. The tort-based theory of breach of duty merges in those cases with a standard common law action for breach of contract. *Cf.* Robert G. Bone, *A New Look at Trade*

---

[3] The *Monsanto* Court attempted to distinguish *Masland* in a footnote, claiming that "Justice Holmes did not deny the existence of a property interest; he simply deemed determination of the existence of that interest irrelevant to the resolution of the case." *Monsanto*, 467 U.S. 1004 n.9.

Secret Law: Doctrine in Search of Justification, 86 CAL. L. REV. 241 (1998) (questioning any distinct theoretical justification for trade secret law and arguing that contract and tort doctrines provide a proper foundation).

Trade secret law has long been grounded in what has been termed "commercial morality." *See* MELVIN F. JAGER, TRADE SECRETS LAW §1:3 (2013) ("[t]he Anglo-American common law . . . began to develop protection for business secrets to enhance commercial morality and good-faith dealings in business"); Bone, 86 CAL. L. REV. at 244 ("Trade secret law is grounded in "relationally specific duties," such as "disloyal employees who use or disclose their employers' secrets in violation of a duty of confidence stemming from the employer-employee relationship").

The *Eastman* case illustrates the principle in action. *See Eastman Co. v. Reichenbach*, 20 N.Y.S. 110, 110, 116 (N.Y. Sup. Ct. 1892), *aff'd sub nom. Eastman Kodak Co. v. Reighenbach*, 29 N.Y.S. 1143 (N.Y. Gen. Term 1894). In the late nineteenth century, Eastman (Kodak), a pioneering developer of photographic technology, brought suit against former high-level employees who departed to start a competing business using secret information that they helped develop at Eastman. They had executed assignment agreements covering all inventions, discoveries, and improvements in photography that they might make, discover, or invent while at Eastman and agreed to maintain company secrets in strict confidence and not to disclose or make improper use of them. The court enjoined defendants' competing venture on the ground that

> [t]his is not legitimate competition, which it is always the policy of the law to foster and encourage, but it is *contra bonos mores* [against good morals], and constitutes a breach of trust which a court of law, and much less a court of equity, should not tolerate.

20 N.Y.S. at 116.

This theme pervades trade secret law. As the Supreme Court recognized in *Kewanee Oil Co. v. Bicron Corp.*, 416 U.S. 470 (1974), its landmark decision holding that federal patent law does not preempt state trade secret protection, "[t]he maintenance of standards of commercial ethics and the encouragement of invention are the broadly stated policies behind trade secret law. 'The necessity of good faith and honest faith dealing is the very life and spirit of the commercial world.'" *Id.* at 481–82 (1974) (quoting *National Tube Co. v. Eastern Tube Co.*, 3 Ohio Cir.Ct.R., N.S., 459, 462 (1902), *aff'd*, 69 Ohio St. 560, 70 N.E. 1127 (1903)).

iii.   *A Third Way?*

Professor Mark Lemley argues that trade secrets make sense not so much as real property, but as *intellectual* property—that is, as government policy designed to promote innovation and, ironically, to encourage efficient disclosure of secrets. Mark A.

Lemley, *The Surprising Virtues of Treating Trade Secrets as IP Rights*, 61 STAN. L. REV. 311 (2008).

The promotion of innovation principle resonates with a property view of trade secrets. Protecting against the theft of proprietary information encourages investment in such information. By contrast, the commercial morality concern aims to deter wrongful acts and is therefore sometimes described as a tort theory. Here the aim of trade secret law is to punish and prevent illicit behavior and even to uphold reasonable standards of commercial behavior. Under the tort theory trade secret protection is not explicitly about encouraging investments. It is plain, however, that one consequence of deterring wrongful behavior would be to encourage investment in trade secrets. Hence, despite their conceptual differences, the tort and property/incentive approaches to trade secrets may well push in the same direction.

The *Kewanee Oil* opinion similarly recognized an IP-related goal of trade secret protection: encouragement of research and development. The Court recognized that

> even though a discovery may not be patentable, that does not destroy the value of the discovery to one who makes it, or advantage the competitor who by unfair means, or as the beneficiary of a broken faith, obtains the desired knowledge without himself paying the price in labor, money, or machines expended by the discoverer.

Id. at 482 (quoting *A. O. Smith Corp. v. Petroleum Iron Works Co.*, 73 F.2d 531, 539 (6th Cir. 1934). The Court emphasized "the importance of trade secret protection to the subsidization of research and development and to increased economic efficiency within large companies through the dispersion of responsibilities for creative developments." *See id.* (citing *Wexler v. Greenberg*, 399 Pa. 569, 578-79, 160 A.2d 430, 434-435 (Penn. S.Ct. 1960)). This aligns with Justice Gray's declaration, in an early seminal case, that "it is the policy of the law, for the advantage of the public, to encourage and protect invention and commercial enterprise." *Peabody v. Norfolk*, 98 Mass. at 458.

3. Overview of Modern Trade Secret Protection

Today, every one of the United States protects trade secrets in some form or another. Improper use or disclosure of a trade secret was traditionally a common law tort. As noted earlier, the Uniform Trade Secrets Act has come to unify trade secret protection notwithstanding its predominately state law foundation. The RESTATEMENT OF TORTS, §§757, 758 as well as the RESTATEMENT (THIRD) OF UNFAIR COMPETITION also serve as valuable sources for navigating trade secret protection.

Only New York, North Carolina, and Massachusetts have not adopted the UTSA, although North Carolina's trade secret statute borrows heavily from the UTSA. New York and Massachusetts protect trade secrets under common law, applying the Restatement of Torts framework. Because of the Uniform Act's importance, we reproduce its primary provisions here.

Uniform Trade Secrets Act, with 1985 Amendments

§1. Definitions

As used in this [Act], unless the context requires otherwise:

(1) "Improper means" includes theft, bribery, misrepresentation, breach or inducement of a breach of a duty to maintain secrecy, or espionage through electronic or other means;

(2) "Misappropriation" means:

(i) acquisition of a trade secret of another by a person who knows or has reason to know that the trade secret was acquired by improper means; or

(ii) disclosure or use of a trade secret of another without express or implied consent by a person who

(A) used improper means to acquire knowledge of the trade secret; or

(B) at the time of disclosure or use, knew or had reason to know that his knowledge of the trade secret was

(I) derived from or through a person who had utilized improper means to acquire it;

(II) acquired under circumstances giving rise to a duty to maintain its secrecy or limit its use; or

(III) derived from or through a person who owed a duty to the person seeking relief to maintain its secrecy or limit its use; or

(C) before a material change of his [or her] position, knew or had reason to know that it was a trade secret and that knowledge of it had been acquired by accident or mistake. . . .

(4) "Trade secret" means information, including a formula, pattern, compilation, program, device, method, technique, or process, that:

(i) derives independent economic value, actual or potential, from not being generally known to, and not being readily ascertainable by proper means by, other persons who can obtain economic value from its disclosure or use, and

(ii) is the subject of efforts that are reasonable under the circumstances to maintain its secrecy.

The federal Defend Trade Secrets Act, enacted in 2016, was "modeled on the Uniform Trade Secrets Act," H. Rep. No. 114-529, 114th Cong., 2d Sess., Defend Trade Secrets Act of 2016, (2016). It defines both trade secret and misappropriation using the language of the UTSA. The DTSA augments the UTSA by defining "improper means":

(A) includes theft, bribery, misrepresentation, breach or inducement of a breach of a duty to maintain secrecy, or espionage through electronic or other means; and

(B) does not include reverse engineering, independent derivation, or any other lawful means of acquisition.

A trade secret claim can be broken down into three essential elements. First, the subject matter involved must qualify for trade secret protection: it must be the type of knowledge or information that trade secret law was meant to protect, and it must not be generally known to all. On eligible subject matter, the current trend, exemplified once again by the UTSA, is to protect as a trade secret any valuable information so long as the information is capable of adding economic value to the plaintiff. The requirement that the information not be generally known follows from the label trade secret. The requirement is meant to ensure that no one claims intellectual property protection for information commonly known in a trade or industry.

The second element to be established by the plaintiff in a trade secret case is that the plaintiff, holder of the trade secret, took *reasonable precautions* under the circumstances to prevent its disclosure. Courts have shown some confusion over the rationale for this requirement. Some see in it evidence that the trade secret is valuable enough to bother litigating; others argue that where the plaintiff has taken reasonable precautions, chances are that a defendant acquired the trade secret wrongfully. Whatever the justification, it is clear that no one may let information about products and operations flow freely to competitors at one time and then later claim that competitors have wrongfully acquired valuable trade secrets. To establish the right to sue later, one must be consistently diligent in protecting information. As always, however, the presence of the term "reasonable" ensures close cases and difficult line-drawing for courts, a theme reflected in several of the cases that follow.

Finally, a trade secret plaintiff also must prove that the defendant acquired the information wrongfully—in a word, that the defendant *misappropriated* the trade secret. Just because a person's information is valuable does not make it wrong for another to use it or disclose it. But use or disclosure is wrong, in the eyes of trade secret law, when the information is acquired through deception, skullduggery, or outright theft. As we will see in the cases that follow, close cases abound in this area because of the creativity of competitors in rooting out information about their rivals' businesses and products.

In many cases, a defendant's use or disclosure is wrongful because of a preexisting obligation to the plaintiff not to disclose or appropriate the trade secret. Such an obligation can arise in either of two ways: explicitly, by contract; and implicitly, because of an *implied duty*. A classic example of an implied duty is the case of an employee. Even in the absence of an explicit contract, most employees are held to have a duty to protect their employers' interests in their secret practices and information. Even where the duty arises by explicit contract, however, public policy limitations on the scope and duration of the agreement will often come into play, in some cases resulting in substantial judicial modification of the explicit obligations laid out in the contract.

B. SUBJECT MATTER

1. Defining Trade Secrets

Metallurgical Industries Inc. v. Fourtek, Inc.
United States Court of Appeals for the Fifth Circuit
790 F.2d 1195 (5th Cir. 1986)

GEE, Circuit Judge:

Today's case requires us to review Texas law on the misappropriation of trade secrets. Having done so, we conclude that the district court misconceived the nature and elements of this cause of action, a misconception that led it to direct a verdict erroneously in favor of appellee Bielefeldt. We also conclude that the court abused its discretion in excluding certain evidence. Accordingly, we affirm in part, reverse in part, and remand the case for a new trial.

I. Facts of the Case

We commence with a brief description of the scientific process concerned. Tungsten carbide is a metallic compound of great value in certain industrial processes. Combined with the metal cobalt, it forms an extremely hard alloy known as "cemented tungsten carbide" used in oil drills, tools for manufacturing metals, and wear-resistant coatings. Because of its great value, reclamation of carbide from scrap metals is feasible. For a long time, however, the alloy's extreme resistance to machining made reclamation difficult. In the late 1960's and early 1970's, a new solution — known as the zinc recovery process — was devised, a solution based on carbide's reaction with zinc at high temperatures. In the crucibles of a furnace, molten zinc will react with the cobalt in the carbide to cause swelling and cracking of the scrap metal. After this has occurred, the zinc is distilled from the crucible, leaving the scrap in a more brittle state. The carbide is then ground into a powder, usable in new products as an alternative to virgin carbide. This process is the generally recognized modern method of carbide reclamation.

Metallurgical Industries has been in the business of reclaiming carbide since 1976, using the more primitive "cold-stream process." In the mid-1970's, Metallurgical began to consider using the zinc recovery process. In that connection, it came to know appellee Irvin Bielefeldt, a representative of Therm-O-Vac Engineering & Manufacturing Company (Therm-O-Vac). Negotiations led to a contract authorizing Therm-O-Vac to design and construct two zinc recovery furnaces, the purchase order for the first being executed in July 1976.

The furnace arrived in April 1977. Dissatisfied with its performance, Metallurgical modified it extensively. First, it inserted chill plates in one part of the furnace to create a better temperature differential for distilling the zinc. Second, Metallurgical replaced the one large crucible then in place with several smaller crucibles to prevent the zinc from dispersing in the furnace. Third, it replaced segmented heating elements which had caused electric arcing with unitary graphite heating elements. Last, it installed a filter in the furnace's vacuum-pumps, which zinc particles had continually clogged. These efforts proved successful and the modified furnace soon began commercial operation.

. . . [M]etallurgical returned to Therm-O-Vac for its second furnace. A purchase order was signed in January 1979, and the furnace arrived that July. Further modifications again had to be made, but commercial production was allegedly achieved in January 1980.

In 1980, after Therm-O-Vac went bankrupt, Bielefeldt and three other former Therm-O-Vac employees — Norman Montesino, Gary Boehm, and Michael Sarvadi — formed Fourtek, Incorporated. Soon thereafter, Fourtek agreed to build a zinc recovery furnace for appellee Smith International, Incorporated (Smith). . . .

Metallurgical . . . brought a diversity action against Smith, Bielefeldt, Montesino, Boehm, and Sarvadi in November 1981. In its complaint, Metallurgical charged the defendants with misappropriating its trade secrets. . . . [Trial] testimony indicated Metallurgical's frequent notices to Bielefeldt that the process was a secret and that the disclosures to him were made in confidence. Another witness recounted meetings in which the modifications were agreed to. Bielefeldt was allegedly unconvinced about the efficacy of these changes and contributed little to the discussion. Metallurgical also presented evidence that it had expended considerable time, effort, and money to modify the furnaces.

[The district court nonetheless granted defendants' motions for directed verdicts.] The principal reason advanced was the court's conclusion that no trade secret is involved. At trial, Metallurgical acknowledged that the individual changes, by themselves, are not secrets; chill plates and pump filters, for example, are well-known. Metallurgical's position instead was that the process, taken as a whole, is a trade secret in the carbide business. The court, however, refused to recognize any protection Texas law provides to a modification process. It also concluded that the information

Bielefeldt obtained from working with Metallurgical is too general to be legally protected. Finally, it ruled that "negative know-how"—the knowledge of what not to do — is unprotected. . . .

III. Defining a "Trade Secret"

We begin by reviewing the legal definition of a trade secret. Of course, to qualify as one, the subject matter involved must, in fact, be a secret; "matters of general knowledge in an industry cannot be appropriated by one as his secret." *Wissman v. Boucher*, 150 Tex. 326, 240 S.W.2d 278, 280 (Tex. 1951); *see also Zoecon Industries v. American Stockman Tag Co.*, 713 F.2d 1174, 1179 (5th Cir. 1983) ("a customer list of readily ascertainable names and addresses will not be protected as a trade secret"). Smith emphasizes the absence of any secret because the basic zinc recovery process has been publicized in the trade. Acknowledging the publicity of the zinc recovery process, however, we nevertheless conclude that Metallurgical's particular modification efforts can be as yet unknown to the industry. A general description of the zinc recovery process reveals nothing about the benefits unitary heating elements and vacuum pump filters can provide to that procedure. That the scientific principles involved are generally known does not necessarily refute Metallurgical's claim of trade secrets.

Metallurgical, furthermore, presented evidence to back up its claim. One of its main witnesses was Arnold Blum, a consultant very influential in the decisions to modify the furnaces. Blum testified as to his belief that Metallurgical's changes were unknown in the carbide reclamation industry. The evidence also shows Metallurgical's efforts to keep secret its modifications. Blum testified that he noted security measures taken to conceal the furnaces from all but authorized personnel. The furnaces were in areas hidden from public view, while signs warned all about restricted access. Company policy, moreover, required everyone authorized to see the furnace to sign a non-disclosure agreement. These measures constitute evidence probative of the existence of secrets. One's subjective belief of a secret's existence suggests that the secret exists. Security measures, after all, cost money; a manufacturer therefore presumably would not incur these costs if it believed its competitors already knew about the information involved. In *University Computing Co. v. Lykes-Youngstown Corp.*, 504 F.2d 518, 535 (5th Cir. 1974), we regarded subjective belief as a factor to consider in determining whether secrecy exists. Because evidence of security measures is relevant, that shown here helps us conclude that a reasonable jury could have found the existence of the requisite secrecy.

Smith argues, however, that Metallurgical's disclosure to other parties vitiated the secrecy required to obtain legal protection. Metallurgical revealed its information to Consarc Corporation in 1978; it also disclosed information in 1980 to La Floridienne, its European licensee of carbide reclamation technology. Because both these disclosures occurred before Bielefeldt allegedly misappropriated the knowledge of modifications, others knew of the information when the Smith furnace was built. This being so, Smith argues, no trade secret in fact existed.

Although the law requires secrecy, it need not be absolute. Public revelation would, of course, dispel all secrecy, but the holder of a secret need not remain totally silent:

> He may, without losing his protection, communicate to employees involved in its use. He may likewise communicate it to others pledged to secrecy. . . . Nevertheless, a substantial element of secrecy must exist, so that except by the use of improper means, there would be difficulty in acquiring the information.

RESTATEMENT OF TORTS, §757 Comment *b* (1939). We conclude that a holder may divulge his information to a limited extent without destroying its status as a trade secret. To hold otherwise would greatly limit the holder's ability to profit from his secret. If disclosure to others is made to further the holder's economic interests, it should, in appropriate circumstances, be considered a limited disclosure that does not destroy the requisite secrecy. The only question is whether we are dealing with a limited disclosure here. . . .

Looking . . . to the policy considerations involved, we glean two reasons why Metallurgical's disclosures to others are limited and therefore insufficient to extinguish the secrecy Metallurgical's other evidence has suggested. First, the disclosures were not public announcements; rather, Metallurgical divulged its information to only two businesses with whom it was dealing. This case thus differs from *Luccous v. J. C. Kinley Co.*, 376 S.W.2d 336 (Tex. 1964), in which the court concluded that the design of a device could not be a trade secret because it had been patented — and thus revealed to all the world — before any dealing between the parties. Second, the disclosures were made to further Metallurgical's economic interests. Disclosure to Consarc was made with the hope that Consarc could build the second furnace. A long-standing agreement gave La Floridienne the right, as a licensee, to the information in exchange for royalty payments. Metallurgical therefore revealed its discoveries as part of business transactions by which it expected to profit.

Metallurgical's case would have been stronger had it also presented evidence of confidential relationships with these two companies, but we are unwilling to regard this failure as conclusively disproving the limited nature of the disclosures. Smith correctly points out that Metallurgical bears the burden of showing the existence of confidential relationships. Contrary to Smith's assertion, however, confidentiality is not a requisite; it is only a factor to consider. Whether a disclosure is limited is an issue the resolution of which depends on weighing many facts. The inference from those facts, construed favorably to Metallurgical, is that it wished only to profit from its secrets in its business dealings, not to reveal its secrets to the public. We therefore are unpersuaded by Smith's argument.

Existing law, however, emphasizes other requisites for legal recognition of a trade secret. In *Huffines*, 314 S.W.2d 763, a seminal case of trade secret law, Texas adopted the widely-recognized pronouncements of the American Law Institute's Restatement of the Law. The Texas Supreme Court quoted the Restatement's definition of a trade secret:

> A trade secret may consist of any formula, pattern, device, or compilation of information which is used in one's business, and which gives him an opportunity to obtain an advantage over competitors who do not know or use it. It may be a chemical compound, a process of manufacturing, treating or preserving materials, a pattern for a machine or other device or a list of customers.

Id. at 776, quoting RESTATEMENT OF TORTS, §757 Comment *b* (1939). From this the criterion of value to the holder of the alleged secret arises. . . .

Metallurgical met the burden of showing the value of its modifications. Lawrence Lorman, the company's vice president, testified that the zinc recovery process gave Metallurgical an advantage over its two competitors by aiding in the production of the highest quality reclaimed carbide powder. The quality of the powder, in fact, makes it an alternative to the more costly virgin carbide. Lorman testified that customers regarded Metallurgical's zinc reclaimed powder as a better product than that reclaimed by the coldstream process used by others. This evidence clearly indicates that the modifications that led to the commercial operation of the zinc recovery furnace provided a clear advantage over the competition.

Another requisite is the cost of developing the secret device or process. In *Huffines'* companion case, *K&G Oil, Tool & Service Co. v. G&G Fishing Tool Service*, 158 Tex. 594, 314 S.W.2d 782, 790, 117 U.S.P.Q. (BNA) 471 (Tex. 1958), the court recognized the cost involved in developing the device in question; "the record shows . . . that much work and ingenuity have been applied to the development of a practical and successful device." *See also Zoecon Industries*, 713 F.2d at 1179 ("even if the names and addresses were readily ascertainable through trade journals as the defendants allege, the other information could be compiled only at considerable expense"). No question exists that Metallurgical expended much time, effort, and money to make the necessary changes. It clearly has met the burden of demonstrating the effort involved in making a complex manufacturing process work.

That the cost of devising the secret and the value the secret provides are criteria in the legal formulation of a trade secret shows the equitable underpinnings of this area of the law. It seems only fair that one should be able to keep and enjoy the fruits of his labor. If a businessman has worked hard, has used his imagination, and has taken bold steps to gain an advantage over his competitors, he should be able to profit from his efforts. Because a commercial advantage can vanish once the competition learns of it, the law should protect the businessman's efforts to keep his achievements secret. As is discussed below, this is an area of law in which simple fairness still plays a large role.

We do not say, however, that all these factors need exist in every case. Because each case must turn on its own facts, no standard formula for weighing the factors can be devised. Secrecy is always required, of course, but beyond that there are no universal requirements. In a future case, for example, should the defendant's breach of confidence be particularly egregious, the injured party might still seek redress in court despite the possibility that the subject matter was discovered at little or no cost or that the object of secrecy is not of great value to him. The definition of "trade secret" will therefore be determined by weighing all equitable considerations. It is easy to recognize the possibility of a trade secret here, however, because Metallurgical presented evidence of all three factors discussed above. . . .

COMMENTS AND QUESTIONS

1. Sales of goods in mass retail markets are made to further the seller's economic interests. Under the rationale in *Fourtek*, why do such sales destroy the value of the secret?

2. If the defendants had acquired information about Metallurgical's process from Consarc or La Floridienne — the Metallurgical licensees — would the case have come out differently? Should it matter whether they acquired the information with knowledge that Metallurgical still considered it a trade secret?

3. The categories of information eligible for protection as trade secrets are quite expansive. As *Fourtek* makes clear, they include secret combinations of items which by themselves are publicly known. They also include both scientific and technical information and business information, such as customer lists and business plans. Can you think of any type of information that should not qualify for trade secret protection?

Note that eligibility for protection is only the first of many hurdles required to establish the existence of a trade secret. Many alleged trade secrets that are *eligible* for protection do not, in fact, receive protection because they do not meet one of the other standards described in this section. Courts have frequently held certain basic ideas or concepts incapable of protection as secrets because they were too well known to derive value from secrecy. For example, in *Buffets, Inc. v. Klinke*, 73 F.3d 765 (9th Cir. 1996), the court held that the plaintiff could not claim its relatively straightforward recipes for barbecued chicken and macaroni and cheese as trade secrets. On the other hand, in *Camp Creek Hospitality Inns v. Sheraton Franchise Corp.*, 139 F.3d 1396 (11th Cir. 1997), the court held that a hotel could protect information about its prices, discounts, and occupancy levels as a trade secret where it was closely guarded information in the industry. And in *Nextdoor.com, Inc. v. Abhyanker*, 2013 WL 3802526 (N.D. Cal. July 19, 2013), the court held that the decision to test a new neighborhood-oriented social network in a particular neighborhood could be a trade secret where the plaintiff did substantial investigation before deciding that that neighborhood was a particularly appropriate one in which to launch the network.

4. Courts have made it clear that trade secrets need not be novel to receive trade secret protection. The idea may have occurred to someone before; it may even be in use by another. But if it is not generally known or readily ascertainable to the competitors in an industry, it may still qualify for trade secret protection. One widely cited decision described the standard for protectable ideas as follows:

> [U]niqueness in the patent law sense is not an essential element of a trade secret, for the patent laws are designed to encourage invention, whereas trade secret law is designed to protect against a breach of faith. However, the trade secret must "possess at least that modicum of originality which will separate it from everyday knowledge." *Cataphote Corporation v. Hudson*, 444 F.2d 1313, 1315 (5th Cir. 1971). As stated in an authoritative treatise on this subject:
>
> > As distinguished from a patent, a trade secret need not be essentially new, novel or unique; therefore, prior art is a less effective defense in a trade secret case than it is in a patent infringement case. The idea need not be complicated; it may be intrinsically simple and nevertheless qualify as a secret, unless it is in common knowledge and, therefore, within the public domain.
>
> 2 CALLMAN, UNFAIR COMPETITION, TRADEMARKS AND MONOPOLIES §52.1 (3d ed. 1968).

Forest Laboratories v. The Pillsbury Co., 425 F.2d 621, 624 (7th Cir. 1971). Some courts have gone even further, suggesting that "[a] trade secret may be no more than 'merely a mechanical improvement that a good mechanic can make.'" *SI Handling Systems, Inc. v. Heisley*, 753 F.2d 1244, 1256 (3d Cir. 1985).

Why not require novelty in order to protect a trade secret? That is, why should the law protect the "secrecy" of a piece of information if others have already discovered it?

5. The Restatement of Torts offers further guidance in determining whether information constitutes a trade secret. It lists six factors to be considered:

- The extent to which the information is known outside the claimant's business.
- The extent to which it is known by employees and others involved in the business.
- The extent of measures taken by the claimant to guard the secrecy of the information.
- The value of the information to the business and its competitors.

- The amount of effort or money expended by the business in developing the information.
- The ease or difficulty with which the information could be properly acquired or duplicated by others.

To be protectable, information must not be "generally known" or "readily ascertainable" by competitors in an industry. *See Burbank Grease Servs. v. Sokolowski*, 693 N.W.2d 89 (Wis. Ct. App. 2005) (Burbank's list of potential customers was readily ascertainable from the Internet, trade associations, and by asking customers whom to contact), *reversed on other grounds*, 717 N.W.2d 781 (Wis. 2006).

6. Why should we bother to protect secrets that were stumbled upon with little or no investment in research but that happen to have "value"? Does the economic rationale for intellectual property suggest that such secrets will be underproduced absent protection?

7. Why is secrecy required at all? Trade secrets are not misappropriated unless information is taken by improper means or from a confidential relationship. Why aren't those tortious elements enough? It is certainly possible to envision a "misappropriation" tort that punishes diversion of information, whether or not it is secret. Indeed, some controversial cases discussed in Chapter VI have created just such a common law tort. In addition to the cases cited there, *see United States Sporting Products v. Johnny Stewart Game Calls*, 865 S.W.2d 214 (Tex. App. 1993) (publicly sold uncopyrighted recordings protectable under a "labor theory"); Note, *The "Genetic Message" from the Cornfields of Iowa: Expanding the Law of Trade Secrets*, 38 Drake L. Rev. 631 (1989) (describing a similar case involving publicly sold grain).

One possible objection to such a scheme is that it may chill the legitimate acquisition of information from competitors. But the only information protected by a misappropriation tort that is not also protected by trade secret law is public information. Since it is public, the need for competitors to acquire it directly from another company or through dubious means is presumably low.[4]

---

[4] Another reason for limiting common law protection to secret information may be concern over preemption of state common law by the federal intellectual property laws. While the course of the law is not completely clear, federal courts have generally held that state laws that create property rights in public information are preempted by the patent and copyright laws. The policy being served by preemption is to protect the balance struck by federal intellectual property laws. *See, e.g., Synercom Technology v. University Computing Co.*, 474 F. Supp. 37 (N.D. Tex. 1979) (state unfair competition laws cannot prevent copying of public information). There are two rationales for such preemption. First, it may be that the federal laws reflect a judgment that unpatentable inventions ought to belong to the public. On this rationale, *see Bonito Boats v. Thunder Craft Boats*, 489 U.S. 141 (1989). Second, preemption may serve to erect barriers between different types of intellectual property protection, "channeling" inventions into one or another form of protection. We discuss federal preemption in more detail in Chapters II(H), III(J), and VI(A).

But there may be a wide gulf between "secret" information and "public" information. If three large companies all use the same process but guard it closely, is it a secret? If a company guards a process closely as a secret, but an account of the process is available in an obscure published source, does the company have a protectable trade secret? Does it matter how obscure the published source is, if the defendant, in fact, obtains the information from the plaintiff rather than going to the public source? What theory of trade secrets would support a finding of liability in such a case? For an argument that the secrecy requirement actually encourages wider disclosure by allowing companies to rely on the law rather than on more stringent physical protections, *see* Mark A. Lemley, *The Surprising Virtues of Treating Trade Secrets as IP Rights*, 61 STAN. L. REV. 311 (2008).

In *Rohm & Haas Co. v. Adco Chemical Co.*, 689 F.2d 424 (3d Cir. 1982), defendant Harvey was a former Rohm & Haas employee who was hired by Adco to duplicate a process for producing "paint delivery vehicles," the chemicals added to paint that allow it to be applied to surfaces easily. There seems no question in the case that Harvey did, in fact, memorize the plaintiff's formula and take it to Adco. In their defense, the defendants offered evidence that a series of prior publications had, in fact, disclosed Rohm & Haas's "secret" process. The court nonetheless concluded that it was a protectable trade secret, in part because the defendants *did not in fact* obtain the information from those publications. Why should this matter? Certainly the defendants' conduct proves that they took the information from the plaintiff, but that should be irrelevant if the plaintiff does not have a protectable secret. Has the *Rohm & Haas* court in effect abolished the requirement of secrecy by requiring only that the defendants in fact obtain the information from the plaintiff?

Rohm & Haas is at the center of a critical debate in trade secret law: whether information must actually be "known" to competitors or merely be "knowable" for the court to conclude that it is not secret. Many courts following the Restatement of Torts have taken the former view, as *Rohm & Haas* does. This view gives broad scope to trade secret law, because it allows a plaintiff to protect information that could have been acquired properly but in fact was not. It also underscores the unfair competition rationale for trade secret protection — the problem is not that the defendant acquired the information at all, but the way in which it was acquired.

In a significant break with the old Restatement rule, the Uniform Trade Secrets Act provides that information is not a trade secret if it is "generally known" or "readily ascertainable by proper means."[5] Under this view, once a secret is readily available through public sources, it loses all trade secret protection. At this point, the defendant is free to obtain the information from the public source *or from the plaintiff herself.* *See* RESTATEMENT (THIRD) OF UNFAIR COMPETITION §39, Comment *f*, at 433 ("When

---

[5] California, by contrast, treats ready ascertainability as a defense, not part of the plaintiff's case. *See* Cal. Civ. Code §3426.1(d)(1); *ABBA Rubber Co. v. Seaquist*, 286 Cal. Rptr. 518 (Ct. App. 1991).

the information is readily ascertainable from such [public] sources, however, actual resort to the public domain is a formality that should not determine liability.").

Even jurisdictions that follow the RESTATEMENT OF TORTS view place some limit on what can qualify for trade secret protection. If information is generally known to the public, or even within a specialized industry, it does not qualify for protection. No company can claim that "$E=mc^2$" is a trade secret, for example, even if it keeps the formula under lock and key, and even if the defendant steals it from the company rather than obtaining it elsewhere. *See Spring Indus. v. Nicolozakes*, 58 U.S.P.Q.2d 1794 (Ohio Ct. App. 2000) (information on gravel mining not a trade secret despite efforts to keep it confidential). We consider the rather different issue of whether two parties could *agree* to treat the formula as a secret in (D), *infra*.

8. What relevance do the competing theories of trade secret protection have for the known vs. knowable debate? If the purpose of trade secret law is to promote innovation, why should a company be entitled to protect an idea that already exists in the literature and can readily be found there? On the other hand, doesn't the tort theory compel the conclusion that a company should be able to protect an idea against being stolen *from it*, even if the idea is commonly known elsewhere?

9. The Restatement factors used in *Forest Labs* seem to focus on how widely the information is known, suggesting that information used by many people cannot be a secret. The secrecy requirement, therefore, may reflect a policy judgment in favor of the distribution of information once it has reached a certain "critical mass." *Metallurgical Industries*, by contrast, focuses on attempts to prevent disclosure of the information. This approach suggests that even widely known information (or published information, as that in *Metallurgical Industries* was) may receive trade secret protection.

Compare the definition of a trade secret offered in the new RESTATEMENT (THIRD) OF UNFAIR COMPETITION:

> A trade secret is any information that can be used in the operation of a business or other enterprise and that is sufficiently valuable and secret to afford an actual or potential economic advantage over others.

RESTATEMENT (THIRD) OF UNFAIR COMPETITION §39. Under the new Restatement, many different companies can possess the same information and each protect it as a secret. *Id.* at illustration 1.[6] In a comment interpreting this provision, the drafters note that "[t]he concept of a trade secret as defined in this Section is intended to be con-

---

[6]. The Restatement does note, however, that "[w]hen information is no longer sufficiently secret to qualify for protection as a trade secret, its use should not serve as a basis for the imposition of liability," *id.* at 433, Comment *f*, suggesting that at some point information is not secret even though companies protect it as if it were.

sistent with the definition of 'trade secret' in §1(4) of the [Uniform Trade Secrets] Act." Is it?

10. Because the definition of trade secrets is so broad, courts are often confronted with arguments that a general combination of information in the plaintiff's product is a secret but that do not specify the actual secrets alleged to be taken. Some courts have required that the plaintiff identify the secrets in question with specificity. *See, e.g.*, *SL Montevideo Tech., Inc. v. Eaton Aerospace, LLC*, 491 F.3d 350, 354 (8th Cir. 2007) ("[s]imply to assert that a trade secret resides in some combination of otherwise known data is not sufficient, as the combination itself must be delineated with some particularity in establishing its trade secret status."); Cal. Code Civ. Proc. 2019.210 (requiring plaintiff to identify the trade secrets with particularity before trial).

PROBLEMS

Problem II-1.   Company *X* possesses a valuable piece of information about the process for making its product. That information is not known at all outside company *X*. Suppose *X* discloses the information to two companies, *A* and *B*. *A* receives the information in confidence, and subject to a written agreement that it will not use or disclose the information outside the bounds of the relationship. *B* receives the information without any restrictions whatever on its use. Does *X* have a protectable trade secret that it can assert against *A*? Against *B*? Against *C*, who steals the information from *X*'s computer network?

Does your answer change if *X*, *A*, *B*, and *C* are the only companies in the industry?

Problem II-2.   StartUp, Inc., is the only participant in a new market. The market is based on a product for which StartUp has a non-exclusive license from the inventor; that is, StartUp cannot prevent others from obtaining a similar license. Nonetheless, StartUp has exhaustively researched the demand for the product, has concluded that a market exists, and has worked to stimulate demand. As a result, it has both "made" a market for the product and developed a comprehensive list of customers.

Thaddeus, a sales representative for StartUp, leaves to found his own company. He gets a license to make the product from its inventor. He takes with him from StartUp the customer list he worked with as an employee, his personal knowledge of and contacts with specific customers, and StartUp's knowledge of the market. StartUp sues Thaddeus for misappropriation of trade secrets. What result?

Problem II-3.   Research Co. is a major pharmaceutical company working on a cure for certain types of cancer. Derek is a molecular biologist employed by Research. After several years on the job, Derek leaves Research for Conglomerate, Inc., another pharmaceutical company, which has decided to work on the same cancer cure. At the time Derek leaves, Research has not been successful in finding a cancer cure. However, as a result of his work at Research, Derek is able to help Conglomerate avoid several unproductive avenues of research. Aided in part by this knowledge, Conglomerate (using scientists other than Derek) develops a cancer cure before Research. Research sues Conglomerate, alleging misappropriation of trade secrets. Does Research have a case?

Problem II-4.   The Church of True Belief is a religious group founded around a set of closely guarded scriptural materials supposedly handed down to Church's elders from Church's deity. After a bitter theological dispute, a group of adherents leaves the church to form the House of Absolute Belief. They take with them a copy of Church's confidential scriptures, which they rely on in gaining adherents and founding the new House. Church sues House for misappropriation of trade secrets.

At trial, the issue is whether the scriptures qualify as a trade secret. The evidence indicates that the scriptures had never before been removed from the confines of Church, that both Church and House are tax-exempt nonprofit organizations which rely on donations for their funding, and that Church (but not House) rations access to the scriptures in proportion to the size of an adherent's donation.

Can the scriptures qualify as a trade secret? Does your answer depend on whether the governing law is the UTSA, the Restatement of Torts, or the Restatement (Third) of Unfair Competition?

Problem II-5.   Pear Computer Corporation, known for its obsessive secrecy, password protects all its files. Can the password itself be a trade secret? Does it matter whether the UTSA or the Restatement applies?

2.   Reasonable Efforts to Maintain Secrecy

Besides the existence of a trade secret, plaintiffs must show under the Uniform Act that they have taken "reasonable measures" to protect the secrecy of their idea. Certainly, a plaintiff cannot publicly disclose the secret and still expect to protect it. But precautions must go further than that. Generally, they must include certain efforts to prevent theft or use of the idea by former employees.

Rockwell Graphic Systems, Inc. v. DEV Industries, Inc.
United States Court of Appeals for the Seventh Circuit
925 F.2d 174 (7th Cir. 1991)

POSNER, Circuit Judge:

This is a suit for misappropriation of trade secrets. Rockwell Graphic Systems, a manufacturer of printing presses used by newspapers, and of parts for those presses, brought the suit against DEV Industries, a competing manufacturer, and against the president of DEV, who used to be employed by Rockwell. . . .

When we said that Rockwell manufactures both printing presses and replacement parts for its presses — "wear parts" or "piece parts," they are called — we were speaking approximately. Rockwell does not always manufacture the parts itself. Sometimes when an owner of one of Rockwell's presses needs a particular part, or when Rockwell anticipates demand for the part, it will subcontract the manufacture of it to an independent machine shop, called a "vendor" by the parties. When it does this it must give the vendor a "piece part drawing" indicating materials, dimensions, tolerances, and methods of manufacture. Without that information the vendor could not manufacture the part. Rockwell has not tried to patent the piece parts. It believes that the purchaser cannot, either by inspection or by "reverse engineering" (taking something apart in an effort to figure out how it was made), discover how to manufacture the part; to do that you need the piece part drawing, which contains much information concerning methods of manufacture, alloys, tolerances, etc. that cannot be gleaned from the part itself. So Rockwell tries — whether hard enough is the central issue in the case — to keep the piece part drawings secret, though not of course from the vendors; they could not manufacture the parts for Rockwell without the drawings. DEV points out that some of the parts are for presses that Rockwell no longer manufactures. But as long as the presses are in service — which can be a very long time — there is a demand for replacement parts.

Rockwell employed Fleck and Peloso in responsible positions that gave them access to piece part drawings. Fleck left Rockwell in 1975 and three years later joined DEV as its president. Peloso joined DEV the following year after being fired by Rockwell when a security guard caught him removing piece part drawings from Rockwell's plant. This suit was brought in 1984, and pretrial discovery by Rockwell turned up 600 piece part drawings in DEV's possession, of which 100 were Rockwell's. DEV claimed to have obtained them lawfully, either from customers of Rockwell or from Rockwell vendors, contrary to Rockwell's claim that either Fleck and Peloso stole them when they were employed by it or DEV obtained them in some other unlawful manner, perhaps from a vendor who violated his confidentiality agreement with Rockwell. Thus far in the litigation DEV has not been able to show which customers or vendors lawfully supplied it with Rockwell's piece part drawings.

The defendants persuaded the magistrate and the district judge that the piece part drawings weren't really trade secrets at all, because Rockwell made only perfunctory efforts to keep them secret. Not only were there thousands of drawings in the hands of the vendors; there were thousands more in the hands of owners of Rockwell presses, the customers for piece parts. The drawings held by customers, however, are not relevant. They are not piece part drawings, but assembly drawings. . . . An assembly drawing shows how the parts of a printing press fit together for installation and also how to integrate the press with the printer's other equipment. Whenever Rockwell sells a printing press it gives the buyer assembly drawings as well. These are the equivalent of instructions for assembling a piece of furniture. Rockwell does not claim that they contain trade secrets. It admits having supplied a few piece part drawings to customers, but they were piece part drawings of obsolete parts that Rockwell has no interest in manufacturing and of a safety device that was not part of the press as originally delivered but that its customers were clamoring for; more to the point, none of these drawings is among those that Rockwell claims DEV misappropriated.

. . . DEV's main argument is that Rockwell was impermissibly sloppy in its efforts to keep the piece part drawings secret.

On this, the critical, issue, the record shows the following. (Because summary judgment was granted to DEV, we must construe the facts as favorably to Rockwell as is reasonable to do.) Rockwell keeps all its engineering drawings, including both piece part and assembly drawings, in a vault. Access not only to the vault, but also to the building in which it is located, is limited to authorized employees who display identification. These are mainly engineers, of whom Rockwell employs 200. They are required to sign agreements not to disseminate the drawings, or disclose their contents, other than as authorized by the company. An authorized employee who needs a drawing must sign it out from the vault and return it when he has finished with it. But he is permitted to make copies, which he is to destroy when he no longer needs them in his work. The only outsiders allowed to see piece part drawings are the vendors (who are given copies, not originals). They too are required to sign confidentiality agreements, and in addition each drawing is stamped with a legend stating that it contains proprietary material. Vendors, like Rockwell's own engineers, are allowed to make copies for internal working purposes, and although the confidentiality agreement that they sign requires the vendor to return the drawing when the order has been filled, Rockwell does not enforce this requirement. The rationale for not enforcing it is that the vendor will need the drawing if Rockwell reorders the part. Rockwell even permits unsuccessful bidders for a piece part contract to keep the drawings, on the theory that the high bidder this round may be the low bidder the next. But it does consider the ethical standards of a machine shop before making it a vendor, and so far as appears no shop has ever abused the confidence reposed in it.

The mere fact that Rockwell gave piece part drawings to vendors—that is, disclosed its trade secrets to "a limited number of outsiders for a particular purpose"— did not forfeit trade secret protection. On the contrary, such disclosure, which is often necessary to the efficient exploitation of a trade secret, imposes a duty of confidentiality on the part of the person to whom the disclosure is made. But with 200 engineers checking out piece part drawings and making copies of them to work from, and numerous vendors receiving copies of piece part drawings and copying them, tens of thousands of copies of these drawings are floating around outside Rockwell's vault, and many of these outside the company altogether. Although the magistrate and the district judge based their conclusion that Rockwell had not made adequate efforts to maintain secrecy in part at least on the irrelevant fact that it took no efforts at all to keep its assembly drawings secret, DEV in defending the judgment that it obtained in the district court argues that Rockwell failed to take adequate measures to keep even the piece part drawings secret. Not only did Rockwell not limit copying of those drawings or insist that copies be returned; it did not segregate the piece part drawings from the assembly drawings and institute more secure procedures for the former. So Rockwell could have done more to maintain the confidentiality of its piece part drawings than it did, and we must decide whether its failure to do more was so plain a breach of the obligation of a trade secret owner to make reasonable efforts to maintain secrecy as to justify the entry of summary judgment for the defendants.

The requirement of reasonable efforts has both evidentiary and remedial significance . . .

[T]he plaintiff must prove that the defendant obtained the plaintiff's trade secret by a wrongful act, illustrated here by the alleged acts of Fleck and Peloso in removing piece part drawings from Rockwell's premises without authorization, in violation of their employment contracts and confidentiality agreements, and using them in competition with Rockwell. Rockwell is unable to prove directly that the 100 piece part drawings it got from DEV in discovery were stolen by Fleck and Peloso or obtained by other improper means. But if it can show that the probability that DEV could have obtained them otherwise — that is, without engaging in wrongdoing — is slight, then it will have taken a giant step toward proving what it must prove in order to recover under the first theory of trade secret protection. The greater the precautions that Rockwell took to maintain the secrecy of the piece part drawings, the lower the probability that DEV obtained them properly and the higher the probability that it obtained them through a wrongful act; the owner had taken pains to prevent them from being obtained otherwise.

. . . . If Rockwell expended only paltry resources on preventing its piece part drawings from falling into the hands of competitors such as DEV, why should the law, whose machinery is far from costless, bother to provide Rockwell with a remedy? The information contained in the drawings cannot have been worth much if Rockwell did not think it worthwhile to make serious efforts to keep the information secret.

The remedial significance of such efforts lies in the fact that if the plaintiff has allowed his trade secret to fall into the public domain, he would enjoy a windfall if permitted to recover damages merely because the defendant took the secret from him, rather than from the public domain as it could have done with impunity. It would be like punishing a person for stealing property that he believes is owned by another but that actually is abandoned property. If it were true, as apparently it is not, that Rockwell had given the piece part drawings at issue to customers, and it had done so without requiring the customers to hold them in confidence, DEV could have obtained the drawings from the customers without committing any wrong. The harm to Rockwell would have been the same as if DEV had stolen the drawings from it, but it would have had no remedy, having parted with its rights to the trade secret. . . .

It is easy to understand therefore why the law of trade secrets requires a plaintiff to show that he took reasonable precautions to keep the secret a secret. If analogies are needed, one that springs to mind is the duty of the holder of a trademark to take reasonable efforts to police infringements of his mark, failing which the mark is likely to be deemed abandoned, or to become generic or descriptive (and in either event be unprotectable). The trademark owner who fails to police his mark both shows that he doesn't really value it very much and creates a situation in which an infringer may have been unaware that he was using a proprietary mark because the mark had drifted into the public domain, much as DEV contends Rockwell's piece part drawings have done.

But only in an extreme case can what is a "reasonable" precaution be determined on a motion for summary judgment, because the answer depends on a balancing of costs and benefits that will vary from case to case and so require estimation and measurement by persons knowledgeable in the particular field of endeavor involved. On the one hand, the more the owner of the trade secret spends on preventing the secret from leaking out, the more he demonstrates that the secret has real value deserving of legal protection, that he really was hurt as a result of the misappropriation of it, and that there really was misappropriation. On the other hand, the more he spends, the higher his costs. The costs can be indirect as well as direct. The more Rockwell restricts access to its drawings, either by its engineers or by the vendors, the harder it will be for either group to do the work expected of it. Suppose Rockwell forbids any copying of its drawings. Then a team of engineers would have to share a single drawing, perhaps by passing it around or by working in the same room, huddled over the drawing. And how would a vendor be able to make a piece part — would Rockwell have to bring all that work in house? Such reconfigurations of patterns of work and production are far from costless; and therefore perfect security is not optimum security.

There are contested factual issues here, bearing in mind that what is reasonable is itself a fact for purposes of Rule 56 of the civil rules. Obviously Rockwell took some precautions, both physical (the vault security, the security guards — one of whom apprehended Peloso in flagrante delicto) and contractual, to maintain the confidentiality of its piece part drawings. Obviously it could have taken more precautions. But at a cost, and the question is whether the additional benefit in security would have exceeded that cost. . . .

Reversed and remanded.

COMMENTS AND QUESTIONS

1. There is an intuitive relationship between the existence of a secret and reasonable efforts to protect a secret. After all, if something is not a secret, there would not seem to be any point to protecting it. And the fact that an idea is well protected may be evidence that it is, in fact, a secret. Nonetheless, the requirements are conceptually distinct. Information in the public domain cannot be turned into a secret merely by treating it as a secret, a point that lawyers and even courts sometimes forget. This distinction is made clear in the Uniform Trade Secrets Act, which defines a trade secret as information that is both "not generally known" *and* the subject of reasonable efforts to maintain secrecy. UTSA §1(4).

Consider whether the opinion in *Rockwell* conflates these two into a single requirement. The court seems to emphasize the evidentiary significance of the precautions Rockwell took in proving misappropriation. Since it was clear (to the court, at least) that the DEV employees did, in fact, take the information from Rockwell, the court did not consider the precautions to be that important. The RESTATEMENT (THIRD) OF UNFAIR COMPETITION seems to follow this approach. Unlike the Uniform Act, the new Restatement does not contain a separate requirement that plaintiffs take reasonable precautions to protect their secrets. The comment to §39 takes the position that, while "[p]recautions taken to maintain the secrecy of information are relevant in determining whether the information qualifies for protection as a trade secret," "if the value and secrecy of the information are clear, evidence of specific precautions taken by the trade secret owner may be unnecessary." RESTATEMENT (THIRD) OF UNFAIR COMPETITION §39, Comment *g*, at 435-36.

Contrast *Rockwell* with the Minnesota Supreme Court's decision in *Electro-Craft Corp. v. Controlled Motion, Inc.*, 332 N.W.2d 890 (Minn. 1983), a case that also involved information taken by former employees and used in starting a competing company. The court found that the information the employees took was not generally known or readily ascertainable in the industry. However, it found that the information did not constitute a trade secret:

(c) Reasonable efforts to maintain secrecy. It is this element upon which [plaintiff Electro-Craft Corp., or "ECC"]'s claim founders. The district court found that, even though ECC had no "meaningful security provisions," ECC showed an intention to keep its data and processes secret. This finding does not bear upon the statutory requirement that ECC use "efforts that are reasonable under the circumstances to maintain . . . secrecy." Minn. Stat. §325C.01, subd. 5(ii). . . . [E]ven under the common law, more than an "intention" was required — the plaintiff was required to show that it had manifested that intention by making some effort to keep the information secret.

This element of trade secret law does not require maintenance of absolute secrecy; only partial or qualified secrecy has been required under the common law. What is actually required is conduct which will allow a court acting in equity to enforce plaintiff's rights. . . .

In the present case, even viewing the evidence most favorably to the findings below, we hold that ECC did not meet its burden of proving that it used reasonable efforts to maintain secrecy as to [the subject matter of the suit, a product called the ECC 1125]. We acknowledge that ECC took minimal precautions in screening its Handbook and publications for confidential information and by requiring some of its employees to sign a confidentiality agreement, but these were not enough.

First, ECC's physical security measures did not demonstrate any effort to maintain secrecy. By "security" we mean the protection of information from discovery by outsiders. Security was lax in this case. For example, the main plant had a few guarded entrances, but seven unlocked entrances existed without signs warning of limited access. Employees were at one time required to wear badges, but that system was abandoned by the time of the events giving rise to this case. The same was generally true of the Amery, Wisconsin plant where ECC 1125 and brushless motors were manufactured. One sign was posted at each plant, however, marking the research and development lab at Hopkins and the machine shop at Amery as restricted to "authorized personnel." Discarded drawings and plans for motors were simply thrown away, not destroyed. Documents such as motor drawings were not kept in a central or locked location, although some design notebooks were kept locked.

The relaxed security by itself, however, does not preclude a finding of reasonable efforts by ECC to maintain secrecy. Other evidence did not indicate that industrial espionage is a major problem in the servo motor industry. Therefore, "security" measures may not have been needed, and the trial court could have found trade secrets if ECC had taken other reasonable measures to preserve secrecy.

However, ECC's "confidentiality" procedures were also fatally lax, and the district court was clearly in error in finding ECC's efforts to be reasonable. By "confidentiality" in this case we mean the procedures by which the employer signals to its employees and to others that certain information is secret and should not be disclosed. Confidentiality was important in this case, for testimony demonstrated that employees in the servo motor business frequently leave their employers in order to produce similar or identical devices for new employers. ECC has hired many employees from other corporations manufacturing similar products.[7] If ECC wanted to prevent its employees from doing the

---

[7] One ECC employee actually prided himself on the information he had brought with him from his former employer. One day, just before that employee left ECC to join another company, the president

same thing, it had an obligation to inform its employees that certain information was secret.

ECC's efforts were especially inadequate because of the non-intuitive nature of ECC's claimed secrets here. The dimensions, etc., of ECC's motors are not trade secrets in as obvious a way as a "secret formula" might be. ECC should have let its employees know in no uncertain terms that those features were secret.

Instead, ECC treated its information as if it were not secret. None of its technical documents were marked "Confidential," and drawings, dimensions and parts were sent to customers and vendors without special marking. Employee access to documents was not restricted. ECC never issued a policy statement outlining what it considered secret. Many informal tours were given to vendors and customers without warnings as to confidential information. Further, two plants each had an "open house" at which the public was invited to observe manufacturing processes. . . .

In summary, ECC has not met its burden of proof in establishing the existence of any trade secrets. The evidence does not show that ECC was ever consistent in treating the information here as secret.

Elsewhere, the *ECC* court noted that the information in question was not in fact known at all outside ECC. Given that, why shouldn't the company be able to prevent its employees from using the information they acquired there? Should the laxity of ECC's precautions matter if no one other than the defendants, in fact, took advantage of it?

2. In *Rockwell,* the court apparently assumed that the manufacturer was in a confidential relationship with the subcontractors to which it sent drawings. Is it reasonable to assume that there was an implied relationship of confidentiality in the absence of an express agreement? Two decisions by the Ninth Circuit set the parameters of this debate. In *Entertainment Research Group v. Genesis Creative Group*, 122 F.3d 1211 (9th Cir. 1997), the court found no confidential relationship between a manufacturer of inflatable costumes and the marketing firm hired to distribute them. By contrast, in *IMAX Corp. v. Cinema Technologies*, 152 F.3d 1161 (9th Cir. 1998), the court concluded that the proprietor of an IMAX movie theater had a duty to IMAX to protect the specifications of the projector as trade secrets from a competitor who was attempting to reverse engineer the IMAX technology.

3. How much effort should be required of trade secret owners? Obviously, the best way to protect a secret is not to tell anyone at all. In the modern commercial world, however, this is normally impractical. Companies with trade secrets must tell

---

of ECC found him copying documents after hours. ECC never questioned the employee or warned him or his new employer that certain information was confidential.

the secret to their employees, their business partners, and often their distributors and customers as well. But the risk of *inadvertent* use or disclosure can be reduced in a number of ways: for example, by requiring employees, licensees, and even customers to sign confidentiality agreements; by investing in physical security measures against theft, such as fences, safes, and guards; and by designing products themselves so that they do not reveal their secrets upon casual (or even detailed) inspection. The First Circuit has held that "affirmative steps" to protect secrecy, not merely "ordinary discretion," are required. *Incase Inc. v. Timex Corp.*, 488 F.3d 46 (1st Cir. 2007).

4. Will reasonable precautions always be a question of fact? Or are certain activities (publishing a secret formula, for example) so inconsistent with trade secret protection that they automatically preclude a successful trade secret suit? *See* Chapter II(B)(3) (discussing disclosure of trade secrets).

One issue that often arises is whether companies that sell products on the open market which embody their trade secret have disclosed the secret. As we shall see, customers who buy a product on the open market are entitled to break it apart to see how it works. This process is called "reverse engineering" the product. Trade secret law does not protect owners against legitimate purchasers who discover the secret through reverse engineering, absent a valid nondisclosure agreement. But does the possibility that a product might be reverse engineered foreclose *any* trade secret protection, even against people who have not actually reverse engineered the product? At least one court has said no. In *Data General Corp. v. Grumman Systems Support Corp.*, 825 F. Supp. 340, 359 (D. Mass. 1993), the court upheld a jury's verdict that Grumman had misappropriated trade secrets contained in object code form in Data General's computer program, despite the fact that many copies of the program had been sold on the open market. The court reasoned: "With the exception of those who lawfully licensed or unlawfully misappropriated MV/ADEX, Data General enjoyed the exclusive use of MV/ADEX. Even those who obtained MV/ADEX and were able to *use* MV/ADEX were unable to discover its trade secrets because MV/ADEX was distributed only in its object code form, which is essentially unintelligible to humans."

Data General suggests that reasonable efforts to protect the secrecy of an idea contained in a commercial product — such as locks, black boxes, or the use of unreadable code—may suffice to maintain trade secret protection even after the product itself is widely circulated. Does this result make sense?

On the basis of the reasoning in *Data General*—that the source code, which contained the secrets, was not widely disclosed—would the distribution of the Data General software in object code form to the general public constitute misappropriation of those trade secrets?

5. If the idea is to encourage investment in trade secrets, why require any degree of "reasonable precautions" at all? One sometimes hears in this regard that *all* "fenc-

ing" expenditures are inefficient. *Cf.* Edmund W. Kitch, *The Law and Economics of Rights in Valuable Information*, 9 J. LEGAL STUD. 683 (1980) (arguing that reasonable precautions make sense only as evidence of the existence of a trade secret). Why not simply require explicit notice — large neon signs, stamps on all documents, or publication of a secrecy policy — in place of physical precautions? For a suggestion that proceeds along these lines to some extent, *see* J.H. Reichman, *Legal Hybrids Between the Patent and Copyright Paradigms*, 94 COLUM. L. REV. 2432 (1994).

Is it appropriate to punish the creator of a valuable secret who has not invested in "reasonable precautions"? What value is there in a legal rule that requires investment in precautions up to the level that would be rational in the absence of the legal rule? Are prospective trade secret thieves actually encouraged by the reasonable precautions argument to steal ideas when they observe a lapse in security, and does this rule give them an incentive to search out such lapses? Professor Kitch asks the related question of why these expenses should be required in addition to the expense of bringing a trade secret lawsuit.

Professor David Friedman, Professor William Landes, and Judge Richard Posner make the related point that a trade secret cause of action which yields a legal remedy ought to be available when it is cheaper than the physical precautions that would be necessary to protect a piece of information. *See* David Friedman, William Landes & Richard Posner, *Some Economics of Trade Secret Law*, 5 J. ECON. PERSPECTIVES 61, 67 (1991). They note further that where "the social costs of enforcing secrecy through the legal system would be high, the benefits of shared information are likely to exceed the net benefits of legal protection."

Should it be a defense to a trade secret action that the plaintiff could more easily have protected the secret through physical precautions?

Professor Kitch notes by way of analogy that we do not prohibit criminal complaints for larceny just because a property owner was careless. (On the other hand, many states do reduce recovery in tort suits for "comparative negligence.") He also suggests that reasonable precautions are required only to put prospective infringers on notice about the existence of a right and to serve as evidence of the fact that the secret is worth protecting legally. The fencing thus serves a notice function, akin to "marking" products with patent numbers, copyright symbols, or trademark symbols. Kitch, *supra*, at 698.

The Court in *duPont & Co. v. Christopher*, 431 F.2d 1012 (5th Cir. 1970), pays significant attention to the role of fencing costs in trade secrets suits. We will return to that case when we consider misappropriation of trade secrets. *See* Chapter II(C).

One might imagine other rationales for requiring reasonable protection. For example, one might treat the requirement of reasonable precautions as serving a gatekeeper function that helps to weed out frivolous trade secret claims by requiring evidence of investment by the plaintiff in protecting the secret.

PROBLEMS

Problem II-6. Smith, a bar owner in rural Alabama, develops by accident one night the relatively simple formula for a new alcoholic beverage. The drink is simply a mixture of three common ingredients. Smith begins selling the drink, which he calls "Mobile Mud," in his bar. However, he instructs his bartenders not to reveal the formula to anyone and has them premix "Mud" in the back of the bar, out of sight of customers. Smith is outraged when he learns that Jimmy Dean, an international distributor of alcoholic beverages, has copied his formula and is marketing it under a different name. At trial, Dean employees and independent experts unanimously testify that it is possible for someone with experience in the beverage industry to determine the formula for Mud by looking at, smelling and tasting the drink.

Has Smith taken reasonable precautions? What more could he have done to protect the "secret formula" of Mobile Mud? Is the secret so obvious to consumers that selling the product on the open market destroys protection? Does your opinion of the case change if you learn that Dean's representative went to Smith's bar and bribed a bartender to disclose the formula?

Problem II-7. MidContinent is a small manufacturer of signs and decals. It has only five employees, two of whom are father and son and two more of whom are family friends. The company describes itself as having a "relaxed, congenial" working atmosphere. In order to avoid what the president considers excessive formality, the employees have never been required to sign confidentiality agreements, and documents kept within the company aren't stamped confidential. The company has never conducted "exit interviews" or instructed its employees about trade secrecy. According to the company president, "we trust our employees, and that trust has never been misplaced." On the other hand, the company does take certain steps to keep outsiders from accessing its customer lists and its adhesive manufacturing process. And there is little history of economic espionage in the decal-manufacturing business. Has MidContinent taken reasonable efforts to protect its secrets? Should it matter whether the party accused of stealing those secrets is an employee or an outsider?

3.   Disclosure of Trade Secrets

It is axiomatic that public disclosure of a trade secret destroys the "secret," and therefore ends protection forever. The corollary to this rule is that as long as a trade secret remains secret, it is protectable. Thus, trade secrets do not last for a specific term of years but continue indefinitely until the occurrence of a particular event — the public disclosure of the secret. Disclosure of a once-protected trade secret can occur in several ways:

i.   *Voluntary Disclosure by the Trade Secret Owner*

A trade secret owner may publish the secret, whether in an academic journal or any other forum. In that case, secrecy is lost, at least provided the publication is accessible to those interested in the subject matter. This loss might reasonably be considered a substantial disincentive to publication of scientific or technical advances. But publication of secret information regularly occurs, either because the inventors have not thought through the consequences of their actions or because the value or prestige of first publication is deemed to outweigh the potential loss of commercial trade secret protection.

One common form of disclosure is the publication of an issued patent. Because (as we shall see) patent law requires the public disclosure of an invention with sufficient specificity to enable one of ordinary skill in the art to make it, obtaining a patent on an invention destroys trade secret protection. *See Tewari De-Ox Sys. v. Mountain States*, 637 F.3d 604 (5th Cir. 2011); *Ferroline Corp. v. General Aniline & Film Corp.*, 207 F.2d 912 (7th Cir. 1953). Thus, an inventor must "elect" either patent or trade secret protection, for the two cannot protect the same invention simultaneously.

The Federal Circuit applied a notable exception to this seemingly absolute rule in *Rhone-Poulenc Agro v. DeKalb Genetics Corp.*, 272 F.3d 1335 (Fed. Cir. 2001). In that case, the defendant had stolen the plaintiff's trade secrets and published them in its own patent application. The court concluded that the trade secret owner never had the opportunity to "elect" to give up trade secret protection, and so ruled that the publication of the defendant's patent had not disclosed plaintiff's trade secrets. This result seems equitable to the plaintiff. But does it really comport with the principle that information must be secret to be protected? For a contrary rule, *see Evans v. General Motors*, 125 F.3d 1448 (Fed. Cir. 1997) (holding that publication by a thief started the one-year clock running for patenting an invention, and reasoning that because the trade secret owner knew of the theft he could have acted to seek patent protection within a reasonable time period).

ii.   *Distributing a Product that Embodies the Trade Secret to the Public*

Selling or distributing a product embodying a trade secret to the public may jeopardize the secret if the secret becomes readily accessible. As one court explained, both the RESTATEMENT OF TORTS and the Uniform Trade Secrets Act "necessarily compel the conclusion that a trade secret is protectable only so long as it is kept secret by the party creating it. If a so-called trade secret is fully disclosed by the products produced by use of the secret then the right to protection is lost." *Vacco Indus. v. Van den Berg*, 6 Cal. Rptr. 2d 602, 611 (Ct. App. 1992) (citations omitted). Further, disclosure may occur even without sale of the product itself, if the secret is disclosed freely and without restriction during the manufacturing or development processes.

However, sales of a product to the public do not necessarily disclose a trade secret simply because the product embodies the trade secret. Rather, the question is whether the secret is apparent from the product itself. Secrets that are apparent to the buyers of a product are considered disclosed by the product, but secrets contained in undecipherable form within the product (such as object code in a computer program) are considered secret even when the product is sold.

In *Data General Corp. v. Digital Computer Controls, Inc.*, 297 A.2d 433 (Del. Ct. Ch. 1971), *aff'd*, 297 A.2d 437 (Del. S. Ct. 1972), Data General sold mainframe computers (Nova 1200) to sophisticated business customers. Data General supplied logic drawings along with the computer to any customers who requested this information so as to enable them to repair or customize them. Digital Computer Controls acquired a Nova 1200 on the open market along with the design drawings. When it launched a business repairing and maintaining Data General Nova 1200 computers, Data General sued for misappropriation of the secrets reflected in the design drawings. The court held that Data General had not forfeited secrecy merely by selling the computers:

> Defendants insist, however, that plaintiff has not maintained that degree of secrecy which will preserve its right to relief, either by publicly selling an article alleged to contain a trade secret, or by failing to restrict access to the design drawings for its device, arguing that matters of common knowledge in an industry may not be claimed as trade secrets.

> It has been recognized in similar cases that even though an unpatented article, device or machine has been sold to the public, and is therefore subject to examination and copying by anyone, the manner of making the article, device or machine may yet constitute a trade secret until such a copy has in fact been made, *Schulenburg v. Signatrol, Inc.*, 33 Ill. 2d 379, 212 N.E.2d 865, and *Tabor v. Hoffman*, N.Y., 118 N.Y. 30, 23 N.E. 12.

> Defendants contend, however, that the issuance by plaintiff of copies of design drawings to its customers was made without safeguards designed properly to maintain the secrecy requisite to the existence of a trade secret. In other words, it is contended that plaintiff's attempts to maintain secrecy merely consisted of (1) not giving copies of the design drawings to those customers who did not need them for maintenance of their computer, (2) obtaining agreements not to disclose the information from those customers who were given copies of the drawings, and (3) printing a legend on the drawings which contained the allegedly confidential information which identified the drawing as proprietary information, the use of which was restricted. Plaintiff argues, however, that disclosure of the design drawings to purchasers of the computer is necessary properly to maintain its device, that such disclosure was required by the very nature of the machine, and that reasonable steps were taken to preserve the secrecy of the material released. I conclude at this preliminary stage of

the case that it cannot be held as a matter of law that such precautions were in-adequate, a factual dispute as to the adequacy of such precautions having clearly been raised. Defendants' motion for summary judgment must accordingly be denied.

Id.

Of what relevance is the motivation behind the disclosure of a secret? Recall that in *Metallurgical Industries,* the court found the fact that Metallurgical had disclosed its secrets only for profit to weigh in favor of trade secret status. Why should this be the case? On the one hand, licensing is evidence that a secret has value and is worth protecting. On the other hand, one could argue that the fact that a secret holder has sold its information for profit suggests that it is not trying to keep this information secret at all but rather is attempting to profit from its disclosure. Which of these arguments you find persuasive may depend on your view of the reasons for trade secret protection.

iii.   *Public Disclosure by a Third Party*

Trade secrets may be publicly disclosed (through publication or the sale of a product) by someone other than the trade secret owner. Commonly, this occurs when someone other than the trade secret owner has independently developed or discovered the secret. Call the first trade secret "owner" *A,* and the independent developer *B. A* has no control over what *B* does with her independent discovery; if she chooses to publish the secret, she defeats not only her rights to trade secret protection, but *A*'s rights as well. Suppose *B* did not develop the secret independently of *A* but in fact stole it from *A.* What happens if *B* publishes the secret? Can *A* still protect it? If so, what happens to *C,* who began using the secret after reading *B*'s publication? This issue was addressed in *Religious Technology Center v. Lerma,* 908 F. Supp. 1362 (E.D. Va. 1995). In that case, the Church of Scientology sued (among others) the Washington Post, which had quoted from part of its confidential scriptures. The court concluded that the fact that the scriptures were posted on a Usenet newsgroup for ten days defeated any claim of trade secrecy:

[For ten days, the documents] remained potentially available to the millions of Internet users around the world.

As other courts who have dealt with similar issues have observed, "posting works to the Internet makes them generally known" at least to the relevant people interested in the newsgroup. Once a trade secret is posted on the Internet, it is effectively part of the public domain, impossible to retrieve. Although the person who originally posted a trade secret on the Internet may be liable for trade secret misappropriation, the party who merely downloads Internet information cannot be liable for misappropriation because there is no misconduct involved in interacting with the Internet.

908 F. Supp. at 1368; *accord American Red Cross v. Palm Beach Blood Bank Inc.*, 143 F.3d 1407 (11th Cir. 1998) (Red Cross donor list lost trade secret status because it was posted on a publicly accessible computer bulletin board). *But see Silicon Image Inc. v. Analogix Semiconductor Inc.*, 2008 WL 166950 (N.D. Cal. Jan. 17, 2008) (presence of information on the Internet does not destroy secrecy, absent evidence that competitors knew about it).

Should the obscurity of the Web site matter? What if it is not indexed in a search engine? In *DVD Copy Control Ass'n v. Bunner*, 116 Cal. App. 4th 241, 10 Cal. Rptr. 3d 185 (Ct. App. 2004), the court found disclosure of a secret on the Internet only because it was "quickly and widely republished to an eager audience," and cautioned that it did not assume that the secrets were lost merely because they were put on the Internet.

Because of the risk of loss of trade secrecy through Internet posting, companies have been more aggressive in suing individuals who post information they consider confidential. *See O'Grady v. Superior Court*, 44 Cal. Rptr. 3d 72 (Ct. App. 2006); *Ford v. Lane*, 67 F. Supp. 2d 745 (E.D. Mich. 1999). In some of these cases, notably *O'Grady*, the company knows only that the information has been disclosed, and not who has done so. Do such lawsuits present First Amendment issues? Several defendants have asserted that they were reporting legitimate news. *See* Franklin B. Goldberg, Ford Motor Co. v. Lane, 16 BERKELEY TECH. L.J. 271 (2001). And *O'Grady* held that bloggers who disclosed Apple's trade secrets were entitled to First Amendment protection as reporters, so their identity could not be disclosed by subpoena.

For an argument that disclosure on the Internet should not destroy a secret irrevocably, *see* Elizabeth A. Rowe, *Introducing a Takedown for Trade Secrets on the Internet*, 2007 WIS. L. REV. 1042; Elizabeth A. Rowe, *Saving Trade Secret Disclosures on the Internet Through Sequential Preservation*, 42 WAKE FOREST L. REV. 1 (2007).

iv.   *Inadvertent Disclosure*

Trade secrets may be disclosed inadvertently (for example, by being left on a train or elsewhere in public view). While the case law on this issue is sparse, it seems reasonable to argue that a truly accidental disclosure should not defeat trade secret protection if reasonable precautions have been taken. On the other hand, if the inadvertent disclosure is widespread, it would seem unfair (as well as impracticable) to require the public as a whole to "give back" the secret. Note that §1(2)(ii)(C) of the Uniform Trade Secrets Act provides that it is misappropriation for someone to disclose a secret that they have reason to know has been acquired "by accident or mistake." THE RESTATEMENT (THIRD) OF UNFAIR COMPETITION §40(b)(4) takes the same position, "unless the [accidental] acquisition was the result of the [trade secret owner]'s failure to take reasonable precautions to maintain the secrecy of the information." *See also Williams v. Curtis-Wright Corp.*, 681 F.2d 161 (3d Cir. 1982) (user of secrets disclosed by mistake was liable for misappropriation because he had constructive notice of the secrecy of the information). But in *DVD Copy Control Ass'n v. Bunner*, 116 Cal. App. 4th 241, 10 Cal. Rptr. 3d 185 (Ct. App. 2004), the court rejected the idea that "once the information became *publicly* available everyone else would be liable under the trade secret laws simply because they knew about its unethical origins." "This," the court said, "is not what trade secret law is designed to do."

v.   *Government Disclosure*

Government agencies sometimes require the disclosure of trade secrets by private parties in order to serve some other social purpose. *See Corn Products Refining Co. v. Eddy*, 249 U.S. 427 (1919) (requiring a food manufacturer to label its product with an accurate list of ingredients). Health and environmental concerns are a very common reason for the government to require disclosure of product contents. For example, the Federal Insecticide, Fungicide and Rodenticide Act (FIFRA), 7 U.S.C. §§136 et seq., requires disclosure of the contents of pesticides as well as a great deal of other information. FIFRA makes two concessions to trade secret protection, however. First, it limits public disclosure of information concerning manufacturing processes and inert (as opposed to active) contents. Second, it provides for compensation to be paid to the inventors of trade secrets which the government appropriates by public disclosure. *See also Ruckelshaus v. Monsanto Co.*, 467 U.S. 986 (1984) (federal requirement that private parties disclose trade secrets may constitute a taking under the Fifth Amendment); *Philip Morris Inc. v. Reilly*, 312 F.3d 24 (1st Cir. 2002) (Massachusetts law requiring labeling of cigarette ingredients was a taking of tobacco companies' trade secrets).

COMMENTS AND QUESTIONS

1. The plaintiff in *Data General* sold over 500 Nova computers to the general public. Data General provided any buyer who requested the "confidential" design drawings with a copy. Why are these drawings still considered a secret? Does widespread disclosure compromise the secrecy claim at some point, even though all disclosures are made under an agreement of confidentiality? This issue often arises in the software industry. As computers have become ubiquitous, the numbers of "secret" programs in circulation may be counted in the millions rather than the hundreds. *Data General* implicitly concludes that even a relatively widespread disclosure to customers does not compromise the secrecy of the computer design. For cases addressing this issue in the context of computer software, compare *Management Science of America v. Cyborg Sys., Inc.*, 1977-1 Trade Cas. (CCH) ¶61,472 (N.D. Ill. 1977) (holding that distribution of 600 copies of a program under a confidentiality agreement did not destroy secrecy) with *Young Dental Mfg. Co. v. Q3 Special Prods., Inc.*,

891 F. Supp. 1345 (E.D. Mo. 1995) (characterizing as "completely frivolous" plaintiff's claim that its publicly sold software was a trade secret).

A closely related question involves attempts by the owners of information to "contract around" the requirement of secrecy. If the parties agree to treat a piece of information as secret, is the licensee bound not to use or disclose the information under contract principles regardless of whether or not it is in fact in the public domain? This issue is a recurring one in intellectual property law, and a problem that has never adequately been addressed. Under what circumstances does the sale of a commercial product embodying a trade secret destroy the secret? Is the answer different for a commercially available product produced by a secret manufacturing process? In this regard, computer software may present a special case. While a particular computer program may be widely distributed, in fact all that is sold to the consumer is a disk containing object code. Object code is virtually impossible for humans to read without machine assistance.[8] Because of this, computer software is in some sense unlike a physical product whose design is evident to the casual observer. Even after it is publicly distributed, object code is meaningless to the casual observer. Only a complex process of reverse engineering (sometimes called "disassembly" or "decompilation") can enable the user to decipher the source code that was originally written for the program.

Should it matter that a computer program is distributed only in object code form? Consider the following case, in which the defendant was accused of misappropriating a computer program in object code form:

The source code can and does qualify as a trade secret. . . .

Whether the object code is a trade secret is a more difficult question.[7] Atkinson first contends that the object code cannot be a trade secret because it does not derive independent economic value from its secrecy, and therefore fails the first definitional requirement of a trade secret. This argument has no merit. Trandes generates most of its revenues by providing computer services. . . . Armed with a copy of the object code, an individual would have the means to offer much the same engineering services as Trandes. . .

---

[8] It is possible to "reverse engineer" object code in some cases to create a kind of rough estimate of what must have been in the original source code. The process, however, is demanding and time consuming even for expert programmers.

[7] This case presents an unusual set of facts. In the ordinary case, the owner of trade secret computer software will maintain the secrecy of the source code but freely distribute the object code. *See, e.g., Q-Co Indus. v. Hoffman*, 625 F. Supp. 608, 617 (S.D.N.Y. 1985) (program secret where source code secret, even though object code not secret). In such cases, the owner of the software cannot claim trade secret protection for the object code because its disclosure to the public destroyed its secrecy. In this case, however, Trandes maintained the secrecy of the source code and the object code, as we explain below.

Atkinson next argues that the object code cannot be a trade secret because Trandes did not keep it secret. . . . Atkinson asserts that the Tunnel System has been widely disclosed as a mass-marketed product and that its existence and its abilities are not secret. [The court concluded that the object code remained secret because it had only been distributed to two customers, and both of them signed licenses agreeing to keep the program a secret.]

Trandes Corp. v. Guy F. Atkinson Co., 996 F.2d 655, 663-64 (4th Cir. 1993). Consider the court's footnote. Can object code be a trade secret if it can easily be duplicated (whether or not the copier understands what he is copying)? Is the plaintiff in this case really trying to leverage copyright protection out of a trade secret claim? In many cases, the alleged trade secret at issue is not the source or object code of the computer program itself but certain high-level design features of the program (its "architecture"). *See Integrated Cash Management Services, Inc. v. Digital Transactions, Inc.*, 920 F.2d 171, 173 (2d Cir. 1990). Suppose that, rather than using what they had learned of the architecture of the program while employed by the company, ICM's former employees had copied the object code of the program altogether. (Leave aside for a moment questions of copyright infringement, and consider only the trade secret issue.) Would they be liable for misappropriating the trade secrets contained in the program architecture on the grounds that copying the program in its entirety necessarily copied the architecture? Or would the fact that the object code was publicly disclosed protect them from liability? *See Silvaco Data Sys. v. Intel Corp.*, 109 Cal. Rptr. 3d 27 (Cal. Ct. App. 2010 (holding that one "does not, by executing machine-readable software, 'use' the underlying source code; nor does one acquire the requisite knowledge of any trade secrets embodied in that code."); *Beacon Wireless Solutions Inc. v. Garmin Int'l*, 894 F. Supp. 2d 727 (W.D. Va. 2012). How would the courts in *Trandes* and the *Data General* cases answer this question? Does the answer suggest a problem with relying on trade secrecy to protect computer programs?

2. Until 1999, patent applications were kept secret by the U.S. Patent Office unless and until the patent issued. *See* 35 U.S.C. §122. If a patent application was not actively prosecuted, or if the patent did not issue, it was declared abandoned by the Patent Office. *See* 37 C.F.R. §1.114 (1995). Abandoned applications were not available to the public. In fact, the application itself was destroyed after 20 years.

In Europe, Japan, and elsewhere, patent applications are published 18 months after they are filed, regardless of whether the patent has yet issued. Normally, however, an applicant is notified before the application is published, allowing him or her to "elect" whether to continue to pursue a patent (and have the application be disclosed to the world) or to forgo prosecuting the patent (and retain the secrecy of the application). In 1999, Congress changed U.S. law to require that some (but not all) patent applications be published after 18 months. Since it takes more than three years on average for a patent to issue, many applicants will face an election not between patent and trade secret protection, but between trade secret protection and the prospect of future patent protection.

The notion of an "election" between trade secret and patent protection assumes that the patent application actually describes all the details of an invention. For more on this issue—known as the "enablement" requirement in patent law—*see* 35 U.S.C. §112, discussed in Chapter III. Certainly there is evidence that firms sometimes make precisely such an election. *See, e.g.*, HENRY PETROSKI, THE PENCIL 114-15 (1990) (describing how the family of Henry David Thoreau kept its pencil-making technology secret rather than disclose it by obtaining a patent). Most patent licenses also allow the licensee to use trade secrets and know-how related to or associated with the patent. If both a patent and its associated secrets are licensed, should there be any limits on the duration of the license? Do these licenses suggest that an inventor can avoid the "election" doctrine and "have it both ways" in some respects? *See United States v. Pilkington plc*, No. 94-345-TUC-WDB (D. Ariz. May 25, 1994) (government antitrust action against a company that sought to enforce trade secrets against competitors after a related patent had expired). For an account of disclosure-related advantages of seeking patents, *see* Robert P. Merges, *A Transactional View of Property Rights*, 20 BERKELEY TECH. L.J. 1477 (2005).

3. To what extent does the incorporation of a secret in a public governmental record preclude trade secret protection? *See Frazee v. U.S. Forest Service*, 97 F.3d 367 (9th Cir. 1996) (information was not a trade secret because it could be obtained from the government under the Freedom of Information Act); *Weygand v. CBS, Inc.*, 43 U.S.P.Q.2d 1120 (C.D. Cal. 1997) (depositing a work with the U.S. Copyright Office destroys trade secrecy).

C.   MISAPPROPRIATION OF TRADE SECRETS

Not all uses of another's trade secrets constitute misappropriation. Acquisition or use of a trade secret is illegal only in two basic situations: where it is done through improper means, or where it involves a breach of confidence. Uniform Trade Secrets Act §1; RESTATEMENT (THIRD) OF UNFAIR COMPETITION §40.

1.   Improper Means

E. I. du Pont deNemours & Co. v. Christopher
United States Court of Appeals for the Fifth Circuit
431 F.2d 1012 (5th Cir. 1970)

GOLDBERG, Circuit Judge:

This is a case of industrial espionage in which an airplane is the cloak and a camera the dagger. The defendants-appellants, Rolfe and Gary Christopher, are photographers in Beaumont, Texas. The Christophers were hired by an unknown third party to take aerial photographs of new construction at the Beaumont plant of E.I. duPont deNemours & Company, Inc. Sixteen photographs of the DuPont facility were taken from the air on March 19, 1969, and these photographs were later developed and delivered to the third party.

DuPont employees apparently noticed the airplane on March 19 and immediately began an investigation to determine why the craft was circling over the plant. By that afternoon the investigation had disclosed that the craft was involved in a photographic expedition and that the Christophers were the photographers. DuPont contacted the Christophers that same afternoon and asked them to reveal the name of the person or corporation requesting the photographs. The Christophers refused to disclose this information, giving as their reason the client's desire to remain anonymous.

Having reached a dead end in the investigation, DuPont subsequently filed suit against the Christophers, alleging that the Christophers had wrongfully obtained photographs revealing DuPont's trade secrets which they then sold to the undisclosed third party. DuPont contended that it had developed a highly secret but unpatented process for producing methanol, a process which gave DuPont a competitive advantage over other producers. This process, DuPont alleged, was a trade secret developed after much expensive and time-consuming research, and a secret which the company had taken special precautions to safeguard. The area photographed by the Christophers was the plant designed to produce methanol by this secret process, and because the plant was still under construction parts of the process were exposed to view from directly above the construction area. Photographs of that area, DuPont alleged, would enable a skilled person to deduce the secret process for making methanol. DuPont thus contended that the Christophers had wrongfully appropriated DuPont trade secrets by taking the photographs and delivering them to the undisclosed third party. In its suit DuPont asked for damages to cover the loss it had already sustained as a result of the wrongful disclosure of the trade secret and sought temporary and permanent injunctions prohibiting any further circulation of the photographs already taken and prohibiting any additional photographing of the methanol plant. . . .

. . . [T]he Christophers argue that for an appropriation of trade secrets to be wrongful there must be a trespass, other illegal conduct, or breach of a confidential relationship. We disagree.

It is true, as the Christophers assert, that the previous trade secret cases have contained one or more of these elements. However, we do not think that the Texas courts would limit the trade secret protection exclusively to these elements. On the contrary, in *Hyde Corporation v. Huffines*, 1958, 158 Tex. 566, 314 S.W.2d 763, the Texas Supreme Court specifically adopted the rule found in the Restatement of Torts which provides:

One who discloses or uses another's trade secret, without a privilege to do so, is liable to the other if

    (a) he discovered the secret by improper means, or

    (b) his disclosure or use constitutes a breach of confidence reposed in him by the other in disclosing the secret to him. . . .

RESTATEMENT OF TORTS §757 (1939). Thus, although the previous cases have dealt with a breach of a confidential relationship, a trespass, or other illegal conduct, the rule is much broader than the cases heretofore encountered. Not limiting itself to specific wrongs, Texas adopted subsection (a) of the Restatement which recognizes a cause of action for the discovery of a trade secret by any "improper" means. . . .

The question remaining, therefore, is whether aerial photography of plant construction is an improper means of obtaining another's trade secret. We conclude that it is and that the Texas courts would so hold. The Supreme Court of that state has declared that "the undoubted tendency of the law has been to recognize and enforce higher standards of commercial morality in the business world." *Hyde Corporation v. Huffines, supra*, 314 S.W.2d at 773. That court has quoted with approval articles indicating that the proper means of gaining possession of a competitor's secret process is "through inspection and analysis" of the product in order to create a duplicate. *K & G Tool & Service Co. v. G & G Fishing Tool Service*, 1958, 158 Tex. 594, 314 S.W.2d 782, 783, 788. Later another Texas court explained:

> The means by which the discovery is made may be obvious, and the experimentation leading from known factors to presently unknown results may be simple and lying in the public domain. But these facts do not destroy the value of the discovery and will not advantage a competitor who by unfair means obtains the knowledge without paying the price expended by the discoverer.

Brown v. Fowler, Tex. Civ. App. 1958, 316 S.W.2d 111, 114, *writ ref'd n.r.e.*

We think, therefore, that the Texas rule is clear. One may use his competitor's secret process if he discovers the process by reverse engineering applied to the finished product; one may use a competitor's process if he discovers it by his own independent research; but one may not avoid these labors by taking the process from the discoverer without his permission at a time when he is taking reasonable precautions to maintain its secrecy. To obtain knowledge of a process without spending the time and money to discover it independently is improper unless the holder voluntarily discloses it or fails to take reasonable precautions to ensure its secrecy.

In the instant case the Christophers deliberately flew over the DuPont plant to get pictures of a process which DuPont had attempted to keep secret. The Christophers delivered their pictures to a third party who was certainly aware of the means by which they had been acquired and who may be planning to use the information contained therein to manufacture methanol by the DuPont process. The third party has a right to use this process only if he obtains this knowledge through his own research efforts, but thus far all information indicates that the third party has gained this knowledge solely by taking it from DuPont at a time when DuPont was making reasonable efforts to preserve its secrecy. In such a situation DuPont has a valid cause of action to prohibit the Christophers from improperly discovering its trade secret and to prohibit the undisclosed third party from using the improperly obtained information.

We note that this view is in perfect accord with the position taken by the authors of the Restatement. In commenting on improper means of discovery the savants of the Restatement said:

> *f. Improper means of discovery.* The discovery of another's trade secret by improper means subjects the actor to liability independently of the harm to the interest in the secret. Thus, if one uses physical force to take a secret formula from another's pocket, or breaks into another's office to steal the formula, his conduct is wrongful and subjects him to liability apart from the rule stated in this Section. Such conduct is also an improper means of procuring the secret under this rule. But means may be improper under this rule even though they do not cause any other harm than that to the interest in the trade secret. Examples of such means are fraudulent misrepresentations to induce disclosure, tapping of telephone wires, eavesdropping or other espionage. A complete catalogue of improper means is not possible. In general they are means which fall below the generally accepted standards of commercial morality and reasonable conduct.

RESTATEMENT OF TORTS §757, Comment *f* at 10 (1939).

In taking this position we realize that industrial espionage of the sort here perpetrated has become a popular sport in some segments of our industrial community. However, our devotion to free-wheeling industrial competition must not force us into accepting the law of the jungle as the standard of morality expected in our commercial relations. Our tolerance of the espionage game must cease when the protections required to prevent another's spying cost so much that the spirit of inventiveness is dampened. Commercial privacy must be protected from espionage which could not have been reasonably anticipated or prevented. We do not mean to imply, however, that everything not in plain view is within the protected vale, nor that all information obtained through every extra optical extension is forbidden. Indeed, for our industrial competition to remain healthy there must be breathing room for observing a competing industrialist. A competitor can and must shop his competition for pricing and examine his products for quality, components, and methods of manufacture. Perhaps ordinary fences and roofs must be built to shut out incursive eyes, but we need not require the discoverer of a trade secret to guard against the unanticipated, the undetectable, or the unpreventable methods of espionage now available.

In the instant case DuPont was in the midst of constructing a plant. Although after construction the finished plant would have protected much of the process from view, during the period of construction the trade secret was exposed to view from the air. To require DuPont to put a roof over the unfinished plant to guard its secret would impose an enormous expense to prevent nothing more than a school boy's trick. We introduce here no new or radical ethic since our ethos has never given moral sanction to piracy. The market place must not deviate far from our mores. We should not require a person or corporation to take unreasonable precautions to prevent another from doing that which he ought not do in the first place. Reasonable precautions against predatory eyes we may require, but an impenetrable fortress is an unreasonable requirement, and we are not disposed to burden industrial inventors with such a duty in order to protect the fruits of their efforts. "Improper" will always be a word of many nuances, determined by time, place, and circumstances. We therefore need not proclaim a catalogue of commercial improprieties. Clearly, however, one of its commandments does say "thou shall not appropriate a trade secret through deviousness under circumstances in which countervailing defenses are not reasonably available." . . .

COMMENTS AND QUESTIONS

1. Improper means has a substantial basis in other torts. *See* Comment *f* to THE RESTATEMENT, cited in *duPont,* and the RESTATEMENT (THIRD) OF UNFAIR COMPETITION §43 (defining improper means as including "theft, fraud, unauthorized interception of communications, inducement of or knowing participation in a breach of confidence, and other means either wrongful in themselves or wrongful under the circumstances of the case.").

DuPont itself provides an example of conduct prohibited by trade secret law that is probably not otherwise tortious. Should otherwise legitimate conduct be prohibited because it will disclose a trade secret? As Judge Posner noted in *Rockwell,* misappropriation of trade secrets is largely redundant if it does not reach any further than other torts. Nonetheless, the reach of the case is troubling. Consider the last sentence of the *duPont* opinion. What is wrong with "deviousness"? Is reverse engineering (which is legal under both the Restatement and the Uniform Act) any less devious than aerial photography? And why should "countervailing defenses" enter the picture?

2. There is general agreement that "reverse engineering" — that is, buying a product and taking it apart to see how it works — is not a misappropriation of a trade secret. As we will see in Chapter III, reverse engineering of a patented invention does permit the discoverer to practice the invention during the patent term. But while it may be easy to see how to reverse engineer a product, how does one reverse engineer a process? Are there realistic alternatives to the sort of espionage condemned in *duPont* for those who seek to reproduce a process? Should there be some legally protected way of discovering a competitor's process?

3. Note how the decision in *duPont* dovetails with the discussion of precautions in II(B)(2). DuPont could have protected itself against aerial photography by building a roof over its plant area before beginning internal construction. The Fifth Circuit rejected this alternative because it would "impose an enormous expense to prevent nothing more than a school boy's trick." On the other hand, the courts are clearly willing to put duPont to *some* expense to protect its secrets from prying eyes. If duPont had allowed its engineers to leave copies of the plant blueprints on subways, the result of the case might be very different.

How much expense is duPont required to incur to protect itself? The uniform answer of the courts is that only "reasonable" precautions must be taken. While this is not a terribly helpful answer, it may be a fairly practical one in any given industry, where companies can protect themselves by taking those precautions that are customary in that industry.

On the other hand, consider the Second Circuit's statement in *Franke v. Wiltschek*, 209 F.2d 493, 495 (2d Cir. 1953):

> It matters not that the defendants could have gained their knowledge from a study of the expired patent and plaintiff's publicly marketed product. The fact is they did not. Instead they gained it from plaintiffs via their confidential relationship, and in doing so incurred a duty not to use it to plaintiff's detriment. This duty they have breached.

Is this consistent with the UTSA?

4. An interesting case involving only circumstantial evidence of misappropriation is *Pioneer Hi-Bred International v. Holden Foundation Seeds, Inc.*, 35 F.3d 1226, 31 U.S.P.Q.2d 1385 (8th Cir. 1994). Plaintiff Pioneer could not establish a specific act of misappropriation, but it did show (through the use of three sophisticated scientific tests) that it was highly unlikely that defendant's hybrid seeds had been developed independently of plaintiff's seeds. Instead, due to genetic similarities, Pioneer showed that it was much more likely that those seeds were "derived from" a popular Pioneer hybrid. Pioneer was found to have maintained reasonable measures to guard against disclosure, including putting experimental seeds in bags marked with a secret code, allowing seeds to be grown only under strict nondisclosure arrangements, and leaving unmarked the fields in which the seeds had been planted. Pioneer was awarded $46.7 million in damages.

By contrast, the Fourth Circuit in *Othentec Ltd. v. Phelan*, 526 F.3d 135 (4th Cir. 2008), made it clear that speculation of theft based on the defendant's speed in entering the market was not enough. The court required "actual objective evidence" of misappropriation.

2. Confidential Relationship

The previous section concerned misappropriation of trade secrets by improperly obtaining them from their owner. But secrets that have been properly obtained may still be misappropriated if they are improperly used or disclosed. Most often, this occurs when the secrets are used or disclosed in violation of a confidential relationship. Confidential relationship cases dominate trade secret litigation; one study found that 93 percent of all trade secret cases are between parties who know each other. *See* David S. Almeling et al., *A Statistical Analysis of Trade Secret Litigation in State Courts*, 46 GONZ. L. REV. 57, 59 (2011).

What is a confidential relationship? Obviously, the easiest way to create a confidential relationship is to sign a contract to that effect. Agreements to keep certain information confidential are generally enforceable, at least if the information meets the definition of a trade secret. *See* RESTATEMENT (THIRD) OF UNFAIR COMPETITION §39, Comment *d*, at 430. But confidential relationships may also arise without any express agreement. Consider the following case.

Smith v. Dravo Corp.
United States Court of Appeals for the Seventh Circuit
203 F.2d 369 (7th Cir. 1953)

LINDLEY, J.

Plaintiffs appeal from a judgment for defendant entered at the close of a trial by the court without a jury. The complaint is in four counts: 1 and 2 charge an unlawful appropriation by defendant of plaintiffs' trade secrets relating to the design and construction and selling and leasing of freight containers; 3 and 4 aver infringement of plaintiffs' patents Nos. 2,457,841 and 2,457,842. . . .

In the early 1940s Leathem D. Smith, now deceased, began toying with an idea which, he believed, would greatly facilitate the ship and shore handling and transportation of cargoes. As he was primarily engaged in the shipbuilding business, it was quite natural that his thinking was chiefly concerned with water transportation and dock handling. Nevertheless his overall plan encompassed rail shipping as well. He envisioned construction of ships especially designed to carry their cargo in uniformly sized steel freight containers. These devices (which, it appears, were the crux of his idea) were: equipped with high doors at one end; large enough for a man to enter easily; weather and pilfer proof; and bore collapsible legs, which (1) served to lock them (a) to the deck of the ship by fitting into recesses in the deck, or (b) to each other, when stacked, by reason of receiving sockets located in the upper four corners of each container, and (2) allowed sufficient clearance between deck and container or container and container for the facile insertion of a fork of a lift tractor, and (3) were equipped with lifting eyelets, which, together with a specially designed hoist, made possible placement of the containers upon or removal from a ship, railroad car or truck, while filled with cargo. The outer dimensions of the devices were such that they would fit compactly in standard gauge North American railroad cars, or narrow gauge South American trains, and in the holds of most water vessels.

[At the end of World War II, Smith's company — Safeway Containers — had some success building and selling such containers.]

On June 23, 1946, Smith died in a sailing accident. The need for cash for inheritance tax purposes prompted his estate to survey his holdings for disposable assets. It was decided that the container business should be sold. Devices in process were completed but no work on new ones was started.

Defendant was interested in the Safeway container, primarily, it appears, for use by its subsidiary, the Union Barge Lines. In October 1946 it contacted Agwilines [one of Smith's customers] seeking information. It watched a loading operation in which Agwilines used the box. At approximately the same time, defendant approached the shipbuilding company and inquired as to the possibility of purchase of a number of the containers. It was told to communicate with Cowan, plaintiffs' eastern representative. This it did, and, on October 29, 1946, in Pittsburgh, Cowan met with defendant's officials to discuss the proposed sale of [containers]. But, as negotiations progressed, defendant demonstrated an interest in the entire container development. Thus, what started as a meeting to discuss the purchase of individual containers ended in the possible foundation for a sale of the entire business.

Based upon this display of interest, Cowan sent detailed information to defendant concerning the business. This included: (1) patent applications for both the "knock-down" and "rigid" crates; (2) blue prints of both designs; (3) a miniature Safeway container; (4) letters of inquiry from possible users; (5) further correspondence with prospective users. In addition, defendant's representatives journeyed to Sturgeon Bay, Wisconsin, the home of the shipbuilding company, and viewed the physical plant, inventory and manufacturing operation.

Plaintiffs quoted a price of $150,000 plus a royalty of $10 per unit. This was rejected. Subsequent offers of $100,000 and $75,000 with royalties of $10 per container were also rejected. Negotiations continued until January 30, 1947, at which time defendant finally rejected plaintiffs' offer.

On January 31, 1947 defendant announced to Agwilines that it "intended to design and produce a shipping container of the widest possible utility" for "coastal steamship application . . . [and] use . . . on the inland rivers and . . . connecting highway and rail carriers." Development of the project moved rapidly, so that by February 5, 1947 defendant had set up a stock order for a freight container which was designed, by use of plaintiffs' patent applications, so as to avoid any claim of infringement. One differing feature was the use of skids and recesses running the length of the container, rather than legs and sockets as employed in plaintiffs' design. However, Agwilines rejected this design, insisting on an adaptation of plaintiffs' idea. In short defendant's final product incorporated many, if not all, of the features of plaintiffs' design. So conceived, it was accepted by the trade to the extent that, by March 1948, defendant had sold some 500 containers. Many of these sales were made to firms who had shown considerable prior interest in plaintiffs' design and had been included in the prospective users disclosed to defendant.

One particular feature of defendant's container differed from plaintiffs: its width was four inches less. As a result plaintiffs' product became obsolete. Their container could not be used interchangeably with defendant's; they ceased production. Consequently the prospects of disposing of the entire operation vanished.

The foregoing is the essence of plaintiffs' cause of action. Stripped of surplusage, the averment is that defendant obtained, through a confidential relationship, knowledge of plaintiffs' secret designs, plans and prospective customers, and then wrongfully breached that confidence by using the information to its own advantage and plaintiffs' detriment.

[The court found that, notwithstanding certain disclosures of information during the operation of Safeway, plaintiffs' information about how to design its containers remained a trade secret.]

(3) Was Defendant in a Position of Trust and Confidence at the Time of the Disclosure?

Mr. Justice Holmes once said that the existence of the confidential relationship is the "starting point" in a cause of action such as this. *E.I. DuPont de Nemours Powder Co. v. Masland*, 244 U.S. 100, 102. While we take a slightly different tack, there is no doubt as to the importance of this element of plaintiffs' case.

Certain it is that a non-confidential disclosure will not supply the basis for a law suit. Plaintiffs' information is afforded protection because it is secret. Promiscuous disclosures quite naturally destroy the secrecy and the corresponding protection. But this is not true where a confidence has been reposed carrying with it communication of an idea.

It is clear that no express promise of trust was exacted from defendant. There is, however, the further question of whether one was implied from the relationship of the parties. Pennsylvania has not provided us with a decision precisely in point but *Pressed Steel Car Co. v. Standard Car Co.*, 210 Pa. 464, 60 A. 4, furnishes abundant guideposts. There plaintiff delivered its blue prints to customers in order that they might acquaint themselves more thoroughly with the railroad cars they were purchasing; from these customers, defendant obtained the drawings. In holding that the customers held the plans as a result of a confidence reposed in them by plaintiff, and that the confidence was breached by delivery of the blue prints to defendant, the court said, 60 A. at page 10: "While there was no expressed restriction placed on the ownership of the prints, or any expressed limitation as to the use to which they were to be put, it is clear . . . that the purpose for which they were delivered by the plaintiff was understood by all parties. . . ."

The quoted language is applicable and determinative. Here plaintiffs disclosed their design for one purpose, to enable defendant to appraise it with a view in mind of purchasing the business. There can be no question that defendant knew and understood this limited purpose. Trust was reposed in it by plaintiffs that the information thus transmitted would be accepted subject to that limitation. "[T]he first thing to be made sure of is that the defendant shall not fraudulently abuse the trust reposed in him. It is the usual incident of confidential relations. If there is any disadvantage in the fact that he knew the plaintiffs' secrets, he must take the burden with the good." *E.I. DuPont de Nemours Powder Co. v. Masland*, 244 U.S. 100,102.

Nor is it an adequate answer for defendant to say that the transactions with plaintiffs were at arm's length. So, too, were the overall dealings between plaintiffs and defendants in *Booth v. Stutz Motor Car Co.*, 7 Cir., 56 F.2d 962; *Allen-Qualley Co. v. Shellmar Products Co.*, D.C., 31 F.2d 293, affirmed, 7 Cir., 36 F.2d 623 and *Schavoir v. American Rebonded Leather Co.*, 104 Conn. 472, 133 A. 582. That fact does not detract from the conclusion that but for those very transactions defendant would not have learned, from plaintiffs, of the container design. The implied limitation on the use to be made of the information had its roots in the "arms-length" transaction.

(4) The Improper Use by Defendant of the Secret Information

Defendant's own evidence discloses that it did not begin to design its container until after it had access to plaintiffs' plans. Defendant's engineers admittedly referred to plaintiffs' patent applications, as they said, to avoid infringement. It is not disputed that, at the urging of Agwilines, defendant revised its proposed design to incorporate the folding leg and socket principles of plaintiffs' containers. These evidentiary facts, together with the striking similarity between defendant's and plaintiffs' finished product, were more than enough to convict defendant of the improper use of the structural information obtained from plaintiffs.

COMMENTS AND QUESTIONS

1. Since the shipping containers were available on the open market, couldn't Dravo have argued that they were not a trade secret? Did Smith's agent, Cowan, disclose anything that was *not* readily apparent from inspection of the containers? For more on the history of containerization, *see* MARC LEVINSON, THE BOX: HOW THE SHIPPING CONTAINER MADE THE WORLD SMALLER AND THE WORLD ECONOMY BIGGER (2008) (mentioning Dravo Corporation container as early precursor of containerization).

2. In *Van Prods. Co. v. General Welding & Fabricating Co.*, 213 A.2d 769, 779-80 (Pa. 1965), the Pennsylvania Supreme Court criticized *Smith* for focusing on the existence of a confidential relationship to the exclusion of whether there was a trade secret at all. The court said: "The starting point in every case of this sort is not whether there was a confidential relationship, but whether, in fact, there was a trade secret to be misappropriated." But where there is a secret, a company that receives the secret in a business negotiation and then uses it without paying is guilty of misappropriating that secret. *See Altavion Inc. v. Konica Minolta Sys. Lab. Inc.*, 171 Cal. Rptr. 3d 714 (Cal. Ct. App. 2014).

3. Compare *Smith v. Dravo* with *Omnitech Int'l v. Clorox Co.*, 29 U.S.P.Q.2d 1665 (5th Cir. 1994), where the court held that it was not an actionable "use" of a trade secret for the defendant to *evaluate* it in the course of trying to decide whether to (a) acquire the company or (b) take a license to use the trade secret. A finding of no liability here makes sense, because it allows the potential licensee to make an informed judgment and therefore promotes efficient licensing. But how far does it extend? Is the potential licensee entitled to replicate the research or build models in an effort to evaluate it? Are there special limits that should be placed on companies engaged in a "make or buy" decision — that is, who are considering *either* licensing the plaintiff's technology *or* entering the market themselves?

Smith and *Omnitech* both involved disclosures in the course of licensing negotiations. Cases such as these form part of the amorphous law of "precontractual liability." *See* E. Allen Farnsworth, *Precontractual Liability and Preliminary Agreements: Fair Dealing and Failed Negotiations*, 87 COLUM. L. REV. 217 (1987). Both the *Smith* and *Omnitech* cases present the problem of Arrow's Information Paradox. What the plaintiff has to sell to the defendant is information that is valuable only because it is secret. If there is no legal protection and if the plaintiff discloses the secret to the defendant, its value will be lost. But the defendant cannot be expected to pay for information unless it can see the information to determine its value. Thus, absent some form of legal protection for confidential disclosures, sale or licensing of trade secrets may not occur. Note that this problem does not arise in other areas of intellectual property, such as patent law, since the inventions being licensed are already publicly disclosed.

4. The RESTATEMENT (THIRD) OF UNFAIR COMPETITION §41 holds that a confidential relationship is established in the following circumstances:

(a) the person made an express promise of confidentiality prior to the disclosure of the trade secret; or

(b) the trade secret was disclosed to the person under circumstances in which the relationship between the parties to the disclosure or the other facts surrounding the disclosure justify the conclusions that, at the time of the disclosure,

(1) the person knew or had reason to know that the disclosure was intended to be in confidence, and

(2) the other party to the disclosure was reasonable in inferring that the person consented to an obligation of confidentiality.

On the issue of knowledge, compare this "had reason to know" standard with the Eleventh Circuit's decision in *Bateman v. Mnemonics, Inc.*, 79 F.3d 1532 (11th Cir. 1996). In that case, the court indicated that it was "wary" of trade secret claims based on implied confidential relationships because they were subject to abuse. The court rejected Bateman's allegation that such a relationship existed because Bateman had not "made it clear to the parties involved that there was an expectation and obligation of confidentiality." Thus, the court seemed to create a standard of actual knowledge on the part of the recipient of confidential information that the discloser of such information intended the disclosure to be confidential. At the other extreme, the Fifth Circuit in *Phillips v. Frey*, 20 F.3d 623, 631-32 (5th Cir. 1994) found an implied confidential relationship to exist in the course of negotiations over the sale of a business, despite the fact that the disclosing party never even requested that the information remain confidential.

Which approach makes more sense? Who is in the best position to clarify the question, the discloser or the recipient?

5. Is there any way for a potential licensee to prevent the formation of a confidential relationship in such a situation?

6. The defendant in *Smith* actually sold a device that was not identical to the plaintiff's. Under what circumstances can a defendant be liable for misappropriation without literally copying the trade secret? In *Mangren Res. & Dev. Corp. v. National Chem. Co.*, 87 F.3d 1339 (7th Cir. 1996), the court defined improper "use" broadly, stating that "the user of another's trade secret is liable even if he uses it with modifications or improvements upon it effected by his own efforts, so long as the substance of the process used by the actor is derived from the other's secret. . . . If trade secret law were not flexible enough to encompass modified or even new products that are substantially derived from the trade secrets of another, the protections that the law provides would be hollow indeed." To similar effect as *Mangren* is *Texas Tanks Inc.*

v. Owens-Corning Fiberglas Corp., 99 F.3d 740 (5th Cir. 1997). In *Texas Tanks,* the Fifth Circuit held that any improper "exercise of control and domination" over a secret constituted a commercial use of that secret. It rejected the defendant's argument that it could not be liable for taking a secret unless the secret was actually incorporated in a commercial product. The court noted that Owens Corning's awareness of the secret would likely influence the development of its own competing product, and that this was enough to demonstrate improper "use" of the secret. And in *Collelo v. Geographic Servs., Inc.*, 283 Va. 56 (2012), the Virginia Supreme Court held that a party could misappropriate trade secrets even though it did not compete with the plaintiff, as long as the plaintiff could show injury.

PROBLEMS

Problem II-9. Solomon, a regular customer of ToolCo's products, comes up with an idea for a new tool. He sends the idea to ToolCo, suggesting that they manufacture it. ToolCo does in fact produce and sell the new tool. Is Solomon entitled to compensation for ToolCo's use of his idea? Does it make any difference if (1) ToolCo actively solicited the idea from Solomon? (2) Solomon sent the suggestion to ToolCo along with a letter saying he wanted to open negotiations over a possible licensing arrangement to use the idea? (3) ToolCo has in the past had an informal, unwritten policy of compensating inventors who submit good ideas?

Problem II-10.   VenCo, a venture capitalist in the business of financing start-up companies, investigates TechCo in an effort to decide whether or not to finance it. To aid in its investigation, VenCo asks for and receives confidential information about TechCo's products and *market* position. VenCo eventually decides not to finance TechCo because of concerns about its management, but it does finance a start-up competitor of TechCo in the same field. Are VenCo or the start-up liable to TechCo? What obligations, if any, does VenCo undertake as a result of its exposure to TechCo's secrets?

Problem II-11.   Falcon Systems employs Kotva as a sales representative. In the course of her work for Falcon, Kotva comes into contact with a large number of actual and potential customers. Some are leads provided by Falcon, while others she develops on her own. To manage her connections, she uses a website called LinkedIn, which allows people to record and build business connections. Kotva uses LinkedIn for all her connections, business as well as personal.

When Kotva leaves Falcon to take a job with a competitor, Falcon argues that her LinkedIn "connections" are effectively a customer list and belong to the company. They insist that she delete her LinkedIn account, or alternatively eliminate any job-related contacts from the site. How should the court rule?

D. DEFENSES

The UTSA lacks any express exceptions to trade secret liability. Yet the definition of misappropriation entails improper acts. And independent discovery or reverse engineering are not improper. Thus, to the extent that a defendant can show that it reverse engineered or independently developed trade secret information, it can avoid liability under state law. The new federal DTSA is even more explicit, expressly providing that reverse engineering and independent invention are not improper means of acquiring a trade secret. Furthermore, courts have long recognized that trade secret protection can "implicate the interest in freedom of expression or advance another significant public interest." *See* RESTATEMENT (THIRD) OF UNFAIR COMPETITION, §40, comment *c*. Section 2 explores this public policy limitation.

1. Independent Discovery and Reverse Engineering

Not all use or disclosure of someone's secret is actionable misappropriation. Rather, as the commissioners who drafted the Uniform Trade Secrets Act noted, there are several categories of "proper means" of obtaining a trade secret. We classify these "proper means" as defenses, because they do not directly deny the existence of a trade secret or the defendant's use of that secret. Rather, they are *legitimate* uses of trade secrets by a competitor.

UTSA Comment to §1 explains that:

One of the broadly stated policies behind trade secret law is "the maintenance of standards of commercial ethics." THE RESTATEMENT OF TORTS, Section 757, Comment (f), notes: "A complete catalogue of improper means is not possible," but Section 1(1) includes a partial listing.

Proper means include:

1. Discovery by independent invention;

2. Discovery by "reverse engineering," that is, by starting with the known product and working backward to find the method by which it was developed. The acquisition of the known product must, of course, also be by a fair and honest means, such as purchase of the item on the open market, for reverse engineering to be lawful;

3. Discovery under a license from the owner of the trade secret;

4. Observation of the item in public use or on public display;

5. Obtaining the trade secret from published literature.

See also RESTATEMENT (THIRD) OF UNFAIR COMPETITION §43 ("Independent discovery and analysis of publicly available products or information are not improper means of acquisition.").

Kadant, Inc. v. Seeley Machine, Inc.
United States District Court for the Northern District of New York
244 F. Supp. 2d 19 (N.D.N.Y. 2003)

HURD, District Judge.

. . .

II.   Facts

Kadant is a publicly traded corporation with yearly sales eclipsing $100 million. Kadant AES ("AES") is a division of Kadant located in Queensbury, New York. For twenty-eight years, AES has manufactured and sold to customers worldwide products that clean and condition papermaking machines and filter water used in the papermaking process. "There are three main products areas of the business of AES: shower and spray devices and nozzles; foil blades to remove water from the paper during the papermaking process; and structures that hold foils and filters for straining water utilized in the papermaking process so that it can be reused." . . . Plaintiff occupies a dominant place in the national papermaking market.

Corlew was hired by AES in July of 1995 as a machinist. Nearly three years later, in April of 1998, he was promoted to a position in the engineering department. In that capacity, Corlew would be provided with a refined customer order, made by an AES engineer and a customer, and it was his job to create a "manufacturing drawing (with instructions and a bill of materials — i.e., the 'recipe') for the order." In order to create such a drawing, Corlew used a computer assisted drawing machine. The computer assisted drawing machine contained "the recipes for the AES products and generate[d] drawings and bills of materials." Plaintiff contends that AES took steps to protect the secrecy of the information contained in the computer assisted drawing machine. In June of 1999, Corlew was promoted again and now had the responsibility to assist the engineers in designing customer orders. Corlew was terminated in the summer of 2001.

During his tenure at AES, Corlew had access to plaintiff's "recipes" ("design specifications") for its products and to plaintiff's computerized database of prospective customers, which includes "names, addresses, and e-mails for all potential customers in the papermaking industry, including the names of individuals key to these companies' purchasing orders." Plaintiff contends that one of Corlew's final assignments while at AES was to coordinate this database with the database containing information on all current AES customers and their purchasing histories. Corlew had access to AES's entire computer system, which apparently included both databases as well as the computer assisted drawing machine containing the design specifications. At the end of his employment, Corlew's access to AES's computer system was terminated, and his laptop was wiped clean of AES information, and/or access thereto. Throughout his employment with AES, Corlew was subject to a signed confidentiality agreement, in which he agreed not to disclose or use to his benefit any confidential information, including information about AES customers.

Following his termination, Corlew formed APE "to outsource the manufacture of his own line of products for sale to the pulp and papermaking industry." According to defendants, APE was not a successful venture, forcing Corlew to begin working for Cambridge Valley Machine, Inc. ("CVM"). In April or May of 2002, Corlew resigned from CVM. Defendants contended in their moving papers that, as a condition of his resignation, Corlew was required to relinquish the rights to the name APE to CVM.

Near the end of April of 2002, Corlew began working for Seeley, "developing and marketing a new line of Seeley products for sale to the pulp and papermaking industry." According to defendants, "[t]he products comprising this new line were reverse-engineered from existing products, freely available in the public domain and unprotected by published patent applications, in-force patents or trade secrets." According to plaintiff, the only way defendants could have developed and put out for sale this new line of products in so short of time is not by reverse engineering, which it alleges is time consuming, expensive, and requiring technical skill, but by Corlew's theft of AES's trade secrets — its design specifications and the customer databases — and infringement of its trademark.

Specifically, claims plaintiff, using as a frame of reference defendants' own expert, it would take defendants 1.7 years to reverse engineer all of plaintiff's nozzles. Defendants maintain, however, that only a small fraction, not all, of plaintiff's products were reverse engineered. The parties also dispute how much time would be associated with the manufacturing process. . . .

III. Discussion

Plaintiff has moved for preliminary injunctive relief pursuant to Fed. R. Civ. P. 52(a). . . .

In order for plaintiff to successfully move for a preliminary injunction, it must demonstrate: 1) a likelihood of irreparable harm if the injunction is not granted; and 2) either a likelihood of success on the merits of its claims, or the existence of serious questions going to the merits of its claims plus a balance of the hardships tipping decidedly in its favor. *Bery v. City of New York*, 97 F.3d 689, 693-94 (2d Cir. 1996). Because the issuance of a preliminary injunction is a drastic remedy, plaintiff is required to make a "clear showing" of these requirements. *See Mazurek v. Armstrong*, 520 U.S. 968, 972 (1997). . . .

B. TRADE SECRET THEFT/MISAPPROPRIATION

. . .

1. Likelihood of Success on the Merits

To establish misappropriation of a trade secret, a plaintiff must prove: 1) that "it possessed a trade secret; and 2) that defendants are using that trade secret in breach of an agreement, confidence, or duty, or as a result of discovery by improper means." *Integrated Cash Management Services, Inc. v. Digital Transactions, Inc.*, 920 F.2d 171, 173 (2d Cir. 1990); *see also Carpetmaster of Latham v. Dupont Flooring Systems*, 12 F. Supp. 2d 257, 261 (N.D.N.Y. 1998). . . .

b. Design Specifications

Secrecy again takes center stage and is dispositive when determining whether plaintiff's product design specifications are entitled to trade secret protection for the purposes of obtaining preliminary injunctive relief. If secrecy is lost when a product is placed on the market, there is no trade secret protection. *See LinkCo*, 230 F. Supp. 2d at 498-99 (collecting cases). The primary issue with respect to this alleged trade secret is whether plaintiff's products could be reverse engineered in the time span between Corlew's hiring at Seeley and defendants' marketing and putting out their products for sale.[9] As will be shown, *infra,* the parties disagree about every material fact that goes toward resolving this debate."

Trade secret law . . . does not offer protection against discovery by . . . so-called reverse engineering[.]" *Kewanee Oil Co. v. Bicron Corp.*, 416 U.S. 470, 476 (1974). However, "the term 'reverse engineering' is not a talisman that may immunize the theft of trade secrets." *Telerate Systems, Inc. v. Caro*, 689 F. Supp. 221, 233 (S.D.N.Y. 1988). The relevant inquiry is whether the means to obtain the alleged trade secret were proper or "honest," as opposed to being obtained by virtue of a confidential relationship with an employer. *See Franke v. Wiltschek*, 209 F.2d 493, 495 (2d Cir. 1953); *Telerate*, 689 F. Supp. at 233. Reverse engineering a product to determine its design specifications is, therefore, permissible so long as the means used to get the information necessary to reverse engineer is in the public domain, and not through the confidential relationship established with the maker or owner of the product.

One court, not satisfied with this distinction, has held that even where a product is out in the public domain, and was thus subject to being reverse engineered by a purchaser, trade secret status remains intact because the defendant's former employment with the plaintiff was the only basis for the defendants being "able to select particular items from a vast sea of public information." *See Monovis, Inc. v. Aquino*, 905 F.

---

[9] "Reverse engineering is the process by which an engineer takes an already existing product and works backward to re-create its design and/or manufacturing process." *United Technologies Corp. by Pratt & Whitney v. F.A.A.*, 102 F.3d 688, 690 n.1 (2d Cir. 1996).

Supp. 1205, 1228 (W.D.N.Y. 1994). This view of the law would effectively eviscerate any benefit reverse engineering would provide in the preliminary injunction analysis as applied to trade secrets, forestall healthy notions of commercial competitiveness, and heavily contribute to an inert marketplace where products can only be developed and sold under an impenetrable cloak of originality. It is therefore rejected.

Plaintiff has presented no evidence that the means used by defendants to obtain the alleged trade secret were improper or dishonest. In short, it has no evidence Corlew actually stole the design specifications. It instead necessarily relies upon an inference — that the only way defendants could develop, market, and sell their products in so short of time is if Corlew stole the design specification information — that is, as far as the evidence to this point shows, is [sic] unjustified. Plaintiff does not seem to argue that reverse engineering is impossible, just that it would take a great deal of time, skill, and expense, and that the lack thereof demonstrates that the design specifications must have been stolen. Defendants have argued that the plaintiff's products were simple, consisting of non-technical and few parts, that reverse engineering would take little time, and that, in any event, they only reverse engineered a small fraction, not all, of plaintiff's products. Plaintiff has not sufficiently rebutted these contentions. Thus, because plaintiff has failed to make a clear showing that defendants improperly obtained and reverse-engineered its products, trade secret protection at this stage of the litigation is improper. *See, e.g., Bridge C.A.T. Scan Associates v. Technicare Corp.*, 710 F.2d 940, 946-47 (2d Cir. 1983) (lack of evidence that means to receive information that plaintiff claimed was trade secret were improper mandated denying preliminary injunctive relief).

COMMENTS AND QUESTIONS

1. Why is reverse engineering lawful? If, as the Commissioners suggested, one purpose of trade secret law is to promote standards of commercial ethics, doesn't there seem to be something wrong with taking apart a competitor's product in order to figure out how to copy it? Does reverse engineering benefit only those competitors who are not smart enough to develop ideas or products for themselves?

In *Chicago Lock Co. v. Fanberg*, 676 F.2d 400 (9th Cir. 1982), the plaintiff, a company that made locks, sued a locksmith who compiled a list of master key codes for the plaintiff's locks by soliciting information from those who had picked the locks on behalf of their clients. The court rejected the claim, holding that the owners of the individual locks had the right to open them, and therefore to authorize others to reverse engineer the key codes:

> A lock purchaser's own reverse-engineering of his own lock, and subsequent publication of the serial number-key code correlation, is an example of the independent invention and reverse engineering expressly allowed by trade

secret doctrine.[4] Imposing an obligation of nondisclosure on lock owners here would frustrate the intent of California courts to disallow protection to trade secrets discovered through "fair and honest means." *See id.* Further, such an implied obligation upon the lock owners in this case would, in effect, convert the Company's trade secret into a state-conferred monopoly akin to the absolute protection that a federal patent affords. Such an extension of California trade secrets law would certainly be preempted by the federal scheme of patent regulation.

Appellants, therefore, cannot be said to have procured the individual locksmiths to breach a duty of nondisclosure they owed to the Company, for the locksmiths owed no such duty.

2. Reverse engineering may be explained as a legal rule designed to weaken trade secret protection relative to patent protection. Can you think of reasons why we would want to weaken trade secret protection? *See Kewanee Oil Co. v. Bicron Corp.*, 416 U.S. 470 (1974) (patent law does not preempt trade secret law, in part because the reverse engineering rule "weakens" trade secret law).

3. Consider the recurring question of whether the parties can agree to override trade secret law. Suppose that the owner of a trade secret includes in a license or sale contract a provision prohibiting the buyer from reverse engineering the product. Is that contractual provision enforceable? The courts are split. *Compare K & G Oil Tool & Serv. Co. v. G & G Fishing Tool Serv.*, 158 Tex. 94, 314 S.W.2d 782, 785-86 (1958) (contract preventing disassembly of tools to protect trade secrets was enforceable), *with Vault Corp. v. Quaid Software Ltd.*, 847 F.2d 255, 265-67 (5th Cir. 1988) (contract provision prohibiting reverse engineering of software void as against public policy).

4. Trade secret law does not protect owners against legitimate purchasers who discover the secret through reverse engineering. But does the possibility that a product might be reverse engineered foreclose *any* trade secret protection? In *Data General Corp. v. Grumman Systems Support Corp.*, 825 F. Supp. 340, 359 (D. Mass. 1993), the court upheld a jury's verdict that Grumman had misappropriated trade secrets contained in object code form in Data General's computer program, despite the fact that many copies of the program had been sold on the open market. The court reasoned: "With the exception of those who lawfully licensed or unlawfully misappropriated MV/ADEX, Data General enjoyed the exclusive use of MV/ADEX. Even those who obtained MV/ADEX and were able to *use* MV/ADEX were unable to discover its trade secrets because MV/ADEX was distributed only in its object code

---

[4] If a group of lock owners, for their own convenience, together published a listing of their own key codes for use by locksmiths, the owners would not have breached any duty owed to the Company. Indeed, the Company concedes that a lock owner's reverse engineering of his own lock is not "improper means."

form, which is essentially unintelligible to humans." The court noted that Data General took significant steps to preserve the secrecy of MV/ADEX, requiring that all users of the program sign licenses agreeing not to disclose the program to third parties. Under this decision, a defendant may have to prove that they had some sort of legitimate access to the plaintiff's information — for example, by demonstrating that they reverse engineered it from a publicly available product — even though the product containing the secret is widely distributed.

Similarly, in *Reingold v. Swiftships*, 126 F.3d 645 (5th Cir. 1997), the court rejected a claim that a boat hull mold could not be a trade secret because it could readily be reverse engineered. While reverse engineering may protect one who engages in it, the court held, it does not protect those who actually acquire the secret by improper means. Should it matter whether the reverse engineering is very difficult or easy enough that any competitor could do it? How many firms have actually reverse engineered the product?

The *Data General* cases suggest that reasonable efforts to protect the secrecy of an idea contained in a commercial product — such as locks, black boxes, or the use of unreadable code — may suffice to maintain trade secret protection even after the product itself is widely circulated. Does this result make sense? For a different approach, *see Videotronics v. Bend Electronics*, 564 F. Supp. 1471, 1476 (D. Nev. 1983) (holding that software cannot be a trade secret if it is publicly distributed and can be readily copied).

5. If a company is looking for a piece of information—say, the solution to a given technical problem—society believes that the company should be allowed free access to information in the public domain. The reason is that minimizing the search costs of the company is thought to be a social good, consistent with some level of protection for the prior investment of others. In a similar vein, suppose the costs of obtaining that information from the public domain are very high, but the costs (to the company) of stealing it from a competitor are very low. Should society punish — and therefore deter — the theft? Wouldn't that simply create an inefficiency, since the company could get the information but would have to incur greater search costs? *Cf.* David Friedman, William Landes & Richard Posner, *Some Economics of Trade Secret Law*, 5 J. ECON. PERSPECTIVES 61, 62 (1991) (arguing that trade secret law prohibits only costly means of obtaining competitors' information, while encouraging cheaper forms of obtaining information such as reverse engineering). Are there other considerations that militate in favor of requiring such a search?

PROBLEMS

Problem II-12. Atech and Alpha both manufacture complex medical devices used in diagnosing a variety of ailments. These devices are sold almost exclusively to hospitals since they cost in excess of $100,000 each. There are several hundred Atech devices currently in use in hospitals throughout the country. Atech, which claims a trade secret in the internal workings of its device, carefully monitors the purchasers of its device. Alpha pays a third party to buy a device from Atech without disclosing that it will be given to Alpha. Once it has obtained the device, Alpha disassembles it and studies it in order to compare it to Alpha's own device. In the course of opening it up, Alpha's engineers pick two internal padlocks on the Atech device. When Atech discovers that Alpha has obtained the device, it demands the unit's return, offering to refund the purchase price. Alpha refuses, and Atech sues for misappropriation of trade secrets.

a) Assume that Atech's trade secrets were worth $5 million. Assume further that the padlocks cost $5 each, and that it costs $100 per lock to pick these padlocks. Has Atech taken reasonable precautions to preserve its secrets? What other security measures must Atech take —and at what cost—both to deter Alpha (and others) from reverse engineering and to preserve its secrecy? Does Atech's sale of the products on the open market automatically preclude a finding of secrecy?

b) Assume Atech has presented the buyer of the machine with a contract that licenses (rather than sells) the machine, subject to the following restrictions: (a) the buyer is prohibited from disclosing anything she learns during the course of using the machine; (b) the buyer is prohibited from reselling the machine; and (c) the buyer is liable for Atech's damages in the event that any third party learns of Atech's secrets from the buyer or the buyer's machine. Is such an agreement enforceable? Would you advise a client thinking of licensing an Atech machine to sign this contract? How would you redraft the agreement to protect the buyer?

c) Assume that after Alpha's engineers picked the padlocks, they gained access to the inner workings of the machine. Assume further that they discovered numerous flaws in the imaging mechanism that caused potentially serious defects in the images (and hence the diagnoses) *stemming* from the Atech machine. Finally, assume that Alpha's engineers not only fixed these problems but significantly improved on Atech's design and hence the reliability of the machine. Should these facts affect Alpha's liability? Atech's remedy?

Problem II-13. Bonnie Bluenote, a world-famous blues guitarist, is noted for her distinctive sound, which she gets by tuning her guitar specially every time before she plays. Although the *guitar* itself is a standard professional model, Bonnie's adjustments of settings on the guitar, amplifier, and sound system combine to produce a distinctive sound. Because the sound is so important to her image, Bonnie guards it carefully. While she is tuning her guitar, only band members and close associates are allowed in the room. When she records in a new studio, she has the sound engineers sign nondisclosure agreements.

One day Freddie Fender-Rhodes, a big fan of Bonnie's and a budding bluesman himself, is hanging around outside the studio where Bonnie is recording her newest album. He happens to see an ID tag, worn by all guests in the studio, in the wastebasket. He fills in his name and walks into the studio. The band members and recording engineers, seeing the tag, let Freddie stay. He observes how Bonnie tunes her guitar, sees the soundboard settings, and makes extensive mental notes.

Five months later, Bonnie is shocked to see in a record store a CD by Freddie titled "The Bonnie Bluenote Sound." Then she discovers that Freddie is planning to publish an article in Blues Guitar magazine revealing the secrets to Bonnie's sound. Does she have any recourse against Freddie? What additional precautions should she have taken?

2. Public Policy Limitation

Courts have long recognized that trade secret protection can "implicate the interest in freedom of expression or advance another significant public interest," RESTATEMENT (THIRD) OF UNFAIR COMPETITION, §40, comment c, and recognized a limited privilege to disclose trade secrets. *See* DAVID W. QUINTO & STUART H. SINGER, 1 TRADE SECRETS: LAW AND PRACTICE §3.02; 1 MELVIN JAGER, TRADE SECRETS LAW §3:14. The RESTATEMENT (THIRD) OF UNFAIR COMPETITION notes that the exception

> depends upon the circumstances of the particular case, including the nature of the information, the purpose of the disclosure, and the means by which the actor acquired the information. A privilege is likely to be recognized, for example, in connection with the disclosure of information that is relevant to public health or safety, or to the commission of a crime or tort, or to other matters of substantial public concern.

§40, comment *c*.

As Professor Peter Menell has explained, this framing offers relatively little clarity or solace to those who seek to report corporate wrongdoing. *See* Peter S. Menell, *Tailoring a Public Policy Exception to Trade Secret Protection*, 105 CAL. L. REV. (forthcoming 2017). Nearly all businesses require their employees to sign NDAs as a condition of employment. Such agreements are essential to being able to establish the reasonable precautions necessary to secure trade secret protection. They are also broad and strict. What if any employee uncovers evidence of regulatory violations, fraud, or even criminal violations at their company? Do they violate their NDA by consulting an attorney or disclosing documents revealing the illegal activity to the government?

At first blush, RESTATEMENT (THIRD) OF UNFAIR COMPETITION, §40, comment *c*, appears to provide some leeway to report the illegal activity. The murky contours of the public policy limitation, however, would give a potential whistleblower pause. How can the employee evaluate "the circumstances of the particular case, including the nature of the information, the purpose of the disclosure, and the means by which the actor acquired the information?" At a minimum, its characterization as a defense that turns on a case-by-case balancing of potentially subjective factors means that an employee or contractor who divulges proprietary information even to the government could be sued for their breach of an NDA. The prospective whistleblower would likely have to consult an attorney, with the attendant costs, and the very act of discussing the allegedly illegal activity with the lawyer could create exposure for violating the NDA. More generally, most prospective whistleblowers will not even be aware of the public policy exception to their NDA absent consulting an attorney.

Cafasso v. Gen. Dynamics C4 Sys., U.S. ex rel. Cafasso v. General Dynamics C4 Systems, Inc., 2009 WL 1457036 (D. Ariz. 2009), *aff'd* 637 F.3d 1047 (9th Cir. 2011), serves as a cautionary tale of the trade secret risks that whistleblowers run. While working as a Chief Scientist at General Dynamics C4 Systems ("GDC4S"), a government aerospace contractor, Mary Cafasso became aware of corporate decisions that she believed to be in violation of the company's obligations under its government contracts. Her reporting of these concerns internally went unheeded. Upon learning that her position was being eliminated, she hurriedly downloaded a large number of confidential files that could support her suspicion. She subsequently filed a whistleblower (qui tam) action against her former employer. Her employer learned of Cafasso's removal of proprietary documents and filed suit against her in state court for breach of contract, misappropriation of trade secrets, and conversion. Shortly thereafter, Cafasso filed a False Claims Act (FCA) action under seal. GDC4S asserted counterclaims in the federal action based on breach of the NDA, misappropriation of trade secrets, and conversion based on her removing computer files as part of FCA action and reviewing these documents with her attorney.

After granting summary judgment to GDC4S on Cafasso's FCA action, the district court determined that Cafasso's disclosure of the documents in question to her attorney breached her NDA. The court rejected a public policy privilege, explaining that

> Public policy does not immunize Cafasso. Cafasso confuses protecting whistleblowers from retaliation for lawfully reporting fraud with immunizing whistleblowers for wrongful acts made in the course of looking for evidence of fraud. The limitation of statutory protection for retaliation to 'lawful acts done by the employee' weighs against any inference of a broad privilege for Cafasso to breach her contract with GDC4S. Statutory incentives encouraging investigation of possible fraud under the FCA do not establish a public policy in favor of

violating an employer's contractual confidentiality and nondisclosure rights by wholesale copying of files admittedly containing confidential, proprietary, and trade secret information.

2009 WL 1457036 at *14. The court ordered Cafasso to pay $300,000 in attorneys' fees for the breach of contract action. The award was based principally on disclosing the proprietary documents to her attorney for purposes of filing a sealed complaint in federal court informing the government of what Ms. Cafasso believed was fraudulent activity.

On appeal, the Ninth Circuit declined to adopt a public exception in a case involving "vast and indiscriminate appropriation" of confidential files, even for the purpose of reporting allegedly illegal activity to her attorney and the government. The court emphasized the overbreadth of the document retrieval, notwithstanding that Cafasso was under substantial time pressure in gathering the documents. The court expressed concern about the sensitivity of the information, yet it was all information to which Cafasso was authorized to view, and she limited disclosure to her attorney (who was also duty-bound to protect the information) and the government through a sealed court filing.

How many employees are willing to run that risk? At a minimum, the RESTATEMENT's characterization of the public policy exception as a defense that turns on a case-by-case balancing of potentially subjective factors means that an employee or contractor who divulges proprietary information even to the government could be sued for their breach of an NDA. Whistleblowers jeopardize their career, financial security, emotional stability, health insurance, and social community. Many struggle to find other positions in their field. *See* Menell, *Tailoring a Public Policy Exception to Trade Secret Protection, supra.* The prospective whistleblower would likely have to consult an attorney, with the attendant costs, and could still face some exposure. More generally, most prospective whistleblowers will not even be aware of this exception to their NDA absent consulting an attorney. As the authors of a recent empirical study examining 230 corporate frauds at large U.S. companies note, "[t]he surprising part is not that most employees do not talk; it is that some talk at all." Alexander Dyck, Adair Morse & Luigi Zingales, *Who Blows the Whistle on Corporate Fraud?*, 65 J. FIN. 2213, 2245 (2010).

As a solution to the problem of reporting illegal activity that might be considered confidential, Professor Menell proposed that Congress adopt a sealed disclosure/trusted intermediary safe harbor that would insulate whistleblowers and their counsel from trade secret liability for disclosing trade secret information *in confidence* to government officials or as part of lawsuit alleging retaliation by an employer. This statutory exception to trade secret liability would provide clear assurance to potential whistleblowers that they do not violate their NDAs merely by consulting legal counsel regarding reporting allegedly illegal conduct to a responsible government official through a confidential channel. In addition, this safe harbor would insulate lawyers advising potential whistleblowers about their options and serving as conduits for presenting evidence of allegedly illegal conduct to the government. Professor Menell further advocated a requirement that NDAs prominently include notice of the law reporting safe harbor to ensure that those with knowledge of illegal conduct are aware of this important public policy limitation on NDAs and exercise due care with trade secrets in reporting such activity.

Congress followed this recommendation in crafting the Defend Trade Secrets Act. *See* James Pooley, *New Federal Trade Secret Law Would Protect Whistleblowers*, Law.com (Feb. 5, 2016). The public policy exception provides:

(B) IMMUNITY FROM LIABILITY FOR CONFIDENTIAL DISCLOSURE OF A TRADE SECRET TO THE GOVERNMENT OR IN A COURT FILING

(1) IMMUNITY.—An individual shall not be held criminally or civilly liable under any Federal or State trade secret law for the disclosure of a trade secret that—

(A) is made—

(i) in confidence to a Federal, State, or local government official, either directly or indirectly, or to an attorney; and

(ii) solely for the purpose of reporting or investigating a suspected violation of law; or

(B) is made in a complaint or other document filed in a lawsuit or other proceeding, if such filing is made under seal.

(2) USE OF TRADE SECRET INFORMATION IN ANTI-RETALIATION LAWSUIT.—An individual who files a lawsuit for retaliation by an employer for reporting a suspected violation of law may disclose the trade secret to the attorney of the individual and use the trade secret information in the court proceeding, if the individual—

(A) files any document containing the trade secret under seal; and

(B) does not disclose the trade secret, except pursuant to court order.

(3) NOTICE.—

(A) IN GENERAL.—An employer shall provide notice of the immunity set forth in this subsection in any contract or agreement with an employee that governs the use of a trade secret or other confidential information.

(B) POLICY DOCUMENT.—An employer shall be considered to be in compliance with the notice requirement in subparagraph (A) if the employer provides a cross-reference to a policy document provided to the employee that sets forth the employer's reporting policy for a suspected violation of law.

(C) NON-COMPLIANCE.—If an employer does not comply with the notice requirement in subparagraph (A), the employer may not be awarded exemplary damages or attorney fees under subparagraph (C) or (D) of section 1836(b)(3) in an action against an employee to whom notice was not provided.

(D) APPLICABILITY.—This paragraph shall apply to contracts and agreements that are entered into or updated after the date of enactment of this subsection.

(4) EMPLOYEE DEFINED.—For purposes of this subsection, the term 'employee' includes any individual performing work as a contractor or consultant for an employer.

(5) RULE OF CONSTRUCTION.—Except as expressly provided for under this subsection, nothing in this subsection shall be construed to authorize, or limit liability for, an act that is otherwise prohibited by law, such as the unlawful access of material by unauthorized means.

DTSA §7, *codified at* 18 U.S.C. §1833.

COMMENTS AND QUESTIONS

1. Professor Menell contends that this new defense properly focuses trade secret protection on commercial morality and promoting legitimate competition, not shielding illegal activity. Do you agree? Could someone who wishes to steal a trade secret abuse this protection? How?

2. The DTSA immunity provision is built upon the idea that lawyers and the government can serve as "trusted intermediaries." *See* Menell, *Tailoring a Public Policy Exception to Trade Secret Protection, supra.* Federal law provides that

> Whoever, being an officer or employee of the United States or. . . any person acting [as an agent thereof including an employee of a private sector organization who is assigned to a government agency] publishes, divulges, discloses, or makes known in any manner or to any extent not authorized by law any. . . trade secrets. . . shall be fined under this title, or imprisoned not more than one year, or both; and shall be removed from office or employment.

18 U.S.C. §1905. This provision is essential to the operation of the federal courts and many agencies, such as the Food and Drug Administration and the Patent and Trademark Office, which routinely handle confidential information.

3. Would the DTSA immunity provision have assisted Edward Snowden in his effort to blow the whistle on the National Security Agency's surveillance activities? As

Professor Menell cautions, the sealed disclosure/trusted intermediary safe harbor depends critically upon the trustworthiness of government officials to whom illegal activity is reported. Corrupting forces can influence government as well as private actors. President Nixon approved the bugging of his political rivals. Contractors can develop cozy relationships with the agencies with whom they work. The revolving door of hiring government officials as well as lobbying of political officials can undermine an agency's objectivity. Various anticorruption laws, such as the Ethics in Government Act of 1978, counteract those forces. *See generally* ROBERT G. VAUGHN, THE SUCCESSES AND FAILURES OF WHISTLEBLOWER LAWS (2012). Nonetheless, a government agency can be the source of the misconduct. The sealed disclosure/trusted intermediary safe harbor is ill-equipped to address such challenges, although it contributes to general awareness of whistleblowing and anti-corruption policies.

4. Should the whistleblower right be broader, allowing for *public disclosure* of trade secrets in some circumstances? Professor David Levine argues that some enterprises, like companies that make voting machines, are so important to the public that the way they work should be transparent. *See* David S. Levine, *Secrecy and Unaccountability: Trade Secrets in Our Public Infrastructure*, 59 FLA. L. REV. 135 (2007).

5. Professor Deepa Varadarajan argues for a broader right to make beneficial uses of a secret, for instance, to improve on the original product or to protect public health. *See* Deepa Varadarajan, *Trade Secret Fair Use*, 83 FORDHAM L. REV. 1401 (2014). Would such a regime be feasible?

E.   AGREEMENTS TO KEEP SECRETS

As we have seen, trade secret law imposes certain limitations on the owner of a trade secret. To qualify for trade secret protection, information must not be generally known, must be valuable, and must not be disclosed. But can an owner of information avoid those restrictions by requiring others to *agree* to keep the information secret, whether or not the information meets the requirements for protection? The question is fundamental in intellectual property law.

Licenses are generally considered good from an economic standpoint because they promote efficiency. The company (or individual) that develops a new product may not be in the best position to market it, particularly if the invention has uses in several different fields. Absent licenses, that company would either have to sell the product outright, use it incompletely or inefficiently, enter a new field itself, or not use it at all. Private contract remedies allow the market to reorder itself efficiently and still determine the appropriate reward for invention. But we cannot always rely on the market to determine an efficient outcome. Indeed, intellectual property in general is an example of pervasive market failure, a failure that may color the role of contract law.

Warner-Lambert Pharmaceutical Co. v. John J. Reynolds, Inc.
United States District Court for the Southern District of New York
178 F. Supp. 655 (S.D.N.Y. 1959)

BRYAN, District Judge.

Plaintiff sues under the Federal Declaratory Judgment Act, 28 U.S.C. §§2201 and 2202, for a judgment declaring that it is no longer obligated to make periodic payments to defendants based on its manufacture or sale of the well known product "Listerine," under agreements made between Dr. J. J. Lawrence and J. W. Lambert in 1881, and between Dr. Lawrence and Lambert Pharmacal Company in 1885. Plaintiff also seeks to recover the payments made to defendants pursuant to these agreements since the commencement of the action.

Plaintiff is a Delaware corporation which manufactures and sells Listerine, among other pharmaceutical products. It is the successor in interest to Lambert and Lambert Pharmacal Company which acquired the formula for Listerine from Dr. Lawrence under the agreements in question. Defendants are the successors in interest to Dr. Lawrence.

Jurisdiction is based on diversity of citizenship.

For some seventy-five years plaintiff and its predecessors have been making the periodic payments based on the quantity of Listerine manufactured or sold which are called for by the agreements in suit. The payments have totaled more than twenty-two million dollars and are presently in excess of one million five hundred thousand dollars yearly. . . .

[J.J. Lawrence developed the formula for Listerine in 1880. He licensed the secret formula exclusively to Lambert (later Warner-Lambert) in 1881 under a contract which provided that

> I, Jordan Lambert, hereby agree for myself, my heirs, executors and assigns to pay monthly to Dr. Lawrence, his heirs, executors or assigns, the sum of twenty dollars for each and every gross of said Listerine hereafter sold by myself, my heirs, executors or assigns.

The amount was reduced by subsequent agreement to $6.00 per gross.]

The agreements between the parties contemplated, it is alleged, "the periodic payment of royalties to Lawrence for the use of a trade secret, to wit, the secret formula for" Listerine. After some modifications made with Lawrence's knowledge and approval, the formula was introduced on the market. The composition of the compound has remained the same since then and it is still being manufactured and sold by the plaintiff.

It is then alleged that the "trade secret" (the formula for Listerine) has gradually become a matter of public knowledge through the years following 1881 and prior to

1949, and has been published in the United States Pharmacopo[e]ia, the National Formulary and the Journal of the American Medical Association, and also as a result of proceedings brought against plaintiff's predecessor by the Federal Trade Commission. Such publications were not the fault of plaintiff or its predecessors. . . .

(1)

The plaintiff seems to feel that the 1881 and 1885 agreements are indefinite and unclear, at least as to the length of time during which they would continue in effect. I do not find them to be so. These agreements seem to me to be plain and unambiguous. . . .

The obligation to pay on each and every gross of Listerine continues as long as this preparation is manufactured or sold by Lambert and his successors. It comes to an end when they cease to manufacture or sell the preparation. . . . The plain meaning of the language used in these agreements is simply that Lambert's obligation to pay is co-extensive with manufacture or sale of Listerine by him and his successors. . . .

(3)

However, plaintiff urges with vigor that the agreement must be differently construed because it involved the conveyance of a secret formula. The main thrust of its argument is that despite the language which the parties used the court must imply a limitation upon Lambert's obligation to pay measured by the length of time that the Listerine formula remained secret.

To sustain this theory plaintiff relies upon a number of cases involving the obligations of licensees of copyrights or patents to make continuing payments to the owner or licensor, and argues that these cases are controlling here. . . .

. . . [A]ll [these cases hold] is that when parties agree upon a license under a patent or copyright the court will assume, in the absence of express language to the contrary, that their actual intention as to the term is measured by the definite term of the underlying grant fixed by statute.

It is quite plain that were it not for the patent and copyright features of such license agreements the term would be measured by use. . . .

In the patent and copyright cases the parties are dealing with a fixed statutory term and the monopoly granted by that term. This monopoly, created by Congress, is designed to preserve exclusivity in the grantee during the statutory term and to release the patented or copyrighted material to the general public for general use thereafter. This is the public policy of the statutes in reference to which such contracts are made and it is against this background that the parties to patent and copyright license agreements contract.

Here, however, there is no such public policy. The parties are free to contract with respect to a secret formula or trade secret in any manner which they determine for their own best interests. A secret formula or trade secret may remain secret indefinitely. It may be discovered by someone else almost immediately after the agreement is entered into. Whoever discovers it for himself by legitimate means is entitled to its use.

But that does not mean that one who acquires a secret formula or a trade secret through a valid and binding contract is then enabled to escape from an obligation to which he bound himself simply because the secret is discovered by a third party or by the general public. I see no reason why the court should imply such a term or condition in a contract providing on its face that payment shall be co-extensive with use. To do so here would be to rewrite the contract for the parties without any indication that they intended such a result. . . .

One who acquires a trade secret or secret formula takes it subject to the risk that there be a disclosure. The inventor makes no representation that the secret is non-discoverable. All the inventor does is to convey the knowledge of the formula or process which is unknown to the purchaser and which in so far as both parties then know is unknown to any one else. The terms upon which they contract with reference to this subject matter are purely up to them and are governed by what the contract they enter into provides.

If they desire the payments or royalties should continue only until the secret is disclosed to the public it is easy enough for them to say so. But there is no justification for implying such a provision if the parties do not include it in their contract, particularly where the language which they use by fair intendment provides otherwise. . . .

COMMENTS AND QUESTIONS

1. The scope of trade secret protection is limited, not by a fixed term of years but by the length of time the information remains secret. Indeed, trade secrets become a part of the public domain once secrecy is lost, and their owner cannot prevent even direct copying. It seems odd that contract law would require royalty payments from Warner-Lambert for 80 years (or presumably 130 or more years, as Listerine is still sold commercially), while every other competitor can copy the formula for free. Are there sound reasons for such a rule?

One such reason may be the economic value of freedom of contract. If a party chooses to contract to pay royalties for as long as it uses a product, it is free to do so, though courts will presume that contract rights over IP expire when the IP expires. *See Nova Chem., Inc. v. Sekisui Plastics Co.*, 579 F.3d 319 (3d Cir. 2009) (distinguishing *Warner-Lambert*: "Here, in contrast, nothing in the License Agreement suggests that the parties intended any ongoing obligations with respect to trade secrets after the 1995 termination of NOVA's obligation to maintain the secrecy of Sekisui's technical information."). Presumably, the amount of the royalty payments as well as their duration will reflect the value of the secret to the buyer, discounted by the likelihood of public disclosure. But doesn't this argument also apply to extensions of the patent or copyright term as well? *Compare Meehan v. PPG Indus.*, 802 F.2d 881, 886 (7th Cir. 1986), *and Boggild v. Kenner Prods.*, 776 F.2d 15, 1320-21 (6th Cir. 1985), which hold that it is illegal to patent or copyright misuse to agree to extend a patent or copyright beyond its term. Why does contract law appear to override trade secret law but not patent or copyright law?

2. The *Warner-Lambert* result is controversial. The RESTATEMENT (THIRD) OF UNFAIR COMPETITION takes the position that nondisclosure agreements which purport to protect information in the public domain may be unenforceable as an unreasonable restraint on trade. *See* §41, Comment *d,* at 472. Further, the Restatement notes that "because of the public interest in preserving access to information that is in the public domain, such an agreement will not ordinarily estop a defendant from contesting the existence of a trade secret." §39, Comment *d,* at 430. A number of cases support this view, which seems at odds with *Warner-Lambert. See, e.g., Gary Van Zeeland Talent, Inc. v. Sandas*, 267 N.W.2d 242 (Wis. 1978); *Sarkes Tarzian, Inc. v. Audio Devices, Inc.*, 166 F. Supp. 250 (S.D. Cal. 1958), *aff'd,* 283 F.2d 695 (9th Cir. 1960). In *Aqua Connect, Inc. v. Code Rebel, Inc.*, 2012 WL 469737 (C.D. Cal. Feb. 13, 2012), for example, the court rejected an effort to prohibit reverse engineering by standard form contract:

> This Court finds that the FAC does not support a legally cognizable trade misappropriation claim because the only improper means pled in the FAC is reverse engineering, which according to California law, "shall not be considered improper means" by itself. Plaintiff argues that the EULA form contract and its alleged breach by Movants can legally convert the alleged reverse engineering into an "improper means" of acquiring Plaintiff's trade secret. The Court finds, however, that Plaintiff's argument lacks merit. Justice Moreno in his concurrence to a California Supreme Court decision, states that "nowhere has it been recognized that a party wishing to protect proprietary information may employ a consumer form contract to, in effect, change the statutory definition of 'improper means' under trade secret law to include reverse engineering, so that an alleged trade secret holder may bring an action." *DVD Copy Control Ass'n, Inc. v. Bunner,* 31 Cal. 4th 864, 901 n.5, 4 Cal. Rptr. 3d 69, 75 P.3d 1 (2003) (Moreno, J., concurring).
>
> An analysis of the statutory language of the California Uniform Trade Secret Act corroborates Justice Moreno's concurrence. Civil Code section 3426.1, subdivision (a) specifically states that "[r]everse engineering alone shall not be considered improper means." Thus, from the plain language of the statute, reverse engineering must be combined with some other improper action in order for it to form the basis of a cognizable misappropriation claim. The Legislative

Committee Comments clarifies that the word "alone" refers to the fact that the reverse engineered item would have to be obtained "by a fair and honest means, such as purchase of the item on the open market for reverse engineering to be lawful." Civil Code §3426.1 (Legislative Committee Comment). Accordingly, reverse engineering is not an improper means of acquiring trade secret information when defendants acquire the item, from which the information is derived, through fair and honest means. Here, the Court finds that the FAC is insufficiently pled because it does not allege that the ACTS trial software was obtained through unfair or dishonest means. FAC ¶8 (alleging that Movants acquired ACTS by downloading a trial version of ACTS). Though a breach of the EULA may support a cognizable breach of contract claim, the Court finds that the mere presence of the EULA does not convert reverse engineering into an "improper means" within the definition of California trade secret law.

On the other hand, the Federal Circuit has seemingly endorsed the *Warner-Lambert* approach, holding that the issuance of a patent did not extinguish the confidentiality obligation imposed by a nondisclosure agreement, even though the issuance of the patent destroyed the trade secret that was the basis for the agreement. *Celeritas Technologies v. Rockwell Int'l Corp.*, 150 F.3d 1354 (Fed. Cir. 1998). The equities in that case might be thought to favor the plaintiff: the patent was held invalid, and so offered the plaintiff no relief against a theft of its technology. *Cf. Aronson v. Quick Point Pencil Co.*, 440 U.S. 257 (1979) (holding that the contract obligated licensee to continue paying royalties on an invention even though licensor's patent application had been rejected). But isn't that the risk a trade secret owner takes in deciding to patent (and therefore disclose) her invention? The Seventh Circuit has held that courts had no power to review business nondisclosure agreements for reasonableness, even though employee agreements were subject to a reasonableness requirement. *IDX Systems v. Epic Systems*, 285 F.3d 581 (7th Cir. 2002). And in *Bernier v. Merrill Air Engineers*, 770 A.2d 97 (Me. 2001), the Maine Supreme Court held that an employee violated a nondisclosure agreement by disclosing information that did not qualify as a trade secret.

3. Should such restrictions be governed by intellectual property law — making them unenforceable — or by contract law, which presumably would enforce them? The answer to that question will determine whether intellectual property laws (including trade secret laws) constitute binding governmental rules balancing competing interests or merely "default" rules that parties may opt to change. In practice, the courts have walked a hazily defined middle line, refusing to hold that intellectual property statutes preempt contracts which alter their terms, but also refusing to enforce certain contracts that go "too far" in upsetting the balance the intellectual property laws have struck.

4. What remedies are appropriate in a case in which a court enforces a contract that extends beyond the scope of trade secret law? Trade secret remedies (which as we will see can include injunctions, punitive damages, and even criminal penalties)? Or only traditional contract remedies?

F. THE SPECIAL CASE OF DEPARTING EMPLOYEES

Many of the thorniest issues in trade secret (and contract) law arise when employees leave a company in order either to start their own business or to take a job elsewhere. Such cases present a fundamental clash of rights between an employee and an employer, as Judge Adams suggests in the following excerpt from *SI Handling Systems v. Heisley*, 753 F.2d 1244, 1266-69 (3d Cir. 1985) (Adams, J., concurring):

When deciding the equitable issues surrounding the request for a trade secret injunction, it would seem that a court cannot act as a pure engineer or scientist, assessing the technical import of the information in question. Rather, the court must also consider economic factors since the very definition of "trade secret" requires an assessment of the competitive advantage a particular item of information affords to a business. Similarly, among the elements to be weighed in determining trade secret status are the value of the information to its owner and to competitors, and the ease or difficulty with which the information may be properly acquired or duplicated.

While the majority may be correct in suggesting that the trial court need not always "engage in extended analysis of the public interest," the court on occasion must apply the elements of sociology. This is so since trade secret cases frequently implicate the important countervailing policies served on one hand by protecting a business person from unfair competition stemming from the usurpation of trade secrets, and on the other by permitting an individual to pursue unhampered the occupation for which he or she is best suited. "Trade secrets are not . . . so important to society that the interests of employees, competitors and competition should automatically be relegated to a lower position whenever trade secrets are proved to exist." Robison, *The Confidence Game: An Approach to the Law About Trade Secrets*, 25 ARIZ. L. REV. 347, 382 (1983).

These observations take on more force, I believe, when a case such as the present one involves the concept of "know-how." Under Pennsylvania law an employee's general knowledge, skill, and experience are not trade secrets. Thus in theory an employer generally may not inhibit the manner in which an employee uses his or her knowledge, skill, and experience — even if these were acquired during employment. When these attributes of the employee are inextricably related to the information or process that constitutes an employer's competitive advantage — as increasingly seems to be the case in newer, high-technology industries — the legal questions confronting the court necessarily become bound up with competing public policies.

It is noteworthy that in such cases the balance struck by the Pennsylvania courts apparently has favored greater freedom for employees to pursue a chosen profession. The courts have recognized that someone who has worked in a particular field cannot be expected to forego the accumulated skills, knowledge, and experience gained before the employee changes jobs. Such qualifications are obviously very valuable to an employee seeking to sell his services in the marketplace. A person leaving one employer and going into the marketplace will seek to compete in the area of his or her greatest aptitude. In light of the highly mobile nature of our society, and as the economy becomes increasingly comprised of highly skilled or high-tech jobs, the individual's economic interests will more and more be buffeted by competitive advantage. Courts must be cautious not to strike a balance that unduly disadvantages the individual worker. . . .

In my view a proper injunction necessarily would impose the minimum restraint upon the free utilization of employee skill consistent with denying unfaithful employees an advantage from misappropriation of information. Thus, as I see it, the district court, on remand, should fashion an injunction that extends only so long as is essential to negate any unfair advantage that may have been gained by the appellants.

The majority opinion in *SI Handling* partially upheld a finding that two former employees had misappropriated trade secrets, but it vacated an injunction against them in order for the district court to reconsider its scope.

Departing employee cases represent over two-thirds of all trade secret cases. *See* David S. Almeling, et al., *A Statistical Analysis of Trade Secret Litigation in State Courts*, 46 GONZ. L. REV. 57, 60 (2011).

1. Employee Trade Secrets

i. *The Common Law Obligation to Assign Inventions*

At common law, ownership of inventions — including ownership of patent rights — was determined according to an employee's status under a long line of common law employee invention cases. In general, employees fall into one of three categories: (1) employees "hired to invent," which results in employer ownership of the invention; (2) employees who invent on the employer's time or using its resources, which results in a limited, nonexclusive "shop right" on the part of the employer to practice the invention; and (3) an employee's "independent invention," in which case the employee owns the invention. *See generally United States v. Dubilier Condenser Corp.*,

289 U.S. 178 (1933); John C. Stedman, *Employer-Employee Relations*, in FREDRIK NEUMEYER, THE EMPLOYED INVENTOR IN THE UNITED STATES 30, 40-41 (1971).

The first category is relatively straightforward. It seems logical to extend this treatment to consultants and others who are not "employees" in the strict sense. *Cf. McElmurry v. Arkansas Power & Light Co.*, 27 U.S.P.Q.2d 1129, 1135 n.15 (Fed. Cir. 1993) (upholding shop right in employer where inventor/patentee was a consultant); Robert P. Merges, *Intellectual Property and the Costs of Commercial Exchange: A Review Essay*, 93 MICH. L. REV. 1570 (1995) (highlighting the role of intellectual property in structuring non-employment-based organizations, such as consulting companies and joint ventures). Category (2) reflects situations where employers have less than a complete claim to the invention, but where the employer's facilities or resources are combined with the inventor's talent and industry to produce the invention. The employee owns it, but the employer is compensated by receiving a limited right to practice the invention. Notably, however, that right to practice does not include the right to sell the invention to others. *Beriont v. GTE Labs., Inc.*, 535 F. App'x 919 (Fed. Cir. 2013). Category (3) covers cases where the employee invents on his or her own time, outside the field of employment. *See Dubilier, supra*.

An employee's obligation to refrain from using an employer's trade secrets looks more onerous when it is the employee herself who came up with the secret. In *Wexler v. Greenberg*, 160 A.2d 430 (Pa. 1960), the Pennsylvania Supreme Court went out of its way to conclude that a departing employee was entitled to take formulas he had himself developed at his prior employer to work for a competitor. Despite the fact that the employee, Greenberg, was the chief chemist at the plaintiff, the court concluded that he was not in fact "hired to invent" and therefore owned the inventions he made.

The *Wexler* result, while it may seem fair, is not the majority rule. Even in Pennsylvania, *Wexler* is not always followed. *See Healthcare Affiliated Services v. Lippancy*, 701 F. Supp. 1142, 1155 (W.D. Pa. 1988) (rejecting *Wexler* analysis, emphasizing that although defendant developed inventions on his own, he did so using knowledge and information made available by the plaintiff employer). *But see Fidelity Fund v. DiSanto*, 500 A.2d 431 (Sup. Ct. Pa. 1985) (denying recovery against ex-employee salesman partly on the basis that he developed client contacts himself during employment).

Does the *Wexler* court confuse an employee's *general* knowledge and skills with specific inventions developed by the employee while at work *based* on that knowledge and skills? If an employee's job involves two tasks, working on established products (covered by trade secrets) and developing new ones, what effect will the *Wexler* rule have on the employee's allocation of time between these tasks?

ii.   Contracts That Restrict the Use of Trade Secrets

Wexler is explicitly based on the absence of a written agreement between employer and employee.[10] Suppose that Greenberg had signed a contract when he was hired which stated that "all discoveries, inventions, or intellectual property rights stemming from employee's work at Buckingham are the exclusive property of Buckingham." Would such a contract be enforceable? Does it matter whether Greenberg's "discoveries" were new formulas or ways to copy competitors' formulas?

An example of the more common situation, in which the court finds either an express or implied agreement to assign an employee's own inventions, is *Winston Research Corp. v. 3M Co.*, 350 F.2d 134 (9th Cir. 1965). There, the court dismissed an argument akin to Greenberg's as follows:

> Winston argues that information is protected from disclosure only if communicated to the employee by the employer who is seeking protection, and that the information involved in this case was not disclosed by [3M] to the employees subsequently hired by Winston, but rather was developed by these employees themselves, albeit while employed by [3M].

> We need not examine the soundness of the rule for which Winston contends, or its applicability to a case such as this in which a group of specialists engaged in related facets of a single development project change their employer. . . . [A]n obligation not to disclose may arise from circumstances other than communication in confidence by the employer. It may also rest upon an express or implied agreement. In the present case, an agreement not to disclose might be implied from [3M]'s elaborate efforts to maintain the secrecy of its development program, and the employees' knowledge of those efforts and participation in them. In any event, [3M] and its employees entered into express written agreements binding the latter not to disclose confidential information, and these agreements did not exclude information which the employee himself contributed.

Id. at 140.

Most companies require their employees to sign some sort of employment agreement, either when they are hired or at some point during their tenure. Employment agreements generally fall into one or more of three categories: confidentiality agreements, invention assignments, and noncompetition agreements. Confidentiality agreements, with which we are concerned here, generally recite that the employee

---

[10] The absence of such an agreement can be significant even in situations in which it might be assumed that the "employer" had a reasonable claim to the employee's invention. *Cf. Lariscey v. United States*, 20 U.S.P.Q.2d 1845 (Fed. Cir. 1991) (prison inmate owns rights to a secret process he developed while working in a prison shop).

will receive confidential information during her employment, and that she undertakes to keep it secret and not to use it for anyone other than the employer. Invention assignments give the employer the right to intellectual property created by the employee while she was employed. Noncompetition agreements limit the circumstances in which former employees can compete for customers with their former employers.

Presumably, employers may require their employees to agree not to use or disclose trade secrets to which they have access during employment. Virtually all employers do so. A variant on the departing employee who wishes to take her own inventions is the departing sales representative who wishes to "take" a list of customers (either a written list or one that they have memorized) in order to call on those customers for a competitor.[11] Customer lists are generally protectable as trade secrets, but enjoining employees from calling on customers with whom they have had longstanding relationships raises serious concerns about employee mobility. Two California cases frame the dispute. In *Moss, Adams & Co. v. Shilling*, 179 Cal. App. 3d 124 (1986), the court drew a line between an employee announcing her departure to start a competing company and actively soliciting old clients to follow her. The former was permissible, but the latter was not. This compromise was thrown into doubt by the decision in *Morlife Inc. v. Perry*, 66 Cal. Rptr. 2d 731 (Ct. App. 1997), where the court held that the passage of the Uniform Trade Secrets Act in California superseded *Moss, Adams* and that continuing personal relationships with former customers could constitute misappropriation of a trade secret. On the other hand, RESTATEMENT (THIRD) OF UNFAIR COMPETITION §41, Comment *d* states:

> The reasonableness of an agreement that merely prohibits the use or disclosure of particular information depends primarily upon whether the information protected by the agreement qualifies as a trade secret. If the information qualifies for protection under the rule stated in §39, a contract prohibiting its use or disclosure is generally enforceable according to its terms. Although in some cases courts have enforced nondisclosure agreements directed at information found ineligible for protection as a trade secret, many of these decisions merely reflect a more narrow definition of trade secret than that adopted in §39. However, a nondisclosure agreement that encompasses information that is generally known or in which the promisee has no protectable interest, such as a former

---

[11] Merely memorizing a trade secret rather than taking physical documents will not preclude a finding of misappropriation, though it may make misappropriation harder to detect. *See Ed Nowogroski Ins. Inc. v. Rucker*, 971 P.2d 936 (Wash. 1999). In *Stampede Tool Warehouse Inc. v. May*, 651 N.E.2d 209 (Ill. Ct. App. 1995), for example, the plaintiff alleged that former employees who started a competing business had misappropriated its trade secrets by memorizing a list of plaintiff's customers and soliciting those customers. The court found the defendants liable, reasoning that "memorization is one method of misappropriation." But if the case involved merely a former employee contacting those she knew from experience to be potential customers, rather than explicitly attempting to memorize a list of customers, it would be hard to fault the employee's conduct.

employee's promise not to use information that is part of the employee's general skill and training (*see* §42, Comment *d*), may be unenforceable as an unreasonable restraint of trade. Agreements that deny the promisor the right to use information that is in the public domain are ordinarily enforceable only if justified on the basis of interests other than the protection of confidential information.

Where should the line be drawn between permissible work and impermissible use of "secret" lists of customers? To whom does the value inherent in personal relationships belong?

A more difficult problem arises when employers attempt to limit an employee's use of information that does not constitute a trade secret under the legal standards described above. Can employers and employees "agree" that the employee will not use *any* information obtained during employment, whether it is public or not? This question parallels the problem of restrictive license provisions — are employers limited by the intellectual property laws to protecting only trade secrets that meet the statutory requirements, or are they free to impose additional restrictions on their employees so long as they do so by agreement? Courts struggle with this issue, with the majority concluding that "reasonable" contract restrictions on employees are enforceable even in the absence of a protectable trade secret. *See Bernier v. Merrill Air Engineers*, 770 A.2d 97 (Me. 2001); 12 ROGER MILGRIM, MILGRIM ON TRADE SECRETS §3.05[1][a], at 3-209 to 3-210. One state has even gone so far as to enact a statute that automatically assigns inventions to an employer provided they were developed in the course of employment and relate to the scope of the employee's work. Nev. Rev. Stat. §600.500.

On the other hand, in an attempt to alleviate the disparity in bargaining power between the employer and the inventor/employee, several states have adopted "freedom to create" statutes restricting the instances in which employers may compel assignment through contract. *See* Minn. Stat. Ann. §181.78 (1980); N.C. Gen. Stat. §66-57.1 to 57.2 (1981); Wash. Rev. Code Ann. §49.44.140 (1987); Cal. Labor Code §2870 (West 1987). These statutes provide that any employee invention assignment agreement that purports to give employers greater rights than they have under the statute is against public policy and unenforceable. The California statute is a good example. It provides that contracts may not require assignment of "invention[s] that the employee developed entirely on his or her own time without using the employer's equipment, supplies, facilities, or trade secret information" unless the invention relates to the employer's current or demonstrably anticipated business. Cal. Labor Code §2870.

Some commentators have argued that the United States is slipping in technological innovation because this country's inventors (the vast majority of whom are employed) have lost their incentive to create partially due to assignment agreements. After labeling the state legislation described above as "a step forward," one author writes: "Comprehensive federal legislation is necessary to provide employed inventors greater control over, and interests in, their inventions in order to create the psychological and financial incentives required to increase technological innovation in the United States. . . . Federal legislation would obviate the need for state reform and would bring uniformity that would solve the potential problem of inventors employed by multistate corporations." Henrik D. Parker, *Reform for Rights of Employed Inventors*, 57 S. CAL. L. REV. 603 (1984). *See also* ORLY LOBEL, TALENT WANTS TO BE FREE (2014) (arguing for an open market for labor). *But see* Robert P. Merges, *The Law and Economics of Employee Inventions*, 13 HARV. J.L. & TECH. 1 (1999) (endorsing some contractual restrictions on employee mobility).

PROBLEM

Problem II-14. Helen, an employee of CarTech, is assigned to work on solving a particular problem in car design. She works for two years on that problem for CarTech, without success. Two months after Helen leaves CarTech to start her own company, she puts out a product that incorporates a solution to the same problem. CarTech sues Helen for misappropriation of trade secrets. At trial, CarTech proves that Helen came up with her system while at CarTech and that she decided to start her own company to exploit her invention rather than disclose it to CarTech. As a result, CarTech had no knowledge of the idea until Helen came out with her product. Should CarTech prevail in its trade secret suit, assuming that there was no employment or invention contract between the parties?

---

iii.   Trailer Clauses

The common law rules just described apply in the absence of contracts, as stated; but they also have some relevance even when written agreements are in place. This is so because, under principles similar to those applied in the law of noncompetition agreements, the law limits the ability of employers to claim ownership by contract of all employee inventions no matter how tenuously related to the employment relationship. A case study in the limits of invention assignment agreements involves the "trailer clause," a contractual provision that requires employees to assign their rights not only in inventions made during the period of employment but also for a certain time thereafter. Trailer clauses developed in response to a number of cases which held that, absent contractual provisions to the contrary, an employee's ideas did not belong to the employer unless they were written down in tangible form (such as a patent disclosure statement) before the employee left work. *See Jamesbury Corp. v. Worcester Valve Co.*, 443 F.2d 205 (1st Cir. 1971).

Of course, even if an employer uses a trailer clause, there is always the risk that the former employee will simply wait out the duration of the term and then conveniently make the discovery upon the trailer clause's expiration. Such a strategy was attempted by an inventor in at least one case. Fortunately for the employer, the court did not believe the defendant inventor's story that the conception date for his flow meter was five days after the expiration of the six months specified in the trailer clause:

> The perfection of a flow meter proved to be a painstakingly intricate process involving extensive testing. It is therefore difficult to believe that after a long and distinguished career with Plaintiff, Mr. Halmi in his musing five days after the trailer clause expired for the first time came up with the idea for the NTV. Although the word "Eureka!" has allegedly been uttered by more than one inventor over the years, the concept at issue does not lend itself to such sudden discovery. The court finds that the concept of the '434 patent must have existed in Mr. Halmi's mind before his employment with GSC ended. Mr. Halmi therefore violated his agreement with GSC.

General Signal Corp. v. Primary Flow Signal, Inc., 1987 U.S. Dist. LEXIS 6929, at *10 (D.R.I. Jul. 27, 1987).

Generally, trailer clauses are enforceable only to the extent that they are "reasonable." Although trailer clauses are generally enforceable, clauses of particularly long or indefinite duration may run afoul of the antitrust laws as well as being unenforceable. *See United Shoe Machinery Co. v. La Chapelle*, 212 Mass. 467, 99 N.E. 289 (1912). One court expressed the requirement of reasonableness as follows:

> Hold-over clauses are simply a recognition of the fact of business life that employees sometimes carry with them to new employers inventions or ideas so related to work done for a former employer that in equity and good conscience the fruits of that work should belong to that former employer. In construing and applying hold-over clauses, the courts have held that they must be limited to *reasonable times* . . . and to *subject matter* which an employee worked on or had knowledge of during his employment. . . . Unless expressly agreed otherwise, an employer has no right under a holdover clause to inventions made outside the scope of the employee's former activities, and made on and with a subsequent employer's time and funds.

Dorr-Oliver, Inc. v. United States, 432 F.2d 447, 452 (Ct. Cl. 1970). Corporations may have trouble enforcing restrictions that are broader in scope. *See Applied Materials, Inc. v. Advanced Micro-Fabrication Equipment (Shanghai) Co.*, 630 F. Supp. 2d 1084 (N.D. Cal. 2009) (rejecting one-year trailer clause as an invalid noncompete agreement). This is particularly true of large conglomerates that attempt to require the assignment of any invention related to their (diverse) fields of business. *See Ingersoll-Rand Co. v. Ciavatta*, 110 N.J. 609, 542 A.2d 879, 896 n.6 (1988).

In addition to controlling inventions made shortly after departure, employers may be able to lay claim to ideas conceived while the defendant was employed, even if those ideas aren't put into practice until years after the defendant leaves her job. *See Motorola Inc. v. Lemko Corp.*, 2012 WL 74319 (N.D. Ill. Jan. 10, 2012) (employment agreement that required assignment of "ideas" as well as "inventions" could cover an idea developed at a former employer that wasn't turned into a patent application until five years later).

2. Noncompetition Agreements

Employees inevitably learn a great deal about a business on the job. They may learn the trade secrets of their employer, but they may also learn such basic information as how many people it takes to make a product, who is likely to buy the product, where to advertise, etc. Further, employees develop personal relationships with vendors, customers, and others that are immensely useful in business. For this reason, many employers would like to prevent their employees from competing against them at all. Such employers often ask their employees to sign "noncompetition agreements," which prevent the employee from competing with his former employer for customers for a set period of time. Should such agreements be enforceable?

 Edwards v. Arthur Andersen LLP
Supreme Court of California
81 Cal. Rptr. 3d 282 (Cal. 2008)

CHIN, J.

We granted review to address the validity of noncompetition agreements in California and the permissible scope of employment release agreements. We limited our review to the following issues: To what extent does Business and Professions Code section 16600 prohibit employee noncompetition agreements. . . .

We conclude that section 16600 prohibits employee noncompetition agreements unless the agreement falls within a statutory exception. . . . We therefore affirm in part and reverse in part the Court of Appeal judgment.

Facts

In January 1997, Raymond Edwards II (Edwards), a certified public accountant, was hired as a tax manager by the Los Angeles office of the accounting firm Arthur Andersen LLP (Andersen). Andersen's employment offer was made contingent upon Edwards's signing a noncompetition agreement, which prohibited him from working for or soliciting certain Andersen clients for limited periods following his termination. The agreement was required of all managers, and read in relevant part: "If you leave the Firm, for eighteen months after release or resignation, you agree not to perform professional services of the type you provided for any client on which you worked during the eighteen months prior to release or resignation. This does not prohibit you from accepting employment with a client. For twelve months after you leave the

Firm, you agree not to solicit (to perform professional services of the type you provided) any client of the office(s) to which you were assigned during the eighteen months preceding release or resignation. You agree not to solicit away from the Firm any of its professional personnel for eighteen months after release or resignation." Edwards signed the agreement.

Between 1997 and 2002, Edwards continued to work for Andersen, moving into the firm's private client services practice group, where he handled income, gift, and estate tax planning for individuals and entities with large incomes and net worth. Over this period he was promoted to senior manager and was on track to become a partner. In March 2002, the United States government indicted Andersen in connection with the investigation into Enron Corporation, and in June 2002, Andersen announced that it would cease its accounting practices in the United States. In April 2002, Andersen began selling off its practice groups to various entities. In May 2002, Andersen internally announced that HSBC USA, Inc. (a New York-based banking corporation), through a new subsidiary, Wealth and Tax Advisory Services (WTAS), would purchase a portion of Andersen's tax practice, including Edwards's group.

In July 2002, HSBC offered Edwards employment. Before hiring any of Andersen's employees, HSBC required them to execute a "Termination of Non-compete Agreement" (TONC) in order to obtain employment with HSBC. Among other things, the TONC required employees to, inter alia, (1) voluntarily resign from Andersen; (2) release Andersen from "any and all" claims, including "claims that in any way arise from or out of, are based upon or relate to Employee's employment by, association with or compensation from" defendant; (3) continue indefinitely to preserve confidential information and trade secrets except as otherwise required by a court or governmental agency; (4) refrain from disparaging Andersen or its related entities or partners; and (5) cooperate with Andersen in connection with any investigation of, or litigation against, Andersen. In exchange, Andersen would agree to accept Edwards's resignation, agree to Edwards's employment by HSBC, and release Edwards from the 1997 noncompetition agreement.

. . .

Edwards signed the HSBC offer letter, but he did not sign the TONC. In response, Andersen terminated Edwards's employment and withheld severance benefits. HSBC withdrew its offer of employment to Edwards.

Procedural History

. . . In the published part of its opinion, the Court of Appeal held: (1) the noncompetition agreement was invalid under section 16600, and requiring Edwards to sign the TONC as consideration to be released from it was an independently wrongful act for purposes of the elements of Edwards's claim for intentional interference with prospective economic advantage. . . .

Discussion

A. Section 16600

Under the common law, as is still true in many states today, contractual restraints on the practice of a profession, business, or trade, were considered valid, as long as they were reasonably imposed. (Bosley Medical Group v. Abramson (1984) 161 Cal. App. 3d 284, 288, 207 Cal. Rptr. 477.) This was true even in California. (Wright v. Ryder (1868) 36 Cal. 342, 357 [relaxing original common law rule that all restraints on trade were invalid in recognition of increasing population and competition in trade].) However, in 1872 California settled public policy in favor of open competition, and rejected the common law "rule of reasonableness," when the Legislature enacted the Civil Code. Today in California, covenants not to compete are void, subject to several exceptions discussed briefly below.

Section 16600 states: "Except as provided in this chapter, every contract by which anyone is restrained from engaging in a lawful profession, trade, or business of any kind is to that extent void." The chapter excepts noncompetition agreements in the sale or dissolution of corporations (§16601), partnerships (*ibid.*; §16602), and limited liability corporations (§16602.5). In the years since its original enactment as Civil Code section 1673, our courts have consistently affirmed that section 16600 evinces a settled legislative policy in favor of open competition and employee mobility. (*See D'sa v. Playhut, Inc.* (2000) 85 Cal. App. 4th 927, 933, 102 Cal. Rptr. 2d 495.) The law protects Californians and ensures "that every citizen shall retain the right to pursue any lawful employment and enterprise of their choice." (*Metro Traffic Control, Inc. v. Shadow Traffic Network* (1994) 22 Cal. App. 4th 853, 859, 27 Cal. Rptr. 2d 573.) It protects "the important legal right of persons to engage in businesses and occupations of their choosing." (Morlife, Inc. v. Perry (1997) 56 Cal. App. 4th 1514, 1520, 66 Cal. Rptr. 2d 731.)

. . .

Under the statute's plain meaning, therefore, an employer cannot by contract restrain a former employee from engaging in his or her profession, trade, or business unless the agreement falls within one of the exceptions to the rule. (§16600.) Andersen, however, asserts that we should interpret the term "restrain" under section 16600 to mean simply to "prohibit," so that only contracts that totally prohibit an employee from engaging in his or her profession, trade, or business are illegal. It would then follow that a mere limitation on an employee's ability to practice his or her vocation would be permissible under section 16600, as long as it is reasonably based.

Andersen contends that some California courts have held that section 16600 (and its predecessor statutes, Civil Code former sections 1673, 1674, and 1675) are the statutory embodiment of prior common law, and embrace the rule of reasonableness in evaluating competitive restraints. (*See, e.g.*, *South Bay Radiology Medical Associates v. Asher* (1990) 220 Cal. App. 3d 1074, 1080, 269 Cal. Rptr. 15 (South Bay Radiology) [§16600 embodies common law prohibition against restraints on trade]; *Vacco Industries, Inc. v. Van Den Berg* (1992) 5 Cal. App. 4th 34, 47-48, 6 Cal. Rptr. 2d 602 (*Vacco*) [§16600 is codification of common law reasonable restraint rule].) Andersen claims that these cases show that section 16600 "prohibits only broad agreements that prevent a person from engaging entirely in his chosen business, trade or profession. Agreements that do not have this broad effect — but merely regulate some aspect of post-employment conduct, e.g., to prevent raiding [employer's personnel] — are not within the scope of [s]ection 16600."

As Edwards observes, however, the cases Andersen cites to support a relaxation of the statutory rule simply recognize that the statutory exceptions to section 16600 reflect the same exceptions to the rule against noncompetition agreements that were implied in the common law. . . .

We conclude that Andersen's noncompetition agreement was invalid. As the Court of Appeal observed, "The first challenged clause prohibited Edwards, for an 18-month period, from performing professional services of the type he had provided while at Andersen, for any client on whose account he had worked during 18 months prior to his termination. The second challenged clause prohibited Edwards, for a year after termination, from 'soliciting,' defined by the agreement as providing professional services to any client of Andersen's Los Angeles office." The agreement restricted Edwards from performing work for Andersen's Los Angeles clients and therefore restricted his ability to practice his accounting profession. (*See Thompson v. Impaxx, Inc.* (2003) 113 Cal. App. 4th 1425, 1429, 7 Cal. Rptr. 3d 427 [distinguishing "trade route" and solicitation cases that protect trade secrets or confidential proprietary information].) The noncompetition agreement that Edwards was required to sign before commencing employment with Andersen was therefore invalid because it restrained his ability to practice his profession. (*See Muggill, supra*, 62 Cal. 2d at pp. 242-243, 42 Cal. Rptr. 107, 398 P.2d 147.)

B. *Ninth Circuit's Narrow-Restraint Exception*

Andersen asks this court to adopt the limited or "narrow-restraint" exception to section 16600 that the Ninth Circuit discussed in Campbell v. Trustees of Leland Stanford Jr. Univ. (9th Cir. 1987) 817 F.2d 499 (*Campbell*), and that the trial court relied on in this case in order to uphold the noncompetition agreement. In *Campbell*, the Ninth Circuit acknowledged that California has rejected the common law "rule of reasonableness" with respect to restraints upon the ability to pursue a profession, but concluded that section 16600 "only makes illegal those restraints which preclude one from engaging in a lawful profession, trade, or business." (*Campbell, supra*, 817 F.2d at p. 502.) The court remanded the case to the district court in order to allow the employee to prove that the noncompetition agreement at issue completely restrained him from practicing his "profession, trade, or business within the meaning of section 16600." (*Campbell*, at p. 503.)

The confusion over the Ninth Circuit's application of section 16600 arose in a paragraph in *Campbell*, in which the court noted that some California courts have excepted application of section 16600 "'where one is barred from pursuing only a small or limited part of the business, trade or profession.'" (*Campbell, supra*, 817 F.2d at p. 502.) . . .

Andersen is correct, however, that *Campbell* has been followed in some recent Ninth Circuit cases to create a narrow-restraint exception to section 16600 in federal court. For example, *International Business Machines Corp. v. Bajorek* (9th Cir. 1999) 191 F. . . .

Contrary to Andersen's belief, however, California courts have not embraced the Ninth Circuit's narrow-restraint exception. Indeed, no reported California state court decision has endorsed the Ninth Circuit's reasoning, and we are of the view that California courts "have been clear in their expression that section 16600 represents a strong public policy of the state which should not be diluted by judicial fiat." (*Scott v. Snelling and Snelling, Inc.* (N.D. Cal. 1990) 732 F. Supp. 1034, 1042.) Section 16600 is unambiguous, and if the Legislature intended the statute to apply only to restraints that were unreasonable or overbroad, it could have included language to that effect. We reject Andersen's contention that we should adopt a narrow-restraint exception to section 16600 and leave it to the Legislature, if it chooses, either to relax the statutory restrictions or adopt additional exceptions to the prohibition-against-restraint rule under section 16600. . . .

DISPOSITION

We hold that the noncompetition agreement here is invalid under section 16600, and we reject the narrow-restraint exception urged by Andersen. Noncompetition agreements are invalid under section 16600 in California even if narrowly drawn, unless they fall within the applicable statutory exceptions of sections 16601, 16602, or 16602.5. . . .

We therefore affirm in part and reverse in part the Court of Appeal judgment, and remand the matter for proceedings consistent with the views expressed above.

In *Comprehensive Technologies Int'l v. Software Artisans, Inc.*, 3 F.3d 730 (4th Cir. 1993), CTI brought suit for copyright infringement and misappropriation of trade secrets against a group of former employees who left the company to form a competing company which shortly thereafter came out with a new product. The court concluded that the departing employees had not infringed CTI's copyrights or misappropriated any CTI trade secrets. Nonetheless, the court enforced an agreement signed by one of the employees, Dean Hawkes. The agreement provided that for a period of twelve months after he left CTI, Hawkes would not engage directly or indirectly in any business within the United States (financially as an investor or lender or as an employee, director, officer, partner, independent contractor, consultant or owner or in any other capacity calling for the rendition of personal services or acts of management, operation or control) which is in competition with the business of CTI. For purposes of this Agreement, the "business of CTI" shall be defined as the design, development, marketing, and sales of CLAIMS EXPRESS- and EDI LINK-type PC-based software with the same functionality and methodology. . . .

The court stated the general legal standard governing covenants not to compete:

Virginia has established a three-part test for assessing the reasonableness of restrictive employment covenants. Under the test, the court must ask the following questions:

1. Is the restraint, from the standpoint of the employer, reasonable in the sense that it is no greater than is necessary to protect the employer in some legitimate business interest?

2. From the standpoint of the employee, is the restraint reasonable in the sense that it is not unduly harsh and oppressive in curtailing his legitimate efforts to earn a livelihood?

3. Is the restraint reasonable from the standpoint of a sound public policy?

Blue Ridge Anesthesia & Critical Care, Inc. v. Gidick, 239 Va. 369, 389 S.E.2d 467, 469 (Va. 1990). If a covenant not to compete meets each of these standards of reasonableness, it must be enforced. As a general rule, however, the Virginia courts do not look favorably upon covenants not to compete, and will strictly construe them against the employer. The employer bears the burden of demonstrating that the restraint is reasonable.

The court found that Hawkes's agreement, which prevented him from competing with CTI anywhere in the United States, was reasonable because CTI had offices, clients, or prospects in many (though not all) states throughout the country. Further, the court noted:

. . . As the individual primarily responsible for the design, development, marketing and sale of CTI's software, Hawkes became intimately familiar with every aspect of CTI's operation, and necessarily acquired information that he could use to compete with CTI in the marketplace. When an employee has access to confidential and trade secret information crucial to the success of the employer's business, the employer has a strong interest in enforcing a covenant not to compete because other legal remedies often prove inadequate. It will often be difficult, if not impossible, to prove that a competing employee has misappropriated trade secret information belonging to his former employer. On the facts of this case, we conclude that the scope of the employment restrictions is no broader than necessary to protect CTI's legitimate business interests.

COMMENTS AND QUESTIONS

1. The California rule set out in §16600 is the minority rule. Most states apply an overarching requirement of "reasonableness" to covenants not to compete, as the Virginia court did in *CTI. See* Mich. Comp. Laws §445.774a (noncompetition agreements enforceable if the agreement is "reasonable as to its duration, geographical area, and type of employment or line of business"). They may disagree, however, on what restrictions are reasonable. In *Gateway 2000 Inc. v. Kelley*, 9 F. Supp. 2d 790 (E.D. Mich. 1998), the court invalidated an agreement that was similar to the one upheld in *CTI*. The court relied in part on the fact that the company had later adopted a less restrictive noncompetition provision, suggesting that the older, broader provision was not necessary to protect its interests. And the Virginia Supreme Court has held unreasonable a noncompetition agreement that prevented the defendant from working for a competitor in any capacity, rather than specifying particular positions the defendant could not take. *Modern Environments, Inc. v. Stinnett*, 561 S.E.2d 694 (Va. 2002).

Some courts have limited the enforcement of noncompetition agreements to situations where trade secrets are likely to be used or disclosed if an employee is allowed to compete. The New York Court of Appeals, for example, took the following view:

> Undoubtedly judicial disfavor of these covenants is provoked by "powerful considerations of public policy which militate against sanctioning the loss of a man's livelihood" (*Purchasing Assoc. v. Weitz. . . .*) Indeed, our economy is premised on the competition engendered by the uninhibited flow of services, talent and ideas. Therefore, no restrictions should fetter an employee's right to apply to his own best advantage the skills and knowledge acquired by the overall experience of his previous employment. This includes those techniques which are but "skillful variations of general processes known to the particular trade" (RESTATEMENT, AGENCY 2d, §396 Comment *b*).

> Of course, the courts must also recognize the legitimate interest an employer has in safeguarding that which has made his business successful and to protect himself against deliberate surreptitious commercial piracy. Thus restrictive covenants will be enforceable to the extent necessary to prevent the disclosure or use of trade secrets or confidential customer information. In addition injunctive relief may be available where an employee's services are unique or extraordinary and the covenant is reasonable. This latter principle has been interpreted to reach agreements between members of the learned professions.

Reed Roberts Assocs. v. Strauman, 40 N.Y.2d 303, 353 N.E.2d 590 (Ct. App. 1976). Does the *Reed Roberts* approach in essence hold noncompetition agreements unenforceable, since it allows them to operate only when trade secret laws also provide relief? Are there sound reasons to enforce an employer-employee agreement that prevents the employee from competing after termination? State statutes which address the issue have generally been interpreted to allow such "reasonable" employee agreements, regardless of how the statutes themselves are worded. Of course, what agreements are "reasonable" is far from clear in this context, and is the subject of considerable litigation. Many states have invalidated noncompetition agreements on the ground that they were unreasonable. *See, e.g., Mutual Service Casualty Ins. Co. v. Brass,* 625 N.W.2d 648 (Wis. Ct. App. 2001); *Brentlinger Enters. v. Curran,* 752 N.E.2d 994 (Ohio Ct. App. 2001); *Harvey Barnett, Inc. v. Shidler,* 143 F. Supp. 2d 1247 (D. Colo. 2001); *Mertz v. Pharmacists Mutual Ins.,* 625 N.W.2d 197 (Neb. 2001); *City Slickers, Inc. v. Douglas,* 40 S.W.3d 805 (Ark. Ct. App. 2001).

If a noncompetition agreement is overbroad, should the courts refuse to enforce it at all, or should they narrow it to make it enforceable? *See Coleman v. Retina Consultants,* 687 S.E.2d 457 (Ga. 2009) (refusing to reform unenforceable agreement).

2. There seems to be no question in the *CTI* court's mind that none of the defendants misappropriated any CTI trade secrets, infringed any copyrights, or otherwise "took" anything belonging to CTI in starting Software Artisans. Why doesn't that dispose of the case? What social purpose is served by enjoining former employees from pursuing their livelihood? Shouldn't the mobility and liberty of individuals be the paramount consideration, as California courts have suggested?

3. Despite the absolute nature of the California statute, California courts have interpreted this statute to bar noncompetition agreements altogether in employee contracts but to permit such agreements if they are ancillary to the sale of a business, so long as the terms of the agreement are "reasonable." *See Monogram Indus., Inc. v. SAR Indus., Inc.,* 64 Cal. App. 3d 692, 134 Cal. Rptr. 714, 718 (1976).[12] Further, while California courts will not enforce a noncompetition agreement, they will prevent departing employees from using or disclosing their former employer's trade secrets. *See State Farm Mutual Automobile Ins. Co. v. Dempster,* 344 P.2d 821 (Cal. Ct. App. 1959); *Gordon v. Landau,* 49 Cal. 2d 690, 321 P.2d 456 (Cal. 1958). Other states, including Alabama, Florida, Louisiana, Montana, and North Dakota, also forbid noncompetition agreements. Still other states, including Colorado, Delaware, Massachusetts, and Tennessee, forbid them in professional settings but allow them in other contexts. *See, e.g., Murfreesboro Med. Clinic v. Udom,* 166 S.W.3d 674 (Tenn. 2005). *But see Central Indiana Podiatry PC v. Krueger,* 882 N.E.2d 723 (Ind. 2008) (noncompete agreement enforceable against physician if reasonable).

---

[12] On the other hand, one court refused to enforce an agreement settling an employment discrimination lawsuit because it included a provision that the plaintiff would not be rehired by the defendant or any of its successors. The court worried that that agreement ran afoul of section 16600. *Golden v. Cal. Emergency Physicians Med. Grp.,* 782 F.3d 1083 (9th Cir. 2015).

4. The strength of California's commitment to the free movement of employees was demonstrated in *The Application Group, Inc. v. The Hunter Group, Inc.*, 72 Cal. Rptr. 2d 73 (Ct. App. 1998). There, the California Court of Appeals held that §16600 precluded the enforcement of a noncompetition agreement entered into in Maryland between a Maryland employer and employee, where the employee subsequently left to take a job telecommuting from Maryland for a California company. Despite the fact that Maryland courts would enforce the agreement, the California court concluded that California's interests were "materially stronger" than Maryland's in this case. *See also D'Sa v. Playhut, Inc.*, 85 Cal. App. 4th 927, 102 Cal. Rptr. 2d 495 (2000) (disregarding choice of law provision in holding a noncompete agreement unenforceable).

California's strong public policy has led to conflicts with other states. The most notable example is *Advanced Bionics v. Medtronic*, 87 Cal. App. 4th 1235 (2001), in which both California and Minnesota courts asserted that their law should control, with the Minnesota court enjoining the departing employee and the California court enjoining the employer from proceeding with the suit. The California Supreme Court ultimately reversed, not because it didn't consider the policy of employee mobility important but because it thought the specter of conflicting judgments unseemly. *Advanced Bionics v. Medtronic*, 29 Cal. 4th 697, 128 Cal. Rptr. 2d 172 (2002). But doing so may simply subjugate California's policy to the law of any other state that would enforce a noncompete agreement, even if the employee doesn't work in that state. *See IBM Corp. v. Bajorek*, 191 F.3d 1033 (9th Cir. 1999) (applying New York law to enjoin competition against New York company by employee in California, and disregarding California policy to the contrary); *Amazon.com, Inc. v. Powers*, 2012 WL 6726538 (W.D. Wash. Dec. 27, 2012) (enforcing Washington choice of law clause in noncompete contract against employee who left Amazon.com to work for Google in California). For a contrary ruling giving nationwide effect to a refusal to enforce a noncompete agreement under Georgia law, *see Palmer & Cay v. Marsh & McLennan*, 404 F.3d 1297 (11th Cir. 2005).

Is there a reasoned way to resolve such conflicts in public policy? Or will the inevitable result be a "race to the courthouse"?

5. What are the competing policy interests at stake in noncompetition clauses? On the one hand, it seems unfair to employers to simply allow their employees to do whatever they want upon leaving. Particularly where the employees were in positions of importance, their knowledge of the employer's trade secrets may leave the former employer at a competitive disadvantage. In a competitive industry, preventing the disclosure of trade secrets is far preferable to suing for misappropriation after they have already been disclosed. A noncompetition agreement may be a reasonable way for an employer to prevent a problem — and a lawsuit — before it starts.

On the other hand, such restrictions seem onerous burdens to impose on employees. Imagine how you would feel as an attorney if you left a firm only to find that you were prevented from practicing law in the same field or geographic region for the next two years. (In this regard, it is significant that even *Reed Roberts* expressed the view that the "learned professions" were properly subject to noncompetition agreements.) In addition, it is not completely clear that such provisions benefit companies in the long run. Strauman, the defendant in *Reed Roberts,* came to Reed Roberts after having worked for a competitor for four years. He was hired in part because of his valuable experience in the industry. What if Strauman's former employer had required him to sign an enforceable noncompete agreement? For scholarly criticism of enforcing noncompetes, *see* Charles Tait Graves, *Analyzing the Non-Competition Covenant as a Category of Intellectual Property Regulation,* 3 HASTINGS SCI. & TECH. L.J. 69 (2010).

Some scholars have suggested that there is a more practical economic motivation for precluding such noncompetition agreements. They argue that the relative success of California's Silicon Valley compared to Boston's Route 128 is directly attributable to the prevalence of noncompetition agreements in Route 128 companies, which prevented the free movement of employees and therefore discouraged start-up companies. *See* ORLY LOBEL, TALENT WANTS TO BE FREE: WHY WE SHOULD LEARN TO LOVE LEAKS, RAIDS, AND FREE RIDING (2015); Ronald J. Gilson, *The Legal Infrastructure of High Technology Industrial Districts: Silicon Valley, Route 128, and Covenants Not to Compete,* 74 N.Y.U. L. REV. 575 (1999); ANNALEE SAXENIAN, REGIONAL ADVANTAGE: CULTURE AND COMPETITION IN SILICON VALLEY AND ROUTE 128 (1994).

6. When a firm requires an existing employee to sign an employment agreement containing a covenant not to compete, the employee is giving up something substantial. What is the employer giving up? Some cases have raised the issue of consideration (in the contract law sense) in such an agreement on the part of the employer; they generally conclude that there is consideration, on one theory or another. *See, e.g., Central Adjustment Bureau v. Ingram,* 678 S.W.2d 28 (Tenn. 1984) (consideration in the form of continuous employment over a long period of time); *Alex Sheshunoff Mgmt. Servs. v. Johnson,* 209 S.W.3d 644, 646 (Tex. 2006) (same; rejecting prior Texas case law); *Lake Land Emp. Grp. v. Columber,* 804 N.E.2d 27 (Ohio 2004) (consideration in the form of continuing to employ an at-will employee; three Justices dissented).

Why not require, out of fairness, that an employer who insists on such a covenant must pay the employee's salary during the term of the noncompete provision? Several other nations follow this approach:

- *Germany*: The German Commercial Code requires that an employer compensate the employee for the complete duration of time that the covenant is in effect up to a maximum duration of two years. *See* WENDI S. LAZAR & GARY R. SINISCALCO (EDS.), RESTRICTIVE COVENANTS AND TRADE SECRETS IN EMPLOYMENT LAW: AN INTERNATIONAL SURVEY, Vol. I, 17-5 (2010) (German Commercial Code §74(a)(1)). Compensation must be at least half of the employee's pay during the previous 12 months of employment.

- *China*: In 2008, China adopted a similar regime. *See* PRC Labor Contract Law of 1 January 2008, Articles 23-24 (2008). Employers may include noncompete restrictions of no more than two years in employment agreements with senior technicians, senior managers, and other employees who have access to trade secrets. Under the law, the employer must compensate the employee throughout the post-employment noncompete period, although the law does not specify the compensation level. It is unclear whether the compensation must be at the prior level or can be as low as minimum wage.

- *United Kingdom*: The UK employs a "garden leave" policy, under which the employee must provide the employer with a long notice period before changing employment. The employer is required to pay full salary and benefits during this period, but cannot force the employee to work. (The employee can stay at home and tend his or her garden.) The garden leave period must be reasonable under the circumstances of the employment.

Some U.S. companies have adopted such approaches on a voluntary basis. *See Marcam Corp. v. Orchard*, 885 F. Supp. 294 (D. Mass. 1995) (enforcing a contractual provision preventing Orchard from working for any competitor in the country for one year, provided that Marcam paid 110 percent of the salary offered by the competitor). *See* Sonya P. Passi, *Compensated Injunctions: A More Equitable Solution to the Problem of Inevitable Disclosure*, 27 BERKELEY TECH. L.J. 927 (2012) (suggesting such an approach). Is the employee likely to be satisfied by that approach? How employable will he be after sitting idle for two years?

7. Does the reasonableness of a noncompete agreement depend on the likelihood of trade secret misappropriation? In *Zodiac Records, Inc. v. Choice Envt'l Servs.*, 112 So.2d 587 (Fla. Ct. App. 2013), the court held that a three-year noncompete was unreasonable and violated due process where the plaintiff stipulated that it could not show that the defendant would use its trade secrets unless the agreement was enforced.

8. Can an employer avoid state laws restricting noncompetition agreements by requiring the employee to sign an agreement that does not forbid employment, but calls for the payment of a "liquidated damage" penalty if the employee goes to work for a competitor? Is such a monetary penalty effectively the same as enforcing a noncompete? What if the employer doesn't forbid employment, but conditions the grant of stock options on not going to work for a competitor? Note that it is common in high-tech industries to grant employees stock options that "vest" over a period of

years, giving the employee an incentive not to leave and abandon the unvested options.

3. The "Inevitable Disclosure" of Trade Secrets

Are there circumstances in which an employee's use or disclosure of trade secrets is "inevitable"? Consider the following case:

PepsiCo, Inc. v. Redmond
United States Court of Appeals for the Seventh Circuit
54 F.3d 1262 (7th Cir. 1995)

Posner, J.:

"[The Seventh Circuit ordered the issuance of a preliminary injunction preventing Quaker Oats Co. from employing Redmond, a former general manager for PepsiCo North America. Redmond was general manager of PepsiCo's California business unit for ten years until, in 1994, he accepted Quaker's offer to become the chief operating officer of its Gatorade and Snapple Co. divisions. The court held that Redmond would inevitably be forced to use PepsiCo trade secrets for his new employer]

PepsiCo asserts that Redmond cannot help but rely on PCNA [PepsiCo North America] trade secrets as he helps plot Gatorade and Snapple's new course, and that these secrets will enable Quaker to achieve a substantial advantage by knowing exactly how PCNA will price, distribute, and market its sports drinks and new age drinks and being able to respond strategically. This type of trade secret problem may arise less often, but it nevertheless falls within the realm of trade secret protection under the present circumstance.

Quaker and Redmond assert that they have not and do not intend to use whatever confidential information Redmond has by virtue of his former employment. They point out that Redmond has already signed an agreement with Quaker not to disclose any trade secrets or confidential information gleaned from his earlier employment. They also note with regard to distribution systems that even if Quaker wanted to steal information about PCNA's distribution plans, they would be completely useless in attempting to integrate the Gatorade and Snapple beverage lines.

The defendants' arguments fall somewhat short of the mark. Again, the danger of misappropriation in the present case is not that Quaker threatens to use PCNA's secrets to create distribution systems or coopt PCNA's advertising and marketing ideas. Rather, PepsiCo believes that Quaker, unfairly armed with knowledge of PCNA's plans, will be able to anticipate its distribution, packaging, pricing, and marketing moves. Redmond and Quaker even concede that Redmond might be faced with a decision that could be influenced by certain confidential information that he obtained while at PepsiCo. In other words, PepsiCo finds itself in the position of a coach, one of whose players has left, playbook in hand, to join the opposing team before the big game. Quaker and Redmond's protestations that their distribution systems and plans are entirely different from PCNA's are thus not really responsive. . . .

Quaker and Redmond do not assert that the confidentiality agreement is invalid; such agreements are enforceable when supported by adequate consideration.[10] Rather, they argue that "inevitable" breaches of these contracts may not be enjoined. The case on which they rely, however, *R. R. Donnelley & Sons Co. v. Fagan*, 767 F. Supp. 1259 (S.D.N.Y. 1991) (applying Illinois law), says nothing of the sort. The *R. R. Donnelley* court merely found that the plaintiffs had failed to prove the existence of any confidential information or any indication that the defendant would ever use it. *Id.* at 1267. The threat of misappropriation that drives our holding with regard to trade secrets dictates the same result here.

. . . In *Teradyne* [v. Clear Communications Corp., 707 F. Supp. 353 (N.D. Ill. 1989)], Teradyne alleged that a competitor, Clear Communications, had lured employees away from Teradyne and intended to employ them in the same field. In an insightful opinion, Judge Zagel observed that "threatened misappropriation can be enjoined under Illinois law" where there is a "high degree of probability of inevitable and immediate . . . use of . . . trade secrets." *Teradyne,* 707 F. Supp. at 356. Judge Zagel held, however, that Teradyne's complaint failed to state a claim because Teradyne did not allege "that defendants have in fact threatened to use Teradyne's secrets or that they will inevitably do so." [The *Teradyne* court held]:

> the defendants' claimed acts, working for Teradyne, knowing its business, leaving its business, hiring employees from Teradyne and entering the same field (though in a market not yet serviced by Teradyne) do not state a claim of threatened misappropriation. All that is alleged, at bottom, is that defendants could misuse plaintiff's secrets, and plaintiffs fear they will. This is not enough. It may be that little more is needed, but falling a little short is still falling short.

Id. at 357.

In *AMP* we affirmed the denial of a preliminary injunction on the grounds that the plaintiff AMP had failed to show either the existence of any trade secrets or the likelihood that defendant Fleischhacker, a former AMP employee, would compromise those secrets or any other confidential business information. AMP, which produced electrical and electronic connection devices, argued that Fleischhacker's new position at AMP's competitor would inevitably lead him to compromise AMP's trade secrets regarding the manufacture of connectors. *AMP,* 823 F.2d at 1207. In rejecting that

---

[10] The confidentiality agreement is also not invalid for want of a time limitation. *See* 765 ILCS 1065/8(b)(1) ("[A] contractual or other duty to maintain secrecy or limit use of a trade secret shall not be deemed to be void or unenforceable solely for lack of durational or geographic limitation on the duty."). Nor is there any question that the confidentiality agreement covers much of the information PepsiCo fears Redmond will necessarily use in his new employment with Quaker.

argument, we emphasized that the mere fact that a person assumed a similar position at a competitor does not, without more, make it "inevitable that he will use or disclose . . . trade secret information" so as to "demonstrate irreparable injury." *Id.*

The ITSA, *Teradyne,* and *AMP* lead to the same conclusion: a plaintiff may prove a claim of trade secret misappropriation by demonstrating that defendant's new employment will inevitably lead him to rely on the plaintiff's trade secrets. *See also* 1 Jager, . . . §7.02[2][a] at 7-20 (noting claims where "the allegation is based on the fact that the disclosure of trade secrets in the new employment is inevitable, whether or not the former employee acts consciously or unconsciously"). . . .

PepsiCo presented substantial evidence at the preliminary injunction hearing that Redmond possessed extensive and intimate knowledge about PCNA's strategic goals for 1995 in sports drinks and new age drinks. The district court concluded on the basis of that presentation that unless Redmond possessed an uncanny ability to compartmentalize information, he would necessarily be making decisions about Gatorade and Snapple by relying on his knowledge of PCNA trade secrets. It is not the "general skills and knowledge acquired during his tenure with" PepsiCo that PepsiCo seeks to keep from falling into Quaker's hands, but rather "the particularized plans or processes developed by [PCNA] and disclosed to him while the employer-employee relationship existed, which are unknown to others in the industry and which give the employer an advantage over his competitors." *AMP,* 823 F.2d at 1202. The Teradyne and AMP plaintiffs could do nothing more than assert that skilled employees were taking their skills elsewhere; PepsiCo has done much more.

COMMENTS AND QUESTIONS

1. What Pepsi trade secrets are threatened by Redmond's "defection" to Quaker? The information Redmond possesses includes (1) new flavor and product packaging information; (2) pricing strategies; (3) Pepsi's "attack plans" for specific markets; and (4) Pepsi's new distribution plan, being pilot tested in California. What advantages would Quaker obtain by knowing this information? How long would it take Quaker to find out about each in the absence of inside knowledge from Redmond? If all these items would become readily apparent the moment Pepsi's plans were implemented, does this circumstance suggest a limit on the appropriate remedy?

Assuming that Quaker will learn of Pepsi's strategies from Redmond unless enjoined, how expensive would it be for Pepsi to develop a new marketing strategy? Could the new strategy take advantage of the fact that Quaker *thinks* it knows what Pepsi will do? How would this possibility affect Quaker's use of the information?

2. Assume that the market for sports and new age drinks is increasingly concentrated in the hands of two companies, Pepsi and Quaker. Should this affect the outcome of the case? Given the court's decision, what can one predict about future salary and benefits negotiations in this industry for employees like Redmond?

3. Is it fair to preclude former employees from doing any work for a competitor simply because they would be incapable of not using the information they obtained from their former employer? Note that the Seventh Circuit upheld an injunction against Redmond's employment for only six months. At the same time, the court issued a permanent injunction against the disclosure of Pepsi's trade secrets. Does this result make sense? If the theory of inevitable disclosure is that Redmond *must* use Pepsi's secrets in his employment, could he go to work for Quaker at the end of six months without violating the permanent injunction? Perhaps the court was implicitly seeking to balance Redmond's interests in employment mobility, reasoning that the business secrets would be less important after that time.

4. Is there any way that that employee can "keep separate" the ideas and projects he was working on for his old employer from the ideas and projects he will be asked to develop for his new employer? If not, should the employer be entitled to prevent the employee from competing even if it cannot show that the employee *intends* to use its trade secrets? *Cf. Al Minor & Assocs. v. Martin*, 881 N.E.2d 850 (Ohio 2008) (holding that the fact that a defendant had the plaintiff's secrets in his memory rather than on a disk or document did not preclude a finding of misappropriation).

IBM made just this argument when one of its disk drive specialists, Peter Bonyhard, left IBM to work for Seagate Technology in the same field. A preliminary injunction granted by the district court against Bonyhard's employment was reversed by the Eighth Circuit in an unpublished decision. IBM v. Bonyhard, 962 F.2d 12 (8th Cir. 1992). Several other decisions have also rejected inevitable disclosure as a basis for an injunction against employment. *Campbell Soup Co. v. Giles*, 47 F.3d 467 (1st Cir. 1995); *FMC Corp. v. Cyprus Foote Mineral Co.*, 899 F. Supp. 1477 (W.D.N.C. 1995). In *Campbell*, the court grounded its rejection of inevitable disclosure theory in the public policy that favors employee mobility. It quoted the district court opinion in the case, holding that public policy "counsels against unilateral conversion of non-disclosure agreements into non-competitive agreements. If Campbell wanted to protect itself against the competition of former employees, it should have done so by contract. This court will not afford such protection after the fact." *See also Carolina Chem. Equip. Co. v. Muckenfuss*, 471 S.E.2d 721 (S.C. Ct. App. 1996) (agreement entitled "Covenant Not to Divulge Trade Secrets" was actually an overly broad and unenforceable covenant not to compete, because the definition of trade secrets in the agreement was so broad that it effectively prevented any competition).

The judicial debate over the appropriateness of the inevitable disclosure doctrine has continued. Several cases have followed *PepsiCo* and enjoined employment absent either proof of trade secret misappropriation or an enforceable noncompetition agreement. *See Uncle B's Bakery v. O'Rourke*, 920 F. Supp. 1405 (N.D. Iowa 1996) (citing *PepsiCo* with approval and enjoining former plant manager at a bagel manufacturer from working for any competing business within a 500-mile radius); *see also*

Nat'l Starch & Chem. Corp. v. Parker Chem. Corp., 530 A.2d 31 (N.J. Super. Ct. App. Div. 1987). By contrast, one court has adopted what might be called a "partial inevitable disclosure" injunction. In *Merck & Co. v. Lyon*, 941 F. Supp. 1443 (M.D.N.C. 1996), the court enjoined a pharmaceutical marketing director from discussing his former employer's products or pricing for a period of two years, but refused to enjoin him from competing employment altogether absent a "showing of bad faith." Another court has accepted an inevitable disclosure theory, but issued an injunction limited to nine months, reasoning that the secrets likely to be disclosed would turn stale over time. *Novell Inc. v. Timpanogos Research Grp.*, 46 U.S.P.Q.2d 1197 (D. Utah 1998).

Other courts, particularly those in California, continue to reject inevitable disclosure altogether. *See, e.g., The Retirement Group v. Galante*, 176 Cal. App. 4th 1226, 1238 (2009); *Holton v. Physician Oncology Servs.*, 742 S.E.2d 702 (Ga. 2013); *GlobeSpan, Inc. v. O'Neill*, 151 F. Supp. 2d 1229 (C.D. Cal. 2001); *Danjaq, LLC v. Sony Corp.*, 50 U.S.P.Q.2d 1638 (C.D. Cal. 1999), *aff'd on other grounds*, 263 F.3d 942 (9th Cir. 2001); *Bayer Corp. v. Roche Molecular Sys.*, 72 F. Supp. 2d 1111, 1120 (N.D. Cal. 1999); *Cardinal Health Staffing Network v. Bowen*, 106 S.W.3d 452 (Tex. App. 2004); *Del Monte Fresh Produce Co. v. Dole Food Co.*, 148 F. Supp. 2d 1326, 1337-39 (S.D. Fla. 2001); *LeJeune v. Coin Acceptors*, 849 A.2d 451 (Md. 2004); *Whyte v. Schlage Lock Co.*, 101 Cal. App. 4th 1443, 125 Cal. Rptr. 2d 277 (Ct. App. 2002).

The federal Defend Trade Secrets Act, enacted in 2016, acknowledges the conflicts but declines to adopt an inevitable disclosure rule that would override the public policy of California and other states. *See* S. Rep., No. 114-220, 114th Cong., 2d Sess., Defend Trade Secrets Act of 2016 12 n.12 (2016). To avoid doing so, the DTSA requires that proof of threatened future misappropriation be based on evidence of conduct and intent and not simply inferred from the employee's position or knowledge. 18 U.S.C. §1836(b)(3)(A)(i). That section provides a court may:

(A) grant an injunction

(i) to prevent any actual or threatened misappropriation described in paragraph (1) on such terms as the court deems reasonable, provided the order does not

(I) prevent a person from entering into an employment relationship, and that the conditions placed on such employment shall be based on evidence of threatened misappropriation and not merely on the information the person knows; or

(II) otherwise conflict with an applicable State law prohibiting restraints on the practice of a lawful profession, trade, or business.

The SENATE REPORT notes that "[t]hese limitations on injunctive relief were included to protect employee mobility, as some have expressed concern that the injunctive relief authorized under the bill could override State-law limitations that safeguard employee mobility and thus could be a substantial departure from existing law in those states." S. REP., S. 1890 at 12. The DTSA would, however, continue to permit state laws to prohibit inevitable disclosure.

5. How inevitable must the disclosure be? In *Bimbo Bakeries v. Botticella*, 613 F.3d 102 (3d Cir. 2010), the court affirmed an injunction preventing a senior executive of Bimbo Bakeries, the maker of Thomas' English Muffins, from going to work for competitor Hostess. Botticella was one of only seven people at Bimbo who knew the formula for the muffins. Notably, the court did not find that it was "virtually impossible" for Botticella to do his job at Hostess without disclosing the formula. Instead, the court found it sufficient that there was a "substantial threat" of misappropriation. Does this result make sense? If the defendant denies any intent to deliver the secret to his new employer, what evidence should a court require before preventing him from going to work? Some courts seek to strike a middle ground, holding that where misappropriation is merely threatened rather than actual, the plaintiff must demonstrate "a high degree of probability of inevitable disclosure. . . . Mere knowledge of a trade secret is not enough, even where the person with such knowledge takes a comparable position with a competitor." *Katch, LLC v. Sweetser*, 2015 WL 6942132 (D. Minn. Nov. 10, 2015).

4. Nonsolicitation Agreements

If the departing employees can avoid using the employer's trade secrets when they leave, the question becomes a rather different one — is it acceptable to hire away a group of employees? In *Diodes, Inc. v. Franzen*, 260 Cal. App. 2d 244, 67 Cal. Rptr. 19 (1968), the president and vice-president of Diodes left to form a competing company, called Semtech. Before they left, the officers solicited a number of Diodes employees to join them. Diodes sued the departing employees, alleging a number of claims centering on unfair competition and breach of fiduciary duty. The court dismissed the complaint, stating:

> As a general principle, one who unjustifiably interferes with an advantageous business relationship to another's damage may be held liable therefor. The product is bottled under a variety of labels, including unfair competition, interference with advantageous relations, contract interference, and inducing breach of contract.
>
> Even though the relationship between an employer and his employee is an advantageous one, no actionable wrong is committed by a competitor who solicits his competitor's employees or who hires away one or more of his competitor's employees who are not under contract, so long as the inducement to leave

is not accompanied by unlawful action. In the employee situation the courts are concerned not solely with the interests of the competing employers, but also with the employee's interest. The interests of the employee in his own mobility and betterment are deemed paramount to the competitive business interests of the employers, where neither the employee nor his new employer has committed any illegal act accompanying the employment change.

67 Cal. Rptr. at 25-26 (citations omitted). *See also Reeves v. Hanlon*, 33 Cal. 4th 1140 (2004) (a competitor who uses only lawful means to solicit at-will employees does not tortiously interfere with economic advantage).

Can employers change this result by forcing their employees to sign "nonsolicitation agreements" that prevent a departing employee from soliciting other employees to join him? What if such agreements also prohibit departing employees from soliciting their former customers? In a case that has been heavily criticized on other grounds, the Ninth Circuit has upheld (albeit without discussion) an injunction against solicitation of employees or customers based on such a nonsolicitation agreement. *See MAI Systems Corp. v. Peak Computing, Inc.*, 991 F.2d 511, 523 (9th Cir. 1993). Other courts and commentators take a more guarded approach, prohibiting solicitation of customers only where there is active inducement to breach an employment contract or where departing employees have taken a customer list which is itself a trade secret. *Cf.* James H. A. Pooley, *Restrictive Employee Covenants in California*, 4 SANTA CLARA COMPUTER & HIGH TECH. L.J. 251, 259 (1988).

If it is legal for an employee to change jobs, why should it be illegal for someone to invite them to do so? *See* ORLY LOBEL, TALENT WANTS TO BE FREE (2014) (arguing against the enforcement of nonsolicitation agreements). Are a group of employees departing together more likely to misappropriate trade secrets?

Should former employees be allowed to compete for the business of their old *customers*? Does your answer depend on whether the employees are using trade secrets in the solicitation? On whether the employee has signed a nonsolicitation agreement? Courts that have allowed agreements preventing the solicitation of customers have nonetheless made it clear that it is only affirmative solicitation of the customer that is forbidden; a departing employee is free to work for a former customer who approaches her. *Paramount Tax v. H&R Block*, 683 S.E.2d 141 (Ga. App. 2009).

Should the dominance of the employer in the industry matter? In *Wood v. Acordia of W. Va., Inc.*, 618 S.E.2d 415 (2005), the court upheld a two-year agreement preventing insurance agents from soliciting any of Acordia's current, former, or prospective customers. In dissent, Justice Starcher pointed out that Acordia was so dominant in the West Virginia insurance market that "every prospect in the market has been spoken for by an Acordia salesman." The agreement at issue thus effectively prevents all competition.

PROBLEM

Problem II-15.   You have been offered a position with a high-technology start-up company. They ask you to sign the following agreement. Do you sign it? Is it enforceable?

EMPLOYMENT, CONFIDENTIAL INFORMATION, AND INVENTION ASSIGNMENT AGREEMENT

As a condition of my employment with Science Company, its subsidiaries, affiliates, successors, or assigns (together the "Company"), and in consideration of my employment with the Company and my receipt of the compensation now and hereafter paid to me by the Company, I agree to the following:

1. *Confidential Information*

(a) *Company Information.* I agree at all times during the term of my employment and thereafter, to hold in strictest confidence, and not to use, except for the benefit of the Company, or to disclose to any person, firm, or corporation without written authorization of the Board of Directors of the Company, any Confidential Information of the Company. I understand that "**Confidential Information**" means any Company proprietary information, technical data, trade secrets or know-how, including, but not limited to, research, product plans, products, services, customer lists and customers (including, but not limited to, customers of the Company on whom I called or with whom I became acquainted during the term of my employment), markets, software, developments, inventions, processes, formulas, technology, designs, drawings, engineering, hardware configuration information, marketing, finances, or other business information disclosed to me by the Company either directly or indirectly in writing, orally, or by drawings or observation of parts or equipment. I further understand that Confidential Information does not include any of the foregoing items which has become publicly known and made generally available through no wrongful act of mine or of others who were under confidentiality obligations as to the item or items involved.

(b) *Third Party Information.* I recognize that the Company has received and in the future will receive from third parties their confidential or proprietary information subject to a duty on the Company's part to maintain the confidentiality of such information and to use it only for certain limited purposes. I agree to hold all such confidential or proprietary information in the strictest confidence and not to disclose it to any person, firm, or corporation or to use it except as necessary in carrying out my work for the Company consistent with the Company's agreement with such third party.

2. *Inventions*

I agree that I will promptly make full written disclosure to the Company, will hold in trust for the sole right and benefit of the Company, and hereby assign to the Company, or its designee, all my right, title, and interest in and to any and all inventions, original works of authorship, developments, concepts, improvements or trade secrets, whether or not patentable or registrable under copyright or similar laws, which I may solely or jointly conceive or develop or reduce to practice, or cause to be conceived or developed or reduced to practice (collectively referred to as "Inventions"), during the period of time I am in the employ of the Company and for three months thereafter, except as provided below. I further acknowledge that all original works of authorship which are made by me (solely or jointly with others) within the scope of and during the period of my employment with the Company and which are protectable by copyright are "works made for hire," as that term is defined in the United States Copyright Act.

3. *Conflicting Employment*

I agree that, during the term of my employment with the Company and for a period of one year thereafter, I will not engage in any other employment, occupation, consulting, or other business activity in competition with or directly related to the business in which the Company is now involved or becomes involved during the term of my employment, nor will I engage in any other activities that conflict with my obligations to the Company.

4. *Returning Company Documents*

I agree that at the time of leaving the employ of the Company, I will deliver to the Company (and will not keep in my possession, recreate or deliver to anyone else) any and all devices, records, data, notes, reports, proposals, lists, correspondence, specifications, drawings, blueprints, sketches, materials, equipment, other documents or property, or reproductions of any aforementioned items developed by me pursuant to my employment with the Company or otherwise belonging to the Company, its successors or assigns.

5. *Notification to New Employer*

In the event that I leave the employ of the Company, I hereby grant consent to notification by the Company to my new employer about my rights and obligations under this Agreement.

6. *Solicitation of Employees*

I agree that for a period of twelve (12) months immediately following the termination of my relationship with the Company for any reason, whether with or without cause, I shall not either directly or indirectly solicit, induce, recruit or encourage any of the Company's employees to leave their employment, or take away such employees, or attempt to solicit, induce, recruit, encourage, or take away employees of the Company, either for myself or for any other person or entity.

G. REMEDIES

As might be expected given the fluidity of doctrine in trade secret law, there are disparate remedies for trade secret misappropriation stemming from different remedial concerns. The Uniform Trade Secrets Act sets forth the following remedies for misappropriation:

Section 2

(a) Actual or threatened misappropriation may be enjoined. Upon application to the court, an injunction shall be terminated when the trade secret has ceased to exist, but the injunction may be continued for an additional reasonable period of time in order to eliminate commercial advantage that otherwise would be derived from the misappropriation.

(b) If the court determines that it would be unreasonable to prohibit future use, an injunction may condition future use upon payment of a reasonable royalty for no longer than the period of time the use could have been prohibited.

(c) In appropriate circumstances, affirmative acts to protect a trade secret may be compelled by court order.

Section 3

(a) In addition to or in lieu of injunctive relief, a complainant may recover damages for the actual loss caused by misappropriation. A complainant also may recover for the unjust enrichment caused by misappropriation that is not taken into account in computing damages for actual loss.

(b) If willful and malicious misappropriation exists, the court may award exemplary damages in an amount not exceeding twice any award made under subsection (a).

Section 4

If (i) a claim of misappropriation is made in bad faith, (ii) a motion to terminate an injunction is made or resisted in bad faith, or (iii) willful and malicious misappropriation exists, the court may award reasonable attorney's fees to the prevailing party.

What motivates this hodgepodge of remedial measures? As we shall see in the chapters to come, most intellectual property statutes operate on the basis of "property rules." That is, as in cases involving real property, the owner of the intellectual property right is entitled to judicial assistance in protecting the right from future interference. Normally, this assistance comes in the form of injunctive relief. By contrast, most tort and contract cases do not involve injunctive relief but rather damages designed to make the plaintiff "whole" in the sense of restoring her to the position she occupied before the tort, or to the position she expected to occupy if the contract had been performed.

Section 2 of the Uniform Trade Secrets Act seems to entitle trade secret plaintiffs to property-like protection, at least so long as their secret remains a secret. But §2(b) holds open the possibility that courts may refuse to grant such an injunction, settling instead for a reasonable "royalty" (presumably a court's attempt to approximate what the parties might have agreed to pay in a licensing transaction). This provision casts some doubt on the "property entitlement" a trade secret owner might expect.

Similar doubt pervades the provisions on damages. Concepts like "reasonable royalty," "lost profits," and limited-time injunctions designed to "eliminate commercial advantage" all sound like restitutionary measures, aimed at making the plaintiff whole after a loss without necessarily punishing or deterring the defendant. But further provisions permit trade secret plaintiffs to recover for "unjust enrichment" on the part of defendants, and to recover treble damages and attorney fees in the case of willful misappropriation. And in some circumstances misappropriation of trade secrets can be a criminal offense, an idea that is certainly more consistent with a property entitlement rule than a tort or contract rule.

Generally, injunctions are available as a remedy in trade secret cases. Since injunctions offer only prospective relief, however, damages for preinjunction activities may also be collected. Since, unlike patents and copyrights, trade secrets have no definite term, the length of the injunction is often a difficult issue. The following case illustrates the use of one important measure of trade secret injunctions, the "head start" theory.

Winston Research Corp. v. 3M Corp.
United States Court of Appeals for the Ninth Circuit
350 F.2d 134 (9th Cir. 1965)

BROWNING, Circuit Judge:

For some uses of precision tape recorder/reproducers, the time interval between coded signals must be recorded and reproduced with great accuracy. To accomplish this, the tape must move at as constant a speed as possible during both recording and reproduction, and any changes in tape speed during recording must be duplicated as nearly as possible during reproduction. The degree to which a particular tape recorder/reproducer accomplishes, this result is measured by its "time-displacement error."

An electronic device known as a "servo" system is commonly used to reduce time-displacement error by detecting fluctuations in tape speed and immediately adjusting the speed of the motor. Machines prior to the Mincom machine employed a flywheel to inhibit fluctuation in tape speed by increasing the inertia of the system. However, the flywheel reduced the effectiveness of the servo system since the increased inertia prevented rapid adjustments in the speed of the motor.

The effectiveness of the servo system in prior machines was also reduced by resonances created by the moving parts. The range of sensitivity of the servo system was limited to exclude the frequencies of the interfering resonances. This had the disadvantage of limiting the capacity of the servo system to respond to a full range of variations in the speed of the tape.

To solve these problems Mincom eliminated the flywheel and reduced the mass of all other rotating parts. This reduced the inertia of the tape transport system, permitting rapid adjustments in tape speed. Interfering resonances were eliminated by mechanical means. This permitted use of a servo system sensitive to a wide range of frequencies, and hence capable of rapid response to a wide range of variations in tape speed. After four years of research and development based upon this approach, Mincom produced a successful machine with an unusually low time-displacement error.

In May 1962, when Mincom had substantially completed the research phase of its program and was beginning the development of a production prototype, Johnson, who was in charge of Mincom's program, left Mincom's employment. He joined Tobias, who had previously been discharged as Mincom's sales manager, in forming Winston Research Corporation. In late 1962, Winston contracted with the government to develop a precision tape reproducer. Winston hired many of the technicians who had participated in the development of the Mincom machine to work on the design and development of the Winston machine.

In approximately fourteen months, Winston completed a machine having the same low time-displacement error as the Mincom machine.

Conflicting policy considerations come into play in deciding what limitations should be imposed upon an employee in the use and disclosure of information acquired in the course of a terminated employment relationship — or, conversely, what protection should be extended to the former employer against use and disclosure of such information.

On the one hand, restrictions upon the use and disclosure of such information limit the employee's employment opportunities, tie him to a particular employer, and weaken his bargaining power with that employer. Such restrictions interfere with the employee's movement to the job in which he may most effectively use his skills. They inhibit an employee from either setting up his own business or from adding his strength to a competitor of his employer, and thus they diminish potential competition. Such restrictions impede the dissemination of ideas and skills throughout industry. The burdens that they impose upon the employee and society increase in proportion to the significance of the employee's accomplishments, and the degree of his specialization.

On the other hand, restrictions upon an employee's disclosure of information that was developed as a result of the employer's initiative and investment, and which was entrusted to the employee in confidence, are necessary to the maintenance of decent standards of morality in the business community. Unless protection is given against unauthorized disclosure of confidential business information by employees, employee-employer relationships will be demoralized; employers will be compelled to limit communication among employees with a consequent loss in efficiency; and business, espionage, deceit, and fraud among employers will be encouraged. . . .

. . . [S]tate law protecting trade secrets cannot be based "on a policy of rewarding or otherwise encouraging the development of secret processes or devices. The protection is merely against breach of faith and reprehensible means of learning another's secret." RESTATEMENT, TORTS §757, comment b.

The district court found, and Winston concedes, that Johnson and the other former Mincom employees based Winston's development program upon the same approach to the problem of achieving a low time-displacement error as they had pursued in developing the Mincom machine. The district court further found that this general approach was not a trade secret of Mincom's. Finally, the district court found that the particular embodiment of these general concepts in the Mincom machine was Mincom's trade secret, and had been improperly utilized by the former Mincom employees in developing the Winston machine.

[The court affirmed the district court's finding that Winston had misappropriated Mincom's trade secrets.]

The district court enjoined Winston Research Corporation, Johnson, and Tobias from disclosing or using Mincom's trade secrets in any manner for a period of two years from the date of judgment. The court also required the assignment of certain patent applications to Mincom. No damages were awarded. . . . Mincom argues that the injunction should have been permanent, or at least for a substantially longer period. Winston contends that no injunctive relief was appropriate.

Mincom was, of course, entitled to protection of its trade secrets for as long as they remained secret. The district court's decision to limit the duration of injunctive relief was necessarily premised upon a determination that Mincom's trade secrets would shortly be fully disclosed, through no fault of Winston, as a result of public announcements, demonstrations, and sales and deliveries of Mincom machines. Mincom has not seriously challenged this implicit finding, and we think the record fully supports it. . . .

We think the district court's approach was sound. A permanent injunction would subvert the public's interest in allowing technical employees to make full use of their knowledge and skill and in fostering research and development. On the other hand, denial of any injunction at all would leave the faithless employee unpunished where, as here, no damages were awarded; and he and his new employer would retain the benefit of a headstart over legitimate competitors who did not have access to the trade secrets until they were publicly disclosed. By enjoining use of the trade secrets for the approximate period it would require a legitimate Mincom competitor to develop a successful machine after public disclosure of the secret information, the district court denied the employees any advantage from their faithlessness, placed Mincom in the position it would have occupied if the breach of confidence had not occurred prior to the public disclosure, and imposed the minimum restraint consistent with the realization of these objectives upon the utilization of the employees' skills. . . .

Winston also challenges the district court's determination that "knowledge of the reasons for" the particular specifications of the Mincom machine, and "knowledge of what not to do . . . and how not to make the same mistakes" as Mincom had made in arriving at these specifications, were Mincom trade secrets. [Although we agree with the district court's conclusion that such "negative know-how" is a trade secret, in the circumstances of this case we can see no way to prohibit Mincom's former employees from using such knowledge without prohibiting them from using their general knowledge and experience at the same time. In an appropriate case, this kind of knowledge can be protected by an injunction or even an award of damages, but this is not such a case.] . . .

Mincom argues that the district court should have awarded money damages as well as injunctive relief. We think the district court acted well within its discretion in declining to do so. Since Winston sold none of its machines, it had no profits to disgorge. The evidence as to possible future profits was at best highly speculative. To enjoin future sales and at the same time make an award based on future profits from the prohibited sales would result in duplicative and inconsistent relief, and the choice that the district court made between these mutually exclusive alternatives was not an unreasonable one. There was evidence that Winston would probably sell its machine and realize profits after the injunction expired, but these sales and profits, as we have seen, would not be tainted by breach of confidence, since Winston could by that time have developed its machine from publicly disclosed information. . . .

Finally, Mincom's employment contracts required its employees to assign to Mincom inventions conceived during employment, and inventions conceived within one year of termination of employment that were "based upon" confidential information. Mincom sought to require the assignment of one patent and a number of patent applications. The district court received evidence as to when each invention was conceived and its relationship to Mincom's secrets.

The district court found that three patent applications involved inventions conceived during the inventors' employment by Mincom, and ordered assignment on that basis. The court also found that a patent and some other patent applications involving inventions conceived after the employees left Mincom and went to Winston were not based on Mincom's confidential trade secrets. [The mere fact that they were conceived after the employees moved to Winston was not the reason for this finding — the reason was that these later inventions simply were not based on Mincom's confidential information.] We think these findings have support in the record and are not clearly erroneous. [Judgment affirmed.]

COMMENTS AND QUESTIONS

1. Should injunctions issue as a matter of course in trade secret cases? The general rule in IP law does not make injunctions automatic, but applies a four-factor balancing test that asks whether the plaintiff will be irreparably injured absent an injunction, whether the grant or denial of an injunction would impose more hardship, and where the public interest lies. *See eBay, Inc. v. MercExchange LLC*, 547 U.S. 388 (2006). Because the public disclosure of a trade secret can destroy the secret altogether, courts and commentators have traditionally thought injunctions appropriate to prevent an injury that truly is irreparable. But in the wake of *eBay* some courts have denied injunctive relief. *See, e.g., Faiveley Transport Malmo AB v. Wabtec Corp.*, 559 F.3d 110 (2d Cir. 2009); *Am. Airlines, Inc. v. Imhof*, 620 F. Supp. 2d 574 (S.D.N.Y. 2009) (refusing to presume irreparable injury; plaintiff did not show that the defendant was likely to disclose the documents he took to his new employer).

Should there be a presumption that injunctive relief is appropriate? Such a presumption is typical of cases involving real property, but no such rule exists in most tort cases, and certainly not in typical contract cases. Are damages sufficient to protect trade secret owners? Perhaps not, since trade secrets are often hard to value, and misappropriation by one party can destroy the secret altogether. On the other hand, the parties could contract for injunctive relief, at least in employment cases, using noncompetition or confidentiality agreements. Should the law impose obligations the parties have not undertaken voluntarily? Should it refuse to enforce contract terms that the parties have agreed to? *See East v. Aqua Gaming Inc.*, 805 So. 2d 932 (Fla. Dist. Ct. App. 2001) (affirming injunction against use of trade secrets, but vacating injunction that prevented competition in the absence of an enforceable noncompete agreement).

One problem with such "automatic" injunctive relief is that it is difficult — and costly — to enforce. Is it an appropriate use of judicial resources to supervise employer-employee relationships on an ongoing basis? Is there a more cost-effective alternative to such supervision?

2. "Head-start injunctions" are available to plaintiffs who have published or otherwise disclosed their secret at some point after it was misappropriated. Suppose Anne possesses a secret that she is in the process of commercializing. Suppose further that it takes Anne two years after developing the secret to bring the product to market, at which point the secret is disclosed. If Benjamin steals Anne's idea during the development process (say, at month 12), Benjamin will be able to get to market one year earlier than if he had waited until the information became public. In such a case, courts will issue a "head-start" injunction for a period of one year, putting Benjamin

in the same position he would have been in without the secret. *See, e.g., Verigy US Inc. v. Mayder*, 2008 WL 564634 (N.D. Cal. Feb. 29, 2008) (granting a five-month injunction to account for the lag time defendant would have faced in getting to market absent misappropriation).

Even if such an injunction is impossible (for example, because Benjamin has already entered the market), courts may allow him to continue using the former secret but require him to pay a "reasonable royalty" to Anne. The reasonable royalty is presumably set by the court, in an effort to approximate the royalty Anne might have charged Benjamin in a voluntary transaction.

Is a reasonable royalty a fair solution in such a situation? *See Mid-Michigan Comp. Sys. v. Marc Glassman Inc.*, 416 F.3d 505 (6th Cir. 2005) (basing damages for misappropriation of computer software on a reasonable royalty). At least one commentator has suggested that such a remedy "is peculiarly inappropriate to redress a situation where injunctive relief ought to be applied." *See* 12 ROGER MILGRIM, MILGRIM ON TRADE SECRETS §1.01[2][a], at 1-36 n.20 (citing a district court decision concluding that limiting relief to a reasonable royalty invites misappropriation).

Is a reasonable royalty always appropriate, even if there is no evidence that the plaintiff lost money (or the defendant gained it) as a result of the misappropriation? In *Ajaxo Inc. v. E*Trade Fin. Corp.*, 115 Cal. Rptr. 3d 168 (Ct. App. 2010), the court held that it was error to refuse to award a reasonable royalty where the plaintiff could not prove damages or unjust enrichment. On the other hand, in *Bianco v. Globus Medical, Inc.*, 53 F. Supp. 3d 929 (E.D. Tex. 2014), the court treated a reasonable royalty as the normal remedy for use of a trade secret when the parties are not in competition, just as it is in patent cases. Notably, the *Bianco* court concluded that the royalty should be paid for fifteen years, well after the secret would have been discovered by independent means, reasoning that when the trade secret owner licensed ideas voluntarily it often signed contracts that required ongoing royalties.

3. Should the idea of "head start" injunctions apply to noncompete agreements as well as trade secret misappropriation? In *EMC Corp. v. Arturi*, 655 F.3d 75 (1st Cir. 2011), Justice Souter, sitting by designation, held that the plaintiff could not extend a noncompete agreement beyond its expiration date, even if the court had not enforced the agreement pending litigation by issuing a preliminary injunction.

If an employee agrees not to compete for a year, and it takes more than a year for the court to decide that agreement is enforceable, what is the plaintiff's remedy? How would damages be calculated in such a case?

4. In *Kewanee Oil Co. v. Bicron Corp.*, 416 U.S. 470, 473 (1974), the former employees had signed confidentiality agreements. The Court upheld the district court's granting of a permanent injunction against the disclosure or use by respondents of 20 of the 40 claimed trade secrets until such time as the trade secrets had been released to the public, had otherwise generally become available to the public, or had been ob-

tained by respondents from sources having the legal right to convey the information. *Id.* at 473-74. *See also Henry Hope X-Ray Prods., Inc. v. Marron Carrel, Inc.*, 674 F.2d 1336, 1342 (9th Cir. 1982) (the limitation on confidential information contains the implicit temporal limitation that information may be disclosed when it ceases to be confidential). *But see Howard Schultz & Assocs. v. Broniec*, 239 Ga. 181, 236 S.E.2d 265, 270 (1977) ("The nondisclosure covenant here contains no time limitation and hence it is unenforceable"); *Gary Van Zeeland Talent, Inc. v. Sandas*, 54 Wis. 2d 202, 267 N.W.2d 242, 250 (1978) (unlimited duration of agreement not to disclose trade secret customer list makes the agreement per se void).

The Eighth Circuit in *Sigma Chemical Co. v. Harris*, 794 F.2d 371, 375 (8th Cir. 1986) explained, in the course of rejecting a "temporally unlimited" injunction, the rationale for limiting injunctions in time:

> [E]xtending the injunction beyond the time needed for independent development would give the employer "a windfall protection and would subvert the public interest in fostering competition and in allowing employees to make full use of their knowledge and ability."

> We believe the part of the injunction prohibiting disclosure of trade secrets must be limited in duration and, accordingly, reverse in part and remand the case to the district court for consideration of the time it would take a "legitimate competitor" to independently reproduce the information contained in the product and vendor files. On remand, the district court should also modify the language of the injunction to expressly state that Harris may use that information which is already in the public domain.

But see Halliburton Energy Servs., Inc. v. Axis Techs., LLC, 444 S.W.3d 251 (Tex. App. 2014) (ordering a perpetual injunction and opining that such perpetual injunctions were the norm). *Halliburton* represents a decidedly minority view among courts to consider the duration of injunctions. *See* Richard F. Dole, Jr., *Permanent Injunctive Relief for Trade Secret Misappropriation Without an Express Limit upon Its Duration: The Uniform Trade Secrets Act Reconsidered*, 17 B.U. J. Sci. & Tech. L. 173, 191-98 (2011) (collecting cases).

5. Who should be enjoined? Several courts have refused to hold the new employer liable for an employee's malfeasance where they were unaware of it. *See Infinity Prods. v. Quandt*, 810 N.E.2d 1028 (Ind. 2004) (no respondeat superior liability for trade secret law); *BEA Sys. v. WebMethods, Inc.*, 595 S.E.2d 87 (Ga. Ct. App. 2004).

1. Criminal Trade Secret Statutes

Misappropriation of trade secrets is not only a tort; in some circumstances, it is a crime. *See generally* Eli Lederman, *Criminal Liability for Breach of Confidential Commercial Information*, 38 Emory L.J. 921 (1989) (summarizing criminal laws governing misappropriation of confidential information). A series of well-publicized criminal prosecutions of computer executives accused of taking trade secrets to their new employers have raised the consciousness of industry professionals about trade secrets. The prosecutions have also raised ethical and political questions about the propriety of trade secret prosecutions "engineered" by the real parties in interest, often major companies such as Intel or Borland.

Criminal trade secret cases differ from civil ones in several respects. The complaining party is the government, rather than the injured company. However, the injured companies are the "real parties in interest" and usually have some presence in the case. Even though they are not parties to the criminal proceeding, they at least supply a significant number of the witnesses and enjoy a high level of communication with the district attorney.

The burden of proof is higher than in a civil case. Some cases that could be won by the plaintiffs as civil cases will be lost in criminal court. This situation is even more likely because several states have definitions of trade secrets in their criminal laws that are more limited than their civil counterparts. For example, Cal. Penal Code §499c, which governs theft of trade secrets, historically limited the definition of a trade secret to "scientific or technical" information. (The constitutionality of this definition of trade secrets was upheld against a vagueness attack in *People v. Serrata*, 133 Cal. Rptr. 144 (Ct. App. 1976).) But in 1996, the California legislature amended its criminal trade secret statute to be coextensive with the broader definition of trade secrets in the Uniform Trade Secrets Act.

Defendants accused of stealing trade secrets may be charged with other offenses as well. For example, defendants who acquire a secret through improper means, as opposed to acquisition in a confidential relationship, may be guilty of larceny, receiving stolen property, or a host of similar crimes. *See People v. Gopal*, 217 Cal. Rptr. 487, 493-94 (Ct. App. 1985). Further, the growth of computer technology has expanded the federal role in prosecuting theft of trade secrets, since data taken over a computer network is considered to cross state lines. *See United States v. Riggs*, 739 F. Supp. 414 (N.D. Ill. 1990) (allowing indictment of computer hackers who published data from a Bell South computer text file for wire fraud and interstate transportation of stolen property).

The prosecution of a criminal (rather than civil) trade secret case has other effects on the parties involved. First, criminal trade secret courtrooms are the scene of constant battles over the publication of information. The real parties in interest will naturally oppose the disclosure in a public courtroom of the very secrets the defendant is accused of stealing. This concern runs headlong into the defendant's constitutional right to a public trial.[13] Second, civil cases are generally stayed pending the outcome of a criminal prosecution. Thus, a criminal prosecution may actually delay injunctive relief — the kind of remedy a civil plaintiff is often most interested in.

COMMENTS AND QUESTIONS

1. Given the stay imposed on a parallel civil action and the higher burden of proof in a criminal case, why would a civil plaintiff ever seek a criminal prosecution?

2. Should theft of trade secrets be a criminal offense? Does the presence of criminal sanctions have any effect on the optimal level of deterrence provided in damages suits, and therefore on the damages that should be awarded in a civil suit?

Do you see any problems with California's inclusion of business information in the criminal trade secret statute? Are there reasons to treat theft of scientific information more harshly than theft of business information?

2. Federal Criminal Liability for Trade Secret Misappropriation

The Economic Espionage Act of 1996, 18 U.S.C. §1831 et seq., makes misappropriation of trade secrets a federal crime. Sections 1831(a) and 1832(a) contain identical language regarding acts of misappropriation, punishing a specified individual who:

(1) steals, or without authorization appropriates, takes, carries away, or conceals, or by fraud, artifice or deception obtains a trade secret;

(2) without authorization copies, duplicates, sketches, draws, photographs, downloads, uploads, alters, destroys, photocopies, replicates, transmits, delivers, sends, mails, communicates, or conveys a trade secret;

(3) receives, buys, or possesses a trade secret, knowing the same to have been stolen or appropriated, obtained, or converted without authorization; . . .

These provisions are significantly broader in some respects than corresponding civil trade secret laws such as the Uniform Act.

In *United States v. Hsu*, 155 F.3d 189 (3d Cir. 1998), the first appellate decision interpreting the Act, the court concluded that the defendants (who were the subject of a sting operation) could be found guilty of conspiring and attempting to misappropri-

---

[13] There is no such right in civil cases. To avoid the very real danger that a misappropriation action will result in disclosure of the very secrets the plaintiff seeks to protect, civil trade secret actions will almost invariably include protective orders limiting the disclosure of information produced in discovery. Such orders are usually agreed to by the parties but may sometimes be imposed by the court. They will sometimes go so far as to prevent the parties themselves (as opposed to the attorneys and hired experts) from reviewing the other side's documents. In such a case, should in-house counsel be given access to discovery documents? *See Brown Bag Software v. Symantec Corp.*, 960 F.2d 1465, 1470 (9th Cir. 1992).

ate information that was not in fact a trade secret, because the crime of attempt did not require proof that the information the defendants tried to steal was in fact a secret. This is an issue that has recurred in the cases. Consider *United States v. Lange*, 312 F.3d 263 (7th Cir. 2002):

§1832(a)(4) makes it a crime to attempt to sell trade secrets without the owner's permission. Even if Lange did not have real trade secrets in his possession, the argument goes, he *thought* he did and therefore may be penalized for an attempted sale. The argument finds support in *Hsu,* which held that in order to avoid graymail — the threat that to obtain a conviction the prosecutor must disclose the secret by putting it in the trial record — a case may be based on §1832(a)(4) without disclosing all details of the trade secret. *Accord, United States v. Pin Yen Yang*, 281 F.3d 534, 543-44 (6th Cir. 2002). We agree with the general approach of these decisions. *Hsu* analogized the attempted sale of information believed to be a trade secret to an attempt such as shooting a corpse, believing it to be alive, or selling sugar, believing it to be cocaine. Events of this sort underlie the maxim that factual impossibility is no defense to a prosecution for attempt. *See United States v. Bailey*, 227 F.3d 792, 797 (7th Cir. 2000); *United States v. Saunders*, 166 F.3d 907, 916 (7th Cir. 1999); *United States v. Cotts*, 14 F.3d 300, 307 (7th Cir. 1994). This does not mean, however, that the defendant's belief *alone* can support a conviction. All attempt prosecutions depend on demonstrating that the defendant took a substantial step toward completion of the offense, which could have been carried out unless thwarted. *Braxton v. United States*, 500 U.S. 344 (1991). Although the American Law Institute recommends a definition of attempt linked closely to intent, Model Penal Code §5.01(1)(c), the Supreme Court has not embraced this view and demands in cases under federal law that the prosecutor establish a probability of success. *See, e.g., Spectrum Sports, Inc. v. McQuillan*, 506 U.S. 447 (1993) ("dangerous probability" of success is an ingredient of attempted monopolization).

An attempted murder may be thwarted by substituting a sack of flour for the intended victim; a sale of drugs may be thwarted by substituting sugar for cocaine, or rock candy for crack. These situations present a good chance of success, but for the intervention. So does "the disgruntled former employee who walks out of his former company with a computer diskette full of engineering schematics" (*Hsu*, 155 F.3d at 201) — a fair description of Lange's conduct (though diskettes are obsolete). *See also United States v. Martin*, 228 F.3d 1, 10-12 (1st Cir. 2000). A sale of trade secrets may be thwarted by substituting a disk with the collected works of Shakespeare for the disk that the defendant believed contained the plans for brake assemblies, or by an inadvertent failure to download the proper file. The attempted sale of the disk is a culpable substantial step. But it is far less clear that sale of information already known to the public could be deemed a substantial step toward the offense, just because the defendant is deluded and does not understand what a trade secret is. Selling a copy of *Zen and the Art of Motorcycle Maintenance* is not attempted economic espionage, even if the defendant thinks that the tips in the book are trade secrets; nor is sticking pins in voodoo dolls attempted murder. Booksellers and practitioners of the occult pose no social dangers, certainly none of the magnitude of those who are tricked into shooting bags of sand that have been substituted for targets of assassination. Lange was more dangerous than our bookseller but much less dangerous than our hypothetical assassin. Perhaps data purloined from an ex-employer is sufficiently *likely* to contain trade secrets to justify calling the preparation for sale a substantial step toward completion of the offense, and thus a culpable attempt, even if the employee stole the wrong data file and did not get his hands on the commercially valuable information. We need not pursue the subject beyond noting the plausibility of the claim and its sensitivity to the facts — what kind of data did the employee think he stole, and so on. For it is not necessary to announce a definitive rule about how dangerous the completed acts must be in trade secret cases: the judge was entitled to (and did) find that Lange had *real* trade secrets in his possession.

Lange wants us to proceed as if all he tried to sell were measurements that anyone could have taken with calipers after disassembling an original-equipment part. Such measurements could not be called trade secrets if, as Lange asserts, the assemblies in question were easy to take apart and measure. But no one would have paid $100,000 for metes and bounds, while Lange told his customers that the data on offer were worth more than that asking price. Which they were. What Lange had, and tried to sell, were the completed specifications and engineering diagrams that reflected all the work completed *after* the measurements had been taken: the metallurgical data, details of the sintering, the results of the tests, the plans needed to produce the finished goods, everything required to get FAA certification of a part supposedly identical to one that had been approved. Those details "derive[d] independent economic value, actual or potential, from not being generally known to, and not being readily ascertainable through proper means by, the public[.]" Every firm other than the original equipment manufacturer and RAPCO had to pay dearly to devise, test, and win approval of similar parts; the details unknown to the rivals, and not discoverable with tape measures, had considerable "independent economic value . . . from not being generally known." A sensible trier of fact could determine that Lange tried to sell trade secrets.

Id. at 268-69.

Some commentators have criticized the EEA for defining misappropriation more broadly in criminal law than the UTSA does in civil law. Nonetheless, Congress, concerned about cybersecurity and foreign hacking of websites, expanded the EEA to create a general federal civil trade secrets law. *See* DEFEND TRADE SECRETS ACT, S. 1890 (2016). While the DTSA generally tracks state law under the UTSA with respect to the definition of trade secrets and misappropriation, one important difference is in the area of remedies. The DTSA permits ex parte seizures of trade secret information and evidence of misappropriation where there was some risk that the secrets would be disclosed or the evidence destroyed before a court could enjoin it during normal legal processes. Those ex parte seizures are subject to a number of conditions and limitations, including proof not only that the plaintiff is likely to win the case and meet the requirements for an injunction but also that the normal process of a temporary restraining order is inadequate because the defendant will not comply with it and that the defendant would destroy or hide the evidence if she were given notice of the proposed seizure. *See* 18 U.S.C. §1836(b)(A)(ii). The SENATE REPORT indicates that "[t]he ex parte seizure provision is expected to be used in instances in which a defendant is seeking to flee the country or planning to disclose the trade secret to a third party immediately or is otherwise not amenable to the enforcement of the court's orders." S. REP. NO. 114-220, 114TH CONG., 2D SESS., DEFEND TRADE SECRETS ACT OF 2016 9-10 (2016).

H. FEDERAL PREEMPTION

The Supremacy Clause of the U.S. CONSTITUTION provides that

> This Constitution, and the Laws of the United States which shall be made in Pursuance thereof; and all Treaties made, or which shall be made, under the Authority of the United States, shall be the supreme Law of the Land; and the Judges in every State shall be bound thereby, any Thing [sic] in the Constitution or Laws of any State to the Contrary notwithstanding

U.S. CONSTITUTION, ART. VI, CL. 2. Thus, the Supremacy Clause nullifies state law attempts to duplicate or interfere with federal intellectual property protection. More difficult cases involve state laws that do not directly conflict with federal authority but instead address interstitial gaps within the federal regime. Courts must grapple with whether Congress intended to leave such gaps unfilled, thereby precluding state protection, or simply allowed state law to fill these voids. The following case addressed the interplay of federal patent law and state trade secret protection.

Kewanee Oil Co. v. Bicron Corp.
Supreme Court of the United States
416 U.S. 470 (1974)

Mr. Chief Justice BURGER delivered the opinion of the Court.

We granted certiorari to resolve a question on which there is a conflict in the courts of appeals: whether state trade secret protection is pre-empted by operation of the federal patent law. In the instant case the Court of Appeals for the Sixth Circuit held that there was preemption. The Courts of Appeals for the Second, Fourth, Fifth, and Ninth Circuits have reached the opposite conclusion. . . .

Petitioner brought this diversity action in United States District Court for the Northern District of Ohio seeking injunctive relief and damages for the misappropriation of trade secrets. The district Court, applying Ohio trade secret law, granted a permanent injunction against the disclosure or use by respondents of 20 of the 40 claimed trade secrets until such time as the trade secrets had been released to the public, had otherwise generally become available to the public, or had been obtained by respondents from sources having the legal right to convey the information.

The Court of Appeals for the Sixth Circuit held that the findings of fact by the District Court were not clearly erroneous, and that it was evident from the record that the individual respondents appropriated to the benefit of Bicron secret information on processes obtained while they were employees at Harshaw. Further, the Court of Appeals held that the District Court properly applied Ohio law relating to trade secrets. Nevertheless, the Court of Appeals reversed the District Court, finding Ohio's trade secret law to be in conflict with the patent laws of the United States. The Court of Appeals reasoned that Ohio could not grant monopoly protection to processes and manufacturing techniques that were appropriate subjects for consideration under 35 U.S.C. §101 for a federal patent but which had been in commercial use for over one year and so were no longer eligible for patent protection under 35 U.S.C. §102(b).

We hold that Ohio's law of trade secrets is not preempted by the patent laws of the United States, and accordingly, we reverse. . . .

III.

The first issue we deal with is whether the States are forbidden to act at all in the area of protection of the kinds of intellectual property which may make up the subject matter of trade secrets.

Article I, §8, cl. 8, of the Constitution grants to the Congress the power

[t]o promote the Progress of Science and useful Arts, by securing for limited Times to Authors and Inventors the exclusive Right to their respective Writings and Discoveries. . . .

In the 1972 Term, in *Goldstein v. California*, 412 U.S. 546 (1973), we held that the cl. 8 grant of power to Congress was not exclusive and that, at least in the case of writings, the States were not prohibited from encouraging and protecting the efforts of those within their borders by appropriate legislation. The States could, therefore, protect against the unauthorized rerecording for sale of performances fixed on records or tapes, even though those performances qualified as "writings" in the constitutional sense and Congress was empowered to legislate regarding such performances and could pre-empt the area if it chose to do so. This determination was premised on the great diversity of interests in our Nation—the essentially nonuniform character of the appreciation of intellectual achievements in the various States. Evidence for this came from patents granted by the States in the 18th century. 412 U.S., at 557.

Just as the States may exercise regulatory power over writings so may the States regulate with respect to discoveries. States may hold diverse viewpoints in protecting intellectual property relating to invention as they do in protecting the intellectual property relating to the subject matter of copyright. The only limitation on the States is that in regulating the area of patents and copyrights they do not conflict with the operation of the laws in this area passed by Congress, and it is to that more difficult question we now turn.

IV.

The question of whether the trade secret law of Ohio is void under the Supremacy Clause involves a consideration of whether that law "stands as an obstacle to the accomplishment and execution of the full purposes and objectives of Congress." *Hines v. Davidowitz*, 312 U.S. 52, 67 (1941). *See Florida Avocado Growers v. Paul*, 373 U.S. 132, 141 (1963). We stated in *Sears, Roebuck & Co. v. Stiffel Co.*, 376 U.S. 225, 229 (1964), that when state law touches upon the area of federal statutes enacted pursuant to constitutional authority, "it is 'familiar doctrine' that the federal policy 'may not be set at naught, or its benefits denied' by the state law. *Sola Elec. Co v. Jefferson Elec. Co.*, 317 U.S. 173, 176 (1942). This is true, of course, even if the state law is enacted in the exercise of otherwise undoubted state power." . . .

The stated objective of the Constitution in granting the power to Congress to legislate in the area of intellectual property is to "promote the Progress of Science and useful Arts." The patent laws promote this progress by offering a right of exclusion for a limited period as an incentive to inventors to risk the often enormous costs in terms of time, research, and development. . . .

The maintenance of standards of commercial ethics and the encouragement of invention are the broadly stated policies behind trade secret law. "The necessity of good faith and honest, fair dealing, is the very life and spirit of the commercial world." . . .

As we noted earlier, trade secret law protects items which would not be proper subjects for consideration for patent protection under 35 U.S.C. §101. As in the case of the recordings in *Goldstein v. California*, Congress, with respect to nonpatentable subject matter, "has drawn no balance; rather, it has left the area unattended, and no reason exists why the State should not be free to act." *Goldstein v. California, supra*, at 570 (footnote omitted).

Since no patent is available for a discovery, however useful, novel, and nonobvious, unless it falls within one of the express categories of patentable subject matter of

35 U.S.C. §101, the holder of such a discovery would have no reason to apply for a patent whether trade secret protection existed or not. Abolition of trade secret protection would, therefore, not result in increased disclosure to the public of discoveries in the area of nonpatentable subject matter. . . .

Congress has spoken in the area of those discoveries which fall within one of the categories of patentable subject matter of 35 U.S.C. §101 and which are, therefore, of a nature that would be subject to consideration for a patent. Processes, machines, manufactures, compositions of matter, and improvements thereof, which meet the tests of utility, novelty, and nonobviousness are entitled to be patented, but those which do not, are not. The question remains whether those items which are proper subjects for consideration for a patent may also have available the alternative protection accorded by trade secret law.

Certainly the patent policy of encouraging invention is not disturbed by the existence of another form of incentive to invention. In this respect the two systems are not and never would be in conflict. Similarly, the policy that matter once in the public domain must remain in the public domain is not incompatible with the existence of trade secret protection. By definition a trade secret has not been placed in the public domain. . . .

. . . Trade secret law will encourage invention in areas where patent law does not reach, and will prompt the independent innovator to proceed with the discovery and exploitation of his invention. Competition is fostered and the public is not deprived of the use of valuable, if not quite patentable, invention. . . .

The final category of patentable subject matter to deal with is the clearly patentable invention, i.e., that invention which the owner believes to meet the standards of patentability. It is here that the federal interest in disclosure is at its peak. . . .

Trade secret law provides far weaker protection in many respects than the patent law. While trade secret law does not forbid the discovery of the trade secret by fair and honest means, e.g., independent creation or reverse engineering, patent law operates "against the world," forbidding any use of the invention for whatever purpose for a significant length of time. The holder of a trade secret also takes a substantial risk that the secret will be passed on to his competitors, by theft or by breach of a confidential relationship, in a manner not easily susceptible of discovery or proof. *Painton & Co. v. Bourns, Inc.*, 442 F.2d, at 224. Where patent law acts as a barrier, trade secret law functions relatively as a sieve. The possibility that an inventor who believes his invention meets the standards of patentability will sit back, rely on trade secret law, and after one year of use forfeit any right to patent protection, 35 U.S.C. §102(b), is remote indeed.

Nor does society face much risk that scientific or technological progress will be impeded by the rare inventor with a patentable invention who chooses trade secret protection over patent protection. The ripeness-of-time concept of invention, developed from the study of the many independent multiple discoveries in history, predicts that if a particular individual had not made a particular discovery others would have, and in probably a relatively short period of time. If something is to be discovered at all very likely it will be discovered by more than one person. . . .

. . . Trade secret law and patent law have co-existed in this country for over one hundred years. Each has its particular role to play, and the operation of one does not take away from the need for the other. . . . Congress, by its silence over these many years, has seen the wisdom of allowing the States to enforce trade secret protection. Until Congress takes affirmative action to the contrary, States should be free to grant protection to trade secrets. . . .

Mr. Justice DOUGLAS, with whom Mr. Justice BRENNAN concurs, dissenting.

Today's decision is at war with the philosophy of *Sears, Roebuck & Co. v. Stiffel Co.*, 376 U.S. 225, and *Compco Corp. v. Day-Brite Lighting, Inc.*, 376 U.S. 234. Those cases involved patents—one of a pole lamp and one of fluorescent lighting fixtures—each of which was declared invalid. The lower courts held, however, that though the patents were invalid the sale of identical or confusingly similar products to the products of the patentees violated state unfair competition laws. We held that when an article is unprotected by a patent, state law may not forbid others to copy it, because every article not covered by a valid patent is in the public domain. Congress in the patent laws decided that where no patent existed, free competition should prevail; that where a patent is rightfully issued, the right to exclude others should obtain for no longer than 17 years, and that the States may not "under some other law, such as that forbidding unfair competition, give protection of a kind that clashes with the objectives of the federal patent laws," 376 U.S., at 231. . . .

The conflict with the patent laws is obvious. The decision of Congress to adopt a patent system was based on the idea that there will be much more innovation if discoveries are disclosed and patented than there will be when everyone works in secret. Society thus fosters a free exchange of technological information at the cost of a limited 17-year monopoly. . . .

A suit to redress theft of a trade secret is grounded in tort damages for breach of a contract—a historic remedy, *Cataphote Corp. v. Hudson*, 422 F.2d 1290. Damages for breach of a confidential relation are not pre-empted by this patent law, but an injunction against use is pre-empted because the patent law states the only monopoly over trade secrets that is enforceable by specific performance; and that monopoly exacts as a price full disclosure. A trade secret can be protected only by being kept secret. Damages for breach of a contract are one thing; an injunction barring disclosure does service for the protection accorded valid patents and is therefore pre-empted. . . .

COMMENTS AND QUESTIONS

1. The rule set forth by *Sears, Roebuck & Co v. Stiffel Co.*, 376 U.S. 225 (1964), was fairly clear: patent law reflects a compromise between the goal of promoting innovation and the danger of condoning monopoly. Supplementing the scope of patent law may upset that balance, and is therefore prohibited. Supplementing *enforcement* of the federal intellectual property laws was condoned in dictum at the end of *Compco Corp. v. Day-Brite Lighting, Inc.*, 376 U.S. 234 (1964), a companion case, and in Justice Harlan's concurrence in both cases. After these cases, state law served a very limited function in the scheme of intellectual property protection. States could work to further the goals of federal protection, but they had to work within the parameters set down by federal law. As a result, both *Sears* and *Compco* struck down state statutes providing design protection to unpatentable utilitarian articles.

The *Kewanee* opinion takes a remarkably different tack. Chief Justice Burger's opinion for the Court emphasizes only one of the two policies shaping the patent laws: the goal of promoting innovation. The opinion does not discuss the dangers intellectual property protection poses for free competition. As a result, the *Kewanee* Court finds no problem with trade secret protection that extends beyond the scope of the patent laws. Note that the Court seems to approve not only of state laws that protect nonpatentable subject matter (an area in which it could be argued that the federal government has no interest),[14] but also the protection of inventions not patentable for some other reason (i.e., suppression, misuse, lack of novelty, or obviousness).

Is *Kewanee* reconcilable with *Sears*? The *Kewanee* court did not overrule *Sears* or *Compco*; indeed, it cited them in support of its holding. Thus state laws preventing copying were treated differently from trade secret laws after *Kewanee*. The latter, although broader in scope (they prevented far more than just outright copying of products), were permissible; the former were not. *See* Paul Goldstein, Kewanee Oil Co. v. Bicron Corp.: *Notes on a Closing Circle*, 1974 SUP. CT. REV. 81 (1974) (arguing that *Kewanee* "closed the circle" on the open-ended preemption analysis of *Sears* and *Compco*); Camilla A. Hrdy, *State Patents As a Solution to Underinvestment in Innovation*, 62 U. KAN. L. REV. 487 (2013) (arguing that state patents, which preceded the adoption of the Constitution in 1789, are still possible and in some cases desirable despite federal nature of patent law).

2. Is preemption a good idea? That depends on what you think of the balance the federal laws have struck. If you are more concerned about injury to competition by conferring monopoly rights on patentees, you are likely to favor the result in *Sears*. If, on the other hand, you think that innovation is underrewarded, it is reasonable to oppose federal preemption. One way to reconcile these cases may be to read *Sears* and

---

[14] Even in this area, though, a federal interest may be discerned. If Congress has declared some subject matter unpatentable, that could reflect a federal determination that that matter is unworthy of protection, a determination that state law should not be allowed to upset.

Compco as expressing a federal policy in favor of reverse engineering of products in the public domain. If that is the overarching federal goal, it is logical to strike down the laws in *Sears* and *Compco* but not *Kewanee,* since trade secrets statutes (unlike the unfair competition laws we have discussed) generally allow reverse engineering. This result is also consistent with the reading of trade secret laws as merely an application of tort and contract principles.

CHAPTER III:
PATENT LAW

A. INTRODUCTION

This chapter explores patent law. After a brief survey of the historical origins and an overview of the main contours, we turn to the elements of patentability. Patent law establishes relatively high thresholds for the granting what can be extremely valuable exclusive rights. We then turn to the delineation of those quasi-property boundaries (claim construction). This provides a bridge to examining patent enforcement: infringement, defenses, and remedies. We then summarize international patent protection. We turn to the increasingly important and controversial area of design patents, which as we will see in Chapters IV and V, overlaps copyright and trademark (trade dress) protection. We conclude the chapter by exploring patent reform and possible futures of patent protection.

1. Historical Background

The first regular administrative apparatus for granting patents—the first real patent "system"—arose during the Renaissance. The term *patent*—from the Latin *patere* (to be open), referring to an open letter of privilege from the sovereign—originated in this period. The Venetian Senate's 1474 Act established the first regularized patent system:

> Be it enacted that, by the authority of this Council, every person who shall build any new and ingenious device in this City, not previously made in this Commonwealth, shall give notice of it to the office of our General Welfare Board when it has been reduced to perfection so that it can be used and operated. It being forbidden to every other person in any of our territories and towns to make any further device conforming with and similar to said one, without the consent and license of the author, for the term of 10 years. And if anybody builds it in violation hereof, the aforesaid author and inventor shall be entitled to have him summoned before any Magistrate of this City, by which Magistrate the said infringer shall be constrained to pay him one hundred ducats; and the device shall be destroyed at once.

Giulio Mandich, *Venetian Patents (1450-1550)*, 30 J. PAT. & TRADEMARK OFF. SOC'Y 166, 177 (1948).

The Venetian Act lays out all the essential features of modern patent protection. It covers "devices"; states that they must be registered with a specific administrative agency; says that they must be "new and ingenious," "reduced to perfection," and "not previously made in this Commonwealth"; provides a fixed term of ten years; and sets forth a procedure to determine infringement, as well as a remedy. Interestingly, the Venetian Act reserved to the Republic the right to use any invention without compensating the inventor. This is an early attempt to reconcile individual interest with the good of the community, a recurring problem in patent law. Indeed, Venetian patents are believed to have originated in part to encourage new entrants (particularly foreigners) to introduce products in competition with the highly structured artisan guilds in Venice. *See* Ted Sichelman & Sean O'Connor, *Patents as Promoters of Competition: The Guild Origins of Patent Law in the Venetian Republic*, 49 SAN DIEGO L. REV. 1267 (2012).

The opening of trade in Europe ensured that the new Venetian concept would spread. As Italian craftsmen—particularly glassworkers—fanned out across Europe, they brought with them the idea of legal protection for inventions.

Patents came to Great Britain by this route in the middle of the sixteenth century. The chief minister under Elizabeth I, William Cecil (Lord Burghley), used patent grants to induce foreign artisans to introduce continental technologies into England. Thus what later became the Anglo-American patent system originated as a mercantilist instrument—what today would be called a "strategic international trade" policy. The idea was to lure immigrants who had desirable skills and know-how with the promise of an exclusive privilege. Ironically, by the mid-eighteenth century, Britain began to show concern over the reverse problem—leakage of its technical prowess to overseas rivals, including the American colonies. *See* DAVID JEREMY, TRANSATLANTIC INDUSTRIAL REVOLUTION 36-49 (1981).

With the accession of James I in England in the early seventeenth century, patents became less an incentive for inventors of new arts and more a royal favor dispensed to well-placed courtiers. Under this rubric, "patents" were granted to such enterprises as running ale-houses. Parliament, whose members represented many trades injured by these special privileges, was displeased. Thus arose the Statute of Monopolies of 1624, which forbade all grants of exclusive privilege except those described in the famous Section 6:

> [B]e it declared and enacted that any declaration before mentioned shall not extend to any letters patent and grants of privilege for the term of fourteen years or under, hereafter to be made, of the sole working or making of any manner of new manufactures within this realm, to the true and first inventor and inventors of such manufacture, which others at the time of making such letters patent shall not use, so as also they be not contrary to law, nor mischievous to the State, by raising prices of commodities at home, or hurt of trade, or generally inconvenient; the said fourteen years to be accounted from the date of the first letters patents, or grant of such privilege hereafter to be made. . . .

This statute called on the common law courts to review all privileges granted by the crown and outlawed all but those based on true inventions. The Statute of Monopolies, with its general ban on exclusive rights to manufacture and sell goods, and its limited exception for the purpose of fostering new inventions, is an early example of both antitrust laws and the complex economic interaction between a desire for competition and a desire for new inventions.

Although the overall contribution of the patent system to the Industrial Revolution has been a matter of debate in historical circles, it seems no coincidence that the patent system matured alongside the early industrial technologies. In his thorough analysis of the Industrial Revolution in Great Britain, H. I. Dutton found that the British patent system was less than water-tight from the inventor's point of view, but that this leakiness redounded to the benefit of the economy in invention and indirectly encouraging innovation (introduction of new products embodying that technology on the market. H. I. DUTTON, THE PATENT SYSTEM AND INVENTIVE ACTIVITY DURING THE INDUSTRIAL REVOLUTION 1750-1852 (1984). In this, the early British experience foreshadows problems that courts struggle with today—how to encourage invention through the use of exclusive rights without stifling the creativity of follow-on inventors.

Patents were among the many British legal concepts introduced to the American colonies. State patents were granted in most of the original thirteen colonies, beginning with a Massachusetts patent in 1641. Even after the Revolution, under the Articles of Confederation, the individual states continued to issue patents.

Conflicts began to arise between the states—most notably over steamboat patents, which were issued to two different inventors during this period. With this problem (among others) in mind, the Constitutional Convention of 1789 resolved to create a national patent system rooted in the Constitution itself. Thus the provision of Article I, Section 8, Clause 8 authorizing Congress to award exclusive rights for a limited time to authors and inventors "for their respective writings and discoveries." One historical footnote is worth mentioning in this connection: An early draft of this provision, set out in James Madison's notes to the Convention, called for both exclusive rights *and* outright subsidies for new inventions. But this was rejected in favor of exclusive rights only. *See* BRUCE BUGBEE, THE GENESIS OF AMERICAN PATENT AND COPYRIGHT LAW 126, 143 (1967). In any event, the first U.S. patent statute was passed in 1790, in the very early days of the first Congress (reflecting the importance of this matter), and the first patent was issued shortly thereafter—to Samuel Hopkins of Pittsford, Vermont, for a process for making potash from wood ashes. Although there may be some limited scope for individual states to issue patents, for all intents and purposes patent law is and has been exclusively federal since 1790. *See* Camilla A. Hrdy, *State Patent Laws in the Age of Laissez Faire*, 28 BERKELEY TECH. L.J. 45, 45 (2013); Camilla A. Hrdy, *State Patents As A Solution to Underinvestment in Innovation*, 62 U. KAN. L. REV. 487 (2013).

The story of Thomas Jefferson's involvement in the early national patent system has often been told. He was a significant contributor to the original statute, and he helped to administer the patent system established in 1790. *See* Edward C. Walterscheid, *The Use and Abuse of History: The Supreme Court's Interpretation of Thomas Jefferson's Influence on the Patent Law*, 39 IDEA 195 (1999); Adam Mossoff, *Who Cares What Thomas Jefferson Thought about Patents? Reevaluating the Patent "Privilege" in Historical Context*, 92 CORNELL L. REV. 953 (2007). Despite this, the strong federal flavor, as well as the emphasis on promotion of industrial technology, owes at least as much to the influence of Alexander Hamilton and other Federalist founders. *See* ALEXANDER HAMILTON, REPORT ON MANUFACTURERS (1791), *reprinted* in 3 ANNALS OF CONG. 971, 980-81 (Dec. 5, 1791), http://www.constitution.org/ ah/rpt_manufactures.pdf (emphasizing the value of promoting specialization in invention relating to machinery).

The nation's first patent act set forth terse general standards for protection, duration, rights, and remedies, but few details. This original institutional structure of the U.S. patent system was, however, short-lived for several reasons. It called upon the

Secretary of State (Thomas Jefferson), the Secretary for the Department of War, and the Attorney General to examine patents, which, in light of their other responsibilities, proved untenable. Second, inventors were displeased with the high and vague threshold for protection: that inventions be deemed "sufficiently useful and important."

As a result, in 1793, Congress struck the requirement that inventions be "sufficiently useful and important" and replaced the examination process with a registration system, leaving the evaluation of patentability entirely to the courts. The Patent Act of 1793 retained a terse standard for patentability: an inventor could patent "any new and useful art, machine, manufacture or composition of matter, or any new and useful improvement on any art, machine, manufacture or composition of matter, not known or used before the application." Patent Act of Feb. 21, 1793, ch. 11, §1, 1 Stat. 318. The inventor was still required to provide a written description of the invention and the manner of use "in such full, clear and exact terms, as to distinguish the same from all other things before known, and to enable any person skilled in the art or science, of which it is a branch, or with which it is most nearly connected, to make, compound, and use the same." *See id.*, §3.

The courts fleshed out this lean statute. In the early years, they filled its gaps with English case law. *See generally* Peter S. Menell, *The Mixed Heritage of Federal Intellectual Property Law and Ramifications for Statutory Interpretation*, in INTELLECTUAL PROPERTY AND THE COMMON LAW 70-71 (Shyam Balganesh, ed., 2013). In 1818, Justice Joseph Story, who wrote 40 patent law opinions between 1813 and 1845, issued a paper stating that "[t]he patent acts of the United States are, in a great degree, founded on the principles and usages which have grown out of the English statute on the same subject." *See* On the Patent Laws, 16 U.S. (3 Wheat.) App. 13-29 (1818).

In his first patent law opinion, Justice Story, sitting as a Circuit Justice, distinguished between unpatentable elements of motion and "the modus operandi, the peculiar device or manner of producing any given effect." The opinion recognized an experimental use defense based on the inference that "it could never have been the intention of the legislature to punish a man, who constructed such a machine merely for philosophical experiments, or for the purpose of ascertaining the sufficiency of the machine to produce its described effects." *See Whittemore v. Cutter*, 29 F.Cas. 1120, 1121-24 (C.C.Mass. 1813). In 1829, Justice Story interpreted the novelty requirement of "not known or used before the application" to pertain only to knowledge or use "by the public." *See Pennock v. Dialogue*, 27 U.S. 1, 19 (1829). The courts also established standards for disclosure, requiring that the patent document identify the patented invention with specificity and distinguish it from the prior art. *See Lowell v. Lewis*, 15 F. Cas. 1018, No. 8568 (C.C.D. Mass. 1817); *Evans v. Eaton*, 20 U.S. 356, 434-35 (1822).

But while the patent system got on its feet under Jefferson and was fleshed out by jurists, it did not grow to its full stature until the 1836 revision, when a formal system of examination, with professional examiners, was substituted for the pro forma registration system of the 1793 Act. The lack of an examination system eroded faith in the patent system due to the proliferation of "unrestrained and promiscuous grants of patent privileges." *See* John Ruggles, Select Committee Report on the State and Condition of the Patent Office, S. Doc. No. 24-338, at 4 (1836). The Senate Report Accompanying the Patent Act of 1836 lamented that "[a] considerable portion of all the patents granted are worthless and void, as conflicting with, and infringing upon one another," the country had become "flooded with patent monopolies, embarrassing to bona fide patentees, whose rights are thus invaded on all sides," and that the "interference and collision of patents and privileges" had produced ruinous vexatious litigation. *See* Senate Report Accompanying Senate Bill No. 239, 24th Cong., 1st Sess. (April 28, 1836).

Since 1836 the patent system has grown dramatically by any standard—number of patents issued, number of cases litigated, or number of significant inventions patented. As greater demands were placed on it, the patent system developed new rules. For example, the requirement that an invention be more than novel, that it reveal an "inventive leap," or what is now called nonobviousness, developed in the mid-nineteenth century to limit the number of patents that were being issued. Late in the nineteenth century the bureaucratic structure of the Patent Office as we know it began to take shape as well.

In Europe, the nineteenth century was a time when a new generation of analytical economists questioned the economic foundations of the patent system. *See* Fritz Machlup & Edith Penrose, *The Patent Controversy in the Nineteenth Century*, 10 J. ECON. HIST. 1 (1950). Indeed, Switzerland and the Netherlands had no patent systems for more than fifty years during this period. E. SCHIFF, INDUSTRIALIZATION WITHOUT NATIONAL PATENTS: THE NETHERLANDS 1869-1912; SWITZERLAND 1850-1907 (1971). *See generally* Petra Moser, *How Do Patent Laws Influence Innovation? Evidence from Nineteenth-Century World's Fairs*, 95 AM. ECON. REV. 1214 (2005) (inventions displayed at 19th-century world's fairs show that national patent laws influenced the variety and types of industries inventors chose to work in). Despite the period of transition and questioning, the patent system was a well-accepted feature of the economic landscape by the beginning of the twentieth century. Key patents on the light bulb, the telephone system, the basic design of the automobile, and the first airplanes symbolized the technical virtuosity and dynamism of the age. *See* B. ZORINA KHAN, THE DEMOCRATIZATION OF INVENTION (2009) (extensive history of U.S. patent law in the nineteenth century). As the scale of industry grew, research and development departments began to appear in the larger companies. *See* THOMAS P. HUGHES, AMERICAN GENESIS: A CENTURY OF INVENTION AND TECHNOLOGICAL ENTHUSIASM 1870-1970, 150-80 (1989); CATHERINE L. FISK, WORKING KNOWLEDGE: EMPLOYEE INNOVATION AND THE RISE OF CORPORATE INTELLECTUAL PROPERTY, 1800-1930 (REISSUE ED., 2014). Patents were not only a valuable output of these departments; they helped measure the productivity of the departments and served to justify their importance.

The history of the U.S. patent system in the twentieth century reflects swings between greater and lesser protection. Following the trust-busting era at the turn of the century, some policymakers and jurists came to believe that large companies with patent portfolios were *too* powerful. Spurred in part by a series of anticompetitive acts by large companies whose patents dominated their respective industries, courts became less willing to enforce patent rights and more willing to punish patentees for exceeding the scope of their patent grant. The pendulum swung back towards patentability during the 1940s. As the nation threw all available resources into the war effort, the armed forces called on engineers and scientists to perfect a vast array of new technologies in short order. By the time the war was over, there was a consensus in Congress in favor of a strong patent system. The 1952 Patent Act, the first major revision of the patent code since the nineteenth century, marked a return to the principles of that century in many respects. *See* Robert P. Merges, *One Hundred Years of Solicitude: Intellectual Property Law, 1900-2000*, 88 Cal. L. Rev. 2187 (2000).

The patent system by general consensus reached a low-water mark during the 1960s, in the wake of this period of strong protection. The PTO issued patents rather freely, without particularly rigorous examination in many circumstances. On the other hand, it was difficult to get a patent upheld in many federal circuit courts, and the circuits diverged widely both as to doctrine and basic attitudes toward patents. As a consequence, industry downplayed the significance of patents.

In 1982 Congress passed the Federal Courts Improvement Act, creating the new Court of Appeals for the Federal Circuit. *See* Rochelle Dreyfuss, *The Federal Circuit: A Case Study in Specialized Courts*, 64 N.Y.U. L. Rev. 1, 25-26 (1989). The Federal Circuit handles several important types of cases, but from the beginning one of its primary functions has been to hear all appeals involving patents. While the Federal Circuit was ostensibly formed strictly to unify patent doctrine, it was no doubt hoped by some (and expected by others) that the new court would make subtle alterations in the doctrinal fabric, with an eye toward expanding the scope of patent protection.

That is exactly what happened over the Federal Circuit's first two decades. *See* John R. Allison & Mark A. Lemley, *Empirical Evidence on the Validity of Litigated Patents*, 26 Am. Intell. Prop. L. Assn Q.J. 185 (1998). The Federal Circuit expanded the scope of patentable subject matter and strengthened patent rights across many dimensions. The result of this stronger protection was a proliferation of low-quality business method and software patents in the late 1990s and early 2000 period. That in turn awakened the Supreme Court, which has issued numerous influential decisions since 2006 tightening patent standards. The Federal Circuit has followed suit, narrowing patent protection in the past several years. Nonetheless, the growth of the patent system continues apace. *See* Mark A. Lemley, *The Surprising Resilience of the Patent System*, Tex. L. Rev.

(2017) (discussing these swings in protection but arguing that they have not greatly affected the overall patent ecosystem).

2. An Overview of the Patent System

It is important to appreciate some basic attributes of the patent system before delving into the cases. This is a complex body of law with its own terminology and tradition, and one must become acquainted with the rudiments before diving into the details.

i. Requirements for Patentability

The Patent and Trademark Office (PTO) reviews each patent application to see if it meets five requirements:

1. **Patentable Subject Matter §101**: The claimed invention fits within one of the four statutory categories ("process, machine, manufacture, or composition of matter") or "improvement thereof" and is not excluded by judicial doctrines barring patents on laws of nature, natural phenomena, and abstract ideas. Recent Supreme Court decisions hold that patents nonetheless cover inventive applications of these ineligible concepts.

2. **Utility §101**: The claimed invention must be useful in two respects: (1) credible utility—it must work for its intended purpose; and (2) specific and substantial utility—it must serve a particular practical purpose. Today, a patent will not be withheld even though the invention works only in an experimental setting and has no proven use in the field or factory. Only if an invention has absolutely no "practical utility" will a patent be denied. The only exception is inventions pertaining to the life sciences, where some cases question whether laboratory promise is enough to establish utility in treating human patients.

3. **Novelty §102**: The invention has not been preceded in identical form in the public prior art. Novelty is evaluated based on technical rules aimed at determining whether the claimed invention was in the prior art. U.S. patent law underwent significant reform of its novelty regime in 2013. For applications filed prior to March 16, 2013, U.S. patent law favors the first to invent so long as the invention was timely filed. For applications filed on or after March 16, 2013, U.S. patent favors the first applicant to have filed, subject to a grace period for prior publication.

4. **Nonobviousness §103**: It represents a nontrivial extension of what was known. This is the most important requirement; it has been called "the ultimate condition of patentability." The reason is that nonobviousness attempts to measure an even more abstract quality than novelty or utility:

the *technical accomplishment* reflected in an invention. This requirement asks whether an invention is a big enough technical advance over the prior art. Even if an invention is new and useful, it will still not merit a patent if it represents merely a trivial step forward in the art.

5. ***Disclosure §112***: The patent specification must convey to a person having ordinary skill in the art: (1) written description—the inventor gave a detailed account of the invention, i.e., demonstrated "possession" as of the time of filing the application; and (2) enablement—that the specification enable a person having ordinary skill in the art to make and use the invention. The disclosure requirements ensures that the patentee has fulfilled the social bargain underlying the patent grant—that those "skilled in the art" of the invention can read and understand the inventor's contribution, and that after the patent expires they will be able to make and use the invention themselves.

ii. *Rights Conferred by a Patent*

"Claims" are the heart of patent law. Claims define the boundaries of the property right that the patent confers. (Innumerable patent cases therefore analogize claims to the "metes and bounds" of a real property deed.) Claims come at the end of the written description of the invention. Most patents also have one or more drawings.

The specification describes the invention. It names all the parts or components of the invention, describes how they work, and illustrates how they work together to perform the invention's function. Only at the end of the specification does the inventor (or, more usually, her patent lawyer) state the precise legal definition of the invention. These are the claims. Here are a few (fanciful) examples of claims:

1. Element 95.
2. A composition comprising
   a. a solid selected from the group consisting of
      i. sodium chloride,
      ii. potassium chloride and
      iii. lithium chloride;
   b. a liquid selected from the group consisting of
      i. sulfuric acid,
      ii. nitric acid. . . .
3. The material wrought tungsten, having a specific gravity of approximately 19 or greater, and capable of being forged and worked.
4. A windmill comprising a wind-catching device, directed to face the oncoming wind force, said device turning a shaft, said shaft acting on gears

or another device to change the direction of said wind force, so as to operate a pump that pumps water.

5. A windmill according to claim 4 wherein the force-changing device is a set of gears.

6. A method for treating baldness comprising applying to the scalp an aqueous solution of the compound minoxidil.

7. An apparatus for playing record albums comprising a cartridge or stylus made from at least 40 percent graphite by weight, a tone arm on which said cartridge or stylus is mounted, a turntable on which said record albums are placed for playing, and means for turning said turntable at appropriate speeds for the playing of said record albums.

Note that all the claims except claim 5 are examples of *independent claims;* they do not refer to any other claim or claims. This is in contrast to a *dependent claim.* You can tell that claim 5 is a dependent claim because it begins with the phrase "A windmill according to claim 4 wherein . . ." A dependent claim incorporates all the limitations of the independent claim on which it depends.

Note also that claim 6 is a claim to a process or method rather than a device, and that the last element of claim 7 is stated in "means plus function" format: the element is not described in detail but is merely listed as "a means" for accomplishing some goal. The importance of this specialized claim format will be discussed in Chapter III(D)(4).

Following a preamble (such as "A composition"), patent claims use a transitional phrase to indicate how the claim limitations define the claim. The phrase "comprising" is an "open" transition: claims using this terminology cover devices that include all the listed elements *plus* any additional elements. The phrase "consisting of," by contrast, is closed: it does not cover devices that include additional elements. "Consisting essentially of" limits the scope of a claim to the specified materials or steps "and those that do not *materially* affect the *basic* and *novel* characteristic(s)" of the claimed invention. *In re Herz,* 537 F.2d 549, 551-52 (CCPA 1976) (emphasis in original).

A patent confers the right to exclude others from making, using, selling, offering for sale, or importing the claimed invention for 20 years from the filing of the patent application

The exclusionary right is in a sense a negative right, for two reasons. First, a patent does not automatically grant an affirmative right to do anything; patented pharmaceuticals, for instance, must still pass regulatory review at the Food and Drug Administration to be sold legally. Second, a patented invention may itself be covered by a preexisting patent. For instance, a broad "pioneering" patent on a product or process may cover later-developed inventions, themselves patented as improvements. In such a case the holder of an improvement patent has the right to exclude everyone from her improvement—including the holder of the broad patent—while at the same time being barred from use of the improvement herself unless the holder of the broad patent authorizes such use. Patents so related are said to be "blocking patents."

iii.   *Patent Prosecution*

The process of obtaining a patent from the Patent Office is known as "prosecution." The time and effort required to prosecute a patent varies immensely from case to case. A few applications are reviewed quickly and issued within a year of the application date. Others languish in the PTO for years and, especially when several inventors claim they were the first to produce a particular invention, even decades. The "average" prosecution takes approximately three to four years. A new program in the U.S. Patent Office allows applicants to pay extra to "fast track" their patent applicants. http://www.uspto.gov/patent/initiatives/usptos-prioritized-patent-examination-program (describing "track one" prosecution; average patent pendency of 1.4 years). It has been estimated that over the course of prosecution, the typical application receives only 18 total hours of attention. *See* John R. Allison & Mark A. Lemley, *Who's Patenting What? An Empirical Exploration of Patent Prosecution*, 53 VAND. L. REV. 2099 (2000). There are, however, significant variations in the length of time and quality of patent examination.

Prosecution begins with the filing of a patent application. Although an inventor or his or her lawyer or patent agent[1] may file a temporary "placeholder" application, called a provisional application, it must be converted into a standard, full-blown "non-provisional" application within one year if it is ever to issue as a patent. *See* §111(b). The basics of an application are: (1) the specification, including a summary of the invention and drawings in most cases; (2) one or more claims, at the end of the specification; (3) an oath, declaring the inventor(s) actually invented what is described in the specification; and (4) applicable filing fees.

New applications are assigned to one of the main examining groups, then to a specific "art unit" that specializes in the relevant technology, and ultimately to one of the roughly 9,000 patent examiners employed at the Patent Office. Applicants may file additional papers, such as an information disclosure statement (IDS), describing prior art known to the applicant at the time of filing, 37 C.F.R. §§1.97, 1.98 (2002), or preliminary amendments, which are changes made to the application before the examiner's first response or "office action." Examiners usually make an initial review of the application, which includes a search of the prior art. The most common office action following this initial review is a rejection of most of the claims in the application, often on grounds of lack of novelty or obviousness. The examiner must state the reasons for each rejection, together with information and references to aid the applicant in judging the desirability of continuing prosecution or overcoming the rejection. §132.

---

[1] Lawyers or non-lawyers with the requisite technical training (science or engineering degree) must pass the Patent Bar Examination administered by the U.S. PTO in order to prosecute patents.

The examiner has the burden to show why an application should not issue as a patent. In response, the applicant can either contest (or "traverse," as patent lawyers say) the rejection or acquiesce in it.

In general, applications can be amended during prosecution. The most common reason for an amendment is to respond to a rejection or other office action. But applicants can also correct mistakes, add or change drawings, and even update the disclosure portion of the specification (though for amendments of this latter type, newly disclosed material does not enjoy the benefit of the initial filing date). Standard amendments are usually permitted up to the time when an examiner issues a final rejection, which may be as early as the second office action.

The label "final rejection" is a misnomer. An applicant can respond to a final rejection in a number of ways, most typically by a continuation or amendment after final rejection under 37 C.F.R. §1.116. (If the applicant feels continued prosecution would not be worthwhile, e.g., because there are clear disagreements with the examiner, he or she may file an appeal to the Patent Trial and Appeal Board (PTAB), an administrative tribunal within the PTO.) A continuation is basically a new version of the application, though continuations come in several flavors.[2] Filing a continuation resets the examination process. A simple continuation application retains the benefit of the initial application's filing date; it therefore may serve much the same role as an amendment. A continuation-in-part ("CIP"), by contrast, adds new matter to the specification. This new matter does not retain the benefit of the earlier filing date, though any information carried over from the original filing does.

Applicants may employ a variation on the continuation theme when the examiner has decided to allow some claims but has issued a final rejection as to others. Typical prosecution strategy is to take the bird in the hand and fight over the contested claims separately. To achieve this, the applicant can file an amendment after final rejection canceling the rejected claims. This puts the remaining claims in condition for allowance. Meanwhile, the rejected claims may be carried over into a separate continuation application. Then the battle over these claims can be joined again; in the meantime, the acceptable claims will become enforceable as soon as the original, slimmed-down application is allowed to issue as a patent.

In addition to these various filings, applicants can communicate with patent examiners by phone or in person, through what is called an examiner interview. Any

---

[2] There are two types of continuations: (1) a "standard" continuation, which may be thought of as a new branch of the patent; and (2) one that completely replaces the prior application and therefore renders it abandoned. Continuations in this second category filed after May 29, 2000, must be filed under a request for continuing examination (RCE). Note that an application prosecuted after an RCE is not technically a new application. *See* 37 C.F.R. §1.114 (2002). A "standard" continuation does not cause the parent application to be abandoned, which is why this is used to split off contested subject matter. The parent application, now minus the contested claims, carries on—and hence can issue as a patent.

notes made during these communications become part of the prosecution history of the patent.

Prior to 2001, U.S. patent applications were not published. They were held in secrecy until the issue date. Long-pending applications, were referred to as "submarine patents" for this reason. These abuses, together with the goal of harmonizing U.S. practice with that of Japan and Europe, led to the publication of patent applications under the American Inventors Protection Act of 1999 ("AIPA"), §122(b). Under the AIPA, most applications are published eighteen months after their filing date.[3] After publication but before the patent issues, the applicant has certain limited legal rights in the invention. So long as the infringer has actual notice of the published patent application, and so long as the claims in the published application are "substantially identical" to the claims in the patent when issued, the applicant/patentee can recover a reasonable royalty from the infringer. Unlike an issued patent, rights in a published application cannot be enforced with an injunction. §154(d).

Interested third parties—in particular, competitors of the applicant—sometimes (although not always) read their competitors' published applications. Regulations put in place after the AIPA permit third parties to submit prior art references to be included in the prosecution file of the application. While third parties have always been permitted to submit prior art during prosecution[4] or after a patent issues, the availability of published applications on the World Wide Web increased interest in pending applications and represented a first step in the direction of a full-blown third party "opposition system" such as those available in Japan and Europe. Significant third party participation is now permitted under various administrative procedures initiated in the America Invents Act (AIA) of 2011, which we discuss below.

The claims section of a patent commonly begins with the broadest claim, which is then "qualified" in a series of dependent claims. This is typically followed by a narrower independent claim, which may itself be qualified by a series of dependent claims. In this way, the general structure of a patent often resembles an inverted pyramid: the broadest claims are first, the narrowest last, and the scope of the claims generally "tapers" from the first to the last.

Prosecution ends when the patent is granted or the application is abandoned. About three-fourths of all applications end up granted as patents. *See* Mark A. Lemley & Bhaven Sampat, *Is the Patent Office a Rubber Stamp?*, 58 EMORY L.J. 181 (2008). The optimal grant rate is a matter of great interest to scholars, though there is no easy way to know for sure exactly how many patent applications should issue as patents. *See*

---

[3] Applicants that only seek protection in the United States can usually keep their applications secret until issued. This leaves trade secret protection if their application never issues.

[4] Under the "public protest" provisions of 37 C.F.R. §1.291 (2002). Note that prior to the publication of applications, third parties had to find out some other way that an application was pending (presumably usually through some disclosure by the applicant him or herself).

Michael D. Frakes and Melissa F. Wasserman, *Does the U.S. Patent and Trademark Office Grant Too Many Bad Patents?: Evidence from a Quasi-Experiment*, 67 STAN. L. REV. 613 (2015). Issued patents are summarized in the Patent Gazette and made available to the public. Prosecution can in a sense continue after a patent has issued. A patentee who comes to believe that her patent claims are either too broad or too narrow can seek a reissue of the patent, so long as the deficiency in the original patent is the result of a bona fide error or omission. Reissues to broaden the scope of claims must be initiated within two years of the original issuance, however.

Once the patent issues, the patent owner can enforce the patent in federal court. Many of the cases that we examine in this chapter are the result of these proceedings. Some of the cases, however, are appeals of patent rejections to the Federal Circuit. Four other forms of patent litigation deserve brief mention here.

- *Patent Interference Proceeding*: A unique form of traditional patent proceeding is a priority dispute between two or more inventors, all of whom claim to have been the first inventor of a particular invention. These are known as interference proceedings. They are an outgrowth of the fact that the United States, until March 15, 2013, awarded a patent to the first inventor, unlike almost every other country, which awards the patent to the first to file a patent application. Interference proceedings are handled by the PTO internally through the Board of Patent Appeals and Interferences (which will become the Patent Trial and Appeal Board under the AIA), again with a right of appeal to the CAFC. For patents that are filed on or after March 16, 2013, interferences will no longer be available – a major change due to the AIA's "first inventor to file" priority rule. However, a patent applicant who files second but who believes the first filer stole (or "derived") the invention from the second filer, may initiate a Derivation Proceeding under the AIA.

- *Post-Grant Review Proceeding*: Beginning in 1980 and now much expanded as result of the America Invents Act of 2011, the Patent Office (through the PTAB) affords patentees and challengers with several post-grant proceedings to ensure that the patent was properly issued. These post-grant proceedings can run in parallel with patent litigation in federal court, although it is common for district judges to stay cases involving patents that are being reviewed by the PTAB. We will discuss these proceedings in the final section on patent reform.

- *Declaratory Relief Action*: Companies that reasonably fear being sued for patent infringement (for example, because the patentee has threatened them with suit) can file declaratory judgment actions seeking to establish that the patent at issue is invalid, or that their conduct does not infringe the patent. Such declaratory judgment actions are typically met with counterclaims charging infringement; these proceed much as normal patent infringement suits.

- *Section 337 Investigation*: The International Trade Commission has jurisdiction to block the importation of products into the United States if they infringe U.S. patents and to block the importation of products made abroad by processes that are patented in the United States. Patent owners can complain to the ITC, which will bring "Section 337" actions against likely infringers. These actions have their own set of procedural rules that operate parallel to district court actions for patent infringement. *See generally* PETER S. MENELL, ET AL., SECTION 337 PATENT INVESTIGATION MANAGEMENT GUIDE (2012).

3. Theories of Patent Law

By contrast with trade secret law, which draws on a number of different (and sometimes contradictory) theoretical bases, the central theory behind patent law is relatively straightforward. This theory posits that inventions are public goods that are costly to make and that are difficult to control once they are released into the world. As a result, absent patent protection inventors will not have sufficient incentive to invest in creating, developing, and marketing new products. Patent law provides a market-driven incentive to invest in innovation, by allowing the inventor to appropriate the full economic rewards of her invention.

Other theories are often advanced to explain intellectual property law. Some scholars look to natural rights justifications. *See* Adam Mossoff, *Rethinking the Development of Patents: An Intellectual History*, 1550-1800, 52 HASTINGS L.J. 1255 (2001); A. Samuel Oddi, *Un-Unified Economic Theories of Patents—The Not-Quite-Holy Grail*, 71 NOTRE DAME L. REV. 267, 274-77 (1996); *cf.* Lawrence C. Becker, *Deserving to Own Intellectual Property*, 68 CHI.-KENT L. REV. 609 (1993) (arguing that entitlement-based rationales for patent law are intuitively appealing, but do not necessarily justify the scope of current patent doctrine). An alternative to classical incentive theory is the prospect theory of patents. *See* Edmund Kitch, *The Nature and Function of the Patent System*, 30 J.L. & ECON. 265 (1977). Kitch offers a property-based vision of patents as entitlements to innovate within a particular field, granted to those who have already started such innovation to encourage, not invention, but commercialization of technology. *See also* Mark F. Grady & Jay I. Alexander, *Patent Law and Rent Dissipation*, 78 VA. L. REV. 305 (1992) (refining Kitch's approach using insights from political economy theory). Professor Merges explores this terrain in JUSTIFYING INTELLECTUAL PROPERTY (2011). *See also* Peter S. Menell, *Property, Intellectual Property, and Social Justice: Mapping the Next Frontier*, 5 BRIGHAM-KANNER PROPERTY CONFERENCE JOURNAL (forthcoming 2016).

Nonetheless, the utilitarian framework serves as the central framework for most patent scholarship. This reflects the utilitarian character of the U.S. Constitution's Intellectual Property Clause as well as the importance of promoting technological innovation for every nation that seeks to meet the needs of its citizens and to defend its sovereignty. It also reflects the patent system's market setting and the broad nature of the patent grant. Patents give the inventor the right to sue not only those who "steal" his or her invention, but those who reverse engineer it and even those who develop the same invention independently. The broad nature of this grant makes it difficult to speak of a "moral entitlement" to a patent. And in part the focus on utilitarian theory mirrors the subject matter of patents, which revolves around mechanical devices, chemical formulae, and the like. It would be anomalous to most to speak of the "personality" invested in stamping machinery or pesticides.

Although the economic incentive story is straightforward, it does not tell us very much about how to design a patent system to provide optimal incentives. For the reasons described in Chapter I, both overprotecting and underprotecting technology can impede innovation. Thus designing the proper economic incentive requires policymakers to balance the length of the patent term, the appropriate standard of invention, and the nature of the rights granted. Resolving these conflicts has occupied courts and legislators since the passage of the first patent statute in 1790. We will reexamine these issues at the end of the chapter.

B. THE ELEMENTS OF PATENTABILITY

The systematic study of intellectual property regimes naturally begins with the requirements for or elements of protectability. This section investigates the five requirements of patentability. In prior editions, we began our coverage with patentable subject matter (§101), which states simply and broadly that

> Whoever invents or discovers any new and useful process, machine, manufacture, or composition of matter, or any new and useful improvement thereof, may obtain a patent therefor, subject to the conditions and requirements of this title.

Until 2012, with some exceptions (notably the brief period between 1978 and 1981), courts interpreted this language relatively expansively. And by the early 2000 period, the Federal Circuit had pretty much lowered the patentable subject matter hurdle to a chalk line on the track. Even non-technological business methods qualified for patentability under *State St. Bank v. Signature Fin. Grp.*, 149 F.3d 1368, 1375 (Fed. Cir. 1998).

Thus, much of the challenge in understanding patentability related to novelty (§102), nonobviousness (§103), and, to a lesser extent, disclosure (§112). The Supreme Court's decision in *Mayo Collaborative Servs. v. Prometheus Labs., Inc.*, 132 S.Ct. 1289 (2012), however, significantly raised and complicated the patent eligibility standard, particularly as relates to business methods, software, genetics, and medical diagnostic methods. This shift has intertwined the patent eligibility inquiry with the nonobviousness and disclosure inquiries. To comprehend nonobviousness, it is necessary to understand novelty. Therefore, we cover patentability in the following order: (1) novelty; (2) nonobviousness; (3) utility; (4) disclosure; and (5) subject matter.

Please bear in mind, however, that courts have indicated that patentable subject matter is a threshold inquiry, and that it is generally decided before issues of novelty or nonobviousness are raised and without directly considering them.

1. Novelty

The concept of novelty, at least as it relates to patent law, seems simple. All we need is a timeline. The first person to invent wins the race. Yet operationalizing this concept into to an administrable and effective system of quasi-property rights in intangible resources raises some challenging policy choices. Even defining the moment of invention—what we call "conception"—introduces significant complications. And proving that moment adds evidentiary complexities.

For most of its history, the U.S. has operated under a first-to-invent system. The old law, Section 102 of the 1952 Patent Act, embodies the principle that only truly new inventions deserve patents, and that as between two claimants it is the first to invent who deserves protection. But even this system required some adaptations so as to encourage prompt filing of applications.

Most of the rest of the world, by contrast, has long operated under a first-to-file system, awarding the patent to the first person to bring the invention to the patent office. After decades of diplomacy, the U.S. significantly shifted toward the international standard through the enactment of the America Invents Act (AIA) of 2011. For all patent applications filed on or after March 16, 2013, the U.S. novelty regime is a variation on the international first-to-file system. We say variation because the AIA regime still permits an inventor a one year grace period under certain conditions. As a result, the U.S. regime still diverges from other first-to-file systems, but is much closer to regimes in other nations than it was under the 1952 Act.

Since part of the goal of the AIA was to both harmonize U.S. law with international law and to simplify the complex mechanics of the 1952 Act regime, you might think that your task in learning patent law is far simpler than prior generations of law students. Unfortunately, the opposite is true. For the next two decades or so, patent lawyers must understand both the 1952 Act novelty regime (which governs patent applications filed prior to March 16, 2013) and the simpler AIA novelty regime, which governs all patents filed since that date.

A bit of good news is that the wording of specific prior art categories used in the AIA was carried over from the 1952 Act, and indeed, many phrases originate in even earlier versions of the Patent Act. Many of the phrases have been the subject of extensive judicial interpretation—making §102 one of many examples of what might be called a strong common law tradition in patent law. Many crucial terms in this body of law should carry with them extensive case law interpretations. It is generally understood, in patent law as elsewhere, that when Congress chooses to preserve legal language with an extensive body of interpretive case law behind it, that choice means that accepted case law interpretations are carried forward into the new legislative enactment. For purposes of the AIA, this general rule has some important consequences. One is that many older cases dealing with prior art will still be relevant when post-AIA patents begin to dominate patent litigation. Thus, many of the cases and principles we discuss in covering the 1952 regime will be important in understanding the AIA as well.

i.   The 1952 Regime

Under the 1952 Act, §102 sets forth two subsets of requirements for a patent to issue: (1) the invention is novel (subsections (a), (e), (f), and (g)); and (2) the application was filed in a timely manner, i.e., it is not subject to a "statutory bar" (subsections (b), (c), and (d)).

The first set of requirements, referred to as anticipation or lack of novelty, seeks to ensure that a patent issues only to the first inventor. This goal is accomplished by using the applicant's date of invention as the relevant baseline for analysis. Prior art—such as published articles (including publicly accessible websites), publicly known techniques, and marketed products—containing all elements of the claimed invention will anticipate, and thereby defeat, the patent claim. The same is true of patent applications filed by a third party before an inventor's application, as long as that earlier third party application is eventually published or issued as a patent.

The second set of requirements, known as statutory bars, promote timely filing by requiring that the patentee file an application within one year of various triggering events. In many cases, the bar arises because of something the inventor does. The classic example is publication of a scientific article. If an inventor fails to file a patent application within one year of the article's publication, she is barred from receiving a patent. She suffers a "loss of right."

Section 102 provides that "A person shall be entitled to a patent unless" various conditions set forth in subsections (a) through (g) stand in the way. Before turning to those conditions, which will occupy much of our study, it is worthwhile noting the evidentiary structure of this statutory provision. By stating that "[a] person shall be entitled to a patent *unless*," (emphasis added), Congress placed the burden of defeating patentability on the PTO. Thus, in rejecting a patent application, the PTO must establish one of the conditions of patentability.

The principal conditions of 102 are printed below, with bracketed insertions. Note that §102(a) is concerned with novelty, while the statutory bars are set forth in §102(b).

1952 Act: 35 U.S.C. §102. Conditions for Patentability; Novelty and Loss of Right to Patent

A person shall be entitled to a patent unless—

(a) [**Novelty**] the invention was known or used by others in this country, or patented or described in a printed publication in this or a foreign country, before the invention thereof by the applicant for patent, or

(b) [**Statutory Bars**] the invention was patented or described in a printed publication in this or a foreign country or in public use or on sale in this country, more than one year prior to the date of the application for patent in the United States, or

(c) [**Abandonment**] [the inventor] has abandoned the invention, or

(d) [**Late filing in the U.S.**] the invention was first patented or caused to be patented . . . by the applicant . . . in a foreign country prior to the date of the application for patent in this country on an application for patent . . . filed more than twelve months before the filing of the application in the United States, or

(e) [**Secret Prior Art: Previously-filed applications**] The invention was described in (1) [a published patent application] by another filed in the United States before the invention by the applicant for patent . . . or (2) a patent granted on an application for patent by another filed in the United States before the invention thereof by the applicant for patent . . . or

(f) [**Derivation**] he did not himself invent the subject matter sought to be patented, or

(g) [**First-to-Invent**] (1) [*inter partes* proceedings] during the course of an interference . . . , another inventor involved therein establishes, to the extent permitted in section 104. . .that before such person's invention thereof the invention was made by such other inventor and not abandoned, suppressed, or concealed, or (2) [*ex parte* prosecution/invalidity defense] before such person's invention thereof, the invention was made in this country by another inventor who had not abandoned, suppressed, or concealed it. In determining priority of invention under this subsection, there shall be considered not only the respective dates of conception and reduction to practice of the invention, but also the reasonable diligence of one who was first to conceive and last to reduce to practice, from a time prior to conception by the other.

ii.   *The Nature of Novelty*

Turning to the specific conditions that stand in the way of obtaining a patent, subsection a provides that

the invention was known or used by others in this country, or patented or described in a printed publication in this or a foreign country, before the invention thereof by the applicant for patent

What does it mean to be "known or used by others"?

Rosaire v. National Lead Co.
United States Court of Appeals for the Fifth Circuit
218 F.2d 72 (5th Cir. 1955)

TUTTLE, Circuit Judge

In this suit for patent infringement there is presented to us for determination the correctness of the judgment of the trial court, based on findings of fact and conclusions of law, holding that the two patents involved in the litigation were invalid and void and that furthermore there had been no infringement by defendant.

The Rosaire and Horvitz patents relate to methods of prospecting for oil or other hydrocarbons. The inventions are based upon the assumption that gases have emanated from deposits of hydrocarbons which have been trapped in the earth and that these emanations have modified the surrounding rock. The methods claimed involve the steps of taking a number of samples of soil from formations which are not themselves productive of hydrocarbons, either over a horizontal area or vertically down a well bore, treating each sample, as by grinding and heating in a closed vessel, to cause entrained or absorbed hydrocarbons therein to evolve as a gas, quantitatively measuring the amount of hydrocarbon gas so evolved from each sample, and correlating the measurements with the locations from which the samples were taken.

Plaintiff claims that in 1936 he and Horvitz invented this new method of prospecting for oil. In due course the two patents in suit, Nos. 2,192,525 and 2,324,085, were issued thereon. Horvitz assigned his interest to Rosaire.

In view of the fact that the trial court's judgment that the patents were invalid, would of course dispose of [this infringement suit] if correct, we turn our attention to this issue. [Appellee argues] that work carried on by one Teplitz for the Gulf Oil Corporation invalidated both patents by reason of the relevant provisions of the patent laws which state that an invention is not patentable if it "was known or used by others in this country" before the patentee's invention thereof, 35 U.S.C.A. §102(a). Appellee contends that Teplitz and his coworkers knew and extensively used in the field the same alleged inventions before any date asserted by Rosaire and Horvitz.

On this point appellant himself in his brief admits that "Teplitz conceived of the idea of extracting and quantitatively measuring entrained or absorbed gas from the samples of rock, rather than relying upon the free gas in the samples. We do not deny that Teplitz conceived of the methods of the patents in suit." And further appellant makes the following admission: "We admit that the Teplitz-Gulf work was done before Rosaire and Horvitz conceived of the inventions. We will show, however, that Gulf did not apply for patent until 1939, did not publish Teplitz's ideas, and did not otherwise give the public the benefit of the experimental work."

The question as to whether the work of Teplitz was "an unsuccessful experiment," as claimed by appellant, or was a successful trial of the method in question and a reduction of that method to actual practice, as contended by appellee, is, of course, a question of fact. On this point the trial court made the following finding of fact:

> I find as a fact that Abraham J. Teplitz and his coworkers with Gulf Oil Corporation and its Research Department during 1935 and early 1936, before any date claimed by Rosaire, spent more than a year in the oil fields and adjacent territory around Palestine, Texas, taking and analyzing samples both over an area and down drill holes, exactly as called for in the claims of the patents which Rosaire and Horvitz subsequently applied for and which are here in suit.

> This Teplitz work was a successful and adequate field trial of the prospecting method involved and a reduction to practice of that method. The work was performed in the field under ordinary conditions without any deliberate attempt at concealment or effort to exclude the public and without any instructions of secrecy to the employees performing the work.

As we view it, if the court's findings of fact are correct then under the statute as construed by the courts, we must affirm the finding of the trial court that appellee's patents were invalid.

[T]here was sufficient evidence to sustain the finding of the trial court that there was more here than an unsuccessful or incomplete experiment. It is clear that the work was not carried forward, but that appears to be a result of two things: (1) that the geographical area did not lend itself properly to the test, and (2) that the "entire gas prospecting program was therefore suspended in September of 1936, in order that the accumulated information might be thoroughly reviewed." It will be noted that the program was not suspended to test the worth of the method but to examine the data that was produced by use of the method involved.

With respect to the argument advanced by appellant that the lack of publication of Teplitz's work deprived an alleged infringer of the defense of prior use, we find no case which constrains us to hold that where such work was done openly and in the ordinary course of the activities of the employer, a large producing company in the oil industry, the statute is to be so modified by construction as to require some affirmative act to bring the work to the attention of the public at large.

While there is authority for the proposition that one of the basic principles underlying the patent laws is the enrichment of the art, and that a patent is given to encourage disclosure of inventions, no case we have found requires a holding that, under the circumstances that attended the work of Teplitz, the fact of public knowledge must be shown before it can be urged to invalidate a subsequent patent.

COMMENTS AND QUESTIONS

1. In *New Railhead Mfg., L.L.C. v. Vermeer Mfg. Co.*, 298 F.3d 1290 (Fed. Cir. 2002), the Federal Circuit considered a similar fact situation. Patentee New Railhead had tested a drill bit in underground drilling that occurred before the critical date for its

patent. In response to the patentee's argument that its use was either nonpublic or experimental, the court followed the reasoning of *Rosaire* and invalidated the patent. Judge Dyk dissented. *See* 298 F.3d at 1300 (Dyk J., dissenting) ("The use actually took place under public land, hidden from view, and there has been no showing whatsoever that the use was anything but confidential. To understand the method of using the drill bit a person at the job site would have to view the drill bit or see it in operation, and this was impossible to do while the drill bit was underground."). In *W.L. Gore & Assocs., Inc. v. Garlock, Inc.*, 721 F.2d 1540 (Fed. Cir. 1983), the Federal Circuit had this to say about "secret" prior use, where patentee Gore argued that prior use by another of a machine conforming to the elements of Gore's claim was nonpublic and therefore nonanticipatory:

> The nonsecret use of a claimed process in the usual course of producing articles for commercial purposes is a public use. Electric Storage Battery Co. v. Shimadzu, 307 U.S. 5, 20 (1939). . . . Thus it cannot be said that the district court erred in determining that the invention set forth in claim 1 of the '566 patent was known or used by others under §102(a), as evidenced by . . . operation of the '401 machine before Dr. Gore's asserted date of that invention.

2. In *Woodland Trust v. Flowertree Nursery, Inc.*, 148 F.3d 1368 (Fed. Cir. 1998), defendant Flowertree argued the invalidity of the patent owned by Woodland based on prior use of a nursery watering system identical to that claimed in the patent:

> Under §102(a), Flowertree stated that the method was previously known and used by each of Joseph Burke and William Hawkins (an owner of Flowertree) in the 1960s and 1970s at their nurseries in Florida, and was then discontinued by these users in 1976 and 1978. The district court found that Hawkins' system at Flowertree was reconstructed in 1988.
>
> Four witnesses testified in support of the defense of prior knowledge and use: Mark Hawkins, Joseph Burke, Charles Hudson, and John Kaufmann. Mark Hawkins is the son of William Hawkins; he testified that his father's system, on which he worked as a child, was destroyed by a tornado in 1978, and was not reconstructed until 1988. Joseph Burke is a nursery owner who has known William Hawkins since the 1960s; he testified that he used the same system as shown in the patent, but tore it down in 1976 and did not rebuild it. Charles Hudson is a nursery owner who had worked for Joseph Burke, and John Kaufmann is a life-long friend of William Hawkins; they testified that they observed the patented system at the Burke or Hawkins nursery, before its use was discontinued.

148 F.3d at 1369. The Federal Circuit reviewed Supreme Court precedent laying down a stringent corroboration requirement, and then concluded:

> This guidance, applied to this case, reinforces the heavy burden when establishing prior public knowledge and use based on long-past events. The

Supreme Court's view of human nature as well as human recollection, whether deemed cynical or realistic, retains its cogency. This view is reinforced, in modern times, by the ubiquitous paper trail of virtually all commercial activity. It is rare indeed that some physical record (e.g., a written document such as notes, letters, invoices, notebooks, or a sketch or drawing or photograph showing the device, a model, or some other contemporaneous record) does not exist.

In this case, despite the asserted many years of commercial and public use, we take note of the absence of any physical record to support the oral evidence. The asserted prior knowledge and use by Hawkins and Burke was said to have begun approximately thirty years ago and to have continued for about a decade. Hawkins testified that his prior use was terminated in 1978, and the district court found that Hawkins' system was not reconstructed until 1988. The relationship of the witnesses and the fact that the asserted prior uses ended twenty years before the trial, and were abandoned until the defendant reportedly learned of the patentee's practices, underscore the failure of this oral evidence to provide clear and convincing evidence of prior knowledge and use. The district court did not rely on the two undated photographs, and indeed their lack of detail and clarity can not have provided documentary support.

With the guidance of precedent, whose cautions stressed the frailty of memory of things long past and the temptation to remember facts favorable to the cause of one's relative or friend, we conclude that this oral evidence, standing alone, did not provide the clear and convincing evidence necessary to invalidate a patent on the ground of prior knowledge and use under §102(a).

Id. at 1373.

Do you agree with the Federal Circuit's implication that in the absence of a strong corroboration requirement for prior public use evidence, there would be a temptation for competitors of a patentee to lie? Is it likely that the witnesses in *Woodland Trust* really made the whole thing up? Note that the alleged prior use was the defendant's own use, so in that particular case the defendant might have had an incentive to lie. With such a strong requirement of documentary evidence, is there much difference between public use evidence and proof that an invention appeared in a prior publication or patent?

3. The very expansive view taken in *Rosaire* of what it means for a disclosure to be "public" was criticized by one scholar:

The term "public" . . . seems merely to mean "not secret." It is unnecessary to show that the previous discovery was ever used commercially, that it was in fact observable by the public if such a process or device would not normally be so viewed, or that it was known to more than a few persons. This construction of the term "public" seems questionable, since it may result in the denial of a patent even though the subsequent inventor has conferred a benefit by filing the invention with the public records.

Comment, *Prior Art in the Patent Law*, 73 HARV. L. REV. 369, 373 (1959). The author goes on to propose a "higher standard of knowledge or use," arguing that

> an invention should be considered "known or used" only if it was so widely known or used that an ordinary skilled worker exercising reasonable diligence to learn the state of the art would have discovered, recognized, and been able to construct the invention.

Id. at 373. In effect, this proposal would apply a trade secret standard of novelty to the patent law—an invention could be "new" even though it had been made before, as long as it was not in general knowledge or use. Are there any problems with applying this weaker standard of novelty to determine whether a patent should be issued? Can it be reconciled with the broad language of section 102(a), precluding patents on inventions that were previously "known or used by others in this country"?

In *Hall v. MacNeale*, 107 U.S. (17 Otto) 90 (1883), Hall had in 1866 received a patent on an improved design for the door and walls of burglar-proof safes. The question before the Court was whether the use of certain earlier-model safes before the critical date was *public* enough to create a statutory bar. The Court held:

> The construction and arrangement and purpose and mode of operation and use of the [hidden feature] in the safes were necessarily known to the workmen who put them in. They were, it is true, hidden from view, after the safes were completed, and it required a destruction of the safe to bring them into view. But this was no concealment of them or use of them in secret. They had no more concealment than was inseparable from any legitimate use of them.

4. One issue in *Rosaire* was the patentee's allegation that the Teplitz work was not prior art because it was incomplete, a mere "abandoned experiment." On this issue, consider *Picard v. United Aircraft Corp.*, 128 F.2d 632 (2d Cir. 1942) (L. Hand, J.):

> It is true that another's experiment, imperfect and never perfected, will not serve either as an anticipation or as part of the prior art, for it has not served to enrich it. The patented invention does not become "known" by such a use or sale, or by anything of which the art cannot take hold and make use as it stands. But the mere fact that an earlier "machine" or "manufacture," sold or used, was an experiment does not prevent its becoming an anticipation or a part of the prior art, provided it was perfected and thereafter became publicly known. Whether it does become so depends upon how far it becomes a part of the stock of knowledge of the art in question. Judged by that standard, the Curtiss engine [prior art reference] was not an "abandoned experiment"; it had been perfected; it had withstood a severer test than was necessary in use; it had been sold; it remained permanently accessible to the art, a contribution to the sum of knowledge so far as it went.

This issue would likely arise today under a different rubric: was the prior art reference "enabled," or capable of teaching one skilled in the art its details. *See, e.g.*, *In re Paulsen*, 30 F.3d 1475 (Fed. Cir. 1994).

5. *Inherency* – Section 102(a) provides that an applicant is not entitled to a patent if her invention was "known or used by others" prior to the date of the applicant's invention. The meaning of this phrase has been called into question in a series of cases involving unintended, "accidental" anticipation of an invention. Most of these cases involve the inherent, unintended production of a particular physical product. When an inventor later *intentionally* makes the product, presumably because she has some use for it, the prior unintended production of the product may be raised as prior art to the invention.

On the one hand, a venerable line of cases holds that where the first, accidental producer was not aware of the product and did not attempt to produce it, the first production did not bar a patent on the "invention" of the product. Thus, in *Tilghman v. Proctor*, 102 U.S. 707 (1880), the Supreme Court held that the accidental separation of fat acids from tallow during operation of a steam engine lubricated by tallow did not anticipate Tilghman's patent for a similar separation process. Of the prior production, the Court said:

> They revealed no process for the manufacture of fat acids. If the acids were accidentally and unwittingly produced, whilst the operators were in pursuit of other and different results, without exciting attention and without it even being known what was done or how it had been done, it would be absurd to say that this was an anticipation of Tilghman's discovery.

Id. at 711. *See also Abbott Labs v. Geneva Pharmaceuticals, Inc.*, 182 F.3d 1315 (Fed. Cir. 1999) (distinguishing *Tilghman* in case where prior art product was appreciated and sold, even though party did not appreciate qualities of product). On the other hand, an equally venerable line of cases holds that if a product is known in the art already, an inventor cannot obtain a patent *on the product* merely by putting it to a new use, "even if the new result had not before been contemplated." *Ansonia Brass & Copper Co. v. Elec. Supply Co.*, 144 U.S. 11 (1892). The inventor could obtain a patent on the new process using that product, however. For more on this distinction, *see Atlas Powder Co. v. Ireco, Inc.*, 190 F.3d 1342 (Fed. Cir. 1999).

Newer Federal Circuit cases have focused on whether an invention was present in the prior art in a way that provided a public benefit. The knowledge of those in the art has been de-emphasized as a factor. In *Schering Corp. v. Geneva Pharms., Inc.*, 339 F.3d 1373, 1377 (Fed. Cir. 2003), the court invalidated a claim to a compound that is necessarily produced in the human body whenever a person ingests the allergy medicine Claritin—even though the patentee Schering-Plough argued that no one knew about the claimed product until Schering characterized it. Another case is *Prima Tek II, L.L.C. v. Polypap, S.A.R.L.*, 412 F.3d 1284 (Fed. Cir. 2005), where the court invalidated a claim to a "potless" floral arrangement holder (see diagram). The claim included, among other things, the elements of (1) a band to hold the floral arrangement; (2) a sheet of decorative material covering the floral arrangement; and (3) "means for forming a crimped portion in the sheet of material." 412 F.3d 1284, 1287 n.1. Polypap, the accused infringer, argued that a published French patent application, the "Charrin reference," inherently anticipated the claim. The patentee Prima Tek countered with the argument that Charrin did not disclose the "crimping" limitation. The court agreed with Polypap, noting that in the drawing below Charrin clearly discloses a string along the top of the floral arrangement holder which necessarily creates crimping in the covering material:

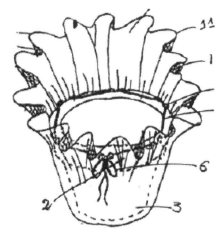

In other words, the invention was already present in the prior art, because the decorative material would be crimped whenever the Charrin device was used, whether or not people recognized or intended that result. *See* Dan L. Burk & Mark A. Lemley, *Inherency*, 47 WM. & MARY L. REV. 371 (2005) (endorsing the move to public benefit, and making the point that if skilled artisans know about the prior use, then there is no need for an inherency doctrine at all).

iii. Statutory Bars

Section 102(b) bars the granting of a patent where

the invention was patented or described in a printed publication in this or a foreign country or in public use or on sale in this country, more than one year prior to the date of the application for patent in the United States.

Recall from the introduction to this section that one difference between statutory bars and novelty is that an inventor can create a statutory bar by her own actions (e.g., publication of an article), whereas she cannot destroy the novelty of her own inventions. In short, an inventor's own work cannot be cited against her (in general) under §102(a), but it is "fair game" under §102(b). Note, however, that the 1952 Act affords the inventor a one year grace period for filing a patent application following one of the statutory bar triggers—patenting, printed publication, public, or public use in the U.S.

Notwithstanding this difference between novelty and statutory bars, subsections 102(a) and (b) are not appreciably different for many purposes. For example, courts interpret "publication"—a term common to both subsections—the same in both contexts. Thus, although the following case involves a §102(b) reference, the reasoning is equally applicable to §102(a).

In re Hall
United States Court of Appeals for the Federal Circuit
781 F.2d 897 (Fed. Cir. 1986)

BALDWIN, Circuit Judge.

This is an appeal from the decision of the U.S. Patent and Trademark Office's (PTO) former Board of Appeals, adhered to on reconsideration by the Board of Patent Appeals and Interferences (board), sustaining the final rejection of claims 1-25 of [Hall's] reissue [a]pplication, based principally on a "printed publication" bar under 35 U.S.C. §102(b). The reference is a doctoral thesis. Because appellant concedes that his claims are unpatentable if the thesis is available as a "printed publication" more than one year prior to the application's effective filing date of February 27, 1979, the only issue is whether the thesis is available as such a printed publication. On the record before us, we affirm the board's decision.

A protest was filed during prosecution of appellant's reissue application which included in an appendix a copy of the dissertation "1,4-α-Glucanglukohydrolase ein amylotylisches Enzym . . ." by Peter Foldi (Foldi thesis or dissertation). The record indicates that in September 1977, Foldi submitted his dissertation to the Department of Chemistry and Pharmacy at Freiburg University in the Federal Republic of Germany, and that Foldi was awarded a doctorate degree on November 2, 1977. . . .

The examiner made a final rejection of the application claims. He said: "On the basis of the instant record it is reasonable to assume that the Foldi thesis was available (accessible) prior to February 27, 197[8]."

By letter, the PTO's Scientific Library asked Dr. Will whether the Foldi dissertation was made available to the public by being cataloged and placed in the main collection. Dr. Will replied in an October 20, 1983 letter, as translated: "Our dissertations, thus also the Foldi dissertation, are indexed in a special dissertations catalogue, which is part of the general users' catalogue. In the stacks they are likewise set apart in a special dissertation section, which is part of the general stacks."

In response to a further inquiry by the PTO's Scientific Library requesting (1) the exact date of indexing and cataloging of the Foldi dissertation or (2) "the time such procedures normally take," Dr. Will replied in a June 18, 1984 letter: "The Library copies of the Foldi dissertation were sent to us by the faculty on November 4, 1977. Accordingly, the dissertation most probably was available for general use toward the beginning of the month of December, 1977."

The board held that the unrebutted evidence of record was sufficient to conclude that the Foldi dissertation had an effective date as prior art more than one year prior to the filing date of the appellant's initial application.

On appeal, appellant raises two arguments: (1) the §102(b) "printed publication" bar requires that the publication be accessible to the interested public, but there is no evidence that the dissertation was properly indexed in the library catalog prior to the critical date; and (2) even if the Foldi thesis were cataloged prior to the critical date, the presence of a single cataloged thesis in one university library does not constitute sufficient accessibility of the publication's teachings to those interested in the art exercising reasonable diligence.

The [printed publication] bar is grounded on the principle that once an invention is in the public domain, it is no longer patentable by anyone.

The statutory phrase "printed publication" has been interpreted to give effect to ongoing advances in the technologies of data storage, retrieval, and dissemination. Because there are many ways in which a reference may be disseminated to the interested public, "public accessibility" has been called the touchstone in determining whether a reference constitutes a "printed publication" bar under 35 U.S.C. §102(b). The §102 publication bar is a legal determination based on underlying fact issues, and therefore must be approached on a case-by-case basis. The proponent of the publication bar must show that prior to the critical date the reference was sufficiently accessible, at least to the public interested in the art, so that such a one by examining the reference could make the claimed invention without further research or experimentation.

[A]ppellant argues that the Foldi thesis was not shown to be accessible because Dr. Will's affidavits do not say when the thesis was indexed in the library catalog and do not chronicle the procedures for receiving and processing a thesis in the library.

[A]ppellant would have it that accessibility can only be shown by evidence establishing a *specific* date of cataloging and shelving before the critical date. While such evidence would be desirable, in lending greater certainty to the accessibility determination, the realities of routine business practice counsel against requiring such evidence. The probative value of routine business practice to show the performance of a specific act has long been recognized. *See, e.g.,* 1 WIGMORE, EVIDENCE §92 (1940); rule 406, FED. R. EVID. Therefore, we conclude that competent evidence of the general library practice may be relied upon to establish an approximate time when a thesis became accessible.

We agree with the board that the evidence of record consisting of Dr. Will's affidavits establishes a prima facie case for unpatentability of the claims under the §102(b) publication bar. It is a case which stands unrebutted.

Accordingly, the board's decision sustaining the rejection of appellant's claims is affirmed.

COMMENTS AND QUESTIONS

1. Note that the issue in this case could arise under either §102(a) or 102(b). If the publication had occurred before the *invention* of the subject matter by the applicant, §102(a) would apply. Section 102(b) applied in this case because the publication occurred more than one year before the applicant *filed* for a patent.

2. Compare the "publicness" standard in *Hall* to the rule in trade secret law (information must be "generally known or readily ascertainable" in an industry). Why is it so much easier to lose patent rights than trade secrets?

3. *Poster Sessions*. In general, a publication becomes public when it becomes available to at least one member of "the general public." In *In re Klopfenstein*, 380 F.3d 1345 (Fed. Cir. 2004), the Federal Circuit addressed whether temporary display of scientific research information at conference "poster session" constituted publication under §102(b). The court held that the determination of whether the display constitutes a publication turns on a balancing of factors, including: (1) the length of time the display was exhibited; (2) the expertise of the target audience; (3) the existence (or lack thereof) of reasonable expectations that the material displayed would not be copied; and (4) the simplicity or ease with which the material displayed could have been copied.

4. A magazine or technical journal is effective as of its date of publication, i.e., when someone first receives it, rather than the date a manuscript was sent to the publisher or the date the journal or magazine was mailed. *See In re Schlittler*, 234 F.2d 882 (C.C.P.A. 1956).

5. *Websites*. How about temporary posting of information on a website? This raises particular problems of *permanent* accessibility, as websites can be taken down at any time; web archiving services may play an important role here. Does *In re Hall* provide any guidance? The Federal Circuit has held that an article posted on the Internet but not indexed in search engines can still be a printed publication. *Voter Verified, INc. v. Premier Election Solutions, Inc.*, 698 F.3d 1374 (Fed. Cir. 2012).

6. *Peer Review of Grant Proposals*. Is a grant proposal sent to a limited number of expert reviewers a publication under §102(a)? *See E. I. du Pont de Nemours & Co. v. Cetus Corp.*, 19 U.S.P.Q.2d (BNA) 1174 (N.D. Cal. 1990) (no).

PROBLEM

Problem III-1. In late 1967 the Navy encountered a problem with its new fighter plane. The Navy's aircraft—stationed on aircraft carriers—were more likely to suffer structural damage than Air Force planes of the same type that were positioned on land. Navy scientists concluded that the widespread problem of fuselage cracking, known as "stress corrosion," was attributable to the harsh marine environment. The Navy presented its problem to the aluminum industry, and Algol Corp. was awarded a research contract to develop a new alloy that would be more resistant to the phenomenon.

Pursuant to the terms of the defense contract, Algol would periodically report on its research results in "progress letters." The Navy drew up a distribution list of 33 designees to receive Algol's progress letters, and each letter bore the following "export control" notice: "This Document Is Subject to Special Export Controls and Each Transmittal to Foreign Governments or Foreign Nationals May Be Made Only with Prior Approval of the Naval Air Systems Command."

The designees included aluminum producers (including Algol's competitors), aircraft manufacturers, government agencies, branches of the military, and academic researchers. Several progress letters were mailed, the last on April 5, 1969. As of the last progress letter, Algol had succeeded in developing a high-strength, stress-corrosion-resistant alloy that met the Navy's needs. Algol successfully applied for a patent covering its process for aging and treating its new alloy on February 5, 1971.

When Algol refused to license the patent to its competitor Richards, the latter began to manufacture and sell a high-strength alloy using Algol's patented technology. Algol filed suit alleging infringement.

You are Senior Counsel for Intellectual Property Matters at Richards Aluminum. Your defense strategy is limited by the fact that if the Algol patent is valid, your company is undeniably engaged in infringement. Algol gathers evidence that the 33 designees who received Algol's progress reports treated them as highly confidential although they contained no express limitation on access other than the export control notice. Depositions of Richards' own executives reveal that your company kept its copies of the letters in a protected area, screened even from some of its own employees. Such procedures were typical in defense industry circles when a report bearing an export control notice was received. Nevertheless, the absence of any other access restrictions on the letters supports Richards' argument that Richards could have shared the report's contents with every American citizen.

Is the patent anticipated by Algol's prior "publication"? If so, under §102(a) or under §102(b)?

iv. *Statutory Bars: Public Use and On Sale*

Egbert v. Lippmann
Supreme Court of the United States
104 U.S. 333 (1881)

Mr. Justice WOODS delivered the opinion of the court.

This suit was brought for an alleged infringement of the complainant's reissued letters-patent, No. 5216, dated Jan. 7, 1873, for an improvement in corset-springs.

The original letters were issued to Samuel H. Barnes. The reissue was made to the complainant, under her then name, Frances Lee Barnes, executrix of the original patentee.

The specification for the reissue declares:—

This invention consists in forming the springs of corsets of two or more metallic plates, placed one upon another, and so connected as to prevent them from sliding off each other laterally or edgewise, and at the same time admit of their playing or sliding upon each other, in the direction of their length or longitudinally, whereby their flexibility and elasticity are greatly increased, while at the same time much strength is obtained.

The bill alleges that Barnes was the original and first inventor of the improvement covered by the reissued letters-patent, and that it had not, at the time of his application for the original letters, been for more than two years in public use or on sale, with his consent or allowance.

The answer takes issue on this averment and also denies infringement. On a final hearing the court dismissed the bill, and the complainant appealed.

We have to consider whether the defence that the patented invention had, with the consent of the inventor, been publicly used for more than two years prior to his application for the original letters, is sustained by the testimony in the record.

[The patent statute] render[s] letters-patent invalid if the invention which they cover was in public use, with the consent and allowance of the inventor, for more than two years prior to his application.[5] Since the passage of the act of 1839 it has been strenuously contended that the public use of an invention for more than two years before such application, even without his consent and allowance, renders the letters-patent therefor void.

It is unnecessary in this case to decide this question, for the alleged use of the invention covered by the letters-patent to Barnes is conceded to have been with his express consent.

The evidence on which the defendants rely to establish a prior public use of the invention consists mainly of the testimony of the complainant.

She testifies that Barnes invented the improvement covered by his patent between January and May, 1855; that between the dates named the witness and her friend Miss Cugier were complaining of the breaking of their corset-steels. Barnes, who was present, and was an intimate friend of the witness, said he thought he could make her a pair that would not break. At their next interview he presented her with a pair of corset-steels which he himself had made. The witness wore these steels a long time. In 1858 Barnes made and presented to her another pair, which she also wore a long time. When the corsets in which these steels were used wore out, the witness ripped them open and took out the steels and put them in new corsets. This was done several times.

It is admitted, and, in fact, is asserted, by complainant, that these steels embodied the invention afterwards patented by Barnes and covered by the reissued letters-patent on which this suit is brought.

---

[5] [This has since been changed to one year.—EDS.]

Joseph H. Sturgis, another witness for complainant, testifies that in 1863 Barnes spoke to him about two inventions made by himself, one of which was a corset-steel, and that he went to the house of Barnes to see them. Before this time, and after the transactions testified to by the complainant, Barnes and [the complainant] had intermarried. Barnes said his wife had a pair of steels made according to his invention in the corsets which she was then wearing, and if she would take them off he would show them to [Sturgis]. Mrs. Barnes went out, and returned with a pair of corsets and a pair of scissors, and ripped the corsets open and took out the steels. Barnes then explained to the witness how they were made and used.

The question for our decision is, whether this testimony shows a public use within the meaning of the statute.

We observe, in the first place, that to constitute the public use of an invention it is not necessary that more than one of the patented articles should be publicly used. The use of a great number may tend to strengthen the proof, but one well-defined case of such use is just as effectual to annul the patent as many. For instance, if the inventor of a mower, a printing press, or a railway-car makes and sells only one of the articles invented by him, and allows the vendee to use it for two years, without restriction or limitation, the use is just as public as if he had sold and allowed the use of a great number.

We remark, secondly, that, whether the use of an invention is public or private does not necessarily depend upon the number of persons to whom its use is known. If an inventor, having made his device, gives or sells it to another, to be used by the donee or vendee, without limitation or restriction, or injunction of secrecy, and it is so used, such use is public, even though the use and knowledge of the use may be confined to one person.

We say, thirdly, that some inventions are by their very character only capable of being used where they cannot be seen or observed by the public eye. An invention may consist of a lever or spring, hidden in the running gear of a watch, or of a rachet, shaft, or cog-wheel covered from view in the recesses of a machine for spinning or weaving. Nevertheless, if its inventor sells a machine of which his invention forms a part, and allows it to be used without restriction of any kind, the use is a public one. So, on the other hand, a use necessarily open to public view, if made in good faith solely to test the qualities of the invention, and for the purpose of experiment, is not a public use within the meaning of the statute.

Tested by these principles, we think the evidence of the complainant herself shows that for more than two years before the application for the original letters there was, by the consent and allowance of Barnes, a public use of the invention, covered by them. He made and gave to her two pairs of corset-steels, constructed according to his device, one in 1855 and one in 1858. They were presented to her for use. He imposed no obligation of secrecy, nor any condition or restriction whatever. They were not presented for the purpose of experiment, nor to test their qualities. No such claim is set up in her testimony. The invention was at the time complete, and there is no evidence that it was afterwards changed or improved. The donee of the steels used them for years for the purpose and in the manner designed by the inventor. They were not capable of any other use. She might have exhibited them to any person, or made other steels of the same kind, and used or sold them without violating any condition or restriction imposed on her by the inventor.

According to the testimony of the complainant, the invention was completed and put to use in 1855. The inventor slept on his rights for eleven years. Letters-patent were not applied for till March, 1866. In the mean time, the invention had found its way into general, and almost universal, use. A great part of the record is taken up with the testimony of the manufacturers and venders [sic] of corset-steels, showing that before he applied for letters-patent the principle of his device was almost universally used in the manufacture of corset-steels. It is fair to presume that having learned from this general use that there was some value in his invention, he attempted to resume, by his application, what by his acts he had clearly dedicated to the public.

We are of opinion that the defence of two years' public use, by the consent and allowance of the inventor, before he made application for letters-patent, is satisfactorily established by the evidence.

Decree affirmed.

Mr. Justice MILLER dissenting.

A private use with consent, which could lead to no copy or reproduction of the machine, which taught the nature of the invention to no one but the party to whom such consent was given, which left the public at large as ignorant of this as it was before the author's discovery, was no abandonment to the public, and did not defeat his claim for a patent. If the little steel spring inserted in a single pair of corsets, and used by only one woman, covered by her outer-clothing, and in a position always withheld from public observation, is a *public* use of that piece of steel, I am at a loss to know the line between a private and a public use.

COMMENTS AND QUESTIONS

1. In what sense was Frances Lee (later Barnes) using the corset steels (i.e., the springs) "publicly"? Why doesn't it matter how many people use the invention, for purposes of deciding if the use was public? Compare this holding to that of the court in *Rosaire* above.

2. The Court emphasizes that Ms. Barnes never entered into a confidentiality agreement with the inventor. But the Court also relates that the two later married. Does Barnes have a reasonable argument that although no *express* "injunction of secrecy" was made, nonetheless an *implied* requirement of secrecy could be inferred from the surrounding circumstances: i.e., an invention of an intimate nature, by a boyfriend (later husband), disclosed to few people? Justice Miller, in dissent, added: "It may well be

imagined that a prohibition to the party so permitted [to use the springs] against her use of the steel spring to public observation, would have been supposed to be a piece of irony." 104 U.S. (14 Otto), at 339. Perhaps the embarrassment of asking was enough to keep Mr. Barnes from requesting that Frances Lee not show the invention to anyone.

3. Subsequent cases have not abandoned *Egbert,* but they have perhaps not read it as broadly as they could. In particular, the Federal Circuit has focused on the nature and purpose of the use in deciding whether it was "public" or not. Use for a commercial purpose is generally a public use, even if it is secret and even if it only occurs once. However, use for personal interest or enjoyment will generally not be considered a "public" use.

A similar rule has developed with respect to the "on sale" prong of the §102(b) statutory bar. A single sale or offer to sell a product will start the clock running, whether or not it was made in secret. On the other hand, discussions that do not rise to the level of a definite offer to sell the invention will not bar a later patent on that invention.

4. The policy behind the statutory bars in §102(b) is to encourage inventors to file patent applications early. The inventor in *Egbert* did not do so. Was it reasonable to bar him from receiving a patent on his invention for this reason? Is anyone entitled to a patent on this invention?

5. *Inventor versus Third Party Use*: While "public use" and "on sale" bars frequently result from the inventor's own conduct, they do not have to. Indeed, sales of the invention by a third party can preclude the inventor from later obtaining a patent, even though the third party had stolen the invention from the inventor. *Evans Cooling Sys., Inc. v. General Motors*, 125 F.3d 1448 (Fed. Cir. 1997). The case arose out of inventor John Evans' demonstration of his aqueous reverse flow cooling system to GM engineers in the spring of 1989. GM, as early as June 13, 1991, received a binding order for sale of a Corvette model car incorporating the aqueous reverse flow cooling system. The district court agreed with GM that this sale created a statutory bar for Evans' subsequent patent application filed July 1, 1992. Evans appealed on two grounds: that no enforceable contract could have been formed in June of 1991 because GM had yet to clear certain requisite regulatory hurdles routinely required for sale of a new car model and that the theft of a trade secret ought to be considered an exception to the general statutory bar rule. The court disposed of the first ground by stating simply that "the mere fact that the offer for sale was illegal or ineffective does not remove it from the purview of the section 102(b) bar." *Id.* at 1452.

The court found the second ground—the "theft exception"—equally unpersuasive in light of existing case law. It wrote:

> While such a result may not seem fair, Evans is not without recourse if GM in fact misappropriated his invention. Evans would have an appropriate remedy in state court for misappropriation of a trade secret. We note as well that the facts Evans alleges in support of its misappropriation claim demonstrate that

Evans knew GM stole the invention at the very time it was allegedly stolen because during the demonstration GM employees allegedly told Mr. Evans they intended to steal the invention and a sealed room was unsealed during the night between the tests. Evans' patent rights would have nevertheless been protected if Mr. Evans had filed a patent application no more than one year from the date of the demonstration. This he did not do; instead Mr. Evans waited for more than two years after the demonstration and some six years after it was reduced to practice.

Id. at 1453-54. For a case involving both a close question of "public accessibility/confidentiality," as well as theft-of-idea issues as in *Evans Cooling, see Delano Farms Co. v. California Table Grape Comm'n*, 778 F.3d 1243, 1249 (Fed. Cir. 2015) (grape variety, stolen from plant patentee, was planted and subsequently transferred to another, under conditions of secrecy; the grape vines were not visible to the public and were generally handled in "an environment of confidentiality'; held, not a public use that bars the patent).

6. *On-Sale Bar—Ready for Patenting*. Must an invention actually be completed and built before it can be sold or "offered for sale"? The Supreme Court has said no. *Pfaff v. Wells Elec., Inc.*, 525 U.S. 55 (1998). The Court reasoned that "invention" occurred when the inventor conceived of the product and did not require proof that the invention has actually been built. Indeed, it noted, many famous inventions (including Alexander Graham Bell's telephone) were patented before a prototype was ever built. *Id.* at 308-09. However, the Court did require evidence that the inventive concept itself was "complete, rather than merely . . . substantially complete":

> [T]he on-sale bar applies when two conditions are satisfied before the critical date. First, the product must be the subject of a commercial offer for sale. . . .

> Second, the invention must be ready for patenting. That condition may be satisfied in at least two ways: by proof of reduction to practice before the critical date; or by proof that prior to the critical date the inventor had prepared drawings or other descriptions of the invention that were sufficiently specific to enable a person skilled in the art to practice the invention. In this case the second condition of the on-sale bar is satisfied because the drawings Pfaff sent to the manufacturer before the critical date fully disclosed the invention.

Id. at 67. *See also Weatherchem Corp. v. J.L. Clark, Inc.*, 163 F.3d 1326 (Fed. Cir. 1998) (applying *Pfaff* to case where detailed drawings had been made in preparation of an offer for sale). Contrast *Pfaff* with *Micro Chem., Inc. v. Great Plains Chem. Co.*, 103 F.3d 1538 (Fed. Cir. 1997) ("Because Pratt was not close to completion of the invention at the time of the alleged offer and had not demonstrated a high likelihood that the invention would work for its intended purpose upon completion, his December 1984 'offer' could not trigger the on-sale bar.").

Several cases have now addressed the relationship between contract law and the "on sale" bar. In *Group One, Ltd. v. Hallmark Cards, Inc.*, 254 F.3d 1041 (Fed. Cir. 2001), the patentee and a third party had conducted correspondence and engaged in other interactions in connection with a later-patented technology. The Federal Circuit refused to find that this exploratory discussion placed the invention "on sale" under §102(b). Only a transaction which "rises to the level of a commercial offer for sale" under the Uniform Commercial Code triggers the on-sale bar, according to the court. 254 F.3d at 1047.

In re Kollar, 286 F.3d 1326 (Fed. Cir. 2002), concerned a licensing transaction involving a chemical process. The Federal Circuit refused to find that the transaction triggered the on-sale bar: "[L]icensing the invention," the court stated, "under which development of the claimed process would have to occur before the process is successfully commercialized, is not . . . a sale." *Id.*, at 1333. *Compare Elan Corp. v. Andrx Pharmaceuticals, Inc.*, 366 F.3d 1336 (Fed. Cir. 2004) (offer to supply potential licensee with limited quantities of bulk tablets not enough to constitute on-sale activity in what otherwise appeared to be a proposed licensing transaction), *with Minton v. National Ass'n of Secs. Dealers, Inc.*, 336 F.3d 1373, 1378 (Fed. Cir. 2003) (inventor's conveyance to lessee of fully operational computer program implementing and thus embodying method subsequently claimed in patent for interactive securities trading system, along with warranty of workability, enabled lessee to practice invention, and thus was "offer for sale" within meaning of on-sale bar).

Does this distinction make sense? Why should those who license a process invention be able to avoid the on-sale bar when those who sell a patented product cannot?

7. *On-Sale Activity Need Not Disclose the Manner in which the Patented Technology Functions.* According to an extensive body of case law, these prior art categories include material that can be quite confidential, or at any rate essentially undiscoverable by members of the general public. A consistent line of cases, for example, holds that confidential sales or offers places an invention "on sale" for purposes of novelty. *See, e.g., Buildex Inc. v. Kason Indus., Inc.*, 849 F.2d 1461, 1464 (Fed. Cir. 1988) (firm offer sent to prospective purchaser was an "on sale" event, even though the offer was marked "confidential"); *Pfaff v. Wells Elecs., Inc.*, 525 U.S. 55 (1998) (nowhere mentioning the need for information about a sale to be publicly available).

8. *Public Use—Informing versus Non-Informing (or Secret) Use/Patentee versus Third-Party Activity.* Although the 1952 Act makes no distinction based whether a public use of a patented product or process reveals the patented invention, the courts have injected a policy basis for distinguishing between patentee and third-party activity based on whether the public use informs the public of how the claimed technology functions. The distinction arises in cases in which the output of an invented machine, or the end product of an invented process, is used in public–so-called "non-informing"

or "secret" "public use" cases. (A use can be "non-informing" because the thing used publicly, the output or end product of a manufacturing process, does not reveal the nature of the actual invention, the machine or process that produced the product.) The cases on non-informing public use have distinguished between the patentee's own activity and the activities of third parties. A patentee's non-informing public use is prior art, whereas a third party's is not. *Compare Metallizing Engineering Co. v. Kenyon Bearing & Auto Parts Co.*, 153 F.2d 516 (2d Cir.1946) (Hand, J.) (patentee's own sales of output from machine is an on sale event barring a patent on the machine) *with W.L. Gore & Associates, Inc. v. Garlock, Inc.*, 721 F.2d 1540 (1983) (third party sale of tape from tape-making machine did not bar a patent to an inventor who filed more than one year after that third party sale); *see generally Woodland Trust v. Flowertree Nursery*, 148 F.3d 1368, 1370-71 (Fed. Cir. 1998) (observing that "[s]ection 102(b), unlike §102(a), is primarily concerned with the policy that encourages an inventor to enter the patent system promptly"). It is based on the policy concern that without such a limit, an inventor could keep his invention secret for years or even decades while profiting from its use, then file a patent application. Because that application was filed later, the patent would expire later, extending the effective life of the inventor's protection. This distinction lacks a textual basis, although it is well-established in Federal Circuit jurisprudence.

PROBLEM

Problem III-2. Scientists involved in the field of spectroscopy were being haunted by ghosts. Spectroscopy is the study and analysis of materials to determine their components and molecular structure. One form of spectroscopy, magnetic resonance spectroscopy, works by observing a material's reaction to imposed radiation. A spectroscope bombards the sample material (usually contained in a test tube) with pulses of radio frequency radiation and then records and analyzes the material's response. If the signal response given by the material was weak, the spectroscope would often confuse interfering noise and static for the material's response. Scientists attempted to solve the problem of unwanted frequencies (or "ghost" frequencies) by various mathematical manipulations.

One such scientist was Daniel Murray, a doctoral candidate studying at Oxford under the supervision of Sir William Akeroyd. In the course of his experiments, Murray arrived at a means of "ghostbusting" through shifting the phase of the frequency transmitter at 90 degree angles between pulses, thus avoiding sophisticated manipulations of data. A patent application embodying the Murray invention was filed in the United Kingdom on April 8, 1999, and in the United States on December 21, 2001. Murray secured patent protection in both countries by 2004.

In the spring of 1998, Akeroyd attended a scientific meeting in Boulder, Colorado. On a bus ride during the conference, Akeroyd engaged Dr. Christopher

Squire in an informal conversation. Squire headed a research team at the U.S.-based Monsanto Company that developed related technology for use in the company's chemical analyses. Akeroyd informed Squire of the promising results of Murray's preliminary research on the phase shifting spectroscope. By mid-2000, Squire had updated his spectrometer at Monsanto to include a similar phase shifting transmitter.

Squire immediately applied his improved spectrometer technology to assess whether a particular Monsanto herbicide was safe for release into the environment. This was a project Squire's team had been working on for a full year prior to the improvement in the lab's spectrometer. Excited by the improved results, Squire invited several of his superiors and fellow employees into the lab to observe his data.

Is Squire's use a public use under §102(b)? Does your analysis depend on any of the following hypothetical facts:

- Dr. Squire was the only person who was permitted access to the Monsanto lab where the updated spectrometer was located.
- Anyone could have entered the lab, but in fact Squire was the only one who did.
- The only person who set eyes upon the updated spectrometer besides Squire was a Monsanto custodian.
- Squire regularly left the door unlocked at night.
- The phase shifting transmitter is located deep inside the apparatus, and cannot be seen without dismantling the spectrometer.

v.   Statutory Bars: The Experimental Use Exception

City of Elizabeth v. Pavement Company
Supreme Court of the United States
97 U.S. 126 (1877)

Mr. Justice BRADLEY delivered the opinion of the court.

This suit was brought by the American Nicholson Pavement Company against the city of Elizabeth, N.J., upon a patent issued to Samuel Nicholson, dated Aug. 20, 1867, for a new and improved wooden pavement. [I]n the specification, it is declared that the nature and object of the invention consists in providing a process or mode of constructing wooden block pavements upon a foundation along a street or roadway with facility, cheapness, and accuracy, and also in the creation and construction of such a wooden pavement as shall be comparatively permanent and durable, by so uniting and combining all its parts, both superstructure and foundation, as to provide against the slipping of the horses' feet, against noise, against unequal wear, and against rot and consequent sinking away from below.

The bill charges that the defendants infringed this patent by laying down wooden pavements in the city of Elizabeth, N.J., constructed in substantial conformity with the process patented, and prays an account of profits, and an injunction.

The defendants . . . averred that the alleged invention of Nicholson was in public use, with his consent and allowance, for six years before he applied for a patent, on a certain avenue in Boston called the Mill-dam; and contended that said public use worked an abandonment of the pretended invention. . . .

The next question to be considered is, whether Nicholson's invention was in public use or on sale, with his consent and allowance, for more than two years prior to his application for a patent, within the meaning of . . . the acts in force in 1854, when he obtained his patent. It is contended by the appellants that the pavement which Nicholson put down by way of experiment, on Mill-dam Avenue in Boston, in 1848, was publicly used for the space of six years before his application for a patent, and that this was a public use within the meaning of the law.

To determine this question, it is necessary to examine the circumstances under which this pavement was put down, and the object and purpose that Nicholson had in view. It is perfectly clear from the evidence that he did not intend to abandon his right to a patent. He had filed a *caveat* in August, 1847, and he constructed the pavement in question by way of experiment, for the purpose of testing its qualities. The road in which it was put down, though a public road, belonged to the Boston and Roxbury Mill Corporation, which received toll for its use; and Nicholson was a stockholder and treasurer of the corporation. The pavement in question was about seventy-five feet in length, and was laid adjoining to the toll-gate and in front of the toll-house. It was constructed by Nicholson at his own expense, and was placed by him where it was, in order to see the effect upon it of heavily loaded wagons, and of varied and constant use; and also to ascertain its durability, and liability to decay. Joseph L. Lang, who was toll-collector for many years, commencing in 1849, familiar with the road before that time, and with this pavement from the time of its origin, testified as follows:

> Mr. Nicholson was there almost daily, and when he came he would examine the pavement, would often walk over it, cane in hand, striking it with his cane, and making particular examination of its condition. He asked me very often how people liked it, and asked me a great many questions about it. I have heard him say a number of times that this was his first experiment with this pavement, and he thought that it was wearing very well. The circumstances that made this locality desirable for the purpose of obtaining a satisfactory test of the durability and value of the pavement were: that there would be a better chance to lay it there; he would have more room and a better chance than in the city; and, besides, it was a place where most everybody went over it, rich and poor. It was a great thoroughfare out of Boston. It was frequently travelled by teams having a load of five or six tons, and some larger. As these teams usually stopped at

the toll-house, and started again, the stopping and starting would make as severe a trial to the pavement as it could be put to.

This evidence is corroborated by that of several other witnesses in the cause; the result of the whole being that Nicholson merely intended this piece of pavement as an experiment, to test its usefulness and durability. Was this a public use, within the meaning of the law?

An abandonment of an invention to the public may be evinced by the conduct of the inventor at any time, even within the two years named in the law. The effect of the law is, that no such consequence will necessarily follow from the invention being in public use or on sale, with the inventor's consent and allowance, at any time within two years before his application; but that, if the invention is in public use or on sale prior to that time, it will be conclusive evidence of abandonment, and the patent will be void.

But, in this case, it becomes important to inquire what is such a public use as will have the effect referred to. That the use of the pavement in question was public in one sense cannot be disputed. But can it be said that the invention was in public use? The use of an invention by the inventor himself, or of any other person under his direction, by way of experiment, and in order to bring the invention to perfection, has never been regarded as such a use. CURTIS, PATENTS, §381; *Shaw v. Cooper*, [32 U.S.] 7 Pet. 292 [1833].

Now, the nature of a street pavement is such that it cannot be experimented upon satisfactorily except on a highway, which is always public.

When the subject of invention is a machine, it may be tested and tried in a building, either with or without closed doors. In either case, such use is not a public use, within the meaning of the statute, so long as the inventor is engaged, in good faith, in testing its operation. He may see cause to alter it and improve it, or not. His experiments will reveal the fact whether any and what alterations may be necessary. If durability is one of the qualities to be attained, a long period, perhaps years, may be necessary to enable the inventor to discover whether his purpose is accomplished. And though, during all that period, he may not find that any changes are necessary, yet he may be justly said to be using his machine only by way of experiment; and no one would say that such a use, pursued with a *bona fide* intent of testing the qualities of the machine, would be a public use, within the meaning of the statute. So long as he does not voluntarily allow others to make it and use it, and so long as it is not on sale for general use, he keeps the invention under his own control, and does not lose his title to a patent.

It would not be necessary, in such a case, that the machine should be put up and used only in the inventor's own shop or premises. He may have it put up and used in the premises of another, and the use may inure to the benefit of the owner of the establishment. Still, if used under the surveillance of the inventor, and for the purpose of enabling him to test the machine, and ascertain whether it will answer the purpose intended, and make such alterations and improvements as experience demonstrates to be necessary, it will still be a mere experimental use, and not a public use, within the meaning of the statute.

Whilst the supposed machine is in such experimental use, the public may be incidentally deriving a benefit from it. If it be a grist-mill, or a carding-machine, customers from the surrounding country may enjoy the use of it by having their grain made into flour, or their wool into rolls, and still it will not be in public use, within the meaning of the law.

But if the inventor allows his machine to be used by other persons generally, either with or without compensation, or if it is, with his consent, put on sale for such use, then it will be in public use and on public sale, within the meaning of the law.

If, now, we apply the same principles to this case, the analogy will be seen at once. Nicholson wished to experiment on his pavement. He believed it to be a good thing, but he was not sure; and the only mode in which he could test it was to place a specimen of it in a public roadway. He did this at his own expense, and with the consent of the owners of the road. Durability was one of the qualities to be attained. He wanted to know whether his pavement would stand, and whether it would resist decay. Its character for durability could not be ascertained without its being subjected to use for a considerable time. He subjected it to such use, in good faith, for the simple purpose of ascertaining whether it was what he claimed it to be. Did he do anything more than the inventor of the supposed machine might do, in testing his invention? The public had the incidental use of the pavement, it is true; but was the invention in public use, within the meaning of the statute? We think not. The proprietors of the road alone used the invention, and used it at Nicholson's request, by way of experiment. The only way in which they could use it was by allowing the public to pass over the pavement.

Had the city of Boston, or other parties, used the invention, by laying down the pavement in other streets and places, with Nicholson's consent and allowance, then, indeed, the invention itself would have been in public use, within the meaning of the law; but this was not the case. Nicholson did not sell it, nor allow others to use it or sell it. He did not let it go beyond his control. He did nothing that indicated any intent to do so. He kept it under his own eyes, and never for a moment abandoned the intent to obtain a patent for it. . . .

It is sometimes said that an inventor acquires an undue advantage over the public by delaying to take out a patent, inasmuch as he thereby preserves the monopoly to himself for a longer period than is allowed by the policy of the law; but this cannot be said with justice when the delay is occasioned by a *bona fide* effort to bring his invention to perfection, or to ascertain whether it will answer the purpose intended. His monopoly only continues for the allotted period, in any event; and it is the interest of the public, as well as himself, that the invention should be perfect and properly tested, before a patent is granted for it. Any attempt to use it for a profit, and not by way of experiment, for a longer period than two years before the application, would deprive the inventor of his right to a patent.

COMMENTS AND QUESTIONS

1. Compare the facts in *City of Elizabeth* to those in *Egbert v. Lippmann, supra*, the "corset case." How did Nicholson's actions in this case differ from those of Barnes in the *Egbert* case? What evidence did Nicholson have regarding his six-year prefiling period that Barnes did not have for his comparably long period?

2. Could Nicholson simply have filed a patent application at the end of year one and prosecuted it while conducting his continued test? Would a patent have been granted on such an application? Note that because Nicholson was able to delay filing his application for six years, he received a patent that expired later and was therefore arguably more valuable to him than the patent he would have received if he had applied at the end of one year.

3. *Factors to Be Considered.* In a 2002 decision, the Federal Circuit provides a list of 13 factors collected from prior cases that are relevant to a finding of experimental use:

> (1) the necessity for public testing, (2) the amount of control over the experiment retained by the inventor, (3) the nature of the invention, (4) the length of the test period, (5) whether payment was made, (6) whether there was a secrecy obligation, (7) whether records of the experiment were kept, (8) who conducted the experiment, (9) the degree of commercial exploitation during testing, (10) whether the invention reasonably requires evaluation under actual conditions of use, (11) whether testing was systematically performed, (12) whether the inventor continually monitored the invention during testing, and (13) the nature of contacts made with potential customers.

Allen Eng'g Corp. v. Bartell Indus., Inc., 299 F.3d 1336, 1353 (Fed. Cir. 2002). The jurisprudence, however, makes clear that even one factor can be decisive. *See Atlanta Attachment Co. v. Leggett & Platt, Inc.*, 516 F.3d 1361, 1366 (Fed. Cir. 2008) (observing that lack of control over the invention during the alleged experiment, while not always dispositive, may be so); *see also Clock Spring, L.P. v. Wrapmaster, Inc.*, 560 F.3d 1317 (Fed. Cir. 2009).

4. A 2005 Federal Circuit case applied the *City of Elizabeth* principles to a case involving "experimental sales." *Electromotive Div. of General Motors Corp. v. Transportation Systems Div. of General Elec. Co.*, 417 F.3d 1203 (Fed. Cir. 2005). In this case, the patentee (GM) claimed planetary compressor bearings for use in turbochargers for diesel train engines. Pursuant to its standard development and testing procedure, GM used prototypes of its new bearing design in numerous train engines before the critical date. It also agreed to supply some bearings covered by one of its patents as spares to one of its customers if it needed them. Defendant GE argued that the sale of the train engines containing the new bearings, and the agreement to supply them as spares, constituted "on sale" activity under §102(b). GM disagreed, and argued that because the bearings were part of its development and testing program, the

customer's use of the engines with the bearings was covered by the "experimental use" of *City of Elizabeth*. The Federal Circuit sided with defendant GE:

When sales are made in an ordinary commercial environment and the goods are placed outside the inventor's control, an inventor's secretly held subjective intent to "experiment," even if true, is unavailing without objective evidence to support the contention. Under such circumstances, the customer at a minimum must be made aware of the experimentation:

We have generally looked to objective evidence to show that a pre-critical date sale was primarily for experimentation. . . . The length of the test period is merely a piece of evidence to add to the evidentiary scale. The same is true with respect to whether payment is made for the device, whether a user agreed to use secretly, whether records were kept of progress, whether persons other than the inventor conducted the asserted experiments, how many tests were conducted, how long the testing period was in relationship to tests of other similar devices.

[*T.P. Laboratories, Inc. v. Professional Positioners, Inc.*, 724 F.2d 965 (Fed. Cir. 1984)], at 971-72.

We agree . . . that a customer's awareness of the purported testing in the context of a sale is a critical attribute of experimentation. If an inventor fails to communicate to a customer that the sale of the invention was made in pursuit of experimentation, then the customer, as well as the general public, can only view the sale as a normal commercial transaction. . . . Accordingly, we hold not only that customer awareness is among the experimentation factors, but also that it is critical.

Our precedent has treated control and customer awareness of the testing as especially important to experimentation. Indeed, this court has effectively made control and customer awareness dispositive. Accordingly, we conclude that control and customer awareness ordinarily must be proven if experimentation is to be found.

417 F.3d 1203, at 1212-15 (citations omitted).

vi.   Priority Rules and First-to-Invent

Having dealt with novelty, we turn now to the closely related topic of *priority*. Section 102(g) of the 1952 Act provides that "[a] person shall be entitled to a patent unless"

(1) [*inter partes* proceedings] during the course of an interference . . ., another inventor involved therein establishes, to the extent permitted in section 104 . . . that before such person's invention thereof the invention was made by such other inventor and not abandoned, suppressed, or concealed, or

(2) [*ex parte* prosecution/invalidity defense] before such person's invention thereof, the invention was made in this country by another inventor who had not abandoned, suppressed, or concealed it.

In determining priority of invention under this subsection, there shall be considered not only the respective dates of conception and reduction to practice of the invention, but also the reasonable diligence of one who was first to conceive and last to reduce to practice, from a time prior to conception by the other.

If this does not make much sense to you upon a first reading, you are not alone. This is one of the most opaque areas of the Patent Act—perhaps the patent law version of the Rule Against Perpetuities. The provision only makes sense with an understanding of substantial jurisprudence that pre-dated the drafting of this provision.

At a structural level, this provision comprises two contexts (interference and prosecution/invalidity defense) and a priority rule that applies to both contexts. Subsection (1) covers *interference proceedings*—formal priority contests between rival claimants to the same patentable subject matter. Subsection (2) covers the use of prior inventions as a source of prior art. One may invoke subsection (2) outside the interference context. The PTO can reject a patent application on this basis; and a defendant in an infringement suit can point to a third party's prior invention as a prior art reference to defeat the validity of the plaintiff's patent.

Besides the different contexts in which they arise, there is a major substantive difference between (g)(1) and (g)(2): their territorial scope. The key phrases are "to the extent permitted in section 104" in (g)(1) and "in this country" in (g)(2). Section 104 allows proof of prior inventive activity in any country that is a signatory to the World Trade Organization (WTO). No proof of conception or reduction to practice in a non-WTO country can be entered in an interference, though this does not matter much since essentially all countries are in the WTO. (And even inventions from non-WTO countries may rely on their U.S. patent application filing date as their date of invention.) Contrast this with the language of (g)(2): only evidence of prior inventions made *in the U.S.* may be introduced outside the interference context.

Putting aside the difference in territorial scope, the basic rules of priority are the same. They are stated in the second sentence. The courts have fleshed out the meaning of this priority rule over many years; the case and notes that follow serve as an introduction. In brief, priority generally goes to the first inventor to (1) reduce an invention to practice, without (2) abandoning the invention. Note in this respect that filing a valid, enabling patent application constitutes a constructive reduction to practice. An exception to this rule is where an inventor is the first to conceive, but the last to reduce to practice: priority may be retained *if* the first conceiver was diligent in reducing to practice, with diligence being measured from a time just prior to the second conceiver's conception date. (Got that? Now you may understand why some famous interferences take a decade or more to work through! *See, e.g., Standard Oil Co.*

(Indiana) v. Montedison, S.P.A., 664 F.2d 356 (3d Cir. 1981) (1981 decision affirming findings of a PTO interference based on a patent application on polypropylene polymer filed in 1953); *U.S. Steel Corp. v. Phillips Petroleum Co.*, 865 F.2d 1247 (Fed. Cir. 1989) (validity of same patent upheld in litigation 36 years after patent was filed). You may also understand some of the appeal of the new, post-2013 AIA "first-to-file" priority system.).

Note also what it means to "abandon, suppress or conceal" an invention. This basically means that the inventor neither pursues a patent nor takes steps to utilize or commercialize an invention. *See Dow Chem. Co. v. Astro-Valcour, Inc.*, 267 F.3d 1334, 1342 (Fed. Cir. 2001). Even a proven first inventor may lose priority if she fails to actively pursue her invention for a long enough time. *See, e.g., Peeler v. Miller*, 535 F.2d 647, 654 (C.C.P.A. 1976) (four year delay between reduction to practice and filing of application constituted abandonment).

Under the AIA, for patents filed on or after March 16, 2013 all this complexity is swept away. All that matters is who files first. (The only exception is cases where an invention is stolen or "derived" from the true inventor—as in the *Evans Cooling* case mentioned earlier.) Even so, because the 1952 Act will continue to apply to patent applications filed prior to March 16, 2013, it is important to understand some of the details of 1952 Act §102(g) until at least March 16, 2033.

In general, priority goes to the first inventor who can show reduction to practice (and who does not abandon, suppress or conceal by waiting too long). Often, this is also the same inventor who can show first conception. Priority in this case is easy: the first to conceive and first to reduce to practice wins, period. A more complicated case arises when one inventor is first to conceive but last to reduce to practice.

Such a case triggers application of the last sentence of §102(g), particularly the "reasonable diligence of one who was first to conceive but last to reduce to practice." In this special situation, as you will see in the following case, the first to conceive must prove an extra element to win priority—the element of diligence. Notice in this case that one of the rival inventors, Kanamaru, introduced only evidence of a patent *filing date* but no evidence regarding dates of conception and reduction to practice. In such cases, the Patent Office effectively collapses the entire sequence of inventive events into the single date of patent filing; it is as if Kanamaru conceived, reduced to practice, and filed a patent application on the invention all on the same day. Comment 2 following the case explains *why* Kanamaru relied only on this date, as opposed to his true conception date.

Griffith v. Kanamaru
United States Court of Appeals for the Federal Circuit
816 F.2d 624 (Fed. Cir. 1987)

NICHOLS, Senior Circuit Judge.

Owen W. Griffith (Griffith) appeals the decision of the Board of Patent Appeals and Interferences (board) that Griffith failed to establish a prima facie case that he is entitled to an award of priority against the filing date of Tsuneo Kanamaru, et al. (Kanamaru) for a patent on aminocarnitine compounds. We affirm.

Background

This patent interference case involves the application of Griffith, an Associate Professor in the Department of Biochemistry at Cornell University Medical College, for a patent on an aminocarnitine compound, useful in the treatment of diabetes, and a patent issued for the same invention to Kanamaru, an employee of Takeda Chemical Industries. The inventors assigned their rights to the inventions to the Cornell Research Foundation, Inc. (Cornell) and to Takeda Chemical Industries respectively.

Griffith had established conception by June 30, 1981, and reduction to practice on January 11, 1984. Kanamaru filed for a United States patent on November 17, 1982. The board found, however, that Griffith failed to establish reasonable diligence for a prima facie case of prior invention. . . .

The board . . . decided that Griffith failed to establish a prima facie case for priority against Kanamaru's filing date. This result was based on the board's conclusion that Griffith's explanation for inactivity between June 15, 1983, and September 13, 1983, failed to provide a legally sufficient excuse to satisfy the "reasonable diligence" requirement of 35 U.S.C. §102(g). [The final sentence of 1952 Act §102(g) reads: "In determining priority of invention under this subsection, there shall be considered not only the respective dates of conception and reduction to practice of the invention, but also the reasonable diligence of one who was first to conceive and last to reduce to practice, from a time prior to conception by the other."] Griffith appeals on the issue of reasonable diligence.

Analysis

This is a case of first impression and presents the novel circumstances of a university suggesting that it is reasonable for the public to wait for disclosure until the most satisfactory funding arrangements are made. The applicable law is the "reasonable diligence" standard contained in 35 U.S.C. §102(g) and we must determine the appropriate role of the courts in construing this exception to the ordinary first-in-time rule. As a preliminary matter we note that, although the board focused on the June 1983 to September 1983 lapse in work, and Griffith's reasons for this lapse, Griffith is burdened with establishing a prima facie case of reasonable diligence from immediately before Kanamaru's filing date of November 17, 1982, until Griffith's reduction to practice on January 11, 1984. 35 U.S.C. §102(g).

On appeal, Griffith presents two grounds intended to justify his inactivity on the aminocarnitine project between June 15, 1983, and September 13, 1983. The first is that . . . it is reasonable, and as a policy matter desirable, for Cornell to require Griffith and other research scientists to obtain funding from outside the university. The second reason Griffith presents is that he reasonably waited for Ms. Debora Jenkins to matriculate in the Fall of 1983 to assist with the project. He had promised her she should have that task which she needed to qualify for her degree. We reject these arguments and conclude that Griffith has failed to establish grounds to excuse his inactivity prior to reduction to practice.

The reasonable diligence standard balances the interest in rewarding and encouraging invention with the public's interest in the earliest possible disclosure of innovation. Griffith must account for the entire period from just before Kanamaru's filing date until his [i.e., Griffith's] reduction to practice. . . .

The board in this case was, but not properly, asked to pass judgment on the reasonableness of Cornell's policy regarding outside funding of research. The correct inquiry is rather whether it is reasonable for Cornell to require the public to wait for the innovation, given the well settled policy in favor of early disclosure. . . . A review of caselaw on excuses for inactivity in reduction to practice reveals a common thread that courts may consider the reasonable everyday problems and limitations encountered by an inventor. *See, e.g., . . . Reed v. Tornqvist*, 436 F.2d 501 (C.C.P.A. 1971) (concluding it is not unreasonable for inventor to delay completing a patent application until after returning from a three week vacation in Sweden, extended by illness of inventor's father). . . . *De Wallace v. Scott*, 15 App. D.C. 157 (1899) (where applicant made bona fide attempts to perfect his invention, applicant's poor health, responsibility to feed his family, and daily job demands excused his delay in reducing his invention to practice).

. . . We first note that, in regard to waiting for a graduate student, Griffith does not even suggest that he faced a genuine shortage of personnel. He does not suggest that Ms. Jenkins was the only person capable of carrying on with the aminocarnitine experiment. We can see no application of precedent to suggest that the convenience of the timing of the semester schedule justifies a three-month delay for the purpose of reasonable diligence. Neither do we believe that this excuse, absent even a suggestion by Griffith that Jenkins was uniquely qualified to do his research, is reasonable.

Griffith's second contention that it was reasonable for Cornell to require outside funding, therefore causing a delay in order to apply for such funds, is also insufficient to excuse his inactivity. The crux of Griffith's argument is that outside funding is desirable as a form of peer review, or monitoring of the worthiness of a given project. He also suggests that, as a policy matter, universities should not be treated as businesses, which ultimately would detract from scholarly inquiry. Griffith states that these considerations, if accepted as valid, would fit within the scope of the caselaw excusing inactivity for "reasonable" delays in reduction to practice and filing.

Griffith's excuses sound more in the nature of commercial development, not accepted as an excuse for delay, than the "hardship" cases most commonly found and discussed *supra*. Delays in reduction to practice caused by an inventor's efforts to refine an invention to the most marketable and profitable form have not been accepted as sufficient excuses for inactivity.

. . . [I]t seems evident that Cornell has consciously chosen to assume the risk that priority in the invention might be lost to an outside inventor, yet, having chosen a noncommercial policy, it asks us to save it the property that would have inured to it if it had acted in single-minded pursuit of gain.

Although we agree with the board's conclusion, it is appropriate to go further and consider other circumstances as they apply to the reasonable diligence analysis of 35 U.S.C. §102(g). The record reveals that from the relevant period of November 17, 1982 (Kanamaru's filing date), to September 13, 1983 (when Griffith renewed his efforts towards reduction to practice), Griffith interrupted and often put aside the aminocarnitine project to work on other experiments. Between June 1982 and June 1983 Griffith admits that, at the request of the chairman of his department, he was primarily engaged in an unrelated research project. . . . Griffith also put aside the aminocarnitine experiment to work on a grant proposal on an unrelated project. . . . Griffith made only minimal efforts to secure funding directly for the aminocarnitine project.

The conclusion we reach from the record is that the aminocarnitine project was second and often third priority in laboratory research as well as the solicitation of funds. We agree that Griffith failed to establish a prima facie case of reasonable diligence or a legally sufficient excuse for inactivity to establish priority over Kanamaru.

COMMENTS AND QUESTIONS

1. What would the result in the interference have been if Professor Griffith had reduced the invention to practice on November 16, 1982? (Recall that Kanamaru's filing date—and therefore, in this case, his effective conception and reduction to practice dates—was November 17, 1982.)

If Griffith had reduced to practice on November 16, 1982, would it matter whether he was diligent between his conception date (June 30, 1981) and his reduction to practice? If not, why not? (Pay attention to the language: "there shall be considered not only the respective dates of conception and reduction to practice of the invention, but also the reasonable diligence of one who was first to conceive and last to reduce to practice." Note that reasonable diligence is mentioned *only in connection with* "one who was first to conceive and last to reduce to practice.")

Assume that Kanamaru introduced the following evidence: a conception date of January 1, 1982, and reduction to practice on November 1, 1982. Assume also, as actually happened, that Griffith's reduction to practice came after Kanamaru's. With

Griffith the first to conceive of the invention, is Kanamaru's diligence an issue under the last sentence of §102(g)(1)? *Should* it be?

2. Since Takeda Chemical, Kanamaru's assignee, is based primarily in Japan, it is reasonable to conclude that Kanamaru did the research leading to his patent application in Japan. This would explain the exclusive reliance on the patent filing date in this priority contest. Before 1995, and thus at the time this case was decided, foreign inventors could not introduce evidence of foreign inventive activity (e.g., conception and reduction to practice). In 1994, however, as part of the legislative package implementing the Trade Related Aspects of Intellectual Property (TRIPs) portion of the Uruguay Round negotiations under the GATT, Congress changed §104 to permit evidence of inventive activity taking place in any country that is a member of the World Trade Organization (the successor organization to the GATT) beginning in 1996. *See* Uruguay Round Agreements Act of 1994, P.L. 103-465, 108 Stat. 4809 (1994), at §531, codified at 35 U.S.C. §104.

3. *Political Economy of First-to-Invent?* As noted at the outset of this section, most countries in the world have long based priority on application filing date—a far simpler and clearer system. The U.S. first-to-invent regime has been premised on a philosophical preference for rewarding true first inventors, not those (presumably large corporations) who have the resources to file quickly. In fact, small inventors were the major lobbying group opposed to international harmonization. Many questioned, however, whether this philosophical benefit outweighed the additional administrative cost, complexity, and lack of clarity about who will win a priority contest. For many years, it was thought that most interferences were won by senior parties anyway. That conventional wisdom proved doubtful. *See* Mark A. Lemley & Colleen V. Chien, Are the U.S. Priority Rules Really Necessary?, 54 HASTINGS L.J. 1299 (2003) ("Of the 100 cases in our population that have final outcomes, junior parties [i.e., those second to file] won 33 (or 33%). More significantly, in the 76 cases that are actually resolved on priority grounds, junior parties won 33 times (or 43%). Thus, it seems that when priority is actually adjudicated, the first to invent is quite frequently not the first to file."). Does this sway your thinking about the desirability of giving up the traditional U.S. "first to invent" standard? As we will see in the next section, the small inventors eventually lost this battle, but were able to retain a U.S. grace period.

4. *Prior User Rights*. Griffith and Kanamaru were well on their way to the same invention at roughly the same time. Under the Federal Circuit's decision, only Kanamaru gets a patent on the invention. What happens to Griffith? Not only is he not entitled to the exclusionary power of a patent on his idea, but Kanamaru can exclude *him* from using his own, independently developed idea. This result seems harsh, particularly where (as here) Griffith was working on his version of the invention long before the patent ever issued to Kanamaru.

To ameliorate this problem, Congress has since granted "prior user rights" to non-patentees if they could show that they were using the invention before it was patented by someone else. *See* AIA of 2011, §5, codified at 35 U.S.C. §273. Under AIA §273, a person who uses an invention commercially more than one year before another applies for a patent or commences the AIA grace period may continue to use the invention despite issuance of a patent to the other person. There are a number of technical restrictions on the new prior user right, including non-transferability. *See* AIA §273(e)(1)(B) (restricting transfer of prior user right to sale of an entire company or line of business). So far the new prior rights provision has seen little use.

Are prior user rights a good idea? Do they unfairly weaken the patent grant? For an argument in favor of prior user rights, *see* Samson Vermont, *Independent Invention as a Defense to Patent Infringement*, 105 Mich. L. Rev. 475 (2006). If a prior user is permitted to continue their use, should the patentee be compensated somehow—say, by receiving a compulsory licensing fee from the prior user? *See generally* Stephen Maurer & Suzanne Scotchmer, *The Independent Inventor Defense in Intellectual Property*, 69 Economica 535 (2002).

vii.   The America Invents Act Regime

Congress shifted the U.S. from the 1952 Act first-to-invent regime toward the international first-to-file standard. The U.S. did not, however, adopt a pure first-to-file system. Importantly, it retained a one year grace period for inventors in certain cases. As a result, it might be more apt to characterize the AIA novelty regime as a modified first to file regime. From a practical standpoint, the new regime makes the following changes: (1) the critical date for most purposes is now the date that a patent application is first filed; (2) the prior art relevant to a given patent claim now consists of all references available under the statute prior to the filing date rather than the invention date, subject to a one-year grace period for the inventor in some cases; and (3) priority contests between rival claimants to an invention will now be determined almost exclusively by looking to when each of the rivals filed their patent application. The discussion that follows elaborates these basic principles and describes how they compare to the operating rules that pertain to the old, 1952 Act, system of priority and novelty. We conclude this section with a series of problems that illustrate the differences between the 1952 Act and AIA regimes.

a.   The AIA: A Simpler Structure

Overall, the AIA provides a simpler structure than the 1952 Act. The distinction between novelty, strictly speaking, and the statutory bars under the 1952 Act is gone. The AIA eliminates the 1952 Act's awkward structure, in which the related but distinct concepts of novelty and statutory bars appeared in successive subsections of §102. This means the end of the repetition of various categories or types of prior art under the two subsections, 1952 Act §102(a) and §102(b)–"patented, printed publications" etc. It also means that the concept of a grace period, which had been buried in the structure and wording of 1952 Act §102(b), is more apparent in the AIA.

The AIA integrates novelty and statutory bars into a unified provision, AIA §102, which first states the rule that prior art appearing before the critical date deprives the inventor of his or her entitlement to a patent; then defines all categories or types of references that qualify as prior art under the AIA (AIA §102(a)(1) and (2)); then defines the critical date as the inventor's filing date (last phrase of AIA §102(a)(1) and (2); and then, finally, identifies the grace period concept as an exception to the general rule that prior art appearing earlier than an inventor's filing date precludes patentability for the inventor's claimed invention.

§102(a) NOVELTY; PRIOR ART. —

A person shall be entitled to a patent unless—

(1) the claimed invention was patented, described in a printed publication, or in public use, on sale, or otherwise available to the public before the effective filing date of the claimed invention; or

(2) the claimed invention was described in a patent issued [to another] . . . or in [another's] application for patent [that is] published . . . [and that] was effectively filed before the effective filing date of the claimed invention.

(b) EXCEPTIONS.—

(1) DISCLOSURES MADE 1 YEAR OR LESS BEFORE THE EFFECTIVE FILING DATE OF THE CLAIMED INVENTION. —disclosure made 1 year or less before the effective filing date of a claimed invention shall not be prior art to the claimed invention under subsection (a)(1) if —

(A) the disclosure was made by the inventor or joint inventor or by another who obtained the subject matter disclosed directly or indirectly from the inventor or a joint inventor; or

(B) the subject matter disclosed had, before such disclosure, been publicly disclosed by the inventor or a joint inventor or another who obtained the subject matter disclosed directly or indirectly from the inventor or a joint inventor.

(2) DISCLOSURES APPEARING IN APPLICATIONS AND PATENTS. — A disclosure shall not be prior art to a claimed invention under subsection (a)(2) if —

(A) the subject matter disclosed was obtained directly or indirectly from the inventor or a joint inventor;

(B) the subject matter disclosed had, before such subject matter was effectively filed under subsection (a)(2), been publicly disclosed by the inventor or a joint inventor or another who obtained the subject matter disclosed directly or indirectly from the inventor or a joint inventor; or

(C) the subject matter disclosed and the claimed invention, not later than the effective filing date of the claimed invention, were owned by the same person or subject to an obligation of assignment to the same person.

[Subsection (c), "COMMON OWNERSHIP UNDER JOINT RESEARCH AGREEMENTS," deems subject matter disclosed and claimed by members of a joint research team to be "owned by the same person" under §102(b)(2)(C) above.]

The phrase "effective filing date" generally refers to the filing of a patent application that establishes priority under U.S. law. This includes an application filed only in the U.S., or at least first in the U.S., and also certain applications filed first in foreign patent systems that are, by virtue of compliance with international treaties and U.S. law, granted the benefit of a U.S. filing date though initially filed elsewhere. *See* AIA §3, at (a)(2)(i) (adding definition of "effective filing date" to §100 of the Patent Act).

b.   No Geographic Restrictions on Prior Art

The AIA continues a longstanding trend by eliminating geographic distinctions in the definition of prior art. Under the 1952 Act, certain types or categories of prior art are within the prior art regardless of where they occur. Patents and printed publications are the best examples. Whether a patent is issued in Germany, Japan, or China, it is still within the prior art; so too with publications. But under the 1952 Act other types of prior art have geographic limits; only "on sale" activities that occurred *within the U.S.*, for example, enter the prior art under the 1952 Act. Foreign sales are not within the prior art. The AIA eliminates geographic distinctions for all categories of prior art. Under the AIA, if an event or activity occurs that meets the definition of prior art, it is within the prior art for U.S. patent law–regardless of where it occurs.

c.   Novelty vs. Priority

The AIA highlights the difference between priority and novelty. Strictly speaking, priority is a question of *who, as between two rival inventors, will obtain a patent for an identical invention.* Priority, in other words, is a matter of "inventor vs. inventor"; whichever of the two is first (under the relevant rule) wins the patent. Novelty is a different matter. Novelty is a question of *whether, as between an inventor and a piece of prior art, the inventor acts before or after the prior art enters the field.* Novelty, then, is a matter of "inventor vs. prior art": if an inventor can show that he or she did whatever is required before a reference enters the prior art, the inventor gets a patent.

The AIA's first-to-file rule eliminates the need to decide which of two rival inventors actually invented first. In most cases, the only relevant question under the AIA is which of the two rival inventors filed first. (One exception is where the first filer learned of or outright stole the invention from another person; when that other person files a rival application, the PTO can undertake a "derivation proceeding" to sort out who is the rightful owner of the invention.) This eliminates the need for the expensive and drawn-out priority contests under the 1952 Act known as patent interferences.

d.   *The AIA Grace Period*

Calling the AIA a "first-to-file" regime is an oversimplification. Section 102(b)(2)(B) provides that an inventor is entitled to a one-year grace period if the inventor discloses their idea first and then files within a year afterwards. This "inventor's own" grace period means that an inventor can do any of a number of acts before filing that would generally constitute prior art–but still preserve the chance for a patent, as long as he or she files within a year. This §102(b)(2)(A) grace period is stated as an "exception" to the general rule that these acts would be prior art because they occur before the filing date. Note, however, that this grace period removes *only* the inventor's acts (i.e., "disclosure[s]") from the prior art. What if a third party performs an act that constitutes prior art after the inventor's act but before the inventor files? The §102(b)(2)(A) grace period is no help to the inventor in this case. Again, that is because the statute only removes the inventor's own "disclosure" from the definition of prior art. §102(1)(A) ("disclosure . . . will not be prior art if . . . made by the inventor").

Is there any way for an inventor to obtain a grace period that prevails even against another person's prior art activity that occurs before the inventor's filing date? Yes; that is the subject of §102(b)(2)(B). This creates a sort of "super grace period" which allows an inventor to file a valid patent application even when a third party prior art event occurs prior to the inventor's filing date. How does the inventor qualify for such a robust grace period? By making a *public disclosure* prior to the third party prior art activity and then filing within one year of the inventor's public disclosure. This effect is created by the language of §102(b)(2)(B) ("disclosure shall not be prior art if . . . the subject matter disclosed had, before [filing] . . . been publicly disclosed by the inventor"). By referring here to "the subject matter disclosed," rather than a disclosure made by the inventor as in (b)(2)(A), §102(b)(2)(B) means that *whoever* discloses the invention, the inventor can preserve novelty by making an earlier *public disclosure*.

Although the courts have yet to rule on what is a public disclosure, it is apparent that Congress intended some sort of distinction here. One reading is that "disclosure" under AIA §102 means any sort of prior art reference as defined by the extensive case law under the 1952 Act. This includes some fairly obscure types of disclosure such as secret sales and items used in public but not in any way discernible. Then "public disclosure," by contrast, would mean only widely and freely available disclosures.

e.   *Scope of Prior Art: Public Use*

As noted earlier, courts have drawn a distinction between patentee and third-party public uses depending on whether they are informing or non-informing/secret. Any public use of the patented technology by the patentee—whether informing or non-informing/secret—constitutes a public use, whereas only informing public uses by third parties qualifies as novelty-defeating public uses. This distinction puts added pressure on patentees to promptly disclose their technology through filing their patent application.

The question remains whether this distinction carries over the AIA. Paralleling the 1952 Act, AIA §102(a) encompasses "on sale" and "public use" within the prior art references that defeat novelty. The normal rule of statutory interpretation is that when Congress reenacts old statutory language, it is assumed to have adopted the meaning that language has acquired in court decisions. *See, e.g., Microsoft Corp. v. i4i* LP, 131 S.Ct. 2238, 2245 (2011); *Erlenbaugh v. United States*, 409 U.S. 239, 243 (1972). That suggests that on sale and public use should mean the same thing in the AIA they did in the 1952 Act. On the other hand, the AIA arguably expands upon the 1952 Act by including "otherwise available to the public." The U.S. PTO has taken the position that the word "otherwise" in that language means that public uses and sales are now limited to transactions and events that are themselves accessible to the public. That interpretation would exclude from the scope of prior art under the AIA not only secret commercial uses like *Metallizing* but the use in *Egbert* and the sale in *Pfaff*.

Professors Merges and Lemley, by contrast, contend that an inventor's non-informing public use is a "disclosure" under AIA §102(a), just as it was under the 1952 Act, by virtue of the facts that (1) the phrase "public use" in AIA §102(a) implicitly incorporates prior case law interpreting this phrase, which includes prior cases on inventor's-own non-informing uses; and (2) "disclosure" in AIA §102(b) means "any legitimate prior art reference under AIA §102(a)," which includes of course "public use" and therefore an inventor's-own non-informing public use prior art. *See* Robert P. Merges, *Priority and Novelty Under the AIA*, 27 BERKELEY TECH. L. J. 1023 (2012); Mark A. Lemley, *Does "Public Use" Mean the Same Thing It Did Last Year?*, 93 TEX. L. REV. 1119 (2015). By the same logic, third party non-informing uses are not "public uses" under the traditional case law. They therefore do not qualify as prior art references under AIA §102(a), and consequently are not "disclosures" under AIA §102(b). It remains to be seen how the courts will grapple with this interpretive question.

PROBLEMS

Problem III-3.

a. Alma conceives of a compound (TAU) in December 2011. She synthesizes the compound in February 2012. Entirely independently of Alma, Edgar publishes an article in NATURE, a scientific journal, describing TAU on December 1, 2012. Alma files a U.S. patent application on April 1, 2013. Assuming that Alma's invention is useful, non-obvious, and adequately described, is her patent valid or invalid based on these facts in the United States?

b. Dylan conceives of a compound (UCB) in December 2011. He synthesizes the compound in February 2012. He publishes this research in SCIENCE, a scientific journal, on June 1, 2012. Entirely independently of Dylan, Katie publishes an article in NATURE describing UCB on December 1, 2012. Dylan files a U.S. patent application on April 1, 2013. Assuming that Dylan's invention is useful, non-obvious, and adequately described, is his patent valid or invalid based on these facts in the United States?

c. Stephanie conceives of a compound (QED) in December 2011. She synthesizes the compound in February 2012. Entirely independently of Stephanie, Klay publishes an article in NATURE describing QED on December 1, 2012. Stephanie files a U.S. patent application on February 1, 2013. Assuming that Stephanie's invention is useful, non-obvious, and adequately described, is her patent valid or invalid based on these facts in the United States?

d. Anna conceives of a compound (MIT) in December 2011. She synthesizes the compound in February 2012. Entirely independently of Anna, Noah places MIT on sale in Europe on December 1, 2012. Anna files a U.S. patent application on April 1, 2013. Assuming that Anna's invention is useful, non-obvious, and adequately described, is her patent valid or invalid based on these facts in the United States?

Problem III-4. Lisa invents a remarkable process for manufacturing circuit boards that reduces the cost by 20% without any diminution in quality. She promptly files a U.S. patent application on April 1, 2013. Much of the electronics industry licenses Lisa's patent. Lisa learns that Drago Corporation is using her patented technology without a license in the United States. She sues Drago for patent infringement. Drago does not deny that it learned of the technology from Lisa's patent. In its trial preparation, however, Drago learns that Mizuki, a small Japanese company, had developed the identical process and used it to manufacture a component of a video game controller that it sold in Japan in 2010. Mizuki has since gone out of business. Based on this information, Drago files a motion for summary judgment asserting that Lisa's patent is invalid for lack of novelty. How should a court decide? What is the basis for the decision?

Suppose instead that Lisa had filed her patent application on March 1, 2013. How should a court decide? Is the analysis any different?

2. Nonobviousness

Section 103(a) of the Patent Act provides that

A patent may not be obtained though the invention is not identically disclosed or described as set forth in section 102 of this title, if the differences between the subject matter sought to be patented and the prior art are such that the subject matter as a whole would have been obvious at the time the invention was made to a person having ordinary skill in the art to which said subject matter pertains. Patentability shall not be negatived by the manner in which the invention was made.

The following case traces the history leading up to this requirement and establishes the modern framework for assessing this most important element of patentability.

Graham v. John Deere Co.
Supreme Court of the United States
383 U.S. 1 (1966)

Mr. Justice CLARK delivered the opinion of the Court.

After a lapse of 15 years, the Court again focuses its attention on the patentability of inventions under the standard of Art. I, §8, cl. 8, of the Constitution and under the conditions prescribed by the laws of the United States. Since our last expression on patent validity, *A. & P. Tea Co. v. Supermarket Corp.*, 340 U.S. 147 (1950), the Congress has for the first time expressly added a third statutory dimension to the two requirements of novelty and utility that had been the sole statutory test since the Patent Act of 1793. This is the test of obviousness, i.e., whether "the subject matter sought to be patented and the prior art are such that the subject matter as a whole would have been obvious at the time the invention was made to a person having ordinary skill in the art to which said subject matter pertains. Patentability shall not be negatived by the manner in which the invention was made." §103 of the Patent Act of 1952, 35 U.S.C. §103 (1964 ed.).

The questions, involved in each of the companion cases before us, are what effect the 1952 Act had upon traditional statutory and judicial tests of patentability and what definitive tests are now required. We have concluded that the 1952 Act was intended to codify judicial precedents embracing the principle long ago announced by this Court in *Hotchkiss v. Greenwood*, 11 How. 248 [52 U.S.] (1851), and that, while the clear language of §103 places emphasis on an inquiry into obviousness, the general level of innovation necessary to sustain patentability remains the same.

I.

(a) Graham v. John Deere Co., an infringement suit by petitioners, presents a conflict between two Circuits over the validity of a single patent on a "Clamp for vibrating Shank Plows." The invention, a combination of old mechanical elements, involves a device designed to absorb shock from plow shanks as they plow through rocky soil and thus to prevent damage to the plow. We granted certiorari. Although we have determined that neither Circuit applied the correct test, we conclude that the patent is invalid under §103. . . .

II.

At the outset it must be remembered that the federal patent power stems from a specific constitutional provision which authorizes the Congress "To promote the Progress of . . . useful Arts, by securing for limited Times to . . . Inventors the exclusive Right to their . . . Discoveries." Art. I, §8, cl. 8. The clause is both a grant of power and a limitation. This qualified authority, unlike the power often exercised in the sixteenth and seventeenth centuries by the English Crown, is limited to the promotion of advances in the "useful arts." It was written against the backdrop of the practices— eventually curtailed by the Statute of Monopolies—of the Crown in granting monopolies to court favorites in goods or businesses which had long before been enjoyed by the public. *See* MEINHARDT, INVENTIONS, PATENTS AND MONOPOLY, pp. 30-35 (London, 1946). The Congress in the exercise of the patent power may not overreach the restraints imposed by the stated constitutional purpose. Nor may it enlarge the patent monopoly without regard to the innovation, advancement or social benefit gained thereby. Moreover, Congress may not authorize the issuance of patents whose effects are to remove existent knowledge from the public domain, or to restrict free access to materials already available. Innovation, advancement, and things which add to the sum of useful knowledge are inherent requisites in a patent system which by constitutional command must "promote the Progress of . . . useful Arts." This is the standard expressed in the Constitution and it may not be ignored. And it is in this light that patent validity "requires reference to a standard written into the Constitution." *A. & P. Tea Co. v. Supermarket Corp.*, *supra*, at 154 (concurring opinion).

Within the limits of the constitutional grant, the Congress may, of course, implement the stated purpose of the Framers by selecting the policy which in its judgment best effectuates the constitutional aim. This is but a corollary to the grant to Congress of any Article I power. *Gibbons v. Ogden*, 9 Wheat. [22 U.S.] 1 [1824]. Within the scope established by the Constitution, Congress may set out conditions and tests for patentability. *McClurg v. Kingsland*, 1 How. [42 U.S.] 202, 206 [1843]. It is the duty of the Commissioner of Patents and of the courts in the administration of the patent system to give effect to the constitutional standard by appropriate application, in each case, of the statutory scheme of the Congress.

Congress quickly responded to the bidding of the Constitution by enacting the Patent Act of 1790 during the second session of the First Congress. It created an agency in the Department of State headed by the Secretary of State, the Secretary of the Department of War and the Attorney General, any two of whom could issue a patent for a period not exceeding 14 years to any petitioner that "hath . . . invented or discovered any useful art, manufacture, . . . or device, or any improvement therein not before known or used" if the board found that "the invention or discovery [was] sufficiently useful and important. . . ." 1 Stat. 110. This group, whose members administered the patent system along with their other public duties, was known by its own designation as "Commissioners for the Promotion of Useful Arts."

Thomas Jefferson, who as Secretary of State was a member of the group, was its moving spirit and might well be called the "first administrator of our patent system." *See* Federico, Operation of the Patent Act of 1790, 18 J. Pat. Off. Soc. 237, 238 (1936). He was not only an administrator of the patent system under the 1790 Act, but was also the author of the 1793 Patent Act. In addition, Jefferson was himself an inventor of great note. His unpatented improvements on plows, to mention but one line of his inventions, won acclaim and recognition on both sides of the Atlantic. Because of his active interest and influence in the early development of the patent system, Jefferson's views on the general nature of the limited patent monopoly under the Constitution, as well as his conclusions as to conditions for patentability under the statutory scheme, are worthy of note.

Jefferson, like other Americans, had an instinctive aversion to monopolies. It was a monopoly on tea that sparked the Revolution and Jefferson certainly did not favor an equivalent form of monopoly under the new government. His abhorrence of monopoly extended initially to patents as well. From France, he wrote to Madison (July 1788) urging a Bill of Rights provision restricting monopoly, and as against the argument that limited monopoly might serve to incite "ingenuity," he argued forcefully that "the benefit even of limited monopolies is too doubtful to be opposed to that of their general suppression," V Writings of Thomas Jefferson, at 47 (Ford ed., 1895).

His views ripened, however, and in another letter to Madison (Aug. 1789) after the drafting of the Bill of Rights, Jefferson stated that he would have been pleased by an express provision in this form: "Art. 9. Monopolies may be allowed to persons for their own productions in literature & their own inventions in the arts, for a term not exceeding—years but for no longer term & no other purpose." *Id.*, at 113. And he later wrote: "Certainly an inventor ought to be allowed a right to the benefit of his invention for some certain time. . . . Nobody wishes more than I do that ingenuity should receive a liberal encouragement." Letter to Oliver Evans (May 1807), V Writings of Thomas Jefferson, at 75-76 (Washington ed.).

Jefferson's philosophy on the nature and purpose of the patent monopoly is expressed in a letter to Isaac McPherson (Aug. 1813), a portion of which we set out in the margin.[2] He rejected a natural-rights theory in intellectual property rights and

---

[2] Stable ownership is the gift of social law, and is given late in the progress of society. It would be curious then, if an idea, the fugitive fermentation of an individual brain, could, of natural right, be claimed in exclusive and stable property. If nature has made any one thing less susceptible than all others of exclusive property, it is the action of the thinking power called an idea, which an individual may exclusively possess as long as he keeps it to himself; but the moment it is divulged, it forces itself into the possession of every one, and the receiver cannot dispossess himself of it. Its peculiar character, too,

clearly recognized the social and economic rationale of the patent system. The patent monopoly was not designed to secure to the inventor his natural right in his discoveries. Rather, it was a reward, an inducement, to bring forth new knowledge. The grant of an exclusive right to an invention was the creation of society—at odds with the inherent free nature of disclosed ideas—and was not to be freely given. Only inventions and discoveries which furthered human knowledge, and were new and useful, justified the special inducement of a limited private monopoly. Jefferson did not believe in granting patents for small details, obvious improvements, or frivolous devices. His writings evidence his insistence upon a high level of patentability.

As a member of the patent board for several years, Jefferson saw clearly the difficulty in "drawing a line between the things which are worth to the public the embarrassment of an exclusive patent, and those which are not." The board on which he served sought to draw such a line and formulated several rules which are preserved in Jefferson's correspondence.[3] Despite the board's efforts, Jefferson saw "with what slow progress a system of general rules could be matured." Because of the "abundance" of cases and the fact that the investigations occupied "more time of the members of the board than they could spare from higher duties, the whole was turned over to the judiciary, to be matured into a system, under which every one might know when his actions were safe and lawful." Letter to McPherson, *supra*, at 181, 182. Apparently Congress agreed with Jefferson and the board that the courts should develop additional conditions for patentability. Although the Patent Act was amended, revised or codified some 50 times between 1790 and 1950, Congress steered clear of a statutory set of

---

is that no one possesses the less, because every other possesses the whole of it. He who receives an idea from me, receives instruction himself without lessening mine; as he who lights his taper at mine, receives light without darkening me. That ideas should freely spread from one to another over the globe, for the moral and mutual instruction of man, and improvement of his condition, seems to have been peculiarly and benevolently designed by nature, when she made them, like fire, expansible over all space, without lessening their density in any point, and like the air in which we breathe, move, and have our physical being, incapable of confinement or exclusive appropriation. Inventions then cannot, in nature, be a subject of property. Society may give an exclusive right to the profits arising from them, as an encouragement to men to pursue ideas which may produce utility, but this may or may not be done, according to the will and convenience of the society, without claim or complaint from any body. VI WRITINGS OF THOMAS JEFFERSON 180-81 (H. A. Washington ed.).

[3] "[A] machine of which we are possessed, might be applied by every man to any use of which it is susceptible." Letter to Isaac McPherson, *id.* at 181.

"[A] change of material should not give title to a patent. As the making a ploughshare of cast rather than of wrought iron; a comb of iron instead of horn or of ivory. . . ." *Id.*

" [A] mere change of form should give no right to a patent, as a high-quartered shoe instead of a low one; a round hat instead of a three-square; or a square bucket instead of a round one." *Id.* at 181-82.

" [A combined use of old implements.] A man has a right to use a saw, an axe, a plane separately; may he not combine their uses on the same piece of wood? "Letter to Oliver Evans (Jan. 1814), *id.* at 298.

requirements other than the bare novelty and utility tests reformulated in Jefferson's draft of the 1793 Patent Act.

III.

The difficulty of formulating conditions for patentability was heightened by the generality of the constitutional grant and the statutes implementing it, together with the underlying policy of the patent system that "the things which are worth to the public the embarrassment of an exclusive patent," as Jefferson put it, must outweigh the restrictive effect of the limited patent monopoly. The inherent problem was to develop some means of weeding out those inventions which would not be disclosed or devised but for the inducement of a patent.

This Court formulated a general condition of patentability in 1851 in *Hotchkiss v. Greenwood*, 11 How. 248 [52 U.S. (1851)]. The patent involved a mere substitution of materials—porcelain or clay for wood or metal in doorknobs—and the Court condemned it, holding:

> [Unless] more ingenuity and skill . . . were required . . . than were possessed by an ordinary mechanic acquainted with the business, there was an absence of that degree of skill and ingenuity which constitute essential elements of every invention. In other words, the improvement is the work of the skilful mechanic, not that of the inventor. At p. 267.

Hotchkiss, by positing the condition that a patentable invention evidence more ingenuity and skill than that possessed by an ordinary mechanic acquainted with the business, merely distinguished between new and useful innovations that were capable of sustaining a patent and those that were not. The *Hotchkiss* test laid the cornerstone of the judicial evolution suggested by Jefferson and left to the courts by Congress. The language in the case, and in those which followed, gave birth to "invention" as a word of legal art signifying patentable inventions. Yet, as this Court has observed, "[t]he truth is the word [invention] cannot be defined in such manner as to afford any substantial aid in determining whether a particular device involves an exercise of the inventive faculty or not." *McClain v. Ortmayer*, 141 U.S. 419, 427 (1891); *A. & P. Tea Co. v. Supermarket Corp., supra*, at 151. Its use as a label brought about a large variety of opinions as to its meaning both in the Patent Office, in the courts, and at the bar. The *Hotchkiss* formulation, however, lies not in any label, but in its functional approach to questions of patentability. In practice, *Hotchkiss* has required a comparison between the subject matter of the patent, or patent application, and the background skill of the calling. It has been from this comparison that patentability was in each case determined.

IV. The 1952 Patent Act

The Act sets out the conditions of patentability in three sections. An analysis of the structure of these three sections indicates that patentability is dependent upon three explicit conditions: novelty and utility as articulated and defined in §101 and §102, and non-obviousness, the new statutory formulation, as set out in §103. The first two sections, which trace closely the 1874 codification, express the "new and useful" tests which have always existed in the statutory scheme and, for our purposes here, need no clarification. The pivotal section around which the present controversy centers is §103. It provides:

§103. Conditions for patentability; non-obvious subject matter

A patent may not be obtained though the invention is not identically disclosed or described as set forth in section 102 of this title, if the differences between the subject matter sought to be patented and the prior art are such that the subject matter as a whole would have been obvious at the time the invention was made to a person having ordinary skill in the art to which said subject matter pertains. Patentability shall not be negatived by the manner in which the invention was made.

The section is cast in relatively unambiguous terms. Patentability is to depend, in addition to novelty and utility, upon the "non-obvious" nature of the "subject matter sought to be patented" to a person having ordinary skill in the pertinent art. . . .

It is undisputed that this section was, for the first time, a statutory expression of an additional requirement for patentability, originally expressed in *Hotchkiss*. It also seems apparent that Congress intended by the last sentence of §103 to abolish the test it believed this Court announced in the controversial phrase "flash of creative genius," used in *Cuno Corp. v. Automatic Devices Corp.*, 314 U.S. 84 (1941).[7] . . .

V

. . . While the ultimate question of patent validity is one of law, *A. & P. Tea Co. v. Supermarket Corp.*, *supra*, at 155, the §103 condition, which is but one of three conditions, each of which must be satisfied, lends itself to several basic factual inquiries. Under §103, the scope and content of the prior art are to be determined; differences between the prior art and the claims at issue are to be ascertained; and the level of ordinary skill in the pertinent art resolved. Against this background, the obviousness or nonobviousness of the subject matter is determined. Such secondary

---

[7] The sentence in which the phrase occurs reads: "[T]he new device, however useful it may be, must reveal the flash of creative genius, not merely the skill of the calling." At p. 91. Although some writers and lower courts found in the language connotations as to the frame of mind of the inventors, none were so intended. The opinion approved Hotchkiss specifically, and the reference to "flash of creative genius" was but a rhetorical embellishment of language going back to 1833. *Cf.* "exercise of genius," *Shaw v. Cooper*, 7 Pet. 292; "inventive genius," *Reckendorfer v. Faber*, 92 U.S. 347 (1876); *Concrete Appliances Co. v. Gomery*, 269 U.S. 177; "flash of thought," *Densmore v. Scofield*, 102 U.S. 375 (1880); "intuitive genius," Potts v. Creager, 155 U.S. 597 (1895). Rather than establishing a more exacting standard, *Cuno* merely rhetorically restated the requirement that the subject matter sought to be patented must be beyond the skill of the calling. It was the device, not the invention, that had to reveal the "flash of creative genius." *See* Boyajian, *The Flash of Creative Genius, An Alternative Interpretation*, 25 J. Pat. & Trademark Off. Soc'y 776, 780, 781 (1943); *Pacific Contact Laboratories, Inc. v. Solex Laboratories, Inc.*, 209 F.2d 529, 533; *Brown & Sharpe Mfg. Co. v. Kar Engineering Co.*, 154 F.2d 48, 51-52; *In re Shortell*, 31 C.C.P.A. (Pat.) 1062, 1069, 142 F.2d 292, 295-96.

considerations as commercial success, long felt but unsolved needs, failure of others, etc., might be utilized to give light to the circumstances surrounding the origin of the subject matter sought to be patented. As indicia of obviousness or nonobviousness, these inquiries may have relevancy. *See* Note, Subtests of "Nonobviousness": A Nontechnical Approach to Patent Validity, 112 U. PA. L. REV. 1169 (1964).

This is not to say, however, that there will not be difficulties in applying the nonobviousness test. What is obvious is not a question upon which there is likely to be uniformity of thought in every given factual context. The difficulties, however, are comparable to those encountered daily by the courts in such frames of reference as negligence and scienter, and should be amenable to a case-by-case development. We believe that strict observance of the requirements laid down here will result in that uniformity and definiteness which Congress called for in the 1952 Act.

While we have focused attention on the appropriate standard to be applied by the courts, it must be remembered that the primary responsibility for sifting out unpatentable material lies in the Patent Office. To await litigation is—for all practical purposes—to debilitate the patent system. We have observed a notorious difference between the standards applied by the Patent Office and by the courts. While many reasons can be adduced to explain the discrepancy, one may well be the free rein often exercised by Examiners in their use of the concept of "invention." In this connection we note that the Patent Office is confronted with a most difficult task. Almost 100,000 applications for patents are filed each year. Of these, about 50,000 are granted and the backlog now runs well over 200,000. 1965 Annual Report of the Commissioner of Patents 13-14. This is itself a compelling reason for the Commissioner to strictly adhere to the 1952 Act as interpreted here. This would, we believe, not only expedite disposition but bring about a closer concurrence between administrative and judicial precedent.

We have been urged to find in §103 a relaxed standard, supposedly a congressional reaction to the "increased standard" applied by this Court in its decisions over the last 20 or 30 years. The standard has remained invariable in this Court. Technology, however, has advanced—and with remarkable rapidity in the last 50 years. Moreover, the ambit of applicable art in given fields of science has widened by disciplines unheard of a half century ago. It is but an evenhanded application to require that those persons granted the benefit of a patent monopoly be charged with an awareness of these changed conditions. The same is true of the less technical, but still useful arts. He who seeks to build a better mousetrap today has a long path to tread before reaching the Patent Office.

VI.

We now turn to the application of the conditions found necessary for patentability to the cases involved here:

A. The Patent in Issue in Graham v. John Deere Co.

This patent, No. 2,627,798 (hereinafter called the '798 patent) relates to a spring clamp which permits plow shanks to be pushed upward when they hit obstructions in the soil, and then springs the shanks back into normal position when the obstruction is passed over. The device . . . is fixed to the plow frame as a unit. The mechanism around which the controversy centers is basically a hinge. The top half of it, known as the upper plate, is a heavy metal piece clamped to the plow frame and is stationary relative to the plow frame. The lower half of the hinge, known as the hinge plate, is connected to the rear of the upper plate by a hinge pin and rotates downward with respect to it. The shank, which is bolted to the forward end of the hinge plate, runs beneath the plate and parallel to it for about nine inches, passes through a stirrup, and then continues backward for several feet curving down toward the ground. The chisel, which does the actual plowing, is attached to the rear end of the shank. As the plow frame is pulled forward, the chisel rips through the soil, thereby plowing it. In the normal position, the hinge plate and the shank are kept tight against the upper plate by a spring, which is atop the upper plate. A rod runs through the center of the spring, extending down through holes in both plates and the shank. Its upper end is bolted to the top of the spring while its lower end is hooked against the underside of the shank [see Figure 3-4].

When the chisel hits a rock or other obstruction in the soil, the obstruction forces the chisel and the rear portion of the shank to move upward. The shank is pivoted against the rear of the hinge plate and pries open the hinge against the closing tendency of the spring. This closing tendency is caused by the fact that, as the hinge is opened, the connecting rod is pulled downward and the spring is compressed. When the obstruction is passed over, the upward force on the chisel disappears and the spring pulls the shank and hinge plate back into their original position. The lower, rear portion of the hinge plate is constructed in the form of a stirrup which brackets the shank, passing around and beneath it. The shank fits loosely into the stirrup (permitting a slight up and down play). The stirrup is designed to prevent the shank from recoiling away from the hinge plate, and thus prevents excessive strain on the shank near its bolted connection. The stirrup also girds the shank, preventing it from fishtailing from side to side.

In practical use, a number of spring-hinge-shank combinations are clamped to a plow frame, forming a set of ground-working chisels capable of withstanding the shock of rocks and other obstructions in the soil without breaking the shanks.

Background of the Patent

Chisel plows, as they are called, were developed for plowing in areas where the ground is relatively free from rocks or stones. Originally, the shanks were rigidly attached to the plow frames. When such plows were used in the rocky, glacial soils of some of the Northern States, they were found to have serious defects. As the chisels hit buried rocks, a vibratory motion was set up and tremendous forces were transmitted to the shank near its connection to the frame. The shanks would break. Graham, one of the petitioners, sought to meet that problem, and in 1950 obtained a patent, U.S. No. 2,493,811 (hereinafter '811), on a spring clamp which solved some of the difficulties. Graham and his companies manufactured and sold the '811 clamps. In 1950, Graham modified the '811 structure and in 1951 filed for a patent. That patent, the one in issue, was granted in 1953. This suit against competing plow manufacturers resulted from charges by petitioners that several of respondents' devices infringed the '798 patent.

The Prior Art

Five prior patents indicating the state of the art were cited by the Patent Office in the prosecution of the '798 application. Four of these patents, 10 other United States patents and two prior-use spring-clamp arrangements not of record in the '798 file wrapper were relied upon by respondents as revealing the prior art. The District Court and the Court of Appeals found that the prior art "as a whole in one form or another contains all of the mechanical elements of the '798 Patent." One of the prior-use clamp devices not before the Patent Examiner—Glencoe—was found to have "all of the elements."

We confine our discussion to the prior patent of Graham, '811, and to the Glencoe clamp device, both among the references asserted by respondents. The Graham '811 and '798 patent devices are similar in all elements, save two: (1) the stirrup and the bolted connection of the shank to the hinge plate do not appear in '811; and (2) the position of the shank is reversed, being placed in patent '811 above the hinge plate, sandwiched between it and the upper plate. The shank is held in place by the spring rod which is hooked against the bottom of the hinge plate passing through a slot in the shank. Other differences are of no consequence to our examination. In practice the '811 patent arrangement permitted the shank to wobble or fishtail because it was not rigidly fixed to the hinge plate; moreover, as the hinge plate was below the shank, the latter caused wear on the upper plate, a member difficult to repair or replace.

Graham's '798 patent application contained 12 claims. All were rejected as not distinguished from the Graham '811 patent. The inverted position of the shank was specifically rejected as was the bolting of the shank to the hinge plate. The Patent Office examiner found these to be "matters of design well within the expected skill of the art and devoid of invention." Graham withdrew the original claims and substituted the two new ones which are substantially those in issue here. His contention was that wear was reduced in patent '798 between the shank and the heel or rear of the upper plate.[11] He

---

[11] In '811, where the shank was above the hinge plate, an upward movement of the chisel forced the shank up against the underside of the rear of the upper plate. The upper plate thus provided the fulcrum about which the hinge was pried open. Because of this, as well as the location of the hinge pin, the shank rubbed against the heel of the upper plate causing wear both to the plate and to the shank. By relocating the hinge pin and by placing the hinge plate between the shank and the upper plate, as in '798, the rubbing

also emphasized several new features, the relevant one here being that the bolt used to connect the hinge plate and shank maintained the upper face of the shank in continuing and constant contact with the underface of the hinge plate.

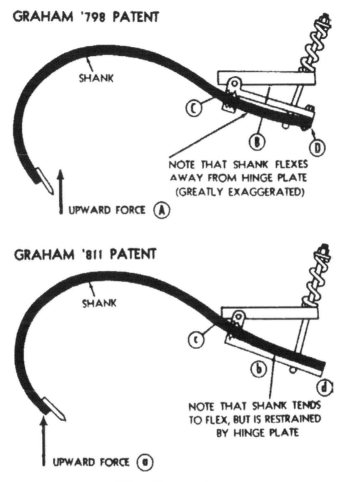

Flex Comparison
Appendix to Opinion of the Court

Graham did not urge before the Patent Office the greater "flexing" qualities of the '798 patent arrangement which he so heavily relied on in the courts. The sole element in patent '798 which petitioners argue before us is the interchanging of the shank and hinge plate and the consequences flowing from this arrangement. The contention is that this arrangement—which petitioners claim is not disclosed in the prior art—permits the shank to flex under stress for its *entire* length. [W]hen the chisel hits an obstruction the resultant force (A) pushes the rear of the shank upward and the shank pivots against

---

was eliminated and the wear point was changed to the hinge plate, a member more easily removed or replaced for repair.

the rear of the hinge plate at (C). The natural tendency is for that portion of the shank between the pivot point and the bolted connection (i.e., between C and D) to bow downward and away from the hinge plate. The maximum distance (B) that the shank moves away from the plate is slight—for emphasis, greatly exaggerated in the sketches. This is so because of the strength of the shank and the short—nine inches or so—length of that portion of the shank between (C) and (D). On the contrary, in patent '811 the pivot point is the upper plate at point (c); and while the tendency for the shank to bow between points (c) and (d) is the same as in '798, the shank is restricted because of the underlying hinge plate and cannot flex as freely. In practical effect, the shank flexes only between points (a) and (c), and not along the entire length of the shank, as in '798. Petitioners say that this difference in flex, though small, effectively absorbs the tremendous forces of the shock of obstructions whereas prior art arrangements failed.

The Obviousness of the Differences

We cannot agree with petitioners. We assume that the prior art does not disclose such an arrangement as petitioners claim in patent '798. Still we do not believe that the argument on which petitioners' contention is bottomed supports the validity of the patent. The tendency of the shank to flex is the same in all cases. If free-flexing, as petitioners now argue, is the crucial difference above the prior art, then it appears evident that the desired result would be obtainable by not boxing the shank within the confines of the hinge. The only other effective place available in the arrangement was to attach it below the hinge plate and run it through a stirrup or bracket that would not disturb its flexing qualities. Certainly a person having ordinary skill in the prior art, given the fact that the flex in the shank could be utilized more effectively if allowed to run the entire length of the shank, would immediately see that the thing to do was what Graham did, i.e., invert the shank and the hinge plate.

Petitioners' argument basing validity on the free-flex theory raised for the first time on appeal is reminiscent of Lincoln Engineering Co. v. Stewart-Warner Corp., 303 U.S. 545 (1938), where the Court called such an effort "an afterthought. No such function . . . is hinted at in the specifications of the patent. If this were so vital an element in the functioning of the apparatus it is strange that all mention of it was omitted." At p. 550. No "flexing" argument was raised in the Patent Office. Indeed, the trial judge specifically found that "flexing is not a claim of the patent in suit . . ." and would not permit interrogation as to flexing in the accused devices. Moreover, the clear testimony of petitioners' experts shows that the flexing advantages flowing from the '798 arrangement are not, in fact, a significant feature in the patent.

We find no nonobvious facets in the '798 arrangement. The wear and repair claims were sufficient to overcome the patent examiner's original conclusions as to the validity of the patent. However, some of the prior art, notably Glencoe, was not before him. There the hinge plate is below the shank but, as the courts below found, all of the elements in the '798 patent are present in the Glencoe structure. Furthermore, even though the position of the shank and hinge plate appears reversed in Glencoe, the mechanical operation is identical. The shank there pivots about the underside of the stirrup, which in Glencoe is *above* the shank. In other words, the stirrup in Glencoe serves exactly the same function as the heel of the hinge plate in '798. The mere shifting of the wear point to the heel of the '798 hinge plate from the stirrup of Glencoe—itself a part of the hinge plate—presents no operative mechanical distinctions, much less nonobvious differences. . . .

The judgment of the Court of Appeals in [Graham v. John Deere] is affirmed. . . .

COMMENTS AND QUESTIONS

1. The Court states that it is proper in interpreting the Graham '798 claims to refer to the prosecution history (or "file wrapper") of the patent. We will see that this is an important tool in the law of infringement later in this chapter. For now, what is important is that the validity of the patent claims is only one part of a larger picture— "claim interpretation." Patentees not only want to have their patents upheld over the prior art, but they also want those patents to be interpreted broadly, to cover a wide range of potential infringements. Because these goals are in tension, it is important to keep them both in mind whenever you interpret the claims of a patent.

2. Without question, the plow design in *Graham* was new, i.e., novel under §102 of the patent code. What policy is served by the detailed inquiry into whether it is "new enough" to deserve a patent, i.e., nonobvious? What would be the effect of a patent system that only required novelty? *See* Robert P. Merges, *Uncertainty and the Standard of Patentability*, 7 HIGH TECH. L.J. 1 (1993). Arguably, §103 requires an "inventive leap" of some degree over what has been done before as a counterbalance to the strong rights given patentholders.

The test established in §103—whether the invention as a whole would be "obvious to one of ordinary skill in the art"—does not itself tell courts very much about how to decide what is obvious. Courts have developed a number of rules to assist in this determination. Two of the most important rules are discussed below.

i. Combining References

To anticipate a patent application under §102, a single prior art reference must disclose every element of what the patentee claims as his invention. If a prior art reference does not disclose all the parts of an invention, it does not "anticipate" the application. Under §103, however, a single reference need not disclose the entire invention to bar a patent. Thus §103 asks whether a researcher who is aware of all the prior art would think to create the claimed invention. In deciding the question of obviousness, it is sometimes permissible to analyze a combination of ideas from different sources of prior art (known as prior art "references").

KSR International Co. v. Teleflex Inc.
Supreme Court of the United States
550 U.S. 398 (2007)

Justice KENNEDY delivered the opinion of the Court.

Teleflex Incorporated and its subsidiary Technology Holding Company—both referred to here as Teleflex—sued KSR International Company for patent infringement. The patent at issue, United States Patent No. 6,237,565 B1, is entitled "Adjustable Pedal Assembly With Electronic Throttle Control." The patentee is Steven J. Engelgau, and the patent is referred to as "the Engelgau patent." Teleflex holds the exclusive license to the patent.

Claim 4 of the Engelgau patent describes a mechanism for combining an electronic sensor with an adjustable automobile pedal so the pedal's position can be transmitted to a computer that controls the throttle in the vehicle's engine. When Teleflex accused KSR of infringing the Engelgau patent by adding an electronic sensor to one of KSR's previously designed pedals, KSR countered that claim 4 was invalid under the Patent Act, 35 U.S.C. §103, because its subject matter was obvious.

Section 103 forbids issuance of a patent when "the differences between the subject matter sought to be patented and the prior art are such that the subject matter as a whole would have been obvious at the time the invention was made to a person having ordinary skill in the art to which said subject matter pertains."

In *Graham v. John Deere Co. of Kansas City,* 383 U.S. 1 (1966), the Court set out a framework for applying the statutory language of §103, language itself based on the logic of the earlier decision in *Hotchkiss v. Greenwood,* 11 How. 248 (1851), and its progeny. *See* 383 U.S., at 15-17. The analysis is objective:

> Under §103, the scope and content of the prior art are to be determined; differences between the prior art and the claims at issue are to be ascertained; and the level of ordinary skill in the pertinent art resolved. Against this background the obviousness or nonobviousness of the subject matter is determined. Such secondary considerations as commercial success, long felt but unsolved needs, failure of others, etc., might be utilized to give light to the circumstances surrounding the origin of the subject matter sought to be patented.

Id., at 17-18.

While the sequence of these questions might be reordered in any particular case, the factors continue to define the inquiry that controls. If a court, or patent examiner, conducts this analysis and concludes the claimed subject matter was obvious, the claim is invalid under §103.

Seeking to resolve the question of obviousness with more uniformity and consistency, the Court of Appeals for the Federal Circuit has employed an approach referred to by the parties as the "teaching, suggestion, or motivation" test (TSM test), under which a patent claim is only proved obvious if "some motivation or suggestion to combine the prior art teachings" can be found in the prior art, the nature of the problem, or the knowledge of a person having ordinary skill in the art. *See, e.g., Al-Site Corp. v. VSI Int'l, Inc.,* 174 F.3d 1308, 1323-1324 (C.A. Fed. 1999). KSR challenges that test, or at least its application in this case. *See* 119 Fed. Appx. 282, 286-290 (C.A. Fed. 2005). Because the Court of Appeals addressed the question of obviousness in a manner contrary to §103 and our precedents, we granted certiorari. We now reverse.

I

A

In car engines without computer-controlled throttles, the accelerator pedal interacts with the throttle via cable or other mechanical link. The pedal arm acts as a lever rotating around a pivot point. In a cable-actuated throttle control the rotation caused by pushing down the pedal pulls a cable, which in turn pulls open valves in the carburetor or fuel injection unit. The wider the valves open, the more fuel and air are released, causing combustion to increase and the car to accelerate. When the driver takes his foot off the pedal, the opposite occurs as the cable is released and the valves slide closed.

In the 1990's it became more common to install computers in cars to control engine operation. Computer-controlled throttles open and close valves in response to electronic signals, not through force transferred from the pedal by a mechanical link. Constant, delicate adjustments of air and fuel mixture are possible. The computer's rapid processing of factors beyond the pedal's position improves fuel efficiency and engine performance.

For a computer-controlled throttle to respond to a driver's operation of the car, the computer must know what is happening with the pedal. A cable or mechanical link does not suffice for this purpose; at some point, an electronic sensor is necessary to translate the mechanical operation into digital data the computer can understand.

Before discussing sensors further we turn to the mechanical design of the pedal itself. In the traditional design a pedal can be pushed down or released but cannot have its position in the footwell adjusted by sliding the pedal forward or back. As a result, a driver who wishes to be closer or farther from the pedal must either reposition himself in the driver's seat or move the seat in some way. In cars with deep footwells these are imperfect solutions for drivers of smaller stature. To solve the problem, inventors, beginning in the 1970's, designed pedals that could be adjusted to change their location in the footwell. Important for this case are two adjustable pedals disclosed in U.S. Patent Nos. 5,010,782 (filed July 28, 1989) (Asano) and 5,460,061 (filed Sept. 17, 1993) (Redding). The Asano patent reveals a support structure that houses the pedal so that even when the pedal location is adjusted relative to the driver, one of the pedal's pivot points stays fixed. The pedal is also designed so that the force necessary to push the pedal down is the same regardless of adjustments to its location. The Redding patent reveals a different, sliding mechanism where both the pedal and the pivot point are adjusted.

We return to sensors. Well before Engelgau applied for his challenged patent, some inventors had obtained patents involving electronic pedal sensors for computer-controlled throttles. These inventions, such as the device disclosed in U.S. Patent No. 5,241,936 (filed Sept. 9, 1991) ('936), taught that it was preferable to detect the pedal's position in the pedal assembly, not in the engine. The '936 patent disclosed a pedal with an electronic sensor on a pivot point in the pedal assembly. U.S. Patent No. 5,063,811 (filed July 9, 1990) (Smith) taught that to prevent the wires connecting the sensor to the computer from chafing and wearing out, and to avoid grime and damage from the driver's foot, the sensor should be put on a fixed part of the pedal assembly rather than in or on the pedal's footpad.

In addition to patents for pedals with integrated sensors inventors obtained patents for self-contained modular sensors. A modular sensor is designed independently of a given pedal so that it can be taken off the shelf and attached to mechanical pedals of various sorts, enabling the pedals to be used in automobiles with computer-controlled throttles. One such sensor was disclosed in U.S. Patent No. 5,385,068 (filed Dec. 18, 1992) ('068). In 1994, Chevrolet manufactured a line of trucks using modular sensors "attached to the pedal support bracket, adjacent to the pedal and engaged with the pivot shaft about which the pedal rotates in operation." 298 F. Supp. 2d 581, 589 (E.D. Mich. 2003).

The prior art contained patents involving the placement of sensors on adjustable pedals as well. For example, U.S. Patent No. 5,819,593 (filed Aug. 17, 1995) (Rixon) discloses an adjustable pedal assembly with an electronic sensor for detecting the pedal's position. In the Rixon pedal the sensor is located in the pedal footpad. The Rixon pedal was known to suffer from wire chafing when the pedal was depressed and released.

This short account of pedal and sensor technology leads to the instant case.

B

KSR, a Canadian company, manufactures and supplies auto parts, including pedal systems. Ford Motor Company hired KSR in 1998 to supply an adjustable pedal system for various lines of automobiles with cable-actuated throttle controls. KSR developed an adjustable mechanical pedal for Ford and obtained U.S. Patent No. 6,151,976 (filed July 16, 1999) ('976) for the design. In 2000, KSR was chosen by General Motors Corporation (GMC or GM) to supply adjustable pedal systems for Chevrolet and GMC light trucks that used engines with computer-controlled throttles. To make the '976 pedal compatible with the trucks, KSR merely took that design and added a modular sensor.

Teleflex is a rival to KSR in the design and manufacture of adjustable pedals. As noted, it is the exclusive licensee of the Engelgau patent. Engelgau filed the patent application on August 22, 2000 as a continuation of a previous application for U.S. Patent No. 6,109,241, which was filed on January 26, 1999. He has sworn he invented the patent's subject matter on February 14, 1998. The Engelgau patent discloses an adjustable electronic pedal described in the specification as a "simplified vehicle control pedal assembly that is less expensive, and which uses fewer parts and is easier to package within the vehicle." Engelgau, col. 2, lines 2-5, Supplemental App. 6. Claim 4 of the patent, at issue here, describes:

> A vehicle control pedal apparatus comprising:
>
> > a support adapted to be mounted to a vehicle structure;
> >
> > an adjustable pedal assembly having a pedal arm moveable in for[e] and aft directions with respect to said support;
> >
> > a pivot for pivotally supporting said adjustable pedal assembly with respect to said support and defining a pivot axis; and
> >
> > an electronic control attached to said support for controlling a vehicle system;
> >
> > said apparatus characterized by said electronic control being responsive to
>
> said pivot for providing a signal that corresponds to pedal arm position as said pedal arm pivots about said pivot axis between rest and applied positions wherein the position of said pivot remains constant while said pedal arm moves in fore and aft directions with respect to said pivot.

Id., col. 6, lines 17-36 (diagram numbers omitted).

We agree with the District Court that the claim discloses "a position-adjustable pedal assembly with an electronic pedal position sensor attached to the support member of the pedal assembly. Attaching the sensor to the support member allows the sensor to remain in a fixed position while the driver adjusts the pedal." 298 F. Supp. 2d, at 586-587.

Before issuing the Engelgau patent the U.S. Patent and Trademark Office (PTO) rejected one of the patent claims that was similar to, but broader than, the present claim 4. The claim did not include the requirement that the sensor be placed on a fixed pivot point. The PTO concluded the claim was an obvious combination of the prior art disclosed in Redding and Smith, explaining:

> Since the prior ar[t] references are from the field of endeavor, the purpose disclosed . . . would have been recognized in the pertinent art of Redding. Therefore it would have been obvious . . . to provide the device of Redding with the . . . means attached to a support member as taught by Smith.

Id., at 595.

In other words Redding provided an example of an adjustable pedal and Smith explained how to mount a sensor on a pedal's support structure, and the rejected patent claim merely put these two teachings together.

Although the broader claim was rejected, claim 4 was later allowed because it included the limitation of a fixed pivot point, which distinguished the design from Redding's. *Ibid*. Engelgau had not included Asano among the prior art references, and Asano was not mentioned in the patent's prosecution. Thus, the PTO did not have before it an adjustable pedal with a fixed pivot point. The patent issued on May 29, 2001 and was assigned to Teleflex.

Upon learning of KSR's design for GM, Teleflex sent a warning letter informing KSR that its proposal would violate the Engelgau patent. "'Teleflex believes that any supplier of a product that combines an adjustable pedal with an electronic throttle control necessarily employs technology covered by one or more'" of Teleflex's patents. *Id.*, at 585. KSR refused to enter a royalty arrangement with Teleflex; so Teleflex sued for infringement, asserting KSR's pedal infringed the Engelgau patent and two other patents. *Ibid*. Teleflex later abandoned its claims regarding the other patents and dedicated the patents to the public. The remaining contention was that KSR's pedal system for GM infringed claim 4 of the Engelgau patent. Teleflex has not argued that the other three claims of the patent are infringed by KSR's pedal, nor has Teleflex argued that the mechanical adjustable pedal designed by KSR for Ford infringed any of its patents.

C

The District Court granted summary judgment in KSR's favor. [That court found the claimed invention obvious in light of the Engelgau and Asano references, and general trends in the field. The Federal Circuit reversed, pointing out that the district court failed to properly apply its TSM test to the prior art and the other facts of the case.]

II

A

We begin by rejecting the rigid approach of the Court of Appeals. Throughout this Court's engagement with the question of obviousness, our cases have set forth an expansive and flexible approach inconsistent with the way the Court of Appeals applied its TSM test here.

The principles underlying [our prior] cases are instructive when the question is whether a patent claiming the combination of elements of prior art is obvious. When a work is available in one field of endeavor, design incentives and other market forces can prompt variations of it, either in the same field or a different one. If a person of ordinary skill can implement a predictable variation, §103 likely bars its patentability. For the same reason, if a technique has been used to improve one device, and a person of ordinary skill in the art would recognize that it would improve similar devices in the same way, using the technique is obvious unless its actual application is beyond his or her skill.

Following these principles may be more difficult in other cases than it is here because the claimed subject matter may involve more than the simple substitution of one known element for another or the mere application of a known technique to a piece of prior art ready for the improvement. Often, it will be necessary for a court to look to interrelated teachings of multiple patents; the effects of demands known to the design community or present in the marketplace; and the background knowledge possessed by a person having ordinary skill in the art, all in order to determine whether there was an apparent reason to combine the known elements in the fashion claimed by the patent at issue. To facilitate review, this analysis should be made explicit. As our precedents make clear, however, the analysis need not seek out precise teachings directed to the specific subject matter of the challenged claim, for a court can take account of the inferences and creative steps that a person of ordinary skill in the art would employ.

B

When it first established the requirement of demonstrating a teaching, suggestion, or motivation to combine known elements in order to show that the combination is obvious, the Court of Customs and Patent Appeals captured a helpful insight. *See* Application of Bergel, 292 F.2d 955, 956-957 (1961). [A] patent composed of several elements is not proved obvious merely by demonstrating that each of its elements was, independently, known in the prior art. Although common sense directs one to look with care at a patent application that claims as innovation the combination of two known devices according to their established functions, it can be important to identify a reason that would have prompted a person of ordinary skill in the relevant field to combine the elements in the way the claimed new invention does. This is so because inventions in most, if not all, instances rely upon building blocks long since uncovered, and claimed discoveries almost of necessity will be combinations of what, in some sense, is already known.

Helpful insights, however, need not become rigid and mandatory formulas; and when it is so applied, the TSM test is incompatible with our precedents. The obviousness analysis cannot be confined by a formalistic conception of the words teaching, suggestion, and motivation, or by overemphasis on the importance of published articles and the explicit content of issued patents. The diversity of inventive pursuits and of modern technology counsels against limiting the analysis in this way. In many fields it may be that there is little discussion of obvious techniques or combinations, and it often may be the case that market demand, rather than scientific literature, will drive design trends. Granting patent protection to advances that would occur in the ordinary course without real innovation retards progress and may, in the case of patents combining previously known elements, deprive prior inventions of their value or utility.

C

The flaws in the analysis of the Court of Appeals relate for the most part to the court's narrow conception of the obviousness inquiry reflected in its application of the TSM test.

The first error of the Court of Appeals in this case was to foreclose this reasoning by holding that courts and patent examiners should look only to the problem the patentee was trying to solve. The question is not whether the combination was obvious to the patentee but whether the combination was obvious to a person with ordinary skill in the art. Under the correct analysis, any need or problem known in the field of endeavor at the time of invention and addressed by the patent can provide a reason for combining the elements in the manner claimed.

The second error of the Court of Appeals lay in its assumption that a person of ordinary skill attempting to solve a problem will be led only to those elements of prior art designed to solve the same problem. *Ibid.* The primary purpose of Asano was solving the constant ratio problem; so, the court concluded, an inventor considering how to put a sensor on an adjustable pedal would have no reason to consider putting it on the Asano pedal. *Ibid.* Common sense teaches, however, that familiar items may have obvious uses beyond their primary purposes, and in many cases a person of ordinary skill will be able to fit the teachings of multiple patents together like pieces of a puzzle. Regardless of Asano's primary purpose, the design provided an obvious example of an adjustable pedal with a fixed pivot point; and the prior art was replete with patents indicating that a fixed pivot point was an ideal mount for a sensor. The idea that a designer hoping to make an adjustable electronic pedal would ignore Asano because Asano was designed to solve the constant ratio problem makes little sense. A person of ordinary skill is also a person of ordinary creativity, not an automaton.

The same constricted analysis led the Court of Appeals to conclude, in error, that a patent claim cannot be proved obvious merely by showing that the combination of elements was "obvious to try." *Id.,* at 289 (internal quotation marks omitted). When there is a design need or market pressure to solve a problem and there are a finite number of identified, predictable solutions, a person of ordinary skill has good reason to pursue the known options within his or her technical grasp. If this leads to the anticipated success, it is likely the product not of innovation but of ordinary skill and common sense. In that instance the fact that a combination was obvious to try might show that it was obvious under §103.

The Court of Appeals, finally, drew the wrong conclusion from the risk of courts and patent examiners falling prey to hindsight bias. A factfinder should be aware, of course, of the distortion caused by hindsight bias and must be cautious of arguments reliant upon *ex post* reasoning. Rigid preventative rules that deny factfinders recourse to common sense, however, are neither necessary under our case law nor consistent with it.

What we hold is that the fundamental misunderstandings identified above led the Court of Appeals in this case to apply a test inconsistent with our patent law decisions.

III

When we apply the standards we have explained to the instant facts, claim 4 must be found obvious. We agree with and adopt the District Court's recitation of the relevant prior art and its determination of the level of ordinary skill in the field. As did the District Court, we see little difference between the teachings of Asano and Smith and the adjustable electronic pedal disclosed in claim 4 of the Engelgau patent. A person having ordinary skill in the art could have combined Asano with a pedal position sensor in a fashion encompassed by claim 4, and would have seen the benefits of doing so. . . .

B

The District Court was correct to conclude that, as of the time Engelgau designed the subject matter in claim 4, it was obvious to a person of ordinary skill to combine Asano with a pivot-mounted pedal position sensor. There then existed a marketplace that created a strong incentive to convert mechanical pedals to electronic pedals, and the prior art taught a number of methods for achieving this advance. The Court of Appeals considered the issue too narrowly by, in effect, asking whether a pedal designer writing on a blank slate would have chosen both Asano and a modular sensor similar to the ones used in the Chevrolet truckline and disclosed in the '068 patent.

In automotive design, as in many other fields, the interaction of multiple components means that changing one component often requires the others to be modified as well. Technological developments made it clear that engines using computer-controlled throttles would become standard. As a result, designers might have decided to design new pedals from scratch; but they also would have had reason to make pre-existing pedals work with the new engines. Indeed, upgrading its own pre-existing model led KSR to design the pedal now accused of infringing the Engelgau patent.

For a designer starting with Asano, the question was where to attach the sensor. The consequent legal question, then, is whether a pedal designer of ordinary skill starting with Asano would have found it obvious to put the sensor on a fixed pivot point. The prior art discussed above leads us to the conclusion that attaching the sensor where both KSR and Engelgau put it would have been obvious to a person of ordinary skill.

Like the District Court, finally, we conclude Teleflex has shown no secondary factors to dislodge the determination that claim 4 is obvious. Proper application of *Graham* and our other precedents to these facts therefore leads to the conclusion that claim 4 encompassed obvious subject matter. As a result, the claim fails to meet the requirement of §103.

We need not reach the question whether the failure to disclose Asano during the prosecution of Engelgau voids the presumption of validity given to issued patents, for claim 4 is obvious despite the presumption. We nevertheless think it appropriate to note that the rationale underlying the presumption—that the PTO, in its expertise, has approved the claim—seems much diminished here.

IV

A separate ground the Court of Appeals gave for reversing the order for summary judgment was the existence of a dispute over an issue of material fact. We disagree with the Court of Appeals on this point as well. To the extent the court understood the *Graham* approach to exclude the possibility of summary judgment when an expert provides a conclusory affidavit addressing the question of obviousness, it misunderstood the role expert testimony plays in the analysis. In considering summary judgment on that question the district court can and should take into account expert testimony, which may resolve or keep open certain questions of fact. That is not the end of the issue, however. The ultimate judgment of obviousness is a legal determination. *Graham,* 383 U.S., at 17. Where, as here, the content of the prior art, the scope of the patent claim, and the level of ordinary skill in the art are not in material dispute, and the obviousness of the claim is apparent in light of these factors, summary judgment is appropriate. Nothing in the declarations proffered by Teleflex prevented the District Court from reaching the careful conclusions underlying its order for summary judgment in this case.

* * *

We build and create by bringing to the tangible and palpable reality around us new works based on instinct, simple logic, ordinary inferences, extraordinary ideas, and sometimes even genius. These advances, once part of our shared knowledge, define a new threshold from which innovation starts once more. And as progress beginning from higher levels of achievement is expected in the normal course, the results of ordinary innovation are not the subject of exclusive rights under the patent laws. Were it otherwise patents might stifle, rather than promote, the progress of useful arts. *See* U.S. Const., Art. I, §8, cl. 8. These premises led to the bar on patents claiming obvious subject matter established in *Hotchkiss* and codified in §103. Application of the bar must not be confined within a test or formulation too constrained to serve its purpose.

KSR provided convincing evidence that mounting a modular sensor on a fixed pivot point of the Asano pedal was a design step well within the grasp of a person of ordinary skill in the relevant art. Its arguments, and the record, demonstrate that claim 4 of the Engelgau patent is obvious. In rejecting the District Court's rulings, the Court of Appeals analyzed the issue in a narrow, rigid manner inconsistent with §103 and our precedents. The judgment of the Court of Appeals is reversed, and the case remanded for further proceedings consistent with this opinion.

It is so ordered.

COMMENTS AND QUESTIONS

1. Consider the opinion's emphasis on predictability: "The combination of familiar elements according to known methods is likely to be obvious when it does no more than yield predictable results." What would it mean for a combination to yield more than a predictable result? *United States v. Adams*, 383 U.S. 39 (1966), offers an example. In that case: (1) the prior art taught that batteries employing the elements claimed by the patentee would probably not work, and indeed might be dangerous; and (2) the claimed combination worked far better than was predicted in the prior art. How might you state an overall test of obviousness that employs "predictability" as its key term? *See generally* Robert P. Merges, *Uncertainty and the Standard of Patentability*, 7 [BERKELEY] HIGH TECH. L.J. 1, 2 (1992) ("The nonobviousness standard encourages researchers to pursue projects whose success appears highly uncertain at the outset. The standard insists that only the results from uncertain research should be rewarded with a patent.").

2. The Court also states: "Granting patent protection to advances that would occur in the ordinary course without real innovation retards progress and may, in the case of patents combining previously known elements, deprive prior inventions of their value or utility." Is there a danger that the Court's opinion may push too far in the opposite direction, awarding patent protection only to a few important and unpredictable innovations? What if the PHOSITA is herself an inventor? Does that mean that "ordinary inventions" are unpatentable? Does the opinion contain anything to alleviate this concern?

3. "The idea that a designer hoping to make an adjustable electronic pedal would ignore Asano because Asano was designed to solve the constant ratio problem makes little sense. A person of ordinary skill is also a person of ordinary creativity, not an automaton." In this passage, the Court rejects a narrow and formalistic notion of "teaching, motivation or suggestion." If you were a litigator seeking to invalidate a patent, how would you use this statement to build your case and structure your argument? Consider especially the Court's additional statements, (1) "When a work is available in one field of endeavor, design incentives and other market forces can prompt variations of it, either in the same field or a different one," and (2) "The proper question to have asked was whether a pedal designer of ordinary skill, facing the wide range of needs created by developments in the field of endeavor, would have seen a benefit to upgrading Asano with a sensor." What evidence would you introduce to establish (a) design incentives, (b) market forces, and (c) the wide range of needs created by developments in the field? How could patent examiners develop evidence of these things during prosecution? How will findings on these issues be handled on appeal? Recall that the Court found summary judgment on nonobviousness appropriate in this case because it is ultimately an issue of law.

In re Kubin
United States Court of Appeals for the Federal Circuit
561 F.3d 1351 (Fed. Cir. 2009)

RADER, Circuit Judge.

Marek Kubin and Raymond Goodwin ("appellants") appeal from a decision of the Board of Patent Appeals and Interferences (the "Board") rejecting the claims of U.S. Patent Application Serial No. 09/667,859 ("'859 Application") as obvious under 35 U.S.C. §103(a). [T]his court affirms.

I

This case presents a claim to a classic biotechnology invention—the isolation and sequencing of a human gene that encodes a particular domain of a protein. Specifically, appellants claim DNA molecules ("polynucleotides") encoding a protein ("polypeptide") known as the Natural Killer Cell Activation Inducing Ligand ("NAIL").

Natural Killer ("NK") cells, thought to originate in the bone marrow, are a class of cytotoxic lymphocytes that play a major role in fighting tumors and viruses. NK cells express a number of surface molecules which, when stimulated, can activate cytotoxic mechanisms. NAIL is a specific receptor protein on the cell surface that plays a role in activating the NK cells.

The specification of the claimed invention recites an amino acid sequence of a NAIL polypeptide. The invention further isolates and sequences a polynucleotide that encodes a NAIL polypeptide. Moreover, the inventors trumpet their alleged discovery of a binding relationship between NAIL and a protein known as CD48. The NAIL-CD48 interaction has important biological consequences for NK cells, including an increase in cell cytotoxicity and in production of interferon. Representative claim 73 of appellants' application claims the DNA that encodes the CD48-binding region of NAIL proteins:

> 73. An isolated nucleic acid molecule comprising a polynucleotide encoding a polypeptide at least 80% identical to amino acids 22-221 of SEQ ID NO:2, wherein the polypeptide binds CD48.

In other words, appellants claim a genus of isolated polynucleotides encoding a protein that binds CD48 and is at least 80% identical to amino acids 22-221 of SEQ ID NO:2—the disclosed amino acid sequence for the CD48-binding region of NAIL.

Appellants' specification discloses nucleotide sequences for two polynucleotides falling within the scope of the claimed genus, namely SEQ ID NO:1 and SEQ ID NO:3. SEQ ID NO: 1 recites the specific coding sequence of NAIL, whereas SEQ ID NO: 3 recites the full NAIL gene, including upstream and downstream non-coding sequences. The specification also contemplates variants of NAIL that retain the same binding properties. However, the specification does not indicate any example variants of NAIL that make [the sorts of] conservative amino acid substitutions [i.e., substitutions that retain the same basic functionality] [that are described as possible in the specification].

II

The Board rejected appellants' claims as invalid under both §103 and §112.

Regarding obviousness, the Board rejected appellants' claims over the combined teachings of U.S. Patent No. 5,688,690 ("Valiante") and 2 Joseph SAMBROOK ET AL., MOLECULAR CLONING: A LABORATORY MANUAL 43-84 (2d ed. 1989) ("Sambrook"). The Board also considered, but found to be cumulative to Valiante and Sambrook, Porunelloor Mathew et al., *Cloning and Characterization of the 2B4 Gene Encoding a Molecule Associated with Non-MHC-Restricted Killing Mediated by Activated Natural Killer Cells and T Cells*, 151 J. IMMUNOLOGY 5328-37 (1993) ("Mathew").

Valiante discloses a receptor protein called "p38" that is found on the surface of human NK cells. Valiante teaches that the p38 receptor is present on virtually all human NK cells and "can serve as an activation marker for cytotoxic NK cells." '690 Patent col.3 ll.3-4. Valiante also discloses and claims a monoclonal antibody specific for p38 called "mAB C1.7." The Board found (and appellants do not dispute) that Valiante's p38 protein is the same protein as NAIL. A monoclonal antibody is an antibody that is mass produced in the laboratory from a single clone and that recognizes only one antigen. Monoclonal antibodies are useful as probes for specifically identifying and targeting a particular kind of cell.

Valiante teaches that "[t]he DNA and protein sequences for the receptor p38 may be obtained by resort to conventional methodologies known to one of skill in the art." '690 Patent col.7 ll.49-51.

Example 12 of Valiante's patent further describes a five-step cloning protocol for "isolating and identifying the p38 receptor." *Id.* at col.18 1.6–col.19 1.28. Valiante discloses neither the amino acid sequence of p38 recognized by mAb C1.7 nor the polynucleotide sequence that encodes p38. Sambrook, incorporated by reference (as cited above) in Valiante, describes methods for molecular cloning. Sambrook does not discuss how to clone any particular gene, but provides detailed instructions on cloning materials and techniques.

The Board found as a factual matter that appellants used conventional techniques "such as those outlined in Sambrook" to isolate and sequence the gene that codes for NAIL. *Id.* The Board also found that appellants' claimed DNA sequence is "isolated from a cDNA library . . . using the commercial monoclonal antibody C1.7 . . . disclosed by Valiante." With regard to the amino acid sequence referred to as SEQ ID NO:2, the Board found that

> Valiante's disclosure of the polypeptide p38, and a detailed method of isolating its DNA, including disclosure of a specific probe to do so, i.e., mAb C1.7, established Valiante's possession of p38's amino acid sequence and provided a reasonable expectation of success in obtaining a polynucleotide

encoding p38, a polynucleotide within the scope of Appellants' claim 73. (*See*Valiante, col.7, l.48 to col.8, l.7.)

Because of NAIL's important role in the human immune response, the Board further found that "one of ordinary skill in the art would have recognized the value of isolating NAIL cDNA, and would have been motivated to apply conventional methodologies, such as those disclosed in Sambrook and utilized in Valiante, to do so." *Id.* at 6-7.

Based on these factual findings, the Board concluded that appellants' claim was "'the product not of innovation but of ordinary skill and common sense,' leading us to conclude NAIL cDNA is not patentable as it would have been obvious to isolate it."

Appellants appeal the Board's decisions both as to obviousness and written description.

III

A

[T]his court determines that the Board had substantial evidence to conclude that appellants used conventional techniques, as taught in Valiante and Sambrook, to isolate a gene sequence for NAIL. In particular, appellants' arguments that Valiante and Sambrook are deficient because they do not provide "any guidance for the preparation of cell culture that will serve as a useful source of mRNA for the preparation of a cDNA library," Appellants' Br. 34, are diminished by appellants' own disclosure.

Kubin and Goodwin cannot represent to the public that their claimed gene sequence can be derived and isolated by "standard biochemical methods" discussed in a well-known manual on cloning techniques, while at the same time discounting the relevance of that very manual to the obviousness of their claims. For this reason as well, substantial evidence supports the Board's factual finding that "[a]ppellants employed conventional methods, 'such as those outlined in Sambrook,' to isolate a cDNA encoding NAIL and determine the cDNA's full nucleotide sequence (SEQ NOS: 1 & 3)."

[Kubin argued that the Mathew reference "teaches away" from the claimed invention.] According to Mathew, "[i]t appears . . . that the 2B4 gene is somewhat conserved during evolution." Mathew at 5335. Mathew's quasi-agnostic stance toward the existence of a human homologue of the 2B4 gene cannot fairly be seen as dissuading one of ordinary skill in the art from combining Mathew's teachings with those of Valiante. Rather, Mathew's disclosure, in light of Valiante's teachings regarding the p38 protein and its role in NK cell activation, would have aroused a skilled artisan's curiosity to isolate the gene coding for p38. Thus, the record supplies ample evidence to support the Board's finding that Mathew "exemplifies how the cDNA encoding 2B4, the mouse version of Valiante's p38 expressed on all NK cells, can be isolated and sequenced."

B

The instant case also requires this court to consider the Board's application of this court's early assessment of obviousness in the context of classical biotechnological inventions, specifically In re Deuel, 51 F.3d 1552 (Fed. Cir. 1995). In *Deuel*, this court reversed the Board's conclusion that a prior art reference teaching a method of gene cloning, together with a reference disclosing a partial amino acid sequence of a protein, rendered DNA molecules encoding the protein obvious. *Id.* at 1559. In reversing the Board, this court in *Deuel* held that "knowledge of a protein does not give one a conception of a particular DNA encoding it." *Id.* Further, this court stated that "obvious to try" is an inappropriate test for obviousness.

> [T]he existence of a general method of isolating cDNA or DNA molecules is essentially irrelevant to the question whether the specific molecules themselves would have been obvious, in the absence of other prior art that suggests the claimed DNAs. . . . "Obvious to try" has long been held not to constitute obviousness. A general incentive does not make obvious a particular result, nor does the existence of techniques by which those efforts can be carried out.

Id. (internal citations omitted) (emphases added). Thus, this court must examine *Deuel*'s effect on the Board's conclusion that Valiante's teaching of the NAIL protein, combined with Va-liante's/Sam brook's teaching of a method to isolate the gene sequence that codes for NAIL, renders claim 73 obvious.

With regard to *Deuel*, the Board addressed directly its application in this case. In particular, the Board observed that the Supreme Court in *KSR* cast doubts on this court's application of the "obvious to try" doctrine:

> To the extent Deuel is considered relevant to this case, we note the Supreme Court recently cast doubt on the viability of Deuel to the extent the Federal Circuit rejected an "obvious to try" test. *See* KSR Int'l Co. v. Teleflex Inc., 550 U.S. 398 (2007) (citing Deuel, 51 F.3d at 1559). Under KSR, it's now apparent "obvious to try" may be an appropriate test in more situations than we previously contemplated.

Insofar as *Deuel* implies the obviousness inquiry cannot consider that the combination of the claim's constituent elements was "obvious to try," the Supreme Court in *KSR* unambiguously discredited that holding. In fact, the Supreme Court expressly invoked *Deuel* as a source of the discredited "obvious to try" doctrine. . . . The Supreme Court repudiated as "error" the *Deuel* restriction on the ability of a skilled artisan to combine elements within the scope of the prior art:

> The same constricted analysis led the Court of Appeals to conclude, in error, that a patent claim cannot be proved obvious merely by showing that the combination of elements was "obvious to try." When there is a design need or market pressure to solve a problem and there are a finite number of identified,

predictable solutions, a person of ordinary skill has good reason to pursue the known options within his or her technical grasp. If this leads to the anticipated success, it is likely the product not of innovation but of ordinary skill and common sense. In that instance the fact that a combination was obvious to try might show that it was obvious under §103.

KSR, 550 U.S. at 421 (internal citation omitted) (emphasis added). The Supreme Court's admonition against a formalistic approach to obviousness in this context actually resurrects this court's own wisdom in In re O'Farrell, which predates the *Deuel* decision by some seven years. This court in *O'Farrell* cautioned that "obvious to try" is an incantation whose meaning is often misunderstood:

> It is true that this court and its predecessors have repeatedly emphasized that "obvious to try" is not the standard under §103. However, the meaning of this maxim is sometimes lost. Any invention that would in fact have been obvious under §103 would also have been, in a sense, obvious to try. The question is: when is an invention that was obvious to try nevertheless nonobvious?

In re O'Farrell, 853 F.2d 894, 903 (Fed. Cir. 1988). To differentiate between proper and improper applications of "obvious to try," this court outlined two classes of situations where "obvious to try" is erroneously equated with obviousness under §103. In the first class of cases,

> what would have been "obvious to try" would have been to vary all parameters or try each of numerous possible choices until one possibly arrived at a successful result, where the prior art gave either no indication of which parameters were critical or no direction as to which of many possible choices is likely to be successful.

Id. In such circumstances, where a defendant merely throws metaphorical darts at a board filled with combinatorial prior art possibilities, courts should not succumb to hindsight claims of obviousness. The inverse of this proposition is succinctly encapsulated by the Supreme Court's statement in *KSR* that where a skilled artisan merely pursues "known options" from a "finite number of identified, predictable solutions," obviousness under §103 arises. 550 U.S. at 421.

The second class of *O'Farrell*'s impermissible "obvious to try" situations occurs where

> what was "obvious to try" was to explore a new technology or general approach that seemed to be a promising field of experimentation, where the prior art gave only general guidance as to the particular form of the claimed invention or how to achieve it.

853 F.2d at 903. Again, *KSR* affirmed the logical inverse of this statement by stating that §103 bars patentability unless "the improvement is more than the predictable use of prior art elements according to their established functions." 550 U.S. at 417.

KSR and *O'Farrell* directly implicate the instant case. Appellants' claim 73 recites a genus of isolated nucleic acid molecules encoding the NAIL protein. As found by the Board, the Valiante reference discloses the very protein of appellants' interest—"p38" as per Valiante. Valiante discloses a monoclonal antibody mAb C1.7 that is specific for p38/NAIL, and further teaches a five-step protocol for cloning nucleic acid molecules encoding p38/NAIL using mAb C1.7. *Id.* In fact, while stating that "[t]he DNA and protein sequences for the receptor p38 may be obtained by resort to conventional methodologies known to one of skill in the art," '690 Patent at col.7 ll.49-51, Valiante cites to the very same cloning manual, Sambrook, cited by Kubin and Goodwin for their proposition that the gene sequence is identified and recovered "by standard biochemical methods." '859 Application at 16. Moreover, the record strongly reinforces (and appellants apparently find no room to dispute) the Board's factual finding that one of ordinary skill would have been motivated to isolate NAIL cDNA, given Valiante's teaching that p38 is "expressed by virtually all human NK cells and thus plays a role in the immune response." The record shows that the prior art teaches a protein of interest, a motivation to isolate the gene coding for that protein, and illustrative instructions to use a monoclonal antibody specific to the protein for cloning this gene. Therefore, the claimed invention is "the product not of innovation but of ordinary skill and common sense." KSR, 550 U.S. at 421. Or stated in the familiar terms of this court's longstanding case law, the record shows that a skilled artisan would have had a resoundingly "reasonable expectation of success" in deriving the claimed invention in light of the teachings of the prior art. *See O'Farrell*, 853 F.2d at 904.

This court also declines to cabin *KSR* to the "predictable arts" (as opposed to the "unpredictable art" of biotechnology). In fact, this record shows that one of skill in this advanced art would find these claimed "results" profoundly "predictable." The record shows the well-known and reliable nature of the cloning and sequencing techniques in the prior art, not to mention the readily knowable and obtainable structure of an identified protein. Therefore this court cannot deem irrelevant the ease and predictability of cloning the gene that codes for that protein. This court cannot, in the face of *KSR*, cling to formalistic rules for obviousness, customize its legal tests for specific scientific fields in ways that deem entire classes of prior art teachings irrelevant, or discount the significant abilities of artisans of ordinary skill in an advanced area of art.

The record in this case shows that Valiante did not explicitly supply an amino acid sequence for NAIL or a polynucleotide sequence for the NAIL gene. In that sense, Kubin and Goodwin's disclosure represents some minor advance in the art. But "[g]ranting patent protection to advances that would occur in the ordinary course without real innovation retards progress." *KSR*, 550 U.S. at 419. "Were it otherwise patents might stifle, rather than promote, the progress of useful arts." *Id.* at 427. In light of the concrete, specific teachings of Sambrook and Valiante, artisans in this field, as found by the Board in its expertise, had every motivation to seek and every reasonable expectation of success in achieving the sequence of the claimed invention. In that sense, the claimed invention was reasonably expected in light of the prior art and "obvious to try."

AFFIRMED.

COMMENTS AND QUESTIONS

1. The *Kubin* case follows a long line of cases that set a fairly relaxed standard of patentability under §103. These cases were often criticized as out of step with what has become fairly routine science in the maturing biotechnology industry. *See, e.g.*, Dan L. Burk, *Biotechnology in the Federal Circuit: A Clockwork Lemon*, 46 ARIZ. L. REV. 441 (2004) (criticizing Federal Circuit nonobviousness doctrine pertaining to biotechnology). *See generally* DAN L. BURK & MARK A. LEMLEY, THE PATENT CRISIS AND HOW THE COURTS CAN SOLVE IT, ch. 12 (2009) (proposing more refined adaptation of patent law to the realities and needs of the biotechnology industry).

2. *Pharmaceutical Patents*. Drug development is the process of taking a candidate drug from identification to marketing approval by the United States Food and Drug Administration. On average, the development of an approved drug takes ten to fifteen years and costs $1.5 billion. *See* Michael Enzo Furrow, *Pharmaceutical Patent Life-Cycle Management After* KSR v. Teleflex, 63 FOOD & DRUG L.J. 275, 278, 283 (2008). Therefore, patent protection plays a critical role in the pharmaceutical industry.

Courts assess the obviousness of chemical compounds by focusing on the identification of a lead compound, which is a compound in the prior art that would be "a natural choice for further development efforts." *Altana Pharma AG v. Teva Pharms. USA, Inc.*, 566 F.3d 999, 1008 (Fed. Cir. 2009). The Federal Circuit uses a three prong prima facie inquiry in assessing obviousness of chemical compounds:

    (a) Whether an artisan of ordinary skill would have selected the asserted prior art as starting point or lead compound;

    (b) Whether the prior art would have provided the PHOSITA with the motivation to alter the lead compound to obtain the claimed compound; and

    (c) Whether the PHOSITA would have had a reasonable expectation of success in making the invention.

Takeda Chem. Indus., Ltd. v. Alphapharm Pty., Ltd., 492 F.3d 1350, 1357 (Fed. Cir. 2007). The first factor depends on the range and properties of potential compounds. The second factor looks to teachings in the prior art as well as structural similarities between the lead compound and the claimed compound. The third factor looks at predictability within the field, unexpected results, the extent to which the prior art teaches away from the compound, and obviousness to try.

What should happen if the invention is obvious to try, but the actual results of trying are unexpected? That often happens with follow-on pharmaceutical patents, for example when scientists follow established protocols to seek an expected variant of an existing chemical (called an "enantiomer") but that variant turns out to be more effective than expected. *See* Mark A. Lemley, *Expecting the Unexpected*, NOTRE DAME L. REV. (2016).

3. A turn toward administrative law principles in Federal Circuit review of the PTO bears closely on the suggestion/motivation issue that was at issue in both *KSR* and *Kubin*. In *In re Gartside*, 203 F.3d 1305 (Fed. Cir. 2000), the Federal Circuit held that the court would review the Patent Office Board of Appeals' fact-findings under the "substantial evidence" standard of the Administrative Procedure Act (APA). This in turn followed in the wake of a Supreme Court decision, *Dickinson v. Zurko*, 527 U.S. 150 (1999), holding that the standards governing judicial review of findings of fact made by federal administrative agencies apply when the Federal Circuit reviews findings of fact made by the Patent and Trademark Office (PTO).

The impact of this "administrative law" turn in PTO review cases has been widely felt. For example, when the *Zurko* case reached the Federal Circuit on remand from the Supreme Court, the Federal Circuit once again reversed the Patent Office Board of Appeals and Interferences. The court stated that the Board's reliance on basic knowledge or common sense was inadequate under the newly imposed standard of review. *In re Zurko*, 258 F.3d 1379 (Fed. Cir. 2001). The court continued the theme in *In re Lee*, 277 F.3d 1338 (Fed. Cir. 2002), holding that the Board's reliance on "common knowledge and common sense" as the motive to combine references did not fulfill the agency's obligation to cite references to support its conclusions:

> Deferential judicial review under the Administrative Procedure Act does not relieve the agency of its obligation to develop an evidentiary basis for its findings. . . . In its decision on Lee's patent application, the Board rejected the need for "any specific hint or suggestion in a particular reference" to support the combination of the . . . references. Omission of a relevant factor required by precedent is both legal error and arbitrary agency action. . . . "Common knowledge and common sense," even if assumed to derive from the agency's expertise, do not substitute for authority when the law requires authority.

277 F.3d at 1344-45. *See also In re Thrift*, 298 F.3d 1357 (Fed. Cir. 2002) (overturning obviousness rejection to claim in speech recognition software invention, which had been premised on ground that "[t]he use of [the claimed element] is old and well known in the art of speech recognition as a means of optimization which is highly desirable."). For a critique of requirements that patent examiners fully document obviousness rejections, *see* Arti K. Rai, *Addressing the Patent Gold Rush: The Role of Deference to PTO Patent Denials*, 2 WASH. U. L. & POL'Y 199 (2000); *see generally* Stuart Minor Benjamin & Arti K. Rai, *Who's Afraid of the APA? What the Patent System Can Learn from Administrative Law*, 95 GEO. L.J. 269 (2007) (offering a comprehensive proposal concerning the integration of patent law and administrative law). For an argument that, after the passage of the AIA, courts should give more deference to the Patent Office's

interpretation of the Patent Act, *see* Melissa F. Wasserman, *The Changing Guard of Patent Law: Chevron Deference for the PTO*, 54 WM. & MARY L. REV. 1959 (2013).

PROBLEMS

Problem III-5. You are a patent lawyer who represents the Deco-Bag Company, a small company that has made a hit by selling decorative trash bags. The best-selling product for Deco-Bag is an orange trash bag, used for holding raked-up leaves and other lawn clippings, that has a traditional Jack-O-Lantern face stenciled onto it. At the same time that competitors have begun selling the bags in large numbers, Deco-Bag has just received an opinion of the Board of Appeals and Interferences at the USPTO. The Board has upheld a final rejection of all claims in a patent application on the bag with Jack-O-Lantern design. Deco-Bag officials are contemplating an appeal of the decision to the Federal Circuit; they have asked for your opinion on the wisdom of this course of action.

Dembiciczak Pumpkin

A representative claim from the application reads as follows:

74. A decorative bag for use by a user with trash filling material, the bag simulating the general outer appearance of an outer surface of a pumpkin having facial indicia thereon, comprising:

a flexible waterproof plastic trash or leaf bag having

an outer surface which is premanufactured orange in color for the user to simulate the general appearance of the outer skin of a pumpkin, and having facial indicia including at least two of an eye, a nose and a mouth on the orange color outer surface for forming a face pattern on said orange color outer surface to simulate the general outer appearance of a decorative pumpkin with a face thereon,

said trash or leaf bag having first and second opposite ends, at least said second end having an opening extending substantially across the full width of said trash or leaf bag for receiving the trash filling material,

wherein when said trash or leaf bag is filled with trash filling material and closed, said trash or leaf bag takes the form and general appearance of a pumpkin with a face thereon.

The prior art cited by the examiner and the Board includes:

• MARY E. PLATTS, A HANDBOOK FOR TEACHERS OF ELEMENTARY ART 24-25 (1966), describing how to teach children to make a "Crepe Paper Jack-O-Lantern" out of a strip of orange crepe paper, construction paper cut-outs in the shape of facial features, and "wadded newspapers" as filling;

• VALERIE INDENBAUM & MARTHA SHAPIRO &, THE EVERYTHING BOOK FOR TEACHERS OF YOUNG CHILDREN 73 (1985), describing a method of making a "paper bag pumpkin" by stuffing a bag with newspapers, painting it orange, and then painting on facial features with black paint;

• U.S. Patent No. 3,349,991 to Leonard Kessler, entitled "Flexible Container" ("Kessler"), describing a bag apparatus wherein the bag closure is accomplished by the use of folds or gussets in the bag material;

• Conventional plastic lawn or trash bags.

Based on this art, the Board affirmed the Examiner's final rejection of all the independent claims (37, 52, 72, 74) under §103, holding that they would have been obvious in light of the conventional trash bags in view of the Platts and Indenbaum/Shapiro references.

What advice would you give to Deco-Bag in this matter?

Problem III-6. You have drafted a patent application for a client claiming a lollipop in the shape of a human thumb. An examiner rejected the claims as obvious over a combination of numerous prior art references. You must now prepare an argument trying to overturn the examiner's decision by appeal to the Board of Patent Appeals and Interferences. The claimed invention consists of a lollipop filled with a plug of gum, chocolate or food-grade wax. A thumb-shaped elastomeric mold served as the product's internal wrapper, and after it was peeled from the candy, the user could wear the mold on his or her own thumb. The examiner relied on the following prior art references in rejecting claims to the thumb-shaped lollipop invention:

• Siciliano shows ice cream in a mold with a stick inserted. The removable mold also serves as the product's wrapper.

> • Copeman shows candy lollipops in elastomeric molds taking "varying shapes, such as fruit or animals." The molds may be used as toy balloons after being removed.
>
> • Harris shows a hollow, thumb-shaped lollipop into which the user's thumb is inserted.
>
> • Webster shows a chewing gum entirely enclosing a liquid syrup product. This patent also suggests the greater appeal to consumers of providing two different components in the same confection.
>
> Although some of the references cite at least one other reference, no reference explicitly suggests combining its teaching with that of any other reference. What is your basis for arguing that the invention is patentable?

ii. *"Secondary" Considerations*

In *Graham,* the Supreme Court stated that the "secondary factors" of commercial success, long-felt need, and so on "may have relevancy." 383 U.S. at 18. The Federal Circuit, by contrast, routinely speaks of these factors—under the rubric "objective evidence"—as a *required* fourth element in the §103 analysis. *See, e.g., Greenwood v. Haitori Seiko Co., Ltd.*, 900 F.2d 238, 241 (Fed. Cir. 1990):

> [C]ertain factual predicates are required before the legal conclusion of obviousness or nonobviousness can be reached. . . . The underlying factual determinations to be made are (1) the scope and content of the prior art, (2) the differences between the claimed invention and the prior art, (3) the level of ordinary skill in the art, and (4) objective evidence of non-obviousness, such as commercial success, long-felt but unsolved need, failure of others, copying, and unexpected results.

Secondary considerations may be useful at times to protect against hindsight bias. "[O]bjective evidence of nonobviousness . . . can often serve as insurance against the insidious attraction of the siren hindsight when confronted with a difficult task of evaluating the prior art." *Gore v. Garlock*, 721 F.2d 1540, 1553 (Fed. Cir. 1983). The Federal Circuit requires that there be a nexus between the proffered secondary consideration and the claimed invention.

Close adherence to this methodology is especially important in the case of less technologically complex inventions, where the very ease with which the invention can be understood may prompt one "to fall victim to the insidious effect of a hindsight syndrome wherein that which only the inventor taught is used against its teacher." *In re Dembiczak*, 175 F.3d 994, 999 (Fed. Cir. 1999) (citing *Gore v. Garlock*, 721 F.2d at 1553).

Secondary considerations include:

- Commercial Success
- Long-Felt Need and Failure by Others

- Awards and Praise
- Skepticism, "Teaching Away," and Unexpected Results
- Licensing Activity
- Copying
- Advances in Collateral Technology
- Near Simultaneous Invention

Should the inventor's cost of making the invention be considered in evaluating obviousness? The statute states that "[p]atentability shall not be negatived by the manner in which the invention was made." That suggests that it would not be improper to consider a high cost of inventing to support nonobviousness, even though a low cost would not bar patentability.

These "secondary considerations" may work as "plus factors," tipping the balance of obviousness one way or the other in a particular case. But the significance of each of these factors has been hotly debated. Consider the following argument from Rochelle Dreyfuss, *The Federal Circuit: A Case Study in Specialized Courts*, 64 N.Y.U. L. REV. 1 (1989):

> Th[e] use of secondary considerations is not new to the CAFC. Rather, these considerations were previously accorded little weight because their appearance can sometimes be attributed to factors other than nonobviousness. For instance, commercial success may be due to the dominant market position of the patentee before the introduction of the new invention; the sudden ability to meet long felt need could derive from other technological advances, unrelated to the inventor's contribution; acquiescence may be attributed to the relative cost of obtaining a license, as opposed to challenging the patent. Rather than reject these considerations entirely, the CAFC has recognized their importance in making the law precise and instead has sought to minimize the extent to which they can be misused. Thus, the court has elaborated a "nexus" requirement, which requires that before secondary considerations can be used to demonstrate nonobviousness, a showing must be made that their appearance is attributable to the inventive characteristics of the discovery as claimed in the patent. . . . Since it is likely that the inconsistent treatment of such inventions was the most destabilizing element of the system, the CAFC has, in this area, made strides in achieving the appearance of precision.

But it is important not to go too far with these factors. For an economically oriented critique of one particular factor, evidence of commercial success, *see* Robert P. Merges, *Economic Perspectives on Innovation: Patent Standards and Commercial Success*, 76 CAL. L. REV. 803, 838 (1988):

> Commercial success is a poor indicator of patentability because it depends for its effectiveness on a long chain of inferences, and because the links in the chain are often subject to doubt. This was one of the central insights of a seminal

article on patentability, *Graham v. John Deere Co.: New Standards for Patents*, [1966 SUP. CT. REV. 293] written by Edmund Kitch in 1966. In it Kitch argued that commercial success was an unreliable indicator of nonobviousness. To make his point, Kitch identified four inferences a judge must make to work backward from evidence of market success to a conclusion of patentable invention:

First, that the commercial success is due to the innovation. Second, that . . . potential commercial success was perceived before its development. Third, the potential commercial success having been perceived, it is likely that efforts were made [by a number of firms] to develop the improvement. Fourth, the efforts having been made by men of skill in the art, they failed because the patentee was the first to reduce his development to practice.

With only this last event as a starting point, a court is asked to reconstruct a long series of events, and, more importantly, to decide how much of the final success is attributable to each factor introduced along the way. Each inference is weak, because there are almost always several explanations why a product was successful or why other firms missed a market opportunity. Only the *last* piece of the puzzle is indisputably established; the goal of the exercise is reached through a series of inferences that only begins with this last piece. It is an altogether extraordinary job of factual reconstruction, one that reveals the falsity of the term "objective evidence," which is often used by proponents of the secondary considerations.

Professor Merges goes on to argue in favor of another "secondary consideration"—failure of others:

Unlike commercial success, the failure of others to make an invention proves directly that parallel research efforts were under way at a number of firms, and that one firm (the patentee) won the race to a common goal. So long as the race was long enough, and so long as there was a clear winner, it is difficult to find fault with such evidence as proof of patentability. In fact, since the failure of others is often one of the inferential steps underlying the commercial success doctrine, it makes sense for courts to adopt a rule of thumb requiring the patentee in most cases to prove failure of others before commercial success will be given substantial weight.

If failure of others is important evidence of nonobviousness, should the *success* of others be evidence of obviousness? In *Merck & Co., Inc. v. Teva Pharmaceuticals USA, Inc.*, 395 F.3d 1364 (Fed. Cir. 2005), the Federal Circuit follows this line of analysis. The court noted that the commercial success of the product in question was a result at least in part of the sale of substitute products was barred by a blocking patent, not on the value of the litigated patent. As a result, there was no nexus between the patentee's commercial success and the obviousness of the invention. Rather, the commercial success was due to regulatory barriers to entry that insulated the patentee from competition regardless how obvious its patent was. *See also Galderma Labs., L.P. v. Tolmar, Inc.*, 737 F.3d 731, 740 (Fed. Cir. 2013) (commercial success no indicator of nonobviousness where blocking patents prevented competitors from marketing product earlier).

That rationale should also give more credence to one of the considerations that point in favor of obviousness – simultaneous invention. One study found that a surprising number of the most prominent inventions in history were developed by multiple inventors at about the same time. *See* Mark A. Lemley, *The Myth of the Sole Inventor*, 110 MICH. L. REV. 709 (2012). Does that suggest those inventions were obvious? Or is there some other explanation?

iii.   The AIA

The new AIA version of §103 shifts the time for determining obviousness from a patent claimant's invention date (i.e., "at the time the invention was made") to the effective filing date ("before the effective filing date of the claimed invention"). This change is tied to the definition of novelty under AIA §102, and is one implication of the shift to a first inventor to file priority system. In theory, moving the relevant date from invention to filing may increase at least slightly the scope of prior art available for obviousness inquiries; but in reality, the change may not make too much difference, especially if inventors adapt their behavior and file soon after invention.

PROBLEM

Problem III-7. Suppose that researchers in a particular pharmaceutical field agree that there are roughly a dozen comparably plausible compounds for attacking a serious disease and that the cost of pursuing regulatory approval for these paths will run into the billions of dollars. Does this set of factors imply that the resulting drug may well be obvious? How can a pharmaceutical company sensibly evaluate this risk? Does this scenario suggest that patent protection is ill-suited for this type of innovation?

---

3.   Utility

Section 101 provides that "[w]hoever invents or discovers any new and *useful* process, machine, manufacture, or composition of matter, or any new and *useful* improvement thereof, may obtain a patent therefor . . ." This is the textual basis for the utility requirement.

At first glance, utility might seem a simple requirement to apply. After all, whether or not something is useful is typically easy to determine. Nonetheless, there are a few areas in which utility is questionable. Chemists often synthesize compounds that they believe might be useful someday but for which no particular use is known or a potential use is highly speculative at the time that they file their patent application. Should they be entitled to a patent before that utility is known?

Brenner v. Manson
Supreme Court of the United States
383 U.S. 519 (1966)

Mr. Justice FORTAS delivered the opinion of the Court.

A Patent Office examiner denied Manson's application, and the denial was affirmed by the Board of Appeals within the Patent Office. The ground for rejection was the failure "to disclose any utility for" the chemical compound produced by the process. This omission was not cured, in the opinion of the Patent Office, by Manson's reference to an article in the November 1956 issue of the Journal of Organic Chemistry, 21 J. ORG. CHEM. 1333-1335, which revealed that steroids of a class which included the compound in question were undergoing screening for possible tumor-inhibiting effects in mice, and that a homologue[3] adjacent to Manson's steroid had proven effective in that role. Said the Board of Appeals, "It is our view that the statutory requirement of usefulness of a product cannot be presumed merely because it happens to be closely related to another compound which is known to be useful."

The Court of Customs and Patent Appeals (hereinafter CCPA) reversed[, stating] "where a claimed process produces a known product it is not necessary to show utility for the product," so long as the product "is not alleged to be detrimental to the public interest."

Our starting point is the proposition, neither disputed nor disputable, that one may patent only that which is "useful." [T]he concept of utility has maintained a central place in all of our patent legislation, beginning with the first patent law in 1790 and culminating in the present [§101] . . .

Respondent does not—at least in the first instance—rest upon the extreme proposition, advanced by the court below, that a novel chemical process is patentable so long as it yields the intended product and so long as the product is not itself "detrimental." Nor does he commit the outcome of his claim to the slightly more conventional proposition that any process is "useful" within the meaning of §101 if it produces a compound whose potential usefulness is under investigation by serious scientific researchers, although he urges this position, too, as an alternative basis for affirming the decision. Rather, he begins with the much more orthodox argument that his process has a specific utility which would entitle him to a declaration of interference even under the Patent Office's reading of §101. The claim is that the supporting affidavits, by reference to Ringold's 1956 article, reveal that an adjacent homologue of the steroid yielded by his process has been demonstrated to have tumor-inhibiting effects in mice, and that this discloses the requisite utility. We do not accept any of

---

[3] "A homologous series is a family of chemically related compounds, the composition of which varies from member to member by CH2 (one atom of carbon and two atoms of hydrogen). . . . Chemists knowing the properties of one member of a series would in general know what to expect in adjacent members."

these theories as an adequate basis for overriding the determination of the Patent Office that the "utility" requirement has not been met.

Even on the assumption that the process would be patentable were respondent to show that the steroid produced had a tumor-inhibiting effect in mice, we would not overrule the Patent Office finding that respondent has not made such a showing. The Patent Office held that, despite the reference to the adjacent homologue, respondent's papers did not disclose a sufficient likelihood that the steroid yielded by his process would have similar tumor-inhibiting characteristics. Indeed, respondent himself recognized that the presumption that adjacent homologues have the same utility has been challenged in the steroid field because of "a greater known unpredictability of compounds in that field." In these circumstances and in this technical area, we would not overturn the finding of the Primary Examiner, affirmed by the Board of Appeals and not challenged by the CCPA.

The second and third points of respondent's argument present issues of much importance. Is a chemical process "useful" within the meaning of §101 either (1) because it works—i.e., produces the intended product? or (2) because the compound yielded belongs to a class of compounds now the subject of serious scientific investigation? These contentions present the basic problem for our adjudication. Since we find no specific assistance in the legislative materials underlying §101, we are remitted to an analysis of the problem in light of the general intent of Congress, the purposes of the patent system, and the implications of a decision one way or the other.

In support of his plea that we attenuate the requirement of "utility," respondent relies upon Justice Story's well-known statement that a "useful" invention is one "which may be applied to a beneficial use in society, in contradistinction to an invention injurious to the morals, health, or good order of society, or frivolous and insignificant"[20]—and upon the assertion that to do so would encourage inventors of new processes to publicize the event for the benefit of the entire scientific community, thus widening the search for uses and increasing the fund of scientific knowledge. Justice Story's language sheds little light on our subject. Narrowly read, it does no more than compel us to decide whether the invention in question is "frivolous and insignificant"—a query no easier of application than the one built into the statute. Read more broadly, so as to allow the patenting of any invention not positively harmful to society, it places such a special meaning on the word "useful" that we cannot accept it in the absence of evidence that Congress so intended. There are, after all, many things in this world which may not be considered "useful" but which, nevertheless, are totally without a capacity for harm.

---

[20] *Note on the Patent Laws*, 3 Wheat. App. 13, 24. *See also* Justice Story's decisions on circuit in *Lowell v. Lewis*, 15 Fed. Cas. 1018 (No. 8568) (C.C.D. Mass.), and *Bedford v. Hunt*, 3 Fed. Cas. 37 (No. 1217) (C.C.D. Mass.).

Whatever weight is attached to the value of encouraging disclosure and of inhibiting secrecy, we believe a more compelling consideration is that a process patent in the chemical field, which has not been developed and pointed to the degree of specific utility, creates a monopoly of knowledge which should be granted only if clearly commanded by the statute. Until the process claim has been reduced to production of a product shown to be useful, the metes and bounds of that monopoly are not capable of precise delineation. It may engross a vast, unknown, and perhaps unknowable area. Such a patent may confer power to block off whole areas of scientific development, without compensating benefit to the public. The basic *quid pro quo* contemplated by the Constitution and the Congress for granting a patent monopoly is the benefit derived by the public from an invention with substantial utility. Unless and until a process is refined and developed to this point—where specific benefit exists in currently available form—there is insufficient justification for permitting an applicant to engross what may prove to be a broad field.

These arguments for and against the patentability of a process which either has no known use or is useful only in the sense that it may be an object of scientific research would apply equally to the patenting of the product produced by the process. Respondent appears to concede that with respect to a product, as opposed to a process, Congress has struck the balance on the side of nonpatentability unless "utility" is shown. Indeed, the decisions of the CCPA are in accord with the view that a product may not be patented absent a showing of utility greater than any adduced in the present case. We find absolutely no warrant for the proposition that although Congress intended that no patent be granted on a chemical compound whose sole "utility" consists of its potential role as an object of use-testing, a different set of rules was meant to apply to the process which yielded the unpatentable product. That proposition seems to us little more than an attempt to evade the impact of the rules which concededly govern patentability of the product itself.

This is not to say that we mean to disparage the importance of contributions to the fund of scientific information short of the invention of something "useful," or that we are blind to the prospect that what now seems without "use" may tomorrow command the grateful attention of the public. But a patent is not a hunting license. It is not a reward for the search, but compensation for its successful conclusion. "[A] patent system must be related to the world of commerce rather than to the realm of philosophy. . . ."

The judgment of the CCPA is Reversed.

Mr. Justice HARLAN, concurring in part and dissenting in part:

. . . Because I believe that the Court's policy arguments are not convincing and that past practice favors the respondent, I would reject the narrow definition of "useful" and uphold the judgment of the CCPA.

The Court's opinion sets out about half a dozen reasons in support of its interpretation. Several of these arguments seem to me to have almost no force. For instance, it is suggested that "[u]ntil the process claim has been reduced to production of a product shown to be useful, the metes and bounds of that monopoly are not capable of precise delineation" and "[i]t may engross a vast, unknown, and perhaps unknowable area." I fail to see the relevance of these assertions; process claims are not disallowed because the products they produce may be of "vast" importance nor, in any event, does advance knowledge of a specific product use provide much safeguard on this score or fix "metes and bounds" precisely since a hundred more uses may be found after a patent is granted and greatly enhance its value. . . .

More to the point, I think, are the Court's remaining, prudential arguments against patentability: namely, that disclosure induced by allowing a patent is partly undercut by patent-application drafting techniques, that disclosure may occur without granting a patent, and that a patent will discourage others from inventing uses for the product. How far opaque drafting may lessen the public benefits resulting from the issuance of a patent is not shown by any evidence in this case but, more important, the argument operates against all patents and gives no reason for singling out the class involved here. The thought that these inventions may be more likely than most to be disclosed even if patents are not allowed may have more force; but while empirical study of the industry might reveal that chemical researchers would behave in this fashion, the abstractly logical choice for them seems to me to maintain secrecy until a product use can be discovered. As to discouraging the search by others for product uses, there is no doubt this risk exists but the price paid for any patent is that research on other uses or improvements may be hampered because the original patentee will reap much of the reward. From the standpoint of the public interest the Constitution seems to have resolved that choice in favor of patentability.

What I find most troubling about the result reached by the Court is the impact it may have on chemical research. Chemistry is a highly interrelated field and a tangible benefit for society may be the outcome of a number of different discoveries, one discovery building upon the next. To encourage one chemist or research facility to invent and disseminate new processes and products may be vital to progress, although the product or process be without "utility" as the Court defines the term, because that discovery permits someone else to take a further but perhaps less difficult step leading to a commercially useful item. In my view, our awareness in this age of the importance of achieving and publicizing basic research should lead this Court to resolve uncertainties in its favor and uphold the respondent's position in this case.

COMMENTS AND QUESTIONS

1. Why does the majority claim that until an applicant shows an invention is useful, the inventor has not supplied the *quid pro quo* for a patent? What harm is there in granting a patent on an invention whose utility only becomes clear later? In granting a patent on a useless device? Who would be harmed by the granting of such a patent? Would granting the patent help the inventor attract investment that could help establish utility?

2. Cases following *Brenner* state that a claimed invention must have a specific and substantial utility that is credible. Asserted uses like "biological activity" or "useful for technical and pharmaceutical purposes" fail the requirement of specific utility; they are too vague. *See, e.g., In re Kirk*, 376 F.2d 936, 941 (C.C.P.A. 1967). The "substantial" utility standard requires proof that an invention serves some practical purpose, and that it is not either generally promising or promising enough to pursue further. "Simply put, to satisfy the 'substantial' utility requirement, an asserted use must show that that claimed invention has a significant and presently available benefit to the public." *Juicy Whip, Inc. v. Orange Bang, Inc.,* 185 F.3d 1364, 1366 (Fed. Cir. 1999).

As a matter of PTO practice, a specification which contains a disclosure of utility which corresponds in scope to the subject matter sought to be patented must be taken as sufficient to satisfy the utility requirement of §101 for the entire claimed subject matter unless there is a reason for one skilled in the art to question the objective truth of the statement of utility or its scope. In other words, claims to utility are assumed to be credible. *In re Langer*, 503 F.2d 1380, 1391 (CCPA 1974). The only time the PTO questions utility, therefore, is when an invention presents a "fantastic claim" to utility such as a perpetual motion machine or cold fusion. *See Newman v. Quigg*, 681 F. Supp. 16 (D. D.C. 1988), *aff'd* 877 F.2d 1575 (Fed. Cir. 1989) (perpetual motion machine); *In re Swartz*, 232 F.3d 862 (Fed. Cir. 2000) ("cold fusion"). The most common application of this requirement comes in chemical and biotechnology cases such as *Brenner* where a chemical compound is identified and is claimed to have utility as a pharmaceutical product. Although it is difficult to predict accurately how the human body will react to a specific compound, some evidence of basic effectiveness can establish utility. *See Ex parte Maas*, 9 U.S.P.Q.2d 1746 (Bd. Pat. App. & Int. 1987) (in vitro or animal test data that is reasonably predictive of utility must be accepted if one skilled in the art would find it predictive of utility).

3. For the steroid compounds at issue in *Brenner*, a practical use discovered some time after the patent application was filed—too late to save the patent. So utility might be thought of as a way to control the *timing* of the patent grant. Why do we require proof of practical utility at the time a patent application is filed? An analogy to land titling might help clarify. An early-stage researcher is akin to a "claim jumper" in the law of mining, or to someone who engages in a "land rush", racing to occupy real property simply to stake a claim, without making any real investment. Because thee kinds of "racing behaviors" can be wasteful, the law often requires substantial

investment before someone is awarded title. This discourages people from making large investments in running from claim to claim – which adds nothing to society's wealth in and of itself – and instead directs investment towards beginning beneficial development of the resources in question. *See* David D. Haddock, *First Possession Versus Optimal Timing: Limiting the Dissipation of Economic Value*, 64 WASH. U. L.Q. 775 (1986); Terry L. Anderson & Peter J. Hill, *The Race for Property Rights*, 33 J.L. & ECON. 177, 184 (1990); Dean Lueck, *The Rule of First Possession and the Design of the Law*, 38 J.L. & ECON. 393 (1995); *see also* Rebecca S. Eisenberg, *Analyze This: A Law and Economics Agenda for the Patent System*, 53 VAND. L. REV. 2081, 2087 (2000) ("Another possible way of understanding the utility requirement is as a timing device, helping to identify when an invention is ripe for patent protection.").

3. The concept of a "use patent" is described in Robert P. Merges & Richard Nelson, *On the Complex Economics of Patent Scope*, 90 COLUM. L. REV. 839 (1990), where the authors discuss an anomaly alluded to in Justice Harlan's dissent in *Brenner:* an inventor who obtains a patent for a product, e.g., a particular molecule, has the right to exclude all others from making, using or selling that product for *any* and all purposes, including purposes that the inventor did not herself discover or invent. For example, a patented compound created for its use as a leather tanning agent might turn out to be an effective treatment for disease. *Cf. In re Thuau*, 135 F.2d 344 (C.C.P.A. 1943). If so, the patentee would have the right to prevent all others from selling the drug as a treatment—including the person who discovered that the leather tanning compound had therapeutic properties. Note that the utility requirement is met so long as the patentee shows *any* specific utility for the chemical when the patent is first filed—in our example, when the leather tanning property of the compound is discovered.

New use patents already exist in a limited way. In our example, discoverer of the disease-fighting property of the leather tanning agent can obtain a *process* patent for "the process of using [the leather tanning compound] to treat disease." *See Rohm & Haas v. Roberts Chem. Co.*, 245 F.2d 693 (4th Cir. 1957) (upholding defendant's patent on a new use of a well-known product as a fungicide); 1 DONALD CHISUM, PATENTS §1.03[8] (collecting other cases on this point). This is in essence only an improvement patent; the discoverer would still have to obtain a license from the patentee to use the compound for the treatment of disease. But the reverse is also true; unlike the example outlined above, if the one who discovered the leather tanning agent's therapeutic properties obtained a process patent, the patentee would have to negotiate a license from the improver to have the right to use the compound to treat disease.

4. Utility for pharmaceutical products can generally be established by animal testing. *See* U.S. PATENT AND TRADEMARK OFFICE, MANUAL OF PATENT EXAMINING PROCEDURES §2107.01. In the past, the biotechnology industry sometimes had trouble overcoming utility rejections without clinical data proving that a particular drug was effective *in humans,* despite Federal Circuit precedent holding that a showing of

efficacy in a laboratory experiment was sufficient to establish the utility of a new drug. *Cross v. Iizuka*, 753 F.2d 1040, 1051 (Fed. Cir. 1985).

The Federal Circuit made it clear that human clinical trials are not necessary to prove the utility of a drug in *In re Brana*, 51 F.3d 1560 (Fed. Cir. 1995). The court held that the results of in vivo tests in mice were sufficiently probative of efficacy in humans to pass the utility threshold:

> The Commissioner, as did the Board, confuses the requirements under the law for obtaining a patent with the requirements for obtaining government approval to market a particular drug for human consumption. . . . FDA approval is not a prerequisite for finding a compound useful within the meaning of the patent laws. . . . Usefulness in patent law, and in particular in the context of pharmaceutical inventions, necessarily includes the expectation of further research and development. . . . Were we to require Phase II testing in order to prove utility, the associated costs would prevent many companies from obtaining patent protection on promising new inventions, thereby eliminating an incentive to pursue, through research and development, potential cures in many crucial areas such as the treatment of cancer.

Brana, 51 F.3d at 1567. On the other hand, in *In re Ziegler*, 992 F.2d 1197, 1203 (Fed. Cir. 1993), the Federal Circuit held that a patent applicant was not entitled to claim priority to a 1954 application for "polypropylene," since at the time of the 1954 application "at best, Ziegler was on the way to discovering a practical utility for polypropylene. . . but in that application Ziegler had not yet gotten there." Are these two cases distinguishable?

5. *Brenner* in many ways represents the "high-water mark" of the utility doctrine. Most applications of the doctrine have been quite limited in the hurdles they place before inventors. Certainly "frivolous" ideas are sometimes patented, suggesting that utility is not an effective mechanism for weeding out economically insignificant inventions. *See* Sean B. Seymore, *Making Patents Useful*, 98 Minn. L. Rev. 1046 (2014) (proposing tightening of the utility requirement).

In re Fisher
United States Court of Appeals for the Federal Circuit
421 F.3d 1365 (2005)

Michel, Chief Judge.

Because we conclude that substantial evidence supports the Board's findings that the claimed invention lacks a specific and substantial utility and that the '643 application does not enable one of ordinary skill in the art to use the invention, we affirm [the decision of the Board of Appeals and Interferences].

The claimed invention relates to five purified nucleic acid sequences that encode proteins and protein fragments in maize plants. The claimed sequences are commonly referred to as "expressed sequence tags" or "ESTs." When a gene is expressed in a cell, the relevant double-stranded DNA sequence is transcribed into a single strand of messenger ribonucleic acid ("mRNA"). Messenger RNA contains three of the same bases as DNA (A, G, and C), but contains uracil ("U") instead of thymine. mRNA is released from the nucleus of a cell and used by ribosomes found in the cytoplasm to produce proteins.

Complementary DNA ("cDNA") is produced synthetically by reverse transcribing mRNA. cDNA, like naturally occurring DNA, is composed of nucleotides containing the four nitrogenous bases, A, T, G, and C. Scientists routinely compile cDNA into libraries to study the kinds of genes expressed in a certain tissue at a particular point in time. One of the goals of this research is to learn what genes and downstream proteins are expressed in a cell so as to regulate gene expression and control protein synthesis.

An EST is a short nucleotide sequence that represents a fragment of a cDNA clone. It is typically generated by isolating a cDNA clone and sequencing a small number of nucleotides located at the end of one of the two cDNA strands. When an EST is introduced into a sample containing a mixture of DNA, the EST may hybridize with a portion of DNA. Such binding shows that the gene corresponding to the EST was being expressed at the time of mRNA extraction.

Claim 1 of the '643 application recites:

> A substantially purified nucleic acid molecule that encodes a maize protein or fragment thereof comprising a nucleic acid sequence selected from the group consisting of SEQ ID NO: 1 through SEQ ID NO: 5.

The ESTs set forth in SEQ ID NO: 1 through SEQ ID NO: 5 are obtained from [a particular] cDNA library. SEQ ID NO:1 through SEQ ID NO:5 consist of 429, 423, 365, 411, and 331 nucleotides, respectively. When Fisher filed the '643 application, he . . .did not know the precise structure or function of either the genes or the proteins encoded for by those genes.

The '643 application generally discloses that the five claimed ESTs may be used in a variety of ways, including: (1) serving as a molecular marker for mapping the entire maize genome, which consists of ten chromosomes that collectively encompass roughly 50,000 genes; (2) measuring the level of mRNA in a tissue sample . . .; (3)providing a source for primers for use in the polymerase chain reaction ("PCR") process to enable rapid and inexpensive duplication of specific genes; (4) identifying the presence or absence of a polymorphism; (5) isolating promoters via chromosome walking; (6) controlling protein expression; and (7) locating genetic molecules of other plants and organisms. [The Board of Appeals and Interferences affirmed a final rejection by the examiner, who found that none of the recited uses for the ESTs satisfied the "substantial utility" standard required for patentability.]

Under the correct application of the law, Fisher argues, the record shows that the claimed ESTs provide seven specific and substantial uses, regardless whether the functions of the genes corresponding to the claimed ESTs are known. . . . Fisher likewise argues that the general commercial success of ESTs in the marketplace confirms the utility of the claimed ESTs. Hence, Fisher avers that the Board's decision was not supported by substantial evidence and should be reversed.

The government contends that . . . Fisher's alleged uses are so general as to be meaningless. What is more, the government asserts that the same generic uses could apply not only to the five claimed ESTs but also to any EST derived from any organism. It thus argues that the seven utilities alleged by Fisher are merely starting points for further research, not the end point of any research effort. . . .

Regarding the seven uses asserted by Fisher, we observe that each claimed EST uniquely corresponds to the single gene from which it was transcribed ("underlying gene"). As of the filing date of the '643 application, Fisher admits that the underlying genes have no known functions. Fisher, nevertheless, claims that this fact is irrelevant because the seven asserted uses are not related to the functions of the underlying genes. We are not convinced by this contention. Essentially, the claimed ESTs act as no more than research intermediates that may help scientists to isolate the particular underlying protein-encoding genes and conduct further experimentation on those genes. The overall goal of such experimentation is presumably to understand the maize genome—the functions of the underlying genes, the identity of the encoded proteins, the role those proteins play during anthesis [i.e., flowering], whether polymorphisms exist, the identity of promoters that trigger protein expression, whether protein expression may be controlled, etc. Accordingly, the claimed ESTs are, in words of the Supreme Court, mere "object[s] of use-testing," to wit, objects upon which scientific research could be performed with no assurance that anything useful will be discovered in the end. *Brenner*, 383 U.S. at 535.

Fisher compares the claimed ESTs to certain other patentable research tools, such as a microscope. Although this comparison may, on first blush, be appealing in that both a microscope and one of the claimed ESTs can be used to generate scientific data about a sample having unknown properties, Fisher's analogy is flawed. As the government points out, a microscope has the specific benefit of optically magnifying an object to immediately reveal its structure. One of the claimed ESTs, by contrast, can only be used to detect the presence of genetic material having the same structure as the EST itself. It is unable to provide any information about the overall structure let alone the function of the underlying gene. Accordingly, while a microscope can offer an immediate, real world benefit in a variety of applications, the same cannot be said for the claimed ESTs. Fisher's proposed analogy is thus inapt. Hence, we conclude that Fisher's asserted uses are insufficient to meet the standard for a "substantial" utility under §101.

We agree with the Board that the facts here are similar to those in *Brenner*. . . .

Here, granting a patent to Fisher for its five claimed ESTs would amount to a hunting license [under *Brenner*] because the claimed ESTs can be used only to gain further information about the underlying genes and the proteins encoded for by those genes. The claimed ESTs themselves are not an end of Fisher's research effort, but only tools to be used along the way in the search for a practical utility. Thus, while Fisher's claimed ESTs may add a noteworthy contribution to biotechnology research, our precedent dictates that the '643 application does not meet the utility requirement of §101 because Fisher does not identify the function for the underlying protein-encoding genes. Absent such identification, we hold that the claimed ESTs have not been researched and understood to the point of providing an immediate, well-defined, real world benefit to the public meriting the grant of a patent.

We conclude that substantial evidence supports the Board's findings that each of the five claimed ESTs lacks a specific and substantial utility and that they are not enabled. Accordingly, the Board's decision affirming the final rejection of claim 1 of the '643 patent for lack of utility under §101 and lack of enablement under §112, first paragraph, is affirmed.

COMMENTS AND QUESTIONS

1. In a dissenting opinion, Judge Rader offers the following analogy in contending that ESTs satisfy the utility requirement as research tools:

> These research tools are similar to a microscope; both take a researcher one step closer to identifying and understanding a previously unknown and invisible structure. Both supply information about a molecular structure. Both advance research and bring scientists closer to unlocking the secrets of the corn genome to provide better food production for the hungry world. If a microscope has §101 utility, so too do these ESTs.

421 F.3d at 1380 (Rader, J., dissenting).

Are you convinced by the majority's argument that a microscope delivers immediate information about a specimen's structure, while ESTs only point to a specimen of interest? *See* Rebecca S. Eisenberg & Robert P. Merges, *Opinion Letter as to the Patentability of Certain Inventions Associated with the Identification of Partial cDNA Sequences*, 23 AM. INTELL. PROP. L. ASS'N Q.J. 1 (1995) (defending the majority's analysis).

2. In an omitted part of his dissenting opinion, Judge Rader notes that:

> In truth, I have some sympathy with the Patent Office's dilemma. The Office needs some tool to reject inventions that may advance the "useful arts" but not sufficiently to warrant the valuable exclusive right of a patent. The Patent Office has seized upon this utility requirement to reject these research tools as contributing "insubstantially" to the advance of the useful arts. The utility requirement is ill suited to that task, however, because it lacks any standard for assessing the state of the prior art and the contributions of the claimed advance. The proper tool for assessing sufficient contribution to the

useful arts is the obviousness requirement of 35 U.S.C. §103. Unfortunately this court has deprived the Patent Office of the obviousness requirement for genomic inventions. *See In re Deuel*, 51 F.3d 1552 (Fed. Cir. 1995); MARTIN J. ADELMAN ET AL., PATENT LAW, 517 (West Group 1998) (commenting that scholars have been critical of *Deuel*, which "overly favored patent applicants in biotech by adopting an overly lax nonobviousness standard."). Nonetheless, rather than distort the utility test, the Patent Office should seek ways to apply the correct test, the test used world wide for such assessments (other than in the United States), namely inventive step or obviousness.

421 F.3d at 1379, 1381-82 (Rader, J., dissenting) (some citations omitted).

3. Will there be incentives to identify ESTs without patent protection for them? Is an intermediate solution possible, such as granting patents on ESTs but limiting the patent to its use as a research tool rather than extending to any use of the DNA sequence?

4. *PTO Utility Guidelines*. Drawing on *Brenner*, the PTO promulgated guidelines requiring that an asserted utility be "specific, credible, and substantial." The credibility element was well known; it is the basis of utility rejections for far-fetched inventions such as perpetual motion machines. The novel aspects of the guidelines were (1) the definition of a "specific" utility and (2) the addition of a new requirement of "substantial" utility. *See* Utility Examination Guidelines, 66 Fed. Reg. 1092 (Jan. 5, 2001).

As regards specific utility, the PTO training materials based on the guidelines give as an example an asserted utility for a gene sequence, claimed to be useful to identify a disease. The Patent Office would now consider this not specific enough. More detail—such as the *specific type* of disease sought to be identified—would be required. As regards "substantial" utility, the guidelines state that the "requirement excludes 'throw-away,' 'insubstantial,' or 'nonspecific' utilities, such as the use of a complex invention as landfill."

The *reason* that "throwaway" utilities are not acceptable is that they permit patents to issue on inventions whose greatest value has yet to be realized. This is particularly acute in the area of gene sequences. The raw sequence information is of only nominal value in itself. The real value lies in identifying the whole genes that include each sequence, and even more importantly, identifying which traits those genes code for. Only then can proteins be mass produced, diseases identified, and gene therapies devised. These are the very "downstream" uses that Heller and Eisenberg are at pains to protect from patent blockages, i.e., "anticommons." Michael A. Heller & Rebecca Eisenberg, *Can Patents Deter Innovation? The Anticommons in Biomedical Research*, 280 SCIENCE 698 (1998); *see also* Michael A. Heller, *The Tragedy of the Anticommons: Property in the Transition from Marx to Markets*, 111 HARV. L. REV. 622 (1998).

5. *The Demise of Moral Utility in U.S. Patent Law.* The concept of immoral subject matter originated in dictum from a Joseph Story opinion. *Lowell v. Lewis*, 15 F. Cas. 1018 (No. 8568) (C.C.D. Mass. 1817). As examples of useless inventions, he cited patents to "poison people, or to promote debauchery, or to facilitate private assassination." 15 F. Cas. 1018, 1019. This doctrine was often invoked in the late nineteenth century to deny patents on gambling devices. Interestingly, it was a successful bar to patentability even where inventions appeared to be useful for things other than gambling. *See, e.g., Schultz v. Holtz*, 82 F. 448 (N.D. Cal. 1897) (patent on coin return device for coin-operated machines denied because it had application to slot machines). Courts struck down patents on this basis well into the twentieth century; *See, e.g., Meyer v. Buckley Mfg. Co.*, 15 F. Supp. 640, 641 (N.D. Ill. 1936) (patent denied on "game of chance" vending machine, where user inserted coin and tried to manipulate miniature steam shovel to scoop up a toy), and even as late as 1941, in a pinball machine patent case, the Seventh Circuit was careful to note the distinction between playing pinball and gambling. *Chic. Patent v. Genco*, 124 F.2d 725, 728 (7th Cir. 1941) (upholding patent on pinball machine). By the 1970s, however, the courts were regularly upholding patents on gambling devices—both because gambling was no longer seen as a major moral issue and because courts had become warier of denying patents on the basis of an indeterminate moral standard. *See, e.g., Ex parte Murphy*, 200 U.S.P.Q. (BNA) 801, 803 (Bd. Pat. App. & Int. 1977) (upholding claim for "one-armed bandit"). *See* Robert P. Merges, *Intellectual Property in Higher Life Forms: the Patent System and Controversial Technologies*, 47 MD. L. REV. 1051 (1988) (reviewing these cases).

The fight against immoral inventions was not limited to patents for gambling devices. Another line of cases denied patents for inventions that could be used only to defraud. In *Juicy Whip, Inc. v. Orange Bang, Inc.*, 185 F.3d 1364 (Fed. Cir. 1999), the inventor claimed a juice dispensing system that only appeared to circulate fresh juice. In actuality, it circulated an undrinkable liquid, while the tanks hidden underneath the glass bowl display dispensed the actual juice. The asserted utilities were this arrangement reduced maintenance costs and avoided contamination.

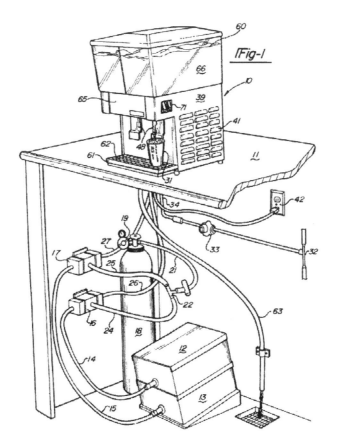

U.S. Patent No. 5,575,405

The defendant in *Juicy Whip*, who had infringed the design, took the remarkable position that the technology at issue was immoral in that it defrauded the public. We say remarkable, in that the defendant was, by infringing the technology, also defrauding the public. The Federal Circuit used the case to remove questions of morality from patent validity analysis. The court observed that "[t]he fact that one product can be altered to make it look like another is in itself a specific benefit sufficient to satisfy the statutory requirement of utility." The court gave the examples of cubic zirconium (designed to simulate a diamond), imitation gold leaf (designed to imitate real gold leaf), synthetic fabrics (designed to simulate expensive natural fabrics), and imitation leather (designed to look like real leather).

In each case, the invention of the product or process that makes such imitation possible has 'utility' within the meaning of the patent statute, and indeed there are numerous patents directed toward making one product imitate another. *See, e.g.*, U.S. Pat. No. 5,762,968 (method for producing imitation grill marks on food without using heat); U.S. Pat. No. 5,899,038 (laminated flooring imitating wood); U.S. Pat. No. 5,571,545 (imitation hamburger). Much of the value of such products resides in the fact that they appear to be something they are not. Thus, in this case the claimed post-mix dispenser meets the statutory requirement of utility by embodying the features of a post-mix dispenser while imitating the visual appearance of a pre-mix dispenser.

The fact that customers may believe they are receiving fluid directly from the display tank does not deprive the invention of utility. . . . [E]ven if the use of a reservoir containing fluid that is not dispensed is considered deceptive, that is not by itself sufficient to render the invention unpatentable. The requirement of 'utility' in patent law is not a directive to the Patent and Trademark Office or the courts to serve as arbiters of deceptive trade practices. Other agencies, such as the Federal Trade Commission and the Food and Drug Administration, are assigned the task of protecting consumers from fraud and deception in the sale of food products. *Cf. In re Watson*, 517 F.2d 465, 474-76 (CCPA 1975) (stating that it is not the province of the Patent Office to determine, under section 101, whether drugs are safe). As the Supreme Court put the point more generally, "Congress never intended that the patent laws should displace the police powers of the States, meaning by that term those powers by which the health, good order, peace and general welfare of the community are promoted." *Webber v. Virginia*, 103 U.S. (13 Otto) 344, 347-48 (1880).

Of course, Congress is free to declare particular types of inventions unpatentable for a variety of reasons, including deceptiveness. *Cf.* 42 U.S.C. §2181(a) (exempting from patent protection inventions useful solely in connection with special nuclear material or atomic weapons). Until such time as Congress does so, however, we find no basis in section 101 to hold that inventions can be ruled unpatentable for lack of utility simply because they have the capacity to fool some members of the public. The district court therefore erred in holding that the invention of the '405 patent lacks utility because it deceives the public through imitation in a manner that is designed to increase product sales.

6. *Patentable Subject Matter as a New Form of Moral Utility.* The AIA, for the first time, expressly excludes patents on specific subject matter categories, namely tax strategies and human organisms. *See* Pub. L. 112-29, §§14, 33, 125 Stat. 284 (2011). These exclusions reflect moral utility concerns. *See* Laura A. Keay, *Morality's Move Within U.S. Patent Law: From Moral Utility to Subject Matter*, 40 AIPLA Q.J. 409 (2012) (describing a recent reemergence in U.S. patent law of the moral utility doctrine as a result of ethical debates surrounding biotechnologies such as human-animal chimeras and genetic diagnostics); Margo A. Bagley, *Patent First, Ask Questions Later: Morality and Biotechnology in Patent Law*, 45 WM. & MARY L. REV. 469 (2003) (arguing for just such a revival of the moral utility doctrine); Thomas A. Magnani, *The Patentability of Human-Animal Chimeras*, 14 BERKELEY TECH. L.J. 443 (1999).

7. *Moral Utility Abroad.* Other nations have integrated moral and ethical considerations more directly into their patent systems. *See* Convention on the Grant of European Patents, Oct. 5, 1973, 13 I.L.M. 268, Art. 53(a) (providing that "European patents shall not be granted in respect of: (a) inventions the publication or exploitation of which would be contrary to ordre public or morality"); Cynthia M. Ho, *Splicing Morality and Patent Law: Issues Arising from Mixing Mice and Men*, 2 WASH. U. J.L. & POL'Y 247 (2000) (discussing the controversy surrounding the patenting of the oncogene mouse and the differences between the U.S. and Europe). *See also* Patent Law of the People's Republic of China, 2008, at Article 5 ("Patent rights shall not be granted for invention-creations that violate the law or social ethics, or harm public interests.").

Should patent examiners serve as moral censors? Do such standards risk subjecting technological advance to special interest politics? *See* Benjamin D. Enerson, *Protecting Society from Patently Offensive Inventions: The Risk of the Moral Utility Doctrine*, 89 CORNELL L. REV. 685 (2004). Consider the controversy surrounding embryonic stem cell research.

PROBLEM

Problem III-8. Acid Look, Inc. (ALI) is a fabric design company that specializes in designing jeans for the high-end fashion market. ALI develops a process for producing a "random faded effect" on the fabric of new jeans, catering to the market for new jeans that appear to be pre-worn. ALI seeks a patent not only on the process of treating the jeans to produce a random faded effect but on jeans treated by this process. The patent examiner rejects the claim to pre-faded jeans on the ground that they lack utility. Is this rejection proper? What test of utility does the patent examiner apply here?

---

4. Disclosure

A patent can be a potent right. In exchange for this government grant, an inventor must disclose the workings of the invention in enough detail to be informative to other people working in the same field. The sufficiency of the patentee's disclosure, and its relationship to the claims of a patent, are the topics we consider in this section.

The overall goal when drafting patent claims is to make them as broad as the Patent Office will allow. There are essentially two constraints on the breadth of the claims you can draft: (a) the mass of publicly available information on your problem—"the prior art" that is essential to novelty and nonobviousness analysis; and (b) the actual work the inventor has done, in the sense that you may not claim beyond what the inventor has invented.

We begin this section with two nineteenth century cases involving iconic inventions—the telegraph and the light bulb. The *Morse* case nicely frames the purposes and balance underlying patent law's disclosure requirements. It also provides valuable background for understanding the contemporary controversy over patentable subject matter (§101), which we cover in Chapter III(B)(5). Before we get there, however, this section will examine the patent disclosure requirements (§112).

O'Reilly v. Morse
Supreme Court of the United States
56 U.S. 62 (1853)

. . .

History of the Invention

[Samuel F.B. Morse] says that he was by profession a historical painter, and had, in 1829, gone to Europe for perfecting himself in that art; that on his return home in October, 1832, there were among the passengers in the ship, the Hon. William C. Rives, Minister of the United States to the court of France, Dr. C. T. Jackson, James Fisher, Esq., of Philadelphia, William Constable, Esq., and other gentlemen of extensive reading and intelligence, and that soon after the voyage commenced, the then experiments and discoveries in relation to electro-magnetism, and the affinity of electricity to magnetism, or their probable identity, became a subject of conversation.

In the course of this discussion, it occurred to him that by means of electricity, signs representing figures, letters, or words, might be legibly written down at any distance, and that the same effect might be produced by bringing the current in contact with paper saturated with some saline solution. These ideas took full possession of his mind, and during the residue of the voyage he occupied himself, in a great measure, in devising means of giving them practical effect.

Before he landed in the United States, he had conceived and drawn out in his sketch book, the form of an instrument for an electro-magnetic telegraph, and had arranged and noted down a system of signs composed of a combination of dots and spaces, which were to represent figures, and these were to indicate words to be found in a telegraphic dictionary, where each word was to have its number. He had also conceived and drawn out the mode of applying the electric or galvanic current, so as to mark signs by its chemical effects. . . .

He specifies what he affirms he had himself discovered or invented, and thus designates his improvement or improvements, a description whereof he had just before given in this his schedule, and which is made part of the patent.

"First. Having thus fully described my invention, I wish it to be understood that I do not claim the use of the galvanic current, or current of electricity, for the purpose of telegraphic communications, generally, but what I specially claim as my invention and improvement is making use of the motive power of magnetism, when developed by the action of such current or currents, substantially as set forth in the foregoing description of the first principal part of my invention, as means of operating or giving motion to machinery, which may be used to imprint signals upon paper or other suitable material or to produce sounds in any desired manner for the purpose of telegraphic communication at any distances."

* * *

"Second. I also claim as my invention and improvement the employment of the machinery called the register or recording instrument, composed of the train of clock-wheels, cylinders, and other apparatus, or their equivalent, for removing the material upon which the characters are to be imprinted, and for imprinting said characters, substantially as set forth in the foregoing description of the second principal part of my invention."

"Third. I also claim as my invention and improvement the combination of machinery herein described, consisting of the generation of electricity, the circuit of conductors, the contrivance for closing and breaking the circuit, the electro-magnet, the pen or contrivance for marking, and the machinery for sustaining and moving the paper, altogether constituting one apparatus of telegraphic machinery, which I denominate the American Electro-Magnetic Telegraph."

"Fourth. I also claim as my invention the combination of two or more galvanic or electric circuits, with independent batteries, substantially by the means herein described, for the purpose of obviating the diminished force of electro-magnetism in long circuits, and enabling me to command sufficient power to put in motion registering or recording machinery at any distance."

"Fifth. I claim as my invention the system of signs, consisting of dots and spaces, and of dots, spaces, and horizontal lines, for numerals, letters, words, or sentences, substantially as herein set forth and illustrated, for telegraphic purposes."

"Sixth. I also claim as my invention the system of signs, consisting of dots and spaces, and of dots, spaces, and horizontal lines, substantially as herein set forth and illustrated, in combination with machinery for recording them, as signals for telegraphic purposes."

"Seventh. I also claim as my invention the types, or their equivalent, and the type rule and post rule, in combination with the signal lever or its equivalent, as herein described, for the purpose of breaking and closing the circuit of galvanic or electric conductors."

"Eighth. I do not propose to limit myself to the specific machinery or parts of machinery described in the foregoing specifications and claims, the essence of my invention being the use of the motive power of the electric or galvanic current, which I call electro-magnetism, however developed, for making or printing intelligible characters, letters, or signs, at any distances, being a new application of that power, of which I claim to be the first inventor or discovered.". . .

"Object of the invention."

"The original and final object of all telegraphing is the communication of intelligence at a distance by signs or signals." . . .

DESCRIPTION OF THE TELEGRAPH

It consists of --

1. The main circuit with its battery

2. The key with the signal lever.

3. The local circuit with its battery.

4. The receiver, or mutator, with its electro-magnet.

5. The register, with its electro-magnet, pen lever, and grooved roller.

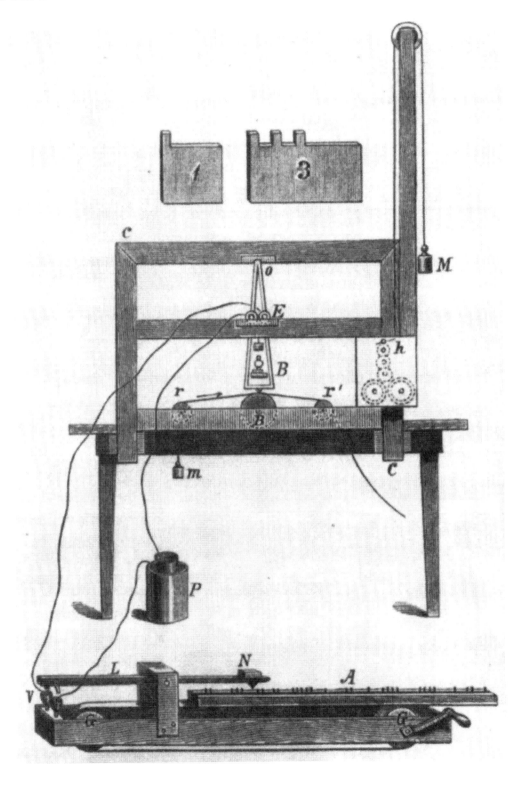

. . . The operator, having been put in possession of the intelligence, and broken the circuit in the lower conductors of his key, and thereby made his signal lever a conductor of the main circuit, applies his hand upon the signal lever and presses it down upon the conductor below, the main circuit is instantly closed, the horseshoe within the helices of this main circuit is a magnet, the armature has drawn its movable lever into contact with the platina point, the local circuit is closed, the horseshoe within the helices of this circuit is an electro-magnet, the armature of the pen lever is upon its heels, the other end of the lever has cast up the pen, and indented an intelligible character upon the paper.

The operator's hand taken off, and the main circuit is broken, the receiver within it is not a magnet, the movable lever has been withdrawn, by its spring, from the platina point, the local circuit is broken, the register magnet is no longer a magnet, and the pen has been sprung down from the paper, and stands ready to repeat and add another character of the intelligence.

The operator's hand upon his lever, and another character is added. And,

These are the characters recorded, and how they are read: .- is A, -... is B, -.-. is C, -.. is D, . is E, ..-. is F, --. is G, ... is H, .. is I, .--- is J, -.- is K, .-.. is L, -- is M, -. is N, --- is O, .--. is P, --.- is Q, .-. is R, ... is S, - is T, ..- is U, ...- is V, .-- is W, -..- is X, -.-- is Y, --.. is Z, and such is the alphabet. Then .---- is 1, ..--- is 2, ...-- is 3, ...- is 4, ... is 5, -.... is 6, --... is 7, ---.. is 8, ----. is 9, ----- is 0; and these are the numerals.

The holding down the lever an instant indented one dot .; the holding it longer made a dash - of a length corresponding to the time. The dots were made at distances corresponding to the time the hand was held off the lever. And,

This is the telegraph and its operations before us.

MR. CHIEF JUSTICE TANEY delivered the opinion of the Court.

In proceeding to pronounce judgment in this case, the Court is sensible not only of its importance, but of the difficulties in some of the questions which it presents for decision. . . .

The appellants take three grounds of defense. In the first place, they deny that Professor Morse was the first and original inventor of the Electro-Magnetic Telegraphs described in his two reissued patents of 1848. Secondly, they insist that if he was the original inventor, the patents under which he claims have not been issued conformably to the acts of Congress, and do not confer on him the right to the exclusive use. And thirdly, if these two propositions are decided against them, they insist that the telegraph of O'Reilly is substantially different from that of Professor Morse, and the use of it, therefore, no infringement of his rights.

[The Court found that Morse was the first and original inventor and then proceeded to assess whether the claims conform to the Patent Acts.]

We perceive no well-founded objection to the description which is given of the whole invention and its separate parts, nor to his right to a patent for the first seven inventions set forth in the specification of his claims. The difficulty arises on the eighth.

It is in the following words:

> "Eighth. I do not propose to limit myself to the specific machinery or parts of machinery described in the foregoing specification and claims, the essence of my invention being the use of the motive power of the electric or galvanic current, which I call electro-magnetism, however developed for marking or printing intelligible characters, signs, or letters, at any distances, being a new application of that power of which I claim to be the first inventor or discoverer."

It is impossible to misunderstand the extent of this claim. He claims the exclusive right to every improvement where the motive power is the electric or galvanic current, and the result is the marking or printing intelligible characters, signs, or letters at a distance.

If this claim can be maintained, it matters not by what process or machinery the result is accomplished. For aught that we now know, some future inventor, in the onward march of science, may discover a mode of writing or printing at a distance by means of the electric or galvanic current, without using any part of the process or combination set forth in the plaintiff's specification. His invention may be less complicated—less liable to get out of order—less expensive in construction, and in its operation. But yet if it is covered by this patent, the inventor could not use it, nor the public have the benefit of it, without the permission of this patentee.

Nor is this all; while he shuts the door against inventions of other persons, the patentee would be able to avail himself of new discoveries in the properties and powers of electro-magnetism which scientific men might bring to light. For he says he does not confine his claim to the machinery or parts of machinery which he specifies, but claims for himself a monopoly in its use, however developed, for the purpose of printing at a distance. New discoveries in physical science may enable him to combine it with new agents and new elements, and by that means attain the object in a manner superior to the present process and altogether different from it. And if he can secure the exclusive use by his present patent, he may vary it with every new discovery and development of the science, and need place no description of the new manner, process, or machinery upon the records of the patent office. And when his patent expires, the public must apply to him to learn what it is. In fine, he claims an exclusive right to use a manner and process which he has not described and indeed had not invented, and therefore could not describe when he obtained his patent. The court is of opinion that the claim is too broad, and not warranted by law.

No one, we suppose will maintain that Fulton could have taken out a patent for his invention of propelling vessels by steam, describing the process and machinery he used, and claimed under it the exclusive right to use the motive power of steam, however developed, for the purpose of propelling vessels. It can hardly be supposed that under such a patent he could have prevented the use of the improved machinery which science has since introduced, although the motive power is steam, and the result is the propulsion of vessels. Neither could the man who first discovered that steam might, by a proper arrangement of machinery, be used as a motive power to grind corn or spin cotton claim the right to the exclusive use of steam as a motive power for the purpose of producing such effects.

Again, the use of steam as a motive power in printing-presses is comparatively a modern discovery. Was the first inventor of a machine or process of this kind entitled to a patent, giving him the exclusive right to use steam as a motive power, however developed, for the purpose of marking or printing intelligible characters? Could he have prevented the use of any other press subsequently invented where steam was used? Yet so far as patentable rights are concerned, both improvements must stand on the same principles. Both use a known motive power to print intelligible marks or letters, and it can make no difference in their legal rights under the patent laws whether the printing is done near at hand or at a distance. Both depend for success not merely upon the motive power, but upon the machinery with which it is combined. And it has never, we believe, been supposed by anyone that the first inventor of a steam printing press was entitled to the exclusive use of steam as a motive power, however developed, for marking or printing intelligible characters. . . .

Many cases have been referred to in the argument which have been decided upon this subject in the English and American courts. We shall speak of those only which seem to be considered as leading ones. And those most relied on, and pressed upon the court in behalf of the patentee, are the cases which arose in England upon Neilson's patent for the introduction of heated air between the blowing apparatus and the furnace in the manufacture of iron.

The leading case upon this patent is that of *Neilson v. Harford* in the English Court of Exchequer. It was elaborately argued, and appears to have been carefully considered by the court. The case was this:

Neilson, in his specification, described his invention as one for the improved application of air to produce heat in fires, forges, and furnaces where a blowing apparatus is required. And it was to be applied as follows: the blast or current of air produced by the blowing apparatus was to be passed from it into an air vessel or receptacle made sufficiently strong to endure the blast, and through or from that vessel or receptacle by means of a tube, pipe, or aperture into the fire, the receptacle be kept artificially heated to a considerable temperature by heat externally applied. He then described in rather general terms the manner in which the receptacle might be constructed and heated and the air conducted through it to the fire, stating that the form of the receptacle was not material nor the manner of applying heat to it. In the action above-mentioned for the infringement of this patent, the defendant, among other defenses, insisted that the machinery for heating the air and throwing it hot into the furnace was not sufficiently described in the specification, and the patent void on that account—and also, that a patent for throwing hot air into the furnace instead of cold, and thereby increasing the intensity of the heat, was a patent for a principle, and that a principle was not patentable.

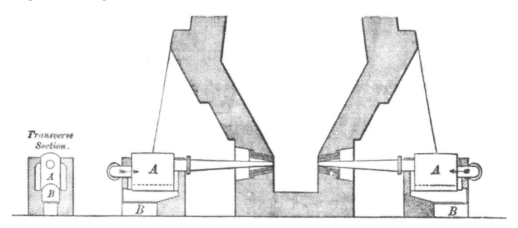

Neilson's Hot Blast Furnace (1829)

Upon the first of these defenses, the jury found that a man of ordinary skill and knowledge of the subject, looking at the specification alone, could construct such an apparatus as would be productive of a beneficial result, sufficient to make it worth while to adapt it to the machinery in all cases of forges, cupolas, and furnaces, where the blast is used.

And upon the second ground of defense, Baron Parke, who delivered the opinion of the court, said:

> "It is very difficult to distinguish it from the specification of a patent for a principle, and this at first created in the minds of the court much difficulty, but after full consideration we think that the plaintiff does not merely claim a principle, but a machine embodying a principle, and a very valuable one. We think the case must be considered as if, the principle being well known, the plaintiff had first invented a mode of applying it by a mechanical apparatus to furnaces, and his invention then consists in this: by interposing a receptacle for heated air between the blowing apparatus and the furnace. In this receptacle he directs the air to be heated by the application of heat externally to the receptacle, and thus he accomplishes the object of applying the blast, which was before cold air, in a heated state to the furnace."

We see nothing in this opinion differing in any degree from the familiar principles of law applicable to patent cases. Neilson claimed no particular mode of constructing the receptacle or of heating it. He pointed out the manner in which it might be done, but admitted that it might also be done in a variety of ways and at a higher or lower temperature, and that all of them would produce the effect in a greater or less degree provided the air was heated by passing through a heated receptacle. And hence it seems that the court at first doubted whether it was a patent for anything more than the discovery that hot air would promote the ignition of fuel better than cold. And if this had been the construction, the court, it appears, would have held his patent to be void because the discovery of a principle in natural philosophy or physical science is not patentable.

But after much consideration it was finally decided that this principle must be regarded as well known, and that the plaintiff had invented a mechanical mode of applying it to furnaces, and that his invention consisted in interposing a heated receptacle between the blower and the furnace, and by this means heating the air after it left the blower and before it was thrown into the fire. Whoever, therefore, used this method of throwing hot air into the furnace used the process he had invented, and thereby infringed his patent, although the form of the receptacle or the mechanical arrangements for heating it might be different from those described by the patentee. For whatever form was adopted for the receptacle or whatever mechanical arrangements were made for heating it, the effect would be produced in a greater or less degree if the heated receptacle was placed between the blower and the furnace and the current of air passed through it.

Undoubtedly the principle that hot air will promote the ignition of fuel better than cold was embodied in this machine. But the patent was not supported because this principle was embodied in it. He would have been equally entitled to a patent if he had invented an improvement in the mechanical arrangements of the blowing apparatus or in the furnace while a cold current of air was still used. But his patent was supported because he had invented a mechanical apparatus by which a current of hot air, instead of cold, could be thrown in. And this new method was protected by his patent. The interposition of a heated receptacle in any form was the novelty he invented.

We do not perceive how the claim in the case before us can derive any countenance from this decision. If the Court of Exchequer had said that Neilson's patent was for the discovery that hot air would promote ignition better than cold, and that he had an exclusive right to use it for that purpose, there might perhaps have been some reason to rely upon it. But the court emphatically denied this right to such a patent. And his claim, as the patent was construed and supported by the court, is altogether unlike that of the patentee before us.

For Neilson discovered that by interposing a heated receptacle between the blower and the furnace and conducting the current of air through it, the heat in the furnace was increased. And this effect was always produced, whatever might be the form of the receptacle or the mechanical contrivances for heating it or for passing the current of air through it and into the furnace.

But Professor Morse has not discovered that the electric or galvanic current will always print at a distance, no matter what may be the form of the machinery or mechanical contrivances through which it passes. You may use electro-magnetism as a motive power and yet not produce the described effect—that is, print at a distance intelligible marks or signs. To produce that effect, it must be combined with, and passed through, and operate upon, certain complicated and delicate machinery, adjusted and arranged upon philosophical principles and prepared by the highest mechanical skill. And it is the high praise of Professor Morse that he has been able, by a new combination of known powers, of which electro-magnetism is one, to discover a method by which intelligible marks or signs may be printed at a distance. And for the method or process thus discovered he is entitled to a patent. But he has not discovered that the electro-magnetic current, used as motive power in any other method, and with any other combination, will do as well. . . .

The 6th section [of the Patent Act] directs who shall be entitled to a patent and the terms and conditions on which it may be obtained. It provides that any person shall be entitled to a patent who has discovered or invented a new and useful art, machine, manufacture, or composition of matter or a new and useful improvement on any previous discovery in either of them. But before he receives a patent, he shall deliver a written description of his invention or discovery, "and of the manner and process of making, constructing, using, and compounding the same" in such exact terms at to enable any person skilled in the art or science to which it appertains or with which it is most nearly connected to make, construct, compound, and use the same. . . .

This Court has decided that the specification required by this law is a part of the patent and that the patent issues for the invention described in the specification. . . .

Indeed, if the eighth claim of the patentee can be maintained, there was no necessity for any specification further than to say that he had discovered that by using the motive power of electro-magnetism, he could print intelligible characters at any distance. We presume it will be admitted on all hands that no patent could have issued on such a specification. Yet this claim can derive no aid from the specification filed. It is outside of it, and the patentee claims beyond it. And if it stands, it must stand simply on the ground that the broad terms above-mentioned were a sufficient description, and entitled him to a patent in terms equally broad. In our judgment, the act of Congress cannot be so construed. . . .

The two reissued patents of 1848, being both valid, with the exception of the eighth claim in the first, the only remaining question is whether they or either of them have been infringed by the defendants.

[The Court proceeded to find that patent was infringed.]

COMMENTS AND QUESTIONS

1. What is the policy rationale for the Court's decision?

2. Why was Morse's specification inadequate to support his eighth claim? Didn't he teach how to use electromagnetism to communicate information at a distance? What more would Morse have had to show to justify that claim?

2. The Court places particular emphasis on *Neilson v. Harford*, an English court decision, which upheld a broad claim to improved hot blast furnaces. What distinguishes Morse's broad eighth claim, which the Court invalidated, from Neilson's broad claim, which the Court of Exchequer upheld.

3. The Court quotes Baron Parke in stating that

> It is very difficult to distinguish [Neilson's patent] from the specification of a patent for a principle, and this at first created in the minds of the court much difficulty, but after full consideration we think that the plaintiff does not merely claim a principle, but a machine embodying a principle, and a very valuable one. *We think the case must be considered as if, the principle being well known,* the plaintiff had first invented a mode of applying it by a mechanical apparatus to furnaces, and his invention then consists in this: by interposing a receptacle for heated air between the blowing apparatus and the furnace.

Neilson v. Harford, 1 Web. P. C. 295, 371 (1841) (emphasis added). Why would the English Court treat Neilson's discovery as "being well known"? As we will see in the next section on patentable subject matter, patent law has long excluded patents on laws of nature in the abstract. As we will see in Chapter III(B)(5) (Patentable Subject Matter), laws of nature, natural phenomena, and abstract ideas are not patentable. An *application* of a law of nature or mathematical formula is eligible. The *Neilson* and *Morse* cases figure prominently in that jurisprudence.

* * * * *

The disclosure requirement of the modern Patent Act parallels the version of the act in play in *Morse*:

> **§112(a)** The specification shall contain a written description of the invention, and of the manner and process of making and using it, in such full, clear, concise, and exact terms as to enable any person skilled in the art to which it pertains, or with which it is most nearly connected, to make and use the same, and shall set forth the best mode contemplated by the inventor of carrying out his invention.

This provision comprises three requirements: (i) enablement; (ii) written description; and (iii) best mode. Only the first two are relevant to modern patent practice. We take each of these sections up in turn. Sections 112(b) – (f) deal with how patents are claimed, as opposed to the adequacy of disclosure.[6] We will cover these issues in the section on claim construction.

i.   Enablement

Many inventions can be deployed in a variety of ways. Patent drafters call them embodiments. Consider the following examples:

- Velcro fasteners can be found on a wide range of products, from shoes to spacesuits to huge industrial storage sacks. All of these embodiments share the same inventive principle: a lineal fuzzy fabric strip with tiny hooks that "mate" with another fabric strip with smaller more rigid loops, attaching temporarily, until pulled apart. Should the person who invented Velcro fasteners be able to patent the entire concept of the new fastener, in whatever context it might be applied?

- In 1861, William Schrafft, a Boston confectioner, invented the jelly bean— small bean-shaped candies with soft candy shells and thick gel interiors. (He urged people to send his jelly beans to soldiers during the American Civil War.) Imagine that he experimented with lemon jelly beans. He might, however, envision a broad array of fruit flavors. Should he be able to claim all fruit-flavored jelly beans?

To claim subsets or all of the embodiments, i.e., all of the species within a genus, the patentee must be in possession of the inventive principle and provide adequate teaching and support for the full range claimed. The reach of this doctrine is explored in the following foundational case.

The Incandescent Lamp Patent
Supreme Court of the United States
159 U.S. 465 (1895)

This was a bill in equity, filed by the consolidated Electric Light Company against the McKeesport Light Company, to recover damages for the infringement of letters patent No. 317,076, issued May 12, 1885, to the Electro-Dynamic Light Company, assignee of Sawyer and Man, for an electric light. The defendants justified [their actions] under certain patents to Thomas A. Edison, particularly No. 223,898, issued January 27, 1880; denied the novelty and utility of the complainants' patent, and averred that the same had been fraudulently and illegally procured. The real defendant was the Edison Electric Light Company, and the case involved a contest between what are known as the Sawyer and Man and the Edison systems of electric lighting.

---

[6] The 1952 Act presented Section 112 as six paragraphs. As a result, court decisions referred to subsections by paragraph number, *e.g.*, §112, ¶1. The AIA relabeled these subsections (a) – (f).

In their application, Sawyer and Man stated that their invention related to "that class of electric lamps employing an incandescent conductor enclosed in a transparent, hermetically-sealed vessel or chamber, from which oxygen is excluded, and . . . more especially to the incandescing conductor, its substance, its form, and its combination with the other elements composing the lamp. Its object is to secure a cheap and effective apparatus; and our improvement consists, first, of the combination, in a lamp chamber, composed wholly of glass, . . . of an incandescing conductor of carbon made from a vegetable fibrous material, in contradistinction to a similar conductor made from mineral or gas carbon, and also in the form of such conductor so made from such vegetable carbon, and combined in the lighting circuit with the exhausted chamber of the lamp."

The specification further stated that:

In the practice of our invention we have made use of carbonized paper, and also wood carbon. We have also used such conductors or burners of various shapes, such as pieces with their lower ends secured to their respective supports, and having their upper ends united so as to form an inverted V-shaped burner. We have also used conductors of varying contours—that is, with rectangular bends instead of curvilinear ones; but we prefer the arch shape.

No especial description of making the illuminating carbon conductors, described in this specification and making the subject-matter of this improvement, is thought necessary, as any of the ordinary methods of forming the material to be carbonized to the desired shape and size, and carbonizing it according to the methods in practice before the date of this improvement, may be adopted in the practice thereof by any one skilled in the arts appertaining to the making of carbons for electric lighting or for other use in the arts. The advantages resulting from the manufacture of the carbon from vegetable fibrous or textile material instead of mineral or gas carbon are many. Among them may be mentioned the convenience afforded for cutting and making the conductor in the desired form and size, the purity and equality of the carbon obtained, its susceptibility to tempering, both as to hardness and resistance, and its toughness and durability.

The claims were as follows:

An incandescing conductor for an electric lamp, of carbonized fibrous or textile material and of an arch or horseshoe shape, substantially as hereinbefore set forth.

The combination, substantially as hereinbefore set forth, of an electric circuit and an incandescing conductor of carbonized fibrous material, included in and forming part of said circuit, and a transparent hermetically sealed chamber in which the conductor is enclosed.

The incandescing conductor for an electric lamp, formed of carbonized paper, substantially as described.

The commercial Edison lamp used by the appellee is composed of a burner made of carbonized bamboo of a peculiar quality discovered by Mr. Edison to be highly useful for the purpose, and having a length of about six inches, a diameter of about five one thousandths of an inch, and an electrical resistance of upwards of 100 ohms. This filament of carbon is bent into the form of a loop, and its ends are secured by good electrical and mechanical connections to two fine platinum wires. . . .

Upon a hearing in the Circuit Court before Mr. Justice Bradley upon pleadings and proofs, the court held the patent to be invalid, and dismissed the bill. 40 Fed. Rep. 21 [C.C.W.D.P.A. (1889)]. Thereupon complainant appealed to this court.

Mr. Justice BROWN, after stating the case as above reported, delivered the opinion of the court.

In order to obtain a complete understanding of the scope of the Sawyer and Man patent, it is desirable to consider briefly the state of the art at the time the application was originally made, which was in January, 1880.

. . . The form of illumination . . . known as the incandescent system . . . consists generally in the passage of a current of electricity through a continuous strip or piece of refractory material, which is a conductor of electricity, but a poor conductor—in other words, a conductor offering a considerable resistance to the flow of the current through it. It was discovered early in this century that various substances might be heated to a white heat by passing a sufficiently strong current of electricity through them. . . .

For many years prior to 1880, experiments had been made by a large number of persons, in various countries, with a view to the production of an incandescent light which could be made available for domestic purposes, and could compete with gas in the matter of expense. Owing partly to a failure to find a proper material, which should burn but not consume, partly to the difficulty of obtaining a perfect vacuum in the globe in which the light was suspended, and partly to a misapprehension of the true principle of incandescent lighting, these experiments had not been attended with success; although it had been demonstrated as early as 1845 that, whatever material was used, the conductor must be enclosed in an air-tight bulb [i.e., vacuum], to prevent it from being consumed by the oxygen in the atmosphere. The chief difficulty was that the carbon burners were subject to a rapid disintegration or evaporation, which electricians assumed was due to the disrupting action of the electric current, and, hence, the conclusion was reached that carbon contained in itself the elements of its own destruction, and was not a suitable material for the burner of an incandescent lamp.

It is admitted that the lamp described in the Sawyer and Man patent is no longer in use, and was never a commercial success; that it does not embody the principle of high resistance with a small illuminating surface; that it does not have the filament burner of the modern incandescent lamp; that the lamp chamber is defective, and that the lamp manufactured by the complainant and put upon the market is substantially the Edison lamp; but it is said that, in the conductor used by Edison (a particular part of the stem of the bamboo lying directly beneath the silicious cuticle, the peculiar fitness for which purpose was undoubtedly discovered by him), he made use of a fibrous or textile material, covered by the patent to Sawyer and Man, and is, therefore, an infringer. It was admitted, however, that the third claim—for a conductor of carbonized paper—was not infringed.

The two main defences to this patent are (1) that it is defective upon its face, in attempting to monopolize the use of all fibrous and textile materials for the purpose of electric illumination; and (2) that Sawyer and Man were not in fact the first to discover that these were better adapted than mineral carbons to such purposes.

Is the complainant entitled to a monopoly of all fibrous and textile materials for incandescent conductors? If the patentees had discovered in fibrous and textile substances a quality common to them all, or to them generally, as distinguishing them from other materials, such as minerals, etc., and such quality or characteristic adapted them peculiarly to incandescent conductors, such claim might not be too broad. If, for instance, minerals or porcelains had always been used for a particular purpose, and a person should take out a patent for a similar article of wood, and woods generally were adapted to that purpose, the claim might not be too broad, though defendant used wood of a different kind from that of the patentee. But if woods generally were not adapted to the purpose, and yet the patentee had discovered a wood possessing certain qualities, which gave it a peculiar fitness for such purpose, it would not constitute an infringement for another to discover and use a different kind of wood, which was found to contain similar or superior qualities. The present case is an apt illustration of this principle. Sawyer and Man supposed they had discovered in carbonized paper the best material for an incandescent conductor. Instead of confining themselves to carbonized paper, as they might properly have done, and in fact did in their third claim, they made a broad claim for every fibrous or textile material, when in fact an examination of over six thousand vegetable growths showed that none of them possessed the peculiar qualities that fitted them for that purpose. Was everybody then precluded by this broad claim from making further investigation? We think not.

The injustice of so holding is manifest in view of the experiments made, and continued for several months, by Mr. Edison and his assistants, among the different species of vegetable growth, for the purpose of ascertaining the one best adapted to an incandescent conductor. Of these he found suitable for his purpose only about three species of bamboo, one species of cane from the Valley of the Amazon, impossible to be procured in quantities on account of the climate, and one or two species of fibres from the agave family. Of the special bamboo, the walls of which have a thickness of about three-eighths of an inch, he used only about twenty-thousandths of an inch in thickness. In this portion of the bamboo the fibres are more nearly parallel, the cell walls are apparently smallest, and the pithy matter between the fibres is at its minimum. It seems that carbon filaments cannot be made of wood—that is, exogenous vegetable growth—because the fibres are not parallel and the longitudinal fibres are intercepted by radial fibres. The cells composing the fibres are all so large that there resulting carbon is very porous and friable. Lamps made of this material proved of no commercial value. After trying as many as thirty or forty different woods of exogenous growth, he gave them up as hopeless. But finally, while experimenting with a bamboo strip which formed the edge of a palmleaf fan, cut into filaments, he obtained surprising results. After microscopic examination of the material, he despatched a man to Japan to make arrangements for securing the bamboo in quantities. It seems that the characteristic of the bamboo which makes it particularly suitable is, that the fibres run more nearly parallel than in other species of wood. Owing to this, it can be cut up into filaments having parallel fibres, running throughout their length, and producing a homogeneous carbon. There is no generic quality, however, in vegetable fibres, because they are fibrous, which adapts them to the purpose. Indeed, the fibres are rather a disadvantage. If the bamboo grew solid without fibres, but had its peculiar cellular formation, it would be a perfect material, and incandescent lamps would last at least six times as long as at present. All vegetable fibrous growths do not have a suitable cellular structure. In some the cells are so large that they are valueless for that purpose. No exogenous, and very few endogenous, growths are suitable. The messenger whom he dispatched to different parts of Japan and China sent him about forty different kinds of bamboo, in such quantities as to enable him to make a number of lamps, and from a test of these different species he ascertained which was best for the purpose. From this it appears very clearly that there is no such quality common to fibrous and textile substances generally as makes them suitable for an incandescent conductor, and that the bamboo which was finally pitched upon, and is now generally used, was not selected because it was of vegetable growth, but because it contained certain peculiarities in its fibrous structure which distinguished it from every other fibrous substance. The question really is whether the imperfectly successful experiments of Sawyer and Man, with carbonized paper and wood carbon, conceding all that is claimed for them, authorize them to put under tribute the results of the brilliant discoveries made by others.

It is required by Rev. Stat. §4888 that the application shall contain a written description of the device "and of the manner and process of making, constructing, compounding, and using it in such full, clear, concise, and exact terms as to enable any person, skilled in the art or science to which it appertains or with which it is most nearly connected, to make, construct, compound, and use the same." The object of this is to apprise the public of what the patentee claims as his own, the courts of what they are called upon to construe, and competing manufacturers and dealers of exactly what they are bound to avoid. *Grant v. Raymond*, 6 Pet. [31 U.S.] 218, 247 [1832]. If the description be so vague and uncertain that no one can tell, except by independent experiments, how to construct the patented device, the patent is void.

It was said by Mr. Chief Justice Taney in *Wood v. Underhill*, 5 How. [46 U.S.] 1, 5 [1857], with respect to a patented compound for the purpose of making brick or tile, which did not give the relative proportions of the different ingredients:

> But when the specification of a new composition of matter gives only the names of the substances which are to be mixed together, without stating any relative proportion, undoubtedly it would be the duty of the court to declare the patent void. And the same rule would prevail where it was apparent that the proportions were stated ambiguously and vaguely. For in such cases it would be evident, on the face of the specification, that no one could use the invention without first ascertaining, by experiment, the exact proportion of the different ingredients required to produce the result intended to be obtained. . . . And if, from the nature and character of the ingredients to be used, they are not susceptible of such exact description, the inventor is not entitled to a patent.

So in *Tyler v. Boston*, 7 Wall. [74 U.S.] 327, 330 [1868], wherein the plaintiff professed to have discovered a combination of fuel oil with the mineral and earthy oils, constituting a burning fluid, the patentee stated that the exact quantity of fuel oil, which is necessary to produce the most desirable compound, must be determined by experiment. And the court observed: "Where a patent is claimed for such a discovery it should state the component parts of the new manufacture claimed with clearness and precision, and not leave a person attempting to use the discovery to find it out 'by experiment.'" *See also Bene v. Jeantet*, 129 U.S. 683 [(1889)].

If Sawyer and Man had discovered that a certain carbonized paper would answer the purpose, their claim to all carbonized paper would, perhaps, not be extravagant; but the fact that paper happens to belong to the fibrous kingdom did not invest them with sovereignty over this entire kingdom, and thereby practically limit other experimenters to the domain of minerals. . . .

We are all agreed that the claims of this patent, with the exception of the third, are too indefinite to be the subject of a valid monopoly. For the reasons above stated the decree of the Circuit Court is Affirmed.

COMMENTS AND QUESTIONS

1. The Court puts forth several rationales for the enablement requirement. For example, the Court asks: "Was everybody then precluded by this broad claim from making further investigation? We think not." What assumption lies behind this statement? Why should the patent system be concerned with "further investigation"? What purpose behind §112 is being served here?

2. Were *all* claims of the Sawyer and Man patent invalidated? Of what relevance, if any, is it that Edison's research resulted in several patents of his own? Does the fact that inventor *A* received a patent suggest anything about whether *A*'s research results are enabled by the specification of a prior patent issued to *B*?

3. Edison's discovery that only a certain type of bamboo plant would work as a filament is an example of his exhaustive research efforts. As we will see in the following section relating to patentable subject matter, the bamboo itself is not patentable, since it is a product of nature. It must be applied.

After isolating the precise type of bamboo that would work, Edison acted with characteristic speed on a characteristically grand scale: he tried to lock up as many acres of production of the bamboo as he could. *See* A. MILLARD, EDISON AND THE BUSINESS OF INNOVATION (1990). *Cf.* Jack Hirshleifer, *The Private and Social Value of Information and the Reward to Inventive Activity*, 61 AM. ECON. REV. 561 (1971) (positing reduced need for intellectual property protection, since inventors have "inside information" about their inventions, so they can reap gains by investing in assets that their inventions will make more valuable and selling short assets that their inventions will make less valuable).

4. The primary argument leveled against the validity of the patent in *Neilson v. Harford*, 1 Web. P. C. 295 (1841), was what modern courts would call lack of enablement. Neilson had disclosed little about the preheating apparatus and said nothing about the need to increase the surface area of the heating vessel when scaling up the process. *Id.* at 339. In rejecting that attack, the Exchequer expressly recognized that Neilson's means of preheating were routine and well known in the art. *Id.* at 344.

5. *Undue Experimentation Standard.* How much would Sawyer and Man have to disclose to justify a patent on all vegetable and fibrous filaments? What if they had tested 100 filaments, and they had all worked about as well? The Federal Circuit in *In re Wands*, 858 F.2d 731 (Fed. Cir. 1988), established that enablement is tested by asking whether the person having ordinary skill in the art would be able to make and use all the species covered by the patent without "undue experimentation." The multi-factor test considers: (1) the quantity of experimentation necessary, (2) the amount of direction or guidance presented, (3) the presence or absence of working examples, (4) the nature of the invention, (5) the state of the prior art, (6) the relative skill of those in the art, (7) the predictability or unpredictability of the art, and (8) the breadth of the claims.

6. *Person Having Ordinary Skill in the Art (PHOSITA) Standard.* As we saw in Section (B)(2) on nonobviousness, patent law employs a hypothetical person, like tort law's reasonable person, in evaluating patentability. As one court has noted:

> A patent specification is not addressed to judges or lawyers, but to those skilled in the art; it must be comprehensible to them, even though the unskilled may not be able to gather from it how to use the invention, and even if it is "all Greek" to the unskilled.

Gould v. Mossinghoff, 229 U.S.P.Q. 1 (D.D.C. 1985), *aff'd in part, vacated in part sub nom. Gould v. Quigg*, 822 F.2d 1074 (Fed. Cir. 1987).

Since relatively few judges or jurors today have science or engineering backgrounds, the parties in the case often must educate the court about the technology at issue.

7. In *Atlas Powder Co. v. E.I. du Pont De Nemours & Co.,* 750 F.2d 1569 (Fed. Cir. 1984), the court affirmed a finding that du Pont, the accused infringer, had not proved lack of enablement on the part of the patentee, Atlas Powder. The patent, for explosive compounds, listed in its specification numerous salts, fuels, and emulsifiers that could form thousands of emulsions, but it gave no commensurate information as to which combinations would work. Du Pont had argued that its tests showed a 40 percent failure rate in constructing various embodiments of the claimed invention. The court rejected this "inoperable species" argument:

> Of course, if the number of inoperative combinations becomes significant, and in effect forces one of ordinary skill in the art to experiment unduly in order to practice the claimed invention, the claims might indeed be invalid. *See, e.g.,* In re Cook, 439 F.2d 730, 735 (1971). That, however, has not been shown to be the case here. . . . The district court also found that one skilled in the art would know how to modify slightly many of [the experimental] "failures" to form a better emulsion.

Id. at 1576-77.

8. *"Analog" Claims in Chemical and Biotechnology Patents.* Many chemicals have "analogs." Two different molecules with almost identical chemical structure will normally behave in approximately the same way. So, too, similar DNA sequences normally have similar effects. The prevalence of analogs creates problems for those who try to patent new chemical or biological products. If they claim only the precise DNA sequence or chemical structure they have identified, it is relatively easy for others to "design around" their invention by varying an insignificant part of the total structure.

To avoid this problem, many patentees claim not only the precise structure they have produced, but its analogs as well. (This is akin to the claims of Sawyer and Man, in the *Incandescent Lamp* case, to fibrous and textile materials other than the paper they had actually experimented with.) To what extent a claim should be allowed to preempt such analogs is a difficult problem in patent law. In *Amgen, Inc. v. Chugai Pharmaceutical Co., Ltd.*, 927 F.2d 1200 (Fed. Cir. 1991), the plaintiff and defendant each held patents on technology related to the production of erythropoietin (EPO), a critical biological protein that stimulates production of red blood cells and is therefore effective in combating anemia and related conditions. Plaintiff Amgen held a patent on a recombinant DNA version of EPO, while defendant Chugai held a license from codefendant Genetics Institute under a product patent for purified EPO made by concentrating trace amounts of the protein from natural sources. The trial court had upheld certain claims in defendant's patent, and it ruled that plaintiff infringed; it also held that certain claims in both patents were invalid for failure to enable.

Plaintiff's recombinant EPO patent included key claim 7, which reads: "A purified and isolated DNA sequence consisting essentially of a DNA sequence encoding a polypeptide having an amino acid sequence sufficiently duplicative of that of erythropoietin to allow possession of the biological property of causing bone marrow cells to increase production of reticulocytes and red blood cells, and to increase hemoglobin synthesis or iron uptake." The "biological property" language, together with the descriptions of the two key functions—blood cell production and iron uptake—was intended to broaden the claim so as to cover any functional substitute or "analog" for the natural EPO protein. The following excerpt comes from the Federal Circuit's discussion of the validity of claim 7 and related claims.

The essential question here is whether the scope of enablement of claim 7 is as broad as the scope of the claim. . . .

The specification of [Amgen's] patent provides that:

> one may readily design and manufacture genes coding for microbial expression of polypeptides having primary conformations [i.e., proteins with a basic shape] which differ from that herein specified for mature EPO in terms of the identity or location of one or more residues [i.e., amino acids] (e.g., substitutions, terminal and intermediate additions and deletions). . . .
>
> DNA sequences provided by the present invention are thus seen to comprehend all DNA sequences suitable for use in securing expression in a procaryotic or eucaryotic host cell of a polypeptide product having at least a part of the primary structural conformation and one or more of the biological properties of erythropoietin. . . .

> The district court found that over 3,600 different EPO analogs can be made by substituting at only a single amino acid position [in the entire protein], and over a million different analogs can be made by substituting three amino acids. The patent indicates that it embraces means for preparation of "numerous" polypeptide analogs of EPO. Thus, the number of claimed DNA encoding sequences that can produce an EPO-like product is potentially enormous.

> In a deposition, Dr. Elliott, who was head of Amgen's EPO analog program, testified that he did not know whether the fifty to eighty EPO analogs Amgen had made "had the biological property of causing bone marrow cells to increase production of reticulocytes and red blood cells, and to increase hemoglobin synthesis or iron uptake" [as required by some of the claims]. Based on this evidence, the trial court [found a lack of enablement]. In making this determination, the court relied in particular on the lack of predictability in the art. . . . After five years of experimentation, the court noted, "Amgen is still unable to specify which analogs have the biological properties set forth in claim 7."

[Although] it is not necessary that a patent applicant test all the embodiments of his invention, *In re Angstadt*, 537 F.2d 498, 502 (C.C.P.A. 1976)[,] what is necessary is that he provide a disclosure sufficient to enable one skilled in the art to carry out the invention commensurate with the scope of his claims. For DNA sequences, that means disclosing how to make and use enough sequences to justify grant of the claims sought. Amgen has not done that here. It is well established that a patent applicant is entitled to claim his invention generically, when he describes it sufficiently to meet the requirements of Section 112. *See Utter v. Hiraga*, 845 F.2d 993, 998 (Fed. Cir. 1988) ("A specification may, within the meaning of 35 U.S.C. §112 ¶1, contain a written description of a broadly claimed invention without describing all species that claim encompasses."). Here, however, despite extensive statements in the specification concerning all the analogs of the EPO gene that can be made, there is little enabling disclosure of particular analogs and how to make them. Details for preparing only a few EPO analog genes are disclosed. Amgen argues that this is sufficient to support its claims; we disagree. This "disclosure" might well justify a generic claim encompassing these and similar analogs, but it represents inadequate support for Amgen's desire to claim all EPO gene analogs. There may be many other genetic sequences that code for EPO-type products. Amgen has told how to make and use only a few of them and is therefore not entitled to claim all of them.

In affirming the district court's [invalidation of these] claims, we do not intend to imply that generic claims to genetic sequences cannot be valid where they are of a scope appropriate to the invention disclosed by an applicant. That is not the case here, where Amgen has claimed every possible analog of a gene containing about 4,000 nucleotides, with a disclosure only of how to make EPO and a very few analogs.

Considering the structural complexity of the EPO gene, the manifold possibilities for change in its structure, with attendant uncertainty as to what utility will be possessed by these analogs, we consider that more is needed concerning identifying the various analogs that are within the scope of the claim, methods for making them, and structural requirements for producing compounds with EPO-like activity. It is not sufficient, having made the gene and a handful of analogs whose activity has not been clearly ascertained, to claim all possible genetic sequences that have EPO-like activity. Under the circumstances, we find no error in the court's conclusion that the generic DNA sequence claims are invalid under Section 112.

PROBLEM

Problem III-9. Suppose William Schrafft received a patent claiming "all food-based flavors" of jelly beans. In his specification, he discloses his method for manufacturing lemon and raspberry varieties. Several years later, during the patent's life, the wizard Bertie Bott (from the Harry Potter series) was experimenting with confections when a pair of dirty socks fell into his concoction. Recognizing the sales potential of sweets that present a "risk with every mouthful," he introduces "Bertie Bott's Every Flavour Beans," which includes "Bogey," "Dirt," "Dirty Sock," "Earthworm," "Earwax," "Envelope Glue," "Dirty Sock," "Phlegm," "Soap," and "Vomit," as well as a broad range of more appetizing flavors—including cherry, lemon, and kale (well, maybe not so appetizing). Can Bertie Bott successfully challenge or circumvent Schrafft's claim? How would you structure the analysis?

---

ii.   *The Written Description Requirement*

In addition to the enablement requirement, a series of cases developed the notion that §112(a) added a "written description" requirement. Originally seen as a doctrine that applied only when claims were amended during prosecution, it has been expanded to form an integral component of the law of patent disclosure. The basic standard is stated clearly enough in the cases: as of the application filing date, the applicant must show the inventor was "in possession" of the invention as later claimed. Courts compare the original disclosure with the final claims of an issued patent, and ask whether the applicant signified that the specific features and embodiments later claimed were in fact important aspects of the invention. As it has evolved, the doctrine has become a way to prevent applicants from claiming subject matter they were not themselves yet aware of, even if skilled artisans could have gleaned it from the patent specification. In recent years, courts have also used written description to test for claim overbreadth in a manner quite reminiscent of the classic enablement test. *See* Dennis Crouch, *An Empirical Study of the Role of the Written Description Requirement in Patent Examination*, 104 Nw. U. L. Rev. 1665, 1667-1668 (2010) (citing studies showing that most written description cases could also be decided on enablement grounds, and finding that in patent appeals at the PTO, written description was almost never used as a ground of invalidity).

The Gentry Gallery, Inc. v. The Berkline Corp.
United States Court of Appeals for the Federal Circuit
134 F.3d 1473 (Fed. Cir. 1998)

LOURIE, Circuit Judge.

The Gentry Gallery appeals from the judgment of the United States District Court for the District of Massachusetts holding that the Berkline Corporation does not infringe U.S. Patent 5,064,244, and declining to award attorney fees for Gentry's defense to Berkline's assertion that the patent was unenforceable. . . . Berkline cross-appeals from the decision that the patent was not shown to be invalid. . . . [B]ecause the court clearly erred in finding that the written description portion of the specification supported certain of the broader claims asserted by Gentry, we reverse the decision that those claims are not invalid under 35 U.S.C. §112, ¶1 (1994).

Background

Gentry owns the '244 patent, which is directed to a unit of a sectional sofa in which two independent reclining seats ("recliners") face in the same direction. Sectional sofas are typically organized in an L-shape with "arms" at the exposed ends of the linear sections. According to the patent specification, because recliners usually have had adjustment controls on their arms, sectional sofas were able to contain two recliners only if they were located at the exposed ends of the linear sections. Due to the typical L-shaped configuration of sectional sofas, the recliners therefore faced in different directions. *See* '244 patent; col. 1, ll. 15-19. Such an arrangement was "not usually comfortable when the occupants are watching television because one or both occupants must turn their heads to watch the same [television] set. Furthermore, the separation of the two reclining seats at opposite ends of a sectional sofa is not comfortable or conducive to intimate conversation." *Id.* at col. 1, ll. 19-25.

The invention of the patent solved this supposed dilemma by, *inter alia,* placing a "console" between two recliners which face in the same direction. This console "accommodates the controls for both reclining seats," thus eliminating the need to position each recliner at an exposed end of a linear section. *Id.* at col. 1, ll. 36-37. Accordingly, both recliners can then be located on the same linear section allowing two people to recline while watching television and facing in the same direction. Claim 1, which is the broadest claim of the patent, reads in relevant part:

A sectional sofa comprising:

a pair of reclining seats disposed in parallel relationship with one another in a double reclining seat sectional sofa section being without an arm at one end . . .,

each of said reclining seats having a backrest and seat cushions and movable between upright and reclined positions . . ., *a fixed console* disposed in the double reclining seat sofa section between the pair of reclining seats and with the console and reclining seats together comprising a unitary structure,

said console including an armrest portion for each of the reclining seats; said arm rests remaining fixed when the reclining seats move from one to another of their positions, and *a pair of control means*, one for each reclining seat, *mounted on the double reclining seat sofa section*. . . .

Id. at col. 4, line 68 to col. 5, ll. 1-27 (emphasis added to most relevant claim language). Claims 9, 10, 12-15, and 19-21 are directed to a sectional sofa in which the control means are specifically located on the console.

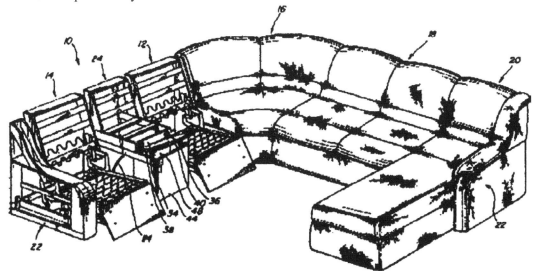

Patent drawing for the Gentry '244 patent.

In 1991, Gentry filed suit . . . alleging that Berkline infringed the patent by manufacturing and selling sectional sofas having two recliners facing in the same direction. In the allegedly infringing sofas, the recliners were separated by a seat which has a back cushion that may be pivoted down onto the seat, so that the seat back may serve as a tabletop between the recliners. . . . The district court granted Berkline's motion for summary judgment of non-infringement, but denied its motions for summary judgment of invalidity and unenforceability. In construing the language "fixed console," the court relied on, *inter alia,* a statement made by the inventor named in the patent, James Sproule, in a Petition to Make Special (PTMS). *See* 37 C.F.R. §1.102 (1997). Sproule had attempted to distinguish his invention from a prior art reference by arguing that the reference, U.S. Patent 3,877,747 to Brennan *et al.* ("Brennan"), "shows a complete center seat with a tray in its back." *Gentry I,* 30 U.S.P.Q.2d at 1137. Based on Sproule's argument, the court concluded that, as a matter of law, Berkline's sofas "contain[] a drop-down tray identical to the one employed by the Brennan product" and therefore did not have a "fixed console" and did not literally infringe the patent. *Id.* The court held that Gentry was also "precluded from recovery" under the doctrine of equivalents. *Id.* at 1138.

Invalidity . . .

Berkline . . . argues that claims 1-8, 11, and 16-18 are invalid because they are directed to sectional sofas in which the location of the recliner controls is not limited to the console. According to Berkline, because the patent only describes sofas having controls on the console and an object of the invention is to provide a sectional sofa "with a console . . . that accommodates the controls for both the reclining seats," '244 patent, col. 1, ll. 35-37, the claimed sofas are not described within the meaning of §112, ¶1. Berkline also relies on Sproule's testimony that "locating the controls on the console is definitely the way we solved it [the problem of building sectional sofa with parallel recliners] on the original group [of sofas]." Gentry responds that the disclosure represents only Sproule's preferred embodiment, in which the controls are on the console, and therefore supports claims directed to a sofa in which the controls may be located elsewhere. Gentry relies on *Ethicon Endo-Surgery, Inc. v. United States Surgical Corp.*, 93 F.3d 1572, 1582 n.7 (Fed. Cir. 1993), and *In re Rasmussen*, 650 F.2d 1212, 1214 (CCPA 1981), for the proposition that an applicant need not describe more than one embodiment of a broad claim to adequately support that claim.

We agree with Berkline that the patent's disclosure does not support claims in which the location of the recliner controls is other than on the console. Whether a specification complies with the written description requirement of §112, ¶1, is a question of fact, which we review for clear error on appeal from a bench trial. *See Vas-Cath Inc. v. Mahurkar*, 935 F.2d 1555, 1563 (Fed. Cir. 1991). To fulfill the written description requirement, the patent specification "must clearly allow persons of ordinary skill in the art to recognize that [the inventor] invented what is claimed." *In re Gosteli*, 872 F.2d 1008, 1012 (Fed. Cir. 1989). An applicant complies with the written description requirement "by describing *the invention,* with all its claimed limitations." *Lockwood v. American Airlines, Inc.*, 107 F.3d 1565, 1572 (Fed. Cir. 1997).

It is a truism that a claim need not be limited to a preferred embodiment. However, in a given case, the scope of the right to exclude may be limited by a narrow disclosure. For example, as we have recently held, a disclosure of a television set with a keypad, connected to a central computer with a video disk player did not support claims directed to "an individual terminal containing a video disk player." *See id.* (stating that claims directed to a "distinct invention from that disclosed in the specification" do not satisfy the written description requirement); *see also Regents of the Univ. of Cal. v. Eli Lilly & Co.*, 119 F.3d 1559, 1568 (Fed. Cir. 1997) (stating that the case law does "not compel the conclusion that a description of a species always constitutes a description of a genus of which it is a part").

In this case, the original disclosure clearly identifies the console as the only possible location for the controls. It provides for only the most minor variation in the location of the controls, noting that the control "may be mounted on top or side surfaces of the console rather than on the front wall . . . without departing from this invention." '244 patent, col. 2, line 68 to col. 3, line 3. No similar variation beyond the console is even suggested. Additionally, the only discernible purpose for the console is to house the controls. As the disclosure states, identifying the only purpose relevant to the console, "[a]nother object of the present invention is to provide . . . a console positioned between [the reclining seats] that accommodates the controls for both of the reclining seats." *Id.* at col. 1, ll. 33-37. Thus, locating the controls anywhere but on the console is outside the stated purpose of the invention. Moreover, consistent with this disclosure, Sproule's broadest original claim was directed to a sofa comprising, *inter alia,* "control means located upon the center console to enable each of the pair of reclining seats to move separately between the reclined and upright positions." Finally, although not dispositive, because one can add claims to a pending application directed to adequately described subject matter, Sproule admitted at trial that he did not consider placing the controls outside the console until he became aware that some of Gentry's competitors were so locating the recliner controls. Accordingly, when viewed in its entirety, the disclosure is limited to sofas in which the recliner control is located on the console.

Gentry's reliance on *Ethicon* is misplaced. It is true, as Gentry observes, that we noted that "an applicant . . . is generally allowed claims, when the art permits, which cover more than the specific embodiment shown." *Ethicon,* 93 F.3d at 1582 n.7 (quoting *In re Vickers*, 141 F.2d 522, 525 (CCPA 1944)). However, we were also careful to point out in that opinion that the applicant "was free to draft claim[s] broadly (within the limits imposed by the prior art) to exclude the lockout precise location as a limitation of the claimed invention" only because he "did not consider the precise location of the lockout to be an element of his invention." *Id.* Here, as indicated above, it is clear that Sproule considered the location of the recliner controls on the console to be an essential element of his invention. Accordingly, his original disclosure serves to limit the permissible breadth of his later-drafted claims.

Similarly, *In re Rasmussen* does not support Gentry's position. In that case, our predecessor court restated the uncontroversial proposition that "a claim may be broader than the specific embodiment disclosed in a specification." 650 F.2d at 1215. However, the court also made clear that "[a]n applicant is entitled to claims as broad as the prior art *and his disclosure* will allow." *Id.* at 1214 (emphasis added). The claims at issue in *Rasmussen,* which were limited to the generic step of "adheringly applying" one layer to an adjacent layer, satisfied the written description requirement only because "one skilled in the art who read [the] specification would understand that it is unimportant how the layers are adhered, so long as they are adhered." Here, on the contrary, one skilled in the art would clearly understand that it was not only important, but essential to Sproule's invention, for the controls to be on the console.

In sum, the cases on which Gentry relies do not stand for the proposition that an applicant can broaden his claims to the extent that they are effectively bounded only by the prior art. Rather, they make clear that claims may be no broader than the supporting disclosure, and therefore that a narrow disclosure will limit claim breadth. Here, Sproule's disclosure unambiguously limited the location of the controls to the console. Accordingly, the district court clearly erred in finding that he was entitled to claims in which the recliner controls are not located on the console. We therefore reverse the judgment that claims 1-8, 11, and 16-18, were not shown to be invalid.

COMMENTS AND QUESTIONS

1. The written description doctrine is more restrictive than the enablement requirement. That is, claims may meet the enablement test but fail the written description test. *See, e.g., Amgen Inc. v. Hoechst Marion Roussel, Inc.,* 314 F.3d 1313, 1334 (Fed. Cir. 2003) ("The enablement requirement is often more indulgent than the written description requirement. The specification need not explicitly teach those in the art to make and use the invention; the requirement is satisfied if, given what they already know, the specification teaches those in the art enough that they can make and use the invention without 'undue experimentation.'"). For example, a patent's disclosure may teach about a certain group of embodiments sufficiently that they can be made without "undue experimentation" under *The Incandescent Lamp Patent*, and yet not single out a specific feature that later appears in a claim. That patent would be invalid under the written description requirement.

2. Berkline's sofa recliners have the reclining controls on arm rests, seat edges, etc. *See www.berkline.com.* The district court stated that Gentry Gallery's amended claims were "'broad' but not unsupported." 939 F. Supp. 98, 105 (D. Mass. 1996). The district court stated that the invention had solved the "control quandary" of removing controls from arm rests and underneath seat cushions, and that this location of the controls on this central console was only one way of implementing the invention.

3. *Critique of the Written Description Doctrine.* Does it make sense to have both an enablement requirement and a written description requirement? If the inventor must teach one of ordinary skill in the art how to make and use the invention, why require them to write down the exact invention as well? *Cf. Moba v. Diamond Automation, Inc.,* 325 F.3d 1306, 1323 (Fed. Cir. 2003) (Rader, J., dissenting) ("Under Federal Circuit case law, [the plaintiff in this case] asked the jury to decide that the patent's disclosure can enable a skilled artisan to make and practice the entire invention, but still not inform that same artisan that the inventor was in possession of the invention. Perplexing."); *see* Harris A. Pitlick, *The Mutation on the Description Requirement Gene,* 80 J. PAT. & TRADEMARK OFF. SOC'Y 209, 222 (1998) (written description cases are "an unmitigated disaster"); Laurence H. Pretty, *The Recline and Fall of Mechanical Genus Claim Scope Under "Written Description" in the Sofa Case,* 80 J. PAT. & TRADEMARK OFF. SOC'Y 469 (1998). Can enablement do the work written description currently does? Robert P. Merges, *Software and Patent Scope: A Report from the Middle Innings,* 85 TEX. L. REV. 1627 (2007) (describing *Gentry Gallery* as an example

of "misappropriation by claim amendment," and suggesting that it could have been decided on enablement, not written description, grounds).

4. *Defense of the Written Description Doctrine*. The separate requirement of adequate written description has been defended on the ground that enablement doctrine is incapable of defining meaningful limits to claim scope. *See* Jeffrey A. Lefstin, *The Formal Structure of Patent Law and the Limits of Enablement*, 23 BERKELEY TECH. L.J. 1141 (2008). Lefstin argues that almost every claim includes in theory an infinite number of embodiments, so that no specification actually teaches how to make all or substantially all claimed embodiments. Written description steps in at this point; its requirement that embodiments be actually described resolves the logical deficiencies of enablement doctrine. Written description, properly understood, is a doctrine of *definition*. One might respond that it is the rigid logic of contemporary enablement doctrine that creates this need, and that an alternative to written description is a relaxing of these doctrinal rigidities—a fix from "within" enablement, which would dispense with the need for a separate doctrine. But for Professor Lefstin, the problem is inherent in the effort to draft a claim to cover a universe of actual and potential embodiments.

5. *Biotechnology Claims and Gun-Jumping*. The application of the written description requirement to biotechnology claims has been a particularly controversial issue. A number of cases beginning in the late 1990s required inventors to disclose specific gene sequences to claim them, even when functional properties of a gene (such as the protein it codes for) were already known. *See Regents of the University of California v. Eli Lilly & Co.*, 119 F.3d 1559 (Fed. Cir. 1997) (claims covering gene sequence for human insulin invalidated under written description requirement, where specification disclosed only sequence of rat insulin); Janice M. Mueller, *The Evolving Application of the Written Description Requirement to Biotechnological Inventions*, 13 BERKELEY TECH. L.J. 615 (1998). If *Gentry Gallery* and its ilk were about late claiming–trying to change the patent to cover things the inventor had not in fact thought of–the biotechnology cases are about "gun-jumping"–leaving the gate before the starter has fired the pistol. The patent race motivates inventors to lay claim to an invention at the earliest possible moment, and sometimes before it is the inventor's grasp. We will see that this same concern arises with regard to the utility requirement, discussed in Chapter III(B)(5).

7. *The Separate Written Description Requirement*. In *Ariad Pharmaceuticals, Inc. v. Eli Lilly & Co.*, 598 F.3d 1336 (Fed. Cir. 2010) (en banc), the Federal Circuit established unequivocally that the written description requirement of §112(a) is separate and apart from enablement. The court based its analysis on a close but controversial textual reading analysis of §112(a), focusing on punctuation and the placement of "and" connectors, as well as precedent, *see Schriber-Schroth Co. v. Cleveland Trust Co.*, 305 U.S. 47, 56-57 (1938); *Vas-Cath Inc. v. Mahurkar*, 935 F.2d 1555, 1562-63 (Fed Cir. 1991).

Ariad clarifies application of the doctrine. The specification must clearly demonstrate to a PHOSITA that the inventor possessed what is claimed as of the filing date. It is a question of fact that depends on the context: nature and scope of the claims; complexity and predictability of relevant technology; extent and content of the prior art; maturity of the science or technology. The requirement has particular relevance to genus claims so as to ensure that the scope is commensurate with the invention. Notably, the Federal Circuit denied that "possession" itself was the touchstone for written description, though it did not articulate an alternative formulation.

The court's application of the test to a breakthrough biotechnology discovery emphasized the "gun-jumping" analysis. The invention at issue was made in a new and unpredictable field. And although Ariad had hypothesized three classes of molecules potentially capable of achieving its broad claim of reducing NF-κB (nuclear factor kappa-light-chain-enhancer of activated B cells) activity, the disclosure was more in the nature of a research plan: Ariad had not actually produced any of those molecules at the time it filed its patent application. Notwithstanding that Ariad's conjectures were ultimately borne out, the court ruled that Ariad was not adequately in possession of the necessary knowledge at the time that they filed their application. A key figure in the file which established the effects was not disclosed until two years after the application date. Ariad sought to salvage the patent by arguing that a PHOSITA could have achieved the result based on the original specification through experimentation. The court concluded, however, that "[i]n the context of this invention, a vague functional description and invitation for further research does not constitute written description of a specific inhibitor [molecule]."

PROBLEM

Problem III-10. Slice-O-Rama is a company that makes food preparation items, including cheese slicers. It owns a U.S. patent covering a cheese slicer with a novel twist: The cutting element is a wire, which can be stretched between an end point and a handle. The slicer is well-received by the public and is even the subject of a national design award. One element in the claim calls for "a cutting wire" stretched between a handle and a fixed point on the base of the cutting element arm.

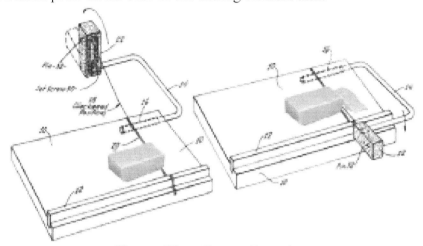

Cheese Slicer Patent Drawing

OmniCorp is a large conglomerate with numerous divisions in various industries. One division, BigChem, Inc., is in the business of developing and manufacturing plastics. In the wake of research on new plastics, BigChem has come up with a plastic that is capable of holding a sharp cutting edge. Deemed "sharpylene," it can be manufactured in a variety of thicknesses, including a very thin version that looks like a wire or piece of string. As part of an internal initiative to encourage various divisions of OmniCorp to work more closely, Fran Fromage, product manager for the food processor and blender product lines in OmniCorp's FoodMulch division, comes across a sample of the BigChem plastic. Being familiar with the popularity of the Slice-O-Rama cheese slicer, she hits on the idea of substituting BigChem's new plastic in place of the metal wire. She believes that this cheese slicer would be an important addition to the FoodMulch product line. She is aware of the Slice-O-Rama patent, but as she puts it, "how can that patent stop us from selling blades made from plastic that *we invented*?! Those folks over at Slice-O-Rama have never even heard of sharpylene!"

You are a member of the patent department at OmniCorp. Assuming that the FoodMulch cheese slicer will meet all limitations other than the "cutting wire" element in the Slice-O-Rama patent, how would you advise Ms. Fromage?

5. Patentable Subject Matter

Section 101 protects "any" "process, machine, manufacture, or composition of matter" or "improvement thereof . . . subject to the conditions and requirements of this title." Essentially the same language has been part of U.S. patent law since 1790. Although the Patent Act has not expressly excluded any subject matter for much of U.S. history,[7] courts have long recognized that there are limits on the types of inventions that are eligible for patenting. These limits emerged during the early to mid-nineteenth century as Anglo-American common law-trained jurists fleshed out the relatively terse requirements for patent eligibility.

Thus, we find the contours of these doctrines not in the text of the Patent Act but in two centuries of jurisprudence that has ebbed and flowed with technological advances, perspectives on scientific discovery, and concerns about whether the patent system encourages or stifles new inventions. Patent eligibility doctrines began to lose salience in the early 1980s as the Federal Circuit substantially liberalized the scope of patentable subject matter. The Supreme Court was silent on patentable subject matter from 1981 until 2010. Since then, the Court has issued four opinions that have redrawn the boundaries of patent eligible subject matter and reinvigorated litigation in the area. *See Bilski v. Kappos*, 561 U.S. 593 (2010); *Mayo Collaborative Servs. v. Prometheus Labs., Inc.*, 132 S.Ct. 1289 (2012); *Ass'n for Molecular Pathology v. Myriad Genetics, Inc.*, 133 S.Ct. 2107 (2013); *Alice Corp. v. CLS Bank Int'l*, 134 S.Ct. 2347 (2014). Most patents in force today issued when the subject matter eligible for patent protection was broader. Consequently, the number of invalidations based on §101 has grown substantially since 2010.

Navigating the boundaries of patentable subject matter requires careful study of the Supreme Court's recent decisions as well as the history that led to these cases.

i. *The Evolution of Patentable Subject Matter Limitations*

Like the modern Patent Act, the nation's first patent statutes authorized granting of patents for a broad range of subject matter—"any new and useful art, machine, manufacture, or composition of matter"—without express limitations. Courts came to recognize that patentability of broad scientific principles and abstract claims created the need for patent eligibility and scope limitations—what we today consider §112 concerns. These concepts were intertwined in the early jurisprudence and continue to overlap today.

---

[7] The AIA, for the first time, expressly excludes specific subject matter categories, namely patents on tax strategies and human organisms. *See* Pub. L. 112-29, §§14, 33, 125 Stat. 284 (2011).

a.   Early Development of Patent Eligibility Limitations

In the years following the nation's founding, English cases greatly influenced American jurisprudence. Intellectual property law followed English statutes and traditions particularly closely.

With the industrial revolution picking up steam (so to speak), courts on both sides of the Atlantic struggled to delineate claims for groundbreaking inventions, such as the steam engine, sewing machine, telegraph, and telephone. Scientific discoveries in metallurgy, chemistry, and electricity fueled the industrial revolution. Patenting of the hot blast process, which historians view as "the most important single innovation in the industry in the age of iron," would prove especially significant to patent eligibility doctrine. *See* ALAN BIRCH, THE ECONOMIC HISTORY OF THE BRITISH IRON AND STEEL INDUSTRY 1784–1879, 181 (1968).

Scottish inventor James Beaumont Neilson challenged the conventional wisdom that hot blast furnaces worked best if they were fed cold air. Instead, Neilson preheated the air entering a furnace which substantially reduced the fuel required and enabled the use of raw coal and lower quality ores. Neilson's patent provided few details. The specification declared broadly that the composition of the air vessel, the manner of applying heat, and "[t]he form or shape of the receptacle" are immaterial to the effect.

Neilson sued numerous ironmakers for patent infringement. The litigation led to the decision in the English Court of the Exchequer, *Neilson v. Harford* (1841), that still reverberates in U.S. patent jurisprudence today. The patent was attacked on the ground that a patent for injecting hot air into the furnace, instead of cold, and thereby increasing the intensity of the heat, was a patent for a principle, and that an abstract (unapplied) principle was not patentable. In upholding the patent, the court reasoned that since the principle worked regardless of the dimensions of the receptacle in which the air was preheated, Neilson's invention did not claim the principle itself but an application of the principle, if a broad one, and thus was patent-eligible.

U.S. courts followed the English approach. They barred protection for a mere "principle," "motive" force, or "new power" in the abstract, but allowed patents on applications of newly discovered laws of nature. The Supreme Court explained in *Le Roy v. Tatham*, where a patent claimed both improved machinery for manufacturing lead pipe and a new property (the manufacture of wrought pipe from solid lead under heat and pressure), that

> [a] principle, in the abstract, is a fundamental truth; an original cause; a motive; these cannot be patented, as no one can claim in either of them an exclusive right. Through the agency of machinery a new steam power may be said to have been generated. But no one can appropriate this power exclusively to himself, under the patent laws. The same may be said of electricity, and of any other power in nature, which is alike open to all, and may be applied to useful purposes by the use of machinery.

In all such cases, the processes used to extract, modify, and concentrate natural agencies, constitute the invention. The elements of the power exist; the invention is not in discovering them, but in *applying* them to useful objects. . . .

55 U.S. (14 How.) 156, 175 (1853) (emphasis added).

As we saw earlier, the Supreme Court addressed *Neilson* again the following year in *O'Reilly v. Morse*, 56 U.S. (15 How.) 62 (1854). While endorsing the requirement that patents must apply a law of nature, the Court nonetheless distinguished Neilson's claim from Morse's final claim. *Id.* Whereas the effect that Neilson claimed (improving the functioning of a hot blast furnace) produced the desired effect for "whatever might be the form of the receptacle, or the mechanical contrivances for heating it, or for passing the current of air through it, and into the furnace," Morse had "not discovered, that the electric or galvanic current will always print at a distance, no matter what may be the form of the machinery or mechanical contrivances through which it passes." *Id.* at 116-17.

By the end of the nineteenth century, American patent eligibility doctrine merely required that the patentee "carry the principle into effect, however simple and self-evident such means may be." *See* DAVID FULTON, THE LAW AND PRACTICE RELATING TO PATENTS, TRADE MARKS AND DESIGNS 41 (1902); *see also* ROBERT FROST, A TREATISE ON THE LAW AND PRACTICE OF LETTERS PATENT FOR INVENTIONS 36 (1891) ("Principles in a concrete form, together with a mode of applying them to a new and useful purpose, may form the subject of a grant of letters patent. . . . It is not necessary that the means, as well as the principle, should be new, for the novelty of the invention consists in applying the new principle by the means specified."). This view continued well into the twentieth century. *See* CAESAR & RIVISE, PATENTABILITY AND VALIDITY, §§33, 34 (1936) (observing that "[i]n the cases where the inventor was required to be also the discoverer of the law or force utilized, it appeared that the application or utilization of the law became self-evident as soon as the principle was formulated").

b. *Funk Brothers: The Emergence of Eligibility Skepticism*

The Supreme Court's decision in *Funk Brothers Seed Co. v. Kalo Inoculant Co.*, 333 U.S. 127 (1948), curtailed patent protection for natural products. The patentee in the case, Kalo Inoculant Company, claimed

An inoculant for leguminous plants comprising a plurality of selected mutually non-inhibitive strains of different species of bacteria of the genus Rhizobium, said strains being unaffected by each other in respect to their ability to fix nitrogen in the leguminous plant for which they are selected.

Such bacteria promote plant growth. When the invention was made, it was known that bacteria of the genus *Rhizobium* naturally exist in symbiosis with leguminous plants, such as peas and beans. Farmers routinely mixed *Rhizobium* cultures with leguminous plants to fix nitrogen from the air into the soil. Unfortunately, particular species of the

Rhizobium genus can colonize only particular legumes. Mixing different *Rhizobium* species into a single commercial product, however, proved unsuccessful. The bacteria species exert inhibitory effects on each other when mixed together. As a result, farmers needed to apply separate cultures to each leguminous crop, adding cost and complication. Kalo discovered that particular combinations of naturally occurring *Rhizobium* bacteria were not inhibitory and, therefore, could be packaged together into a product to be applied across leguminous plants more conveniently. He claimed, however, not a specific combination of bacteria but the idea of combining noninhibitory strains, whatever they turned out to be.

A divided Supreme Court invalidated the patent on eligibility grounds: it did "not disclose an invention or discovery within the meaning of the patent statutes." *Funk Bros.*, 333 U.S. at 132. The Court explained:

> [P]atents cannot issue for the discovery of phenomena of nature. The qualities of these bacteria, like the heat of the sun, electricity, or the quality of metals, are part of the storehouse of knowledge of all men. They are manifestations of laws of nature, free to all men and reserved exclusively to none. He who discovers a hitherto unknown phenomenon of nature has no claim to a monopoly of it which the law recognizes. If there is to be invention from such a discovery, it must come from the *application* of the law of nature to a new and useful end. . . .

> Discovery of the fact that certain strains of each species of these bacteria can be mixed without harmful effect to the properties of either is a discovery of their qualities of non-inhibition. It is no more than the discovery of some of the handiwork of nature and hence is not patentable. *The aggregation of select strains of the several species into one product is an application of that newly-discovered natural principle.* But however ingenious the discovery of that natural principle may have been, the application of it is hardly more than an advance in the packaging of the inoculants.

Id. at 131 (emphasis added). Justice Douglas acknowledged that the inventor had applied the law of nature, but nonetheless invalidated the claim as insufficiently inventive in its application of the newly-discovered natural principle. The Court noted that

> a product must be more than new and useful to be patented; it must also satisfy the requirements of invention or discovery. *Cuno Eng'g Corp. v. Automatic Devices Corp.*, 314 U.S. 84, 90, 91 (1941), and cases cited; 35 U.S.C. §31. The application of this newly-discovered natural principle to the problem of packaging of inoculants may well have been an important commercial advance. But once nature's secret of the non-inhibitive quality of certain strains of the species of Rhizobium was discovered, the state of the art made the production of a mixed inoculant a simple step. Even though it may have been the product of skill, it certainly was not the product of invention.

Id. at 131-32.

In a concurring opinion, Justice Frankfurter offered an alternate basis for invalidation reminiscent of the *Morse* decision. In his view, the patent was invalid not for unpatentable subject matter but rather for want of adequate identification of successful combinations of mutually non-inhibitory bacteria. *Funk Bros.*, 333 U.S. at 133. He went on to observe

> It only confuses the issue . . . to introduce such terms as 'the work of nature' and the 'laws of nature.' For these are vague and malleable terms infected with too much ambiguity and equivocation. Everything that happens may be deemed 'the work of nature,' and any patentable composite exemplifies in its properties 'the laws of nature.' Arguments drawn from such terms for ascertaining patentability could fairly be employed to challenge almost every patent.

Id. at 134-35.[8]

Following Funk Brothers, several appellate decisions implemented its holding. They hold newly discovered scientific principles to be unpatentable and require inventive application of such principles. *See, e.g., Davison Chem. Corp. v. Joliet Chems., Inc.*, 179 F.2d 793 (7th Cir. 1950); *In re Arnold*, 185 F.2d 686 (C.C.P.A. 1950); *Nat'l Lead Co. v. W. Lead Prods. Co.*, 324 F.2d 539 (9th Cir. 1963).

c. The New Technological Age

The dawn of the digital age presented new patent eligibility issues for the Supreme Court. The inventor in *Gottschalk v. Benson*, 409 U.S. 63 (1972), claimed an algorithm for converting binary-coded decimal numerals into pure binary numerals. In upholding the PTO's rejection of the patent on subject matter grounds, a unanimous Court, drawing upon *Le Roy*, *Morse*, and *Funk Brothers*, articulated three principles for determining whether a process is patentable: (1) "[p]henomena of nature, though just discovered, mental processes, and abstract intellectual concepts are not patentable, as they are the basic tools of scientific and technological work," *id.* at 67; (2) "[t]ransformation and reduction of an article 'to a different state or thing' is the clue to the patentability of a process claim that does not include particular machines," *id.* at 70; and (3) algorithms may not be patented so as to avoid the practical effect of "wholly pre-empt[ing a] mathematical formula," *id.* at 71. Echoing concerns raised by various amicus briefs, the Court concluded by calling on Congress to take up the question of whether and to what extent computer programs ought to be patentable. *See id.* at 71-73.

Six years later in *Parker v. Flook*, 437 U.S. 584 (1978), the Supreme Court addressed whether a procedure for updating an alarm limit—measuring the present value of a process variable (such as temperature), using an algorithm to calculate an

---

[8] Justices Burton and Jackson dissented, finding the product claims within the scope of patentable subject matter and adequately disclosed. *Funk Bros.*, at 136.

updated alarm-limit value, and adjusting the updated value—was eligible for patent protection. Writing for the majority in a sharply divided opinion, Justice Stevens expressly embraced an *inventive* application doctrine in upholding the PTO's rejection of the claim. The Court grounded the doctrine on the statement in *Neilson* that "'*the case must be considered as if the principle being well known, the plaintiff had first invented a mode of applying it . . . .*'" *Flook*, 437 U.S. at 592 (quoting *Morse*, quoting *Neilson*). Based on this sentence from *Neilson*, the Supreme Court reasoned that "this case must also be considered as if the principle or mathematical formula were well known" and that patent eligibility required sufficient inventiveness beyond the application of the algorithm to be within the scope of patentable subject matter. *Id.* at 592, 594-95. The Court declared:

> Even though a phenomenon of nature or mathematical formula may be well known, an *inventive application* of the principle may be patented. Conversely, the discovery of such a phenomenon cannot support a patent unless there is some other inventive concept in its application.

Id. at 594 (emphasis added).

Query: Did the Court interpret *Neilson* (and *Morse*'s interpretation of *Neilson*) correctly?

Justice Stewart, with whom Chief Justice Burger and Justice Rehnquist joined, dissenting, did not see the patent at issue as pre-empting use of the algorithm, but rather as a potentially patentable application of it. *Id.* at 599. He criticized the majority opinion for excluding a process from the scope of patentable subject matter because "*one step* in the process would not be patentable subject matter if considered in isolation." The dissent observed that "thousands of processes and combinations have been patented that contained one or more steps or elements that themselves would have been unpatentable subject matter." *Id.* (citation omitted; emphasis in original). The majority opinion responded to this contention by noting that the process is unpatentable "not because it contains a mathematical algorithm as one component, but because once that algorithm is assumed to be within the prior art, the application, considered as a whole, contains no patentable invention," *id.* at 594—the *inventive* application doctrine.

As the Court grappled with the patentability of computer software, it also confronted the patentability of genetically modified organisms. *See Diamond v. Chakrabarty*, 447 U.S. 303 (1980). The inventor claimed a self-replicating bacterium into which he had injected oil-degrading plasmids that could be used in dispersing oil spills. *Id.* at 305. The PTO rejected the claim on the grounds that microorganisms are "products of nature" and living things, both of which make them ineligible for patent protection under §101. *Id.* at 306. The Court of Customs and Patent Appeals reversed, upholding the claim under the standards set forth in *Flook*.

The Supreme Court affirmed the appellate court decision, opening the way for patent protection for genetically modified organisms. *Id.* at 318. Writing for the majority, Chief Justice Burger characterized the Constitution's grant of patent legislative authority and §101's text broadly. *Chakrabarty*, 447 U.S. at 307-08. While recognizing the unpatentability of "laws of nature, physical phenomena, and abstract ideas," the Court judged Chakrabarty's claim to a "nonnaturally occurring manufacture or composition of matter—a product of human ingenuity "having a distinctive name, character [and] use"—to "plainly" qualify for patent eligibility. *Id.* at 309-10 (quoting *Hartranft v. Wiegmann*, 121 U.S. 609, 615 (1887)). Drawing a contrast to *Funk Brothers*, the Court noted that Chakrabarty "has produced a new bacterium with markedly different characteristics from any found in nature and one having the potential for significant utility. His discovery is not nature's handiwork, but his own." *Id.* at 310.[9]

Moreover, *Chakrabarty* interpreted the scope of patent-eligible subject matter expansively, stressing that §101 encompasses any invention falling within the four designated categories. *Id.* at 308-09. The Supreme Court also looked to the legislative history of the 1952 Patent Act, from which it concluded that "Congress intended statutory subject matter to 'include anything under the sun that is made by man.'"[10] *Id.* at 309.

Propelled in part by *Chakrabarty*'s broad reading of patent eligibility, the pendulum swung decisively away from *Flook* the next year. Writing for the majority, Justice Rehnquist explained that processes have been eligible for patent protection since the 1793 Act and referenced the statement from *Benson* that "[t]ransformation and reduction of an article 'to a different state or thing' is the clue to the patentability of a process claim that does not include particular machines." *Diamond v. Diehr*, 450 U.S. 175, 184 (1981) (quoting *Benson*, 409 U.S. at 70). The Court concluded that "a physical and chemical process for molding precision synthetic rubber products falls within the §101 categories of possibly patentable subject matter." *Id.* Justice Rehnquist purported to distinguish *Benson* and *Flook* before proclaiming that "[o]ur earlier opinions lend support to our present conclusion that a claim drawn to subject matter otherwise statutory does not become nonstatutory simply because it uses a mathematical formula, computer program, or digital computer." *Id.* at 187. The Court emphasized that process claims are properly analyzed

---

[9] Justice Brennan, joined by Justices White, Marshall, and Powell, dissented on the grounds that the 1930 and 1970 plant patent statutes indicate that that Congress did not believe that newly developed living organisms were patentable under §101. *Id.* at 320-21.

[10] The full passage from which this quotation was taken is arguably less expansive. *See* Brief Amici Curiae of Professors Peter S. Menell and Michael J. Meurer In Support of Respondent, Bilski v. Kappos, U.S. S.Ct. No 08-964, at 19-22, http://papers.ssrn.com/sol3/papers.cfm?abstract_id=1482022.

as a whole. It is inappropriate to dissect the claims into old and new elements and then to ignore the presence of the old elements in the analysis. This is particularly true in a process claim because a new combination of steps in a process may be patentable even though all the constituents of the combination were well known and in common use before the combination was made. The 'novelty' of any element or steps in a process, or even of the process itself, is of no relevance in determining whether the subject matter of a claim falls within the §101 categories of possibly patentable subject matter.

Id. at 188-89. In so holding, Justice Rehnquist seemed to overrule *Flook*'s requirement of *inventive* application. He reiterated, however, that "a mathematical formula as such" is not patentable nor is limiting the use of a formula to a particular technological environment, citing *Benson* and *Flook. Id.* at 191. The touchstone for patentability of a process embodying a mathematical formula, according to the majority opinion, is significant post-solution activity—i.e., "transforming or reducing an article to a different state or thing." *Id.* at 191-92.

Justice Stevens, joined by Justices Brennan, Marshall, and Blackmun, dissented, emphasizing that the majority eviscerated *Flook*'s inventive application requirement. To the dissenters, if the inventor's "method is regarded as an 'algorithm' as that term was used" in *Benson* and *Flook*, "and if no other inventive concept is disclosed in the patent application," then the claim falls outside the scope of patentable processes under §101. *Id.* at 213-14. Moreover, the dissenters contended that "the postsolution activity described in the *Flook* application was no less significant than the automatic opening of the curing mold involved in [*Diehr*]." *Id.* at 215.

d. The Rise of the Federal Circuit and Dismantling of Patentable Subject Matter Limitations

In the ensuing three decades, the Federal Circuit gradually eroded patent eligibility limitations. Building off of *Diehr*, the Federal Circuit chipped away at the post-solution activity necessary to bring software-related claims within §101. *See, e.g., In re Alappat*, 33 F.3d 1526 (Fed. Cir. 1994) (holding that the display of data on a computer screen could suffice). Similarly, the Federal Circuit endorsed the PTO's policy of permitting the patenting of isolated DNA molecules. *See Amgen, Inc. v. Chugai Pharm. Co.*, 927 F.2d 1200 (Fed. Cir. 1991). In a departure from prior jurisprudence—see *Hotel Sec. Checking Co. v. Lorraine Co.*, 160 Fed. 467, 469, 479 (2nd Cir. 1908); WILLIAM ANTHONY DELLER, 1 WALKER ON PATENTS: DELLER'S EDITION, 62, 69 (1937)—the Federal Circuit "la[id the] ill-conceived [business method] exception to rest." *State St. Bank v. Signature Fin. Grp.*, 149 F.3d 1368, 1375 (Fed. Cir. 1998). At the time, the Supreme Court declined to weigh in on these controversies.

The Federal Circuit's loosening of patent eligibility standards expanded the range of patents being issued. The PTO shifted its position from skepticism about expansive patent eligibility to openness and even enthusiasm. Patents for software, DNA, and business methods flooded the PTO. Entrepreneurs and venture capitalists saw patenting as a valuable tool for developing (or at least claiming) Internet businesses. The late 1990s witnessed unprecedented growth of start-up businesses based on speculative initial public offerings secured, in part, on patent portfolios.

The bursting of the Internet (dot-com) stock bubble in 2000 produced a dramatic shake-out. Bankruptcies and subsequently, the auctioning and trading of Internet-related patents, became widespread. Entities whose sole purpose was to assert these patents emerged. Patent holding companies and non-practicing entities sought to monetize their Internet patents, purchased at fire sales. Lawsuits by patent assertion entities produced a tidal wave of patent validity challenges as well as calls by Silicon Valley companies, policymakers, and scholars for policy reform.

In the late 2000s the Federal Circuit issued several decisions that cautiously reintroduced limits on patent eligibility. *See, e.g.*, *In re Nuijten*, 500 F.3d 1346 (Fed. Cir. 2007) (holding that a watermarked electromagnetic signal does not fall into any of the four categories of patent-eligible subject matter); *In re Comiskey*, 499 F.3d 1365 (Fed. Cir. 2007), *amended by* 554 F.3d 967 (Fed. Cir. 2009) (affirming rejection of a business method patent under §101 as merely relying on mental steps). Most notably, the Federal Circuit, sitting en banc, attempted to clarify the boundaries of patentable subject matter under §101. *See In re Bilski*, 545 F.3d 943 (Fed. Cir. 2008) (en banc).

Bilski claimed a method of managing risk of commodity prices—a business method that a computer could implement:

> A method for managing the consumption risk costs of a commodity sold by a commodity provider at a fixed price comprising the steps of:
>
> > (a) initiating a series of transactions between said commodity provider and consumers of said commodity wherein said consumers purchase said commodity at a fixed rate based upon historical averages, said fixed rate corresponding to a risk position of said consumer;
> >
> > (b) identifying market participants for said commodity having a counter-risk position to said consumers; and
> >
> > (c) initiating a series of transactions between said commodity provider and said market participants at a second fixed rate such that said series of market participant transactions balances the risk position of said series of consumer transactions.

Claim 1, U.S. Patent Application No. 08/833,892. In an effort to harmonize the Supreme Court's *Benson*, *Flook*, and *Diehr* precedents, the Federal Circuit articulated the "machine-or-transformation" (MoT) test "to determine whether a process claim is tailored narrowly enough to encompass only a particular application of a fundamental principle rather than to pre-empt the principle itself." Under the MoT test, a claimed process is patent-eligible under §101 if: "(1) it is tied to a particular machine or apparatus, or (2) it transforms a particular article into a different state or thing." The court concluded that the Bilski patent failed both prongs and hence was unpatentable: it was not tied to a "particular" machine. Further, the transformation of legal obligations or relationships, business risks, or other abstractions is not a tangible change, eligible for patent protection.

ii.   *The Supreme Court's Revival of Subject Matter Limitations*

The Supreme Court opened a new chapter in patent eligibility jurisprudence with its grant of review in the *Bilski* case. The majority ruled that Bilski's broad independent claim to hedging was "an unpatentable abstract idea, just like the algorithms at issue in *Benson* and *Flook*. Allowing petitioners to patent risk hedging would pre-empt use of this approach in all fields, and would effectively grant a monopoly over an abstract idea." *Id.* at 611-12. The Court further rejected Bilski's narrower dependent claims as unpatentable by reference to *Flook*, which "established that limiting an abstract idea to one field of use or adding token postsolution components did not make the concept patentable." *Id.*

While affirming the Federal Circuit's decision holding Bilski's hedging patent application invalid, the Supreme Court rejected the MoT test as the sole test of patent eligibility of process claims. Nonetheless, the Supreme Court characterized the MoT test as a "useful and important clue, an investigative tool, for determining whether some claimed inventions are processes under §101," but too rigid given the broad statutory definition in §100(b) of "process." *Id.* at 603-04. While recognizing the jurisprudentially developed exclusions for laws of nature, natural phenomena, and abstract ideas, the Court nonetheless warned that the judiciary does not have "*carte blanche* to impose other limitations that are inconsistent with the text and the statute's purpose and design." *Id.* at 603. On similar grounds, the majority rejected the argument that business methods are categorically excluded from patent eligibility. *Id.* at 606-08.

Justice Stevens, joined by Justices Ginsburg, Breyer, and Sotomayor, concurred in the judgment, but contended that the Patent Act and jurisprudence have long categorically excluded business methods from patent eligibility. *Id.* at 613. The opinion grounded its conclusion in constitutional limits on legislative power. Article I, §8, cl. 8 authorizes Congress to grant patents for discoveries so as to promote "useful Arts." The "useful Arts" translate to "technology" in modern parlance. Justice Stevens did not believe that innovations in business methods fell within this domain. "During the 17th and 18th centuries, Great Britain saw innovations in business organization, business models, management techniques, and novel solutions to the challenges of operating global firms[, yet f]ew if any of these methods of conducting business were patented." *Id.* at 631 (footnotes omitted).

The Supreme Court then turned to patents on medical diagnostic processes.

Mayo Collaborative Services v. Prometheus Laboratories, Inc.
Supreme Court of the United States
132 S.Ct. 1289 (2012)

BREYER, J. (for a unanimous Court):

Section 101 of the Patent Act defines patentable subject matter. It says:

> Whoever invents or discovers any new and useful process, machine, manufacture, or composition of matter, or any new and useful improvement thereof, may obtain a patent therefor, subject to the conditions and requirements of this title.

The Court has long held that this provision contains an important implicit exception. "[L]aws of nature, natural phenomena, and abstract ideas" are not patentable. *Diamond v. Diehr*, 450 U.S. 175, 185 (1981); *Le Roy v. Tatham*, 14 How. 156, 175 (1853); *O'Reilly v. Morse*, 15 How. 62, 112–120 (1854); *cf. Neilson v. Harford*, Webster's Patent Cases 295, 371 (1841) (English case discussing same). Thus, the Court has written that "a new mineral discovered in the earth or a new plant found in the wild is not patentable subject matter. Likewise, Einstein could not patent his celebrated law that E=mc²; nor could Newton have patented the law of gravity. Such discoveries are 'manifestations of . . . nature, free to all men and reserved exclusively to none.'" *Chakrabarty, supra*, at 309 (quoting *Funk Brothers Seed Co. v. Kalo Inoculant Co.*, 333 U.S. 127, 130 (1948)).

> "Phenomena of nature, though just discovered, mental processes, and abstract intellectual concepts are not patentable, as they are the basic tools of scientific and technological work." *Gottschalk v. Benson*, 409 U.S. 63, 67 (1972). And monopolization of those tools through the grant of a patent might tend to impede innovation more than it would tend to promote it.

The Court has recognized, however, that too broad an interpretation of this exclusionary principle could eviscerate patent law. For all inventions at some level embody, use, reflect, rest upon, or apply laws of nature, natural phenomena, or abstract ideas. Thus, in *Diehr* the Court pointed out that "'a process is not unpatentable simply because it contains a law of nature or a mathematical algorithm.'" 450 U.S., at 187 (quoting *Parker v. Flook*, 437 U.S. 584, 590 (1978)). It added that "an *application* of a law of nature or mathematical formula to a known structure or process may well be deserving of patent protection." *Diehr, supra*, at 187. And it emphasized Justice Stone's similar observation in *Mackay Radio & Telegraph Co. v. Radio Corp. of America*, 306 U.S. 86 (1939):

> "'While a scientific truth, or the mathematical expression of it, is not a patentable invention, a novel and useful structure created with the aid of knowledge of scientific truth may be.'" 450 U.S., at 188 (quoting *Mackay Radio, supra*, at 94).

See also Funk Brothers, supra at 130 ("If there is to be invention from [a discovery of a law of nature], it must come from the application of the law of nature to a new and useful end").

Still, as the Court has also made clear, to transform an unpatentable law of nature into a patent-eligible *application* of such a law, one must do more than simply state the law of nature while adding the words "apply it." *See, e.g., Benson, supra,* at 71–72.

The case before us lies at the intersection of these basic principles. It concerns patent claims covering processes that help doctors who use thiopurine drugs to treat patients with autoimmune diseases determine whether a given dosage level is too low or too high. The claims purport to apply natural laws describing the relationships between the concentration in the blood of certain thiopurine metabolites and the likelihood that the drug dosage will be ineffective or induce harmful side-effects. We must determine whether the claimed processes have transformed these unpatentable natural laws into patent-eligible applications of those laws. We conclude that they have not done so and that therefore the processes are not patentable.

Our conclusion rests upon an examination of the particular claims before us in light of the Court's precedents. Those cases warn us against interpreting patent statutes in ways that make patent eligibility "depend simply on the draftsman's art" without reference to the "principles underlying the prohibition against patents for [natural laws]." *Flook, supra,* at 593. They warn us against upholding patents that claim processes that too broadly preempt the use of a natural law. *Morse, supra,* at 112–120; *Benson, supra,* at 71–72. And they insist that a process that focuses upon the use of a natural law also contain other elements or a combination of elements, sometimes referred to as an "inventive concept," sufficient to ensure that the patent in practice amounts to significantly more than a patent upon the natural law itself. *Flook, supra,* at 594; *see also Bilski, supra,* at 3218, 130 S.Ct. at 3230 ("[T]he prohibition against patenting abstract ideas 'cannot be circumvented by attempting to limit the use of the formula to a particular technological environment' or adding 'insignificant postsolution activity' " (quoting *Diehr, supra,* at 191–192)).

We find that the process claims at issue here do not satisfy these conditions. In particular, the steps in the claimed processes (apart from the natural laws themselves) involve well-understood, routine, conventional activity previously engaged in by researchers in the field. At the same time, upholding the patents would risk disproportionately tying up the use of the underlying natural laws, inhibiting their use in the making of further discoveries.

I

A

The patents before us concern the use of thiopurine drugs in the treatment of autoimmune diseases, such as Crohn's disease and ulcerative colitis. When a patient ingests a thiopurine compound, his body metabolizes the drug, causing metabolites to form in his bloodstream. Because the way in which people metabolize thiopurine compounds varies, the same dose of a thiopurine drug affects different people differently, and it has been difficult for doctors to determine whether for a particular patient a given dose is too high, risking harmful side effects, or too low, and so likely ineffective.

At the time the discoveries embodied in the patents were made, scientists already understood that the levels in a patient's blood of certain metabolites, including, in particular, 6–thioguanine and its nucleotides (6–TG) and 6–methyl–mercaptopurine (6–MMP), were correlated with the likelihood that a particular dosage of a thiopurine drug could cause harm or prove ineffective. *See* U.S. Patent No. 6,355,623, col.8, ll.37–40, 2 App. 10. ("Previous studies suggested that measurement of 6–MP metabolite levels can be used to predict clinical efficacy and tolerance to azathioprine or 6–MP" (citing Cuffari, Théorêt, Latour, & Seidman, *6–Mercaptopurine Metabolism in Crohn's Disease: Correlation with Efficacy and Toxicity*, 39 GUT 401 (1996))). But those in the field did not know the precise correlations between metabolite levels and likely harm or ineffectiveness. The patent claims at issue here set forth processes embodying researchers' findings that identified these correlations with some precision.

More specifically, the patents—U.S. Patent No. 6,355,623 ('623 patent) and U.S. Patent No. 6,680,302 ('302 patent)—embody findings that concentrations in a patient's blood of 6–TG or of 6–MMP metabolite beyond a certain level (400 and 7000 picomoles per 8×10^8 red blood cells, respectively) indicate that the dosage is likely too high for the patient, while concentrations in the blood of 6–TG metabolite lower than a certain level (about 230 picomoles per 8×10^8 red blood cells) indicate that the dosage is likely too low to be effective.

The patent claims seek to embody this research in a set of processes. Like the Federal Circuit we take as typical claim 1 of the '623 Patent, which describes one of the claimed processes as follows:

> "A method of optimizing therapeutic efficacy for treatment of an immune-mediated gastrointestinal disorder, comprising:
>
> "(a) administering a drug providing 6–thioguanine to a subject having said immune-mediated gastrointestinal disorder; and
>
> "(b) determining the level of 6–thioguanine in said subject having said immune-mediated gastrointestinal disorder,
>
> "wherein the level of 6–thioguanine less than about 230 pmol per 8x108 red blood cells indicates a need to increase the amount of said drug subsequently administered to said subject and
>
> "wherein the level of 6–thioguanine greater than about 400 pmol per 8x108 red blood cells indicates a need to decrease the amount of said drug subsequently administered to said subject." '623 patent, col.20, ll.10–20, 2 App. 16.

For present purposes we may assume that the other claims in the patents do not differ significantly from claim 1. . . .

II

Prometheus' patents set forth laws of nature—namely, relationships between concentrations of certain metabolites in the blood and the likelihood that a dosage of a thiopurine drug will prove ineffective or cause harm. Claim 1, for example, states that if the levels of 6–TG in the blood (of a patient who has taken a dose of a thiopurine drug) exceed about 400 pmol per 8×10^8 red blood cells, then the administered dose is likely to produce toxic side effects. While it takes a human action (the administration of a thiopurine drug) to trigger a manifestation of this relation in a particular person, the relation itself exists in principle apart from any human action. The relation is a consequence of the ways in which thiopurine compounds are metabolized by the body—entirely natural processes. And so a patent that simply describes that relation sets forth a natural law.

The question before us is whether the claims do significantly more than simply describe these natural relations. To put the matter more precisely, do the patent claims add enough to their statements of the correlations to allow the processes they describe to qualify as patent-eligible processes that apply natural laws? We believe that the answer to this question is no.

A

If a law of nature is not patentable, then neither is a process reciting a law of nature, unless that process has additional features that provide practical assurance that the process is more than a drafting effort designed to monopolize the law of nature itself. A patent, for example, could not simply recite a law of nature and then add the instruction "apply the law." Einstein, we assume, could not have patented his famous law by claiming a process consisting of simply telling linear accelerator operators to refer to the law to determine how much energy an amount of mass has produced (or vice versa). Nor could Archimedes have secured a patent for his famous principle of flotation by claiming a process consisting of simply telling boat builders to refer to that principle in order to determine whether an object will float.

What else is there in the claims before us? The process that each claim recites tells doctors interested in the subject about the correlations that the researchers discovered. In doing so, it re-cites an "administering" step, a "determining" step, and a "wherein" step. These additional steps are not themselves natural laws but neither are they sufficient to transform the nature of the claim.

First, the "administering" step simply refers to the relevant audience, namely doctors who treat patients with certain diseases with thiopurine drugs. That audience is a pre-existing audience; doctors used thiopurine drugs to treat patients suffering from autoimmune disorders long before anyone asserted these claims. In any event, the "prohibition against patenting abstract ideas 'cannot be circumvented by attempting to limit the use of the formula to a particular technological environment.'" *Bilski, supra,* 130 S.Ct., at 3230 (quoting *Diehr,* 450 U.S., at 191–192).

Second, the "wherein" clauses simply tell a doctor about the relevant natural laws, at most adding a suggestion that he should take those laws into account when treating his patient. That is to say, these clauses tell the relevant audience about the laws while trusting them to use those laws appropriately where they are relevant to their decisionmaking (rather like Einstein telling linear accelerator operators about his basic law and then trusting them to use it where relevant).

Third, the "determining" step tells the doctor to determine the level of the relevant metabolites in the blood, through whatever process the doctor or the laboratory wishes to use. As the patents state, methods for determining metabolite levels were well known in the art. '623 patent, col.9, ll.12–65, 2 App. 11. Indeed, scientists routinely measured metabolites as part of their investigations into the relationships between metabolite levels and efficacy and toxicity of thiopurine compounds. '623 patent, col.8, ll.37–40, *id.,* at 10. Thus, this step tells doctors to engage in well-understood, routine, conventional activity previously engaged in by scientists who work in the field. Purely "conventional or obvious" "[pre]-solution activity" is normally not sufficient to transform an unpatentable law of nature into a patent-eligible application of such a law. *Flook,* 437 U.S., at 590; *see also Bilski,* 130 S.Ct., at 3230 ("[T]he prohibition against patenting abstract ideas 'cannot be circumvented by' . . . adding 'insignificant post-solution activity'" (quoting *Diehr,* supra, at 191–192)).

Fourth, to consider the three steps as an ordered combination adds nothing to the laws of nature that is not already present when the steps are considered separately. *See Diehr, supra,* at 188 ("[A] new combination of steps in a process may be patentable even though all the constituents of the combination were well known and in common use before the combination was made"). Anyone who wants to make use of these laws must first administer a thiopurine drug and measure the resulting metabolite concentrations, and so the combination amounts to nothing significantly more than an instruction to doctors to apply the applicable laws when treating their patients.

The upshot is that the three steps simply tell doctors to gather data from which they may draw an inference in light of the correlations. To put the matter more succinctly, the claims inform a relevant audience about certain laws of nature; any additional steps consist of well-understood, routine, conventional activity already engaged in by the scientific community; and those steps, when viewed as a whole, add nothing significant beyond the sum of their parts taken separately. For these reasons we believe that the steps are not sufficient to transform unpatentable natural correlations into patentable applications of those regularities.

B

1

A more detailed consideration of the controlling precedents reinforces our conclusion. The cases most directly on point are *Diehr* and *Flook,* two cases in which the Court reached opposite conclusions about the patent eligibility of processes that embodied the equivalent of natural laws. The *Diehr* process (held patent eligible) set forth a method for molding raw, uncured rubber into various cured, molded products. The process used a known mathematical equation, the Arrhenius equation, to determine when (depending upon the temperature inside the mold, the time the rubber had been in the mold, and the thickness of the rubber) to open the press.

The Court pointed out that the basic mathematical equation, like a law of nature, was not patentable. But it found the overall process patent eligible because of the way the additional steps of the process integrated the equation into the process as a whole. Those steps included "installing rubber in a press, closing the mold, constantly determining the temperature of the mold, constantly recalculating the appropriate cure time through the use of the formula and a digital computer, and automatically opening the press at the proper time." *Id.,* at 187. It nowhere suggested that all these steps, or at least the combination of those steps, were in context obvious, already in use, or purely conventional. And so the patentees did not "seek to pre-empt the use of [the] equation," but sought "only to foreclose from others the use of that equation in conjunction with all of the other steps in their claimed process." *Ibid.* These other steps apparently added to the formula something that in terms of patent law's objectives had significance— they transformed the process into an inventive application of the formula.

The process in *Flook* (held not patentable) provided a method for adjusting "alarm limits" in the catalytic conversion of hydrocarbons. Certain operating conditions (such as temperature, pressure, and flow rates), which are continuously monitored during the conversion process, signal inefficiency or danger when they exceed certain "alarm limits." The claimed process amounted to an improved system for updating those alarm limits through the steps of: (1) measuring the current level of the variable, e.g., the temperature; (2) using an apparently novel mathematical algorithm to calculate the current alarm limits; and (3) adjusting the system to reflect the new alarm-limit values. 437 U.S., at 585–587.

The Court, as in *Diehr,* pointed out that the basic mathematical equation, like a law of nature, was not patentable. But it characterized the claimed process as doing nothing other than "provid[ing] a[n unpatentable] formula for computing an updated alarm limit." *Flook, supra,* at 586. Unlike the process in *Diehr,* it did not "explain how the variables used in the formula were to be selected, nor did the [claim] contain any disclosure relating to chemical processes at work or the means of setting off an alarm or adjusting the alarm limit." *Diehr, supra,* at 192, n. 14; *see also Flook,* 437 U.S., at 586. And so the other steps in the process did not limit the claim to a particular application. Moreover, "[t]he chemical processes involved in catalytic conversion of hydrocarbons[,] . . . the practice of monitoring the chemical process variables, the use of alarm limits to trigger alarms, the notion that alarm limit values must be recomputed and readjusted, and the use of computers for 'automatic monitoring-alarming'" were all "well known," to the point where, putting the formula to the side, there was no "inventive concept" in the claimed application of the formula. *Id.,* at 594. "[P]ost-solution activity" that is purely "conventional or obvious," the Court wrote, "can[not] transform an unpatentable principle into a patentable process." *Id.,* at 589, 590.

The claim before us presents a case for patentability that is weaker than the (patent-eligible) claim in *Diehr* and no stronger than the (unpatentable) claim in *Flook.* Beyond picking out the relevant audience, namely those who administer doses of thiopurine drugs, the claim simply tells doctors to: (1) measure (somehow) the current level of the relevant metabolite, (2) use particular (unpatentable) laws of nature (which the claim sets forth) to calculate the current toxicity/inefficacy limits, and (3) reconsider the drug dosage in light of the law. These instructions add nothing specific to the laws of nature other than what is well-understood, routine, conventional activity, previously engaged in by those in the field. And since they are steps that must be taken in order to apply the laws in question, the effect is simply to tell doctors to apply the law somehow when treating their patients. The process in *Diehr* was not so characterized; that in *Flook* was characterized in roughly this way.

2

Other cases offer further support for the view that simply appending conventional steps, specified at a high level of generality, to laws of nature, natural phenomena, and abstract ideas cannot make those laws, phenomena, and ideas patentable. This Court has previously discussed in detail an English case, *Neilson,* which involved a patent claim that posed a legal problem very similar to the problem now before us. The patent applicant there asserted a claim

> "for the improved application of air to produce heat in fires, forges, and furnaces, where a blowing apparatus is required. [The invention] was to be applied as follows: The blast or current of air produced by the blowing apparatus was to be passed from it into an air-vessel or receptacle made sufficiently strong to endure the blast; and through or from that vessel or receptacle by means of a tube, pipe, or aperture into the fire, the receptacle be kept artificially heated to a considerable temperature by heat externally applied." *Morse,* 15 How., at 114–15.

The English court concluded that the claimed process did more than simply instruct users to use the principle that hot air promotes ignition better than cold air, since it explained how the principle could be implemented in an inventive way. Baron Parke wrote (for the court):

> "It is very difficult to distinguish [Neilson's claim] from the specification of a patent for a principle, and this at first created in the minds of some of the

court much difficulty; but after full consideration, we think that the plaintiff does not merely claim a principle, but a machine embodying a principle, and a very valuable one. We think the case must be considered as if the principle being well known, the plaintiff had first invented a mode of applying it by a mechanical apparatus to furnaces; and his invention then consists in this—by interposing a receptacle for heated air between the blowing apparatus and the furnace. In this receptacle he directs the air to be heated by the application of heat externally to the receptacle, and thus he accomplishes the object of applying the blast, which was before of cold air, in a heated state to the furnace." *Neilson v. Harford*, Webster's Patent Cases, at 371.

Thus, the claimed process included not only a law of nature but also several unconventional steps (such as inserting the receptacle, applying heat to the receptacle externally, and blowing the air into the furnace) that confined the claims to a particular, useful application of the principle.

In *Bilski* the Court considered claims covering a process for hedging risks of price changes by, for example, contracting to purchase commodities from sellers at a fixed price, reflecting the desire of sellers to hedge against a drop in prices, while selling commodities to consumers at a fixed price, reflecting the desire of consumers to hedge against a price increase. One claim described the process; another reduced the process to a mathematical formula. 130 S.Ct., at 3223–3224. The Court held that the described "concept of hedging" was "an unpatentable abstract idea." *Id.*, 130 S.Ct., 3239. That some claims limited hedging to use in commodities and energy markets and specified that "well-known random analysis techniques [could be used] to help establish some of the inputs into the equation." did not undermine this conclusion, for "*Flook* established that limiting an abstract idea to one field of use or adding token postsolution components did not make the concept patentable." *Id.*, 130 S.Ct., at 3231.

Finally, in *Benson* the Court considered the patentability of a mathematical process for converting binary-coded decimal numerals into pure binary numbers on a general purpose digital computer. The claims "purported to cover any use of the claimed method in a general-purpose digital computer of any type." 409 U.S., at 64. The Court recognized that "'a novel and useful structure created with the aid of knowledge of scientific truth'" might be patentable. *Id.*, at 673 (quoting *Mackay Radio*, 306 U.S., at 94). But it held that simply implementing a mathematical principle on a physical machine, namely a computer, was not a patentable application of that principle. For the mathematical formula had "no substantial practical application except in connection with a digital computer." *Benson, supra*, at 71. Hence the claim (like the claims before us) was overly broad; it did not differ significantly from a claim that just said "apply the algorithm."

3

The Court has repeatedly emphasized [the] concern that patent law not inhibit further discovery by improperly tying up the future use of laws of nature. Thus, in

Morse the Court set aside as unpatentable Samuel Morse's general claim for "'the use of the motive power of the electric or galvanic current ... however developed, for making or printing intelligible characters, letters, or signs, at any distances,'" 15 How., at 86. The Court explained:

> "For aught that we now know some future inventor, in the onward march of science, may discover a mode of writing or printing at a distance by means of the electric or galvanic current, without using any part of the process or combination set forth in the plaintiff's specification. His invention may be less complicated—less liable to get out of order—less expensive in construction, and in its operation. But yet if it is covered by this patent the inventor could not use it, nor the public have the benefit of it without the permission of this patentee." *Id.,* at 113.

Similarly, in *Benson* the Court said that the claims before it were "so abstract and sweeping as to cover both known and unknown uses of the [mathematical formula]." 409 U.S., at 67, 68. In *Bilski* the Court pointed out that to allow "petitioners to patent risk hedging would pre-empt use of this approach in all fields." 130 S.Ct., at 3231. And in *Flook* the Court expressed concern that the claimed process was simply "a formula for computing an updated alarm limit," which might "cover a broad range of potential uses." 437 U.S., at 586.

These statements reflect that, even though rewarding with patents those who discover new laws of nature and the like might well encourage their discovery, those laws and principles, considered generally, are "the basic tools of scientific and technological work." *Benson, supra,* at 67. And so there is a danger that the grant of patents that tie up their use will inhibit future innovation premised upon them, a danger that becomes acute when a patented process amounts to no more than an instruction to "apply the natural law," or otherwise forecloses more future invention than the underlying discovery could reasonably justify. *See generally* Lemley, Risch, Sichelman, & Wagner, *Life After* Bilski, 63 STAN. L .REV. 1315 (2011) (hereinafter Lemley) (arguing that §101 reflects this kind of concern); *see also* C. BOHANNAN & H. HOVENKAMP, CREATION WITHOUT RESTRAINT: PROMOTING LIBERTY AND RIVALRY IN INNOVATION 112 (2012) ("One problem with [process] patents is that the more abstractly their claims are stated, the more difficult it is to determine precisely what they cover. They risk being applied to a wide range of situations that were not anticipated by the patentee"); W. LANDES & R. POSNER, THE ECONOMIC STRUCTURE OF INTELLECTUAL PROPERTY LAW 305–306 (2003) (The exclusion from patent law of basic truths reflects "both . . . the enormous potential for rent seeking that would be created if property rights could be obtained in them and ... the enormous transaction costs that would be imposed on would-be users [of those truths]").

The laws of nature at issue here are narrow laws that may have limited applications, but the patent claims that embody them nonetheless implicate this concern. They tell a treating doctor to measure metabolite levels and to consider the resulting measurements in light of the statistical relationships they describe. In doing so, they tie up the doctor's subsequent treatment decision whether that treatment does, or does not, change in light of the inference he has drawn using the correlations. And they threaten to inhibit the development of more refined treatment recommendations (like that embodied in Mayo's test), that combine Prometheus' correlations with later discovered features of metabolites, human physiology or individual patient characteristics. The "determining" step too is set forth in highly general language covering all processes that make use of the correlations after measuring metabolites, including later discovered processes that measure metabolite levels in new ways.

We need not, and do not, now decide whether were the steps at issue here less conventional, these features of the claims would prove sufficient to invalidate them. For here, as we have said, the steps add nothing of significance to the natural laws themselves. Unlike, say, a typical patent on a new drug or a new way of using an existing drug, the patent claims do not confine their reach to particular applications of those laws. The presence here of the basic underlying concern that these patents tie up too much future use of laws of nature simply reinforces our conclusion that the processes described in the patents are not patent eligible, while eliminating any temptation to depart from case law precedent.

III

We have considered several further arguments in support of Prometheus' position. But they do not lead us to adopt a different conclusion. First, the Federal Circuit, in upholding the patent eligibility of the claims before us, relied on this Court's determination that "[t]ransformation and reduction of an article 'to a different state or thing' is *the clue* to the patentability of a process claim that does not include particular machines." *Benson, supra,* at 70–71 (emphasis added). It reasoned that the claimed processes are therefore patent eligible, since they involve transforming the human body by administering a thiopurine drug and transforming the blood by analyzing it to determine metabolite levels. 628 F.3d, at 1356–1357.

The first of these transformations, however, is irrelevant. As we have pointed out, the "administering" step simply helps to pick out the group of individuals who are likely interested in applying the law of nature. And the second step could be satisfied without transforming the blood, should science develop a totally different system for determining metabolite levels that did not involve such a transformation. Regardless, in stating that the "machine-or-transformation" test is an "*important and useful clue*" to patentability, we have neither said nor implied that the test trumps the "law of nature" exclusion. *Bilski,* 130 S.Ct., at 3225–3227 (emphasis added). That being so, the test fails here.

Second, Prometheus argues that, because the particular laws of nature that its patent claims embody are narrow and specific, the patents should be upheld. Thus, it encourages us to draw distinctions among laws of nature based on whether or not they will interfere significantly with innovation in other fields now or in the future. Brief for Respondent 42–46; *see also* Lemley 1342–1344 (making similar argument).

But the underlying functional concern here is a *relative* one: how much future innovation is foreclosed relative to the contribution of the inventor. A patent upon a narrow law of nature may not inhibit future research as seriously as would a patent upon Einstein's law of relativity, but the creative value of the discovery is also considerably smaller. And, as we have previously pointed out, even a narrow law of nature (such as the one before us) can inhibit future research.

In any event, our cases have not distinguished among different laws of nature according to whether or not the principles they embody are sufficiently narrow. *See, e.g., Flook,* 437 U.S. 584 (holding narrow mathematical formula unpatentable). And this is understandable. Courts and judges are not institutionally well suited to making the kinds of judgments needed to distinguish among different laws of nature. And so the cases have endorsed a bright-line prohibition against patenting laws of nature, mathematical formulas and the like, which serves as a somewhat more easily administered proxy for the underlying "building-block" concern.

Third, the Government argues that virtually any step beyond a statement of a law of nature itself should transform an unpatentable law of nature into a potentially patentable application sufficient to satisfy §101's demands. Brief for United States as Amicus Curiae. The Government does not necessarily believe that claims that (like the claims before us) extend just minimally beyond a law of nature should receive patents. But in its view, other statutory provisions—those that insist that a claimed process be novel, 35 U.S.C. §102, that it not be "obvious in light of prior art," §103, and that it be "full[y], clear[ly], concise[ly], and exact[ly]" described, §112—can perform this screening function. In particular, it argues that these claims likely fail for lack of novelty under §102.

This approach, however, would make the "law of nature" exception to §101 patentability a dead letter. The approach is therefore not consistent with prior law. The relevant cases rest their holdings upon section 101, not later sections.

We recognize that, in evaluating the significance of additional steps, the §101 patent-eligibility inquiry and, say, the §102 novelty inquiry might sometimes overlap. But that need not always be so. And to shift the patent-eligibility inquiry entirely to these later sections risks creating significantly greater legal uncertainty, while assuming that those sections can do work that they are not equipped to do.

What role would laws of nature, including newly discovered (and "novel") laws of nature, play in the Government's suggested "novelty" inquiry? Intuitively, one would suppose that a newly discovered law of nature is novel. The Government, however, suggests in effect that the novelty of a component law of nature may be disregarded when evaluating the novelty of the whole. *See* Brief for United States as Amicus Curiae 27. But §§102 and 103 say nothing about treating laws of nature as if they were part of the prior art when applying those sections. *Cf. Diehr,* 450 U.S., at 188 (patent claims "must be considered as a whole"). And studiously ignoring *all* laws of nature when evaluating a patent application under §§102 and 103 would "make all inventions unpatentable because all inventions can be reduced to underlying principles of nature which, once known, make their implementation obvious." *Id.,* at 189, n. 12, 101 S.Ct. 1048. *See also* Eisenberg, *Wisdom of the Ages or Dead–Hand Control? Patentable Subject Matter for Diagnostic Methods After* In re Bilski, 3 CASE W. RES. J.L. TECH. & INTERNET 1, [62-63] (2012).

Section 112 requires only a "written description of the invention TTT in such full, clear, concise, and exact terms as to enable any person skilled in the art to make and use the same." It does not focus on the possibility that a law of nature (or its equivalent) that meets the[] [disclosure] conditions will nonetheless create [a] risk that a patent on the law would significantly impede future innovation.

These considerations lead us to decline the Government's invitation to substitute §§102, 103, and 112 inquiries for the better established inquiry under §101.

Fourth, Prometheus, supported by several amici, argues that a principle of law denying patent coverage here will interfere significantly with the ability of medical researchers to make valuable discoveries, particularly in the area of diagnostic research. That research, which includes research leading to the discovery of laws of nature, is expensive; it "ha[s] made the United States the world leader in this field"; and it requires protection. Brief for Respondent 52.

Other medical experts, however, argue strongly against a legal rule that would make the present claims patent eligible, invoking policy considerations that point in the opposite direction. [Various medical organizations] tell us that if "claims to exclusive rights over the body's natural responses to illness and medical treatment are permitted to stand, the result will be a vast thicket of exclusive rights over the use of critical scientific data that must remain widely available if physicians are to provide sound medical care." Brief for American College of Medical Genetics et al. as Amici Curiae 7.

We do not find this kind of difference of opinion surprising. Patent protection is, after all, a two-edged sword. On the one hand, the promise of exclusive rights provides monetary incentives that lead to creation, invention, and discovery. On the other hand, that very exclusivity can impede the flow of information that might permit, indeed spur, invention, by, for example, raising the price of using the patented ideas once created, requiring potential users to conduct costly and time-consuming searches of existing patents and pending patent applications, and requiring the negotiation of complex licensing arrangements. . . .

* * *

For these reasons, we conclude that the patent claims at issue here effectively claim the underlying laws of nature themselves. The claims are consequently invalid. And the Federal Circuit's judgment is reversed.

COMMENTS AND QUESTIONS

1. The Supreme Court summarized the representative patent claim at issue as comprising three components: (1) an administering step; (2) a determining step; and (3) a wherein clause. The Court declares that "to transform an unpatentable law of nature into a patent-eligible application of such a law, one must do more than simply state the law of nature while adding the words 'apply it.' Could the patentee have cured its eligibility problem by claiming that the thiopurine dosage be modified based on the blood chemistry change, rather than merely "indicating" a change in the "wherein" clause? Would that have changed the claim from being merely a glorified observation of a natural fact into a true process that leads to actions that cause some effects? Why might the patentee have claimed its invention in such an oblique way?

2. *Inventive Application.* The decision revives the inventive application framework set forth in *Flook*, a test that appeared to have been overridden by *Diehr*. In so doing, the Court based the decision, as it did in *Flook*, on *Neilson v. Harford*, stating that "the claimed process [in *Neilson*] included not only a law of nature but also several unconventional steps (such as inserting the receptacle, applying heat to the receptacle externally, and blowing the air into the furnace) that confined the claims to a particular, useful application of the principle." Did the *Mayo* Court interpret *Neilson* (and *Morse*'s interpretation of *Neilson*) correctly? What is unconventional about inserting a receptacle, applying heat to the receptacle externally, and blowing air into the furnace? As noted in note 4 following the *Incandescent Lamp Patent* case (relating to enablement), the Court of Exchequer considered the Neilson's application of discovery (preheating air prior to injection into the furnace) to be "perfectly well known."

So why would Baron Parke have said "[w]e think the case must be considered as if the principle being well known, ..."? The answer lies in the prior sentence: "we think that the plaintiff does not merely claim a principle, but a machine embodying a principle, and a very valuable one." The Court of Exchequer was drawing an analogy to *Minter v. Wells*, Carpmael's Patent Cases 622 (1834), which held that a broad claim to a reclining chair embodying a well-known scientific principle (the self-adjusting leverage) was drawn to a machine as opposed to merely claiming a principle of mechanics in the abstract. The *Neilson* decision was merely postulating a counter-factual scenario so as to analogize to *Minter*. *See* Brief of Professors Jeffrey A. Lefstin & Peter S. Menell as Amici Curiae in Support of Petition for a Writ of Certiorari, *Sequenom, Inc. v. Ariosa Diagnostics, Inc.*, No. 15-1182 (Apr. 29, 2016), http://papers.ssrn.com/sol3/papers.cfm?abstract_id=2767904. The Exchequer concluded that Neilson's claim, like Minter's, was to a machine and not merely an abstract scientific principle. Neilson's discovery, that preheating air before injecting into a blast furnace would improve combustion over the prior art (injecting unheated air), was in fact new and, as the court noted, very valuable. *See generally* Jeffrey A. Lefstin, *Inventive Application: A History*, 67 FLA. L. REV. 565 (2015). Thus, both *Flook* and *Mayo* based the inventive application requirement on a profound misunderstanding of the *Neilson* case.

3. How does §101 patentable subject matter eligibility analysis compare with §103 nonobviousness analysis? How does determination of whether application of a law of nature is "well-understood, routine, conventional" compare with whether "the differences between the subject matter sought to be patented and the prior art are such that the subject matter as a whole would have been obvious at the time the invention was made to a person having ordinary skill in the art to which said subject matter pertains"?

4. *Inventions and Discoveries.* Art. I, §8, Cl. 8 of the U.S. CONSTITUTION grants Congress power to establish patent protection for "Discoveries." U.S. patent law has, since its inception in 1790, authorized the granting of patents for "inventions and discoveries." The 1952 Patent Act defines "invention" to mean "invention or discovery." §100(a). Does the judicially-established inventive application standard override legislative intent as reflected in the text of the patent acts? Under *Mayo*, are conventional applications of new discoveries patentable?

5. *Preemption Rationale.* Citing *Morse*, the *Mayo* Court emphasizes that its limits on patent eligibility are based on concerns about preempting the use of a natural law, i.e., conferring overbroad monopoly power and interfering with cumulative creativity. Isn't *Morse* better understood as a case about overbroad claiming—the specification did not support a claim to all methods of communicating at a distance using electromagnetism? How does §101 patentable subject matter eligibility analysis compare with the §112(a) written description requirement? In *Dolbear v. Am. Bell Tel. Co.*, 126 U.S. 1, 535 (1888), the Supreme Court explained that an inventor's claim might practically preempt all of a discovery. Such breadth would "show []the great importance of [the] discovery, but it will not invalidate [the] patent." Does §112 provide sufficient tools for ensuring that patents do not extend beyond their proper scope? Or is there room for patentable subject matter to police patent overreaching? *See* Mark A. Lemley et al., *Life After Bilski*, 63 STAN. L. REV. 1315 (2011) (arguing that the proper role for patentable subject matter is in policing overbreadth).

Recall Justice Frankfurter's concurrence in *Funk Brothers* that introducing "such terms as 'the work of nature' and the 'laws of nature'" only confuse the issue as "[a]rguments drawn from such terms for ascertaining patentability could fairly be employed to challenge almost every patent." 333 U.S. at 134-35.

How are patentees, the PTO, and lower courts to make sense of the inventive application doctrine? Aren't most innovations in the burgeoning field of personalized medicine—the determination of correlations between an individual's genetic makeup and the probabilities of his or her responsiveness to particular treatments such as chemotherapy—likely to fall within the "law of nature" exclusion? Is the Court suggesting that such application of breakthrough scientific discoveries—even though potentially life-saving and worthy of a Nobel Prize—are unpatentable because they risk "inhibit[ing] further discovery by improperly tying up the future use of laws of nature"? Wouldn't it better, as Justice Frankfurter suggested in his *Funk Bros.* concurrence, to address the preemption concern by policing claim breadth? Can §112 serve that purpose? How would a §112 challenge have fared in *Mayo*?

Subsequent decisions have made clear that while preemption is the concern that motivates the patentable subject matter cases, the legal test is not whether a law of nature or an abstract idea is preempted.

7. What does the Supreme Court mean by a "law of nature"? Is a mathematical algorithm the same as the relationship between blood-borne drug (or metabolite) levels and the efficacy of the drug? Is a formula such as the one in *Flook* the product of observation, such as the correlation in *Mayo*? Do mathematical relationships exist "in nature" where engineers and mathematicians discover them, or are they human creations? A more apt description of what the Court has in mind may be "facts about the world." The optimal metabolic level of thiopurine in the human body isn't a "law of nature" in a classical sense. But it is a fact to be discovered, not invented. That seems enough to bring it within the ambit of *Mayo*. As for the algorithms in cases such as *Flook*, there is a longstanding tradition that sees mathematical relationships as preexisting facts about the world that are merely discovered, rather than invented. *See Platonism in the Philosophy of Mathematics*, STANFORD ENCYCLOPEDIA OF PHILOSOPHY, http://plato.stanford.edu/entries/platonism-mathematics/. On the other hand, there is an alternative tradition that sees mathematics as a very useful set of descriptive aids that are more properly described as inventions rather than pre-existing truths. *See* MARK BALAGUER, PLATONISM AND ANTI-PLATONISM IN MATHEMATICS (2001). In any event, computer software code can hardly be described as pure mathematics–it is written in a complex, human-invented programming language that is used to solve real-world problems. It would surprise most coders to be told that the complex piece of programming they worked on for three months was merely "discovered"!

8. *The* Alice *Decision*. In *Alice Corp. v. CLS Bank International*, 134 S.Ct. 2347 (2014), the Supreme Court addressed patent claims reminiscent of those at issue in *Bilski*. A representative claim stated:

A method of exchanging obligations as between parties, each party holding a credit record and a debit record with an exchange institution, the credit records and debit records for exchange of predetermined obligations, the method comprising the steps of:

(a) creating a shadow credit record and a shadow debit record for each stakeholder party to be held independently by a supervisory institution from the exchange institutions;

(b) obtaining from each exchange institution a start-of-day balance for each shadow credit record and shadow debit record;

(c) for every transaction resulting in an exchange obligation, the supervisory institution adjusting each respective party's shadow credit record or shadow debit record, allowing only these transactions that do not result in the value of the shadow debit record being less than the value of the shadow credit record at any time, each said adjustment taking place in chronological order, and

(d) at the end-of-day, the supervisory institution instructing on[e] of the exchange institutions to exchange credits or debits to the credit record and debit record of the respective parties in accordance with the adjustments of the said permitted transactions, the credits and debits being irrevocable, time invariant obligations placed on the exchange institutions.

U.S. Patent No. 5,970,479, Claim 33. The en banc Federal Circuit divided 5-5 on the interpretation of *Bilski* and *Mayo*. Writing for a unanimous Supreme Court, Justice Thomas reaffirmed the inventive application approach revived in *Mayo*. The decision characterized *Mayo* as a two-step inquiry:

Step 1: Does the patent claim a patent-ineligible law of nature, natural
phenomena, or abstract idea?

Step 2: If so, does the claim contain an *inventive* concept sufficient to
transform the ineligible law of nature, natural phenomena, or abstract
idea into a patent-eligible *application* of the ineligible subject matter?

The *Alice* decision characterized step two of this analysis as a search for an "inventive concept"—i.e., an element or combination of elements that is "sufficient to ensure that the patent in practice amounts to significantly more than a patent upon the [ineligible concept] itself." *Id.* at 2355. Applying this framework, the Court concluded that the representative method claim does no more than implement the abstract idea of intermediated settlement on a generic computer and that the system and media claims add nothing of substance to the underlying abstract idea. *Id.* at 2355-60. Echoing Justice Stevens' concurrence in *Bilski*, Justice Sotomayor, joined by Justices Ginsburg and Breyer, concurred in the holding based on the view that business methods do not qualify as a "process" under §101. *Id.* at 2360; *see* Peter S. Menell, *Forty Years of Wondering in the Wilderness and No Closer to the Promised Land:* Bilski*'s Superficial Textualism and the Missed Opportunity to Return Patent Law to its Technology Mooring*, 63 STAN. L. REV. 1289 (2011)

9. *Implementing the Mayo/Alice Framework.* The two-step *Alice* test has become the definitive test for patentable subject matter since 2014. Lower courts have struggled to make much sense of the Supreme Court's decisions. *See DDR Holdings, LLC v. Hotels.com, L.P.*, 773 F.3d 1245 (Fed. Cir. 2014) (emphasizing under step 1 that the claim is "rooted in the computer technology" and hence not abstract; and basing step 2

analysis on a bald assertion that the claimed invention is "not merely the routine or conventional use of the Internet" without discussion of prior art); *Ultramercial, Inc. v. Hulu, LLC*, 772 F.3d 709, 715 (2014) (noting that "[a]s the Court stated in *Alice*, '[a]t some level, "all inventions . . . embody, use, reflect, rest upon, or apply laws of nature, natural phenomena, or abstract ideas"); *Ameritox Ltd. v. Millennium Health, LLC*, 88 F.Supp.3d 885 (W.D. Wisc. Feb. 18, 2015); *Cal. Inst. of Tech. v. Hughes Commc'ns. Inc.*, 59 F. Supp. 3d 974 (C.D. Cal. 2014); *Cogent Med., Inc. v. Elsevier Inc.*, 70 F.Supp.3d 1058 (N.D. Cal. Sept. 30, 2014). Nonetheless, they appear to have gotten the message from four straight Supreme Court rulings in five years on the issue. At this writing, the Federal Circuit had decided 39 patentable subject matter cases since *Alice* in the fields of software, business methods, and genetics, and 38 of the 39 invalidated the patents. In the software domain, those decisions have made it clear that adding ordinary computer hardware such as processors, servers, scanners, or the Internet to an abstract idea (i.e., an algorithm) will not suffice.

One significant practical effect of *Mayo* and *Alice* has been that software and business method patents are increasingly evaluated for patentable subject matter at the outset of a case. While we have reserved patentable subject matter for last because it is intertwined with both obviousness and disclosure, many courts speak of it as a "threshold" requirement that is resolved as a matter of law.

Courts applying *Alice* increasingly do so on a motion to dismiss, considering whether the implementation of an abstract idea is inventive by looking only within the four corners of the patent. This approach has had the practical consequence of making it quicker and cheaper to weed out bad patents, and it has cut back significantly on the leverage exercised by so-called "patent trolls" that use the cost of litigation itself to extort a settlement. But does it make sense as a matter of doctrine? How can a court know whether the implementation of an abstract idea is inventive (i.e., well-understood, conventional or routine) without collecting evidence on what is known in the art? *Cf.* Dennis D. Crouch & Robert P. Merges, *Operating Efficiently Post-*Bilski *by Ordering Patent Doctrine Decision-Making*, 25 BERKELEY TECH. L.J. 1673 (2010) (arguing that §101 should be used only as a last resort).

One possible rationale for the current approach to §101 is that it gives courts a quick way to screen out weak patents. In this sense it might be analogized to the "quick look" doctrine in antitrust law, under which courts are asked to make a cursory analysis of an alleged violation to determine if it will harm competition. *Cal. Dental Ass'n v. FTC*, 526 U.S. 756 (1999). The software patents the Supreme Court invalidated in *Bilski* and *Alice* certainly seem to fit the description of weak, "dot com era" patents. On the other hand, there are many other fairly rapid ways to dispose of cases. To take one example: the *KSR* case on nonobviousness was decided on summary judgment at the district court level. In addition, the recent cases under §101 were decided before the new AIA administrative patent revocation proceedings (inter partes review, covered business methods) had taken effect. With the availability of these other alternative ways to weed out weak patents, there may be less of a case for the new §101 summary analysis. In which case the confusion and concern over the current application of §101 might not have been strictly necessary.

10. *Patent Policy and Promoting Advances in Personalized Medicine.* Is *Mayo* good patent policy? Is it good health care policy? Is it good overall policy? On what does your answer depend? The cost of personalized medicine research? The riskiness of personalized medicine research? The extent to which it constrains medical practitioners and downstream innovators? Suppose that the costs of collecting and evaluating DNA, which are falling precipitously, drive the cost of personalized medicine research. Does that affect your view?

Suppose Congress were to decide that the determination of novel and non-obvious correlations between known drug treatments and individual responsiveness based on molecular biology research merited patent protection. Similarly, suppose Congress were to decide that the determination of novel and non-obvious algorithms merited patent protection. Could Congress amend §101 to include the following: "Applications of newly discovered laws of nature and algorithms shall be eligible for patent protection so long as the claimed invention is new, non-obvious, and useful when viewed as a whole." Alternatively, would such patent protection extend beyond Congress's constitutional authority? What is the foundation for the patentable subject matter exclusions—Constitutional, statutory, or jurisprudential?

11. *Medical and Surgical Procedure Patents and Political Economy.* In 1992, Dr. Samuel L. Pallin obtained U.S. Patent No. 5,080,111 on a method of making self-sealing incisions as part of cataract surgery. Prior to this patent, medical professionals did not generally seek patents on surgical procedures. After word of this patent spread, the American Medical Association ("AMA") unanimously adopted a resolution at its 1994 Annual Meeting "vigorously condemn[ing] the patenting of medical and surgical procedures and [vowing to] work with Congress to outlaw this practice." The uproar increased after Dr. Pallin sued another doctor for infringement. *See Pallin v. Singer*, 36 U.S.P.Q.2d 1050 (D. Vt. 1995). A broad coalition of medical associations successfully enlisted several legislators with medical backgrounds to block such patents. The biotechnology and pharmaceutical industry, in conjunction with patent law associations, vigorously opposed any effort to restrict patent eligibility. The ultimate compromise left §101 unchanged. Instead, Congress added §287(c) which bars infringement actions against any medical practitioner or a related health care entity. The provision does not, however, bar lawsuits against makers of devices specially designed to infringe a medical procedure patent. *See* §271(c) (contributory infringement). As noted earlier, an analogous compromise led to the establishment of a prior user right for methods of doing business following the Federal Circuit's *State Street Bank* decision opening the way for business method patents. The political economy surrounding reforming patentable subject matter (and patent law more generally) is complicated by entrenched interests.

iii.   *Patenting of Molecular Biology/Biotechnology*

Path-breaking discoveries in the field of genetic engineering have posed substantial challenges for patent eligibility. As noted earlier, the Supreme Court held in *Diamond v. Chakrabarty*, 447 U.S. 303 (1980), that newly invented genetically modified organisms were patentable.

But this precedent did not resolve the question of whether isolated sequences of DNA are patentable. Since the late 19th century, following Gregor Mendel's discovery of the basic principles of heredity from plant experiments and Swiss physician Friedrich Miescher's discovery of a microscopic substance in the pus of discarded surgical bandages, scientists have suspected that chemical compounds in the nuclei of cells played a role in human biology. In 1953, James Watson and Francis Crick proposed the double-helix model of DNA structure. Within a few years, they and others had begun to unravel the relationship among DNA, RNA, and proteins that form the foundation of molecular biology.

Although this early basic research was not patented, methods for combining and replicating DNA were. Stanford University and the University of California patented the first gene splicing methods, invented by Professors Stanley Cohen and Herbert Boyer, in the early 1970s and licensed them broadly, earning more than $200 million for the universities. Boyer would go on to co-found Genentech, which became a major patent-based enterprise. The polymerase chain reaction (PCR) technique for amplifying a single copy of a piece of DNA, invented by Dr. Kary Mullis of Cetus Corporation was patented in the late 1980s, *see* U.S. Patent Nos. 4,683,202, 4,683,195, 4,965,188. It greatly expanded biotechnology research. These method patents fit well within the mold of traditional scientific process inventions and did not encounter serious patentable subject matter eligibility challenges.

The use of these and other techniques to map the human (and other) genomes and isolate regions of the DNA structure associated with particular traits and disease propensities generated significant controversy over the patenting of natural substances and life. Could scientists patent particular, isolated, naturally-occurring sequences of DNA?

To appreciate this question, we need to examine earlier jurisprudence relating to claims to isolated natural substances. In *American Wood-Paper Co. v. The Fibre Disintegrating Co.*, 90 U.S. (23 Wall.) 566 (1874), the patentee claimed "as a new article of manufacture" "a pulp suitable for the manufacture of paper, made from wood or other vegetable substances, by boiling the wood or other vegetable substance in an alkali under pressure, substantially as described." In essence, the patentee sought to patent the cellulose product (and not just the process) of a paper production technology. The Supreme Court rejected the claim, noting that "There are many things well known and valuable in medicine or in the arts which may be extracted from divers[e] substances. But the extract is the same, no matter from what it has been taken. A process to obtain it from a subject from which it has never been taken may be the creature of invention, but the thing itself when obtained cannot be called a new manufacture." *Id.* at 593-94.

Notwithstanding (and apparently unaware of) this decision, Judge Learned Hand issued a highly influential decision several decades later upholding a claim to purified adrenaline. *See Parke-Davis & Co. v. H.K. Mulford & Co.*, 189 F. 95 (C.C.S.D.N.Y. 1911) (Hand, J.), *aff'd in part, rev'd in part*, 196 F. 496 (2nd Cir. 1912); Linda J. Demaine & Aaron Xavier Fellmeth, *Reinventing the Double Helix: A Novel and Nonobvious Reconceptualization of the Biotechnology Patent*, 55 STAN. L. REV. 303, 334-39 (2002). Judge Hand established a pragmatic test: "Takamine was the first to make [purified adrenaline] available for any use by removing it from the other gland-tissue. . . . [I]t became for every practical purpose a new thing commercially and therapeutically." 189 F. at 102-03.

With the advances in biotechnology following Watson and Crick's path-breaking discoveries, mapping the human genome became a realistic goal by the mid-1980s. In 1988, Congress funded the Department of Energy and the National Institutes of Health (NIH) to undertake the Human Genome Project. Private company also entered the competition, which quickly led to the filing of patent claims on sequences of cDNA called expressed sequence tags (ESTs). After reviewing the patent jurisprudence, the PTO issued a series of guidelines essentially following Judge Hand's approach. In its 2001 Utility Examination Guidelines, the PTO explained:

> An inventor can patent a discovery when the patent application satisfies the statutory requirements. The U.S. Constitution uses the word 'discoveries' where it authorizes Congress to promote progress made by inventors. . . .
>
> . . . Thus, an inventor's discovery of a gene can be the basis for a patent on the genetic composition isolated from its natural state and processed through purifying steps that separate the gene from other molecules naturally associated with it.

PTO, Utility Examination Guidelines, 66 Fed. Reg. 1092, 1092-93 (Jan. 5, 2001) (citing Parke-Davis and a patent issued to Louis Pasteur on a yeast used in beer brewing, U.S. Patent No. 141,072 (1873)). Patenting of isolated genetic compounds quickly took off, with the principal focus on the utility requirement, which we covered in Chapter III(B)(3).

The patentable subject matter question, however, was simmering and would come to a boil over a decade later over the patenting of genes associated with breast and ovarian cancer. In the early 1990s human gene discovery was incredibly challenging. The human genome contains about 3 billion nucleotides and the average gene contains about 10,000-15,000 nucleotides making the search for a specific gene without a map akin to finding a needle in the haystack. In 1990, a UC Berkeley team led by Professor Mary-Claire King made the first major step towards identifying the breast cancer 1

(BRCA1) gene by using linkage analysis[11] to locate BRCA1 to a 22-million nucleotide region on chromosome 17. *See* Mary-Claire King. *"The Race" to Clone BRCA1*, 343 SCIENCE 1462 (Mar. 28, 2014).

This region was too large to directly sequence or clone but set off a race between competing teams of scientists to pinpoint the exact location and sequence of BRCA1. Mark Skolnick, a population geneticist, assembled a team and co-founded Myriad Genetics to discover the BRCA1 gene. Myriad's had two key advantages—strong ability to raise capital to undertake this labor-intensive work and access to the Utah Cancer registry and an extensive database of Mormon pedigrees living in Utah. These factors led Myriad to pinpoint the BRCA1 gene to a 600,000-nucleotide region, which was small enough for physical mapping. Myriad used several positional cloning strategies to map this region using libraries of random human genomic DNA fragments and cDNA. But others, including King, were also racing to sequence the BRCA1 and BRCA2 genes. In 1994, Myriad discovered the precise location of BRCA1, the BRCA1 cDNA sequence, and a partial sequence of BRCA1 genomic DNA. Myriad subsequently filed a patent containing composition and method claims stemming from this discovery including isolated DNA claims. A competing company, Oncor, also filed patents on the BRCA1 gene, and the two sued each other for infringement. Myriad published the gene sequence for BRCA2 in 1995, just one day before a competing group published partial sequence data for the same gene. *See* E. Richard Gold & Julia Carbone, *Myriad Genetics: In the Eye of the Policy Storm*, 12 GENET. MED. S39 (2010).

After over a decade of paying to use Myriad's test for the gene, the Association for Molecular Pathology, a consortium of individuals from academic and community medical centers, government, and industry, challenged the patentability of DNA compounds.

Association for Molecular Pathology v. Myriad Genetics, Inc., Supreme Court of the United States 133 S.Ct. 2107 (2013)

THOMAS, J.

Respondent Myriad Genetics, Inc. (Myriad), discovered the precise location and sequence of two human genes, mutations of which can substantially increase the risks of breast and ovarian cancer. Myriad obtained a number of patents based upon its discovery. This case involves claims from three of them and requires us to resolve

---

[11] Genetic linkage analysis is based on the tendency for genes and other genetic markers to be inherited together because of their location near one another on the same chromosome. A gene is a functional physical unit of heredity that can be passed from parent to child. Because DNA segments that lie near each other on a chromosome tend to be inherited together, markers are often used as tools for tracking the inheritance pattern of a gene that has not yet been identified but whose approximate location is known. Linkage analysis uses statistical measures to estimate linkage of DNA and genetic traits.

whether a naturally occurring segment of deoxyribonucleic acid (DNA) is patent eligible under 35 U.S.C. §101 by virtue of its isolation from the rest of the human genome. We also address the patent eligibility of synthetically created DNA known as complementary DNA (cDNA), which contains the same protein-coding information found in a segment of natural DNA but omits portions within the DNA segment that do not code for proteins. For the reasons that follow, we hold that a naturally occurring DNA segment is a product of nature and not patent eligible merely because it has been isolated, but that cDNA is patent eligible because it is not naturally occurring. We, therefore, affirm in part and reverse in part the decision of the United States Court of Appeals for the Federal Circuit.

I
A

Genes form the basis for hereditary traits in living organisms. The human genome consists of approximately 22,000 genes packed into 23 pairs of chromosomes. Each gene is encoded as DNA, which takes the shape of the familiar "double helix" that Doctors James Watson and Francis Crick first described in 1953. Each "cross-bar" in the DNA helix consists of two chemically joined nucleotides. The possible nucleotides are adenine (A), thymine (T), cytosine (C), and guanine (G), each of which binds naturally with another nucleotide: A pairs with T; C pairs with G. The nucleotide cross-bars are chemically connected to a sugar-phosphate backbone that forms the outside framework of the DNA helix. Sequences of DNA nucleotides contain the information necessary to create strings of amino acids, which in turn are used in the body to build proteins. Only some DNA nucleotides, however, code for amino acids; these nucleotides are known as "exons." Nucleotides that do not code for amino acids, in contrast, are known as "introns."

Creation of proteins from DNA involves two principal steps, known as transcription and translation. In transcription, the bonds between DNA nucleotides separate, and the DNA helix unwinds into two single strands. A single strand is used as a template to create a complementary ribonucleic acid (RNA) strand. The nucleotides on the DNA strand pair naturally with their counterparts, with the exception that RNA uses the nucleotide base uracil (U) instead of thymine (T). Transcription results in a single strand RNA molecule, known as pre-RNA, whose nucleotides form an inverse image of the DNA strand from which it was created. Pre-RNA still contains nucleotides corresponding to both the exons and introns in the DNA molecule. The pre-RNA is then naturally "spliced" by the physical removal of the introns. The resulting product is a strand of RNA that contains nucleotides corresponding only to the exons from the original DNA strand. The exons-only strand is known as messenger RNA (mRNA), which creates amino acids through translation. In translation, cellular structures known as ribosomes read each set of three nucleotides, known as codons, in the mRNA. Each codon either tells the ribosomes which of the 20 possible amino acids to synthesize or provides a stop signal that ends amino acid production.

DNA's informational sequences and the processes that create mRNA, amino acids, and proteins occur naturally within cells. Scientists can, however, extract DNA from cells using well known laboratory methods. These methods allow scientists to isolate specific segments of DNA—for instance, a particular gene or part of a gene—which can then be further studied, manipulated, or used. It is also possible to create DNA synthetically through processes similarly well known in the field of genetics. One such method begins with an mRNA molecule and uses the natural bonding properties of nucleotides to create a new, synthetic DNA molecule. The result is the inverse of the mRNA's inverse image of the original DNA, with one important distinction: Because the natural creation of mRNA involves splicing that removes introns, the synthetic DNA created from mRNA also contains only the exon sequences. This synthetic DNA created in the laboratory from mRNA is known as complementary DNA (cDNA).

Changes in the genetic sequence are called mutations. Mutations can be as small as the alteration of a single nucleotide—a change affecting only one letter in the genetic code. Such small-scale changes can produce an entirely different amino acid or can end protein production altogether. Large changes, involving the deletion, rearrangement, or duplication of hundreds or even millions of nucleotides, can result in the elimination, misplacement, or duplication of entire genes. Some mutations are harmless, but others can cause disease or increase the risk of disease. As a result, the study of genetics can lead to valuable medical breakthroughs.

B

This case involves patents filed by Myriad after it made one such medical breakthrough. Myriad discovered the precise location and sequence of what are now known as the BRCA1 and BRCA2 genes. Mutations in these genes can dramatically increase an individual's risk of developing breast and ovarian cancer. The average American woman has a 12- to 13-percent risk of developing breast cancer, but for women with certain genetic mutations, the risk can range between 50 and 80 percent for breast cancer and between 20 and 50 percent for ovarian cancer. Before Myriad's discovery of the BRCA1 and BRCA2 genes, scientists knew that heredity played a role in establishing a woman's risk of developing breast and ovarian cancer, but they did not know which genes were associated with those cancers.

Myriad identified the exact location of the BRCA1 and BRCA2 genes on chromosomes 17 and 13. Chromosome 17 has approximately 80 million nucleotides, and chromosome 13 has approximately 114 million. Within those chromosomes, the BRCA1 and BRCA2 genes are each about 80,000 nucleotides long. If just exons are counted, the BRCA1 gene is only about 5,500 nucleotides long; for the BRCA2 gene, that number is about 10,200. Knowledge of the location of the BRCA1 and BRCA2 genes allowed Myriad to determine their typical nucleotide sequence. That information, in turn, enabled Myriad to develop medical tests that are useful for detecting mutations in a patient's BRCA1 and BRCA2 genes and thereby assessing whether the patient has an increased risk of cancer.

Once it found the location and sequence of the BRCA1 and BRCA2 genes, Myriad sought and obtained a number of patents. Nine composition claims from three of those patents are at issue in this case. [From Fn. 2: At issue are claims 1, 2, 5, 6, and 7 of U.S. Patent 5,747,282 (the '282 patent), claim 1 of U.S. Patent 5,693,473 (the '473 patent), and claims 1, 6, and 7 of U.S. Patent 5,837,492 (the '492 patent).] Claims 1, 2, 5, and 6 from [U.S. Patent 5,747,282] are representative. The first claim asserts a patent on "[a]n isolated DNA coding for a BRCA1 polypeptide," which has "the amino acid sequence set forth in SEQ ID NO:2." App. 822. SEQ ID NO:2 sets forth a list of 1,863 amino acids that the typical BRCA1 gene encodes. See id., at 785—790. Put differently, claim 1 asserts a patent claim on the DNA code that tells a cell to produce the string of BRCA1 amino acids listed in SEQ ID NO:2.

Claim 2 of the '282 patent operates similarly. It claims "[t]he isolated DNA of claim 1, wherein said DNA has the nucleotide sequence set forth in SEQ ID NO:1." Like SEQ ID NO:2, SEQ ID NO:1 sets forth a long list of data, in this instance the sequence of cDNA that codes for the BRCA1 amino acids listed in claim 1. Importantly, SEQ ID NO:1 lists only the cDNA exons in the BRCA1 gene, rather than a full DNA sequence containing both exons and introns. As a result, the Federal Circuit recognized that claim 2 asserts a patent on the cDNA nucleotide sequence listed in SEQ ID NO:1, which codes for the typical BRCA1 gene.

Claim 5 of the '282 patent claims a subset of the data in claim 1. In particular, it claims "[a]n isolated DNA having at least 15 nucleotides of the DNA of claim 1." App. 822. The practical effect of claim 5 is to assert a patent on any series of 15 nucleotides that exist in the typical BRCA1 gene. Because the BRCA1 gene is thousands of nucleotides long, even BRCA1 genes with substantial mutations are likely to contain at least one segment of 15 nucleotides that correspond to the typical BRCA1 gene. Similarly, claim 6 of the '282 patent claims "[a]n isolated DNA having at least 15 nucleotides of the DNA of claim 2." *Ibid.* This claim operates similarly to claim 5, except that it references the cDNA-based claim 2. The remaining claims at issue are similar, though several list common mutations rather than typical BRCA1 and BRCA2 sequences. *See ibid.* (claim 7 of the '282 patent); *id.*, at 930 (claim 1 of the '473 patent); *id.*, at 1028 (claims 1, 6, and 7 of the '492 patent).

C

Myriad's patents would, if valid, give it the exclusive right to isolate an individual's BRCA1 and BRCA2 genes (or any strand of 15 or more nucleotides within the genes) by breaking the covalent bonds that connect the DNA to the rest of the individual's genome. The patents would also give Myriad the exclusive right to synthetically create BRCA cDNA.

But isolation is necessary to conduct genetic testing, and Myriad was not the only entity to offer BRCA testing after it discovered the genes. The University of Pennsylvania's Genetic Diagnostic Laboratory (GDL) and others provided genetic testing services to women. Petitioner Dr. Harry Ostrer, then a researcher at New York

University School of Medicine, routinely sent his patients' DNA samples to GDL for testing. After learning of GDL's testing and Ostrer's activities, Myriad sent letters to them asserting that the genetic testing infringed Myriad's patents. App. 94—95 (Ostrer letter). In response, GDL agreed to stop testing and informed Ostrer that it would no longer accept patient samples. Myriad also filed patent infringement suits against other entities that performed BRCA testing, resulting in settlements in which the defendants agreed to cease all allegedly infringing activity. Myriad, thus, solidified its position as the only entity providing BRCA testing.

Some years later, petitioner Ostrer, along with medical patients, advocacy groups, and other doctors, filed this lawsuit seeking a declaration that Myriad's patents are invalid under 35 U.S.C. §101. The District Court . . . granted summary judgment to petitioners on the composition claims at issue in this case based on its conclusion that Myriad's claims, including claims related to cDNA, were invalid because they covered products of nature. The Federal Circuit reversed, and this Court granted the petition for certiorari, vacated the judgment, and remanded the case in light of *Mayo Collaborative Services v. Prometheus Laboratories, Inc.*, 566 U.S. ___ (2012).

II

A

Section 101 of the Patent Act provides:

> "Whoever invents or discovers any new and useful . . . composition of matter, or any new and useful improvement thereof, may obtain a patent therefor, subject to the conditions and requirements of this title."

35 U.S.C. §101.

We have "long held that this provision contains an important implicit exception[:] Laws of nature, natural phenomena, and abstract ideas are not patentable." *Mayo*, 566 U.S., at ___. Rather, "'they are the basic tools of scientific and technological work'" that lie beyond the domain of patent protection. As the Court has explained, without this exception, there would be considerable danger that the grant of patents would "tie up" the use of such tools and thereby "inhibit future innovation premised upon them." This would be at odds with the very point of patents, which exist to promote creation.

The rule against patents on naturally occurring things is not without limits, however, for "all inventions at some level embody, use, reflect, rest upon, or apply laws of nature, natural phenomena, or abstract ideas," and "too broad an interpretation of this exclusionary principle could eviscerate patent law." 566 U.S., at ___. As we have recognized before, patent protection strikes a delicate balance between creating "incentives that lead to creation, invention, and discovery" and "imped[ing] the flow of information that might permit, indeed spur, invention." *Id.*, at ___. We must apply this well-established standard to determine whether Myriad's patents claim any "new and useful . . . composition of matter," §101, or instead claim naturally occurring phenomena.

B

It is undisputed that Myriad did not create or alter any of the genetic information encoded in the BRCA1 and BRCA2 genes. The location and order of the nucleotides existed in nature before Myriad found them. Nor did Myriad create or alter the genetic structure of DNA. Instead, Myriad's principal contribution was uncovering the precise location and genetic sequence of the BRCA1 and BRCA2 genes within chromosomes 17 and 13. The question is whether this renders the genes patentable.

Myriad recognizes that our decision in [*Diamond v.*] *Chakrabarty*, 447 U.S. 303 (1980)] is central to this inquiry. In *Chakrabarty*, scientists added four plasmids to a bacterium, which enabled it to break down various components of crude oil. 447 U.S., at 305, and n.1. The Court held that the modified bacterium was patentable. The Chakrabarty bacterium was new "with markedly different characteristics from any found in nature," 447 U.S., at 310, due to the additional plasmids and resultant "capacity for degrading oil." *Id.*, at 305, n.1. In this case, by contrast, Myriad did not create anything. To be sure, it found an important and useful gene, but separating that gene from its surrounding genetic material is not an act of invention.

Groundbreaking, innovative, or even brilliant discovery does not by itself satisfy the §101 inquiry. In *Funk Brothers Seed Co. v. Kalo Inoculant Co.*, 333 U.S. 127 (1948), this Court considered a composition patent that claimed a mixture of naturally occurring strains of bacteria that helped leguminous plants take nitrogen from the air and fix it in the soil. The Court held that the composition was not patent eligible because the patent holder did not alter the bacteria in any way. His patent claim thus fell squarely within the law of nature exception. So do Myriad's. Myriad found the location of the BRCA1 and BRCA2 genes, but that discovery, by itself, does not render the BRCA genes "new . . . composition[s] of matter," §101, that are patent eligible.

Indeed, Myriad's patent descriptions highlight the problem with its claims. For example, a section of the '282 patent's Detailed Description of the Invention indicates that Myriad found the location of a gene associated with increased risk of breast cancer and identified mutations of that gene that increase the risk. In subsequent language Myriad explains that the location of the gene was unknown until Myriad found it among the approximately eight million nucleotide pairs contained in a subpart of chromosome 17. Many of Myriad's patent descriptions simply detail the "iterative process" of discovery by which Myriad narrowed the possible locations for the gene sequences that it sought. Myriad seeks to import these extensive research efforts into the §101 patent-eligibility inquiry. But extensive effort alone is insufficient to satisfy the demands of §101.

Nor are Myriad's claims saved by the fact that isolating DNA from the human genome severs chemical bonds and thereby creates a nonnaturally occurring molecule. Myriad's claims are simply not expressed in terms of chemical composition, nor do they rely in any way on the chemical changes that result from the isolation of a particular section of DNA. Instead, the claims understandably focus on the genetic information encoded in the BRCA1 and BRCA2 genes. If the patents depended upon the creation of a unique molecule, then a would-be infringer could arguably avoid at least Myriad's patent claims on entire genes (such as claims 1 and 2 of the '282 patent) by isolating a DNA sequence that included both the BRCA1 or BRCA2 gene and one additional nucleotide pair. Such a molecule would not be chemically identical to the molecule "invented" by Myriad. But Myriad obviously would resist that outcome because its claim is concerned primarily with the information contained in the genetic sequence, not with the specific chemical composition of a particular molecule.

Finally, Myriad argues that the PTO's past practice of awarding gene patents is entitled to deference, citing *J.E.M. Ag Supply, Inc. v. Pioneer Hi-Bred Int'l, Inc.*, 534 U.S. 124 (2001). We disagree. Congress has not endorsed the views of the PTO in subsequent legislation.

Further undercutting the PTO's practice, the United States argued in the Federal Circuit and in this Court that isolated DNA was not patent eligible under §101, Brief for United States as Amicus Curiae 20-33, and that the PTO's practice was not "a sufficient reason to hold that isolated DNA is patent-eligible." *Id.*, at 26. *See also id.*, at 28-29. These concessions weigh against deferring to the PTO's determination.

C

cDNA does not present the same obstacles to patentability as naturally occurring, isolated DNA segments. As already explained, creation of a cDNA sequence from mRNA results in an exons-only molecule that is not naturally occurring. Petitioners concede that cDNA differs from natural DNA in that "the non-coding regions have been removed." They nevertheless argue that cDNA is not patent eligible because "[t]he nucleotide sequence of cDNA is dictated by nature, not by the lab technician." That may be so, but the lab technician unquestionably creates something new when cDNA is made. cDNA retains the naturally occurring exons of DNA, but it is distinct from the DNA from which it was derived. As a result, cDNA is not a "product of nature" and is patent eligible under §101, except insofar as very short series of DNA may have no intervening introns to remove when creating cDNA. In that situation, a short strand of cDNA may be indistinguishable from natural DNA.

III

It is important to note what is not implicated by this decision. First, there are no method claims before this Court. Had Myriad created an innovative method of manipulating genes while searching for the BRCA1 and BRCA2 genes, it could possibly have sought a method patent. But the processes used by Myriad to isolate DNA were well understood by geneticists at the time of Myriad's patents [and so method claims were not available].

Similarly, this case does not involve patents on new applications of knowledge about the BRCA1 and BRCA2 genes. Judge Bryson aptly noted that, "[a]s the first party with knowledge of the [BRCA1 and BRCA2] sequences, Myriad was in an excellent position to claim applications of that knowledge. Many of its unchallenged claims are limited to such applications." 689 F.3d, at 1349.

Nor do we consider the patentability of DNA in which the order of the naturally occurring nucleotides has been altered. Scientific alteration of the genetic code presents a different inquiry, and we express no opinion about the application of §101 to such endeavors. We merely hold that genes and the information they encode are not patent eligible under §101 simply because they have been isolated from the surrounding genetic material.

COMMENTS AND QUESTIONS

1. In invalidating Myriad's isolated DNA claims, the Court noted that the isolated DNA contained the same genetic information as naturally occurring genomic DNA and that Myriad did not create or alter this information. The Court also noted that "[a]s the first party with knowledge of the [BRCA1] sequences, Myriad was in an excellent position to claim applications of that knowledge." One very useful application is sequencing BRCA1 DNA for mutations to diagnose or prognose breast cancer. Should the patentee's identification of the function of the sequence and listing the sequence mean that the sequence is patentable? How about a method claim limited to the use of the sequence to diagnose susceptibility to breast cancer?

2. The Court affirmed the validity of Myriad's BRCA1 cDNA claims on the ground that BRCA1 cDNA was not naturally occurring and therefore not drawn to a judicial exception: "the lab technician unquestionably creates something new when cDNA is made." cDNA, however, contains the same genetic information as naturally occurring mRNA and Myriad did not create or alter this information. The act of reverse-transcribing natural mRNA into cDNA was known, routine, and conventional when the Myriad patents were filed in 1994. *See* Jeffrey A. Lefstin, *The Three Faces of Prometheus: A Post-*Alice *Jurisprudence of Abstractions*, 16 N.C. J.L. & TECH. 647, 678-79 (2015). Are the chemical differences between cDNA and mRNA sufficient to make cDNA patentable? Would your answer change if you were presented evidence that isolated DNA is similarly chemically different from genomic DNA? (This was in fact an emphasis in some of the Federal Circuit opinions in *Myriad*.) How can the conventional (non-inventive) application of an unpatentable product of nature (genomic DNA) result in a patentable composition (cDNA)? Note that the Court does not mention *Mayo* and the "inventive concept" test in distinguishing cDNA from gDNA.

Lower courts have not read *Myriad*'s discussion of cDNA expansively. They have refused to patent human gene sequences modified with other standard but non-naturally-occurring material like primers. *In re BRCA1- and BRCA2-Based Heredity Cancer Test Patent Litig.*, 774 F.3d 755 (Fed. Cir. 2014).

3. Justice Scalia concurred in part and concurred in the judgment. Here is the entirety of his opinion:

I join the judgment of the Court, and all of its opinion except Part I-A and some portions of the rest of the opinion going into fine details of molecular biology. I am unable to affirm those details on my own knowledge or even my own belief. It suffices for me to affirm, having studied the opinions below and the expert briefs presented here, that the portion of DNA isolated from its natural state sought to be patented is identical to that portion of the DNA in its natural state; and that complementary DNA (cDNA) is a synthetic creation not normally present in nature.

Is Justice Scalia concerned that his colleagues on the Court lack the capacity to resolve patent cases involving advanced scientific issues? As just noted, arguably he was right to be so concerned. The majority did not appear to understand the relationship between gDNA and cDNA. It is notable that Judge Learned Hand, widely considered one of the most accomplished intellectual property jurists, voiced a similar sentiment in the concluding paragraph of the *Parke-Davis* opinion.

I cannot stop without calling attention to the extraordinary condition of the law which makes it possible for a man without any knowledge of even the rudiments of chemistry to pass upon such questions as these. The inordinate expense of time is the least of the resulting evils, for only a trained chemist is really capable of passing upon such facts . . . In Germany, where the national spirit eagerly seeks for all the assistance it can get from the whole range of human knowledge, they do quite differently. The court summons technical judges to whom technical questions are submitted and who can intelligently pass upon the issues without blindly groping among testimony upon matters wholly out of their ken. How long we shall continue to blunder along without the aid of unpartisan and authoritative scientific assistance in the administration of justice, no one knows; but all fair persons not conventionalized by provincial legal habits of mind ought, I should think, unite to effect some such advance.

Parke-Davis & Co. v. H.K. Mulford Co., 189 F. 95, 115 (C.C.S.D.N.Y 1911). Germany uses a three-judge panel, including a technical expert, on its patent cases. What are the benefits and drawbacks of employing technically trained judges instead of generalists to adjudicate patent cases?

4. Courts and the PTO considered DNA compositions to be patent-eligible (subject to meeting the separate utility requirement, which we will turn to in Chapter III(B)(5)) beginning in the 1980s. By the time *Myriad* was decided, the era of new human gene patents was effectively over; the human genome had been sequenced more than a decade before. In what ways do you think the history of the BRCA1 discovery might have been different if isolated DNA was not considered patent-eligible subject matter in the 1990s? What about the development of genetic tests for breast cancer?

PROBLEMS

Problem III-11. Expectant parents have long sought to know about the health of their fetus. Through amniocentesis, doctors have been able to extract fluid from the amniotic sac surrounding the developing fetus to conduct various tests to determine genetic disorders, such as Down Syndrome. Amniocentesis is usually done when a woman is between fourteen and sixteen weeks pregnant. The procedure is typically limited to women who have an elevated risk for genetic or chromosomal problems. The test is invasive and poses small but significant risks to the fetus and mother, such as miscarriage, needle injury to the fetus, and transmission of infection such as HIV or hepatitis C from an infected mother to fetus.

In 1996, Drs. Dennis Lo and James Wainscoat discovered cell-free fetal DNA ("cffDNA") in maternal plasma and serum. cffDNA is non-cellular fetal DNA that circulates freely in a pregnant woman's blood. Drs. Lo and Wainscoat implemented a method for detecting the small fraction of paternally inherited cffDNA in maternal plasma or serum to determine fetal characteristics, such as gender and genetic abnormalities. The invention, commercialized by Sequenom as its MaterniT21 test, created a non-invasive alternative technique to analyze fetal DNA that avoids the risks of amniocentesis.

In 1999, they filed a patent application that claimed these non-invasive prenatal diagnosis methods:

1. A method for detecting a paternally inherited nucleic acid of fetal origin performed on a maternal serum or plasma sample from a pregnant female, which method comprises amplifying a paternally inherited nucleic acid from the serum or plasma sample and detecting the presence of a paternally inherited nucleic acid of fetal origin in the sample.

The specification provides, in pertinent part:

SUMMARY AND OBJECTS OF THE INVENTION

It has now been discovered that foetal DNA is detectable in maternal serum or plasma samples. This is a surprising and unexpected finding; maternal plasma is the very material that is routinely discarded by investigators studying noninvasive prenatal diagnosis using foetal cells in maternal blood.

DETAILED DESCRIPTION OF THE PREFERRED EMBODIMENTS

The preparation of serum or plasma from the maternal blood sample is carried out by standard techniques. . . . Standard nucleic acid amplification systems can be used, including PCR [polymerase chain reaction], the ligase chain reaction, nucleic acid sequence based amplification (NASBA), branched DNA methods, and so on.

[O]ne skilled in the art is aware of a variety of techniques which might be used to detect different nucleic acid species. . . . These techniques are a matter of routine for one skilled in the art for the analysis of DNA.

The PTO granted Drs. Lo and Wainscoat U.S. Patent No. 6,258,540 in 2001. When Sequenom learned that Ariosa Diagnostics was offering non-invasive fetal diagnostic testing, it threatened to sue. Ariosa filed a declaratory relief action seeking to invalidate the '540 patent as invalid under §101. How should this case be decided under the applicable Supreme Court decisions?

Problem III-12. You were just hired as chief IP counsel to the Senate Judiciary Committee. Following the chaos surrounding the patent system over the past two decades, the Committee Chair would like to rethink the archaic language of the current §101. She believes that the provision is "out of step in an era of computers and biotechnology."

Several lobbyists have seized on the occasion to introduce their pet revisions. Environmentalists have asked that "newly discovered natural products" be added to the categories of patentable subject matter; they believe this addition will create an incentive to identify and preserve rare species with potential benefits, e.g., plants used as ingredients in medicines. In addition, bioscience companies, some software companies, and academic institutions believe that scientific breakthroughs and inventive algorithms should be patentable even if they merely apply merely conventional (as opposed to inventive) methods. Some enterprising business entrepreneurs advocate patent protection for inventive business methods. And some athletic stars have called for patent protection on inventive athletic techniques.

Is there any justification in refusing to change the current language—e.g., because it has shown enough flexibility to adapt to computer technology and biotechnology and the like? Is there anything special about traditional technology—machines, manufactures, etc.—that makes it more valuable, or more in need of protection, than other "innovations" such as newly discovered natural products, new "pure" science results, new academic theories, or new techniques for doing business (such as the leveraged buyout, or the multidivisional corporate structure)? Why not grant property rights over all sorts of new things, and let the market figure out which ones are truly worthwhile?

C. ADMINISTRATIVE PATENT REVIEW

In 1980, Congress established the *ex parte* reexamination process to enable patent owners and third parties to request the PTO to review the validity of issued patents. *See* J. Steven Baughman, *Reexamination Reexaminations: A Fresh Look at the Ex Parte and Inter Partes Mechanisms for Reviewing Issued Patents*, 89 J. PAT & TRADEMARK OFF. SOC'Y 349 (2007); §303(a); PTO Ex Parte Reexamination Rules, 37 C.F.R. §1.515(a). The review process was limited to novelty and nonobviousness and a limited range of prior art (patents and printed publications). The process was conducted *ex parte*—i.e., only the patent owner participated. And the process could and often did take years to complete. Courts were reluctant to stay enforcement proceedings pending completion of reexamination. Most accused infringers did not consider *ex parte* reexamination to be a viable alternative to litigation. As a result, the ex parte reexamination was only sparsely utilized.

In 1999, Congress established a more balanced *inter partes* reexamination procedure which allowed third party challengers to comment on patent owner responses. This procedure also failed to gain much traction. The process was slow and barred challengers from raising any ground that could have been raised during the reexamination during subsequent civil litigation. In 2005, the PTO established the Central Reexamination Unit ("CRU"), which expedited reexaminations and resulted in greater usage of the reexamination. Nonetheless, district courts were still reluctant to stay parallel cases, leading to costly duplication.

As the patent reform efforts gained momentum in the post dot-com period, the logic of a more robust administrative review process paralleling the European Patent Office's opposition system gained support. *See* Joseph Farrell and Robert P. Merges, *Incentives to Challenge and Defend Patents: Why Litigation Won't Reliably Fix Patent Office Errors and Why Administrative Patent Review Might Help*, 19 BERKELEY TECH. L.J. 9430 (2004). Much of the AIA focused on expanding and expediting review.

The AIA established three principal review procedures: (1) *inter partes* review (IPR)— *inter partes* reexamination was phased out and folded into IPR, §§311-19; (2) covered business method review (CBMR)—a transitional review proceeding focused on weeding out dubious business method patents, AIA §18; and (3) post-grant review (PGR), §§321-29. The AIA left *ex parte* reexamination in place. *See* §§301-07; Jonathan Tamimi, *Breaking Bad Patents: The Formula for Quick, Inexpensive Resolution of Patent Validity*, 29 BERKELEY TECH. L.J. 587 (2014). The following table compares the key characteristics of the AIA review systems.

Comparison of Administrative Patent Review Proceedings

AIA Review	IPR	PGR	CBMR
Evidentiary Standard	Petitioner to prove invalidity by the preponderance of the evidence		
Grounds for Review	§102, §103	Any defense relating to invalidity	
Prior Art Limited to:	Patents and printed publications	No Limits	
Threshold to Institute Review	Reasonable likelihood that one or more claims is invalid	More likely than not at least one claim is unpatentable, or petition raises a novel legal question of patentability	
Time to Institution	w/i 9 months of grant or reissue		
Time to Decision	Maximum of 12–18 months from institution decision		
Claim Amendments	Patent owner may cancel claims, or propose a reasonable number of substitute claims Presumption that only one substitute claim will be required for each challenged claim		
Claim Construction	"Broadest reasonable construction in light of specification"		
Stay Considerations:	1) Stay simplify issues and streamline trial? 2) Is Discovery complete, trial date set? 3) Stay tactically advantage moving party or unduly burden nonmoving party?		*AIA Consideration:* 4) Stay reduce burden on the parties and the court? Stays presumptively granted
Estoppel in Subsequent Civil Action	Any ground raised or reasonably could have been raised		Any ground *actually* raised
Effect of Settlement	Estoppel provisions do not apply		

1.   Post-Grant Review

The AIA's new Post-Grant Review (PGR) procedure parallels the European-style "patent oppositions." A PGR permits anyone to challenge the validity of a patent within nine months of its issuance (or nine months of a patent reissue). The challenger—or "petitioner," in the words of the statute—may "request to cancel as unpatentable [one] or more claims of a patent on any ground that could be raised" in a district court proceeding. *See* §321, citing §282(b) (relating to grounds for invalidity). Unlike pre-AIA reexamination procedures, which were focused on prior art in the form of patents and printed publications, PGR significantly widens the grounds for challenge, creating in effect a mini-trial on patent validity. A PGR permits evidence of on-sale activities, public uses, prior-filed but not-yet-issued patents, and other types of disclosures, as well as issues such as enablement.

PGRs (as well as other review proceedings) are heard by three administrative patent judge (APJ) panels of the Patent Trial and Appeal Board (PTAB), successor to the pre-AIA Board of Patent Appeals and Interferences.

Congress expressed its hope that the PGR proceeding would come to be seen as a viable alternative to traditional ex parte reexaminations, and to district court litigation as well:

> The initial reexamination statute [in 1980] had several limitations that later proved to make it a less viable alternative to litigation for evaluating patent validity than Congress intended. First, a reexamination request could only be based on prior art, and could not be based on prior public use or prior sales. Moreover, the requestor could not raise any challenge based on §101 (utility, eligibility) or §112 (indefiniteness, enablement, written description, best mode). A third party alleging a patent is invalid, therefore, had fewer challenges it could raise in the proceeding and, therefore, may instead opt to risk infringement and litigate the validity of the patent in court. Second, in the original reexamination system, the third-party challenger had no role once the proceeding was initiated, while the patent holder had significant input throughout the entire process. Third, a challenger that lost at the USPTO under reexamination had no right to appeal an examiner's, or the Patent Board's, decision either administratively or in court. Restrictions such as these made reexamination a much less favored avenue to challenge questionable patents than litigation. Reexamination proceedings are also often costly, taking several years to complete, . . . and are first conducted by examiners and, if the patent is rejected, then by Patent Board judges. Thus, many patents must go through two rounds of administrative review (one by the examiner, and a second by the Patent Board) adding to the length of the proceeding.

Committee on the Judiciary, U.S. Cong., America Invents Act, H.R. Rep. No 112-98, 112th Cong., 1st Sess., at 45 (June 1, 2011). The House Report goes on to say:

The Committee believes that this new, early-stage process for challenging patent validity and its clear procedures for submission of art will make the patent system more efficient and improve the quality of patents and the patent system. This new, but time-limited, post-grant review procedure will provide a meaningful opportunity to improve patent quality and restore confidence in the presumption of validity that comes with issued patents in court.

Id. at 48.

i.   *Timing and Sequencing*

PGR requests must be filed within a statutory nine-month "window" after the patent issues. §321(c). The PTO's regulations accompanying the AIA provide a timeline for PGR proceedings. In general, these proceedings are expected to move quickly in keeping with the notion that a PGR is intended to be a streamlined, cheaper alternative to district court litigation for assessing patent validity.

The PGR process begins with a request from a petitioner.

[T]he petition [must] identify each claim being challenged, the specific grounds on which each claim is challenged, how the claims are to be construed, how the claims as construed are unpatentable, why the claims as construed are unpatentable under the identified grounds, and . . . [citations to] evidence relied upon . . . to support the challenge.

USPTO, Notice of Proposed Rulemaking, Changes to Implement Post-Grant Review Proceedings, 77 Fed. Reg. 7060, 7064 (Feb. 10, 2012) (proposing new provision to be codified at 37 C.F.R. §42.204(b)).

The patent owner then has two months to respond. The patent owner may set forth reasons why the PGR should not be instituted, but cannot at this point present new evidence of patentability such as expert declarations. After this filing, the PTO has three months to decide if a PGR is warranted. §324(c).

The Director may not authorize a post-grant review to be instituted unless the Director determines that the information presented in the petition filed under section 321, if such information is not rebutted, would demonstrate that it is more likely than not that at least [one] of the claims challenged in the petition is unpatentable.

An additional criterion is described in §324(b): "The determination required under subsection (a) may also be satisfied by a showing that the petition raises a novel or unsettled legal question that is important to other patents or patent applications." Under §324(e), the PTO Commissioner's decision whether or not to institute a PGR proceeding is final and non-appealable.

Once a PGR is instituted, the PTO can, by regulation, require the "patent owner [to] file with [a PGR] response, through affidavits or declarations, any additional factual evidence and expert opinions on which the patent owner relies in support of the response." §326(a)(8). The patent owner can respond in a number of ways, including the filing of substituted or amended claims, as long as the new claims (1) find support in the originally filed specification, (2) respond in some way to the ground for the PGR request, and (3) do not broaden the scope of coverage of the original claims. *See* Proposed Rules to be codified at 37 C.F.R. §§42.220(b) and (c), 77 Fed. Reg. 7060, 7066. The AIA envisions a focused discovery process in connection with PGR proceedings; "such discovery shall be limited to evidence directly related to factual assertions advanced by either party in the proceeding," and these limits are backed by sanctions "should a party to a PGR misuse discovery to harass or to cause unnecessary delay or an unnecessary increase in the cost of the proceeding. . . ." §326(a)(5) and (6).

The limits on discovery are one way that the drafters of the AIA hoped to make PGRs effective but efficient. In general, the goal is for the PTO to reach a final decision in a PGR proceeding within one year of deciding the PGR may proceed. There is the possibility of a six-month extension "for good cause." 77 Fed. Reg. 7060, 7064.

ii. *Coordination with Other Proceedings*

The AIA reduces the burden of parallel proceedings by barring PGR proceedings if a requestor has already filed a civil action. §325(a)(1) If a civil action is filed after a PGR petition, that action will be stayed until the patent owner requests that the stay be lifted or the patent owner files a counterclaim. Furthermore, the AIA authorizes the PTAB to streamline and coordinate different administrative proceedings by consolidating diverse challenges involving a single patent into one proceeding. §315(d). Pursuant to the AIA's estoppel provisions, any issue that was raised or could reasonably have been raised in a PGR may not be further contested in another PTO proceeding (such as an Inter Partes Review) or in a district court or ITC proceeding. *See* §§325(e)(1) and (2). In these ways, the AIA PGR process discourages duplicative proceedings and channels validity determinations issues toward the PGR process in the first instance.

Final PGR decisions can be appealed to the Federal Circuit. §329. (PGR institution decisions are not appealable. §324(e)). It should be noted that even with a very efficient Federal Circuit disposition, a PGR could well run three years through appeal, which is a long time in light of the stated goal of providing an efficient procedure for weeding out weak patent claims.

2. Inter Partes Review: Successor to Inter Partes Reexaminations

The new Inter Partes Review (IPR) procedure replaces the Inter Partes Reexamination system. As of September 16, 2012, anyone—patent owner or third party—may request a review of an issued patent. The requestor must show that there is "a reasonable likelihood that the requester would prevail with respect to at least [one] of the claims challenged in the request." The new IPR system replaces only existing *inter partes reexaminations*—not the parallel system of *ex parte reexamination*.

Existing ex parte reexamination rules provide a different threshold for initiating a proceeding;[12] require the proceeding to be conducted by an examiner with a right of appeal to the PTAB; and allow for limited participation by third parties. These ex parte reexaminations were left essentially intact; the new IPR system will run in conjunction with them.

An IPR proceeding is subject to the same limits as to prior art that apply in current reexamination proceedings: only patents and printed publications can be cited to initiate an IPR. *See* §311(b). The AIA, in §316(a)(9), permits the patent owner to submit substitute claims, or to cancel claims, in light of an IPR proceeding.

Unlike the PGR process, which can raise any invalidity ground, IPRs may only challenge lack of novelty or obviousness. Furthermore, the challenger may only present patents or printed publications.

i. *Timing and Sequencing*

The AIA seeks to avoid duplicative litigation by estopping an IPR requestor from challenging a patent claim in district court or an ITC enforcement action on the basis of "any ground that the petitioner raised or reasonably could have raised during that inter partes review." §315(e)(2). Similarly, the requestor may not file a second IPR or pursue any other administrative proceeding on any ground that was raised or could have been raised in the IPR. §315(e)(1).

The IPR process was designed to dovetail with the PGR process. Therefore, IPRs cannot be filed until after the PGR filing period (nine months after patent issuance) has passed or until after a PGR proceeding has been completed. Thus, an IPR can follow directly after an unsuccessful PGR request, although it is unlikely such a petition will be successful. §311(c).

ii. *Coordination with Other Proceedings*

An IPR must be filed before a declaratory action is filed in district court by the patent challenger. §315(a)(1). If district court litigation is filed after an IPR, that litigation will be automatically stayed during the IPR proceeding. §315(a)(2). The stay can be lifted only if (a) the patent owner asks the court to lift the stay; (b) the patent owner files a district court counterclaim alleging patent infringement; or (c) the declaratory judgment plaintiff-patent challenger terminates the district court litigation. However, if a patent owner sues an infringer for patent infringement and the infringer defends with a counterclaim asserting patent invalidity, this does not trigger the

---

[12] Section 303(a), which applies to ex parte reexaminations, says in part: "[T]he [PTO] Director will determine whether a substantial new question of patentability affecting any claim of the patent concerned is raised by the request," and if so, a reexamination will be instituted. The "substantial new question of patentability" standard is lower than the "reasonable likelihood that the requestor would prevail" standard under the AIA's IPR procedure, which means it should be easier to initiate a reexamination than an IPR.

automatic stay provision of §315. *See* §315(a)(3). An accused infringer who has been sued by the patentee for patent infringement must file a request to initiate an IPR within one year after the patentee files an infringement action. §315(b).

3. Covered Business Method Review (CBMR)

With the tightening of patent validity standards by the courts, Congress established a broader review proceeding than IPRs to deal with the large stock of questionable business method patents. AIA §18. The AIA defines covered business method patents as "a method or corresponding apparatus for performing data processing or other operations used in the practice, administration, or management of a financial product or service," not including "technological invention[s]." AIA §18(d)(1). In determining whether a patent claims a "technological invention," the PTAB assesses "whether the claimed subject matter as a whole recites a technological feature that is novel and unobvious . . . and solves a technical problem using a technical solution." *See* 37 C.F.R. §42.301(b) (2013).

The standards for instituting CBMR, like that for PGR, is higher than for IPR. A CBMR proceeding will be instituted if it is more likely than not that at least one claim is unpatentable or that there is a "novel or unsettled legal question that is important to other patents or patent applications." §324(a)–(b). As with the other proceedings, the institution decision is not appealable.

In contrast to IPR, CBMR allows the challenger to assert any ground of invalidity, not only under §§102 or 103, and does not limit the evidentiary basis to patents and printed publications. CBMR also has a weaker estoppel provision than the other review processes. CBMR petitioners are estopped only on grounds that the petitioner raised during the review in subsequent civil and ITC litigation. CBMR petitioners cannot, however, raise any ground that they "reasonably could have raised" in the CBMR in later proceedings at the PTO for the same patent. AIA §18(a)(1)(A).

Congress built a sunset provision for CBMR into the AIA. The program ends on September 16, 2020. AIA §18(a)(3)(a).

4. Derivation Proceeding

By shifting from a first-to-invent to a modified first-to-file priority system, the AIA eliminates the interference proceedings for patents filed after March 15, 2013. Nevertheless, due to concern that unscrupulous claimants might steal an invention and beat the true inventor to the Patent Office by filing first, Congress established a special administrative proceeding to sort out claims that the applicant stole or "derived" an invention from another.

Under AIA §135, a Derivation Proceeding begins when a petitioner alleges that "an inventor named in an earlier application derived the claimed invention from an inventor named in the petitioner's application and, without authorization, the earlier application claiming such invention was filed." AIA §135. The challenge must be brought within one year of the publication of the claim to the invention that the petitioner says was derived (i.e., one year after patent publication, or one year after patent issuance if the application was never published under §122).

COMMENTS AND QUESTIONS

1. The IPR and CBMR procedures have proven very popular among accused infringers and district judges. In its first full year of operation, the PTAB received over 1,000 petitions. The PTAB instituted review in over 80% of these petitions, and invalidated many of the reviewed claims. *See* Brian J. Love & Shawn Ambwani, Inter Partes Review: *An Early Look at the Numbers*, 81 UNIV. OF CHI. L. REV. DIALOGUE 93 (2014) (reporting that the PTAB invalidated all claims in 77.5% of the first 160 petitions instituted). The number of petitions has since doubled to nearly 2,000 petitions per year in 2014 and 2015. The PTAB has hired over 200 APJs to handle the load.

2. *Claim Construction.* During patent prosecution, the PTO applies "the broadest reasonable interpretation" (BRI) in construing claims. The rationale for using this standard, as opposed the meaning that a PHOSITA would give a claims term (as articulated in *Phillips*), is that it facilitates the exploration of the "metes and bounds to which the applicant may be entitled, and thus to aid in sharpening and clarifying the claims during the application stage, when claims are readily changed." *See In re Skvorecz*, 580 F.3d 1262, 1267 (Fed. Cir. 2009); U.S. PATENT AND TRADEMARK OFFICE, MANUAL OF PATENT EXAMINING PROCEDURE §2111 (9th ed. Mar. 2014). The applicant has wide latitude to amend claims during examination.

The PTO chose to carry over the BRI standard to PTAB review. Patentees complained that this standard is inappropriate in view of the different nature of post grant review and the far more limited ability to amend claims during IPR. They contended that BRI conflicts with the standard that district courts apply in parallel proceedings. Nonetheless, the Supreme Court upheld the use of BRI in IPR proceedings as a reasonable exercise of the PTO's rulemaking authority under the AIA. *See Cuozzo Speed Techs., LLC, v. Lee*, ___ U.S. ___ (2016).

3. *Success or Death Panel.* The relatively high invalidation rate for PTAB petitions has been hailed as an indicator of success in reducing litigation costs, delay, and uncertainty and as an indication that PTAB is far too prone to invalidating patents. One explanation for this pattern is that there are many dubious patents—some that issued prior to the Supreme Court's higher nonobviousness standard and many for which the PTO did not have the full prior art. Time will tell whether this early period is simply weeding out a large stock of dubious patents or changing the standards for patentability.

4. *Expertise versus Due Process.* Recall our discussion following the *Myriad* case of whether the patent system should use decisionmakers with technical experience to resolve patent disputes. The PTAB system has partially shifted more of the invalidity decisions to such a group. PTAB APJs have technical training and patent system

expertise. In addition, they sit in panels of three, which presumably provides a broader range of perspectives. Should all reviews of patent validity be handled through such a process?

D.   CLAIMS AND CLAIM CONSTRUCTION

Patent claims define a patent owner's legal rights; they have been analogized to the "metes and bounds" of a real property deed. Thus, the meaning of words in the claim determine the claim boundaries. As we saw in our analysis of the novelty requirement, a claim is anticipated if the claim limitations "read on" a prior art reference. As we will see in Chapter III(E)(1), direct infringement analysis is the mirror image of novelty analysis: an accused device or process that "reads on" the claimed invention infringes the patent.

Thus, claim boundaries are critical to patent validity and infringement determinations. They are also critical to patent law's notice function. In the words of the late Federal Circuit Judge Giles Rich, one of the most influential patent lawyers (he co-drafted the 1952 Patent Act) and jurists of the 20th century, "the name of the game is the claim." Giles S. Rich, *Extent of Protection and Interpretation of Claims— American Perspectives*, 21 INT'L REV. INDUS. PROP. & COPYRIGHT L. 497, 499 (1990).

Linguistically minor variations in phraseology and meaning can be the difference between a finding of infringement (and thus exclusion of the competitor, and perhaps damages) and non-infringement (and thus open entry in at least part of the patentee's market). To the hard-headed businessperson, claim interpretation defines the intangible real estate that belongs exclusively to a patentee. To a patent lawyer, precision (or a lack of precision, in some cases) is a tool of the trade. The typical businessperson looks straight to the bottom line: can the patentee exclude a competitor (expanding the reach of its exclusive legal franchise) or will it have to share shelf space and profits? That validity pushes in the opposite direction from infringement makes the analysis even more complex: a broader claim is easier to invalidate since it encompasses more potential prior art. As Judge Rich put it: "the stronger a patent the weaker it is and the weaker a patent the stronger it is." Giles S. Rich, *The Proposed Patent Legislation: Some Comments*, 35 GEO. WASH. L. REV. 641, 644 (1967).

This section begins with an overview of patent claiming and claim formats. It then examines claim construction jurisprudence. We then explore functional claiming. We conclude with the claim indefiniteness doctrine.

1.   Patent Claiming and Claim Formats

i.   *The Evolution of Patent Claiming: From Central Claims to Peripheral Claims*

The practice of claiming inventions, as opposed to merely describing them, traces back to the early nineteenth century. *See* J. Jonas Anderson & Peter S. Menell, *Informal*

Deference: A Historical, Empirical, and Normative Analysis of Patent Claim Construction, 108 Nw. U. L. Rev. 1, 8-21 (2014). Historians credit Robert Fulton, developer of the first commercially successful steamboat, with "inventing" the patent claim. *See* Karl B. Lutz, *Evolution of the Claims of U.S. Patents,* 20 J. Pat. Off. Soc'y 134, 137 (1938). His 1811 patent stated:

> Having been the first to demonstrate the superior advantages of a water wheel or wheels, I claim as my exclusive right, the use of two wheels, one over each side of the boat to take the purchase on the water . . . .

See also Camilla A. Hrdy, *State Patent Laws in the Age of Laissez Faire,* 28 Berkeley Tech. L.J. 45, 78 (2013) (describing patent-like right granted to Fulton by New York State, and subsequent litigation). Although there were sporadic examples in the first two decades of the nineteenth century of patents expressly claiming inventions, such explicit claiming was not the general practice.

Justice Joseph Story, who would emerge as the leading patent jurist of the first half of the nineteenth century, immediately came to see the problems with vague and conclusory descriptions of inventions. Sitting in his first patent case (and the first case to focus on the question of distinguishing a patented invention from the prior art), he noted the "intrinsic difficulty . . . to ascertain . . . the exact boundaries between what was known and used before, and what is new." *See Whittemore v. Cutter,* 29 F. Cas. 1123, 1124 (C.C.D. Mass. 1813) (No. 17,601); *see also Odiorne v. Winkley,* 18 F. Cas. 581, 582 (C.C.D. Mass. 1814) (No. 10,432) (noting the "intrinsic difficulty"). Justice Story explicated this principle more fully four years later, charging the jury that:

> A patent is grantable only for a new and useful invention; and, unless it be distinctly stated, in what that invention specifically consists, it is impossible to say, whether it ought to be patented or not; and it is equally difficult to know, whether the public infringe upon or violate the exclusive right secured by the patent.

Lowell v. Lewis, 15 F. Cas. 1018, 1020 (C.C.D. Mass. 1817) (No. 8568).

In 1828, the Superintendent of the Patent Office instructed applicants that many patents had been vacated for failure to claim what is new and is the invention or discovery:

> In the specification it is perfectly proper to describe an entire machine, although most parts of it may have been long known and used, as, otherwise, it may be difficult to make known the improvements; but after doing this, the patentee should distinctly set forth what he claims as new; and this is best done in a separate paragraph, at the end of the specification . . . .

Thomas P. Jones, *Information to Persons Applying for Patents, or Transacting Other Business at the Patent Office,* 6 Franklin J. & Am. Mechanics' Mag. 332, 334 (1828).

Thus, by the late 1820s, it had become common practice for patent applicants to include a formal designation of the claimed invention in a separate paragraph at the end of the specification. The 1836 Patent Act, which reinstituted patent examination, required applicants to "particularly specify and point out the part, improvement, or combination, which he claims as his own invention or discovery." Patent Act of 1836, ch. 357, §6.

The form of patent claiming that emerged during this period—which has come to be known as "central" claiming—differs substantially from the "peripheral" format in common usage today. Central claiming was directed at identifying the thing the patentee built as the invention – a "sign post" indicating that this, and things sufficiently similar to it, were protected by patent. *See* Dan L. Burk & Mark A. Lemley, *Fence Posts or Sign Posts? Rethinking Patent Claim Construction*, 157 U. PA. L. REV. 1743 (2009). The early claiming format responded to the invalidation of overbroad claiming by using "reference characters"—alpha-numeric labels for patent drawings—to specify particular structural components illustrating their improvement.

Even before the 1836 Act, some applicants began using a more radical claiming format that would come to be known as "peripheral" claiming. These claims used linguistic formulations, rather than references to specific improvements, to delineate the metes and bounds of the claimed invention. If central claims were sign posts, peripheral claims are "fence posts" that attempt to define the outer bounds of the patent right. Burk & Lemley, *supra*. In a series of pamphlets issued in the 1860s, the Patent Office pushed applicants toward the use of peripheral claiming. The Patent Office began publishing its decision at this time. These decisions upheld claims lacking reference characters, permitted "genus claiming," and signaled receptivity to multiple claims in stating that "claims in different forms . . . prevent misconstructions." *See Ex parte Perry & Lay*, 1869 Dec. Comm'r Pat. 1, 1.

The courts also played a critical role in the shift toward peripheral claiming. In two 1877 Supreme Court decisions—*Merrill v. Yeomans*, 94 U.S. 568, 573-74 (1876) and *Keystone Bridge Co. v. Phoenix Iron Co.*, 95 U.S. 274, 278 (1877)—the Supreme Court embraced patent law's public notice function by linking the scope of patent protection to the metes and bounds set forth in patent claims. This contributed to the decline of central claiming and eventually made claim construction an essential step in infringement analysis. In a watershed passage in *Merrill*, the Court explained the critical role of clearly identifiable patent boundaries for technological and economic advance:

> The genius of the inventor, constantly making improvements in existing patents--a process which gives to the patent system its greatest value,--should not be restrained by vague and indefinite descriptions of claims in existing patents from the salutary and necessary right of improving on that which has already been invented. It seems to us that nothing can be more just and fair, both to the patentee and to the public, than that the former should understand,

and correctly describe, just what he has invented, and for what he claims a patent.

The patent claim quickly emerged as the defining feature of the patent. *See Burns v. Meyer*, 100 U.S. 671, 672 (1879) ("The courts, therefore, should be careful not to enlarge, by construction, the claim which the Patent Office has admitted, and which the patentee has acquiesced in, beyond the fair interpretation of its terms."). In his seminal 1890 treatise, William C. Robinson characterized it as "the office of the Claim to define the limits of that exclusive use which is secured to the inventor by the patent"; "[t]he Claim is thus the life of the patent so far as the rights of the inventor are concerned." 2 WILLIAM C. ROBINSON, THE LAW OF PATENTS FOR USEFUL INVENTIONS §§504, 505 (1890). This shift brought claim construction to a prominent role in patent litigation. As Robinson explained, "The paramount importance of the Claim, and the necessity for such exactness and completeness in its statements as will precisely define the invention to be protected by the patent, have led to the establishment of numerous rules for framing it." *Id.* at §507.

ii. *Claim Formats*

The challenge in drafting patent claims is to make them as broad as the prior art and other patent doctrines will allow. Because of this, and because drafting claims is time-consuming and expensive, patent drafters are always on the lookout for convenient ways to broadly cover the elements of inventions. Section 112(b)-(f) guide the drafting of patent claims:

(b) CONCLUSION.—The specification shall conclude with one or more claims particularly pointing out and distinctly claiming the subject matter which the inventor or a joint inventor regards as the invention .

(c) FORM.—A claim may be written in independent or, if the nature of the case admits, in dependent or multiple dependent form.

(d) REFERENCE IN DEPENDENT FORMS.—Subject to subsection (e), a claim in dependent form shall contain a reference to a claim previously set forth and then specify a further limitation of the subject matter claimed. A claim in dependent form shall be construed to incorporate by reference all the limitations of the claim to which it refers.

(e) REFERENCE IN MULTIPLE DEPENDENT FORM.—A claim in multiple dependent form shall contain a reference, in the alternative only, to more than one claim previously set forth and then specify a further limitation of the subject matter claimed. A multiple dependent claim shall not serve as a basis for any other multiple dependent claim. A multiple dependent claim shall be construed to incorporate by reference all the limitations of the particular claim in relation to which it is being considered.

(f) ELEMENT IN CLAIM FOR A COMBINATION.—An element in a claim for a combination may be expressed as a means or step for performing a specified function without the recital of structure, material, or acts in support thereof, and such claim shall be construed to cover the corresponding structure, material, or acts described in the specification and equivalents thereof.

These provisions establish formatting rules to avoid confusion and promote clarity. We will be focusing on §§112(b) and (f) in subsections 4 and 3 respectively. Before doing so, it will be useful to review the basic principles of patent claim construction.

2.   Judicial Claim Construction

The construction of patent claims plays a critical role in nearly every patent case. It is central to the evaluation of infringement and validity, and can affect or determine the outcome of other significant issues such as unenforceability, enablement, and remedies. The process by which courts interpret patent claims represents one of the most distinctive aspects of patent litigation.

In patent cases, as elsewhere, the distinction between questions of law and fact is an important issue. As we have seen so far, patent cases often center on scientific or technical details such as how an invention differs from the prior art, or how it works compared to a competitor's product. Whether a judge or a jury decides these key issues may make a significant difference in the outcome of a patent infringement case.

As the use of juries in patent cases became more prevalent in the 1980s, whether the judge or the jury should construe the terms of patent claims emerged as a pressing issue. It was common for judges to charge juries with claim construction. Resolving the scope of patent claims in this manner, however, significantly increased the complexity and uncertainty of trials. By 1995, approximately 75% of patent cases were tried to juries. One effect of this practice was to shroud the jury's claim construction in the black box of jury deliberations, making jury patent decisions especially difficult to review. Federal Circuit Judge Paul Michel lamented that "[w]hen the court delegates both construction and infringement to the jury's discretion, the jury is free to do almost anything it wishes." *See* Paul R. Michel, *The Challenge Ahead: Increasing Predictability in Federal Circuit Jurisprudence for the New Century*, 43 AM. U. L. REV. 1231, 1239 (1994). The question of who should determine the meaning of patent claims came before the Supreme Court in the seminal case of *Markman v. Westview Instruments*, 517 U.S. 370 (1996).

Markman sued Westview Instruments for infringement of its patent on a system for tracking articles of clothing in a dry-cleaning operation. After a jury found infringement, Westview Instruments moved for judgment as a matter of law on the ground that the patent and its prosecution history made it clear that the patent claims at issue did not extend to the Westview's accused device. The trial court granted the motion based on its examination of the relevant documentation. On appeal, the patentee asserted that the trial court's judgment violated its Seventh Amendment right to a jury trial on claim construction. Markman stressed that it had introduced expert testimony on the issue. Based largely on functional considerations, the Supreme Court held that claim construction is a matter for the court and hence beyond the province of the jury. The Court emphasized that judges are better equipped than juries to construe the meaning of patent claim terms, given their training and experience interpreting written instruments (such as contracts and statutes). Even though cases may arise in which the credibility of competing experts affects the determination of claim meaning "in the main," the Court anticipated that claim construction determinations will be "subsumed within the necessarily sophisticated analysis of the whole document, required by the standard construction rule that a term can be defined only in a way that comports with the instrument as a whole." *Id.* at 389. The Court also emphasized that judges can better promote uniformity and certainty in claim construction.

The *Markman* decision ushered in a new era and quickly led to the emergence of pre-trial "Markman hearings" to construe disputed claim terms. Following the lead of the Northern District of California, many of the most patent-intensive districts have adopted Patent Local Rules providing for joint, sequenced, staged, and timely disclosure of claim construction and other contentions, paving the way to a claim construction hearing within about eight months of the first case management conference. *See generally* PETER S. MENELL, ET AL., PATENT CASE MANAGEMENT JUDICIAL GUIDE, chs. 2 and 5 (Federal Judicial Center) (3rd ed. 2016). Most courts conduct a separate Markman hearing and issue a claim construction order before trial. Such hearings are often held in conjunction with a technology tutorial provided by the attorneys or technical experts. In many cases, such rulings provide the basis for summary judgment determinations on issues of validity and infringement.

Another effect of the *Markman* ruling was to bring claim construction out into the open. This has produced voluminous jurisprudence on how to construe claims. Within a few years, many litigants, lower court judges, scholars, and even some Federal Circuit jurists perceived claim construction law to be in chaos. Between 2000 and 2005, the reversal rate for district court claim constructions hovered in the mid-40 percent range. *See J. Jonas Anderson & Peter S. Menell, Informal Deference: A Historical, Empirical, and Normative Analysis of Patent Claim Construction*, 108 NW. U. L. REV. 1, 40-41 (2014). A respected district court judge observed that given such a high reversal rate, "you might as well throw darts." *See* Anandashankar Mazumdar, *Federal District Courts Need Experts that Are Good 'Teachers,' Judges Tell Bar*, 70 PAT. TRADEMARK & COPYRIGHT J. (BNA) 536, 537 (Sept. 16, 2005) (quoting Judge Marsha J. Pechman of the U.S. District Court of Western Washington).

"Proceduralist" jurists on the Federal Circuit gave primary weight to the claim language, focusing on ordinary meaning derived from dictionaries. "Holistic" jurists drew upon the full range of interpretive tools—claim language, specification, prosecution history, dictionaries, and expert testimony. Many perceived the outcome of claim construction decisions to be highly panel-specific. *See* R. Polk Wagner & Lee

Petherbridge, *Is the Federal Circuit Succeeding? An Empirical Assessment of Judicial Performance*, 152 U. PA. L. REV. 1105 (2004).

The Federal Circuit granted en banc review in the following case to clarify and harmonize claim construction jurisprudence.

Phillips v. AWH Corporation
United States Court of Appeals for the Federal Circuit
415 F.3d 1303 (Fed. Cir. 2005) (en banc)

BRYSON, Circuit Judge:

Edward H. Phillips invented modular, steel-shell panels that can be welded together to form vandalism-resistant walls. The panels are especially useful in building prisons because they are load-bearing and impact-resistant, while also insulating against fire and noise. Mr. Phillips obtained a patent on the invention, U.S. Patent No. 4,677,798 ("the '798 patent"). . . .

In February 1997, Mr. Phillips brought suit in the United States District Court for the District of Colorado charging AWH with . . . infringement. . . .

[In deciding] the patent infringement issue, the district court focused on the language of claim 1, which recites "further means disposed inside the shell for increasing its load bearing capacity comprising internal steel baffles extending inwardly from the steel shell walls.". . . [Finding that the accused product did not contain "baffles" as that term is used in claim 1,] the district court granted summary judgment of non-infringement.

Mr. Phillips appealed [and a divided] panel of this court affirmed. *Phillips v. AWH Corp.*, 363 F.3d 1207 (Fed. Cir. 2004). The majority [Judge Lourie, joined by Judge Newman] sustained the district court's summary judgment of noninfringement, although on different grounds. The dissenting judge [Judge Dyk] would have reversed the summary judgment of noninfringement . . .

[T]he [original Federal Circuit] panel concluded that the patent uses the term "baffles" in a restrictive manner. Based on the patent's written description, the panel held that the claim term "baffles" excludes structures that extend at a 90 degree angle from the walls. The panel noted that the specification repeatedly refers to the ability of the claimed baffles to deflect projectiles and that it describes the baffles as being "disposed at such angles that bullets which might penetrate the outer steel panels are deflected." '798 patent, col. 2, ll. 13-15; *see also id.* at col. 5, ll. 17-19 (baffles are "disposed at angles which tend to deflect the bullets"). In addition, the panel observed that nowhere in the patent is there any disclosure of a baffle projecting from the wall at a right angle and that baffles oriented at 90 degrees to the wall were found in the prior art. Based on "the specification's explicit descriptions," the panel concluded "that the patentee regarded his invention as panels providing impact or projectile resistance and that the baffles must be oriented at angles other than 90 [degrees]." *Phillips*, 363 F.3d at 1213. The panel added that the patent specification "is intended to support and inform the claims, and here it makes it unmistakably clear that the invention involves baffles angled at other than 90 [degrees]." The panel therefore upheld the district court's summary judgment of noninfringement.

The dissenting judge argued that the panel had improperly limited the claims to the particular embodiment of the invention disclosed in the specification, rather than adopting the "plain meaning" of the term "baffles."[T]he dissenting judge contended, the specification "merely identifies impact resistance as one of several objectives of the invention." In sum, the dissent concluded that "there is no reason to supplement the plain meaning of the claim language with a limitation from the preferred embodiment." Consequently, the dissenting judge argued that the court should have adopted the general purpose dictionary definition of the term baffle, i.e., "something for deflecting, checking, or otherwise regulating flow," and therefore should have reversed the summary judgment of noninfringement.

This court agreed to rehear the appeal en banc and vacated the judgment of the panel. We now . . . reverse the portion of the court's judgment addressed to the issue of infringement.

I

Claim 1 of the '798 patent is representative of the asserted claims with respect to the use of the term "baffles." It recites:

> Building modules adapted to fit together for construction of fire, sound and impact resistant security barriers and rooms for use in securing records and persons, comprising in combination, an outer shell . . ., sealant means . . . and further means disposed inside the shell for increasing its load bearing capacity comprising internal steel baffles extending inwardly from the steel shell walls. . . .

II

The first paragraph of section 112 of the Patent Act states that the specification shall contain a written description of the invention, and of the manner and process of making and using it, in such full, clear, concise, and exact terms as to enable any person skilled in the art to which it pertains . . . to make and use the same. . . .

The second paragraph of section 112 provides that the specification shall conclude with one or more claims particularly pointing out and distinctly claiming the subject matter which the applicant regards as his invention.

Those two paragraphs of section 112 frame the issue of claim interpretation for us. The second paragraph requires us to look to the language of the claims to determine what "the applicant regards as his invention." On the other hand, the first paragraph requires that the specification describe the invention set forth in the claims. The principal question that this case presents to us is the extent to which we should resort to and rely on a patent's specification in seeking to ascertain the proper scope of its claims. . . .

A

It is a "bedrock principle" of patent law that "the claims of a patent define the invention to which the patentee is entitled the right to exclude." *Innova[/Pure Water, Inc. v. Safari Water Filtration Systems, Inc.*, 381 F.3d 1111 (Fed. Cir. 2004)], at 1115. That principle has been recognized since at least 1836, when Congress first required that the specification include a portion in which the inventor "shall particularly specify and point out the part, improvement, or combination, which he claims as his own invention or discovery." Act of July 4, 1836, ch. 357, §6, 5 Stat. 117, 119. In the following years, the Supreme Court made clear that the claims are "of primary importance, in the effort to ascertain precisely what it is that is patented." *Merrill v. Yeomans*, 94 U.S. 568, 570 (1876). . . . We have frequently stated that the words of a claim "are generally given their ordinary and customary meaning." *Vitronics [Corp. v. Conceptronic, Inc.*, 90 F.3d 1576 (Fed. Cir. 1996)], at 1582. We have made clear, moreover, that the ordinary and customary meaning of a claim term is the meaning that the term would have to a person of ordinary skill in the art in question at the time of the invention, i.e., as of the effective filing date of the patent application.

The inquiry into how a person of ordinary skill in the art understands a claim term provides an objective baseline from which to begin claim interpretation. . . . That starting point is based on the well-settled understanding that inventors are typically persons skilled in the field of the invention and that patents are addressed to and intended to be read by others of skill in the pertinent art.

Importantly, the person of ordinary skill in the art is deemed to read the claim term not only in the context of the particular claim in which the disputed term appears, but in the context of the entire patent, including the specification.

B

In some cases, the ordinary meaning of claim language as understood by a person of skill in the art may be readily apparent even to lay judges, and claim construction in such cases involves little more than the application of the widely accepted meaning of commonly understood words. *See Brown v. 3M*, 265 F.3d 1349, 1352 (Fed Cir. 2001) (holding that the claims did "not require elaborate interpretation"). In such circumstances, general purpose dictionaries may be helpful. In many cases that give rise to litigation, however, determining the ordinary and customary meaning of the claim requires examination of terms that have a particular meaning in a field of art. Because the meaning of a claim term as understood by persons of skill in the art is often not immediately apparent, and because patentees frequently use terms idiosyncratically, the court looks to "those sources available to the public that show what a person of skill in the art would have understood disputed claim language to mean." *Innova*, 381 F.3d at 1116. Those sources include "the words of the claims themselves, the remainder of the specification, the prosecution history, and extrinsic evidence concerning relevant scientific principles, the meaning of technical terms, and the state of the art." *Id.* . . .

1

Quite apart from the written description and the prosecution history, the claims themselves provide substantial guidance as to the meaning of particular claim terms. *See Vitronics*, 90 F.3d at 1582.

To begin with, the context in which a term is used in the asserted claim can be highly instructive. To take a simple example, the claim in this case refers to "steel baffles," which strongly implies that the term "baffles" does not inherently mean objects made of steel. . . .

Other claims of the patent in question, both asserted and unasserted, can also be valuable sources of enlightenment as to the meaning of a claim term. *Vitronics*, 90 F.3d at 1582. Because claim terms are normally used consistently throughout the patent, the usage of a term in one claim can often illuminate the meaning of the same term in other claims. . . . Differences among claims can also be a useful guide in understanding the meaning of particular claim terms. . . . For example, the presence of a dependent claim that adds a particular limitation gives rise to a presumption that the limitation in question is not present in the independent claim. *See Liebel-Flarsheim Co. v. Medrad, Inc.*, 358 F.3d 898, 910 (Fed. Cir. 2004).

2

The claims, of course, do not stand alone. Rather, they are part of "a fully integrated written instrument," *Markman*, 52 F.3d at 978, consisting principally of a specification that concludes with the claims. For that reason, claims "must be read in view of the specification, of which they are a part." *Id.* at 979. As we stated in *Vitronics*, the specification "is always highly relevant to the claim construction analysis. Usually, it is dispositive; it is the single best guide to the meaning of a disputed term." 90 F.3d at 1582.

This court and its predecessors have long emphasized the importance of the specification in claim construction. In *Autogiro Co. of America v. United States*, 384 F.2d 391, 397-98 (Ct. Cl. 1967*)*, the Court of Claims characterized the specification as "a concordance for the claims," based on the statutory requirement that the specification "describe the manner and process of making and using" the patented invention. . . . That principle has a long pedigree in Supreme Court decisions as well. [Citations omitted.]

3

In addition to consulting the specification, we have held that a court "should also consider the patent's prosecution history, if it is in evidence." *Markman*, 52 F.3d at 980. Like the specification, the prosecution history provides evidence of how the PTO and the inventor understood the patent. Furthermore, like the specification, the prosecution history was created by the patentee in attempting to explain and obtain the patent. Yet because the prosecution history represents an ongoing negotiation between the PTO and the applicant, rather than the final product of that negotiation, it often lacks the clarity of the specification and thus is less useful for claim construction purposes. Nonetheless, the prosecution history can often inform the meaning of the claim language by demonstrating how the inventor understood the invention and whether the inventor limited the invention in the course of prosecution, making the claim scope narrower than it would otherwise be.

C

Although we have emphasized the importance of intrinsic evidence in claim construction, we have also authorized district courts to rely on extrinsic evidence, which "consists of all evidence external to the patent and prosecution history, including expert and inventor testimony, dictionaries, and learned treatises." *Markman*, 52 F.3d at 980, citing *Seymour v. Osborne*, 78 U.S. (11 Wall.) 516, 546 (1870). Within the class of extrinsic evidence, the court has observed that dictionaries and treatises can be useful in claim construction. . . . We have especially noted the help that technical dictionaries may provide to a court "to better understand the underlying technology" and the way in which one of skill in the art might use the claim terms. *Vitronics*, 90 F.3d at 1584 n.6. Because dictionaries, and especially technical dictionaries, endeavor to collect the accepted meanings of terms used in various fields of science and technology, those resources have been properly recognized as among the many tools that can assist the court in determining the meaning of particular terminology to those of skill in the art of the invention.

We have also held that extrinsic evidence in the form of expert testimony can be useful to a court for a variety of purposes, such as to provide background on the technology at issue, to explain how an invention works, to ensure that the court's understanding of the technical aspects of the patent is consistent with that of a person of skill in the art, or to establish that a particular term in the patent or the prior art has a particular meaning in the pertinent field. . . . However, conclusory, unsupported assertions by experts as to the definition of a claim term are not useful to a court. . . .

[U]ndue reliance on extrinsic evidence poses the risk that it will be used to change the meaning of claims in derogation of the "indisputable public records consisting of the claims, the specification and the prosecution history," thereby undermining the public notice function of patents. *Southwall Techs.[, Inc. v. Cardinal IG Co.,*] 54 F.3d [1570] at 1578 [Fed. Cir. 1995].

III

Although the principles outlined above have been articulated on numerous occasions, some of this court's cases have suggested a somewhat different approach to claim construction, in which the court has given greater emphasis to dictionary definitions of claim terms and has assigned a less prominent role to the specification and the prosecution history. The leading case in this line is *Texas Digital Systems, Inc. v. Telegenix, Inc.*, 308 F.3d 1193 (Fed. Cir. 2002).

A

In *Texas Digital*, the court noted that "dictionaries, encyclopedias and treatises are particularly useful resources to assist the court in determining the ordinary and customary meanings of claim terms." 308 F.3d at 1202. Those texts, the court explained, are "objective resources that serve as reliable sources of information on the established meanings that would have been attributed to the terms of the claims by those of skill in the art," and they "deserve no less fealty in the context of claim construction" than in any other area of law. *Id.* at 1203. The court added that because words often have multiple dictionary meanings, the intrinsic record must be consulted to determine which of the different possible dictionary meanings is most consistent with the use of the term in question by the inventor. If more than one dictionary definition is consistent with the use of the words in the intrinsic record, the court stated, "the claim terms may be construed to encompass all such consistent meanings." *Id.*

The *Texas Digital* court further explained that the patent's specification and prosecution history must be consulted to determine if the patentee has used "the words [of the claim] in a manner clearly inconsistent with the ordinary meaning reflected, for example, in a dictionary definition." 308 F.3d at 1204. The court identified two circumstances in which such an inconsistency may be found. First, the court stated, "the presumption in favor of a dictionary definition will be overcome where the patentee, acting as his or her own lexicographer, has clearly set forth an explicit definition of the term different from its ordinary meaning." Second, "the presumption also will be rebutted if the inventor has disavowed or disclaimed scope of coverage, by using words or expressions of manifest exclusion or restriction, representing a clear disavowal of claim scope."

The court concluded that it is improper to consult "the written description and prosecution history as a threshold step in the claim construction process, before any effort is made to discern the ordinary and customary meanings attributed to the words themselves." *Texas Digital*, 308 F.3d at 1204. To do so, the court reasoned, "invites a violation of our precedent counseling against importing limitations into the claims." *Id.*

B

Although the concern expressed by the court in *Texas Digital* was valid, the methodology it adopted placed too much reliance on extrinsic sources such as dictionaries, treatises, and encyclopedias and too little on intrinsic sources, in particular the specification and prosecution history. In effect, the *Texas Digital* approach limits the role of the specification in claim construction to serving as a check on the dictionary meaning of a claim term. . . . That approach, in our view, improperly restricts the role of the specification in claim construction.

Assigning such a limited role to the specification, and in particular requiring that any definition of claim language in the specification be express, is inconsistent with our rulings that the specification is "the single best guide to the meaning of a disputed term," and that the specification "acts as a dictionary when it expressly defines terms used in the claims or when it defines terms by implication." *Vitronics*, 90 F.3d at 1582.

The main problem with elevating the dictionary to such prominence is that it focuses the inquiry on the abstract meaning of words rather than on the meaning of claim terms within the context of the patent. Properly viewed, the "ordinary meaning" of a claim term is its meaning to the ordinary artisan after reading the entire patent. Yet heavy reliance on the dictionary divorced from the intrinsic evidence risks transforming the meaning of the claim term to the artisan into the meaning of the term in the abstract, out of its particular context, which is the specification. Thus, there may be a disconnect between the patentee's responsibility to describe and claim his invention, and the dictionary editors' objective of aggregating all possible definitions for particular words.

The problem is that if the district court starts with the broad dictionary definition in every case and fails to fully appreciate how the specification implicitly limits that definition, the error will systematically cause the construction of the claim to be unduly expansive. The risk of systematic overbreadth is greatly reduced if the court instead focuses at the outset on how the patentee used the claim term in the claims, specification, and prosecution history, rather than starting with a broad definition and whittling it down.

Thus, the use of the dictionary may extend patent protection beyond what should properly be afforded by the inventor's patent. . . . .

Even technical dictionaries or treatises, under certain circumstances, may suffer from some of these deficiencies. There is no guarantee that a term is used in the same way in a treatise as it would be by the patentee. In fact, discrepancies between the patent and treatises are apt to be common because the patent by its nature describes something novel.

Moreover, different dictionaries may contain somewhat different sets of definitions for the same words. A claim should not rise or fall based upon the preferences of a particular dictionary editor, or the court's independent decision, uninformed by the specification, to rely on one dictionary rather than another. Finally, the authors of dictionaries or treatises may simplify ideas to communicate them most effectively to the public and may thus choose a meaning that is not pertinent to the understanding of particular claim language. The resulting definitions therefore do not necessarily reflect the inventor's goal of distinctly setting forth his invention as a person of ordinary skill in that particular art would understand it.

As we have noted above, however, we do not intend to preclude the appropriate use of dictionaries. Dictionaries or comparable sources are often useful to assist in understanding the commonly understood meaning of words and have been used both by our court and the Supreme Court in claim interpretation. . . .

We also acknowledge that the purpose underlying the *Texas Digital* line of cases— to avoid the danger of reading limitations from the specification into the claim—is sound. Moreover, we recognize that the distinction between using the specification to interpret the meaning of a claim and importing limitations from the specification into the claim can be a difficult one to apply in practice. *See Comark Communic'ns, Inc. v. Harris Corp.*, 156 F.3d 1182, 1186–87 (Fed. Cir. 1998) ("there is sometimes a fine line between reading a claim in light of the specification, and reading a limitation into the claim from the specification"). However, the line between construing terms and importing limitations can be discerned with reasonable certainty and predictability if the court's focus remains on understanding how a person of ordinary skill in the art would understand the claim terms. For instance, although the specification often describes very specific embodiments of the invention, we have repeatedly warned against confining the claims to those embodiments. *See, e.g., Nazomi Communic'ns, Inc. v. ARM Holdings, PLC*, 403 F.3d 1364, 1369 (Fed. Cir. 2005) (claims may embrace "different subject matter than is illustrated in the specific embodiments in the specification. In particular, we have expressly rejected the contention that if a patent describes only a single embodiment, the claims of the patent must be construed as being limited to that embodiment. That is not just because section 112 of the Patent Act requires that the claims themselves set forth the limits of the patent grant, but also because persons of ordinary skill in the art rarely would confine their definitions of terms to the exact representations depicted in the embodiments.

To avoid importing limitations from the specification into the claims, it is important to keep in mind that the purposes of the specification are to teach and enable those of skill in the art to make and use the invention and to provide a best mode for doing so. . . . One of the best ways to teach a person of ordinary skill in the art how to make and use the invention is to provide an example of how to practice the invention in a particular case. Much of the time, upon reading the specification in that context, it will become clear whether the patentee is setting out specific examples of the invention to accomplish those goals, or whether the patentee instead intends for the claims and the embodiments in the specification to be strictly coextensive. . . . . . The manner in which the patentee uses a term within the specification and claims usually will make the distinction apparent. . . .

In the end, there will still remain some cases in which it will be hard to determine whether a person of skill in the art would understand the embodiments to define the outer limits of the claim term or merely to be exemplary in nature. While that task may present difficulties in some cases, we nonetheless believe that attempting to resolve that problem in the context of the particular patent is likely to capture the scope of the actual invention more accurately than either strictly limiting the scope of the claims to the embodiments disclosed in the specification or divorcing the claim language from the specification.

In *Vitronics*, we did not attempt to provide a rigid algorithm for claim construction, but simply attempted to explain why, in general, certain types of evidence are more valuable than others. Today, we adhere to that approach and reaffirm the approach to claim construction outlined in that case, in *Markman*, and in *Innova*. We now turn to the application of those principles to the case at bar.

IV

A

The critical language of claim 1 of the '798 patent—"further means disposed inside the shell for increasing its load bearing capacity comprising internal steel baffles extending inwardly from the steel shell walls"—imposes three clear requirements with respect to the baffles. First, the baffles must be made of steel. Second, they must be part of the load-bearing means for the wall section. Third, they must be pointed inward from the walls. Both parties, stipulating to a dictionary definition, also conceded that the term "baffles" refers to objects that check, impede, or obstruct the flow of something. The intrinsic evidence confirms that a person of skill in the art would understand that the term "baffles," as used in the '798 patent, would have that generic meaning.

The other claims of the '798 patent specify particular functions to be served by the baffles. For example, dependent claim 2 states that the baffles may be "oriented with the panel sections disposed at angles for deflecting projectiles such as bullets able to penetrate the steel plates." The inclusion of such a specific limitation on the term "baffles" in claim 2 makes it likely that the patentee did not contemplate that the term "baffles" already contained that limitation. *See Dow Chem. Co. v. United States*, 226 F.3d 1334, 1341-42 (Fed. Cir. 2000) (concluding that an independent claim should be given broader scope than a dependent claim to avoid rendering the dependent claim redundant). Independent claim 17 further supports that proposition. It states that baffles are placed "projecting inwardly from the outer shell at angles tending to deflect projectiles that penetrate the outer shell." That limitation would be unnecessary if persons of skill in the art understood that the baffles inherently served such a function. . . . Dependent claim 6 provides an additional requirement for the baffles, stating that "the internal baffles of both outer panel sections overlap and interlock at angles providing deflector panels extending from one end of the module to the other." If the baffles recited in claim 1 were inherently placed at specific angles, or interlocked to form an intermediate barrier, claim 6 would be redundant.

The specification further supports the conclusion that persons of ordinary skill in the art would understand the baffles recited in the '798 patent to be load-bearing objects that serve to check, impede, or obstruct flow. At several points, the specification discusses positioning the baffles so as to deflect projectiles. *See* '798 patent, col. 2, ll.

13-15; *id.*, col. 5, ll. 17-19. The patent states that one advantage of the invention over the prior art is that "there have not been effective ways of dealing with these powerful impact weapons with inexpensive housing." *Id.*, col. 3, ll. 28-30. While that statement makes clear the invention envisions baffles that serve that function, it does not imply that in order to qualify as baffles within the meaning of the claims, the internal support structures must serve the projectile-deflecting function in all the embodiments of all the claims. The specification must teach and enable all the claims, and the section of the written description discussing the use of baffles to deflect projectiles serves that purpose for claims 2, 6, 17, and 23, which specifically claim baffles that deflect projectiles. . . .

The specification discusses several other purposes served by the baffles. For example, the baffles are described as providing structural support. The patent states that one way to increase load-bearing capacity is to use "at least in part inwardly directed steel baffles 15, 16." '798 patent, col. 4, ll. 14-15. The baffle 16 is described as a "strengthening triangular baffle." *Id.*, col. 4, line 37. Importantly, Figures 4 and 6 do not show the baffles as part of an "intermediate interlocking, but not solid, internal barrier." In those figures, the baffle 16 simply provides structural support for one of the walls, as depicted below:

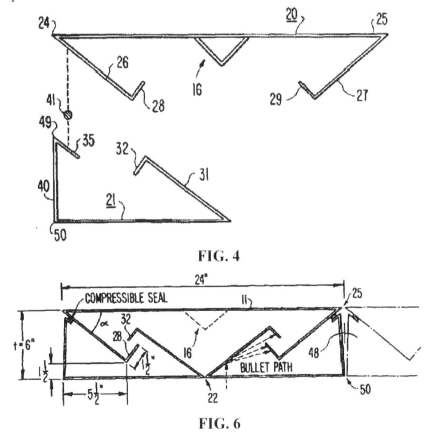

FIG. 4

FIG. 6

Other uses for the baffles are listed in the specification as well. In Figure 7, the overlapping flanges "provide for overlapping and interlocking the baffles to produce substantially an intermediate barrier wall between the opposite [wall] faces":

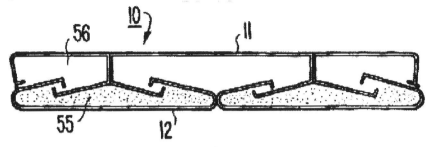

FIG. 7.

'798 patent, col. 5, ll. 26-29. Those baffles thus create small compartments that can be filled with either sound and thermal insulation or rock and gravel to stop projectiles. *Id.*, col. 5, ll. 29-34. By separating the interwall area into compartments (*See, e.g.*, compartment 55 in Figure 7), the user of the modules can choose different types of material for each compartment, so that the module can be "easily custom tailored for the specific needs of each installation." *Id.*, col. 5, ll. 36-37. When material is placed into the wall during installation, the baffles obstruct the flow of material from one compartment to another so that this "custom tailoring" is possible.

The fact that the written description of the '798 patent sets forth multiple objectives to be served by the baffles recited in the claims confirms that the term "baffles" should not be read restrictively to require that the baffles in each case serve all of the recited functions. We have held that "the fact that a patent asserts that an invention achieves several objectives does not require that each of the claims be construed as limited to structures that are capable of achieving all of the objectives." *Liebel-Flarsheim*, 358 F.3d at 908. . . . Although deflecting projectiles is one of the advantages of the baffles of the '798 patent, the patent does not require that the inward extending structures always be capable of performing that function. Accordingly, we conclude that a person of skill in the art would not interpret the disclosure and claims of the '798 patent to mean that a structure extending inward from one of the wall faces is a "baffle" if it is at an acute or obtuse angle, but is not a "baffle" if it is disposed at a right angle.

B

Invoking the principle that "claims should be so construed, if possible, as to sustain their validity," *Rhine v. Casio*, Inc., 183 F.3d 1342, 1345 (Fed. Cir. 1999), AWH argues that the term "baffles" should be given a restrictive meaning because if the term is not construed restrictively, the asserted claims would be invalid.

While we have acknowledged the maxim that claims should be construed to preserve their validity, we have not applied that principle broadly, and we have certainly not endorsed a regime in which validity analysis is a regular component of claim construction. . . . Instead, we have limited the maxim to cases in which "the court concludes, after applying all the available tools of claim construction, that the claim is still ambiguous." *Liebel-Flarsheim*, 358 F.3d at 911. In such cases, we have looked to whether it is reasonable to infer that the PTO would not have issued an invalid patent, and that the ambiguity in the claim language should therefore be resolved in a manner that would preserve the patent's validity.

In this case . . . the claim term at issue is not ambiguous. Thus, it can be construed without the need to consider whether one possible construction would render the claim invalid while the other would not. The doctrine of construing claims to preserve their validity, a doctrine of limited utility in any event, therefore has no applicability here.

In sum, we reject AWH's arguments in favor of a restrictive definition of the term "baffles." Because we disagree with the district court's claim construction, we reverse the summary judgment of noninfringement. In light of our decision on claim construction, it is necessary to remand the infringement claims to the district court for further proceedings.

MAYER, Circuit Judge, with whom NEWMAN, Circuit Judge, joins, dissenting.

Now more than ever I am convinced of the futility, indeed the absurdity, of this court's persistence in adhering to the falsehood that claim construction is a matter of law devoid of any factual component. Because any attempt to fashion a coherent standard under this regime is pointless, as illustrated by our many failed attempts to do so, I dissent.

This court was created for the purpose of bringing consistency to the patent field. *See* H.R. REP. NO 312, 97th Cong., 1st Sess. 20-23 (1981). Instead, we have taken this noble mandate, to reinvigorate the patent and introduce predictability to the field, and focused inappropriate power in this court. In our quest to elevate our importance, we have, however, disregarded our role as an appellate court; the resulting mayhem has seriously undermined the legitimacy of the process, if not the integrity of the institution.

In the name of uniformity, *Cybor Corp. v. FAS Technologies, Inc.*, 138 F.3d 1448 (Fed. Cir. 1998) (en banc), held that claim construction does not involve subsidiary or underlying questions of fact and that we are, therefore, unbridled by either the expertise or efforts of the district court. What we have wrought, instead, is the substitution of a black box, as it so pejoratively has been said of the jury, with the black hole of this court. Out of this void we emit "legal" pronouncements by way of "interpretive necromancy"; these rulings resemble reality, if at all, only by chance. Regardless, and with a blind eye to the consequences, we continue to struggle under this irrational and reckless regime, trying every alternative — dictionaries first, dictionaries second, never dictionaries, etc., etc., etc.

Again today we vainly attempt to establish standards by which this court will interpret claims. But after proposing no fewer than seven questions, receiving more than thirty amici curiae briefs, and whipping the bar into a frenzy of expectation, we say nothing new, but merely restate what has become the practice over the last ten years

— that we will decide cases according to whatever mode or method results in the outcome we desire, or at least allows us a seemingly plausible way out of the case. I am not surprised by this. Indeed, there can be no workable standards by which this court will interpret claims so long as we are blind to the factual component of the task.

While this court may persist in the delusion that claim construction is a purely legal determination, unaffected by underlying facts, it is plainly not the case. Claim construction is, or should be, made in context: a claim should be interpreted both from the perspective of one of ordinary skill in the art and in view of the state of the art at the time of invention. . . . These questions, which are critical to the correct interpretation of a claim, are inherently factual. They are hotly contested by the parties, not by resort to case law as one would expect for legal issues, but based on testimony and documentary evidence. During so called *Markman* "hearings," which are often longer than jury trials, parties battle over experts offering conflicting evidence regarding who qualifies as one of ordinary skill in the art; the meaning of patent terms to that person; the state of the art at the time of the invention; contradictory dictionary definitions and [specifically] which [particular dictionary to use, when more than one was available at the time] would be consulted by the skilled artisan; the scope of specialized terms; the problem a patent was solving; what is related or pertinent art; whether a construction was disallowed during prosecution; how one of skill in the art would understand statements during prosecution; and on and on. In order to reconcile the parties' inconsistent submissions and arrive at a sound interpretation, the district court is required to sift through and weigh volumes of evidence. While this court treats the district court as an intake clerk, whose only role is to collect, shuffle and collate evidence, the reality, as revealed by conventional practice, is far different.

* * *

If we persist in deciding the subsidiary factual components of claim construction without deference, there is no reason why litigants should be required to parade their evidence before the district courts or for district courts to waste time and resources evaluating such evidence. . . . If the proceedings before the district court are merely a "tryout on the road," [citation omitted] . . . as they are under our current regimen, it is wasteful to require such proceedings at all. Instead, all patent cases could be filed in this court; we would determine whether claim construction is necessary, and, if so, the meaning of the claims. Those few cases in which claim construction is not dispositive can be remanded to the district court for trial. In this way, we would at least eliminate the time and expense of the charade currently played out before the district court.

Eloquent words can mask much mischief. The court's opinion today is akin to rearranging the deck chairs on the Titanic — the orchestra is playing as if nothing is amiss, but the ship is still heading for Davey Jones' locker.

COMMENTS AND QUESTIONS

1. *Clarifying Claim Construction Standards.* The *Phillips* case represents the most comprehensive statement of claim construction principles:

Perspective: Claims are construed from the standpoint of the PHOSITA.

Time Period: Claims are construed as of the time of the invention (or the effective filing date; the court treats the two dates as interchangeable, although they are not)

Evidentiary Sources:

- *Intrinsic Evidence* (specification and prosecution history) shall be the principal basis for construing claims
- *Extrinsic Evidence* (expert testimony, dictionaries) are permissible sources, but cannot contradict intrinsic evidence
    - The is no presumption in favor of dictionary definitions
    - The is no heavy presumption in favor of ordinary meaning

---

2. *Are Embodiments Merely Examples or Limitations?* In many construction disputes, including *Phillips*, the dispute boils down to whether the claimed invention is limited to the embodiments (i.e., the examples set forth in the specification) or are those embodiments merely illustrative. While recognizing that "[t]here is sometimes a fine line between reading a claim in light of the specification, and reading a limitation into the claim from the specification," the court nonetheless observes that "[m]uch of the time, upon reading the specification [from the perspective of a PHOSITA], it will become clear whether the patentee is setting out specific examples of the invention to [teach how to make and use the invention], or whether the patentee instead intends for the claims and the embodiments in the specification to be strictly coextensive. The manner in which the patentee uses a term within the specification and claims usually will make the distinction apparent." In reality, however, patent drafters are intentionally vague about this issue so as to leave flexibility to argue either that the claim should not be limited so to ensnare the alleged infringer or should be limited to the embodiments to avoid prior art.

The *Phillips* court emphasized that "although the specification often describes very specific embodiments of the invention, we have repeatedly warned against confining the claims to those embodiments. In particular, we have expressly rejected the contention that if a patent describes only a single embodiment, the claims of the patent must be construed as being limited to that embodiment."

3. *Meaning and Certainty.* Federal Circuit cases have had to decide plausible disagreements over the meanings of the words "a," *North American Vaccine, Inc. v. American Cyanamid Co.*, 7 F.3d 1571, 1581 (Fed. Cir. 1993); "or," *Kustom Signals, Inc. v. Applied Concepts, Inc.*, 264 F.3d 1326 (Fed. Cir. 2001) "to," *Cybor Corp. v. FAS Technologies, Inc.*, 138 F.3d 1448, 1459 (Fed. Cir. 1998); "including," *Toro Co. v. White Consolidated Industries, Inc.*, 199 F.3d 1295 (Fed. Cir. 1999); and "through,"

Sage Products, Inc. v. Devon Industries, Inc., 126 F.3d 1420 (Fed. Cir. 1997), to name but a few, suggesting that even words we think have clear meanings may be subject to interpretation.

Given this, does the focus on the words of the claim make sense at all? Some scholars have argued that the claim construction process is irretrievably broken because it focuses on malleable words chosen by lawyers rather than on what the patentee actually invented. *See* Dan L. Burk & Mark A. Lemley, *Fence Posts or Sign Posts? Rethinking Patent Claim Construction*, 157 U. Pa. L. Rev. 1743 (2009).

4. *Does a Court Have to Construe Each and Every Word in a Disputed Claim?* The answer has traditionally been no. *See* U.S. Surgical Corp. v. Ethicon, Inc., 103 F.3d 1554, 1568 (Fed. Cir. 1997) ("Claim construction is a matter of resolution of disputed meanings and technical scope, to clarify and when necessary to explain what the patentee covered by the claims, for use in the determination of infringement. It is not an obligatory exercise in redundancy."); *Acumed LLC v. Stryker Corp.*, 483 F.3d 800, 806 (Fed. Cir. 2007) ("[A] sound claim construction need not always purge every shred of ambiguity. The resolution of some line-drawing problems—especially easy ones like this one—is properly left to the trier of fact."). Federal judges regularly limit the number of disputed terms they will construe. *See* Peter S. Menell, et al., Patent Case Management Judicial Guide §5.1.2. (Federal Judicial Center) (3rd ed. 2016) (mechanisms for limiting the number of claim terms to construe).

Increasingly, however, the Federal Circuit has emphasized that when the parties have a dispute over the scope of the claim, it is the district court, not the jury, that must resolve that dispute. See O2 Micro Int'l v. Beyond Innovation Tech. Co., 521 F.3d 1351, 1362 (Fed. Cir. 2008) (although "district courts are not (and should not be) required to construe every limitation present in a patent's asserted claims," the court must interpret the scope of any claim term for which the parties have presented a "fundamental dispute."); *EON IP Corp. v. Silver Spring Networks*, 815 F.3d 1314 (Fed. Cir. 2016) (reversing district court for failing to construe the terms "mobile" and "portable" when it was evident the parties gave those terms different meanings).

Does it make sense to construe ordinary English terms, as opposed to technical terms a jury might not be expected to understand? Does construing non-technical terms encroach upon the jury's prerogative?

5. *Meaning as of When?* At what point in time should a court consider the meaning of a claim term — when the claim was filed in a patent application, at the time the infringement took place, or some other time? *PC Connector Solutions LLC v. SmartDisk Corp.*, 406 F.3d 1359 (Fed. Cir. 2005), holds that the claim words "conventional," "traditional," and "standard" should be interpreted as being temporally limited to the conventions, traditions, and standards that existed at the time when the patent was filed. The patent at issue covered a device for connecting peripheral devices to a computer via the computer's disk drive. Claim 1 of the patent is representative:

1. In combination a computer having a diskette drive, an end user computer peripheral device having an input/output port normally connectible to a *conventional* computer input/output port, and a coupler which couples the computer with the end user computer peripheral device without using a *conventional* computer input/output port: said coupler being sized and shaped for insertion within the diskette drive of the computer . . . whereby data is transferred from said computer to said end user computer peripheral device via said read/write head of said computer, said coupler, and said input/output port of said end user computer peripheral device.

The accused devices in the case were couplers to link peripheral devices through a computer disk drive, but the couplers were designed to handle a particular class of peripheral devices—flash memories and smart cards that have flat, planar surface contact electrodes as their normal connecting elements (connectors radically different from the sort of multi-pronged connectors conventional in 1988). The court held that the accused devices could not infringe the patent because the relevant claim language limited the invention to an adapter for peripheral devices having 1988-style connectors:

We find nothing in the written description that amounts to a clear attempt by the patentee to impart any special meaning to the words "normally," "conventional," "traditionally," or "standard." Likewise, in the prosecution history, we do not read the patentability arguments that were made specifically to distinguish a test fixture as having effected the particular redefinition now advanced on appeal. As a consequence, the terms "normally," "conventional," "traditionally," and "standard" are governed by their ordinary and customary meanings, and that, in view of their implicit time-dependence, the district court did not err in construing the literal scope of the claim limitations qualified by those terms as being limited to technologies existing at the time of the invention.

PC Connector's argument that the dictionary definitions of "normally," "conventional," "traditionally," and "standard" contain no explicit reference to a time limitation is not persuasive, as their time-related significance is implicit from their ordinary usage—just as other words are implicitly not time-related. A comparison of the words "conventional" and "dedicated" is instructive in this regard, as PC Connector's briefs appear to treat them as interchangeable and coterminous in claim scope, when, in fact, they are not. To illustrate, a present-day USB port may be described as a "dedicated" I/O port within the ordinary meaning of "dedicated" as that word would be used to characterize the I/O ports found on a computer built in 1988, yet it would not be considered "conventional" back then, even though it is "conventional" today. Thus, unlike the word "dedicated," the word "conventional" necessarily has a meaning specific to the time of filing.

406 F.3d at 1363-64. Do these words have "implicit" time-related significance? Why did the patentee invite this discussion by limiting the claim to an adapter for peripherals

having "conventional" connectors? For more on this important issue, *see* Mark A. Lemley, *The Changing Meaning of Patent Claim Terms*, 104 MICH. L. REV. 101 (2005) (arguing that patent claim terms should have a fixed meaning throughout time, and that that meaning should be fixed at the time the patent application is first filed).

6. *Standard of Appellate Review*. One of the most controversial issues briefed, but not resolved, in *Phillips* was whether the Federal Circuit should review district court decisions de novo, i.e., without deference to underlying factual findings. Judge Mayer's dissent took the issue up, but did not bring along enough of his colleagues.

District Judge Pechman's barb that "you might as well throw darts" in construing claims took aim at the Federal Circuit's lack of deference to district judges' determinations. The issue turns on whether claim construction entails underlying factual findings. Fed. R. Civ. Pro. 52(a)(6) requires a court of appeals to uphold a district court's findings of fact unless they are clearly erroneous.

Following the Supreme Court's *Markman* decision, the Federal Circuit took the position that claim construction was a pure question of law and hence Rule 52(a)(6) did not apply to review of claim construction rulings. *See Cybor Corp. v. FAS Technologies, Inc.*, 138 F.3d 1448 (Fed. Cir. 1998) (en banc). The Supreme Court did not expressly resolve this question in *Markman*, but nonetheless characterized claim construction as a "mongrel [or mixed fact/law] practice." *Markman v. Westview Instruments, Inc.*, 517 U.S. 370, 378 (1996). If the parties offer conflicting evidence as to how a PHOSITA would understand the disputed claim term, would a district court need to make a factual finding?

The deference issue continued to reverberate in the Federal Circuit after the *Phillips* decision. Even though the claim construction reversal rate dropped significantly, *see* J. Jonas Anderson & Peter S. Menell, *Informal Deference: A Historical, Empirical, and Normative Analysis of Patent Claim Construction*, 108 NW. U. L. REV. 1, 41-42, 48-56 (2014), judges within the circuit remained split on the proper standard of review. The Supreme Court finally resolved the controversy in *Teva Pharmaceuticals USA, Inc. v. Sandoz, Inc.*, 135 S.Ct. 831 (2015). The Court held that claim construction can entail fact-finding and restored the fundamental juridical principle—reflected in Federal Rule of Civil Procedure 52(a)(6)—that the Federal Circuit, like other appellate courts, must "give due regard to the trial court's opportunity to judge the witnesses' credibility" and defer to the trial court's factual determinations unless "clearly erroneous." Nonetheless, the Court recognized the primacy of the intrinsic evidence. Thus, while factual determinations underlying claim construction rulings are subject to the "clearly erroneous" (or "abuse of discretion") standard of review, the Federal Circuit exercises *de novo* review over the ultimate claim construction decision. In this manner, district judges can use their distinctive vantage point and evidentiary tools to ferret out factual underpinnings while the Federal Circuit can operate as a check on fidelity to the patent instrument.

As a practical matter, however, very little has changed since *Teva*. Courts overwhelmingly focus on intrinsic evidence, following *Phillips*, and so the Federal Circuit has not had occasion to defer to district court factfinding on claim construction. This may change if district judges begin to hold evidentiary hearings as part of claim construction and make formal factual findings as to the meaning of disputed claim terms. *See* J. Jonas Anderson & Peter S. Menell, *Restoring the Fact/Law Distinction in Patent Claim Construction*, 109 Nw. U. L. Rev. Online 187 (2015).

3. Canons of Claim Construction

Courts have established a set of rules, or canons, of interpretation to help guide the claim construction process. *See generally* Peter S. Menell, Matthew D. Powers, & Steven C. Carlson, *Patent Claim Construction: A Modern Synthesis and Structured Framework*, 25 Berkeley Tech. L.J. 711 (2010).

i. Ordinary vs. Contextual or "Particular" Meaning

Reliance on context is actually a collection of rules and sub-doctrines, rather than a single canon. The general issue is this: claims are skeletal, employing as few words as possible. (Remember that in general the fewer the words, the broader the claim; and breadth is the goal of all claim drafters.) Specifications, by contrast, are written to put flesh on these bones — to provide background and depth to explain how an invention works. The goal in drafting a specification is to satisfy the enablement and written description requirements of §112—to tell people in the art how to "make and use" the invention. Often a word used in a claim will also be used in the specification — in context. These contrasting uses provide the grist for many a hard-fought contest over claim interpretation.

As a starting point, the Federal Circuit has often stated its presumption that the meaning of words in a claim is the "ordinary," i.e., non-contextual, meaning that would be assigned to those words. *Phillips v. AWH Corp.* 415 F.3d 1303, 1312-13 (Fed. Cir. 2005) (en banc).

ii. Contextual Meaning

Despite starting with ordinary meaning, most claim interpretation cases turn on contextual (or, as the *Phillips* court called them, "particular") meanings. The dispute in *Nystrom v. TREX Co., Inc.*, 424 F.3d 1136 (Fed. Cir. 2005), concerned the term "board." Nystrom, the patentee, claimed "[a] board for use in constructing a flooring surface for exterior use. . . ." Nystrom's specification as well as the prosecution history consistently described his decking invention with respect to *wooden* boards. The accused infringer, TREX, sold exterior decking planks made from composites of wood fibers and recycled plastic. Nystrom argued for the plain or ordinary meaning of "board" and cited various dictionary definitions to prove that the "ordinary" or "plain" meaning of "board" is not limited to a thing made of wood. Nystrom's specification, however, consistently described his decking invention with respect to *wooden* boards. The court limited Nystrom to the context and background of the specification to flesh out—and hence limit—the meaning of the word in the claim.

iii.   *"Lexicographer" Rule*

The "ordinary meaning" approach has a further limitation: patentees are free to be their own lexicographers—i.e., to define claim terms in any way they wish. *Phillips v. AWH Corp.*, 415 F.3d 1303, 1316 (Fed. Cir. 2005) (en banc) ("[O]ur cases recognize that the specification may reveal a special definition given to a claim term by the patentee that differs from the meaning it would otherwise possess. In such cases, the inventor's lexicography governs."); *Jack Guttman, Inc. v. Kopykake Enterprises, Inc.*, 302 F.3d 1352 (Fed. Cir. 2002) (providing a rare example of a patentee expressly defining a term). *Jack Gutman Enterprises* is a very rare case: the vast majority of cases that cite the "lexicographer rule" do *not* involve an explicit definition. *Cf. Martek Biosciences Corp. v. Nutrinova, Inc.*, 579 F.3d 1363 (Fed. Cir. 2009) (unusual five-judge panel case, in which majority and dissent disagreed about the effectiveness of a definition of "animal" that included humans; dissent argued that this definition conflicted with consistent usage in the specification). Because of this, the "lexicographer rule" is very often invoked in service of the routine search for contextual or "particular" meaning, as described above.

In an effort to promote claim clarity, the PTO instituted a pilot program to encourage applicants to provide glossaries by offering accelerated examination. The program ended as a result of the relatively low participation. *See* USPTO, Glossary Initiative, http://www.uspto.gov/patent/initiatives/glossary-initiative.

iv.   *Disclaimer of Subject Matter*

Accused infringers often contend that language in a patent's specification forms a special contextual meaning for a word used in a patent claim. At times, "meaning through context" involves the more specific argument that a patentee has affirmatively *disclaimed* a certain meaning. This can arise through language in the specification or, commonly, statements made during patent prosecution. If successful, this argument establishes that certain interpretations of claim language are foreclosed by the patentee's own explicit statements.

AstraZeneca AB, Inc. v. Mutual, 384 F.3d 1333 (Fed. Cir. 2004) illustrates the disavowal doctrine. The principal claim in the key patent at issue reads as follows:

> 1. A solid preparation providing extended release of an active compound with very low solubility in water comprising a solution or dispersion of an effective amount of the active compound in a semi-solid or liquid nonionic solubilizer, wherein the amount by weight of the solubilizer is at least equal to the amount by weight of the active compound, and a release controlling system to provide extended release.

The dispute centered on the term "solubilizer." The Federal Circuit observed that "[t]he parties agree that as a general matter, artisans would understand the term 'solubilizer' to embrace three distinct types of chemicals: (1) surface active agents (also known as "surfactants"), (2) co-solvents, and (3) complexation agents." 384 F.3d 1333, 1336 (footnote omitted). The district court, looking to "ordinary meaning," held that "solubilizer" comprised three types of chemicals noted above based on a dictionary definition. The Federal Circuit reversed on the ground that the patentee had specifically "disavowed" the latter two categories of chemicals.

> [W]e hold that the inventors deliberately acted as their own lexicographers. The 'Description of the Invention' states that '[t]he solubilizers suitable according to the invention *are defined below*' (emphasis added), and two paragraphs later, states that '[t]he solubilizers suitable for the preparations according to the invention are semi-solid or liquid non-ionic *surface active agents*' (emphasis added). Astrazeneca maintains that these statements simply refer to preferred embodiments of 'suitable' solubilizers. We might agree if the specification stated, for example, '*a solubilizer* suitable for the preparations according to the invention,' but in fact, the specification definitively states '*the solubilizers* suitable for the preparations according to the invention' (emphasis added). Astrazeneca seems to suggest that lexicography requires a statement in the form 'I define _____ to mean _____,' but such rigid formalism is not required. . . Certainly the '081 specification's statement that '[t]he solubilizers suitable according to the invention are defined below' provides a strong signal of lexicography.

384 F.3d 1333, 1340. The court then turned to "disavowal":

> Second, we hold the specification clearly disavows nonsurfactant solubilizers. The inventors' lexicography alone works an implicit disavowal of nonsurfactant solubilizers, but the rest of the specification goes further. The 'Description of the Invention' twice describes micelle structures as a feature of the novel formulation structure conceived by the inventors. . . . It is undisputed that surfactants are the only solubilizers believed to form micelle structures in watery environments. Indeed, immediately after the reference to the 'micelle-structure formed by the solubilizer' of the invention, the specification criticizes other types of solubilizers—and specifically co-solvents—as leading to undesirable precipitation. . . . AstraZeneca contends that these statements in the specification simply address the features of preferred embodiments. Astrazeneca seems to suggest that clear disavowal requires an 'expression of manifest exclusion or restriction' in the form of 'my invention does not include _____.' But again, such rigid formalism is not required: Where the general summary or description of the invention describes a feature of the invention (here, micelles formed by the solubilizer) and criticizes other products (here, other solubilizers, including co-solvents) that lack that same feature, this

operates as a clear disavowal of these other products (and processes using these products).

384 F.3d 1333, 1340.

The Federal Circuit requires that any such disavowal be "clear and unambiguous" to alter claim scope. *See Microsoft Corp. v. Multi-Tech Sys., Inc.*, 357 F.3d 1340 (Fed. Cir. 2004). It regularly resists efforts to change the ordinary meaning of claim terms through disclaimer, particularly when it is based on the prosecution history rather than the specification.

v. *"Claim Differentiation": Contextual Meaning from Other Claims*

The doctrine of claim differentiation is the patent law version of a general principle of legal interpretation: the non-redundancy principle. *See, e.g., Bailey v. United States*, 516 U.S. 137, 146 (1995) ("We assume that Congress used two terms because it intended each term to have a particular, nonsuperfluous meaning."); *Reiter v. Sonotone Corp.*, 442 U.S. 330, 339 (1979) ("In construing a statute we are obliged to give effect, if possible, to every word Congress used."); *Colautti v. Franklin*, 439 U.S. 379, 392 (1979) (explaining that an "elementary canon of construction [is] that a statute should be interpreted so as not to render one part inoperative"). The court relied on the claim differentiation doctrine in *Phillips*. Do you agree with its analysis?

Recall that the issue in *Nystrom* was the meaning of the word "board." The accused infringer, TREX, wanted to limit the meaning of the claim to "wooden boards," so as to exclude TREX's composite boards from the definition and therefore from legal liability for infringement. Nystrom argued that the meaning of "board" in claim 1 could not logically be limited to "wooden boards," because claim 16 of the Nystrom patent specifically claimed "a wooden board." Interpreting "board" in claim 1 as implicitly meaning "wooden board" would render meaningless the language of claim 16. If "board" in this patent means "wooden board," claim 16 would mean "wooden wooden board"—a ridiculous proposition. Why might that argument not have prevailed? *Cf.* Mark A. Lemley, *The Limits of Claim Differentiation*, 22 BERKELEY TECH. L.J. 1389 (2007) (arguing that claim differentiation should be applied with caution because patent drafters are often aiming for redundancy).

vi. *Purpose or Goal of the Invention*

One contextual clue that courts have used to supply meaning for a claim term is the purpose or goal of an invention. In *Minnesota Mining & Manufacturing Co. v. Johnson & Johnson Orthopaedics, Inc.*, 976 F.2d 1559 (Fed. Cir. 1992), *Minnesota Mining* held a series of patents related to orthopedic casting tapes and, more specifically, to resin-based casting systems which have replaced the old-fashioned plaster casts. The claimed casts were formed from curable sheets of material. Several key claims required that each sheet have a "lubricant" or be "pre-lubricated." Polyethylene and silicon were identified in the patent as effective lubricants. This posed a problem, given that certain references in the prior art disclosed identical lubricants, but those lubricants were said to be directed to other functions, and when used they resulted in a "tacky" surface that would not serve the purpose of making a smooth orthopedic cast. The Federal Circuit interpreted the claims at issue so as to find no anticipation. The district court had found that the lubricants disclosed in the patent specification were designed to make the sheet's resin slippery when activated. The Federal Circuit held that it was absolutely correct to "use the specification . . . to determine what the inventor meant by terms and phrases in the claims." And, more importantly: "The fundamental purpose and significance of the [patented] invention is to produce a non-sticky or non-tacky resin (i.e., a slippery resin) to permit smoothing and forming of the casting tapes, thereby overcoming the 'tacky resin' problem of the prior art. . . . This is evident throughout the patent specification."

Related to this idea is the canon that a construction that excludes the patentee's preferred embodiment is ordinarily improper. *Vitronics Corp. v. Conceptronic, Inc.,* 90 F.3d 1576, 1578 (Fed. Cir. 1996) ("Such an interpretation is rarely, if ever, correct and would require highly persuasive evidentiary support.").

vii.   *Construing Claims to Preserve Their Validity*

A traditional maxim of claim construction was that claims should be construed, where possible, to preserve their validity. *See, e.g., Rhine v. Casio, Inc.,* 183 F.3d 1342, 1345 (Fed. Cir. 1999) ("claims should be so construed, if possible, as to sustain their validity"). This canon too has its roots in statutory interpretation—the rule that statutes are to be construed where possible to avoid raising constitutional questions. Similarly, courts sought to construe claims to avoid raising questions of validity. Almost always, that maxim counseled in favor of construing those claims narrowly.

Since *Markman,* however, courts have shied away from applying this doctrine. In part the problem is procedural: a court construing patent claims pretrial cannot know how a jury will rule on the question of validity. *Phillips* was dismissive of the canon, and it has fallen into general disuse in the wake of that opinion. The courts have warned that this canon is "a last resort, not a first principle." *MBO Labs., Inc. v. Becton, Dickinson & Co.,* 474 F.3d 1323, 1331 (Fed. Cir. 2007). And in any event, patent claim drafters should not rely on courts to save their patents from inadvertent drafting errors. This was the sad lesson of the drafter in *Chef America, Inc. v. Lamb-Weston, Inc.,* 358 F.3d 1371, 1371 (Fed. Cir. 2004), who made the mistake of claiming that its cookie dough product should be baked "to" a temperature of 450–800 degrees Fahrenheit. Though the drafter obviously meant to claim a process of baking by heating *the oven* to this temperature, and then baking for a brief time, the court would not change the clearly stated claim language; so the inventor ended up with a patent that covered only charred hunks of blackened dough.

viii.   *Narrow Construction Preferred*

Some have suggested, drawing upon the *contra proferentem* contract law principle, that the claims should be interpreted against the draftsperson, i.e., the patentee. *See 3M Innovative Properties Cos. v. Tredegar Corp.*, 725 F.3d 1315, 1336 (Fed. Cir. 2013). Does this analogy make sense? Should it matter whether (as is normally true) the patentee wants the claim construed broadly or whether (as it sometimes the case) it is the accused infringer who wants the broad construction? The final canon of construction may be expressed as a tie-breaker rule: when two interpretations are equally plausible, choose the narrower interpretation. Hence, the rule is to be deployed sparingly, only in cases that remain close after all other interpretive resources have been exhausted. But sometimes after all the rules are applied, two equally plausible interpretations of a claim — one broader, one narrower — are possible. In such a case, the Federal Circuit has held that the "notice function" of claims requires that the narrower interpretation prevail. *See Athletic Alternatives, Inc. v. Prince Manufacturing, Inc.*, 73 F.3d 1573, 1581 (Fed. Cir. 1996).

An argument can be made that the *contra proferentem* rule ought to be applied routinely so as to encourage more clarity and less opportunism by patent drafters. *See* Peter S. Menell & Michael J. Meurer, *Notice Failure and Notice Externalities*, 5 J. LEGAL ANALYSIS 1 (2013).

The following chart summarizes the principal claim construction principles and canons:

FOUNDATIONAL PRINCIPLES

- Construe from perspective of one of ordinary skill in the art
- Construe from time period of invention (i.e., effective filing date)
- Interpret claim terms by reference to patent and prosecution history as a whole
- Appropriate to consider extrinsic evidence, but it cannot contradict intrinsic evidence
  - No "presumption in favor of dictionary definition"
  - No "heavy presumption" of ordinary meaning

ORDINARY MEANING

FACTORS THAT FAVOR NARROWER CONSTRUCTION

DESCRIPTION OF INVENTION

- Characterization of "the present invention"
- Distinctions over the prior art
- Consistent usage of claim terms in patent and prosecution history

PROSECUTION DISCLAIMER

- Surrendering claim scope during prosecution narrows claim interpretation
- "Clear and unmistakable disavowal" required for prosecution disclaimer

SPECIAL CASES

- Inventors may expressly define terms differently than ordinary meaning
- Specification may disclaim coverage to embodiments
- Ambiguity in claim term may permit limiting scope to preferred embodiment
- Means-plus-function terms are limited to structures in specification, and equivalents

FACTORS THAT FAVOR BROADER CONSTRUCTION

CLAIM DIFFERENTIATION

- "Pure" claim differentiation creates a presumption that independent claims are broader than dependent claims
- Presumption may be rebutted based on specification or prosecution history, or where §112, ¶6 involved

PREFERRED EMBODIMENT GENERALLY NOT LIMITING

Peter S. Menell, et al., Patent Case Management Judicial Guide §5.2.3.2.1 (Federal Judicial Center) (3rd ed. 2016).

PROBLEM

Problem III-13. Pizza King holds U.S. Patent No. 4,498,686 pertaining to a "package saver" invention.

Abstract

A temperature resistant molded plastic device is described for use in boxes or packages such as pizza boxes where there is a tendency of large cover portions to sag downwardly to damage the soft pizza or other packaged products. In use, the saver is positioned near the center of the package to support the box cover for protecting the contents.

Background of the Invention

[T]he invention relates to such a package saver which is molded from plastic to have minimal size, weight, and cost and which is suitable for supporting large carton covers such as those used for pizza pies. The molded plastic saver is positioned centrally of the completed pie or other product to support the cover during storage and delivery. * * *

[A]n object of the present invention is to provide an easily manufactured, relatively inexpensive, lightweight article which is placed on the pie or cake within the package to support the central portion of the package cover during delivery.

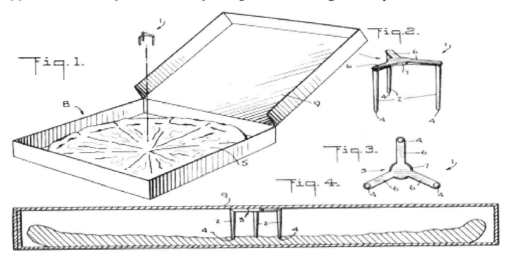

Description of the Preferred Embodiment

To provide a lightweight and inexpensive device for the purpose discussed above, the saver is preferably molded as a unitary device from one of the plastics which is heat resistant such as the thermo set plastics and which will resist temperatures of as high as about 500° F.

In its preferred form, as illustrated, the saver 1 has spaced vertical legs 2 connected to a cover support 3. The lower portions of the legs 4 have a minimal cross section to minimize any marking of the protected article 5 and they are also made thin for minimizing the volume of plastic required. The cover support 3 of the saver 1 also preferably has a minimum volume by consisting of a spoke-like arrangement of radially oriented leg supports 6 molded to extend from a central portion 7.

This construction of portion support 3 provides a suitable broad and stable support for box 8 cover 9 which is of minimal volume and thus has minimal cost. A disposable saver 1 is provided which may be used in the boxes or cartons without damage to the packaged pizza pie or other product.

As various changes may be made in the form, construction and arrangement of the invention and without departing from the spirit and scope of the invention, and without sacrificing any of its advantages, it is to be understood that all matters herein is to be interpreted as illustrative and not in a limiting sense.

Claims

Having thus described my invention, I claim:

1. in combination a package having a flexible cover, a food article packaged therein and spaced downwardly from the cover, a unitary molded plastic package saving device for positioning between the cover and the article for supporting the package cover thereby preventing damage to the packaged food article by the cover, said device comprising the combination of three or more spaced legs, each leg having one relatively flat end adapted for engaging the packaged article and having its opposite end attached to a device cover portion.

2. The combination as claimed in claim 1 in which said device cover portion comprises a number of flat cover sections radiating from a common flat central portion.

3. The combination as claimed in claim 1 wherein said device is formed of heat resistant plastic.

4. The combination as claimed in claim 1 wherein said device is formed of thermo-setting plastic.

* * * * *

Giuseppe's Pizza develops its own package saver device by fusing together two plastic pieces.

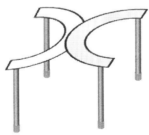

Pizza King sues for patent infringement. The court schedules a Markman hearing to construe the patent claim. What is Giuseppe's best claim construction? What is Pizza King's best response? On what do you base the argument and counter-argument? If you were the judge, what would you decide?

4. The Special Case (and Problems) of Functional Claims – §112(f)

Patent scope plays a critical role in patent law. Beginning in the middle of the nineteenth century, inventors sought greater breadth in the boundaries of their invention by attempting to define their invention at a higher level of abstraction. Rather than claiming the device they actually built or described, inventors sought to identify the inventive contribution and to claim any device that incorporated that inventive contribution, even if it was not identical to the patentee's device. These patentees were using claim language to define a conceptual area rather than identify specific patent boundaries. *See* Mark A. Lemley, *Software Patents and the Return of Functional Claiming*, 2013 WIS. L. REV. 905. An inventor of a new chemical might, for instance, claim a group of related chemicals—a genus—rather than specify each of the species.

The Wright Brothers, for instance, invented only a particular improvement to flying machines, albeit a critical one: they came up with a way of warping a wing to control the direction of flight while turning a rear rudder to counterbalance the effect of bending the wing, maintaining the stability of the plane. JOHN ANDERSON, JR., INVENTING FLIGHT: THE WRIGHT BROTHERS AND THEIR PREDECESSORS 101 (2004). The Wrights solved the stability problem by having a single cable warp the wing and turn the rudder at the same time. Their patent, however, was written using functional language, claiming "means for simultaneously moving the lateral portions [of a wing] into different angular relations" and "means whereby said rudder is caused to present to the wind that side thereof . . . having the smaller angle of incidence." U.S. Patent No. 821,393 claim 7 (filed Mar. 23, 1903). Glenn Curtiss improved the design of the wing by using ailerons, movable portions of the wing. Ailerons could be moved independently of the rudder by the pilot; the two were not connected, as they were in the Wright's design. But the Wright Brothers nonetheless successfully asserted the patent against subsequent inventors such as Glenn Curtiss. Judge Learned Hand held that the ailerons under separate control were literally within the scope of the patent. *Wright Co. v. Paulhan*, 177 F. 261, 264 (C.C.S.D.N.Y. 1910) (holding the Wrights' patent to be pioneering and so entitled to broad scope). A frustrated Curtiss was reported to have said that the Wright brothers believed their patent was so broad that anyone who jumped up and down and flapped their arms infringed it. The Wrights successfully enforced their patent to defeat all alternative aircraft, including many that surpassed the technical achievement of the Wrights.

By the 1940s, functional claiming of this sort had become widespread. The Supreme Court rejected the practice in 1946 in *Halliburton Oil Well Cementing Co. v. Walker*, 329 U.S. 1 (1946); *cf. Funk Bros. Seed Co. v. Kalo Inoculant Co.*, 333 U.S. 127, 133 (1948) (Frankfurter, J., concurring) (arguing that claims to groups of bacteria that are "not identified and are identifiable only by their compatibility" should be rejected because similar efforts to claim by function in other areas are impermissible). In *Halliburton*, the patentee had drafted its claim entirely in functional terms, referring to "means for" performing various functions. The Court held that the patent claim was indefinite because it did not specify how the patent performed the function or limited the invention to the particular means the patentee actually invented. Substituting broad functional language at the very point of novelty, the Court said, did not sufficiently put the world on notice of what the patentee was removing from the world.

Patent lawyers took their case to Congress. When Congress passed the Patent Act of 1952 six years after *Halliburton*, it overruled Halliburton insofar as that decision had prevented functional claiming at the point of novelty. Patentees could once again use functional language such as "means for processing data" even if the data processing means was the novel part of the invention. Nonetheless, Congress limited the scope of "means-plus-function" claim elements. Section 112(f) provides:

> An element in a claim for a combination may be expressed as a means or step for performing a specified function without the recital of structure, material, or acts in support thereof, and such claim shall be construed to cover the corresponding structure, material, or acts described in the specification and equivalents thereof.

This "means-plus-function" claiming represents a significant departure from the normal rules of patent claim construction. Patent claim construction starts with the plain meaning of the claim language. While the description of the invention can be read to help understand what the claims mean, the fundamental rule of patent claim construction is that the claim terms are not to be narrowed by reference to what the patentee actually invented or described. A patentee can, for example, claim a group of chemicals without having described, much less tested, all or even many of the chemicals in the group. Similarly, a patent claim to a "chair comprising a seat, legs, and a back" would cover a nearly infinite array of chairs, regardless of how many legs it has, whether it has wheels on the legs, and whether it is made of wood, metal, plastic, or upholstery. *See* Jeffrey A. Lefstin, *The Formal Structure of Patent Law and the Limits of Enablement*, 23 BERKELEY TECH. L.J. 1141, 1169-70 (2008). Further, if the patentee uses the magic word "comprising" (and virtually all do) the patent claim must include the listed elements but is not limited to those elements; adding additional elements (such as arms) will not avoid infringement.

Against this backdrop, §112(f) actually represents a significant narrowing of claim scope. While the 1952 Act rejected *Halliburton* and permitted functional claiming, in fact the sort of functional claiming the statutory text allows is far different from the functional claiming that was the norm in 1940. A means-plus-function claim element is not interpreted to cover every means of performing the function. Instead, the courts apply a different rule of claim construction, limiting the scope of these claims by reading in the particular technologies described in the patent specification.

To take an example, suppose that the patent claim includes as an element a "means for processing data." Read literally, without reference to §112(f), this language would encompass any possible means for processing data, including any computer, but also a calculator, an abacus, pencil and paper, and perhaps even the human brain. Section

112(f) permits the use of such functional language but doesn't permit it to cover any means of performing the data-processing function. Instead, the claim would be limited to the particular "means for processing data" actually described in the patent specification (say, an iPad) "and equivalents thereof."

While the last phrase in the statute—"and equivalents thereof"—permits some broadening of both means-plus-function and step-plus-function claims, such equivalents must have been known as of the time of the invention. (As we will see in (D)(1)(a)(ii), *infra*, the doctrine of equivalents can provide an additional stretch to "equivalents" based on after-arising advances, i.e., based on technologies that emerge after the time of the invention claimed using functional language.) The first stage in the analysis is whether the term in question is "mean-plus-function." *See DePuy Spine, Inc. v. Medtronic Sofamor Danek, Inc.*, 469 F.3d 1005, 1023 (Fed. Cir. 2006) (Means-plus-function claiming applies only to "purely functional limitations that do not provide the structure that performs the recited function."). The Federal Circuit applied a rebuttable presumption that §112(f) applies "[i]f the word 'means' appears in a claim element in association with a function." *Callicrate v. Wadsworth Mfg., Inc.*, 427 F.3d 1361, 1368 (Fed. Cir. 2005). As illustrated in *Phillips*, however, the presumption is rebutted where the claim language itself provides the structure that performs the recited function.

This presumption against construing such limitations under §112(f) used to be characterized as a "strong" presumption. *See Inventio AG v. ThyssenKrupp Elevator Americas Corp.*, 649 F.3d 1350, 1358 (Fed. Cir. 2011). To rein in vague claims, the Federal Circuit revoked this characterization of the presumption as "strong" in *Williamson v. Citrix Online LLC*, 792 F.3d 1339 (Fed. Cir. 2015) (en banc): a term lacking "means" will nonetheless be construed under §112(f) if the "challenger demonstrates that the claim fails to recite sufficiently definite structure or else recites function without reciting sufficient structure for performing that function." The focus is on the claim language as a whole, not just the isolated term that is akin to "means." Generic terms such as "mechanism," "element," "device" and other such terms that do not connote sufficiently definite structure in the context of the overall claim are tantamount to stating "means," and therefore may be construed pursuant to §112(f) if nothing else in the claim provides sufficient structure. The Federal Circuit referred to such "black box" words as "nonce" words. The focus should remain on whether the term, in the context of the claim as a whole, connotes a class (even a broad class) of specific structures. If so, then the term should not be construed under §112(f).

Once it is determined that §112(f) applies, then the court proceeds through three steps: (1) identifying the function of the term based upon claim term language (but not embodiments); (2) identifying the corresponding structure, material, or act based on disclosed embodiments; and (3) at the infringement stage, the fact-finder determines whether the accused device falls within "equivalents thereof" as of the time of patent issuance. *See* PETER S. MENELL, ET AL., PATENT CASE MANAGEMENT JUDICIAL GUIDE, §5.2.3.5 (Federal Judicial Center 3rd ed. 2016).

PROBLEM

Problem III-14. Ernest Kahlert obtained a patent for in-line skates in 1953. His breakthrough related to cushioning the wheels. To avoid cluttering his apparatus claim with detailed explanation of the upper portion of the device, he began his claim as follows: "An in-line roller skate, comprising an upper portion adapted to receive the skater's foot, a means for fastening said upper portion . . ." His specification notes that "[t]he upper portion of the roller blade can be fastened with laces, zippers, buckles, and snaps."

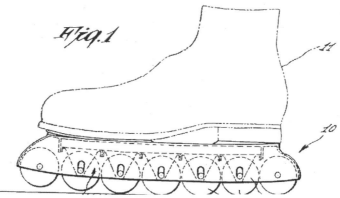

Unbeknownst to Kahlert, a Swiss electrical engineer George de Mestral had been experimenting with a new method of fastening. While walking in the woods, he wondered if the burrs that clung to his trousers—and dog—could be turned into something useful. This led him to develop a hook and loop fastener, which he patented in 1955. The fastener consisted of two components: a lineal fabric strip with tiny hooks that could "mate" with another fabric strip with smaller loops, attaching temporarily, until pulled apart. The early prototypes were made of cotton, which proved impractical. He eventually landed on the idea of using nylon and polyester, which became a great success. De Mestral gave the name Velcro, combining the French words *velours* ("velvet"), and *crochet* ("hook").

In 1958, Rollerglide introduced an inline skate that had all of the elements of Kahlert's claimed invention except that it used a compression strap combined with a buckle as well as Velcro (duly licensed) to fasten the upper portion of the shoe. The compression strap/buckle and Velcro fasteners held the foot snuggly, while providing flexibility. Inline skate enthusiasts loved it and it quickly displaced sales of Kaglert's product. Kahlert seeks your advice on whether Rollerglide's product falls within the scope of Kahlert's claim. Does Rollerglide's product come within Kahlert's claim? Explain how you reached this conclusion.

5.   Claim Indefiniteness

Nautilus, Inc. v. Biosig Instruments, Inc.
U.S. Supreme Court
134 S.Ct. 2120 (2014)

Justice GINSBURG delivered the opinion of the Court.

The Patent Act requires that a patent specification "conclude with one or more claims *particularly pointing out and distinctly claiming* the subject matter which the applicant regards as [the] invention." 35 U.S.C. §112[(b)] (emphasis added). This case, involving a heart-rate monitor used with exercise equipment, concerns the proper reading of the statute's clarity and precision demand. According to the Federal Circuit, a patent claim passes the §112[(b)] threshold so long as the claim is "amenable to construction," and the claim, as construed, is not "insolubly ambiguous." 715 F.3d 891, 898-899 (2013). We conclude that the Federal Circuit's formulation, which tolerates some ambiguous claims but not others, does not satisfy the statute's definiteness requirement. In place of the "insolubly ambiguous" standard, we hold that a patent is invalid for indefiniteness if its claims, read in light of the specification delineating the patent, and the prosecution history, fail to inform, with reasonable certainty, those skilled in the art about the scope of the invention. Expressing no opinion on the validity of the patent-in-suit, we remand, instructing the Federal Circuit to decide the case employing the standard we have prescribed.

I

Authorized by the Constitution "[t]o promote the Progress of Science and useful Arts, by securing for limited Times to . . . Inventors the exclusive Right to their . . . Discoveries," Art. I, §8, cl. 8, Congress has enacted patent laws rewarding inventors with a limited monopoly. "Th[at] monopoly is a property right," and "like any property right, its boundaries should be clear." *Festo Corp. v. Shoketsu Kinzoku Kogyo Kabushiki Co.*, 535 U.S. 722, 730 (2002). *See* also *Markman v. Westview Instruments, Inc.*, 517 U.S. 370, 373 (1996) ("It has long been understood that a patent must describe the exact scope of an invention and its manufacture. . . ."). Thus, when Congress enacted the first Patent Act in 1790, it directed that patent grantees file a written specification "containing a description . . . of the thing or things . . . invented or discovered," which "shall be so particular" as to "distinguish the invention or discovery from other things before known and used." Act of Apr. 10, 1790, §2, 1 Stat. 110.

The patent laws have retained this requirement of definiteness even as the focus of patent construction has shifted. Under early patent practice in the United States, we have recounted, it was the written specification that "represented the key to the patent."*Markman*, 517 U.S., at 379. Eventually, however, patent applicants began to set out the invention's scope in a separate section known as the "claim." *See* generally 1 R. MOY, WALKER ON PATENTS §4.2, pp. 4—17 to 4—20 (4th ed. 2012). The Patent Act of 1870 expressly conditioned the receipt of a patent on the inventor's inclusion of one or more such claims, described with particularity and distinctness. *See* Act of July 8, 1870, §26, 16 Stat. 201 (to obtain a patent, the inventor must "particularly point out and distinctly claim the part, improvement, or combination which [the inventor] claims as his invention or discovery").

The 1870 Act's definiteness requirement survives today, largely unaltered. Section 112 of the Patent Act of 1952, applicable to this case, requires the patent applicant to conclude the specification with "one or more claims particularly pointing out and distinctly claiming the subject matter which the applicant regards as his invention." 35 U.S.C. §112[(b)]. A lack of definiteness renders invalid "the patent or any claim in suit." §282, ¶2(3).

II

A

The patent in dispute, U.S. Patent No. 5,337,753 ('753 patent), issued to Dr. Gregory Lekhtman in 1994 and assigned to respondent Biosig Instruments, Inc., concerns a heart-rate monitor for use during exercise. Previous heart-rate monitors, the patent asserts, were often inaccurate in measuring the electrical signals accompanying each heartbeat (electrocardiograph or ECG signals). The inaccuracy was caused by electrical signals of a different sort, known as electromyogram or EMG signals, generated by an exerciser's skeletal muscles when, for example, she moves her arm, or grips an exercise monitor with her hand. These EMG signals can "mask" ECG signals and thereby impede their detection.

Dr. Lekhtman's invention claims to improve on prior art by eliminating that impediment. The invention focuses on a key difference between EMG and ECG waveforms: while ECG signals detected from a user's left hand have a polarity opposite to that of the signals detected from her right hand,[2] EMG signals from each hand have the same polarity. The patented device works by measuring equalized EMG signals detected at each hand and then using circuitry to subtract the identical EMG signals from each other, thus filtering out the EMG interference.

As relevant here, the '753 patent describes a heart-rate monitor contained in a hollow cylindrical bar that a user grips with both hands, such that each hand comes into contact with two electrodes, one "live" and one "common." The device is illustrated in figure 1 of the patent, *id.*, at 41, reproduced [at the end of] this opinion.

Claim 1 of the '753 patent, which contains the limitations critical to this dispute, refers to a "heart rate monitor for use by a user in association with exercise apparatus and/or exercise procedures." *Id.*, at 61. The claim "comprise[s]," among other elements, an "elongate member" (cylindrical bar) with a display device; "electronic circuitry including a difference amplifier"; and, on each half of the cylindrical bar, a live electrode and a common electrode "mounted . . . in spaced relationship with each

---

[2] This difference in polarity occurs because the heart is not aligned vertically in relation to the center of the body; the organ tilts leftward from apex to bottom.

other." *Ibid.* [In Figure 1 from the patent, the live electrodes are identified by numbers 9 and 13, and the common electrodes, by 11 and 15. The spaced relationship is the area between 9 and 11 on the left side and between 11 and 15 on the right side of the elongate member.]

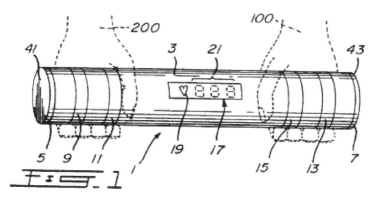

The claim sets forth additional elements, including that the cylindrical bar is to be held in such a way that each of the user's hands "contact[s]" both electrodes on each side of the bar. Further, the EMG signals detected by the two electrode pairs are to be "of substantially equal magnitude and phase" so that the difference amplifier will "produce a substantially zero [EMG] signal" upon subtracting the [EMG from the ECG] signals.

B

The dispute between the parties arose in the 1990s, when Biosig allegedly disclosed the patented technology to StairMaster Sports Medical Products, Inc. According to Biosig, StairMaster, without ever obtaining a license, sold exercise machines that included Biosig's patented technology, and petitioner Nautilus, Inc., continued to do so after acquiring the StairMaster brand. In 2004, based on these allegations, Biosig brought a patent infringement suit against Nautilus in the U.S. District Court for the Southern District of New York.

With Biosig's lawsuit launched, Nautilus asked the U.S. Patent and Trademark Office (PTO) to reexamine the '753 patent. The reexamination proceedings centered on whether the patent was anticipated or rendered obvious by prior art—principally, a patent issued in 1984 to an inventor named Fujisaki, which similarly disclosed a heart-rate monitor using two pairs of electrodes and a difference amplifier. Endeavoring to distinguish the '753 patent from prior art, Biosig submitted a declaration from Dr. Lekhtman. The declaration attested, among other things, that the '753 patent sufficiently informed a person skilled in the art how to configure the detecting electrodes so as "to produce equal EMG [signals] from the left and right hands." *Id.*, at 160. Although the electrodes' design variables—including spacing, shape, size, and material—cannot be standardized across all exercise machines, Dr. Lekhtman explained, a skilled artisan could undertake a "trial and error" process of equalization.

This would entail experimentation with different electrode configurations in order to optimize EMG signal cancellation. [Dr. Lekhtman's declaration also referred to an expert report prepared by Dr. Henrietta Galiana, Chair of the Department of Biomedical Engineering at McGill University, for use in the infringement litigation. That report described how Dr. Galiana's laboratory technician, equipped with a wooden dowel, wire, metal foil, glue, electrical tape, and the drawings from the '753 patent, was able in two hours to build a monitor that "worked just as described in the . . . patent." *Id.*, at 226.] In 2010, the PTO issued a determination confirming the patentability of the '753 patent's claims.

Biosig thereafter reinstituted its infringement suit, which the parties had voluntarily dismissed without prejudice while PTO reexamination was underway. In 2011, the District Court conducted a hearing to determine the proper construction of the patent's claims, *see Markman v. Westview Instruments, Inc.*, 517 U.S. 370 (1996) (claim construction is a matter of law reserved for court decision), including the claim term "in spaced relationship with each other." According to Biosig, that "spaced relationship" referred to the distance between the live electrode and the common electrode in each electrode pair. Nautilus, seizing on Biosig's submissions to the PTO during the reexamination, maintained that the "spaced relationship" must be a distance "greater than the width of each electrode." The District Court ultimately construed the term to mean "there is a defined relationship between the live electrode and the common electrode on one side of the cylindrical bar and the same or a different defined relationship between the live electrode and the common electrode on the other side of the cylindrical bar," without any reference to the electrodes' width.

Nautilus moved for summary judgment, arguing that the term "spaced relationship," as construed, was indefinite under §112[(b)]. The District Court granted the motion. Those words, the District Court concluded, "did not tell [the court] or anyone what precisely the space should be," or even supply "any parameters" for determining the appropriate spacing.

The Federal Circuit reversed and remanded. A claim is indefinite, the majority opinion stated, "only when it is 'not amenable to construction' or 'insolubly ambiguous.'" 715 F.3d 891, 898 (2013) (quoting *Datamize, LLC v. Plumtree Software, Inc.*, 417 F.3d 1342, 1347 (C.A. Fed. 2005)). Under that standard, the majority determined, the '753 patent survived indefiniteness review. Considering first the "intrinsic evidence"—i.e., the claim language, the specification, and the prosecution history—the majority discerned "certain inherent parameters of the claimed apparatus, which to a skilled artisan may be sufficient to understand the metes and bounds of 'spaced relationship.'" 715 F.3d at 899. These sources of meaning, the majority explained, make plain that the distance separating the live and common electrodes on each half of the bar "cannot be greater than the width of a user's hands"; that is so "because claim 1 requires the live and common electrodes to independently detect electrical signals at two distinct points of a hand." Furthermore, the majority noted, the intrinsic evidence teaches that this distance cannot be "infinitesimally small, effectively merging the live and common electrodes into a single electrode with one detection point." The claim's functional provisions, the majority went on to observe, shed additional light on the meaning of "spaced relationship." Surveying the record before the PTO on reexamination, the majority concluded that a skilled artisan would know that she could attain the indicated functions of equalizing and removing EMG signals by adjusting design variables, including spacing.

In a concurring opinion, Judge Schall reached the majority's result employing "a more limited analysis." *Id.* at 905. Judge Schall accepted the majority's recitation of the definiteness standard, under which claims amenable to construction are nonetheless indefinite when "the construction remains insolubly ambiguous." *Ibid.* (internal quotation marks omitted). The District Court's construction of "spaced relationship," Judge Schall maintained, was sufficiently clear: the term means "there is a fixed spatial relationship between the live electrode and the common electrode" on each side of the cylindrical bar. *Ibid.* Judge Schall agreed with the majority that the intrinsic evidence discloses inherent limits of that spacing. But, unlike the majority, Judge Schall did not "presum[e] a functional linkage between the 'spaced relationship' limitation and the removal of EMG signals." *Id.* at 906. Other limitations of the claim, in his view, and not the "'spaced relationship' limitation itself," "included a functional requirement to remove EMG signals." *Ibid.*

We granted certiorari, and now vacate and remand.

III

A

Although the parties here disagree on the dispositive question—does the '753 patent withstand definiteness scrutiny—they are in accord on several aspects of the §112[(b)] inquiry. First, definiteness is to be evaluated from the perspective of someone skilled in the relevant art. *See, e.g., General Elec. Co. v. Wabash Appliance Corp.*, 304 U.S. 364, 371 (1938). *See also* §112[(a)] (patent's specification "shall contain a written description of the invention, and of the manner and process of making and using it, in such full, clear, concise, and exact terms as to enable *any person skilled in the art* to which it pertains, or with which it is most nearly connected, to make and use the same" (emphasis added)). Second, in assessing definiteness, claims are to be read in light of the patent's specification and prosecution history. *See, e.g., United States v. Adams*, 383 U.S. 39, 48—49 (1966) (specification); *Festo Corp. v. Shoketsu Kinzoku Kogyo Kabushiki Co.*, 535 U.S. 722, 741 (2002) (prosecution history). Third, "[d]efiniteness is measured from the viewpoint of a person skilled in [the] art *at the time the patent was filed*." Brief for Respondent 55 (emphasis added).

The parties differ, however, in their articulations of just how much imprecision §112[(b)] tolerates. In Nautilus' view, a patent is invalid when a claim is "ambiguous, such that readers could reasonably interpret the claim's scope differently." Biosig and the Solicitor General would require only that the patent provide reasonable notice of the scope of the claimed invention.

Section 112, we have said, entails a "delicate balance." *Festo*, 535 U.S., at 731. On the one hand, the definiteness requirement must take into account the inherent limitations of language. Some modicum of uncertainty, the Court has recognized, is the "price of ensuring the appropriate incentives for innovation." *Id.* at 732. One must bear in mind, moreover, that patents are "not addressed to lawyers, or even to the public generally," but rather to those skilled in the relevant art. *Carnegie Steel Co. v. Cambria Iron Co.*, 185 U.S. 403, 437 (1902) (also stating that "any description which is sufficient to apprise [steel manufacturers] in the language of the art of the definite feature of the invention, and to serve as a warning to others of what the patent claims as a monopoly, is sufficiently definite to sustain the patent").

At the same time, a patent must be precise enough to afford clear notice of what is claimed, thereby "'appris[ing] the public of what is still open to them.'" *Markman*, 517 U.S., at 373 (quoting *McClain v. Ortmayer*, 141 U.S. 419, 424 (1891)). Otherwise there would be "[a] zone of uncertainty which enterprise and experimentation may enter only at the risk of infringement claims." *United Carbon Co. v. Binney & Smith Co.*, 317 U.S. 228, 236 (1942). And absent a meaningful definiteness check, we are told, patent applicants face powerful incentives to inject ambiguity into their claims. *See* Brief for Petitioner 30—32 (citing patent treatises and drafting guides). *See also* FEDERAL TRADE COMMISSION, THE EVOLVING IP MARKETPLACE: ALIGNING PATENT NOTICE AND REMEDIES WITH COMPETITION 85 (2011) (quoting testimony that patent system fosters "an incentive to be as vague and ambiguous as you can with your claims" and "defer clarity at all costs"). Eliminating that temptation is in order, and "the patent drafter is in the best position to resolve the ambiguity in . . . patent claims." *Halliburton Energy Servs., Inc. v. M-I LLC*, 514 F.3d 1244, 1255 (C.A. Fed. 2008). *See also Hormone Research Foundation, Inc. v. Genentech, Inc.*, 904 F.2d 1558, 1563 (C.A. Fed. 1990) ("It is a well-established axiom in patent law that a patentee is free to be his or her own lexicographer. . . .").

To determine the proper office of the definiteness command, therefore, we must reconcile concerns that tug in opposite directions. Cognizant of the competing concerns, we read §112[(b)] to require that a patent's claims, viewed in light of the specification and prosecution history, inform those skilled in the art about the scope of the invention with reasonable certainty. The definiteness requirement, so understood, mandates clarity, while recognizing that absolute precision is unattainable. The standard we adopt accords with opinions of this Court stating that "the certainty which the law requires in patents is not greater than is reasonable, having regard to their subject-matter." *Minerals Separation, Ltd. v. Hyde*, 242 U.S. 261, 270 (1916). *See also United Carbon*, 317 U.S., at 236 ("claims must be reasonably clear-cut"); *Markman*, 517 U.S., at 389 (claim construction calls for "the necessarily sophisticated analysis of the whole document," and may turn on evaluations of expert testimony).

B

In resolving Nautilus' definiteness challenge, the Federal Circuit asked whether the '753 patent's claims were "amenable to construction" or "insolubly ambiguous." Those formulations can breed lower court confusion,[8] for they lack the precision §112[(b)] demands. It cannot be sufficient that a court can ascribe some meaning to a patent's claims; the definiteness inquiry trains on the understanding of a skilled artisan at the time of the patent application, not that of a court viewing matters post hoc. To tolerate imprecision just short of that rendering a claim "insolubly ambiguous" would diminish the definiteness requirement's public-notice function and foster the innovation-discouraging "zone of uncertainty," *United Carbon*, 317 U.S. at 236, against which this Court has warned.

Appreciating that "terms like 'insolubly ambiguous' may not be felicitous," Brief for Respondent 34, Biosig argues the phrase is a shorthand label for a more probing inquiry that the Federal Circuit applies in practice. The Federal Circuit's fuller explications of the term "insolubly ambiguous," we recognize, may come closer to tracking the statutory prescription. *See, e.g.*, 715 F.3d, at 898 (case below) ("[I]f reasonable efforts at claim construction result in a definition that does not provide sufficient particularity and clarity to inform skilled artisans of the bounds of the claim, the claim is insolubly ambiguous and invalid for indefiniteness." (internal quotation marks omitted)). But although this Court does not "micromanag[e] the Federal Circuit's particular word choice" in applying patent-law doctrines, we must ensure that the Federal Circuit's test is at least "probative of the essential inquiry." *Warner-Jenkinson Co. v. Hilton Davis Chemical Co.*, 520 U.S. 17, 40 (1997). Falling short in that regard, the expressions "insolubly ambiguous" and "amenable to construction" permeate the Federal Circuit's recent decisions concerning §112[(b)]'s requirement. We agree with Nautilus and its amici that such terminology can leave courts and the patent bar at sea without a reliable compass.

The parties nonetheless dispute whether factual findings subsidiary to the ultimate issue of definiteness trigger the clear-and-convincing-evidence standard and, relatedly, whether deference is due to the PTO's resolution of disputed issues of fact. We leave these questions for another day. The court below treated definiteness as "a legal issue [the] court reviews without deference," 715 F.3d at 897, and Biosig has not called our attention to any contested factual matter—or PTO determination thereof—pertinent to its infringement claims.

---

[8] *See, e.g., Every Penny Counts, Inc. v. Wells Fargo Bank, N.A.*, 4 F. Supp. 3d 1286, 1292 (M.D. Fla. 2014) (finding that "the account," as used in claim, "lacks definiteness," because it might mean several different things and "no informed and confident choice is available among the contending definitions," but that "the extent of the indefiniteness . . . falls far short of the 'insoluble ambiguity' required to invalidate the claim").

IV

Both here and in the courts below, the parties have advanced conflicting arguments as to the definiteness of the claims in the '753 patent. Nautilus maintains that the claim term "spaced relationship" is open to multiple interpretations reflecting markedly different understandings of the patent's scope, as exemplified by the disagreement among the members of the Federal Circuit panel.[11]

Notably, however, all three panel members found Nautilus' arguments unavailing.

Biosig responds that "spaced relationship," read in light of the specification and as illustrated in the accompanying drawings, delineates the permissible spacing with sufficient precision.

"[M]indful that we are a court of review, not of first view," *Cutter v. Wilkinson*, 544 U.S. 709, 718, n.7 (2005), we decline to apply the standard we have announced to the controversy between Nautilus and Biosig. As we have explained, the Federal Circuit invoked a standard more amorphous than the statutory definiteness requirement allows. We therefore follow our ordinary practice of remanding so that the Court of Appeals can reconsider, under the proper standard, whether the relevant claims in the '753 patent are sufficiently definite.

* * *

For the reasons stated, we vacate the judgment of the United States Court of Appeals for the Federal Circuit and remand the case for further proceedings consistent with this opinion.

It is so ordered.

COMMENTS AND QUESTIONS

1. *Interaction with Claim Construction*. Given its close connection to claim construction, the claim indefiniteness issue typically arises in conjunction with claim construction. As a result, we present it here, rather than with the rest of the §112 validity doctrines.

2. The Court states the new test for indefiniteness: a claim is indefinite if it "fail[s] to inform, with reasonable certainty, those skilled in the art about the scope of the invention." It is left to the Federal Circuit to apply the new test to the patent at issue in this case. Does the claim term "spaced relationship" fail to inform about the scope of the invention? What about the evidence regarding what this term would mean to one skilled in the art, discussed especially by the Federal Circuit judges in their opinions below? How much should the stated purpose of the invention bear on the question of reasonable certainty regarding claim scope?

3. *Terms of Degree*. In footnote 5 of the opinion (omitted in the excerpt above), the Court mentions some cases involving the common issue of claims that include terms of degree:

    See also Eibel Process Co. v. Minnesota & Ontario Paper Co., 261 U.S. 45, 58, 65-66 (1923) (upholding as definite a patent for an improvement to a paper-making machine, which provided that a wire be placed at a "high" or "substantial elevation," where "readers . . . skilled in the art of paper making and versed in the use of the . . . machine" would have "no difficulty . . . in determining . . . the substantial [elevation] needed" for the machine to operate as specified).

134 S.Ct. at 2129 n.5. It is important to remember, as the Court emphasizes in *Nautilus*, that definiteness is to be viewed from the PHOSITA's perspective. Hence the "reasonable certainty" required by the opinion is the reasonable certainty of an expert in the field. This may render many terms of approximation definite, because knowledge of the field may often supply implicit parameters in areas where the layperson would be quite uncertain about claim scope.

    4. *Nautilus Remand*. The Federal Circuit upheld the patent under the Supreme Court's indefiniteness standard, but suggested somewhat cynically that "we may now steer by the bright star of 'reasonable certainty,' rather than the unreliable compass of 'insoluble ambiguity.'" *Biosig Instruments, Inc.v. Nautilus, Inc.*, 783 F.3d 1374, 1379 (Fed. Cir. 2015). Nautilus again sought Supreme Court review, but the Court declined. It remains to be seen whether the Supreme Court's intervention will alter the stringency of the indefiniteness standard. It does perhaps send a message to district courts that they have a greater role to play in policing the clarity of patent claims.

    5. *Interaction with Presumption of Validity*. In footnote 10 (omitted), the Court says:

        The Federal Circuit suggests that a permissive definiteness standard "'accord[s] respect to the statutory presumption of patent validity.'" 715 F.3d 891, 902 (2013) (quoting Exxon Research, 265 F.3d, at 1375). *See also* §282, ¶1 ("[a] patent shall be presumed valid," and "[t]he burden of establishing invalidity of a patent or any claim thereof shall rest on the party asserting such invalidity"); *Microsoft Corp. v. i4i Ltd. Partnership*, 131 S.Ct. 2238, 2242 (2011) (invalidity defenses must be proved by "clear and convincing evidence"). As the parties appear to agree, however, this presumption of validity does not alter the degree of clarity that §112[(b)] demands from patent applicants; to the contrary, it incorporates that definiteness requirement by reference. *See* §282, ¶2(3) (defenses to infringement actions include "[i]nvalidity of the patent or any claim in suit for failure to comply with . . . any requirement of [§112]").

134 S.Ct. 2120, at 2130 n.10. It is worth pondering how one attacking a patent for indefiniteness can go about establishing the invalidity case. How does one establish a lack of reasonable certainty regarding claim scope, in clear and convincing terms, so as to overcome the statutory presumption of validity? Does that standard even apply, since indefiniteness is theoretically a question of law based on interpretation of the

document? *See* J. Jonas Anderson & Peter S. Menell, *Restoring the Fact/Law Distinction in Patent Claim Construction*, 109 Nw. U. L. Rev. Online 187, 198-200 (2015) (challenging the court's characterization of indefiniteness as a pure question of law after *Teva*). In view of the Supreme Court's rejection of *Cybor*'s *de novo* standard of review of patent claim construction in *Teva*, there is good reason to believe that a district judge's determination of claim indefiniteness would also fall within the Rule 52(a)(6) framework on which the Supreme Court relied. The same functional considerations that led the Court to place claim construction within the province of the court apply to indefiniteness. Therefore, even if claim indefiniteness ought not be characterized as a pure question of law, it nonetheless likely falls exclusively "within the province of the court." In any event, the Federal Circuit does not hesitate to reverse district courts on indefiniteness. *See, e.g.*, *Eidos Display, LLC v. AU Optronics Corp.*, 779 F.3d 1360 (Fed. Cir. 2015) (reversing district court invalidation of patent on indefiniteness grounds).

E.   INFRINGEMENT

Just as trespass on a real property interest constitutes a tort, infringement of a patent has long viewed as tort—a form of trespass upon an intangible property interest. Section 271 sets forth the basic standards for patent infringement.

There are several levels of infringement. We begin with the most basic level: direct infringement. For infringement to occur, there must be at least one act of direct infringement. After exploring this terrain, we examine various forms of indirect infringement.

1.   Direct Infringement

Direct infringement can occur literally—where a person squarely carries out all of the elements of the claimed invention—as well as non-literally.

i.   *Literal Infringement*

Section 271(a) provides that "whoever without authority makes, uses, offers to sell, or sells any patented invention, within the United States or imports into the United States any patented invention during the term of the patent therefor, infringes the patent." To prove literal infringement, the patent owner must prove that the alleged infringer carries out all of the elements of the claimed invention. This is essentially the mirror image of novelty analysis. If what comes before the patent filing would anticipate the patent claim, it infringes the claim if it comes after the invention date. Thus we have already covered the test of literal infringement. The analysis often boils down to a dispute over claim interpretation. The following case illustrates the importance of claim construction.

Larami Corp. v. Amron
United States District Court for the Eastern District of Pennsylvania
27 U.S.P.Q.2d 1280 (1993)

REED, J.

This is a patent case concerning toy water guns manufactured by plaintiff Larami Corporation ("Larami"). [The patent claim by defendant appears to have grown out of a counterclaim to plaintiff's action for various Lanham Act and state law violations, predicated on threats made by defendants to various of plaintiff's customers and business associates.] Currently before me is Larami's motion for partial summary judgment of noninfringement of [defendant's] United States Patent No. 4,239,129 ("the '129 patent"). . . .

For the reasons discussed below, the motion will be granted.

I. Background

Larami manufactures a line of toy water guns called "SUPER SOAKERS." This line includes five models: SUPER SOAKER 20, SUPER SOAKER 30, SUPER SOAKER 50, SUPER SOAKER 100, and SUPER SOAKER 200. All use a hand-operated air pump to pressurize water and a "pinch trigger" valve mechanism for controlling the ejection of the pressurized water. All feature detachable water reservoirs prominently situated outside and above the barrel of the gun. . . .

Defendants Alan Amron and Talk To Me Products, Inc. (hereinafter referred to collectively as "TTMP") claim that the SUPER SOAKER guns infringe on the '129 patent which TTMP obtained by assignment from Gary Esposito ("Esposito"), the inventor. The '129 patent covers a water gun which, like the SUPER SOAKERS, operates by pressurizing water housed in a tank with an air pump. In the '129 patent, the pressure enables the water to travel out of the tank through a trigger-operated valve into an outlet tube and to squirt through a nozzle. Unlike the SUPER SOAKERS, the '129 patent also contains various electrical features to illuminate the water stream and create noises. Also, the water tank in the '129 patent is not detachable, but is contained within a housing in the body of the water gun.

The "Background of the Invention" contained in the '129 patent reads as follows:

Children of all ages, especially boys, through the years have exhibited a fascination for water, lights and noise and the subject invention deals with these factors embodied in a toy simulating a pistol.

An appreciable number of U.S. patents have been issued which are directed to water pistols but none appear to disclose a unique assembly of components which can be utilized to simultaneously produce a jet or stream of water, means for illuminating the stream and a noise, or if so desired, one which can be operated without employing the noise and stream illuminating means. A reciprocal pump is employed to obtain sufficient pressure whereby the pistol can eject a stream an appreciable distance in the neighborhood of thirty feet and this stream can be illuminated to more or less simulate a lazer [sic] beam. . . .

Larami has moved for partial summary judgment of noninfringement of the '129 patent. . . .

II. Discussion . . .

B. Infringement and Claim Interpretation

A patent owner's right to exclude others from making, using or selling the patented invention is defined and limited by the language in that patent's claims. *Corning Glass Works v. Sumitomo Electric U.S.A., Inc.*, 868 F.2d 1251, 1257 (Fed. Cir. 1989). Thus, establishing infringement requires the interpretation of the "elements" or "limitations" of the claim and a comparison of the accused product with those elements as so interpreted. Because claim interpretation is a question of law, it is amenable to summary judgment.

The words in a claim should be given their "ordinary or accustomed" meaning. Senmed, Inc. v. Richard-Allan Medical Industries, Inc., 888 F.2d 815, 819 & n.8 (Fed. Cir. 1989). An inventor's interpretations of words in a claim that are proffered after the patent has issued for purposes of litigation are given no weight. . . .

A patent holder can seek to establish patent infringement in either of two ways: by demonstrating that every element of a claim (1) is literally infringed or (2) is infringed under the doctrine of equivalents. To put it a different way, because every element of a claim is essential and material to that claim, a patent owner must, to meet the burden of establishing infringement, "show the presence of every element or its substantial equivalent in the accused device." If even one element of a patent's claim is missing from the accused product, then "[t]here can be no infringement as a matter of law." . . . *London v. Carson Pirie Scott & Co.*, 946 F.2d 1534, 1538-39 (Fed. Cir. 1991).

Larami contends, and TTMP does not dispute, that twenty-eight (28) of the thirty-five (35) claims in the '129 patent are directed to the electrical components that create the light and noise. Larami's SUPER SOAKER water guns have no light or noise components. Larami also contends, again with no rebuttal from TTMP, that claim 28 relates to a "poppet valve" mechanism for controlling the flow of water that is entirely different from Larami's "pinch trigger" mechanism. Thus, according to Larami, the six remaining claims (claims 1, 5, 10, 11, 12 and 16) are the only ones in dispute. Larami admits that these six claims address the one thing that the SUPER SOAKERS and the '129 patent have in common—the use of air pressure created by a hand pump to dispense liquid. Larami argues, however, that the SUPER SOAKERS and the '129 patent go about this task in such fundamentally different ways that no claim of patent infringement is sustainable as a matter of law.

1. Literal Infringement of Claim 1

TTMP claims that SUPER SOAKER 20 literally infringes claim 1 of the '129 patent. Claim 1 describes the water gun as:

[a] toy comprising an elongated housing [case] having a chamber therein for a liquid [tank], a pump including a piston having an exposed rod [piston rod] and extending rearwardly of said toy facilitating manual operation for building up an appreciable amount of pressure in said chamber for ejecting a stream of liquid therefrom an appreciable distance substantially forwardly of said toy, and means for controlling the ejection.

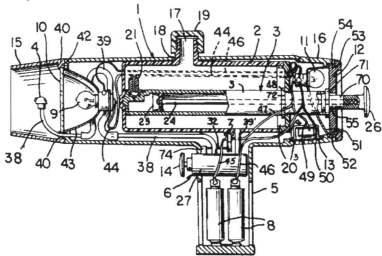

Patent drawing showing the preferred embodiment of TTMP's water pistol and/or flash light structure. (Figure 5 in the '129 patent)

Claim 1 requires, among other things, that the toy gun have "an elongated housing having a chamber therein for a liquid." The SUPER SOAKER 20 water gun, in contrast, has an external water reservoir (chamber) that is detachable from the gun housing, and not contained within the housing. TTMP argues that SUPER SOAKER 20 contains a "chamber therein for a liquid" as well as a detachable water reservoir. It is difficult to discern from TTMP's memorandum of law exactly where it contends the "chamber therein" is located in SUPER SOAKER 20. Furthermore, after having examined SUPER SOAKER 20 . . . , I find that it is plain that there is no "chamber" for liquid contained within the housing of the water gun. The only element of SUPER SOAKER 20 which could be described as a "chamber" for liquid is the external water reservoir located atop the housing. Indeed, liquid is located within the housing only when the trigger causes the liquid to pass from the external water reservoir through the tubing in the housing and out of the nozzle at the front end of the barrel. SUPER SOAKER 20 itself shows that such a transitory avenue for the release of liquid is clearly not a "chamber therein for liquid." Therefore, because the absence of even one element of a patent's claim from the accused product means there can be no finding of literal infringement, London, 946 F.2d at 1538-39, I find that SUPER SOAKER 20 does not infringe claim 1 of the '129 patent as a matter of law. . . .

Accordingly, I conclude that the SUPER SOAKER 20 water gun does not literally infringe claim 1 of the '129 patent.

2. Infringement by Equivalents of Claim 10

[The court further found that defendants TTMP failed to produce evidence which would support a finding that there was a genuine issue of material fact as to whether the Super Soaker guns infringed claim 10 under the doctrine of equivalents.

The court began its analysis by noting that successful use of the doctrine to show infringement requires the patent owner to prove that the accused product has the "substantial equivalent" of every limitation or element of a patent claim. TTMP argued that claim 10 teaches an arrangement of the tank, air pump and outlet nozzle along the same axis. The court, citing a previous decision regarding this same claim, denied that claim 10 required the three components to be located on the same axis; thus the axial placement of these components on the Super Soakers "cannot infringe claim 10 of the '129 patent because there is nothing in the language of claim 10 to which it could be substantially equivalent."

Additionally, Super Soakers' use of an external, detachable water reservoir was found to be such a dramatic improvement over the traditional design—benefiting both the manufacturer and user—that it could not be held to be the "substantial equivalent" of the claim 10 requirement of "a tank in the barrel for a liquid."]

III. Conclusion

In patent cases, summary judgment is appropriate where the accused product does not literally infringe the patent and where the patent owner does not muster evidence that is "sufficient to satisfy the legal standard for infringement under the doctrine of equivalents." *London*, 946 F.2d at 1538. Thus, and for the foregoing reasons, Larami's motion for partial summary judgment of noninfringement of the '129 patent will be granted.

COMMENTS AND QUESTIONS

1. Suppose TTMP had drafted claim 1 using the following phrase: "an elongated housing having a chamber for a liquid." If the specification failed to attach any special meaning to this term, would the court's holding regarding literal infringement of claim 1 have been affected?

2. As in Comment 1, assume that the specification did not discuss further the phrase "having a chamber for a liquid." But suppose that Larami discovers that claim 1 was originally rejected by an examiner because a prior art reference showed a squirt gun with an oversized chamber on top of the body of the gun. The patent applicant successfully overcame this rejection by pointing out that in the invention the chamber is inside the housing of the gun. The face of the '129 patent would not, however, give a clue to potential infringers such as Larami as to the potentially narrower definition of the claim language conceded during the prosecution history. To find out what the

inventor argued during prosecution, one would need to obtain the prosecution history, or "file wrapper," for the patent.

3. The elements of a patent claim are of considerable importance in determining its scope. For an accused product to literally infringe a patent, *every* element contained in the patent claim must also be present in the accused product or device. If a claimed apparatus has five parts, or "elements," and the allegedly infringing apparatus has only four of those five, it does not literally infringe. This is true even though the defendant may have copied the four elements exactly, and regardless of how significant or insignificant the missing element is.

What happens if an alleged infringer *adds* elements? The outcome then depends on the wording of the patentee's claim. If the patentee has drafted an "open" claim, usually indicated by the term "comprising," the additional elements do not circumvent the claim. *See, e.g., Genentech, Inc. v. Chiron Corp.*, 112 F.3d 495, 501 (Fed. Cir. 1997) ("'Comprising' is a term of art used in claim language which means that the named elements are essential, but other elements may be added and still form a construct within the scope of the claim."). But if the claim stated "consisting of," then the alleged infringer would not literally infringe. *See Norian Corp. v. Stryker Corp.*, 363 F.3d 1321 (Fed. Cir. 2004) (claims to dental repair kit "consisting of" certain chemicals not infringed by infringer's kit, which also included mixing spatula).

This rule has an important consequence for the process of innovation. Patentees who have properly claimed a fundamental technology can assert their patent against anyone who uses that technology, even if the defendants have improved it or put it to different use. A broad basic patent therefore gives its owner a great deal of control not only over potential direct competitors, but over a number of derivative or ancillary markets during the term of the patent.

ii.   *Literal Infringement: The Doctrine of Equivalents*

If competitors could circumvent patents through insubstantial changes in the design of a product, then many patents would lose their value, and patent drafters would expend unreasonable efforts trying to include every possible variation. Patent claims are supposed to describe the "metes and bounds" of the invention, just as deeds do for real property. But unlike geophysical measurement, the English language lacks numerical precision. The doctrine of equivalents exists to prevent defendants from taking the essence of the patented invention while skirting the literal language of the claims.

Graver Tank & Mfg. Co. v. Linde Air Products Co.
Supreme Court of the United States
339 U.S. 605 (1950)

Mr. Justice JACKSON delivered the opinion of the Court.

Linde Air Products Co., owner of the Jones patent for an electric welding process and for fluxes to be used therewith, brought an action for infringement against Lincoln and the two Graver companies. . . .

In determining whether an accused device or composition infringes a valid patent, resort must be had in the first instance to the words of the claim. If accused matter falls clearly within the claim, infringement is made out and that is the end of it.

But courts have also recognized that to permit imitation of a patented invention which does not copy every literal detail would be to convert the protection of the patent grant into a hollow and useless thing. Such a limitation would leave room for—indeed encourage—the unscrupulous copyist to make unimportant and insubstantial changes and substitutions in the patent which, though adding nothing, would be enough to take the copied matter outside the claim, and hence outside the reach of law. One who seeks to pirate an invention, like one who seeks to pirate a copyrighted book or play, may be expected to introduce minor variations to conceal and shelter the piracy. Outright and forthright duplication is a dull and very rare type of infringement. To prohibit no other would place the inventor at the mercy of verbalism and would be subordinating substance to form. It would deprive him of the benefit of his invention and would foster concealment rather than disclosure of inventions, which is one of the primary purposes of the patent system.

The doctrine of equivalents evolved in response to this experience. The essence of the doctrine is that one may not practice a fraud on a patent. Originating almost a century ago in the case of *Winans v. Denmead*, 15 How. 330 [(1853)], it has been consistently applied by this Court and the lower federal courts, and continues today ready and available for utilization when the proper circumstances for its application arise. "To temper unsparing logic and prevent an infringer from stealing the benefit of the invention" a patentee may invoke this doctrine to proceed against the producer of a device "if it performs substantially the same function in substantially the same way to obtain the same result." *Sanitary Refrigerator Co. v. Winters*, 280 U.S. 30, 42 [(1929)]. The theory on which it is founded is that "if two devices do the same work in substantially the same way, and accomplish substantially the same result, they are the same, even though they differ in name, form or shape." *Union Paper-Bag Machine Co. v. Murphy*, 97 U.S. 120, 125 [(1877)]. The doctrine operates not only in favor of the patentee of a pioneer or primary invention, but also for the patentee of a secondary invention consisting of a combination of old ingredients which produce new and useful results, although the area of equivalence may vary under the circumstances. The wholesome realism of this doctrine is not always applied in favor of a patentee but is sometimes used against him. Thus, where a device is so far changed in principle from a patented article that it performs the same or a similar function in a substantially different way, but nevertheless falls within the literal words of the claim, the doctrine of equivalents may be used to restrict the claim and defeat the patentee's action for infringement. *Westinghouse v. Boyden Power Brake Co.*, 170 U.S. 537, 568 [(1898)]. . . .

What constitutes equivalency must be determined against the context of the patent, the prior art, and the particular circumstances of the case. Equivalence, in the patent law, is not the prisoner of a formula and is not an absolute to be considered in a vacuum. It does not require complete identity for every purpose and in every respect. In determining equivalents, things equal to the same thing may not be equal to each other and, by the same token, things for most purposes different may sometimes be equivalents. Consideration must be given to the purpose for which an ingredient is used in a patent, the qualities it has when combined with the other ingredients, and the function which it is intended to perform. An important factor is whether persons reasonably skilled in the art would have known of the interchangeability of an ingredient not contained in the patent with one that was. . . .

In the case before us, we have two electric welding compositions or fluxes: the patented composition, Unionmelt Grade 20, and the accused composition, Lincolnweld 660. The patent under which Unionmelt is made claims essentially a combination of alkaline earth metal silicate and calcium fluoride; Unionmelt actually contains, however, silicates of calcium and magnesium, two alkaline earth metal silicates. Lincolnweld's composition is similar to Unionmelt's, except that it substitutes silicates of calcium and manganese—the latter not an alkaline earth metal—for silicates of calcium and magnesium. In all other respects, the two compositions are alike. The mechanical methods in which these compositions are employed are similar. They are identical in operation and produce the same kind and quality of weld.

The question which thus emerges is whether the substitution of the manganese which is not an alkaline earth metal for the magnesium which is, under the circumstances of this case, and in view of the technology and the prior art, is a change of such substance as to make the doctrine of equivalents inapplicable; or conversely, whether under the circumstances the change was so insubstantial that the trial court's invocation of the doctrine of equivalents was justified.

Without attempting to be all-inclusive, we note the following evidence in the record: Chemists familiar with the two fluxes testified that manganese and magnesium were similar in many of their reactions. There is testimony by a metallurgist that alkaline earth metals are often found in manganese ores in their natural state and that they serve the same purpose in the fluxes; and a chemist testified that "in the sense of the patent" manganese could be included as an alkaline earth metal. Much of this testimony was corroborated by reference to recognized texts on inorganic chemistry. Particularly important, in addition, were the disclosures of the prior art, also contained in the record. The Miller patent, No. 1,754,566, which preceded the patent in suit, taught the use of manganese silicate in welding fluxes. Manganese was similarly disclosed in the Armor patent, No. 1,467,825, which also described a welding composition. And the record contains no evidence of any kind to show that Lincolnweld was developed as the result of independent research or experiments.

It is not for this Court to even essay an independent evaluation of this evidence. This is the function of the trial court. . . .

The trial judge found on the evidence before him that the Lincolnweld flux and the composition of the patent in suit are substantially identical in operation and in result. He found also that Lincolnweld is in all respects equivalent to Unionmelt for welding purposes. And he concluded that "for all practical purposes, manganese silicate can be efficiently and effectively substituted for calcium and magnesium silicates as the major constituent of the welding composition." These conclusions are adequately supported by the record; certainly they are not clearly erroneous.

It is difficult to conceive of a case more appropriate for application of the doctrine of equivalents. The disclosures of the prior art made clear that manganese silicate was a useful ingredient in welding compositions. Specialists familiar with the problems of welding compositions understood that manganese was equivalent to and could be substituted for magnesium in the composition of the patented flux and their observations were confirmed by the literature of chemistry. Without some explanation or indication that Lincolnweld was developed by independent research, the trial court could properly infer that the accused flux is the result of imitation rather than experimentation or invention. Though infringement was not literal, the changes which avoid literal infringement are colorable only. We conclude that the trial court's judgment of infringement respecting the four flux claims was proper, and we adhere to our prior decision on this aspect of the case.

Affirmed.

Mr. Justice BLACK, with whom Mr. Justice DOUGLAS concurs, dissenting.

I heartily agree with the Court that "fraud" is bad, "piracy" is evil, and "stealing" is reprehensible. But in this case, where petitioners are not charged with any such malevolence, these lofty principles do not justify the Court's sterilization of Acts of Congress and prior decisions, none of which are even mentioned in today's opinion. . . .

[The Patent Act] provides that an applicant "shall particularly point out and distinctly claim the part, improvement, or combination which he claims as his invention or discovery." . . . "[I]t is the claim which measures the grant to the patentee." What is not specifically claimed is dedicated to the public. *See, e.g., Miller v. Brass Co.*, 104 U.S. 350, 352 [(1881)]. . . . Today the Court tacitly rejects those cases. It departs from the underlying principle which, as the Court pointed out in *White v. Dunbar*, 119 U.S. 47, 51 [(1886)], forbids treating a patent claim "like a nose of wax, which may be turned and twisted in any direction, by merely referring to the specification, so as to make it

include something more than, or something different from, what its words express."
. . . Giving this patentee the benefit of a grant that it did not precisely claim is no less
"unjust to the public" and no less an evasion of [the Patent Act] merely because done
in the name of the "doctrine of equivalents."

In seeking to justify its emasculation of [the Patent Act] by parading potential
hardships which literal enforcement might conceivably impose on patentees who had
for some reason failed to claim complete protection for their discoveries, the Court fails
even to mention the program for alleviation of such hardships which Congress itself
has provided [for reissue of patents where a patent is "wholly or partly inoperative"
due to certain errors arising from "inadvertence, accident, or mistake" of the
patentee.] . . .

Mr. Justice DOUGLAS, dissenting.

The Court applies the doctrine of equivalents in a way which subverts the
constitutional and statutory scheme for the grant and use of patents.

The claims of the patent are limited to a flux "containing a major proportion of
alkaline earth metal silicate." Manganese silicate, the flux which is held to infringe, is
not an alkaline earth metal silicate. It was disclosed in the application and then excluded
from the claims. It therefore became public property. *See Mahn v. Harwood*, 112 U.S.
354, 361 [(1884)]. It was, to be sure, mentioned in the specifications. But the measure
of the grant is to be found in the claims, not in the specifications. The specifications
can be used to limit but never to expand the claim.

The Court now allows the doctrine of equivalents to erase those time-honored rules.
Moreover, a doctrine which is said to protect against practicing "a fraud on a patent" is
used to extend a patent to a composition which could not be patented. For manganese
silicate had been covered by prior patents, now expired. Thus we end with a strange
anomaly: a monopoly is obtained on an unpatented and unpatentable article.

COMMENTS AND QUESTIONS

1. The doctrine of equivalents (DOE) has a long pedigree, dating back to *Winans v.
Denmead*, (1853). Do you read the dissents to be questioning the DOE or the majority's
application of the DOE to this case?

2. *Fair Reward vs. Public Notice*. Justice Black complains that the DOE
undermines the disclosure requirement. He notes that the patentee could have sought
re-issuance of the patent to expand coverage, but broadening reissues may only be
obtained within two years of patent issuance. *See* §251(d). Who should bear the risk of
failing to do so—the patentee or the public?

3. *Subject Matter Disclosed But Not Claimed/Dedication to the Public*. Justice
Douglas rebukes the majority for overriding a venerable doctrine that bars reclaiming
of knowledge that has fallen into the public domain. He notes that the patentee
disclosed both magnesium and manganese silicates in its specification, yet only

claimed magnesium silicates were claimed. (He also notes manganese silicates were in the prior art.) Do you find his criticism persuasive?

The Federal Circuit revisited this question in *Johnson & Johnston Associates Inc. v. R.E. Service Co., Inc.*, 285 F.3d 1046 (Fed. Cir. 2002) (en banc) and sided with Justice Douglas. The court squarely held that the DOE cannot be used to reach subject matter that was disclosed, but not claimed. The only option for the patentee is to reclaim that matter through reissuance of the patent within two years of the patent's issuance. The Federal Circuit emphasized the importance of public notice.

4. *All-Elements Rule*. In *Warner-Jenkinson v. Hilton Davis Chemical Co.*, 520 U.S. 17 (1997), the Supreme Court revisited the doctrine of equivalents for the first time since *Graver Tank*. *Warner-Jenkinson* involved a claim to a process for purifying dyes. The claim had three key limitations: (1) the pore diameter of the filtration screen; (2) a pressure range under which the filtration took place; and (3) a requirement that the filtration take place in an aqueous solution having a pH range "from approximately 6.0 to 9.0." Limitation (3), the pH range, was added by the patentee during the prosecution of the patent. The accused infringer, Warner-Jenkinson, used a filtration process that met the first two limitations, but operated at a pH of 5.0.

The Supreme Court first affirmed the continued viability of the doctrine of equivalents, as it had in *Graver Tank*. Next, it laid down some basic principles regarding the doctrine. The Court did not reject the venerable "triple identity" test of *Graver Tank*—i.e., that equivalence may be found where the accused product produces substantially the same function, in substantially the same way, to achieve substantially the same result as the device of the patent claim. But it noted that this test might be more suitable to mechanical inventions than to chemical processes such as the one in this case. On the ultimate question of the proper standard in a doctrine of equivalents case, the Court held:

> In our view, the particular linguistic framework used is less important than whether the test is probative of the essential inquiry: Does the accused product or process contain elements identical or equivalent to each claimed element of the patented invention? Different linguistic frameworks may be more suitable to different cases, depending on their particular facts. A focus on individual elements and a special vigilance against allowing the concept of equivalence to eliminate completely any such elements should reduce considerably the imprecision of whatever language is used. An analysis of the role played by each element in the context of the specific patent claim will thus inform the inquiry as to whether a substitute element matches the function, way, and result of the claimed element, or whether the substitute element plays a role substantially different from the claimed element.

520 U.S. at 40. This approach is known as the "all elements rule." A corollary of the rule states that an accused device cannot be infringing if it would effectively vitiate (or

eliminate) any claim limitation. *See Freedman Seating Co. v. Am. Seating Co.*, 420 F.3d 1350, 1358 (Fed. Cir. 2005).

5. *Prosecution History Estoppel.* Another central issue in *Warner-Jenkinson* was the addition of the pH limit to the claim during prosecution of the patent. This triggered application of the doctrine of "prosecution history estoppel." The accused infringer argued that that doctrine prevented the patentee from arguing infringement under the doctrine of equivalents because the patentee had surrendered coverage for any pH under 6.0 when the "6.0 to 9.0" range was added to the claim during prosecution. The Court in *Warner-Jenkinson* created a presumption under these circumstances that the claim had been amended to avoid prior art, and thus that prosecution history estoppel did indeed apply. 520 U.S. at 33. But it permitted the patentee to rebut this presumption with evidence that the claim had been amended for some other purpose, unrelated to avoiding the prior art. The status of this presumption, and the doctrine of prosecution history estoppel generally, was the key issue in *Festo Corp. v. Shoketsu Kinzoku Kogyo Kabushiki Co., Ltd.*, 535 U.S. 722 (2002).

The Federal Circuit ruled in *Festo* that the narrowing of a claim limitation during prosecution barred any recourse to the DOE with regard to that limitation. This was a departure from its prior jurisprudence applying a flexible standard for how prosecution history estoppel affected invocation of the DOE to reach non-literal infringement.

Recognizing both the difficulties faced by patentees of anticipating unimportant and insubstantial substitutes for elements of their invention as well as the need for clear public notice, the Supreme Court adopted a rebuttable presumption that amendments made to narrow a claim limitation foreclose later stretching of that limitation to reach an accused technology under the doctrine of equivalents. The patentee can rebut this presumption under three scenarios: (1) the equivalent was unforeseeable to a person having ordinary skill in the art at the time of the amendment; (2) the rationale for the amendment was no more than tangentially related to the equivalent at issue; or (3) another reason suggesting that the patentee could not reasonably be expected to have described the alleged equivalent.

If the Court sought to encourage public notice optimally, why not limit the DOE to unforeseeable equivalents—i.e., after-arising technology? Isn't the patentee the least-cost-avoider? Isn't such a foreseeability rule consistent with the *contra preferentem* (interpret against the draftsperson) doctrine?

6. *Prior Art Rule.* A patentee may not use the doctrine of equivalents to obtain coverage of subject matter in the prior art, i.e., "coverage which he could not lawfully have obtained from the USPTO by literal claims." *Wilson Sporting Goods Co. v. David Geoffrey & Assocs.*, 904 F.2d 677, 683-84 (Fed. Cir. 1990). Accordingly, an accused infringer who merely practices the prior art cannot infringe under the doctrine of equivalents. This principle is applied by constructing a hypothetical claim based on the accused technology. If the PTO could have allowed the hypothetical claim over the prior art (i.e., if the prior art did not anticipate or render the hypothetical claim obvious,

Abbott Labs v. Dey, L.P., 287 F.3d 1097, 1105-06 (Fed. Cir. 2002)), the prior art does not preclude infringement under the doctrine of equivalents.

7. *§112(f) Equivalents and the Doctrine of Equivalents: After-Arising Technology.* Recall in Problem III-14 (in-line skates) and the Rollerglide's use of Velcro to secure the shoe portion of its in-line skate. At that problem explained, Velcro was not invented until after the patentee's in-line skate invention. Therefore, the use of Velcro as a fastening method could not be equivalent to the corresponding structure, material, or acts described in the specification as of time of the in-line skate invention. But could it be equivalent under the DOE? Can a means-plus-function claim that is not literally infringed be infringed under the doctrine of equivalents?

The cases say yes, but only in two limited circumstances. Specifically, the Federal Circuit has found separate ground for the doctrine of equivalents in §112(f) cases where the *function* (as opposed to the corresponding structure) was equivalent but not identical, and where the accused device contained *after-arising technology* that was equivalent to the patented structure, but was not known at the time the patent application was filed. *See WMS Gaming, Inc. v. International Game Technology*, 184 F.3d 1339 (Fed. Cir. 1999).

8. *Reverse Doctrine of Equivalents.* The majority in *Graver Tank* notes that the DOE also works in reverse: "where a device is so far changed in principle from a patented article that it performs the same or a similar function in a substantially different way, but nevertheless falls within the literal words of the claim, the doctrine of equivalents may be used to restrict the claim and defeat the patentee's action for infringement." The Court cites *Westinghouse v. Boyden Power Brake Co.*, 170 U.S. 537, 568 (1898) which has never been overruled, but largely stands alone as a case of literal infringement for which liability did not attach.

The case traces back to a time when trains were the most important overland transportation system. In 1869, George Westinghouse invented a train brake that used a central reservoir of compressed air for stopping power. Further advances in his design, primarily the addition of an air reservoir in each brake cylinder, resulted in a brake that was patented in 1887. An improvement on this 1887 brake, invented by George Boyden, added an ingenious mechanism for pushing compressed air into the brake piston both from the central reservoir *and* from a local reservoir in each brake cylinder. (Westinghouse's brake required a complicated series of passageways to supply air from the two sources.) With the added stopping power of the Boyden brake, engineers could safely operate the increasingly long trains of the late nineteenth century.

The Westinghouse patent included a claim for "the combination of a main air-pipe, an auxiliary reservoir, a brake-cylinder, a triple valve [the device that coordinated the airflows from the main reservoir and the individual brake reservoir] and an auxiliary-valve device, actuated by the piston of the triple-valve . . . for admitting air in the application of the brake." The Court noted that the literal wording of the Westinghouse patent could be read to cover Boyden's brake, since it included what could be described as a "triple valve." But it refused to find infringement, on the ground that Boyden's was a significant contribution that took the invention outside the equitable bounds of the patent:

> We are induced to look with more favor upon this device, not only because it is a novel one and a manifest departure from the principle of the Westinghouse patent, but because it solved at once in the simplest manner the problem of quick [braking] action, whereas the Westinghouse patent did not prove to be a success until certain additional members had been incorporated in it.

Id. at 572.

According to the Federal Circuit, "because products on which patent claims are readable word for word often are in fact the same, perform the same function in the same way, and achieve the same result, as the claimed invention, a defense based on the reverse doctrine of equivalents is rarely offered." *SRI Int'l v. Matsushita Electric Corp. of America*, 775 F.2d 1107, 1123 n.19 (Fed. Cir. 1985); *see also Tate Access Floors, Inc. v. Interface Architectural Resources, Inc.*, 279 F.3d 1357 (Fed. Cir. 2002) (coming close to sounding the death knell for the reverse DOE). No case since *Westinghouse* has squarely applied the doctrine to excuse infringement.

The Federal Circuit has, however, applied the doctrine to reverse a finding of infringement in *Scripps Clinic & Research Foundation v. Genentech, Inc.*, 927 F.2d 1565 (Fed. Cir. 1991), a case typical of an early wave of biotechnology patent actions. Genentech invented and patented the recombinant DNA form of the blood protein Factor VIII:C, a blood clotting agent made by the body and useful in treating patients with clotting disorders. Scripps had previously obtained a patent on purified Factor VIII:C, which it made by isolating and purifying the protein from raw human blood. Scripps sued Genentech for infringement of its product patent, citing the conventional rule that a product patent covers the product no matter how it is made. After attempting to distinguish its recombinant version from Scripps' purified natural protein, Genentech ultimately relied on a pragmatic defense: that the recombinant version was by far cheaper to make, and therefore ought not to be deemed an infringement. The Federal Circuit remanded the case for a determination whether the reverse doctrine of equivalents applied in these circumstances. Since *Tate Access,* the Federal Circuit has gone out of its way on several occasions to make it clear that the reverse doctrine of equivalents, while rare, does still have viability. *See, e.g., Amgen, Inc. v. Hoechst Marion Roussel*, 314 F.3d 1313, 1351 (Fed. Cir. 2003); *Plant Genetic Systems, N.V. v. DeKalb Genetics Corp.*, 315 F.3d 1335, 1341 (Fed. Cir. 2003) ("[T]he judicially-developed 'reverse doctrine of equivalents,' requiring interpretation of claims in light of the specification, may be safely relied upon to preclude improper enforcement against later developers.").

Summary: Non-Literal Infringement

Limiting Principles

- The All-Elements (All-Limitations) Rule
- Prosecution History Estoppel
    - *Festo* Rebuttable Presumption: amendments made to narrow a claim limitation foreclose application of the DOE unless:
        1. Unforeseeable Equivalents—principally after-arising art
        2. Tangential Amendments
        3. Amendments for "Other Reasons"
- Prior Art Rule (*Wilson Sporting Goods*)
- The Public Dedication Rule (*Johnson & Johnston*)

Means-Plus-Function Claims (applies to after-arising art)

The Reverse Doctrine of Equivalents

PROBLEM

Problem III-15. Mike Molar, a production engineer for Tasty Toothpaste Corp. (Tasty) hit upon a way to make a sanitary, cheap, and small disposable toothbrush. The problem he had been running into was how to keep the toothbrush small while still providing a feature he thought necessary to make it attractive—a built-in supply of toothpaste. The solution: a small reservoir for holding toothpaste in the handle of the toothbrush. Then the user could squeeze the toothpaste from the reservoir to the brush bristles.

He quickly built a prototype of the invention. To build it, he bought a fountain pen, pulled out the ink cartridge and other parts from the interior, tore the bristles off a toothbrush and glued them onto a hollow tube, poked two holes in the top of the tube between two rows of bristles, fitted up a plastic plunger that slid in and out at the back of the fountain pen body, pulled the plunger all the way out, filled the tube with toothpaste, glued the tube inside the fountain pen body, and pushed the plunger. Voilà! Toothpaste came out of the holes more or less onto the bristles, ready for brushing. It worked! He drafted a patent specification that included this passage:

It is one important object of the present invention to provide a portable toothbrush which is easily carried in the pocket and which is thus available whenever it is required for brushing teeth.

The open end of the device includes a reduced section portion which carries the bristles. The cylindrical body shaft includes an interior passage that extends into the reduced section end (i.e., the one with the bristles). The passage includes two termination openings which are in the area at the base of the toothbrush bristles.

An open space for placing toothpaste is provided within the interior passage, and a movable plunger is provided for forcing the toothpaste from this space through the narrow part of the passage and out through the termination openings into the toothpaste bristles for use.

In the preferred embodiment, the body shaft is made of plastic. The invention may be made so as to be disposable. Various means for filling the space with toothpaste are envisioned, including pressure-injection through a small hole in the top of the body, which hole can then be sealed. This would make the toothbrush usable only once; it would then be disposed.

He concluded with the following claim.

1. A pocket toothbrush having an exterior structure resembling a traditional fountain pen case comprising

   a. a removable cylindrical end cap cover,

   b. a main cylindrical body shaft over at least one end of which said end cap cover fits and having means for engaging the interior of said end cap cover to retain said end cap cover,

   c. said cylindrical body shaft having one end which contains toothbrush bristles [the "bristle end"] extending transversely and capable of being confined within said end cap,

   d. said cylindrical body shaft including an interior passage extending into said bristle end and having at least one termination opening in the area at the base of said bristles,

   e. a movable plunger extending into said cylindrical body shaft in said main cylindrical body shaft,

   f. said body shaft including an interior space for the accommodation of a charge of toothpaste to be fed to said bristles by the operation of said movable plunger, said space being at least big enough to hold a charge for a single application of toothpaste.

Once the patent issues, Tasty begins selling a disposable, portable toothbrush that garners a loyal following. Soon competitors begin entering the market. One, KopyCat Industries, Inc. (KCI), begins selling a portable toothbrush that includes a replaceable toothpaste cartridge so that the brush can be used over and over if the user wishes. The cartridges are designed to have a weak plastic closure that easily breaks when the plunger is pushed against the cartridge. This keeps the toothpaste from hardening in the openings to the bristles. Also, instead of a cap, the KCI design has a telescoping retractable cover that remains attached to the non-bristle end of the brush. The cover is collapsed down, the brush used, and then the cover is pulled back into place. The retractable cover is attached very firmly with two tiny screws. The screws can be taken out and the cover removed, but it takes a tiny jewelers screwdriver and is difficult.

Tasty has threatened to sue KCI for infringement of the Molar patent. KCI has come to you for advice. Does KCI runs a serious risk of being found liable for infringing the Molar patent, either literally or under the doctrine of equivalents? What changes might KCI make in its product to avoid a future infringement action by Tasty?

Problem III-16. In the early 1960s, Hughes Aircraft invented an apparatus for maintaining a satellite in geosynchronous orbit (i.e., maintaining a constant position relative to a location on earth). Claim 1 of its 1964 patent claimed an apparatus comprising:

a. a body adapted to spin about an axis;

b. fluid supply means associated with said body;

c. a valve connected to said fluid supply means;

d. fluid expulsion means disposed on said body and coupled with said valve and oriented to expel said fluid substantially along a line parallel to said axis and separated therefrom;

e. means disposed on said body for providing an indication to a location external to said body of the instantaneous spin angle position of said body about said axis and the orientation of said axis with reference to a fixed external coordinate system;

f. and means disposed on said body for receiving from said location control signals synchronized with said indication;

g. said valve being coupled to said last-named means and responsive to said control signals for applying fluid to said fluid expulsion means in synchronism therewith for precessing said body to orient said axis in a predetermined desired relationship with said fixed external coordinate system.

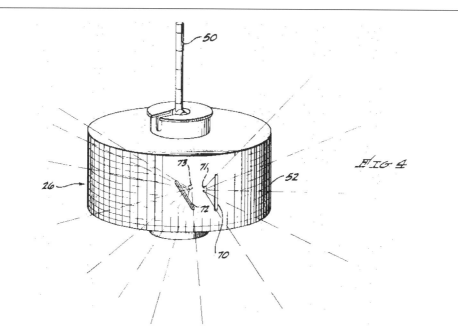

Step e refers to "means disposed on said body for providing an indication to a location external to said body of the instantaneous spin angle position." Step f refers to "means disposed on said body for receiving from said location control signals synchronized with said indication." At the time that the invention was made, computer technology was relatively primitive. Consequently, it needed to perform the complex calculations necessary to maintain geosynchronous orbit using a mainframe computer located on earth. The patent issued in 1973.

By that time, microprocessor technology had advanced to the point that computers could be substantially reduced in size. NASA developed a satellite that utilized key elements of the Hughes Aircraft system –i.e., taking "instantaneous spin angle position of said body about said axis and the orientation of said axis with reference to a fixed external coordinate system"—and determining the necessary precession of jets to maintain geosynchronous orbit. But due to advances in microprocessor technology, it could do the entire position adjustment process on board the satellite, i.e., it did not need to send positional information to the earth and receive the adjustment information. Hughes sued for infringement. Under modern infringement doctrines, what are NASA's best arguments to defeat the infringement claim? What are Hughes best counterarguments? How should the judge/jury resolve the case?

2.   Indirect Infringement

Tort law principles have long extended liability beyond those who directly commit a tort to those who aid, abet, contribute, and induce violations of property and personal interests. Since patent law traces its infringement principles to tort law, inducement and contributory infringement evolved to address infringing activity that lacked the element of a direct making, using, or selling of the patented invention. These doctrines were codified in the 1952 Act, yet they still retain a common law character. They bring into play the mental state—knowledge and intent—of the alleged infringer.

i.   *Inducement*

Section 271(b) provides that "Whoever actively induces infringement of a patent shall be liable as an infringer." Inducement involves behavior that omits any direct making, using, or selling of the patented invention but that nevertheless amounts to an attempt to appropriate the value of an invention. It is often described as activity that "aids and abets" infringement. Although inducing infringement commonly involves instructing another to violate a patent, this branch of liability is broad enough to ensnare a host of diverse activities.

Global-Tech Appliances, Inc. v. SEB S.A.
Supreme Court of the United States
563 U.S. 754 (2011)

Justice ALITO delivered the opinion of the Court.

We consider whether a party who "actively induces infringement of a patent" under 35 U.S.C. §271(b) must know that the induced acts constitute patent infringement.

I

This case concerns a patent for an innovative deep fryer designed by respondent SEB S.A., a French maker of home appliances. In the late 1980's, SEB invented a "cool-touch" deep fryer, that is, a deep fryer for home use with external surfaces that remain cool during the frying process. The cool-touch deep fryer consisted of a metal frying pot surrounded by a plastic outer housing. Attached to the housing was a ring that suspended the metal pot and insulated the housing from heat by separating it from the pot, creating air space between the two components. SEB obtained a U.S. patent for its design in 1991, and sometime later, SEB started manufacturing the cool-touch fryer and selling it in this country under its well-known "T–Fal" brand. Superior to other products in the American market at the time, SEB's fryer was a commercial success.

In 1997, Sunbeam Products, Inc., a U.S. competitor of SEB, asked petitioner Pentalpha Enterprises, Ltd., to supply it with deep fryers meeting certain specifications. Pentalpha is a Hong Kong maker of home appliances and a wholly owned subsidiary of petitioner Global–Tech Appliances, Inc.

In order to develop a deep fryer for Sunbeam, Pentalpha purchased an SEB fryer in Hong Kong and copied all but its cosmetic features. Because the SEB fryer bought in Hong Kong was made for sale in a foreign market, it bore no U.S. patent markings. After copying SEB's design, Pentalpha retained an attorney to conduct a right-to-use study, but Pentalpha refrained from telling the attorney that its design was copied directly from SEB's.

The attorney failed to locate SEB's patent, and in August 1997 he issued an opinion letter stating that Pentalpha's deep fryer did not infringe any of the patents that he had found. That same month, Pentalpha started selling its deep fryers to Sunbeam, which resold them in the United States under its trademarks. By obtaining its product from a manufacturer with lower production costs, Sunbeam was able to undercut SEB in the U.S. market.

After SEB's customers started defecting to Sunbeam, SEB sued Sunbeam in March 1998, alleging that Sunbeam's sales infringed SEB's patent. Sunbeam notified Pentalpha of the lawsuit the following month. Undeterred, Pentalpha went on to sell deep fryers to Fingerhut Corp. and Montgomery Ward & Co., both of which resold them in the United States under their respective trademarks.. . .

II

Pentalpha argues that active inducement liability under §271(b) requires more than deliberate indifference to a known risk that the induced acts may violate an existing patent. Instead, Pentalpha maintains, actual knowledge of the patent is needed.

A

In assessing Pentalpha's argument, we begin with the text of §271(b)—which is short, simple, and, with respect to the question presented in this case, inconclusive. Section 271(b) states: "Whoever actively induces infringement of a patent shall be liable as an infringer."

Although the text of §271(b) makes no mention of intent, we infer that at least some intent is required. The term "induce" means "[t]o lead on; to influence; to prevail on; to move by persuasion or influence." WEBSTER'S NEW INTERNATIONAL DICTIONARY 1269 (2d ed.1945). The addition of the adverb "actively" suggests that the inducement must involve the taking of affirmative steps to bring about the desired result, *see id.*, at 27.

When a person actively induces another to take some action, the inducer obviously knows the action that he or she wishes to bring about. If a used car salesman induces a customer to buy a car, the salesman knows that the desired result is the purchase of the car. But what if it is said that the salesman induced the customer to buy a damaged car? Does this mean merely that the salesman induced the customer to purchase a car that happened to be damaged, a fact of which the salesman may have been unaware? Or does this mean that the salesman knew that the car was damaged? The statement that the salesman induced the customer to buy a damaged car is ambiguous.

1

So is §271(b). In referring to a party that "induces infringement," this provision may require merely that the inducer lead another to engage in conduct that happens to amount to infringement, i.e., the making, using, offering to sell, selling, or importing of a patented invention. *See* §271(a).[2] On the other hand, the reference to a party that "induces infringement" may also be read to mean that the inducer must persuade another to engage in conduct that the inducer knows is infringement. Both readings are possible. . . .

While both the language of §271(b) and the pre-1952 case law that this provision was meant to codify are susceptible to conflicting interpretations, our decision in [*Aro Mfg. Co. v. Convertible Top Replacement Co.*, 377 U.S. 476 (1964) (*Aro II*)] resolves the question in this case. In *Aro II*, a majority held that a violator of §271(c) must know "that the combination for which his component was especially designed was both patented and infringing," 377 U.S., at 488, and as we explain below, that conclusion compels this same knowledge for liability under §271(b).

C

As noted above, induced infringement was not considered a separate theory of indirect liability in the pre-1952 case law. Rather, it was treated as evidence of "contributory infringement," that is, the aiding and abetting of direct infringement by another party. *See* Lemley, *Inducing Patent Infringement*, 39 U.C.D.L.REV. 225, 227 (2005). When Congress enacted §271, it separated what had previously been regarded as contributory infringement into two categories, one covered by §271(b) and the other covered by §271(c).

Aro II concerned §271(c), which states in relevant part:

> "Whoever offers to sell or sells ... a component of a patented [invention] . . ., constituting a material part of the invention, knowing the same to be especially made or especially adapted for use in an infringement of such patent, and not a staple article or commodity of commerce suitable for substantial noninfringing use, shall be liable as a contributory infringer." (Emphasis added.)

This language contains exactly the same ambiguity as §271(b). The phrase "knowing [a component] to be especially made or especially adapted for use in an infringement" may be read to mean that a violator must know that the component is "especially adapted for use" in a product that happens to infringe a patent. Or the phrase may be read to require, in addition, knowledge of the patent's existence.

---

[2] Direct infringement has long been understood to require no more than the unauthorized use of a patented invention. *See Aro Mfg. Co. v. Convertible Top Replacement Co.*, 377 U.S. 476, 484 (1964); 3 A. DELLER, WALKER ON PATENTS §453, p. 1684 (1937). Thus, a direct infringer's knowledge or intent is irrelevant.

This question closely divided the *Aro II* Court. In a badly fractured decision, a majority concluded that knowledge of the patent was needed. 377 U.S., at 488, and n. 8 (White, J., concurring); *id.*, at 524–527 (Black, J., dissenting).5 Justice Black's opinion, which explained the basis for the majority's view, concluded that the language of §271(c) supported this interpretation. *See id.*, at 525. His opinion also relied on an amendment to this language that was adopted when the bill was in committee. *Id.*, at 525–527.

Four Justices disagreed with this interpretation and would have held that a violator of §271(c) need know only that the component is specially adapted for use in a product that happens to infringe a patent. *See id.*, at 488–490, n. 8. These Justices thought that this reading was supported by the language of §271(c) and the pre–1952 case law, and they disagreed with the inference drawn by the majority from the amendment of §271(c)'s language. *Ibid.*

While there is much to be said in favor of both views expressed in Aro II, the "holding in Aro II has become a fixture in the law of contributory infringement under [section] 271(c)," 5 R. MOY, WALKER ON PATENTS §15:20, p. 15–131 (4th ed.2009)— so much so that SEB has not asked us to overrule it. Nor has Congress seen fit to alter §271(c)'s intent requirement in the nearly half a century since Aro II was decided. In light of the "'special force'" of the doctrine of stare decisis with regard to questions of statutory interpretation, *see John R. Sand & Gravel Co. v. United States*, 552 U.S. 130, 139 (2008), we proceed on the premise that §271(c) requires knowledge of the existence of the patent that is infringed.

Based on this premise, it follows that the same knowledge is needed for induced infringement under §271(b). As noted, the two provisions have a common origin in the pre–1952 understanding of contributory infringement, and the language of the two provisions creates the same difficult interpretive choice. It would thus be strange to hold that knowledge of the relevant patent is needed under §271(c) but not under §271(b).

2

Accordingly, we now hold that induced infringement under §271(b) requires knowledge that the induced acts constitute patent infringement.

III

Returning to Pentalpha's principal challenge, we agree that deliberate indifference to a known risk that a patent exists is not the appropriate standard under §271(b). We nevertheless affirm the judgment of the Court of Appeals because the evidence in this case was plainly sufficient to support a finding of Pentalpha's knowledge under the doctrine of willful blindness.

A

The doctrine of willful blindness is well established in criminal law. Many criminal statutes require proof that a defendant acted knowingly or willfully, and courts applying the doctrine of willful blindness hold that defendants cannot escape the reach of these statutes by deliberately shielding themselves from clear evidence of critical facts that are strongly suggested by the circumstances. The traditional rationale for this doctrine is that defendants who behave in this manner are just as culpable as those who have actual knowledge. Edwards, *The Criminal Degrees of Knowledge*, 17 MOD. L. REV. 294, 302 (1954) (hereinafter Edwards) (observing on the basis of English authorities that "up to the present day, no real doubt has been cast on the proposition that [willful blindness] is as culpable as actual knowledge"). It is also said that persons who know enough to blind themselves to direct proof of critical facts in effect have actual knowledge of those facts. *See United States v. Jewell*, 532 F.2d 697, 700 (C.A.9 1976) (en banc).

This Court's opinion more than a century ago in *Spurr v. United States*, 174 U.S. 728 (1899),[6] while not using the term "willful blindness," endorsed a similar concept. . . . Following our decision in *Spurr*, several federal prosecutions in the first half of the 20th century invoked the doctrine of willful blindness. Later, a 1962 proposed draft of the Model Penal Code, which has since become official, attempted to incorporate the doctrine by defining "knowledge of the existence of a particular fact" to include a situation in which "a person is aware of a high probability of [the fact's] existence, unless he actually believes that it does not exist." ALI, MODEL PENAL CODE §2.02(7) (Proposed Official Draft 1962). . . .

Given the long history of willful blindness and its wide acceptance in the Federal Judiciary, we can see no reason why the doctrine should not apply in civil lawsuits for induced patent infringement under 35 U.S.C. §271(b). . . .

B

. . .

3

While the Courts of Appeals articulate the doctrine of willful blindness in slightly different ways, all appear to agree on two basic requirements: (1) the defendant must subjectively believe that there is a high probability that a fact exists and (2) the defendant must take deliberate actions to avoid learning of that fact. We think these requirements give willful blindness an appropriately limited scope that surpasses recklessness and negligence. Under this formulation, a willfully blind defendant is one who takes deliberate actions to avoid confirming a high probability of wrongdoing and who can almost be said to have actually known the critical facts. *See* G. WILLIAMS, CRIMINAL LAW §57, p. 159 (2d ed. 1961) ("A court can properly find wilful blindness only where it can almost be said that the defendant actually knew"). By contrast, a reckless defendant is one who merely knows of a substantial and unjustified risk of such wrongdoing, *see* ALI, MODEL PENAL CODE §2.02(2)(c) (1985), and a negligent

---

[6] The doctrine emerged in English law almost four decades earlier and became firmly established by the end of the 19th century. *Edwards* 298–301. . . .

defendant is one who should have known of a similar risk but, in fact, did not, *see* §2.02(2)(d).

The test applied by the Federal Circuit in this case departs from the proper willful blindness standard in two important respects. First, it permits a finding of knowledge when there is merely a "known risk" that the induced acts are infringing. Second, in demanding only "deliberate indifference" to that risk, the Federal Circuit's test does not require active efforts by an inducer to avoid knowing about the infringing nature of the activities.

4

In spite of these flaws, we believe that the evidence when viewed in the light most favorable to the verdict for SEB is sufficient under the correct standard. The jury could have easily found that before April 1998 Pentalpha willfully blinded itself to the infringing nature of the sales it encouraged Sunbeam to make.

SEB's cool-touch fryer was an innovation in the U.S. market when Pentalpha copied it. As one would expect with any superior product, sales of SEB's fryer had been growing for some time. Pentalpha knew all of this, for its CEO and president, John Sham, testified that, in developing a product for Sunbeam, Pentalpha performed "market research" and "gather[ed] information as much as possible." Pentalpha's belief that SEB's fryer embodied advanced technology that would be valuable in the U.S. market is evidenced by its decision to copy all but the cosmetic features of SEB's fryer.

Also revealing is Pentalpha's decision to copy an overseas model of SEB's fryer. Pentalpha knew that the product it was designing was for the U.S. market, and Sham—himself a named inventor on numerous U.S. patents—was well aware that products made for overseas markets usually do not bear U.S. patent markings. Even more telling is Sham's decision not to inform the attorney from whom Pentalpha sought a right-to-use opinion that the product to be evaluated was simply a knockoff of SEB's deep fryer. On the facts of this case, we cannot fathom what motive Sham could have had for withholding this information other than to manufacture a claim of plausible deniability in the event that his company was later accused of patent infringement. Nor does Sham's testimony on this subject provide any reason to doubt that inference. Asked whether the attorney would have fared better had he known of SEB's design, Sham was nonresponsive. All he could say was that a patent search is not an "easy job" and that is why he hired attorneys to perform them.

Taken together, this evidence was more than sufficient for a jury to find that Pentalpha subjectively believed there was a high probability that SEB's fryer was patented, that Pentalpha took deliberate steps to avoid knowing that fact, and that it therefore willfully blinded itself to the infringing nature of Sunbeam's sales.

* * *

The judgment of the United States Court of Appeals for the Federal Circuit is *Affirmed.*

COMMENTS AND QUESTIONS

1. Inducement, like contributory infringement, requires that direct patent infringement. Someone must actually "make, use, sell, offer for sale, or import" under §271(a). The inducer is "indirectly liable" for encouraging, aiding, and abetting the direct infringer. Because the alleged inducer is not a direct infringer, it may be liable for acts that do not themselves directly violate the patent statute. This explains why some level of knowledge or intent is required: only if the inducer did what it did with the aim and plan of causing an infringing act is it reasonable to find the inducer liable under the patent statute. (There is no knowledge or intent requirement for a direct infringer; this is why an innocent independent inventor can still be liable for patent infringement. *See* Robert P. Merges, *A Few Kind Words for Absolute Infringement Liability in Patent Law*, 30 BERKELEY TECH. L. J., forthcoming 2016.)

Who were the direct infringers in the Globaltech case? Why did SEB, the patentee, not sue them? If they were foreign manufacturers, perhaps no one "made" an infringing product within the U.S. Hence, such entities would not be liable under U.S. patent law due to the patent law's territoriality limits. How about the retailers selling the infringing fryers in stores in the U.S.? Perhaps SEB did not want to antagonize them, hoping they would sell its fryers at some point. The point is that sometimes, the party the patentee may want to sue is not itself a direct infringer. This means that a complex interplay of strategy and legal principles may be involved. Perhaps SEB wanted to go after the design company that prepared the plans for the infringing fryer – this potential defendant was reachable in the U.S., and perhaps SEB wanted to send a warning not to copy future SEB designs. Whatever the motivation, the point is that by choosing to sue an indirect infringer SEB brought issues of knowledge and intent into the case that are not a problem when suit is brought against a direct infringer.

2. This case illustrates both the similarities and the differences between indirect liability in patent law and tort law. Although the Court begins with the terse statutory standard as well as a dictionary definition, it draws heavily upon the knowledge/intent standards in tort and criminal law in developing the mental state requirement for active inducement under patent law. At the same time, the focus of intent is different. In patent law, unlike tort law, the defendant must know its act is unlawful. Why the difference?

3. *Imputed Knowledge.* Notwithstanding the Court's conclusion that patent inducement "requires knowledge that the induced acts constitute patent infringement," the court nonetheless opens up a broad inquiry by considering willful blindness to establish such knowledge. In dissent, Justice Kennedy contends that "[w]illful blindness is not knowledge; and judges should not broaden a legislative proscription by analogy." *Global-Tech*, 131 S.Ct. at 2072 (Kennedy, J., dissenting). He concludes by noting that "[i]f willful blindness is as close to knowledge and as far from the 'knew or should have known' jury instruction provided in this case as the Court suggests, then reviewing the record becomes all the more difficult. I would leave that task to the Court of Appeals in the first instance on remand." *Id.* at 2074.

4. *Belief of Invalidity Not a Defense to Inducement*. Since the Global-Tech Court concluded that "induced infringement . . . requires knowledge that the induced acts constitute patent infringement," it could reasonably be inferred that a good faith belief that the patent is invalid would negate the requisite intent for inducement liability. After all, how could one have an intent to infringe an invalid patent? Cisco Systems successfully made this defense in defending Commil USA's induced infringement claim. *See Commil USA, LLC v. Cisco Systems, Inc.*, 720 F.3d 1361, 1368-69 (Fed. Cir. 2013) (holding that evidence of an accused inducer's good-faith belief of invalidity may negate the requisite intent for induced infringement). Yet the Supreme Court, in a decision authored by Justice Kennedy, the lone dissenter in Global-Tech, held that a defendant's belief as to validity does not have any bearing on induced infringement. Commil USA, LLC v. Cisco Systems, Inc., 135 S.Ct. 1920 (2015). The Court reasoned

> The scienter element for induced infringement concerns infringement; that is a different issue than validity. Section 271(b) requires that the defendant "actively induce[d] infringement." That language requires intent to "bring about the desired result," which is infringement. And because infringement and validity are separate issues under the Act, belief regarding validity cannot negate the scienter required under §271(b).

> When infringement is the issue, the validity of the patent is not the question to be confronted. . . .

> Indeed, the issues of infringement and validity appear in separate parts of the Patent Act. . . . Further, noninfringement and invalidity are listed as two separate defenses . . .

> Allowing this new defense would also undermine [patent law's presumption of validity]. . . .

Id. at 1928. Does this make sense to you? Justice Scalia was not persuaded: "[i]nfringing a patent means invading a patentee's exclusive right to practice his claimed invention. Only valid patents confer exclusivity—invalid patents do not. It follows, as night the day, that only valid patents can be infringed. To talk of infringing an invalid patent is to talk nonsense." *Id.* at 1931 (Scalia, J. dissenting, joined by Roberts, C.J.).

ii.   Contributory Infringement

Section 271(c) provides that

> Whoever offers to sell or sells within the United States or imports into the United States a component of a patented machine, manufacture, combination or composition, or a material or apparatus for use in practicing a patented process, constituting a material part of the invention, knowing the same to be especially made or especially adapted for use in an infringement of such patent, and not a

staple article or commodity of commerce suitable for substantial noninfringing use, shall be liable as a contributory infringer.

C.R. Bard, Inc. v. Advanced Cardiovascular Systems, Inc.
United States Court of Appeals for the Federal Circuit
911 F.2d 670 (Fed. Cir. 1990)

This is a case of claimed infringement of a method patent for a medical treatment. Defendant-Appellant Advanced Cardiovascular Systems, Inc. (ACS) was marketing [a] perfusion catheter for use in coronary angioplasty. Plaintiff-Appellee C.R. Bard, Inc. (Bard) sued ACS for alleged infringement of U.S. Patent No. 4,581,017 ('017), which Bard had purchased all rights to as of December 31, 1986. The '017 patent relates to a method for using a catheter in coronary angioplasty. The district court granted plaintiff Bard summary judgment against ACS, finding infringement of claim 1 of the '017 patent. We reverse the grant of summary judgment and remand the case for further proceedings.

Plaintiff Bard alleges that the ACS catheter is especially adapted for use by a surgeon in the course of administering a coronary angioplasty in a manner that infringes claim 1 of the '017 patent, that therefore ACS is a contributory infringer, and that ACS actively induces infringement. Of course, a finding of induced or contributory infringement must be predicated on a direct infringement of claim 1 by the users of the ACS catheter.

For purposes of this case, the statute requires that ACS sell a catheter for use in practicing the '017 process, which use constitutes a material part of the invention, knowing that the catheter is especially made or adapted for use in infringing the patent, and that the catheter is not a staple article or commodity of commerce suitable for substantial noninfringing use.

In asserting ACS's contributory infringement of claim 1, Bard seeks to establish the requisite direct infringement by arguing that there is no evidence that any angioplasty procedures using the ACS catheter would be noninfringing. Testing this assertion requires a two step analysis. First is a determination of the scope of the claim at issue. Second is an examination of the evidence before the court to ascertain whether, under §271(c), use of the ACS catheter would infringe the claim as interpreted.

Bard argues that [a] prior art patent teaches the use of the catheter with the inlets (side openings) where the blood enters the tube placed only in the aorta, whereas the '017 method in suit involves insertion of the catheter into the coronary artery in such a manner that the openings "immediately adjacent [the] balloon fluidly connect locations within [the] coronary artery surrounding [the] proximal and distal portions of [the] tube." Thus, Bard argues, a surgeon, inserting the ACS catheter into a coronary artery to a point where an inlet at the catheter's proximal end draws blood from the artery, infringes the '017 patent.

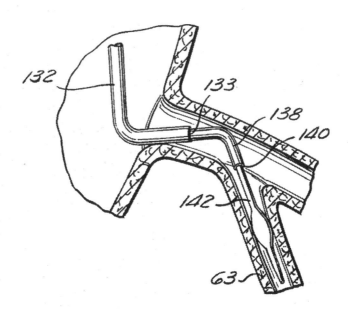

[The aorta is the large blood vessel on top; the coronary artery, labeled 63, is below it.]

[I]t is important to note that the ACS catheter has a series of ten openings in the tube near, and at the proximal end of, the balloon. The first of these openings—the one closest to the balloon [42b in Figure 2 below]—is approximately six millimeters (less than one inch) from the edge of the proximal end of the balloon. The remainder are located along the main lumen at intervals, the furthest from the balloon being 6.3 centimeters (approximately 2½ inches) away [past 40b in Figure 2].

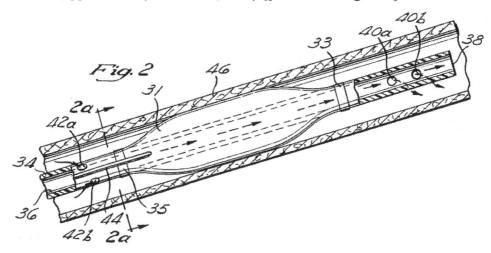

It would appear that three possible fact patterns may arise in the course of using the ACS catheter. The first pattern involves positioning the catheter such that all of its side openings are located only in the aorta. This is clearly contemplated by the prior art '725 patent cited by the examiner. In the second of the possible fact patterns, all of the side openings are located within the coronary artery. This situation appears to have been contemplated by the '017 patent, the method patent at issue. In the third fact pattern, some of the side openings are located in the aorta and some are located in the artery.

There is evidence in the record that 40 to 60 percent of the stenoses that require angioplasty are located less than three centimeters from the entrance to the coronary artery. ACS argues that therefore the ACS catheter may be used in such a way that all of the openings are located in the aorta. Even assuming that the trial judge's conclusion is correct that claim 1 is applicable to the third of the fact patterns, it remains true that on this record a reasonable jury could find that, pursuant to the procedure described in the first of the fact patterns (a noninfringing procedure), there are substantial noninfringing uses for the ACS catheter.

Whether the ACS catheter "has no use except through practice of the patented method," *Dawson Chemical Co. v. Rohm & Haas Co.*, is thus a critical issue to be decided in this case. As the Supreme Court recently noted, "[w]hen a charge of contributory infringement is predicated entirely on the sale of an article of commerce that is used by the purchaser [allegedly] to infringe a patent, the public interest in access to that article of commerce is necessarily implicated." *Sony Corp. v. Universal City Studios, Inc.*, 464 U.S. 417, 440 (198[4]) [declining to find contributory copyright infringement in sale of video cassette recorders]. Viewing the evidence in this case in a light most favorable to the nonmoving party, and resolving reasonable inferences in ACS's favor, it cannot be said that Bard is entitled to judgment as a matter of law. The grant of summary judgment finding ACS a contributory infringer under §271(c) is not appropriate.

A person induces infringement under §271(b) by actively and knowingly aiding and abetting another's direct infringement. Bard argues that ACS induced infringement under §271(b) by: 1) providing detailed instructions and other literature on how to use its catheter in a manner which would infringe claim 1; and 2) having positioned the inlets near the balloon's proximal end so as to allow a user of the ACS catheter to infringe claim 1. Because a genuine issue of material fact exists, a grant of summary judgment finding ACS induced infringement is also not appropriate.

COMMENTS AND QUESTIONS

1. While Bard sued ACS, a competing manufacturer of catheters, the "real" infringer in this case is the doctor who completed the catheterization under circumstances that violated Bard's patent. What should doctors do in such a situation? Refuse to perform procedures that infringe a patent? Seek a license? In 1996, Congress amended the patent laws to exempt doctors who perform medical processes from liability for infringement, rendering this problem moot. However, Congress apparently

intended to leave device manufacturers liable for contributory infringement of such patents. *See* §287.

2. A classic example of inducement/contributory infringement is the sale of device components or "replacement parts" for a patented device, even though the parts themselves constitute less than the complete device and hence do not directly infringe. Contributory infringement is often used to attack sellers of parts where the actual ultimate infringers are end-users who replace parts or assemble components. *See, e.g., Aro Mfg. Corp. v. Convertible Top Co.*, 377 U.S. 176 (1964); *Husky Injection Molding Systems, Ltd. v. R&D Tool Engineering Co.*, 291 F.3d 780 (Fed. Cir. 2002). Another example is the sale of products with instructions that assist buyers in employing a process that infringes a process patent. *See Dawson Chem. Co. v. Rohm & Haas, Inc.*, 448 U.S. 176 (1980).

3. If an unpatented product has no other use except in conjunction with the patented machine, process or product, is it reasonable automatically to presume that making, using or selling the *unpatented* product is contributory infringement? Or should companies be allowed to compete in the market for non-staple products that work with the patented invention? For a discussion of these issues, *see Dawson Chem. Co. v. Rohm & Haas, Inc.*, 448 U.S. 176 (1980); *Husky Injection Molding Systems, Ltd. v. R&D Tool Engineering Co.*, 291 F.3d 780 (Fed. Cir. 2002). Section 271(c) says that whoever sells or imports a component "constituting a material part of the invention, knowing the same to be especially made or especially adapted for use in an infringement of such patent, and not a staple article or commodity of commerce suitable for substantial noninfringing use" will be an infringer. Notice how this parallels the knowledge or intent requirement for inducement, which was the subject of the *Globaltech* case.

iii.   Joint Infringement

How does patent law handle situations where no single person or entity performs all the acts required to infringe a claim? In *BMC Resources, Inc. v. Paymentech, L.P.*, 498 F.3d 1373 (Fed. Cir. 2007), the patent owner brought suit for infringement of its patented method for processing debit transactions without a personal identification number (PIN). The accused infringer, Paymentech, showed that the claimed process involved performance of the following steps:

1. The customer calls a merchant to pay a bill;
2. The merchant collects payment information from the customer and sends it to Paymentech;
3. Paymentech routes the information to a participating debit network;
4. The debit network forwards the information to an affiliated financial institution;

5. The financial institution authorizes or declines the transaction, and if authorized, charges the customer's account according to the payment information collected by the merchant; and

6. Information regarding the status of the transaction moves from the financial institution to the debit network and then, through Paymentech, to the merchant who informs the customer of the status of the transaction.

Because some of these steps were neither performed by Paymentech nor with its active guidance or control, no single entity performed all the steps of the claim. Therefore, no direct infringement occurred. The court pointed out that more attentive claim drafting might have produced a claim that was infringed by a single entity such as Paymentech, *see* Mark A. Lemley, David O'Brien, Ryan M. Kent, Ashok Ramani, & Robert Van Nast, *Divided Infringement Claims*, 33 AIPLA Q.J. 255, 272-75 (2005), although not all inventions involving multiple actions can feasibly be confined to a single actor. The court further observed that if a single "mastermind" had centrally coordinated all the infringing steps among multiple actors, that mastermind would be liable for inducement under vicarious liability principles. 498 F.3d at 1381.

The next year, another Federal Circuit panel held that when multiple actors belonging to distinct enterprises collectively practice the steps of a process patent, there is no infringement liability unless one organization controls, directly or via contract, the actions of the others. Furthermore, a mere relationship between parties—such as providing access to a system and instructing users on the system's use—cannot establish "control or direction" required for inducement. *Muniauction, Inc. v. Thomson Corp.*, 532 F.3d 1318 (Fed. Cir. 2008).

This standard for liability did not sit well with several members of the Federal Circuit. In 2012, the court reconsidered this rule en banc and concluded that an actor could be held liable for *inducing* infringement even if all of the steps in patented process were not committed by a single entity. *See Akamai Technologies, Inc. v. Limelight Networks, Inc.*, 692 F.3d 1301 (Fed. Cir. 2012) (per curiam) (en banc). The majority based its analysis on legislative history of the 1952 Act, quoting testimony by Giles Rich, one of the principal drafters:

> Improvements in such arts as radio communication, television, etc., sometimes involve the new combinations of elements which in use are normally owned by different persons. Thus, a new method of radio communication may involve a change in the transmitter and a corresponding change in the receiver. To describe such an invention in patent claims, it is necessary either to specify *a new method which involves both transmitting and receiving*, or a new combination of an element in the receiver and an element in the transmitter. There are patents with such claims covering television inventions of importance.

The recent decisions of the Supreme Court [the cases targeted by the statutory changes] appear to make it impossible to enforce such patents in the usual case where a radio transmitter and a radio receiver are owned and operated by different persons, *for, while there is obvious infringement of the patent, there is no direct infringer of the patent but only two contributory infringers.*

Contributory Infringement of Patents: Hearings Before the Subcomm. on Patents, Trade-marks, and Copyrights of the H. Comm. on the Judiciary, 80th Cong. 5 (1948) (statement of G. Rich on behalf of the New York Patent Law Association) (emphasis added) (quoted in *Akamai*, 692. F.4d at 1310). Mr. (later Judge) Rich's statement indicates that "the 'obvious infringement' should be remediable, even though 'there is no direct infringer' of the patent." *Akamai*, 692. F.3d at 1311.

Judge Linn, joined by three colleagues, accused the majority of "assum[ing] the mantle of policy maker." The dissenters emphasized that both the Patent Act and Supreme Court precedent—*Aro Mfg. Co. v. Convertible Top Replacement Co.*, 365 U.S. 336, 341 (1961); *Deepsouth Packing Co. v. Laitram Corp.*, 406 U.S. 518, 526 (1972)—clearly establish that there can be no indirect liability of a patent without direct infringement. "Section 271, paragraph (a), is *a declaration of what constitutes infringement*," H.R. REP. NO. 82–1923, at 9 (1952) (emphasis added), and §271(b) and (c) liability is built on that foundation. *Akamai*, 692. F.3d at 1338 (Linn, J., dissenting). It also criticized the majority for reading the term "infringement" to mean two different things in two different subsections of the statute.

This split prompted the Supreme Court to weigh in. The Supreme Court reversed the Federal Circuit for the reasons articulated by Judge Linn. *See Limelight Networks, Inc. v. Akamai Technologies, Inc.*, 134 S.Ct. 2111 (2014). Nonetheless, the Court noted that the "problem" sought to be resolved by the Federal Circuit's en banc opinion in *Akamai* was created by the Federal Circuit in its decision in *Muniauction*—the rule that when multiple actors belonging to distinct enterprises collectively practice the steps of a process patent, there is no infringement liability unless one organization exercises direct supervisory or contractual control direct supervisory or contractual control over the actions of the other actor(s).

On remand, the full court, *sua sponte*, issued the following opinion.

Akamai Technologies, Inc v. Limelight Networks, Inc.,
Court of Appeals for the Federal Circuit
797 F.3d 1020 (Fed. Cir. 2015) (en banc)

PER CURIAM.

This case was returned to us by the United States Supreme Court, noting "the possibility that [we] erred by too narrowly circumscribing the scope of §271(a)" and suggesting that we "will have the opportunity to revisit the §271(a) question. . . ." We hereby avail ourselves of that opportunity.

Sitting en banc, we unanimously set forth the law of divided infringement under 35 U.S.C. §271(a). We conclude that, in this case, substantial evidence supports the jury's finding that Limelight Networks, Inc. ("Limelight") directly infringes U.S. Patent 6,108,703 (the "'703 patent") under §271(a). We therefore reverse the district court's grant of judgment of noninfringement as a matter of law.

I. DIVIDED INFRINGEMENT

Direct infringement under §271(a) occurs where all steps of a claimed method are performed by or attributable to a single entity. *See BMC Res., Inc. v. Paymentech, L.P.*, 498 F.3d 1373, 1379–81 (Fed. Cir. 2007). Where more than one actor is involved in practicing the steps, a court must determine whether the acts of one are attributable to the other such that a single entity is responsible for the infringement. We will hold an entity responsible for others' performance of method steps in two sets of circumstances: (1) where that entity directs or controls others' performance, and (2) where the actors form a joint enterprise.

To determine if a single entity directs or controls the acts of another, we continue to consider general principles of vicarious liability. In the past, we have held that an actor is liable for infringement under §271(a) if it acts through an agent (applying traditional agency principles) or contracts with another to perform one or more steps of a claimed method. *See BMC*, 498 F.3d at 1380–81. We conclude, on the facts of this case, that liability under §271(a) can also be found when an alleged infringer conditions participation in an activity or receipt of a benefit upon performance of a step or steps of a patented method and establishes the manner or timing of that performance. *Cf. Metro–Goldwyn–Mayer Studios Inc. v. Grokster, Ltd.*, 545 U.S. 913, 930 (2005) (stating that an actor "infringes vicariously by profiting from direct infringement" if that actor has the right and ability to stop or limit the infringement). In those instances, the third party's actions are attributed to the alleged infringer such that the alleged infringer becomes the single actor chargeable with direct infringement. Whether a single actor directed or controlled the acts of one or more third parties is a question of fact, reviewable on appeal for substantial evidence, when tried to a jury.

Alternatively, where two or more actors form a joint enterprise, all can be charged with the acts of the other, rendering each liable for the steps performed by the other as if each is a single actor. *See* RESTATEMENT (SECOND) OF TORTS §491 cmt. b ("The law ... considers that each is the agent or servant of the others, and that the act of any one within the scope of the enterprise is to be charged vicariously against the rest."). A joint enterprise requires proof of four elements:

(1) an agreement, express or implied, among the members of the group;

(2) a common purpose to be carried out by the group;

(3) a community of pecuniary interest in that purpose, among the members; and

(4) an equal right to a voice in the direction of the enterprise, which gives an equal right of control.

Id. §491 cmt.c. As with direction or control, whether actors entered into a joint enterprise is a question of fact, reviewable on appeal for substantial evidence. *Id.* ("Whether these elements exist is frequently a question for the jury, under proper direction from the court.").

We believe these approaches to be most consistent with the text of §271(a), the statutory context in which it appears, the legislative purpose behind the Patent Act, and our past case law. Section 271(a) is not limited solely to principal-agent relationships, contractual arrangements, and joint enterprise, as the vacated panel decision held. Rather, to determine direct infringement, we consider whether all method steps can be attributed to a single entity.

II. APPLICATION TO THE FACTS OF THIS CASE

Today we outline the governing legal framework for direct infringement and address the facts presented by this case. In the future, other factual scenarios may arise which warrant attributing others' performance of method steps to a single actor. Going forward, principles of attribution are to be considered in the context of the particular facts presented.

. . . In 2006, Akamai Technologies, Inc. ("Akamai") filed a patent infringement action against Limelight alleging infringement of several patents, including the ′703 patent, which claims methods for delivering content over the Internet.

[Claim 34 provides:

A content delivery method, comprising:

distributing a set of page objects across a network of content servers managed by a domain other than a content provider domain, wherein the network of content servers are organized into a set of regions;

for a given page normally served from the content provider domain, tagging at least some of the embedded objects of the page so that requests for the objects resolve to the domain instead of the content provider domain;

in response to a client request for an embedded object of the page:

resolving the client request as a function of a location of the client machine making the request and current Internet traffic conditions to identify a given region; and

returning to the client an IP address of a given one of the content servers within the given region that is likely to host the embedded object and that is not overloaded.

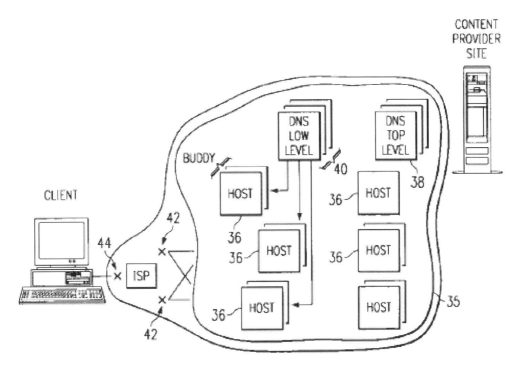

Figure 3

The case proceeded to trial, at which the parties agreed that Limelight's customers—not Limelight—perform the "tagging" and "serving" steps in the claimed methods. For example, as for claim 34 of the '703 patent, Limelight performs every step save the "tagging" step, in which Limelight's customers tag the content to be hosted and delivered by Limelight's content delivery network. After the close of evidence, the district judge instructed the jury that Limelight is responsible for its customers' performance of the tagging and serving method steps if Limelight directs or controls its customers' activities. The jury found that Limelight infringed claims 19, 20, 21, and 34 of the '703 patent. Following post-trial motions, the district court first denied Limelight's motion for judgment of noninfringement as a matter of law, ruling that Akamai had presented substantial evidence that Limelight directed or controlled its customers. After we decided *Muniauction, Inc. v. Thomson Corp.*, 532 F.3d 1318 (Fed. Cir. 2008), the district court granted Limelight's motion for reconsideration, holding as a matter of law that there could be no liability.

We reverse and reinstate the jury verdict. The jury heard substantial evidence from which it could find that Limelight directs or controls its customers' performance of each remaining method step, such that all steps of the method are attributable to Limelight. Specifically, Akamai presented substantial evidence demonstrating that Limelight conditions its customers' use of its content delivery network upon its customers' performance of the tagging and serving steps, and that Limelight establishes the manner or timing of its customers' performance. We review the evidence supporting "conditioning use of the content delivery network" and "establishing the manner or timing of performance" in turn.

First, the jury heard evidence that Limelight requires all of its customers to sign a standard contract. The contract delineates the steps customers must perform if they use the Limelight service. These steps include tagging and serving content. As to tagging, Limelight's form contract provides: "Customer shall be responsible for identifying via the then current [Limelight] process all [URLs] of the Customer Content to enable such Customer Content to be delivered by the [Limelight network]." In addition, the contract requires that Limelight's customers "provide [Limelight] with all cooperation and information reasonably necessary for [Limelight] to implement the [Content Delivery Service]." As for the serving step, the form contract states that Limelight is not responsible for failures in its content delivery network caused by its customers' failure to serve content. If a customer's server is down, Limelight's content delivery network need not perform. Thus, if Limelight's customers wish to use Limelight's product, they must tag and serve content. Accordingly, substantial evidence indicates that Limelight conditions customers' use of its content delivery network upon its customers' performance of the tagging and serving method steps.

Substantial evidence also supports finding that Limelight established the manner or timing of its customers' performance. Upon completing a deal with Limelight, Limelight sends its customer a welcome letter instructing the customer how to use Limelight's service. In particular, the welcome letter tells the customer that a Technical Account Manager employed by Limelight will lead the implementation of Limelight's services. The welcome letter also contains a hostname assigned by Limelight that the customer "integrate[s] into [its] webpages." This integration process includes the tagging step. Moreover, Limelight provides step-by-step instructions to its customers telling them how to integrate Limelight's hostname into its webpages if the customer wants to act as the origin for content. If Limelights customers do not follow these precise steps, Limelight's service will not be available. Limelight's Installation Guidelines give Limelight customers further information on tagging content. Lastly, the jury heard evidence that Limelight's engineers continuously engage with customers' activities. Initially, Limelight's engineers assist with installation and perform quality assurance testing. The engineers remain available if the customer experiences any problems. In sum, Limelight's customers do not merely take Limelight's guidance and act independently on their own. Rather, Limelight establishes the manner and timing of its customers' performance so that customers can only avail themselves of the service upon their performance of the method steps.

We conclude that the facts Akamai presented at trial constitute substantial evidence from which a jury could find that Limelight directed or controlled its customers' performance of each remaining method step. As such, substantial evidence supports the jury's verdict that all steps of the claimed methods were performed by or attributable to Limelight. Therefore, Limelight is liable for direct infringement.

III. CONCLUSION

At trial, Akamai presented substantial evidence from which a jury could find that Limelight directly infringed the '703 patent. Therefore, we reverse the district court's grant of judgment of noninfringement as a matter of law. Because issues in the original appeal and cross-appeal remain, we return the case to the panel for resolution of all residual issues consistent with this opinion.

COMMENTS AND QUESTIONS

1. Does this standard fundamentally change the law to allow joint infringement theories, or merely broaden the scope of §271(a) to ensnare a relatively small subset of joint enterprises? The new joint enterprise theory of vicarious infringement attaches liability "when an alleged infringer conditions participation in an activity or receipt of a benefit upon performance of a [method step] and establishes the manner or timing of that performance." This is a looser type of control than the more rigid tests rejected by the Federal Circuit on remand from the Supreme Court. *See* Olajumoke Obayanju, *What Next? Exploring the Federal Circuit's Expansion of Direct Infringement Liability Post-Akamai v. Limelight and the Process It Took to Get There*, 25 FED. CIRCUIT B.J. 319, 332 (2016). Because of the looser standard, more product sellers and service providers may be liable than under the previous test. Is there any way for these parties and their clients to contractually allocate the risk of infringement?

2. Suppose the contract had been silent on what the customers would do. Would the result change? Should it? What if the software were designed so that the customer had no choice; the software "pulled" information on tagged objects directly from the customer. Would the customer's assent to the overall service constitute acceptance of the service provider's control over the "manner and timing of performance"?

PROBLEM

Problem III-17. Nichols, a scientist who enjoys puzzles, designs a "rotating cube" puzzle in which each face of the cube is composed of a number of smaller cubes, each face is initially of a different color, and the object of the puzzle is to restore the original color scheme once it has been disturbed. Nichols obtains a patent on a method of solving this puzzle, but not on the physical puzzle itself.

Rubik builds and sells puzzles similar to the ones Nichols has designed. Has Rubik infringed the Nichols patent, either directly or indirectly? Does it matter whether Nichols's patent covers the only known solution to the puzzle, or only one among many possible solutions? What if Rubik's product includes a "cheat" sheet advising buyers how to solve the puzzle using a number of methods, including Nichols's? What if Rubik includes a copy of the Nichols patent with each cube sold, ostensibly to advise users how to avoid infringement, but arguably with the intent of encouraging them to use the Nichols method?

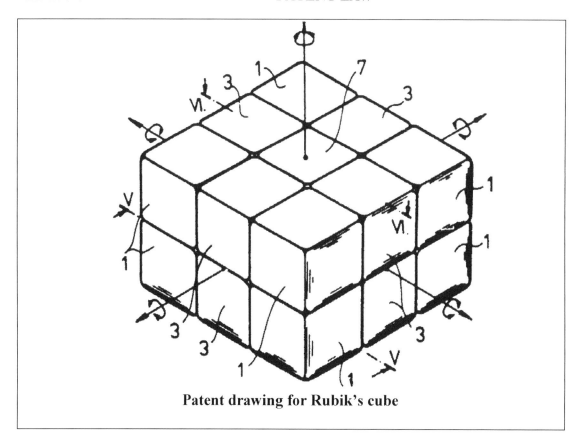

Patent drawing for Rubik's cube

F. DEFENSES

Section 282(b) of the Patent Act provides for the following defenses:

(1) Noninfringement, absence of liability for infringement or unenforceability;

(2) Invalidity of the patent or any claim in suit on any ground specified in part II [of the Patent Act] as a condition for patentability;

(3) Invalidity of the patent or any claim in suit for failure to comply with—

    (A) any requirement of section 112, except that the failure to disclose the best mode shall not be a basis on which any claim of a patent may be canceled or held invalid or otherwise unenforceable; or

    (B) any requirement of section 251 [relating to reissue of defective patents];

(4) Any other fact or act made a defense by [the Patent Act].

In addition to these statutory defenses, courts have recognized a variety of other defenses, including experimental use, inequitable conduct, patent misuse, laches, and equitable estoppel.

1. Invalidity and the Presumption of Validity

In a conventional patent enforcement action, where a patent owner seeks to hold an alleged infringer liable, the patent owner does not have to prove the validity of the patent. Under §282(a), a patent is presumed valid. We discussed the grounds for invalidity in Chapter III(B). They are the same whether the PTO or the courts are considering validity. Once a patent has issued, though, "[t]he burden of establishing invalidity . . . rest[s] on the party asserting such invalidity." *Id.* This presumption aims to secure the patentee's quasi-property right and reflects the role of the PTO in examining the application. The party disputing the patent's validity must prove invalidity by "clear and convincing evidence," a higher standard than the typical civil law standard—preponderance of the evidence.

COMMENTS AND QUESTIONS

1. Should this standard apply where the alleged infringer brings forth prior art that the Patent Office did not consider during examination? The Supreme Court noted in *KSR Int'l Co. v. Teleflex Inc.*, 550 U.S. 398, 426 (2007) "the rationale underlying the presumption—that the PTO, in its expertise, has approved the claim—seems much diminished." Yet the Court ruled in *Microsoft Corp. v. i4i Ltd.*, 564 U.S. 91 (2011), that the presumption still applies, but "the challenger's burden to persuade the jury of its invalidity defense by clear and convincing evidence may be easier to sustain. . . . [T]he jury may be instructed to consider that it has heard evidence that the PTO had no opportunity to evaluate before granting the patent."

2. *Assignor Estoppel.* A seller of a patent or patent application may not, absent exceptional circumstances, attack the validity of that patent in a subsequent patent infringement litigation. *See Mentor Graphics Corp. v. Quickturn Design Systems, Inc.*, 150 F.3d 1374, 1378 (Fed. Cir. 1998). The doctrine derives from legal estoppel (or estoppel by deed), which prohibits a grantor of property from challenging the validity of the grant. *See Westinghouse Elec. & Mfg. Co. v. Formica Insulation Co.*, 266 U.S. 342, 348-49 (1924). It applies to bar inventors who later move to a competing company or start one of their own, preventing them from challenging the patent they invented, even if they did not sell the patent to its current owner but simply signed an employment agreement assigning all rights in their inventions.

The doctrine of assignor estoppel has been applied quite broadly by the Federal Circuit, which has never refused to apply the doctrine and has extended it to a wide array of groups in privity with the inventor. *See* Mark A. Lemley, *Rethinking Assignor Estoppel*, 54 HOUS. L. REV. (forthcoming 2016). Exceptional circumstances that might theoretically allow an invalidity challenge by an inventor include: an express reservation by the assignor of the right to challenge the validity of the patent or an express waiver by the assignee of the right to assert assignor estoppel, *cf. Mentor Graphics Corp. v. Quickturn Design Systems, Inc.*, 150 F.3d 1374, 1378 (Fed. Cir.

1998), or where the assignor's participation was under duress, *cf. Shamrock Technologies, Inc. v. Medical Sterilization, Inc.*, 903 F.2d 789, 793 (Fed. Cir. 1990).

3. No Licensee Estoppel. Under traditional contract and property principles, "one receiving bargained-for benefits under a contract may not question the consideration he has received." *See* Robert B. Orr, Note, *The Doctrine of Licensee Repudiation in Patent Law*, 63 YALE L.J. 125 (1953). Courts have applied this doctrine to bar patent licensees from challenging the validity of the patents supporting their bargain since the mid-19th century. *See Automatic Radio Manufacturing Co. v. Hazeltine Research, Inc.*, 339 U.S. 827, 836 (1950). In a break from this tradition, the Supreme Court ruled in *Lear, Inc. v. Adkins*, 395 U.S. 653 (1969) looked to "the strong federal policy favoring free competition in ideas which do not merit patent protection" reflected in these cases in refusing to honor contractual restrictions on licensees challenging patent validity. The Court emphasized

> Licensees may often be the only individuals with enough economic incentive to challenge the patentability of an inventor's discovery. If they are muzzled, the public may continually be required to pay tribute to would-be monopolists without need or justification. We think it plain that the technical requirements of contract doctrine must give way before the demands of the public interest in the typical situation involving the negotiation of a license after a patent has issued.

Id. at 670-71. Can you think of any circumstances in which it might be economically efficient to allow parties to restrict licensee patent challenges? If licensees are free to challenge patents for public policy reasons, why not inventors? *See generally* Rochelle Cooper Dreyfuss, *Dethroning Lear: Licensee Estoppel and the Incentive to Innovate*, 72 VA. L. REV. 677, 694-95 (1986); Rochelle Cooper Dreyfuss & Lawrence S. Pope, *Dethroning Lear? Incentives to Innovate After Medimmune*, 24 BERKELEY TECH. L.J. 971, 1007 (2009).

2.   "With Authority"

Recall that §271(a) (Infringement of patent) refers to "whoever without authority makes, sells, . . ." (emphasis added). Thus, an important set of defenses to infringement relate to authorization—either through agreement or by operation of law. Patent licenses can be express or implied.

i.   *Express or Implied License*

Obviously, an express license to practice a patented invention would preclude a patent suit, since the defendant was using the invention "with authority" from the patent owner. An implied license arises by acquiescence, conduct, equitable estoppel, or legal estoppel. *Wang Labs., Inc. v. Mitsubishi Elecs. Am., Inc.*, 103 F.3d 1571, 1580 (Fed. Cir. 1997). Such licenses are generally revocable. The existence and scope of licenses are generally governed by state contract law.

ii. The Exhaustion Principle/First Sale Doctrine

Under the exhaustion principle (also referred to as the first sale doctrine), the first unrestricted sale of a patented product exhausts the patentee's control over that product and it can be resold and repaired without implicating the patent owner's rights. The doctrine traces back to the nineteenth century. "[T]he patentee or his assignee having in the act of sale received all the royalty or consideration which he claims for the use of his invention in that particular machine or instrument, it is open to the use of the purchaser without further restriction on account of the monopoly of the patentees." *Adams v. Burke*, 84 U.S. 453 (1873); *see Aro Mfg. Co. v. Convertible Top Replacement Co.*, 377 U.S. 476, 484 (1964) (stating that "it is fundamental that sale of a patented article by the patentee . . . carries with it an 'implied license to use.'").

The Supreme Court reaffirmed the principle of exhaustion in *Quanta Computer, Inc. v. LG Electronics, Inc.*, 533 U.S. 617 (2008). It strongly suggested that once a patentee sold or authorized the sale of a product in this country, its control over that particular product ended, at least as a matter of patent law. It acknowledged that parties could contract for post-sale restrictions, but noted that those restrictions would be evaluated and enforced as a matter of contract, not patent, law. *Id.* n.7. Nonetheless, the Federal Circuit in *Lexmark Int'l, Inc. v. Impression Products, Inc.*, 816 F.3d 721 (Fed. Cir. 2016) (en banc), refused to follow the suggestion in *Quanta*, instead holding that even a sticker that purported to limit use of a product once sold could make anyone who violated the terms of that "contract" a patent infringer. The case involved a defendant that refilled and refurbished printer toner cartridges in spite of a "single use only" label on the cartridges. Such a "label license" pushes hard against the line that separates a bilateral contract from a unilateral restriction on personal property that purports to "run with the goods," i.e., a restriction that applies to all subsequent transferees who receive notice of the restriction. Such "personal property servitudes" have traditionally been disfavored, on the theory that they gum up free flowing markets for goods.

COMMENTS AND QUESTIONS

1. *Method Claims.* The doctrine of patent exhaustion applies to method claims and the method patent is exhausted by sale of the item that embodies the method. *See Quanta Computer, Inc. v. LG Electronics, Inc.*, 533 U.S. 617 (2008). Although repair of a patented product that has been sold is permissible, reconstruction of the patented technology crosses the line into the patentee's "make" right.

2. *Permissible Repair/Impermissible Reconstruction Doctrine.* The line between permitted repair and impermissible reconstruction is not easily determined, resulting in vague, context-specific rulings. *See, e.g., Hewlett-Packard Co. v. Repeat-O-Type Stencil Mfg. Co.*, 123 F.3d 1445 (Fed. Cir. 1997) (dealing with refilling of printer cartridges). Such issues frequently arise in the context of contributory infringement claims, where the alleged infringer is providing specialized replacement parts. *See, e.g.,*

Everpure v. Cuno, Inc., 875 F.3d 300 (Fed. Cir. 1989) ("Here it is the combination that is protected. The cartridge is not. . . . A purchaser of [Everpure's] filter unit is free to replace the worn out filter cartridge and the fact that it requires a particular cartridge configuration to mate it to the head does not alter the legal principle."). Contractual restrictions on resale or reuse can provoke patent misuse allegations and antitrust counterclaims. *See Lexmark Int'l, Inc., v. Impression Prods.*, Inc., 816 F.3d 721 (Fed. Cir. 2016) (en banc); *Monsanto Co. v. McFarling*, 363 F.3d 1336, 1341 (Fed. Cir. 2004); *Mallinckrodt, Inc. v. Medipart, Inc.*, 976 F.2d 700 (Fed. Cir. 1992).

3. *Policy Rationale*. The exhaustion doctrine has been criticized for interfering with freedom of contract. *See* Richard A. Epstein, *The Disintegration of Intellectual Property? A Classical Liberal Response to a Premature Obituary*, 62 STAN. L. REV. 455, 502-09 (2010). Professor Glen Robinson contends that

> the traditional hostility to use and resale restraints on personal property is misguided in both the common law and intellectual property contexts. While there may be legitimate reasons for limiting an owner's right to impose post-transfer restrictions on use and resale, those reasons are more exceptional than has been commonly assumed. Moreover, in the new digital world where servitude-type restrictions can be engineered into the architecture of the property itself, public policy restrictions on contractual 'servitudes' may prove to be ineffectual, creating a new reason to take a fresh look at old conceptions of personal property servitudes.

Glen O. Robinson, *Personal Property Servitudes,* 71 U. CHI. L. REV. 1449 (2004).

Other scholars (and the Supreme Court, in the copyright context) worry that contractual restrictions on the use of personal property, like non-possessory interests in real property, can greatly complicate the use of resources over time. *See Kirtsaeng v. John S. Wiley & Sons*, 133 S.Ct. 1351 (2013); Molly Shaffer Van Houweling, *The New Servitudes*, 96 GEO. L.J. 885 (2007); Zechariah Chafee, Jr., *Equitable Servitudes on Chattels*, 41 HARV. L. REV. 945 (1928); *see generally* MICHAEL HELLER, THE GRIDLOCK ECONOMY: HOW TOO MUCH OWNERSHIP WRECKS MARKETS, STOPS INNOVATION, AND COSTS LIVES (2008). Others have suggested that the issue turns on the optimal standardization of legal regimes. *See* Thomas W. Merrill & Henry E. Smith, *Optimal Standardization in the Law of Property: The* Numerus Clausus *Principle*, 110 YALE L.J. 1 (2000).

4. *Territoriality, Price Discrimination/Gray Goods/Parallel Imports, and International Exhaustion*. Patent protection is territorial. Suppose that a patentee decides to sell its patented widget for a high price in the United States and a lower price in Asia. Drug companies often follow this model, with lower prices in lesser developed nations.

Economists refer to this phenomenon as price discrimination. Although it sounds evil, it has various virtues. First, it ensures that the patented good reaches a larger population, thereby reducing the deadweight loss of a single monopoly price. Second, it facilitates companies to provide different levels of services in different regions.

Does the Patent Act bar the authorized purchaser of a U.S. patented good in Asia from importing it to the United States without authorization—i.e., does the sale abroad exhaust the patent rights in the U.S.? As we will see in Chapter IV, the Supreme Court has interpreted the Copyright Act to hold that such a foreign sale does exhaust copyright protection and such good can lawfully be imported into the United States even though the copyright owner has not authorized importation of the good into the United States. *See Kirtsaeng v. John Wiley & Sons, Inc.*, 133 S.Ct. 1351 (2013). In *Lexmark Int'l, Inc., v. Impression Prods.*, Inc., 816 F.3d 721 (Fed. Cir. 2016) (en banc), the Federal Circuit declined to apply the international exhaustion principle to patent protection. In distinguishing the Supreme Court's treatment of copyright protection, the Federal Circuit emphasized that "Section 271(a) connects 'make,' 'sell,' 'use,' and the other terms [including 'importing'] with the disjunction 'or,' . . ."

PROBLEM

Problem III-18. Big Soya, Inc. is a large agricultural chemicals firm that sells a widely used herbicide named WEEDAWAY. Beginning in the 1980s, Big Soya began investing heavily in agricultural biotechnology research, with an eye toward developing advanced herbicides and related products. One of the problems that Big Soya faces, like all herbicide firms, is "selectivity": designing products that kill weeds, but do little or no damage to farm crops. In the mid-1990s, Big Soya researchers hit on the idea of developing a genetically engineered strain of soybeans that is particularly immune to the effects of the popular WEEDAWAY herbicide. By the late 1990s, they had perfected—and patented—special strains of soybean seeds with just these properties, which they called "WEEDAWAY-PROOF" seeds. As part of its strategy to protect the market for its proprietary seeds, Big Soya asks farmers using the seeds to sign a contract restricting the farmers' activities in a number of ways. Specifically, the farmers agree: (1) To use the seed containing Big Soya gene technologies for planting a commercial crop only in a single season; (2) Not to supply any of the seed to any other person or entity for planting, and to not save any crop produced from this seed for replanting, or supply saved seed to anyone for replanting; (3) Not to use the seed or provide it to anyone for crop breeding, research, generation of herbicide registration data, or seed production. The farmers' agreement also contains a clause specifying damages in the event of breach by the farmer:

In the event that the Grower saves, supplies, sells or acquires seed for replant in violation of this Agreement and license restriction, in addition to other remedies available to the technology provider(s), the Grower agrees that damages will include a claim for liquidated damages, which will be based on 120 times the applicable Technology Fee.

In a lawsuit brought against a farmer, Betty Overall, Big Soya alleges that Betty saved seeds from a batch of WEEDAWAY-PROOF soybeans, and used them again the next season. Betty argues that she bought the seeds outright, despite having signed the agreement (which she claims neither to have read nor understood); that farmers have traditionally had the right to plant "saved seed" from the previous year's crops, and that the Plant Variety Protection Act (see below) even enshrines that tradition in a "saved seed" exemption. Betty argues that Big Soya's farmers' agreement and the assertion of its patents against farmers such as Betty is patent misuse. Do you agree? How would you argue the case, based on Motion Picture and the other materials in this chapter?

3.   The "Experimental Use" Defense

Notwithstanding the absolute language of §271(a), there is a judicially created exception to infringement that is commonly known as the "experimental use" exception. The doctrine had its origins in Justice Joseph Story's opinion in *Whittemore v. Cutter*, 29 F. Cas. 1120 (C.C.D. Mass. 1813) (No. 17,600). In that case, the defendant appealed a jury instruction to the effect that the "making of a machine . . . with a design to use it for profit" constituted infringement. Justice Story upheld the trial judge's instruction and stated that "it could never have been the intention of the legislature to punish a man, who constructed such a machine merely for philosophical experiments, or for the purpose of ascertaining the sufficiency of the machine to produce its described effects." 29 F. Cas. at 1121.

Madey v. Duke University
United States Court of Appeals for the Federal Circuit
307 F.3d 1351 (Fed. Cir. 2002)

GAJARSA, Circuit Judge.

* * *

BACKGROUND

In the mid–1980s Madey was a tenured research professor at Stanford University. At Stanford, he had an innovative laser research program, which was highly regarded in the scientific community. An opportunity arose for Madey to consider leaving Stanford and take a tenured position at Duke. Duke recruited Madey, and in 1988 he left Stanford for a position in Duke's physics department. In 1989 Madey moved his free electron laser ("FEL") research lab from Stanford to Duke. The FEL lab contained substantial equipment, requiring Duke to build an addition to its physics building to house the lab. In addition, during his time at Stanford, Madey had obtained sole ownership of two patents practiced by some of the equipment in the FEL lab.

At Duke, Madey served for almost a decade as director of the FEL lab. During that time the lab continued to achieve success in both research funding and scientific breakthroughs. However, a dispute arose between Madey and Duke. Duke contends that, despite his scientific prowess, Madey ineffectively managed the lab. Madey contends that Duke sought to use the lab's equipment for research areas outside the allocated scope of certain government funding, and that when he objected, Duke sought to remove him as lab director. Duke eventually did remove Madey as director of the lab in 1997. The removal is not at issue in this appeal, however, it is the genesis of this unique patent infringement case. As a result of the removal, Madey resigned from Duke in 1998. Duke, however, continued to operate some of the equipment in the lab. Madey then sued Duke for patent infringement of his two patents, and brought a variety of other claims. . . .

II. DISCUSSION

. . .

The Experimental Use Defense

. . . Madey contends that the Supreme Court's opinion in *Warner–Jenkinson Co. v. Hilton Davis Chem. Co.*, 520 U.S. 17 (1997) eliminates the experimental use defense. The Supreme Court held in *Warner–Jenkinson* that intent plays no role in the application of the doctrine of equivalents. *Warner–Jenkinson*, 520 U.S. at 36. Madey implicitly argues that the experimental use defense necessarily incorporates an intent inquiry, and thus is inconsistent with *Warner–Jenkinson*. . . . [W]e do not view such an inconsistency as inescapable, and conclude the experimental use defense persists albeit in the very narrow form articulated by this court in *Embrex* [*v. Service Engineering Corp.*], 216 F.3d [1343, 1349 [(Fed. Cir. 2000)].

The District Court Improperly Shifted the Burden to Madey

As a precursor to the burden-shifting issue, Madey argues that the experimental use defense is an affirmative defense that Duke must plead or lose. We disagree. Madey points to no source of authority for its assertion that experimental use is an affirmative defense. Indeed, we have referred to the defense in a variety of ways. *See Roche* [*Products, Inc. v. Bolar Pharmaceutical Co., Inc.*, 733 F.2d 858, 862, 221 (Fed. Cir. 1984)] (referring to experimental use as both an exception and a defense). Given this lack of precise treatment in the precedent, Madey has no basis to support its affirmative defense argument. . . .

The district court held that in order for Madey to overcome his burden to establish actionable infringement, he must establish that Duke did not use the patent-covered free electron laser equipment solely for experimental or other non-profit purposes. Madey argues that this improperly shifts the burden to the patentee and conflates the experimental use defense with the initial infringement inquiry.

We agree with Madey that the district court improperly shifted the burden to him. The district court folded the experimental use defense into the baseline assessment as to whether Duke infringed the patents. . . . [The district court] erroneously required Madey to show as a part of his initial claim that Duke's use was not experimental. The defense, if available at all, must be established by Duke.

The District Court's Overly Broad Conception of Experimental Use

Madey argues, and we agree, that the district court had an overly broad conception of the very narrow and strictly limited experimental use defense. The district court stated that the experimental use defense inoculated uses that "were solely for research, academic, or experimental purposes," and that the defense covered use that "is made for experimental, non-profit purposes only." Both formulations are too broad and stand in sharp contrast to our admonitions in *Embrex* and *Roche* that the experimental use defense is very narrow and strictly limited. In *Embrex*, we followed the teachings of *Roche* and *Pitcairn* [*v. United States*, 212 Ct.Cl. 168, 547 F.2d 1106 (1976)) to hold that the defense was very narrow and limited to actions performed "for amusement, to satisfy idle curiosity, or for strictly philosophical inquiry." *Embrex*, 216 F.3d at 1349. Further, use does not qualify for the experimental use defense when it is undertaken in the "guise of scientific inquiry" but has "definite, cognizable, and not insubstantial commercial purposes." *Id.* (*quoting Roche*, 733 F.2d at 863). The concurring opinion in *Embrex* expresses a similar view: use is disqualified from the defense if it has the "slightest commercial implication." *Id.* at 1353. Moreover, use in keeping with the legitimate business of the alleged infringer does not qualify for the experimental use defense. *See Pitcairn*, 547 F.2d at 1125–26. The district court supported its conclusion with a citation to *Ruth v. Stearns–Roger Mfg. Co.*, 13 F.Supp. 697, 713 (D.Colo. 1935), a case that is not binding precedent for this court.

The *Ruth* case represents the conceptual dilemma that may have led the district court astray. Cases evaluating the experimental use defense are few, and those involving non-profit, educational alleged infringers are even fewer. In *Ruth*, the court concluded that a manufacturer of equipment covered by patents was not liable for contributory infringement because the end-user purchaser was the Colorado School of Mines, which used the equipment in furtherance of its educational purpose. Thus, the combination of apparent lack of commerciality, with the non-profit status of an educational institution, prompted the court in *Ruth*, without any detailed analysis of the character, nature and effect of the use, to hold that the experimental use defense applied. This is not consistent with the binding precedent of our case law postulated by *Embrex*, *Roche* and *Pitcairn*.

Our precedent clearly does not immunize use that is in any way commercial in nature. Similarly, our precedent does not immunize any conduct that is in keeping with the alleged infringer's legitimate business, regardless of commercial implications. For example, major research universities, such as Duke, often sanction and fund research projects with arguably no commercial application whatsoever. However, these projects unmistakably further the institution's legitimate business objectives, including educating and enlightening students and faculty participating in these projects. These projects also serve, for example, to increase the status of the institution and lure lucrative research grants, students and faculty.

In short, regardless of whether a particular institution or entity is engaged in an endeavor for commercial gain, so long as the act is in furtherance of the alleged infringer's legitimate business and is not solely for amusement, to satisfy idle curiosity, or for strictly philosophical inquiry, the act does not qualify for the very narrow and strictly limited experimental use defense. Moreover, the profit or non-profit status of the user is not determinative.

In the present case, the district court attached too great a weight to the non-profit, educational status of Duke, effectively suppressing the fact that Duke's acts appear to be in accordance with any reasonable interpretation of Duke's legitimate business objectives.[7] On remand, the district court will have to significantly narrow and limit its conception of the experimental use defense. The correct focus should not be on the non-profit status of Duke but on the legitimate business Duke is involved in and whether or not the use was solely for amusement, to satisfy idle curiosity, or for strictly philosophical inquiry. . . .

COMMENTS AND QUESTIONS

1. *Is the Ivory Tower Just Another Office Building?* Do the aggressive patent acquisition, licensing, and enforcement activities of universities undermine the legitimacy of their claims to "special treatment" under the research exemption? *See* DEREK BOK, UNIVERSITIES IN THE MARKETPLACE: THE COMMERCIALIZATION OF HIGHER EDUCATION 201 (2003) ("Universities may not yet be willing to trade all of their values for money, but they have proceeded much further down that road than they are generally willing to acknowledge."); Mark A. Lemley, *Are Universities Patent Trolls?*, 16 FORDHAM INTELL. PROP., MEDIA, & ENT. L.J. 611 (2008).

2. *Scope of Experimental Use.* Do you think that experimental use should be broader? Note that the Patent Act permits patents on "improvements thereof."

Based on the history and rationale of the experimental use doctrine, Professor Rebecca Eisenberg contends that research to check the adequacy of the specification and the validity of the patent holder's claims about the invention should be exempt from infringement liability. Rebecca Eisenberg, *Patents and the Progress of Science: Exclusive Rights and Experimental Use*, 56 U. CHI. L. REV. 1017 (1989). By contrast, research use of a patented invention with a primary or significant market among research users should not be exempt from infringement liability when the research user is an ordinary consumer of the patented invention.

---

[7] Duke's patent and licensing policy may support its primary function as an educational institution. *See Duke University Policy on Inventions, Patents, and Technology Transfer* (1996), available at http://www.ors.duke.edu/policies/patpol.htm (last visited Oct. 3, 2002). Duke, however, like other major research institutions of higher learning, is not shy in pursuing an aggressive patent licensing program from which it derives a not insubstantial revenue stream.

Professor Eisenberg argues for a middle ground where a researcher uses a patented invention in a way that could potentially lead to improvements in the patented technology or to the development of alternative means of achieving the same purpose. In those scenarios, it might be appropriate to award a reasonable royalty after the fact to be sure that the patent holder receives an adequate return on the initial investment in developing the patented invention. The patent holder should not, however, be entitled to enjoin the use of a patented invention in such efforts to improve upon the patented technology. How would you go about setting the reasonable royalty in a case where a subsequent improver infringed a patent in the course of developing a superior alternative that destroys the patentee's market?

3. The European Patent Convention provides that patent protection "does not extend to acts done for experimental purposes relating to the subject matter of the patented invention." Art. 27(b), European Patent Convention (implemented in all EU states except Austria). *See also* Patent Act of the People's Republic of China, Article 69(4) (shall not be patent infringement "(4) Any person uses the relevant patent specially for the purpose of scientific research and experimentation"). Would these provisions have immunized Duke University?

4. *Use of Patented Technology for Drug Testing.* Generic drug companies would like to enter the market as soon as a patent expires. This is also valuable for drug consumers who benefit from competitive pricing. To be ready to hit the ground running, however, the generic company needs FDA approval to market the drug. In *Roche Products, Inc. v. Bolar Pharmaceutical Co.*, 733 F.2d 858 (Fed. Cir. 1984), the Federal Circuit held that the experimental use exception did not include "the limited use of a patented drug for testing and investigation strictly related to FDA drug approval requirements. . . . Bolar may intend to perform "experiments," but unlicensed experiments conducted with a view to the adaption of the patented invention to the experimentor's business are a violation of the rights of the patentee to exclude others from using his patented invention."733 F.2d at 861, 863.

5. *Bolar Amendment: Statutory Experimental Use Exception for Drug Testing.* Congress passed the Drug Price Competition and Patent Term Restoration Act, Pub. L. 98-417 (1984), informally known as the Hatch-Waxman Act. The Act establishes an Abbreviated New Drug Application (ANDA) process to speed entry of generic drugs onto the marketplace after a patent expires. Congress overturned the *Bolar* decision by enacting §271(e)(1):

> it shall not be an act of infringement to make, use, offer to sell, or sell within the United States or import into the United States a patented invention . . . solely for uses reasonably related to the development and submission of information under a Federal law which regulates the manufacture, use, or sale of drugs or veterinary biological products.

The Supreme Court held in *Merck KGaA v. Integra Life Sciences I Ltd.*, 545 U.S. 193 (2005), that the exemption broadly protects any pre-clinical testing of patented compounds that is reasonably related to the submission of information to a regulatory agency, and not just late-stage safety and efficacy testing in human subjects. Integra owned five patents to "RGD peptides," small proteins that attach tightly to certain binding sites on the surfaces of blood vessel cells. Researchers working in cooperation with Merck discovered that RGD peptides could be used to block receptors active during the proliferation of blood vessel cells. Because this has the effect of slowing down blood vessel growth, it is an effective way to inhibit the growth of tumors. Merck and its research collaborators used RGD peptides in two different ways: (1) to test them directly as tumor-inhibiting agents; and (2) as "benchmarks" against which to measure other compounds they were developing for tumor inhibition.

The Supreme Court held that the Bolar Amendment immunized Merck's use of Integra's patents:

> Congress did not limit §271(e)(1)'s safe harbor to the development of information for inclusion in a submission to the FDA; nor did it create an exemption applicable only to the research relevant to filing an ANDA for approval of a generic drug. Rather, it exempted from infringement all uses of patented compounds "reasonably related" to the process of developing information for submission under any federal law regulating the manufacture, use, or distribution of drugs. We decline to read the "reasonable relation" requirement so narrowly as to render §271(e)(1)'s stated protection of activities leading to FDA approval for all drugs illusory. Properly construed, §271(e)(1) leaves adequate space for experimentation and failure on the road to regulatory approval: At least where a drugmaker has a reasonable basis for believing that a patented compound may work, through a particular biological process, to produce a particular physiological effect, and uses the compound in research that, if successful, would be appropriate to include in a submission to the FDA, that use is "reasonably related" to the "development and submission of information under . . . Federal law."

545 U.S. 206-07. Some have suggested that this result discourages pharmaceutical companies from disclosing their research. *See* Lawrence B. Ebert, *In Favor of the Federal Circuit Position in* Merck v. Integra, 87 J. PAT. & TRADEMARK OFF. SOC'Y 321, 339-40 (2005).

4. Prior User Rights

Congress established the §273 prior user defense as a safe harbor for the financial community in 1999 following *State St. Bank v. Signature Fin. Grp.*, 149 F.3d 1368 (Fed. Cir. 1998), the controversial decision opening the way for business method patents. Congress expanded the prior user defense significantly in the AIA to include "subject matter consisting of a process, or consisting of a machine, manufacture, or composition of matter used in a manufacturing or other commercial process." §273(a). One who secures a prior user right does not invalidate the patent at issue; the right is a personal defense that shields only this one party from liability. For this defense to apply, the invention must have been used commercially in the U.S. by the party asserting the defense at least one year before the earlier of either: (1) the effective filing date, or (2) the date of the first public disclosure of the claimed invention. The prior use defense must be established by clear and convincing evidence. This defense is subject to various limitations and exceptions, including that it may not be asserted against "an institution of higher education . . . or technology transfer organization whose primary purpose is to facilitate the commercialization of technologies developed by one or more such institutions of higher education." §273(e)(5).

5. Inequitable Conduct

Where a patent applicant breaches the duty to prosecute a patent application in good faith and candor, it may result in a finding of inequitable conduct. *See* 37 C.F.R. §1.56 (2013); *Purdue Pharma L.P. v. Endo Pharm. Inc.*, 410 F.3d 690, 695 (Fed. Cir. 2005). Inequitable conduct may "arise from an affirmative misrepresentation of a material fact, failure to disclose material information, or submission of false material information, coupled with an intent to deceive or mislead the USPTO." *Id.* A determination that inequitable conduct occurred in relation to one or more claims will render the entire patent unenforceable. *Kingsdown Med. Consultants, Ltd. v. Hollister, Inc.*, 863 F.2d 867, 877 (Fed. Cir. 1988) (en banc in relevant part).

This doctrine came under scrutiny as defendants routinely alleged inequitable conduct in the hopes that they could uncover some shred of evidence casting doubt on the patentee's candor during prosecution. Such allegations provided a basis for costly and time-consuming discovery. Well-funded defendants could use the cost and delay as leverage in settling patent litigation. The threat of inequitable conduct also contributed to patentees flooding the PTO with prior art references out of concern that any article in their files could be used as part of a future inequitable conduct defense.

Therasense, Inc. v. Becton-Dickinson, Inc.
United States Court of Appeals for the Federal Circuit
649 F.3d 1276 (Fed. Cir. 2011) (en banc)

RADER, Chief Judge.

[Therasense, a subsidiary of Abbott Laboratories, obtained several patents on disposable glucose test strips for diabetes management. Becton, Dickenson and Co. sued for a declaratory judgment that Abbott's patents were invalid. Abbott countersued Becton and Bayer Healthcare LLC for infringement. After the cases were consolidated for trial in the Northern District of California, the district court held all of the litigated patent claims either invalid or not infringed. The court also held one of the patents, U.S. Patent No. 5,820,551 ("the '551 patent"), unenforceable due to inequitable conduct. On appeal, a panel of the Federal Circuit unanimously affirmed all of the district court's holdings of noninfringement and invalidity, including the district court's ruling that all litigated claims in the '551 patent were invalid for obviousness. The panel also affirmed the district court's holding that the '551 patent was unenforceable due to inequitable conduct, but the panel was divided on that issue. The full court granted rehearing en banc solely on the inequitable conduct issue.]

The '551 patent claims a test strip with an electrochemical sensor . . . *"configured to be exposed to said whole blood sample without an intervening membrane or other whole blood filtering member . . . ."* '551 patent [claim 1] (emphasis added). "Whole blood," an important term in the claim, means blood that contains all of its components, including red blood cells.

In the prior art, some sensors employed diffusion-limiting membranes to control the flow of glucose to the electrode because the slower mediators of the time could not deal with a rapid in-flux of glucose. Other prior art sensors used protective membranes to prevent "fouling." Fouling occurs when red blood cells stick to the active electrode and interfere with electron transfer to the electrode. Protective membranes permit glucose molecules to pass, but not red blood cells.

Abbott filed the original application leading to the '551 patent in 1984. Over thirteen years, that original application saw multiple rejections for anticipation and obviousness, including repeated rejections over U.S. Patent No. 4,545,382 ("the '382 patent"), another patent owned by Abbott. The '382 patent specification discussed protective membranes in the following terms: "Optionally, but preferably when being used on live blood, a protective membrane surrounds both the enzyme and the mediator layers, permeable to water and glucose molecules." Col.4 ll.63–66. "Live blood" refers to blood within a body.

In 1997, Lawrence Pope, Abbott's patent attorney, and Dr. Gordon Sanghera, Abbott's Director of Research and Development, studied the novel features of their application and decided to present a new reason for a patent. Pope presented new claims to the examiner based on a new sensor that did not require a protective membrane for whole blood. Pope asserted that this distinction would overcome the prior art '382 patent, whose electrodes allegedly required a protective membrane. The examiner requested an affidavit to show that the prior art required a membrane for whole blood at the time of the invention.

To meet this evidentiary request, Dr. Sanghera submitted a declaration to the U.S. Patent and Trademark Office ("PTO") stating:

> [O]ne skilled in the art would have felt that an active electrode comprising an enzyme and a mediator would require a protective membrane if it were to be used with a whole blood sample. . . .

J.A. 7637. Pope, in submitting Sanghera's affidavit, represented:

> The art continued to believe [following the '382 patent] that a barrier layer for [a] whole blood sample was necessary. . . .

[O]ne skilled in the art would *not* read lines 63 to 65 of column 4 of U.S. Patent No. 4,545,382 to teach that the use of a protective membrane with a whole blood sample is option-ally or merely preferred. One skilled in the art would not have read the disclosure of the ['382 patent] as teaching that the use of a protective membrane with whole blood samples was optional. He would not, especially in view of the working examples, have read the "optionally, but preferably" language at line 63 of column [4] as a technical teaching but rather mere patent phraseology. . . .

There is no teaching or suggestion of unprotected active electrodes for use with whole blood specimens in [the '382 patent]. . . .

J.A. 7645–46.

Several years earlier, while prosecuting the European counterpart to the '382 patent, European Patent EP 0 078 636 ("EP '636"), Abbott made representations to the European Patent Office ("EPO") regarding the same "optionally, but preferably" language in the European specification. On January 12, 1994, to distinguish a German reference labeled D1, which required a diffusion-limiting membrane, Abbott's European patent counsel argued that their invention did not require a diffusion-limiting membrane:

> *Contrary to the semipermeable membrane of D1, the protective membrane optionally utilized with the glucose sensor of the patent is [sic] suit is not controlling the permeability of the substrate* . . . Rather, in accordance with column 5, lines 30 to 33 of the patent in suit:
>
> > "Optionally, but preferably when being used on live blood, a protective membrane surrounds both the enzyme and the mediator layers, permeable to water and glucose molecules."
>
> *See also* claim 10 of the patent in suit as granted according to which the sensor electrode has an outermost protective membrane (11) permeable to water and glucose molecules. . . . Accordingly, the purpose of the protective membrane of the patent in suit, preferably to be used with in vivo measurements, is a safety measurement to prevent any course [sic] particles coming off during use but not a permeability control for the substrate.

J.A. 6530–31 (emphases added).

On May 23, 1995, Abbott's European patent counsel submitted another explanation about the D1 reference and EP '636.

> "Optionally, but preferably when being used on live blood, a protective membrane surrounds both the enzyme and the mediator layers, permeable to water and glucose molecules."
>
> *It is submitted that this disclosure is unequivocally clear. The protective membrane is optional, however, it is preferred when used on live blood in order to prevent the larger constituents of the blood, in particular erythrocytes from*

interfering with the electrode sensor. Furthermore it is said, that said protective membrane should not prevent the glucose molecules from penetration, the membrane is "permeable" to glucose molecules. This teaches the skilled artisan that, whereas the [D1 membrane] must . . . control the permeability of the glucose . . . the purpose of the protective membrane in the patent in suit is not to control the permeation of the glucose molecules. For this very reason *the sensor electrode as claimed does not have (and must not have) a semipermeable membrane in the sense of D1.*

J.A. 6585 (first and third emphases added).

III

Inequitable conduct is an equitable defense to patent infringement that, if proved, bars enforcement of a patent. This judge-made doctrine evolved from a trio of Supreme Court cases that applied the doctrine of unclean hands to dismiss patent cases involving egregious misconduct: *Keystone Driller Co. v. General Excavator Co.*, 290 U.S. 240, 54 (1933), . . .

Keystone involved the manufacture and suppression of evidence. The patentee knew of "a possible prior use" by a third party prior to filing a patent application but did not inform the PTO. After the issuance of the patent, the patentee paid the prior user to sign a false affidavit stating that his use was an abandoned experiment and bought his agreement to keep secret the details of the prior use and to suppress evidence. With these preparations in place, the patentee then asserted this patent, along with two other patents, against Byers Machine Co. ("Byers"). *Keystone Driller Co. v. Byers Mach. Co.*, 4 F.Supp. 159 (N.D. Ohio 1929). Unaware of the prior use and of the cover-up, the court held the patents valid and infringed and granted an injunction.

The patentee then asserted the same patents against General Excavator Co. and Osgood Co. and sought a temporary injunction based on the decree in the previous Byers case. *Keystone*, 290 U.S. at 242. The district court denied the injunctions but made the defendants post bonds. The defendants discovered and introduced evidence of the corrupt transaction between the patentee and the prior user. The district court declined to dismiss these cases for unclean hands. On appeal, the Sixth Circuit reversed and remanded with instructions to dismiss the complaints. The Supreme Court affirmed.

The Supreme Court explained that if the corrupt transaction between the patentee and the prior user had been discovered in the previous *Byers* case, "the court undoubtedly would have been warranted in holding it sufficient to require dismissal of the cause of action." *Id.* at 246. Because the patentee used the *Byers* decree to seek an injunction in the cases against General Excavator Co. and Osgood Co., it did not come to the court with clean hands, and dismissal of these cases was appropriate.

[The Federal Circuit then summarized similar facts from subsequent Supreme Court cases, *Hazel–Atlas Glass Co. v. Hartford–Empire Co.*, 322 U.S. 238 (1944), *overruled on other grounds by Standard Oil Co. v. United States*, 429 U.S. 17 (1976), and *Precision Instrument Manufacturing Co. v. Automotive Maintenance Machinery Co.*, 324 U.S. 806 (1945).]

IV

The unclean hands cases of *Keystone, Hazel–Atlas*, and *Precision* formed the basis for a new doctrine of inequitable conduct that developed and evolved over time. As the inequitable conduct doctrine evolved from these unclean hands cases, it came to embrace a broader scope of misconduct, including not only egregious affirmative acts of misconduct intended to deceive both the PTO and the courts but also the mere nondisclosure of in-formation to the PTO. Inequitable conduct also diverged from the doctrine of unclean hands by adopting a different and more potent remedy— unenforceability of the entire patent rather than mere dismissal of the instant suit.

In line with this wider scope and stronger remedy, inequitable conduct came to require a finding of both intent to deceive and materiality. *Star Scientific Inc. v. R.J. Reynolds Tobacco Co.*, 537 F.3d 1357, 1365 (Fed. Cir. 2008). To prevail on the defense of inequitable conduct, the accused infringer must prove that the applicant misrepresented or omitted material information with the specific intent to deceive the PTO. *Id.* The accused infringer must prove both elements – intent and materiality – by clear and convincing evidence. *Id.* If the accused infringer meets its burden, then the district court must weigh the equities to determine whether the applicant's conduct before the PTO warrants rendering the entire patent unenforceable. *Id.*

This court recognizes that the early unclean hands cases do not present any standard for materiality. Needless to say, this court's development of a materiality requirement for inequitable conduct does not (and cannot) supplant Supreme Court precedent. Though inequitable conduct developed from these cases, the unclean hands doctrine remains available to supply a remedy for egregious misconduct like that in the Supreme Court cases.

As inequitable conduct emerged from unclean hands, the standards for intent to deceive and materiality have fluctuated over time. In the past, this court has espoused low standards for meeting the intent requirement, finding it satisfied based on gross negligence or even negligence. This court has also previously adopted a broad view of materiality, using a "reasonable examiner" standard based on the PTO's 1977 amendment to Rule 56. *See Am. Hoist & Derrick Co. v. Sowa & Sons, Inc.*, 725 F.2d 1350, 1362 (Fed.Cir.1984); *see also* 37 C.F.R. §1.56 (1977) (a reference is material if "there is a substantial likelihood that a reasonable examiner would consider it important in deciding whether to allow the application to issue as a patent"). Further weakening the showing needed to establish inequitable conduct, this court then placed intent and materiality together on a "sliding scale." *Am. Hoist*, 725 F.2d at 1362. This modification to the inequitable conduct doc-trine held patents unenforceable based on a reduced showing of intent if the record contained a strong showing of materiality, and vice versa. In effect, this change conflated, and diluted, the standards for both intent and materiality.

Perhaps most importantly, the remedy for inequitable conduct is the "atomic bomb" of patent law. *Aventis Pharma S.A. v. Amphastar Pharm., Inc.*, 525 F.3d 1334, 1349 (Fed. Cir. 2008) (Rader, J., dissenting). Unlike validity defenses, which are claim specific, *see* 35 U.S.C. §288, inequitable conduct regarding any single claim renders the entire patent unenforceable. *Kingsdown Med. Consultants, Ltd. v. Hollister Inc.*, 863 F.2d 867, 877 (Fed. Cir. 1988). Unlike other deficiencies, inequitable conduct cannot be cured by reissue or reexamination. Moreover, the taint of a finding of inequitable conduct can spread from a single patent to render unenforceable other related patents and applications in the same technology family. Thus, a finding of inequitable conduct may endanger a substantial portion of a company's patent portfolio. . . .

A finding of inequitable conduct may also spawn antitrust and unfair competition claims. Further, prevailing on a claim of inequitable conduct often makes a case "exceptional," leading potentially to an award of attorneys' fees under 35 U.S.C. §285. A finding of inequitable conduct may also prove the crime or fraud exception to the attorney-client privilege.

With these far-reaching consequences, it is no wonder that charging inequitable conduct has become a common litigation tactic. One study estimated that eighty percent of patent infringement cases included allegations of inequitable conduct. Committee Position Paper[,Committee Position Paper, *The Doctrine of Inequitable Conduct and the Duty of Candor in Patent Prosecution: Its Current Adverse Impact on the Operation of the United States Patent System*, 16 AIPLA Q.J. 74, 75 (1988)]; *see also* Christian Mammen, *Controlling the "Plague": Reforming the Doctrine of Inequitable Conduct*, 24 BERKELEY TECH. L.J. 1329, 1358 (2009). Inequitable conduct "has been overplayed, is appearing in nearly every patent suit, and is cluttering up the patent system." *Kimberly–Clark Corp. v. Johnson & Johnson*, 745 F.2d 1437, 1454 (Fed.Cir.1984). "[T]he habit of charging inequitable conduct in almost every major patent case has become an absolute plague. Reputable lawyers seem to feel compelled to make the charge against other reputable lawyers on the slenderest grounds, to represent their client's interests adequately, perhaps." *Burlington Indus., Inc. v. Dayco Corp.*, 849 F.2d 1418, 1422 (Fed.Cir.1988).

Left unfettered, the inequitable conduct doctrine has plagued not only the courts but also the entire patent system. Because allegations of inequitable conduct are routinely brought on "the slenderest grounds," *Burlington Indus.*, 849 F.2d at 1422, patent prosecutors constantly confront the specter of inequitable conduct charges. With inequitable conduct casting the shadow of a hangman's noose, it is unsurprising that patent prosecutors regularly bury PTO examiners with a deluge of prior art references, most of which have marginal value. *See* Brief for the United States as Amicus Curiae at 17 (submission of nine hundred references without any indication which ones were most relevant); Brief of the Biotechnology Industry Organization as Amicus Curiae at 7 (submission of eighteen pages of cited references, including five pages listing references to claims, office actions, declarations, amendments, interview summaries, and other communications in related applications). "Applicants disclose too much prior art for the PTO to meaningfully consider, and do not explain its significance, all out of fear that to do otherwise risks a claim of inequitable conduct." ABA Section of Intellectual Property Law, *A Section White Paper: Agenda for 21st Century Patent Reform* 2 (2009). This tidal wave of disclosure makes identifying the most relevant prior art more difficult. *See* Brief for the United States as Amicus Curiae at 1 (submission of "large numbers of prior art references of questionable materiality . . . harms the effectiveness of the examination process"). "This flood of information strains the agency's examining resources and directly contributes to the backlog." *Id.* at 17–18.

While honesty at the PTO is essential, low standards for intent and materiality have inadvertently led to many unintended consequences, among them, increased adjudication cost and complexity, reduced likelihood of settlement, burdened courts, strained PTO resources, increased PTO backlog, and impaired patent quality. This court now tightens the standards for finding both intent and materiality in order to redirect a doctrine that has been overused to the detriment of the public.

V

To prevail on a claim of inequitable conduct, the accused infringer must prove that the patentee acted with the specific intent to deceive the PTO. A finding that the misrepresentation or omission amounts to gross negligence or negligence under a "should have known" standard does not satisfy this intent requirement. *Kingsdown*, 863 F.2d at 876. In other words, the accused infringer must prove by clear and convincing evidence that the applicant knew of the reference, knew that it was material, and made a deliberate decision to withhold it. . . .

Intent and materiality are separate requirements. *Hoffmann–La Roche, Inc. v. Promega Corp.*, 323 F.3d 1354, 1359 (Fed.Cir. 2003). A district court should not use a "sliding scale," where a weak showing of intent may be found sufficient based on a strong showing of materiality, and vice versa. Moreover, a district court may not infer intent solely from materiality. Instead, a court must weigh the evidence of intent to deceive independent of its analysis of materiality. Proving that the applicant knew of a reference, should have known of its materiality, and decided not to submit it to the PTO does not prove specific intent to deceive.

Because direct evidence of deceptive intent is rare, a district court may infer intent from indirect and circumstantial evidence. *Larson Mfg. Co. of S.D., Inc. v. Aluminart Prods. Ltd.*, 559 F.3d 1317, 1340 (Fed. Cir. 2009). However, to meet the clear and convincing evidence standard, the specific intent to deceive must be "the single most reasonable inference able to be drawn from the evidence." *Star*, 537 F.3d at 1366. Indeed, the evidence "must be sufficient to *require* a finding of deceitful intent in the light of all the circumstances." *Kingsdown*, 863 F.2d at 873 (emphasis added). Hence, when there are multiple reasonable inferences that may be drawn, intent to deceive cannot be found. This court reviews the district court's factual findings regarding what reasonable inferences may be drawn from the evidence for clear error.

VI

This court holds that, as a general matter, the materiality required to establish inequitable conduct is but-for materiality. When an applicant fails to disclose prior art to the PTO, that prior art is but-for material if the PTO would not have allowed a claim had it been aware of the undisclosed prior art. Hence, in assessing the materiality of a withheld reference, the court must determine whether the PTO would have allowed the claim if it had been aware of the undisclosed reference. In making this patentability determination, the court should apply the preponderance of the evidence standard and give claims their broadest reasonable construction. *See* MANUAL OF PATENT EXAMINING PROCEDURE ("MPEP") §§706, 2111 (8th ed. Rev.8, July 2010). Often the patentability of a claim will be congruent with the validity determination—if a claim is properly invalidated in district court based on the deliberately withheld reference, then that reference is necessarily material because a finding of invalidity in a district court requires clear and convincing evidence, a higher evidentiary burden than that used in prosecution at the PTO. However, even if a district court does not invalidate a claim based on a deliberately withheld reference, the reference may be material if it would have blocked patent issuance under the PTO's different evidentiary standards.

Because inequitable conduct renders an entire patent (or even a patent family) unenforceable, as a general rule, this doctrine should only be applied in instances where the patentee's misconduct resulted in the unfair benefit of receiving an unwarranted claim.

After all, the patentee obtains no advantage from misconduct if the patent would have issued anyway. Moreover, enforcement of an otherwise valid patent does not injure the public merely because of misconduct, lurking somewhere in patent prosecution, that was immaterial to the patent's issuance.

Although but-for materiality generally must be proved to satisfy the materiality prong of inequitable conduct, this court recognizes an exception in cases of affirmative egregious misconduct. When the patentee has engaged in affirmative acts of egregious misconduct, such as the filing of an unmistakably false affidavit, the misconduct is material. *See Rohm & Haas Co. v. Crystal Chem. Co.*, 722 F.2d 1556, 1571 (Fed.Cir.1983) ("there is no room to argue that submission of false affidavits is not material"). After all, a patentee is unlikely to go to great lengths to deceive the PTO with a falsehood unless it believes that the falsehood will affect issuance of the patent.

[T]he general rule requiring but-for materiality provides clear guidance to patent practitioners and courts, while the egregious misconduct exception gives the test sufficient flexibility to capture extraordinary circumstances. Thus, not only is this court's approach sensitive to varied facts and equitable considerations, it is also consistent with the early unclean hands cases—all of which dealt with egregious misconduct.

VII

On remand, the district court should determine whether the PTO would not have granted the patent but for Abbott's failure to disclose the EPO briefs. In particular, the district court must determine whether the PTO would have found Sanghera's declaration and Pope's accompanying submission unpersuasive in overcoming the obviousness rejection over the '382 patent if Abbott had disclosed the EPO briefs. Because the district court did not find intent to deceive under the knowing and deliberate standard set forth in this opinion, this court vacates the district court's findings of intent. On remand, the district court should determine whether there is clear and convincing evidence demonstrating that Sanghera or Pope knew of the EPO briefs, knew of their materiality, and made the conscious decision not to disclose them in order to deceive the PTO.

COMMENTS AND QUESTIONS

1. On remand, the district court once again found inequitable conduct under the new standard.

2. Why is the penalty for inequitable conduct stronger than the penalty for invalidity—rendering the patent as a whole unenforceable rather than just the tainted claim? Who has more information about the inventor's work and the precise prior art it relates to—the examiner or the inventor? Who has more to gain from the issuance (or rejection) of a patent?

How harsh is unenforceability really? If a patentee knows their application will be rejected in its entirety if they disclose a key piece of prior art, are they any worse off with unenforceability than if they had never obtained the patent in the first place? *See* Tun-Jen Chiang, *The Upside-Down Inequitable Conduct Doctrine*, 107 Nw. U. L. Rev. 1243 (2013) (arguing that inequitable conduct under-deters the most egregious cases of abuse while overdeterring marginal ones).

3. Many inequitable conduct cases involve suppressing a key prior art reference. It is important to note, however, that only prior art that was *known* by the inventor or the patent lawyer gives rise to a duty of disclosure. This rule is embodied not only in the doctrine of inequitable conduct in the courts, but also in Rule 56 of the rules of the patent practice, pertaining to the duty of patent applicants during prosecution. *See* 37 C.F.R. §1.56(a) ("Each individual associated with the filing and prosecution of a patent application has a duty of candor and good faith in dealing with the [patent] office, which includes a duty to disclose to the office all information *known to that individual* to be material to patentability . . .") (emphasis added). Note that this means that patentees do *not* have to conduct a prior art search. But if they know about prior art, it must be

disclosed. Do you think it should matter whether (1) the reference was in a class or group that the Examiner *should* have searched? (2) that it was disclosed, but in a long "string cite" of less relevant prior art? (3) that the patentee didn't know of the key reference, but *should have*?

4. *Supplemental Examination*. Patent owners have long sought to reduce the impact of the inequitable conduct defense. The AIA provides a procedure for doing so. According to the House Report accompanying the AIA:

> The Act addresses the inequitable conduct doctrine by authorizing supplemental examination of a patent to correct errors or omissions in proceedings before the Office. Under this new procedure, information that was not considered or was inadequately considered or was incorrect can be presented to the Office. If the Office determines that the information does not present a substantial new question of patentability or that the patent is still valid, that information cannot later be used to hold the patent unenforceable or invalid on the basis for an inequitable-conduct attack in civil litigation.

Committee on the Judiciary, U.S. Cong., "America Invents Act," H.R. REP. NO 112-98, 112th Cong., 1st Sess., at 50 (June 1, 2011). Section 257(c)(1) provides that

> A patent shall not be held unenforceable on the basis of conduct relating to information that had not been considered, was inadequately considered, or was incorrect in a prior examination of the patent if the information was considered, reconsidered, or corrected during a supplemental examination of the patent.

If the PTO decides that the newly submitted information in supplemental examination presents a substantial new question of patentability with respect to one or more of the petitioner's claims, it may order a reexamination of those claims.

6. Prosecution Laches

The practice of "submarine patenting"—deliberately keeping a secret patent application pending for years in the PTO, only to spring it on an unsuspecting industry—has periodically been challenged under a variety of patent law doctrines. Submarine patenting has survived charges of inequitable conduct in some notable district court cases. *See Ford Motor Co. v. Lemelson*, 42 U.S.P.Q.2d 1706 (D. Nev. 1997); *Advanced Cardiovascular Sys. v. Medtronic Inc.*, 1996 WL 467293 (N.D. Cal. 1996) (both rejecting inequitable conduct claims). But one court has held that allegations of submarine patenting may state an *antitrust* claim against the patentee. *See Discovision Assocs. v. Disc Mfg. Inc.*, 42 U.S.P.Q.2d 1749 (D. Del. 1997).

In *Symbol Technologies v. Lemelson*, 277 F.3d 1361 (Fed. Cir. 2002), the Federal Circuit adopted a theory of "prosecution laches" under which excessive delay in prosecuting a patent could preclude its enforcement against an unsuspecting industry. *Symbol Technologies* involved notorious submarine patentee Jerome Lemelson, who had amassed well over 1,000 paper patents and had kept some applications pending for over 40 years. The Federal Circuit concluded that unreasonable and unexplained delay in prosecuting a patent could be grounds to bar enforcement of that patent. For subsequent opinions after remand, *see* 301 F. Supp. 2d 1147 (D. Nev. 2004), *aff'd*, 422 F.3d 1378 (Fed. Cir. 2005). Judge Newman, dissenting in the original opinion, argued that because Lemelson had followed the rules for filing continuation applications set out in the patent statute, he should not be barred from enforcing his long-pending patents. *See also In re Bogese*, 303 F.3d 1362 (Fed. Cir. 2002) (upholding examiner's final rejection of patent due to applicant's unreasonable delay). On the problem of successive continuations in patent applications, *see* Mark A. Lemley & Kimberly Moore, *Ending Abuse of Patent Continuations*, 84 B.U. L. Rev. 63 (2004).

Does *Symbol Technologies* solve the problem of submarine patents by effectively discouraging strategic refiling? Would a bright-line rule serve this purpose better than a reasonableness standard? How can the courts distinguish between delay caused by the patentee and delay that is the fault of the PTO?

7. Patent Misuse

Patent misuse is a judicially created doctrine that bars patentees from enforcing their patent against infringers when they have "misused" the patent. It was first adopted by the Supreme Court in 1917.

Motion Picture Patents Co. v. Universal Film Manufacturing Co. et al.
Supreme Court of the United States
243 U.S. 502 (1917)

Mr. Justice CLARKE delivered the opinion of the court.

In this suit relief is sought against three defendant corporations as joint infringers of claim number seven of United States letters patent No. 707,934 granted to Woodville Latham, assignor, on August 26, 1902, for improvements in Projecting-Kinetoscopes. It is sufficient description of the patent to say that it covers a part of the mechanism used in motion picture exhibiting machines for feeding a film through the machine with a regular, uniform and accurate movement and so as not to expose the film to excessive strain or wear.

The defendants in a joint answer do not dispute the title of the plaintiff to the patent but they deny the validity of it, deny infringement, and claim an implied license to use the patented machine.

Evidence which is undisputed shows that the plaintiff on June 20, 1912, in a paper styled "License Agreement" granted to The Precision Machine Company a right and license to manufacture and sell machines embodying the inventions described and claimed in the patent in suit, and in other patents, throughout the United States, its territories and possessions. This agreement contains a covenant on the part of the grantee that every machine sold by it, except those for export, shall be sold "under the restriction and condition that such exhibiting or projecting machines shall be used solely for exhibiting or projecting motion pictures containing the inventions of reissued letters patent No. 12,192, leased by a licensee of the licensor while it owns said patents, and upon other terms to be fixed by the licensor and complied with by the user while the said machine is in use and while the licensor owns said patents (which other terms shall only be the payment of a royalty or rental to the licensor while in use)." . . .

The agreement further provides that the grantee shall not sell any machine at less than the plaintiff's list price, except to jobbers and others for purposes of resale and that it will require such jobbers and others to sell at not less than plaintiff's list price. . . .

It was admitted at the bar that 40,000 of the plaintiff's machines are now in use in this country and that the mechanism covered by the patent in suit is the only one with which motion picture films can be used successfully.

This state of facts presents two questions for decision: . . .

Second. May the assignee of a patent, which has licensed another to make and sell the machine covered by it, by a mere notice attached to such machine, limit the use of it by the purchaser or by the purchaser's lessee to terms not stated in the notice but which are to be fixed, after sale, by such assignee in its discretion? . . .

Since *Pennock v. Dialogue*, 2 Pet. 1, was decided in 1829 this court has consistently held that the primary purpose of our patent laws is not the creation of private fortunes for the owners of patents but is "to promote the progress of science and useful arts" (Constitution, Art. I, §8). . . .

Plainly, this language of the statute and the established rules to which we have referred restrict the patent granted on a machine, such as we have in this case, to the mechanism described in the patent as necessary to produce the described results. It is not concerned with and has nothing to do with the materials with which or on which the machine operates. The grant is of the exclusive right to use the mechanism to produce the result with any appropriate material, and the materials with which the machine is operated are no part of the patented machine or of the combination which produces the patented result. The difference is clear and vital between the exclusive right to use the machine which the law gives to the inventor and the right to use it exclusively with prescribed materials to which such a license notice as we have here seeks to restrict it. . . . Both in form and in substance the notice attempts a restriction upon the use of the supplies only and it cannot with any regard to propriety in the use of language be termed a restriction upon the use of the machine itself.

Whatever right the owner may have to control by restriction the materials to be used in operating the machine must be derived through the general law from the ownership of the property in the machine and it cannot be derived from or protected by the patent law. . . .

This construction gives to the inventor the exclusive use of just what his inventive genius has discovered. It is all that the statute provides shall be given to him and it is all that he should receive, for it is the fair as well as the statutory measure of his reward for his contribution to the public stock of knowledge. If his discovery is an important one his reward under such a construction of the law will be large, as experience has abundantly proved, and if it be unimportant he should not be permitted by legal devices to impose an unjust charge upon the public in return for the use of it. For more than a century this plain meaning of the statute was accepted as its technical meaning, and that it afforded ample incentive to exertion by inventive genius is proved by the fact that under it the greatest inventions of our time, teeming with inventions, were made. . . .

The construction of the patent law which justifies as valid the restriction of patented machines, by notice, to use with unpatented supplies necessary in the operation of them, but which are no part of them, is believed to have originated in *Heaton-Peninsular Button-Fastener Co. v. Eureka Specialty Co.*, 77 Fed. Rep. 288 (which has come to be widely referred to as the *Button-Fastener Case*), decided by the Circuit Court of Appeals of the Sixth Circuit in 1896. In this case the court, recognizing the pioneer character of the decision it was rendering, speaks of the "novel restrictions" which it is considering and says that it is called upon "to mark another boundary line around the patentee's monopoly, which will debar him from engrossing the market for an article not the subject of a patent," which it declined to do.

This decision proceeds upon the argument that, since the patentee may withhold his patent altogether from public use he must logically and necessarily be permitted to impose any conditions which he chooses upon any use which he may allow of it. The defect in this thinking springs from the substituting of inference and argument for the language of the statute and from failure to distinguish between the rights which are given to the inventor by the patent law and which he may assert against all the world through an infringement proceeding and rights which he may create for himself by private contract which, however, are subject to the rules of general as distinguished from those of the patent law. While it is true that under the statutes as they were (and now are) a patentee might withhold his patented machine from public use, yet if he consented to use it himself or through others, such use immediately fell within the terms of the statute and as we have seen he is thereby restricted to the use of the invention as it is described in the claims of his patent and not as it may be expanded by limitations as to materials and supplies necessary to the operation of it imposed by mere notice to the public.

. . .The perfect instrument of favoritism and oppression which such a system of doing business, if valid, would put into the control of the owner of such a patent should make courts astute, if need be, to defeat its operation. If these restrictions were sustained plainly the plaintiff might, for its own profit or that of its favorites, by the obviously simple expedient of varying its royalty charge, ruin anyone unfortunate enough to be dependent upon its confessedly important improvements for the doing of business.

. . . [F]ollowing the decision of the *Button-Fastener Case,* it was widely contended as obviously sound, that the right existed in the owner of a patent to fix a price at which the patented article might be sold and resold under penalty of patent infringement. But this court, when the question came before it in *Bauer v. O'Donnell,* 229 U.S. 1, . . . decided that the owner of a patent is not authorized by either the letter or the purpose of the law to fix, by notice, the price at which a patented article must be sold after the first sale of it, declaring that the right to vend is exhausted by a single, unconditional sale, the article sold being thereby carried outside the monopoly of the patent law and rendered free of every restriction which the vendor may attempt to put upon it. The statutory authority to grant the exclusive right to "use" a patented machine is not greater, indeed it is precisely the same, as the authority to grant the exclusive right to "vend," and, looking to that authority, for the reasons stated in this opinion we are convinced that the exclusive right granted in every patent must be limited to the invention described in the claims of the patent and that it is not competent for the owner of a patent by notice attached to its machine to, in effect, extend the scope of its patent monopoly by restricting the use of it to materials necessary in its operation but which are no part of the patented invention, or to send its machines forth into the channels of trade of the country subject to conditions as to use or royalty to be paid to be imposed thereafter at the discretion of such patent owner. The patent law furnishes no warrant for such a practice and the cost, inconvenience and annoyance to the public which the opposite conclusion would occasion forbid it.

It is argued as a merit of this system of sale under a license notice that the public is benefitted by the sale of the machine at what is practically its cost and by the fact that the owner of the patent makes its entire profit from the sale of the supplies with which it is operated. This fact, if it be a fact, instead of commending, is the clearest possible condemnation of, the practice adopted, for it proves that under color of its patent the owner intends to and does derive its profit, not from the invention on which the law gives it a monopoly but from the unpatented supplies with which it is used and which are wholly without the scope of the patent monopoly, thus in effect extending the power to the owner of the patent to fix the price to the public of the unpatented supplies as effectively as he may fix the price on the patented machine. . . .

Coming now to the terms of the notice attached to the machine sold to the Seventy-Second Street Amusement Company under the license of the plaintiff and to the first question as we have stated it.

This notice first provides that the machine, which was sold to and paid for by the Amusement Company may be used only with moving picture films containing the invention of reissued patent No. 12,192, so long as the plaintiff continues to own this reissued patent.

Such a restriction is invalid because such a film is obviously not any part of the invention of the patent in suit; because it is an attempt, without statutory warrant, to continue the patent monopoly in this particular character of film after it has expired, and because to enforce it would be to create a monopoly in the manufacture and use of moving picture films, wholly outside of the patent in suit and of the patent law as we have interpreted it. . . .

A restriction which would give to the plaintiff such a potential power for evil over an industry which must be recognized as an important element in the amusement life of the nation, under the conclusions we have stated in this opinion, is plainly void, because wholly without the scope and purpose of our patent laws and because, if sustained, it would be gravely injurious to that public interest, which we have seen is more a favorite of the law than is the promotion of private fortunes. . . .

Mr. Justice HOLMES, dissenting.

I suppose that a patentee has no less property in his patented machine than any other owner, and that in addition to keeping the machine to himself the patent gives him the further right to forbid the rest of the world from making others like it. In short, for whatever motive, he may keep his device wholly out of use. *Continental Paper Bag Co. v. Eastern Paper Bag Co.*, 210 U.S. 405, 422. So much being undisputed, I cannot understand why he may not keep it out of use unless the licensee, or, for the matter of that, the buyer, will use some unpatented thing in connection with it. Generally speaking the measure of a condition is the consequence of a breach, and if that consequence is one that the owner may impose unconditionally, he may impose it conditionally upon a certain event. *Ashley v. Ryan*, 153 U.S. 436, 443. *Lloyd v. Dollison*, 194 U.S. 445, 449. . . .

No doubt this principle might be limited or excluded in cases where the condition tends to bring about a state of things that there is a predominant public interest to prevent. But there is no predominant public interest to prevent a patented tea pot or film feeder from being kept from the public, because, as I have said, the patentee may keep them tied up at will while his patent lasts. Neither is there any such interest to prevent the purchase of the tea or films that is made the condition of the use of the machine. The supposed contravention of public interest sometimes is stated as an attempt to extend the patent law to unpatented articles, which of course it is not, and more accurately as a possible domination to be established by such means. But the domination is one only to the extent of the desire for the tea pot or film feeder, and if the owner prefers to keep the pot or the feeder unless you will buy his tea or films, I cannot see in allowing him the right to do so anything more than an ordinary incident of ownership, or at most, a consequence of the *Paper Bag Case,* on which, as it seems to me, this case ought to turn. *See Grant v. Raymond*, 6 Pet. 218, 242. . . .

COMMENTS AND QUESTIONS

1. The asserted justification for the patent misuse doctrine lies in the public policy underpinning the patent laws. It is no coincidence, however, that the doctrine first developed around 1900, shortly after the antitrust laws were passed. Patent misuse and antitrust are strikingly similar in the sorts of conduct they prohibit. For example, in

Motion Picture, the conduct at issue was (among other things) resale price maintenance, which is *per se* illegal under the antitrust laws. Patent misuse as originally conceived, however, was broader than the antitrust laws. Neither market power nor actual effect on competition need be proven to show patent misuse, as they would to prove an antitrust violation.

2. The Court continually expanded the scope of the patent misuse doctrine in the decades that followed *Motion Picture.* That expansion culminated in the cases of *Mercoid Corp. v. Mid-Continent Inv. Co.,* 320 U.S. 661 (1944) and *Carbice Corp. v. American Patents Dev. Corp.,* 283 U.S. 27 (1931). *Mercoid* held that it was patent misuse to tie a patented product to a non-staple product. A staple product is one which has an existing market, beyond use with the patent. A non-staple product has no substantial commercial use except in connection with the patent. *Carbice* held that a showing of patent misuse (which does not require proof of market power or impact) was prima facie evidence of an antitrust violation.

Both of these rules were short-lived. Congress amended the patent laws in 1952 by adding the following provisions:

35 U.S.C. §271. Infringement of Patent

. . .

(c) Whoever offers to sell or sells within the United States or imports into the United States a component of a patented machine, manufacture, combination or composition, or a material or apparatus for use in practicing a patented process, constituting a material part of the invention, knowing the same to be especially made or especially adapted for use in an infringement of such patent, and *not a staple article or commodity of commerce suitable for substantial noninfringing use,* shall be liable as a contributory infringer.

(d) No patent owner otherwise entitled to relief for infringement or contributory infringement of a patent shall be denied relief or deemed guilty of misuse or illegal extension of the patent right by reason of his having done one or more of the following:

(1) derived revenue from acts which if performed by another without his consent would constitute contributory infringement of the patent;

(2) licensed or authorized another to perform acts which if performed without his consent would constitute contributory infringement of the patent;

(3) sought to enforce his patent rights against infringement or contributory infringement;

(emphasis added). The Supreme Court explicated the importance of this statutory limit on the patent misuse doctrine in *Dawson Chem. Co. v. Rohm & Haas Co.,* 448 U.S. 176, 200-01 (1980):

Section 271(c) identifies the basic dividing line between contributory infringement and patent misuse. It adopts a restrictive definition of contributory infringement that distinguishes between staple and nonstaple articles of commerce. It also defines the class of nonstaple items narrowly. In essence, this provision places materials like the dry ice of the *Carbice* case outside the scope of the contributory infringement doctrine. As a result, it is no longer necessary to resort to the doctrine of patent misuse in order to deny patentees control over staple goods used in their inventions.

The limitations on contributory infringement written into §271(c) are counterbalanced by limitations on patent misuse in §271(d). Three species of conduct by patentees are expressly excluded from characterization as misuse. First, the patentee may "deriv[e] revenue" from acts that "would constitute contributory infringement" if "performed by another without his consent." This provision clearly signifies that a patentee may make and sell nonstaple goods used in connection with his invention. Second, the patentee may "licens[e] or authoriz[e] another to perform acts" which without such authorization would constitute contributory infringement. This provision's use in the disjunctive of the term "authoriz[e]" suggests that more than explicit licensing agreements is contemplated. Finally, the patentee may "enforce his patent rights against . . . contributory infringement." This provision plainly means that the patentee may bring suit without fear that his doing so will be regarded as an unlawful attempt to suppress competition. The statute explicitly states that a patentee may do "one or more" of these permitted acts, and it does not state that he must do any of them.

In our view, the provisions of §271(d) effectively confer upon the patentee, as a lawful adjunct of his patent rights, a limited power to exclude others from competition in nonstaple goods. A patentee may sell a nonstaple article himself while enjoining others from marketing that same good without his authorization. By doing so, he is able to eliminate competitors and thereby to control the market for that product. Moreover, his power to demand royalties from others for the privilege of selling the nonstaple item itself implies that the patentee may control the market for the nonstaple good; otherwise, his "right" to sell licenses for the marketing of the nonstaple good would be meaningless, since no one would be willing to pay him for a superfluous authorization.

3. Congress has shown continued dissatisfaction with the scope of the patent misuse doctrine. In 1988, it passed the Patent Misuse Reform Act, which added an additional limitation on the patent misuse doctrine.

§271(d) No patent owner otherwise entitled to relief for infringement or contributory infringement of a patent shall be denied relief or deemed guilty of misuse or illegal extension of the patent right by reason of his having done one or more of the following: . . . (4) refused to license or use any rights to the patent;

or (5) conditioned the license of any rights to the patent or the sale of the patented product on the acquisition of a license to rights in another patent or purchase of a separate product, unless, in view of the circumstances, the patent owner has market power in the relevant market for the patent or patented product on which the license or sale is conditioned.

There is obviously a great deal of overlap between the policies of the patent misuse doctrine and those underlying the antitrust laws. If misuse claims are not tested by conventional antitrust principles, what principles apply?

4. *Differences in Patent Misuse and Conventional Antitrust Doctrines.* Patent misuse extends (or may extend) to a number of practices that do not fall within the antitrust laws at all. Here are the principal contexts:

- *Nonmetered Licenses.* Patentees are entitled to charge royalties on the patents they license to others. What form may those license payments take? Hazeltine Research, a consumer electronics patent consortium, charged a royalty based on a flat percentage of a purchaser's sales, regardless of how many patents the purchaser needed or how important they were to the end product. The Court upheld this arrangement in 1950 in *Automatic Radio Mfg. Co. v. Hazeltine Research, Inc.*, 339 U.S. 827, 833-34 (1950). But in *Zenith Radio Corp. v. Hazeltine Research, Inc.*, 395 U.S. 100 (1969), the Court struck down the royalty provision: "We also think patent misuse inheres in a patentee's insistence on a percentage-of-sales royalty, regardless of use, and his rejection of licensee proposals to pay only for actual use. Unquestionably, a licensee must pay if he uses the patent. . . . There is nothing in the right granted the patentee to keep others from using, selling, or manufacturing his invention which empowers him to insist on payment not only for use but also for producing products which do not employ his discoveries at all."

  What is wrong with nonmetered royalties? *See* ROBERT BORK, THE ANTITRUST PARADOX (1978); RICHARD A. POSNER, ANTITRUST LAW: AN ECONOMIC PERSPECTIVE (1976). If a licensee is only willing to pay a fixed amount for a license, should it matter how that amount is collected? Certainly the "percentage of sales" formula is not itself anticompetitive, and it may be far more convenient than more exact measures of how much a licensee uses a patent. Should the transaction costs of royalty accounting come into play in deciding whether a practice amounts to misuse? One problem with agreements requiring licensees to pay a percentage of all sales is that they also provide an effective source of information for policing a cartel.

- *Grantback Clauses.* As a condition to a license agreement, a patentee will sometimes require the licensee to grant him rights to any "improvement patents" the licensee is issued while using the licensed patent. Courts have been fairly lenient with respect to such "grantback clauses." *See Transparent-Wrap Mach. Corp. v. Stokes & Smith Co.*, 329 U.S. 637 (1947). But grantbacks may sometimes run afoul of the patent misuse doctrine. Grantbacks are common in agreements among independent patent holders to bundle their patents together for "one stop licensing"—an arrangement called a patent pool. Because pools constitute agreements amongst would-be competitors, they have traditionally been suspect under antitrust law, though a fair number have been approved. For a discussion of pool formation, and the proper way to determine whether they are useful or anticompetitive, *see* Robert P. Merges and Michael Mattioli, *Measuring the Costs and Benefits of Patent Pools*, OHIO ST. L.J. (forthcoming 2016-2017).

- *Field-of-Use Restrictions.* Most patent licenses contain some sort of restriction on how the patent may be used by the licensee. Restrictions that attempt to control the price at which the licensee sells products made using the patented process or equipment are illegal per se under Sherman Act §1. Other restrictions, however, control not the price but the geographic or product market in which the licensee sells. These agreements have generally been upheld, unless they are part of a tying arrangement.

- *Patent Suppression.* For a variety of reasons, most patents are never commercialized. The reasons can include lack of adequate financing, absence of commercial value, or simply bad business judgment. Inventions may be patented as a matter of course, in case they turn out to be useful. Many biotechnology companies follow this practice. There are less benign reasons as well. Inventions may be deliberately patented and then not used so as to deny competitors the opportunity that the technology presents.

  Commentators have long argued over whether suppression actually occurs, and whether it is an economically rational strategy. *See, e.g.,* Kurt M. Saunders, *Patent Nonuse and the Role of Public Interest as a Deterrent to Technology Suppression*, 15 HARV. J.L. & TECH. 389, 392 (2002) ("There is evidence to suggest that products as obscure as artificial caviar and as important as photocopiers have been strategically shelved."); Mark Clark, *Suppressing Innovation: Bell Laboratories and Magnetic Recording*, 34 TECH. & CULT. 516, 532 (1993) (documenting suppression of Hickman patents covering magnetic recording, a policy that the author argues was pursued by AT&T to preserve markets and for "ideological reasons," i.e., the threat to privacy from recorded phone conversations); Charles Allen Black, *The Cure for Deadly Patent Practices: Preventing Technology Suppression and Patent Shelving in the Life Sciences*, 14 ALB. L.J. SCI. & TECH. 397 (2004) (reporting that manufacturers of pantyhose may have suppressed their design for "no-run" hose to maintain the lucrative market for disposable hose).

In all these cases (and numerous others), patents for the allegedly suppressed products exist. What is uncertain is *why* the products were never commercialized. The companies involved often claim that the products do not, in fact, work as promised. Those claims are bolstered by the argument of economists that suppression simply makes no sense. If a new invention is truly superior to current products, they argue, the patentee could sell that invention and more than make up for any losses it might sustain in the market for its current products. Indeed, economists continue, that is the definition of a superior product.

This argument has substantial force when the allegedly suppressed invention is in the same market as the patentee's current products. Thus pantyhose manufacturers could presumably switch from selling disposable hose to selling no-run hose and, assuming the no-run hose was really a better product, charge prices high enough to make up for the fact that they would sell fewer pairs of hose. This argument is not completely convincing, however. If the process for producing no-run hose requires different machinery from that which the manufacturers currently use, there will be substantial fixed costs associated with the switch. Manufacturers may prefer to delay introducing the new product until they have to replace their machines anyway; they will suppress the invention until then. By contrast, if a new entrant into the market could use the patented process, he would choose to build the new machines immediately. By suppressing the patent, therefore, the patentee causes society to lose the benefits of the immediate production of the new process.[13] An example of this occurred in the rubber industry, when Standard Oil admitted in a 1942 consent decree to inhibiting the introduction of synthetic rubber. The reason was clearly to preserve its extensive investment in natural rubber production processes. *See* D.R.B. Ross, *Patents and Bureaucrats: U.S. Synthetic Rubber Development Before Pearl Harbor*, in BUSINESS AND GOVERNMENT 119, 120 (J.R. Frese & J. Judd eds., 1985). *See generally* Dunford, *Suppression of Technology*, 32 ADMIN. SCI. Q. 512 (1987).

This "retooling" problem is even more serious when the patentee is not in the same market as the patented invention but rather in an upstream or downstream market that would be affected by the patent. Consider the rumor that Exxon purchased and buried the design for the "momentum

---

[13] Of course, the patentee could always license the patent to the new entrant. However, innovation is associated with strong first-mover advantages, so the first company to manufacture and sell a product is likely to maintain a dominant position even after the patent expires and after further inventions supersede the original one. Thus licensing to competitors may not be an attractive option for many patentees.

engine," which would tremendously increase automobile engine efficiency (and therefore tremendously decrease the demand for gasoline). It could produce and sell the momentum engine, using the revenues from those sales to offset its loss in gasoline revenues. However, Exxon is not in the engine business and is likely to be less efficient at that business than it is at refining and selling gasoline. Its profit-maximizing course may therefore be to conceal the invention, so that no one else can use it, and to continue to sell gasoline. On the other hand, there is evidence of a more robust corporate market for patent licenses in the contemporary economy—suggesting that perhaps Exxon would license such a technology today. *See* ASHISH ARORA ET AL., MARKETS FOR TECHNOLOGY: THE ECONOMICS OF INNOVATION AND CORPORATE STRATEGY (2001).

In any event, Congress—and the courts before it—deemed that the costs of determining when nonuse or suppression is actionable, together with potential strategic uses of any remedies for it, outweigh the benefits of rooting out actual cases of suppression. *See* §271(d)(4) (protecting nonuse).

- *Post-Expiration Royalties.* The Supreme Court held in *Brulotte v. Thys Co.*, 379 U.S. 29, 32 (1964), that license agreements providing for payment of patent royalties beyond the expiration of a patent are per se patent unlawful. The Supreme Court reaffirmed that decision in *Kimble v. Marvel Entertainment, LLC*, 135 S.Ct. 2401 (2015).

5. *Equitable Estoppel and Laches.* Equitable estoppel arises where a patentee misleads an alleged infringer into believing that she would not be sued for using the patented technology. The defense may bar all relief on an infringement claim. *See A.C. Aukerman Co. v. R.L. Chaides Constr. Co.*, 960 F.2d 1020, 1041 (Fed. Cir. 1992) (en banc). Three elements must be established to prove equitable estoppel:

(1) The actor, who usually must have knowledge of the true facts, communicates something in a misleading way, either by words, conduct or silence.

(2) The other relies upon that communication.

(3) And the other would be harmed materially if the actor is later permitted to assert any claim inconsistent with his earlier conduct.

Id. (quoting D.B. Dobbs, HANDBOOK ON THE LAW OF REMEDIES §2.3, at 42 (1973)). In the patent infringement context, the "something" communicated is that the plaintiff will not bring an infringement claim against the accused infringer. Accordingly, the defendant must not only be aware of the patentee and/or his patent but also know or reasonably be able to infer that the patentee has been aware of the accused infringer's acts for some time. A plaintiff's inaction may give rise to the inference that the infringement claim was abandoned based on other facts regarding the parties' relationship or contracts with each other. Regarding the third factor, material harm may include a change of economic position or loss of evidence.

Even where the defendant proves all three elements of the estoppel defense, the court must consider "any other evidence and facts respecting the equities of the parties in exercising its discretion and deciding whether to allow the defense of equitable estoppel to bar the suit." *Id.* at 1043. The defense does not require an unreasonable delay in filing suit. However, such a delay may be evidence relevant to determining whether the plaintiff's conduct was misleading. For an argument that the estoppel concept ought to be extended to situations where the holder of a standard-essential patent, discussed in Chapter III(G)(2)(ii)(d), leads third parties into adopting a standard with promises of non-enforcement, and then enforces vigorously when those parties are "locked in" to the standard. *See* Robert P. Merges and Jeffery M. Kuhn, *An Estoppel Doctrine for Patented Standards*, 97 CAL. L. REV. 1 (2009).

The equitable defense of laches may be available where the plaintiff unreasonably delayed filing her infringement suit. *See SCA Hygiene Products Aktiebolag v. First Quality Baby Products, LLC*, 807 F.3d 1311 (Fed. Cir. 2015) (en banc); *A.C. Aukerman Co.*, 960 F.2d at 1032. The defense is applicable where the accused infringer proves two factors:

(1) [T]he plaintiff delayed filing suit for an unreasonable and inexcusable length of time from the time the plaintiff knew or reasonably should have known of its claim against the defendant, and

(2) [T]he delay operated to the prejudice or injury of the defendant.

Id. The period of delay is defined as the time from when the plaintiff knew or reasonably should have known of the defendant's alleged infringing acts until the date of suit. This period may not begin until after the patent issues. Regarding the second factor, prejudice to the defendant may be either economic or evidentiary. A laches defense may be defeated where the infringer "has engaged in particularly egregious conduct which would change the equities significantly in plaintiff's favor." *Id.* at 1033 (quoting *TWM Mfg. Co. v. Dura Corp.*, 592 F.2d 346, 349 (6th Cir. 1979)). Laches only bars damages accrued prior to suit. *See id.* at 1041.

A rebuttable presumption of laches exists where the accused infringer proves that the plaintiff delayed filing suit for more than six years after actual or constructive knowledge of the defendant's alleged infringing acts. *See id.* at 1035-36, 1038. A patentee guilty of laches typically does not surrender its right to an ongoing royalty. *SCA Hygiene Products Aktiebolag*, 807 F.3d at 1331. Laches will only foreclose an ongoing royalty in extraordinary circumstances. Equitable estoppel bars the entire suit; laches does not. *Id.* at 1333.

G. REMEDIES

1. Injunctions

As we have seen, the rights conferred by a patent are different from those that grow out of real property rights. On the other hand, there are a number of similarities between patent law and real property law. With patents, as with most other legal entitlements that share the label "property," the traditional rule has been that the owner of the property right may obtain an injunction to prevent ongoing "trespasses." Indeed, in one important conceptual framework used to describe many types of legal entitlements, it is the injunctive remedy that distinguishes the property right from other entitlements. *See* Guido Calabresi & A. Douglas Melamed, *Property Rules, Liability Rules, and Inalienability: One View of the Cathedral*, 85 HARV. L. REV. 1089 (1972).

According to Calabresi and Melamed, the extent and nature of transaction costs in a particular case dictate whether one of the parties ought to have an absolute property right or simply the right to collect damages caused by the other party's encroachment. Within this framework, several factors point toward a property rule: few parties, difficult valuation problems, and otherwise low transaction costs. Other factors indicate that a liability rule might better effectuate the bargain: many parties (especially where any one has the power to "hold up" the whole enterprise), likelihood of strategic bargaining, and otherwise high transaction costs.

The holder of a legal entitlement other than a property right can obtain compensation when the right is violated but cannot prevent violations. Because those who violate such a right must pay damages, this form of entitlement is referred to as a *liability rule.* Classic examples of liability rule entitlements (which we will call "liability rights") are the rights of tort victims, the rights of parties to a contract in the face of a breach, and landowners whose parcels are taken by the government for public use pursuant to eminent domain. In breach of contract scenario, for example, it is generally understood that the normal remedy for breach of contract is damages—a monetary payment—rather than compelling the breaching party to perform the contract. Contracting parties cannot usually obtain injunctions to prevent breach. ("Specific performance" is an exception to this rule.)

Comparing patent rights to contract rights illuminates the challenges of compensating patentees for infringement. Take, for example, a contract for delivery of 100 bushels of wheat at $5.00 per bushel. If the seller breaches, contract law provides the buyer the difference between the contract price and the market price at the time of breach. Since wheat is a standard commodity, the market price can be easily determined based on commodity exchanges at the time.

By contrast, patent infringement poses a valuation challenge: Patent rights are unique. A patent might not be co-extensive with a particular product (e.g., a smartphone comprises many patented technologies). Infringing activity can affect the trajectory of the patentee's business over the remaining life of the patent.

The effect of injunctive remedies goes beyond allowing the rightholder to prevent activities of the infringer. To the extent that a rightholder will consider negotiating a license with the infringer, the threat of an injunction will heavily influence the *terms* of the license. Specifically, it allows the rightholder to set her own price for the injury. In intellectual property cases, it allows the rightholder, and not a court, to set the terms of a license agreement settling the infringement litigation. This is assumed to be the efficient result, as a court called on to set the terms of the exchange would have a difficult time doing so quickly and cheaply given the specialized nature of the assets and the varied and complex business environments in which they are deployed. Hence the parties are left to make their own deal.

On the other hand, a property right is a potent weapon. Sometimes this causes problems. Especially where courts may have a difficult time determining how much of a composite product's value is attributable to a (perhaps small) patented component, the availability of property right may lead to what economists call a "holdup problem"—an entitlement holder who uses his rights strategically to extract more than the fair market value of his or her asset. *See* Mark A. Lemley & Philip J. Weiser, *Should Property or Liability Rules Govern Information?*, 85 TEX. L. REV. 783 (2007). A classic example is the owner of the last of many parcels being assembled for a large real estate project. Should injunctions be readily available when holdup is a potential problem? Calabresi and Melamed suggest not; their framework calls for a liability rule, not a property rule, in that situation. For a general discussion of the desirability of adjusting property rights when economic conditions give rightholders "undue leverage" (i.e., make those rights more valuable than their intrinsic worth), *see* ROBERT P. MERGES, JUSTIFYING INTELLECTUAL PROPERTY ch. 6 (2011).

The Supreme Court confronted this issue in 2006. But it did not limit its decision to holdup situations.

eBay, Inc. v. MercExchange, LLC
Supreme Court of the United States
547 U.S. 388 (2006)

Justice THOMAS delivered the opinion of the Court.

Ordinarily, a federal court considering whether to award permanent injunctive relief to a prevailing plaintiff applies the four-factor test historically employed by courts of equity. Petitioner[] eBay Inc. argue[s] that this traditional test applies to disputes arising under the Patent Act. We agree and, accordingly, vacate the judgment of the Court of Appeals.

I

Petitioner eBay operates a popular Internet Web site that allows private sellers to list goods they wish to sell, either through an auction or at a fixed price. . . . Respondent MercExchange, L.L.C., holds a number of patents, including a business method patent for an electronic market designed to facilitate the sale of goods between private individuals by establishing a central authority to promote trust among participants. *See* U.S. Patent No. 5,845,265. MercExchange sought to license its patent to eBay . . ., as it had previously done with other companies, but the parties failed to reach an agreement. MercExchange subsequently filed a patent infringement suit against eBay . . .A jury found that MercExchange's patent was valid, that eBay . . . had infringed that patent, and that an award of damages was appropriate.

Following the jury verdict, the District Court denied MercExchange's motion for permanent injunctive relief. The Court of Appeals for the Federal Circuit reversed, applying its "general rule that courts will issue permanent injunctions against patent infringement absent exceptional circumstances." We granted certiorari to determine the appropriateness of this general rule.

II

According to well-established principles of equity, a plaintiff seeking a permanent injunction must satisfy a four-factor test before a court may grant such relief. A plaintiff must demonstrate: (1) that it has suffered an irreparable injury; (2) that remedies available at law, such as monetary damages, are inadequate to compensate for that injury; (3) that, considering the balance of hardships between the plaintiff and defendant, a remedy in equity is warranted; and (4) that the public interest would not be disserved by a permanent injunction. *See, e.g., Weinberger v. Romero-Barcelo*, 456 U.S. 305, 311-313 (1982); *Amoco Production Co. v. Gambell*, 480 U.S. 531, 542, (1987). The decision to grant or deny permanent injunctive relief is an act of equitable discretion by the district court, reviewable on appeal for abuse of discretion. *See, e.g., Romero-Barcelo*, 456 U.S., at 320.

These familiar principles apply with equal force to disputes arising under the Patent Act. As this Court has long recognized, "a major departure from the long tradition of equity practice should not be lightly implied." *Ibid.* Nothing in the Patent Act indicates that Congress intended such a departure. To the contrary, the Patent Act expressly provides that injunctions "may" issue "in accordance with the principles of equity." 35 U.S.C. §283.

To be sure, the Patent Act also declares that "patents shall have the attributes of personal property," §261, including "the right to exclude others from making, using, offering for sale, or selling the invention," §154(a)(1). According to the Court of Appeals, this statutory right to exclude alone justifies its general rule in favor of permanent injunctive relief. But the creation of a right is distinct from the provision of remedies for violations of that right. Indeed, the Patent Act itself indicates that patents shall have the attributes of personal property "[s]ubject to the provisions of this title," 35 U.S.C. §261, including, presumably, the provision that injunctive relief "may" issue only "in accordance with the principles of equity," §283.

This approach is consistent with our treatment of injunctions under the Copyright Act. Like a patent owner, a copyright holder possesses "the right to exclude others from using his property." *Fox Film Corp. v. Doyal*, 286 U.S. 123, 127 (1932); *see also id.*, at 127-128, 52 S.Ct. 546 ("A copyright, like a patent, is at once the equivalent given by the public for benefits bestowed by the genius and meditations and skill of individuals, and the incentive to further efforts for the same important objects" (internal quotation marks omitted)). Like the Patent Act, the Copyright Act provides that courts "may" grant injunctive relief "on such terms as it may deem reasonable to prevent or restrain infringement of a copyright." 17 U.S.C. §502(a). And as in our decision today, this Court has consistently rejected invitations to replace traditional equitable considerations with a rule that an injunction automatically follows a determination that a copyright has been infringed. *See, e.g., New York Times Co. v. Tasini*, 533 U.S. 483, 505 (2001) (citing *Campbell v. Acuff-Rose Music, Inc.*, 510 U.S. 569, 578 n. 10 (1994)); *Dun v. Lumbermen's Credit Ass'n*, 209 U.S. 20, 23-24 (1908).

Neither the District Court nor the Court of Appeals below fairly applied these traditional equitable principles in deciding respondent's motion for a permanent injunction. Although the District Court recited the traditional four-factor test, it appeared to adopt certain expansive principles suggesting that injunctive relief could not issue in a broad swath of cases. Most notably, it concluded that a "plaintiff's willingness to license its patents" and "its lack of commercial activity in practicing the patents" would be sufficient to establish that the patent holder would not suffer irreparable harm if an injunction did not issue. But traditional equitable principles do not permit such broad classifications. For example, some patent holders, such as university researchers or self-made inventors, might reasonably prefer to license their patents, rather than undertake efforts to secure the financing necessary to bring their works to market themselves. Such patent holders may be able to satisfy the traditional four-factor test, and we see no basis for categorically denying them the opportunity to do so. To the extent that the District Court adopted such a categorical rule, then, its analysis cannot be squared with the principles of equity adopted by Congress. The court's categorical rule is also in tension with *Continental Paper Bag Co. v. Eastern Paper Bag Co.*, 210 U.S. 405, 422-430 (1908), which rejected the contention that a court of equity has no jurisdiction to grant injunctive relief to a patent holder who has unreasonably declined to use the patent.

In reversing the District Court, the Court of Appeals departed in the opposite direction from the four-factor test. The court articulated a "general rule," unique to patent disputes, "that a permanent injunction will issue once infringement and validity have been adjudged." The court further indicated that injunctions should be denied only in the "unusual" case, under "exceptional circumstances" and "'in rare instances . . . to protect the public interest.'" Just as the District Court erred in its categorical denial of injunctive relief, the Court of Appeals erred in its categorical grant of such relief. *Cf. Roche Products v. Bolar Pharmaceutical Co.*, 733 F.2d 858, 865 (C.A. Fed. 1984) (recognizing the "considerable discretion" district courts have "in determining whether the facts of a situation require it to issue an injunction").

Because we conclude that neither court below correctly applied the traditional four-factor framework that governs the award of injunctive relief, we vacate the judgment of the Court of Appeals, so that the District Court may apply that framework in the first instance. In doing so, we take no position on whether permanent injunctive relief should or should not issue in this particular case, or indeed in any number of other disputes arising under the Patent Act. We hold only that the decision whether to grant or deny injunctive relief rests within the equitable discretion of the district courts, and that such discretion must be exercised consistent with traditional principles of equity, in patent disputes no less than in other cases governed by such standards.

Accordingly, we vacate the judgment of the Court of Appeals, and remand for further proceedings consistent with this opinion.

It is so ordered.

Chief Justice ROBERTS, with whom Justice SCALIA and Justice GINSBURG join, concurring.

I agree with the Court's holding that "the decision whether to grant or deny injunctive relief rests within the equitable discretion of the district courts, and that such discretion must be exercised consistent with traditional principles of equity, in patent disputes no less than in other cases governed by such standards," and I join the opinion of the Court. That opinion rightly rests on the proposition that "a major departure from the long tradition of equity practice should not be lightly implied." *Weinberger v. Romero-Barcelo*, 456 U.S. 305, 320 (1982).

From at least the early 19th century, courts have granted injunctive relief upon a finding of infringement in the vast majority of patent cases. This "long tradition of equity practice" is not surprising, given the difficulty of protecting a right to exclude through monetary remedies that allow an infringer to use an invention against the patentee's wishes—a difficulty that often implicates the first two factors of the traditional four-factor test. This historical practice, as the Court holds, does not entitle a patentee to a permanent injunction or justify a general rule that such injunctions should issue. The Federal Circuit itself so recognized in *Roche Products, Inc. v. Bolar Pharmaceutical Co.*, 733 F.2d 858, 865-867 (1984). At the same time, there is a difference between exercising equitable discretion pursuant to the established four-factor test and writing on an entirely clean slate. "Discretion is not whim, and limiting discretion according to legal standards helps promote the basic principle of justice that like cases should be decided alike." *Martin v. Franklin Capital Corp.*, 546 U.S. 132, 139 (2005). When it comes to discerning and applying those standards, in this area as others, "a page of history is worth a volume of logic." *New York Trust Co. v. Eisner*, 256 U.S. 345, 349 (1921) (opinion for the Court by Holmes, J.).

Justice KENNEDY, with whom Justice STEVENS, Justice SOUTER, and Justice BREYER join, concurring.

The Court is correct, in my view, to hold that courts should apply the well-established, four-factor test—without resort to categorical rules—in deciding whether to grant injunctive relief in patent cases. The Chief Justice is also correct that history may be instructive in applying this test. (concurring opinion). The traditional practice of issuing injunctions against patent infringers, however, does not seem to rest on "the difficulty of protecting a right to exclude through monetary remedies that allow an infringer to use an invention against the patentee's wishes." (Roberts, C.J., concurring). Both the terms of the Patent Act and the traditional view of injunctive relief accept that the existence of a right to exclude does not dictate the remedy for a violation of that right. To the extent earlier cases establish a pattern of granting an injunction against patent infringers almost as a matter of course, this pattern simply illustrates the result of the four-factor test in the contexts then prevalent. The lesson of the historical practice, therefore, is most helpful and instructive when the circumstances of a case bear substantial parallels to litigation the courts have confronted before.

In cases now arising trial courts should bear in mind that in many instances the nature of the patent being enforced and the economic function of the patent holder present considerations quite unlike earlier cases. An industry has developed in which firms use patents not as a basis for producing and selling goods but, instead, primarily for obtaining licensing fees. *See* FTC, TO PROMOTE INNOVATION: THE PROPER BALANCE OF COMPETITION AND PATENT LAW AND POLICY, ch. 3, pp. 38-39 (Oct. 2003). For these firms, an injunction, and the potentially serious sanctions arising from its violation, can be employed as a bargaining tool to charge exorbitant fees to companies that seek to buy licenses to practice the patent. *See ibid.* When the patented invention is but a small component of the product the companies seek to produce and the threat of an injunction is employed simply for undue leverage in negotiations, legal damages may well be sufficient to compensate for the infringement and an injunction may not serve the public interest. In addition injunctive relief may have different consequences for the burgeoning number of patents over business methods, which were not of much economic and legal significance in earlier times. The potential vagueness and suspect validity of some of these patents may affect the calculus under the four-factor test.

The equitable discretion over injunctions, granted by the Patent Act, is well suited to allow courts to adapt to the rapid technological and legal developments in the patent system. For these reasons it should be recognized that district courts must determine whether past practice fits the circumstances of the cases before them. With these observations, I join the opinion of the Court.

COMMENTS AND QUESTIONS

1. This Supreme Court ruling has had an immediate and profound impact on patent litigation. *See* Christopher B. Seaman, *Permanent Injunctions in Patent Litigation After eBay: An Empirical Study*, 101 IOWA L. REV. (forthcoming 2016) (noting that non-practicing entities are much less likely to obtain injunctions after *eBay*.)

2. Leading remedies scholars question whether the Supreme Court's *eBay* test comports with long-standing remedial standards for *permanent* injunctions. Their research indicates that the Supreme Court aligns more closely with the test for *preliminary* injunctions, a judgment which is rendered before the violation has been conclusively established. *See* Mark P. Gergen, John M. Golden & Henry E. Smith, *The Supreme Court's Accidental Revolution? The Test for Permanent Injunctions*, 112 COLUM. L. REV. 203, 208 (2012).

3. Should the availability of injunctions depend on whether the patentee manufactures the patented product or is simply in the business of licensing (and litigating) patents? What if the plaintiff has as its business model the acquisition of third-party patents, strictly with an eye toward maximizing patent-related revenue by suing as many actual manufacturers as possible? As patents have become more valuable, these and related issues are finding their way into legal arguments regarding the desirability of injunctions and other remedies. Most lower court decisions have split along these lines, granting injunctive relief to patentees who participate in the market but denying injunctive relief to non-practicing entities because they cannot satisfy *eBay*'s four-factor test.

4. *Ongoing Royalties.* In *Paice LLC v. Toyota Motor Corp.*, 609 F.Supp.2d 620 (E.D.Tex 2009), the court found that Toyota's hybrid automobiles infringed Paice's patent on a microprocessor and controllable torque transfer unit that accepts input from both an internal combustion engine and an electric motor. The court determined that a permanent injunction is not warranted and awarded a running royalty of $98 per vehicle, nearly four times the award of past damages. Does it make sense to deny an injunction but at the same time punish the defendant by charging a higher royalty rate going forward? *See* Mark A. Lemley, *The Ongoing Confusion Over Ongoing Royalties*, 76 Mo. L. REV. (2011).

2. Damages

Section 284 of the Patent Act provides:

Upon finding for the claimant the court shall award the claimant damages adequate to compensate for the infringement but in no event less than a reasonable royalty for the use made of the invention by the infringer, together with interest and costs as fixed by the court.

When the damages are not found by a jury, the court shall assess them. In either event the court may increase the damages up to three times the amount found or assessed. Increased damages under this paragraph shall not apply to provisional rights under section 154(d) of this title.

The court may receive expert testimony as an aid to the determination of damages or of what royalty would be reasonable under the circumstances.

Section 286 establishes a six-year statute of limitations, barring patentees from recovering damages for any infringing acts committed more than six years prior to the filing of the complaint or counterclaim for infringement.

Courts apply two principal approaches for measuring damages "adequate to compensate" for a defendant's infringement: lost profits and reasonable royalties.

i.   *Lost Profits*

Courts have struggled with the problem of setting appropriate measures of damages for past infringement. In *Panduit Corp. v. Stahlin Bros. Fibre Works, Inc.*, 575 F.2d 1152, 1158 n.5 (6th Cir. 1978), the court adopted an oft-used four-factor test for determining lost profits:

To obtain as damages the profits on sales he would have made absent the infringement, i.e., the sales made by the infringer, a patent owner must prove:

(1) demand for the patented product,

(2) absence of acceptable noninfringing substitutes,

(3) his manufacturing and marketing capability to exploit the demand, and

(4) the amount of the profit he would have made.

Price Erosion. The per-unit profit that the patentee would have earned can be difficult to estimate because the infringer's activity has created competition that would not have otherwise occurred in the market. Consequently, the patentee may also recover additional lost profits damages under a price erosion theory. *See Crystal Semiconductor Corp. v. TriTech Microelectronics Int'l, Inc.*, 246 F.3d 1336, 1357 (Fed. Cir. 2001). To recover for price erosion damages, a patentee is required to prove that "but for" the infringement, she would have sold her patented invention at a higher price. Furthermore, the patentee must prove the number of products she would have sold at this price. Accordingly, "the patentee's price erosion theory must account for the nature, or definition, of the market, similarities between any benchmark market and the market in which price erosion is alleged, and the effect of the hypothetically increased price on the likely number of sales at that price in that market."

What assumption does this theory make about the demand for the patentee's product? Wouldn't you expect the number of units sold to decline as the price increases?

Market-Share Rule. When more than two sellers share a market and at least one seller is a non-infringing competitor of the patentee, it would appear that one element in the *Panduit* test is missing: the absence of noninfringing substitutes. Courts can, however, inquire into what would have happened if the infringer had not been in the market. Under this theory, the court is asked to assume that the patentee's market share relative to the noninfringer would have remained the same in the absence of the infringer. Consequently, it is assumed that the patentee would have made the same percentage of the infringer's sales as the patentee made in the overall market. *See, e.g., State Indus. v. Mor-Flo, Inc.,* 883 F.2d 1573 (Fed. Cir. 1988); Roy J. Epstein, *The Market Share Rule with Price Erosion: Patent Infringement Lost Profits Damages After* Crystal, 31 AIPLA Q.J. 1 (2003).

Lost Sales of Unpatented Components or Products. A patentee may also recover for lost profits on unpatented components sold with a patented product, so-called "convoyed sales." *See Rite-Hite Corp. v. Kelley Co.,* 56 F.3d 1538, 1546 (Fed. Cir. 1995) (en banc) ("[i]f a particular injury was or should have been reasonably foreseeable by an infringing competitor in the relevant market, broadly defined, that injury is generally compensable absent a persuasive reason to the contrary.")

COMMENTS AND QUESTIONS

1. The Federal Circuit decision in *Grain Processing Corp. v. American Maize Products Co.,* 185 F.3d 1341 (Fed. Cir. 1999) elucidates the requirement that there be no acceptable noninfringing substitutes. Plaintiff Grain Processing was the holder of a patent on a form of maltodextrin, a food additive used in frostings, syrups, drinks, cereals, and frozen foods. After finding infringement, Judge Frank Easterbrook of the Seventh Circuit (sitting by designation on the district court) denied the patentee lost profits damages. Judge Easterbrook found that although the infringer did not in fact sell a noninfringing alternative during the damages period, it easily *could have.* The Federal Circuit affirmed, opening the way for accused infringers to argue more freely about hypothetical scenarios that might have played out if they had known they were infringing.

In summary, this court requires reliable economic proof of the market that establishes an accurate context to project the likely results "but for" the infringement. The availability of substitutes invariably will influence the market forces defining this "but for" marketplace, as it did in this case. Moreover, a substitute need not be openly on sale to exert this influence. Thus, with proper economic proof of availability, as American Maize provided the district court in this case, an acceptable substitute not on the market during the infringement may nonetheless become part of the lost profits calculus and therefore limit or preclude those damages.

185 F.3d at 1356.

It should be noted that the facts in *Grain Processing* made it particularly easy to make a persuasive case that the noninfringing substitute would very likely have been employed by the infringer. The technology was well understood — so much so that the infringer switched to a noninfringing version of the product within two weeks of being ordered to do so by the district court; buyers and consumers of maltodextrin did not value the features of the claimed product in a way that set it apart from other versions, making other versions good substitutes; and the accused infringer had especially convincing proof that it could easily have ramped up production of the noninfringing alternative.

The Federal Circuit reaffirmed and applied *Grain Processing* in *Crystal Semiconductor Corp. v. Tritech Microelectronics Int'l, Inc.*, 246 F.3d 1336, 1358-60 (Fed. Cir. 2001) (affirming trial court findings and emphasizing need to analyze market reaction to patented technology). But the court also made clear in a subsequent case that it was serious about the need for the infringer to prove that the noninfringing substitute was *readily* available. *See Micro Chemical, Inc. v. Lextron, Inc.*, 318 F.3d 1119, 1123 (Fed. Cir. 2003) (reversing a trial court finding of ready availability under *Grain Processing*); John W. Schlicher, *Measuring Patent Damages by the Market Value of Inventions — The* Grain Processing, Rite-Hite, *and* Aro *Rules*, 82 J. PAT. & TRADEMARK OFF. SOC'Y 503 (2000).

ii.   *Reasonable Royalty*

a.   *The Basic Inquiry*

Section 284 provides that the patent owner is entitled to "damages adequate to compensate for the infringement, but in no event less than a reasonable royalty for the use made of the invention by the infringer." Thus, when lost profits cannot be proved, the patent owner is entitled to a reasonable royalty. A reasonable royalty is an amount "which a person, desiring to manufacture and sell a patented article, as a business proposition, would be willing to pay as a royalty and yet be able to make and sell the patented article, in the market, at a reasonable profit." *Goodyear Tire and Rubber Co. v. Overman Cushion Tire Co.*, 95 F.2d 978 at 984 (6th Cir. 1937) (citing *Rockwood v. General Fire Extinguisher Co.*, 37 F.2d 62 at 66 (2d Cir. 1930)), *appeal dismissed*, 306 U.S. 665 (1938).

"A "reasonable royalty" contemplates a hypothetical negotiation between the patentee and the infringer at a time before the infringement began. [T]his analysis necessarily involves some approximation of the market as it would have hypothetically developed absent infringement. This analysis, in turn, requires sound economic and factual predicates." *Riles v. Shell Exploration and Production Co.*, 298 F.3d 1302, 1311 (Fed. Cir. 2002). "In a normal negotiation, the potential licensee has three basic choices: forgo all use of the invention; pay an agreed royalty; infringe the patent and risk litigation." *Fromson v. Western Litho Plate and Supply Co.*, 853 F.2d 1568, 1576 (Fed. Cir. 1988). In a hypothetical negotiation, however, the factfinder "presumes that the licensee has made the second choice, when in fact it made the third." *Id.* Commentators—and some courts—have noted that this standard would disadvantage a patentee if a court were "to pretend that the infringement never happened." *TWM Mfg. Co. v. Dura Corp.*, 789 F.2d 895, 900 (Fed. Cir. 1986). As a consequence, courts keep in mind that the hypothetical negotiation approach "must be flexibly applied as a device in the aid of justice." *Id.* (internal quotations omitted).

In practice, however, the choice is only rarely between infringing and taking a license. Most patent defendants are not copiers but independent inventors. Had they been aware of the patent when they developed their product, these independent inventors might have had another choice: pick an alternative way of implementing the invention that is not subject to the patent. For that reason, the reasonable royalty should logically be limited by the value of the patent over the available noninfringing alternatives, just as those alternatives constrain the ability to recover lost profits. *See Grain Processing Corp. v. American Maize-Prods. Co.*, 185 F.3d 1341 (Fed. Cir. 1999).

This means that courts walk a fine line when awarding reasonable royalties: between undercompensating the patentee by resort to a purely fictional negotiation which takes place outside the shadow of any actual infringement and awarding damages far removed from industry standards, the negotiating positions of the parties, and other real world constraints. In addition, although the cases sometimes hint at a quasi-punitive component in a reasonable royalty calculation, the statute provides for an explicit "multiplier" *only* in the case of willful infringement.

If the right measure of royalty is based on the value of the patented invention over the available noninfringing alternatives, the true value of the invention might be zero in many cases. *See* Daniel L. Brean, *Ending Unreasonable Royalties: Why Nominal Damages are Adequate to Compensate Patent Assertion Entities for Infringement*, 39 Vt. L. Rev. 867 (2015). Indeed, a number of commentators and industry representatives have argued that the problem is not undercompensation, but overcompensation, particularly where a patentee owns a patent on a small component but can measure damages based on the sale of a large, multi-component product. *See* Mark A. Lemley & Carl Shapiro, *Patent Holdup and Royalty Stacking*, 85 Tex. L. Rev. 1991 (2007). Nevertheless, courts always award some royalty, *Apple Corp. v. Motorola, Inc.*, 757 F.3d 1286 (Fed. Cir. 2014), and they have been unsympathetic to infringers who argue that the patentee's proposed royalty would have meant that the infringer would have lost money on sales of the product. *See, e.g., Golight, Inc. v. Wal-Mart Stores, Inc.*, 355 F.3d 1327, 1338 (Fed. Cir. 2004); *Monsanto Co. v. Ralph*, 382

F.3d 1374, 1384 (Fed. Cir. 2004) ("[T]he law does not require that an infringer be permitted to make a profit. And, where, as here, a patentee is unwilling to grant an unlimited license, the hypothetical negotiation process has its limits.").

Several problems have emerged in determining a reasonably royalty. The principal methodology relies on a broad and open-ended set of factors. Beyond these factors, courts have struggled with apportioning value within patented products. A third issue relates to valuation of patents that are part of a pool of patents governed by fair, reasonable, and non-discriminatory (FRAND) licensing agreements.

b. The Georgia-Pacific Factors

Setting reasonable royalties entails a detailed review of the technology at issue, the bargaining positions of the parties, and other factors that might have been relevant if the hypothetical negotiation had actually taken place. The district court in *Georgia-Pacific v. U.S. Plywood Corp.*, 318 F. Supp. 1116, 1120 (S.D.N.Y. 1970), enumerated a broad list of factors that has been widely followed:

1. The royalties received by the patentee for the licensing of the patent in suit, proving or tending to prove an established royalty.

2. The rates paid by the licensee for the use of other patents comparable to the patent in suit.

3. The nature and scope of the license, as exclusive or non-exclusive; or as restricted or non-restricted in terms of territory or with respect to whom the manufactured product may be sold.

4. The licensor's established policy and marketing program to maintain his patent monopoly by not licensing others to use the invention or by granting licenses under special conditions designed to preserve that monopoly.

5. The commercial relationship between the licensor and licensee, such as, whether they are competitors in the same territory in the same line of business; or whether they are inventor and promoter.

6. The effect of selling the patented specialty in promoting sales of other products of the licensee; that existing value of the invention to the licensor as a generator of sales of his non-patented items; and the extent of such derivative or convoyed sales.

7. The duration of the patent and the term of the license.

8. The established profitability of the product made under the patent, its commercial success, and its current popularity.

9. The utility and advantages of the patent property over the old modes or devices, if any, that had been used for working out similar results.

10. The nature of the patented invention, the character of the commercial embodiment of it as owned and produced by the licensor, and the benefits to those who have used the invention.

11. The extent to which the infringer has made use of the invention, and any evidence probative of the value of that use.

12. The portion of the profit or of the selling price that may be customary in the particular business or in comparable businesses to allow for the use of the invention or analogous inventions.

13. The portion of the realizable profit that should be credited to the invention as distinguished from non-patented elements, the manufacturing process, business risks, or significant features or improvements added by the infringer.

14. The opinion testimony of qualified experts.

15. The amount that a licensor (such as the patentee) and a licensee (such as the infringer) would have agreed upon (at the time the infringement began) if both had been reasonably and voluntarily trying to reach an agreement; that is, the amount which a prudent licensee—who desired, as a business proposition, to obtain a license to manufacture and sell a particular article embodying the patented invention—would have been willing to pay as a royalty and yet be able to make a reasonable profit and which amount would have been acceptable by a prudent patentee who was willing to grant a license.

Id. at 1120.

COMMENTS AND QUESTIONS

1. Is the reasonable royalty approach circular? While it seems to make sense to base a royalty on what other parties were negotiating for similar rights, those license negotiations themselves will be driven by what the parties think will happen if they don't come to terms and the dispute goes to court, not what parties would have agreed to under the assumption that the patent was valid and infringed. *See* Jonathan Masur, *The Use and Misuse of Patent Licenses*, 110 NORTHWESTERN UNIV. L. REV. 1115 (2015).

2. Application of the *Georgia-Pacific* factors was once again endorsed in a 2009 Federal Circuit case that also required district court judges to reject inadequate evidence in reasonable royalty cases. *See Lucent Techs., Inc. v. Gateway, Inc.*, 580 F.3d 1301 (Fed. Cir. 2009). The *Lucent* case involved a patent on a minor component (the pop-up calendar, or "date picker" function) of a complex software product (Microsoft's Outlook scheduling and calendaring program). The jury had awarded over $500 million in damages, in part on the basis of licensing agreements from the computer industry that bore little relationship to the hypothetical license negotiation that served as the

foundation of the damages award in the case. The Federal Circuit reversed the trial court's denial of a post-trial motion to reject the jury verdict. Henceforth, the court instructed, judges must actively supervise the introduction of "comparable licensing" evidence so that it is truly comparable, and therefore capable of grounding a truly reasonable royalty finding.

3. The *Georgia-Pacific* factors are so numerous, complex, and mind-numbing that jurors have difficulty understanding how to juggle so many considerations. The Federal Circuit Bar Association's January 2016 Model Jury Instructions have boiled down the factors:

> *6.7 Reasonable Royalty—Relevant Factors*
>
> In determining the reasonable royalty, you should consider all the facts known and available to the parties at the time the infringement began. Some of the kinds of factors that you may consider in making your determination are:
>> (1) The value that the claimed invention contributes to the accused product.
>> (2) The value that factors other than the claimed invention contribute to [the accused product].
>> (3) Comparable license agreements, such as those covering the use of the claimed invention or similar technology.

This concise and focused instruction provides a more balanced and comprehensible set of considerations than the *Georgia-Pacific* laundry list. Does it leave any important considerations out? *Cf.* Norman Siebrasse and Thomas Cotter, *A New Framework for Determining Reasonable Royalties in Patent Litigation*, FLA. L. REV. (forthcoming 2016); William Lee and A. Douglas Melamed, *Breaking the Vicious Cycle of Patent Damages*, 101 CORNELL L. REV. 385 (2016); David O. Taylor, *Using Reasonable Royalties to Value Patented Technology*, 49 GA. L. REV. 79 (2014); Daralyn J. Durie & Mark A. Lemley, *A Structured Approach to Calculating Reasonable Royalties*, 14 LEWIS & CLARK L. REV. 627 (2010).

c. Damages Theories and Evidence

A reasonable royalty calculation will typically require determining the royalty base and the royalty rate. The determination is relatively straightforward where the demand for a final product comprises a single patented technology, such as a drug with a patented active ingredient. The most sensible royalty base would typically be total sales revenue for the final product, what is often referred to as the entire market value. *See Fonar Corp. v. Gen. Elec. Co.*, 107 F.3d 1543, 1552 (Fed. Cir. 1997) (citing *Rite–Hite Corp. v. Kelley Co.*, 56 F.3d 1538, 1549 (Fed. Cir. 1995) (en banc)). The royalty rate would account for alternative treatments (of which there may be few), marketing costs, and manufacturing costs.

Patent law has long struggled to deal with apportioning patent value where a patent covers only one component of a larger product. *See Cincinnati Car Co. v. New York*

Rapid Transit Corp., 66 F.2d 592, 593 (2d Cir. 1933) (Learned Hand, J.) (observing that the allocation of profits among multiple components "is in its nature unanswerable"). The problem has become particularly acute in modern patent litigation as a result of the growing use of juries called upon to apportion value based on complex and often widely divergent economic expert analyses.

In theory, a wide range of royalty bases can be appropriate with an appropriated calibrated royalty rate to account for the myriad factors affecting consumer demand. In practice, however, the open-ended nature of the *Georgia-Pacific* framework can lead to wildly divergent royalty calculations by expert economists. Especially in a jury trial, such testimony can produce outsize damage awards. As the Supreme Court recognized long ago, it would be "very grave error to instruct a jury 'that as to the measure of damages the same rule is to govern, whether the patent covers an entire machine or an improvement on a machine.'" *Seymore v. McCormick*, 57 U.S. 480, 491 (1853); *see also Westinghouse Elec. & Mfg. Co. v. Wagner Co.*, 225 U.S. 604, 614-15 (1912) ("[The] invention may have been used in combination with valuable improvements made, or other patents appropriated by the infringer, and each may have jointly, but unequally contributed to the profits. In such case, if plaintiff's patent only created a part of the profits, he is only entitled to recover that part of the net gains."); *Garretson v. Clark*, 111 U.S. 120, 121 (1884) ("When a patent is for an improvement, and not for an entirely new machine or contrivance, the patentee must show in what particulars his improvement has added to the usefulness of the machine or contrivance.)

While estimating a reasonable royalty is not an "exact science" in that there may be more than one reliable method, *Apple Inc. v. Motorola, Inc.*, 757 F.3d 1286, 1315 (Fed. Cir. 2014), the Federal Circuit has enhanced the judge's gatekeeping role to prevent excessive awards. Recent decisions have sought to align the royalty base to the patented component of a product, exclude unreliable damage theories, scrutinize the admissibility of various forms of evidence, and provide limiting jury instructions.

In general, a patent holder seeking a reasonable royalty must provide substantial evidence supporting both its choice of royalty base and royalty rate. "[W]here multi-component products are involved, the governing rule is that the ultimate combination of royalty base and royalty rate must reflect the value attributable to the infringing features of the product, and no more." *Ericsson, Inc., v. D-Link Sys., Inc.*, 773 F.3d 1201, 1226 (Fed. Cir. 2014) (citing *VirnetX, Inc. v. Cisco Sys., Inc.*, 767 F.3d 1308 (Fed. Cir. 2014)).

As the Federal Circuit has warned, "reliance on the entire market value might mislead the jury, who may be less equipped to understand the extent to which the royalty rate would need to do the work in such instances." *Ericsson*, 773 F.3d at 1227 (citing *LaserDynamics, Inc. v. Quanta Computer, Inc.*, 694 F.3d 51, 67, 68 (Fed. Cir. 2012) (barring the use of too high a royalty base—even if mathematically offset by a "'low enough royalty rate'"—because such a base "carries a considerable risk" of misleading a jury into overcompensating, stating that such a base "'cannot help but skew the damages horizon for the jury'" and "make a patentee's proffered damages amount appear modest by comparison" (quoting *Uniloc USA, Inc. v. Microsoft Corp.*, 632 F.3d 1292, 1320 (Fed. Cir. 2011))).

To cabin the risk of outsize awards in multi-component cases, the Federal Circuit has pushed the royalty base toward the smallest salable patent practicing unit or "SSPPU." *See Cornell Univ. v. Hewlett-Packard Co.*, 609 F. Supp. 2d 279 (N.D.N.Y. 2009) (Rader, J., sitting by designation). The Federal Circuit embraced the SSPPU framework in *LaserDynamics Inc. v. Quanta Computer, Inc.*, 694 F.3d 51 (Fed. Cir. 2012), holding that "it is generally required that royalties be based not on the entire product, but instead on the 'smallest salable patent-practicing unit.' . . . The entire market value rule is a narrow exception to this general rule." *Id.* at 67; *see also VirnetX, Inc., v. Cisco Sys., Inc.*, 767 F.3d 1308, 1328-29 (Fed. Cir. 2014); *LaserDynamics, Inc., v. Quanta Comput., Inc.*, 694 F.3d 51, 66-70 (Fed. Cir. 2012); *Uniloc USA, Inc. v. Microsoft Corp.*, 632 F.3d 1292, 1320 (Fed. Cir. 2011); *Lucent Techs., Inc. v. Gateway, Inc.*, 580 F.3d 1301, 1336 (Fed. Cir. 2009).

Beyond calibrating the royalty base to the scale of the patent practicing unit, courts seek to ensure that the royalty rate is based on sound economic methodology and grounded in reliable and pertinent evidence. Using the construct of the hypothetical negotiation between a willing licensor and licensee, experts use the *Georgia-Pacific* factors to determine a license rate that would have been agreed upon just before the infringement began (and based on the assumption that the patent was valid, infringed, and enforceable). The proof of an appropriate royalty rate using this method allows for necessary "approximation and uncertainty." *Aqua Shield v. Inter Pool Cover Team*, 774 F.3d 766, 771 (Fed. Cir. 2014). Nevertheless, it must be supported by substantial evidence, which usually will be based on the application of the relevant, but not necessarily the complete list of fifteen, *Georgia-Pacific* factors. *See WhitServe, LLC, v. Computer Packages, Inc.*, 694 F.3d 10, 31-32 (Fed. Cir. 2012).

The open-ended *Georgia-Pacific* framework affords economic experts substantial leeway in determining a royalty rate. The most pertinent evidence usually comprises past licenses to the infringing or comparable technology, the value of comparable features in the marketplace, an estimate of the value of the benefit provided by the infringed features by comparison to non-infringing alternatives, or an estimate of the cost to design around the patent. *See, e.g., Ericsson*, 773 F.3d at 1227 (citing *Monsanto Co. v. McFarling*, 488 F.3d 973, 978 (Fed. Cir. 2007) ("An established royalty is usually the best measure of a 'reasonable' royalty for a given use of an invention . . . ."). However, license agreements that are unrelated to the claimed invention cannot form the basis of a reasonable royalty calculation. *See, e.g., Lucent*, 580 F.3d at 1327; *see also ResQNet*, 594 F.3d at 869 ("Any evidence unrelated to the claimed invention does not support compensation for infringement but punishes beyond the reach of the statute."). The Federal Circuit has observed that licenses arising out of litigation might be reliable in certain circumstances, but has cautioned that "litigation itself can skew the results of the hypothetical negotiation." *ResQNet*, 594 F.3d at 872.

In many cases, the technology either has not been previously licensed or the licenses cover a broader range of technologies than the patented invention and/or multiple product or product components. As an alternative or shortcut to considering the *Georgia-Pacific* factors, some patentees have put forward general royalty theories such as the 25% rule and the Nash Bargaining Solution (50% split of net product value). The Federal Circuit has rejected the application of these generalized "rules of thumb." *See Apple*, 757 F.3d at 1324-25; *VirnetX*, 767 F.3d at 1331-34 (rejecting the Nash Bargaining Solution); *Uniloc*, 632 F.3d at 1312 (rejecting the "25% Rule"). Such evidence is inadmissible.

Damages experts have begun to deploy consumer surveys to allocate value within multi-component patented products. *See* Zelin Yang, Note, *Damaging Royalties: An Overview of Reasonable Royalty Damages*, 29 BERKELEY TECH. L.J. 647, 664 (2014); S. Christian Platt & Bob Chen, *Recent Trends and Approaches in Calculating Patent Damages: Nash Bargaining Solution and Conjoint Surveys*, 86 PATENT, TRADEMARK & COPYRIGHT J. (BNA) 909 (Aug. 30, 2013). Marketing researchers have long used "conjoint analysis" to differentiate value within product configurations. *See* Paul E. Green, Abba M. Krieger & Yoram Wind, *Thirty Years of Conjoint Analysis: Reflections and Prospects*, 31 INTERFACES 56 (2001); Paul E. Green & V. Srinivasan, *Conjoint Analysis in Marketing: New Developments with Implications for Research and Practice*, 54(4) J. OF MARKETING 3 (1990).

Conjoint analysis draws upon consumer ranking of products with different features. Researchers use statistical methods to estimate consumers' willingness to pay for particular attributes. While these methods provide a logical framework for differentiating value, the technique can be limited in practice. *See* Patricia Dyck, *Beyond Confusion—Survey Evidence of Consumer Demand and the Entire Market Value Rule*, 4 HASTINGS SCI. & TECH. L.J. 209, 226 (2012) (noting sensitivity to data collection methods and algorithms and the problem of combinatorial explosion); Lisa Cameron, Michael Cragg & Daniel McFadden, *The Role of Conjoint Surveys in Reasonable Royalty Cases*, LAW360 (Oct. 16, 2013).

Courts have been cautiously receptive to conjoint analysis. Recognizing the general admissibility of consumer surveys, *Oracle Am., Inc. v. Google, Inc.*, No. C 10-03571 WHA, 2012 WL 850705, at *10 (N.D. Cal. Mar. 13, 2012), Judge Alsup nonetheless rejected some of Oracle's expert's conjoint analysis as unreliable while allowing some of it to be admitted. *Id.* *10-*14. In *TV Interactive Data Corp. v. Sony Corp.*, 929 F. Supp. 2d 1006 (N.D. Cal. 2013), Magistrate Judge Joseph Spero held the patentee's expert testimony using conjoint analysis to be admissible. *Id.* at 1019-25.

d. FRAND Licenses

A growing number of technologies arise within the context of network industries in which standard protocols and interfaces promote technological innovation and greater consumer value. Industry standard-setting organizations such as the Institute of Electrical Electronics Engineers (IEEE) and the International Telecommunication Union (ITU) bring together company representatives to develop industry standards. To ensure that the industry standards reflect the best technologies while avoiding (or at least postponing) licensing disputes, the participants typically commit to license standard-essential patents (SEPs) on "reasonable and non-discriminatory" (RAND) or "fair, reasonable and non-discriminatory" (FRAND) terms. The standard-setting organizations have typically left the parameters for determining FRAND license terms undefined, *see* Mark A. Lemley, *Intellectual Property Rights and Standard-Setting Organizations*, 90 CAL. L. REV. 1889, 1906 (2002), leaving courts with the difficult task of determining licensing rates for highly complex products involving potentially hundreds of patents.

The valuation of SEPs presents distinct problems. Industry standards can encompass hundreds of patented technologies of carrying significance. Not surprisingly, owners of patents within a SEP pool often see their patents as particularly valuable, thereby risking hold-up and undue royalty stacking. The challenge lies in separating the value of the particular technology from the often tremendous value from standardization. Once consumers adopt a product, they become locked into the standard to varying degrees. This could provide the patentee tremendous leverage in a negotiation. With potentially hundreds of SEPs and dozens of patent owners, the problem becomes intractable if patent owners stake out aggressive positions or refuse to propose licensing terms.

In a series of recent cases, courts have surmounted this challenge by interpreting the principal goal of standard-setting agreements to be widespread adoption of the standard by barring FRAND licensors from capturing the coordination and network value of the standard. *See Microsoft Corp. v. Motorola, Inc.*, No. C10-1823JLR, 2013 U.S. Dist. LEXIS 60233, 2013 WL 2111217 (W.D. Wash. Apr. 25, 2013); *see also Ericsson*, 773 F.3d at 1229-35; *In re Innovatio IP Ventures LLC Patent Litig.*, No. 11 C 9308, 2013 U.S. Dist. LEXIS 144061, 2013 WL 5593609 (N.D. Ill. Oct. 3, 2013). The courts have adapted the *Georgia-Pacific* factors to serve the standard-setting context.

3. Enhanced Damages

Halo Electronics, Inc. v. Pulse Electronics, Inc.
Stryker Corp. v. Zimmer, Inc.
Supreme Court of the United States
__ U.S. ___ (2016)

ROBERTS, Chief Justice

Section 284 of the Patent Act provides that, in a case of infringement, courts "may increase the damages up to three times the amount found or assessed." 35 U.S.C. §284. In *In re Seagate Technology, LLC*, 497 F. 3d 1360 (2007) (en banc), the United States Court of Appeals for the Federal Circuit adopted a two-part test for determining when a district court may increase damages pursuant to §284. Under *Seagate*, a patent owner must first "show by clear and convincing evidence that the infringer acted despite an objectively high likelihood that its actions constituted infringement of a valid patent." *Id.*, at 1371. Second, the patentee must demonstrate, again by clear and convincing evidence, that the risk of infringement "was either known or so obvious that it should have been known to the accused infringer." *Ibid.* The question before us is whether this test is consistent with §284. We hold that it is not.

I

A

Enhanced damages are as old as U.S. patent law. The Patent Act of 1793 mandated treble damages in any successful infringement suit. *See* Patent Act of 1793, §5, 1 Stat. 322. In the Patent Act of 1836, however, Congress changed course and made enhanced damages discretionary, specifying that "it shall be in the power of the court to render judgment for any sum above the amount found by [the] verdict . . . not exceeding three times the amount thereof, according to the circumstances of the case." Patent Act of 1836, §14, 5 Stat. 123. In construing that new provision, this Court explained that the change was prompted by the "injustice" of subjecting a "defendant who acted in ignorance or good faith" to the same treatment as the "wanton and malicious pirate." *Seymour* v. *McCormick*, 16 How. 480, 488 (1854). There "is no good reason," we observed, "why taking a man's property in an invention should be trebly punished, while the measure of damages as to other property is single and actual damages." *Id.*, at 488–489. But "where the injury is wanton or malicious, a jury may inflict vindictive or exemplary damages, not to recompense the plaintiff, but to punish the defendant." *Id.*, at 489. . . .

In 1870, Congress amended the Patent Act, but preserved district court discretion to award up to treble damages "according to the circumstances of the case." Patent Act of 1870, §59, 16 Stat. 207. We continued to describe enhanced damages as "vindictive or punitive," which the court may "inflict" when "the circumstances of the case appear to require it." *Tilghman* v. *Proctor*, 125 U.S. 136, 143–144 (1888); *Topliff* v. *Topliff*, 145 U.S. 156, 174 (1892) (infringer knowingly sold copied technology of his former employer). At the same time, we reiterated that there was no basis for increased damages where "[t]here is no pretence of any wanton and wilful breach" and "nothing that suggests punitive damages, or that shows wherein the defendant was damnified other than by the loss of the profits which the plaintiff received." *Cincinnati Siemens-Lungren Gas Illuminating Co.* v. *Western Siemens-Lungren Co.*, 152 U.S. 200, 204 (1894). . . .

Some early decisions did suggest that enhanced damages might serve to compensate patentees as well as to punish infringers. *See, e.g., Clark* v. *Wooster*, 119 U.S. 322, 326 (1886) (noting that "[t]here may be damages beyond" licensing fees "but these are more properly the subjects" of enhanced damage awards). Such statements, however, were not for the ages, in part because the merger of law and equity removed certain procedural obstacles to full compensation absent enhancement. *See generally* 7 CHISUM ON PATENTS §20.03[4][b][iii] (2011). In the main, moreover, the references to compensation concerned costs attendant to litigation. *See Clark*, 119 U.S., at 326 (identifying enhanced damages as compensation for "the expense and trouble the plaintiff has been put to"). That concern dissipated with the enactment in 1952 of 35 U.S.C. §285, which authorized district courts to award reasonable attorney's fees to prevailing parties in "exceptional cases" under the Patent Act. *See Octane Fitness, LLC* v. *ICON Health & Fitness Inc.*, 572 U.S. ___, ___ (2014).

It is against this backdrop that Congress, in the 1952 codification of the Patent Act, enacted §284. "The stated purpose" of the 1952 revision "was merely reorganization in language to clarify the statement of the statutes." *Aro Mfg. Co.* v. *Convertible Top Replacement Co.*, 377 U.S. 476, 505, n.20 (1964) (internal quotation marks omitted). This Court accordingly described §284—consistent with the history of enhanced damages under the Patent Act—as providing that "punitive or 'increased' damages" could be recovered "in a case of willful or bad-faith infringement." *Id.*, at 508; *see also Dowling* v. *United States*, 473 U.S. 207, 227, n.19 (1985) ("willful infringement"); *Florida Prepaid Postsecondary Ed. Expense Bd.* v. *College Savings Bank*, 527 U.S. 627, 648, n. 11 (1999) (describing §284 damages as "punitive").

B

In 2007, the Federal Circuit decided *Seagate* and fashioned the test for enhanced damages now before us. Under *Seagate*, a plaintiff seeking enhanced damages must show that the infringement of his patent was "willful." 497 F. 3d, at 1368. The Federal Circuit announced a two-part test to establish such willfulness: First, "a patentee must show by clear and convincing evidence that the infringer acted despite an objectively high likelihood that its actions constituted infringement of a valid patent," without regard to "[t]he state of mind of the accused infringer." *Id.*, at 1371. This objectively defined risk is to be "determined by the record developed in the infringement proceedings." *Ibid.* "Objective recklessness will not be found" at this first step if the accused infringer, during the infringement proceedings, "raise[s] a 'substantial question' as to the validity or noninfringement of the patent." *Bard Peripheral*

Vascular, Inc. v. *W. L. Gore & Assoc., Inc.*, 776 F. 3d 837, 844 (CA Fed. 2015). That categorical bar applies even if the defendant was unaware of the arguable defense when he acted. *See Seagate*, 497 F. 3d, at 1371.

Second, after establishing objective recklessness, a patentee must show—again by clear and convincing evidence—that the risk of infringement "was either known or so obvious that it should have been known to the accused infringer." *Seagate*, 497 F. 3d, at 1371. Only when both steps have been satisfied can the district court proceed to consider whether to exercise its discretion to award enhanced damages. *Ibid.*

Under Federal Circuit precedent, an award of enhanced damages is subject to trifurcated appellate review. The first step of *Seagate*—objective recklessness—is reviewed *de novo*; the second—subjective knowledge—for substantial evidence; and the ultimate decision—whether to award enhanced damages—for abuse of discretion. *See Bard Peripheral Vascular, Inc.* v. *W. L. Gore & Assoc., Inc.*, 682 F. 3d 1003, 1005, 1008 (CA Fed. 2012).

C

1

Petitioner Halo Electronics, Inc., and respondents Pulse Electronics, Inc. supply electronic components. 769 F. 3d 1371, 1374–1375 (CA Fed. 2014). Halo alleges that Pulse infringed its patents for electronic packages containing transformers designed to be mounted to the surface of circuit boards. *Id.*, at 1374. In 2002, Halo sent Pulse two letters offering to license Halo's patents. *Id.*, at 1376. After one of its engineers concluded that Halo's patents were invalid, Pulse continued to sell the allegedly infringing products. *Ibid.*

In 2007, Halo sued Pulse. *Ibid.* The jury found that Pulse had infringed Halo's patents, and that there was a high probability it had done so willfully. *Ibid.* The District Court, however, declined to award enhanced damages under §284, after determining that Pulse had at trial presented a defense that "was not objectively baseless, or a 'sham.'" App. to Pet. for Cert. in No. 14–1513, p. 64a (quoting *Bard*, 682 F. 3d, at 1007). Thus, the court concluded, Halo had failed to show objective recklessness under the first step of *Seagate*. The Federal Circuit affirmed.

2

Petitioners Stryker Corporation, Stryker Puerto Rico, Ltd., and Stryker Sales Corporation (collectively, Stryker) and respondents Zimmer, Inc., and Zimmer Surgical, Inc. (collectively, Zimmer), compete in the market for orthopedic pulsed lavage devices. A pulsed lavage device is a combination spray gun and suction tube, used to clean tissue during surgery. In 2010, Stryker sued Zimmer for patent infringement. The jury found that Zimmer had willfully infringed Stryker's patents and awarded Stryker $70 million in lost profits. The District Court added $6.1 million in supplemental damages and then trebled the total sum under §284, resulting in an award of over $228 million.

Specifically, the District Court noted, the jury had heard testimony that Zimmer had "all-but instructed its design team to copy Stryker's products," and had chosen a "high-risk/high-reward strategy of competing immediately and aggressively in the pulsed lavage market," while "opt[ing] to worry about the potential legal consequences later." "[T]reble damages [were] appropriate," the District Court concluded, "[g]iven the one-sidedness of the case and the flagrancy and scope of Zimmer's infringement."

The Federal Circuit affirmed the judgment of infringement but vacated the award of treble damages. 782 F. 3d, at 662. Applying *de novo* review, the court concluded that enhanced damages were unavailable because Zimmer had asserted "reasonable defenses" at trial. We granted certiorari in both cases and now vacate and remand.

II

A

The pertinent text of §284 provides simply that "the court may increase the damages up to three times the amount found or assessed." 35 U.S.C. §284. That language contains no explicit limit or condition, and we have emphasized that the "word 'may' clearly connotes discretion." *Martin* v. *Franklin Capital Corp.*, 546 U.S. 132, 136 (2005) (quoting *Fogerty* v. *Fantasy, Inc.*, 510 U.S. 517, 533 (1994)).

At the same time, "[d]iscretion is not whim." *Martin*, 546 U.S., at 139. "[I]n a system of laws discretion is rarely without limits," even when the statute "does not specify any limits upon the district courts' discretion." *Flight Attendants* v. *Zipes*, 491 U.S. 754, 758 (1989). "[A] motion to a court's discretion is a motion, not to its inclination, but to its judgment; and its judgment is to be guided by sound legal principles." *Martin*, 546 U S., at 139 (quoting *United States* v. *Burr*, 25 F. Cas. 30, 35 (No. 14,692d) (CC Va. 1807) (Marshall, C. J.); alteration omitted). Thus, although there is "no precise rule or formula" for awarding damages under §284, a district court's "discretion should be exercised in light of the considerations" underlying the grant of that discretion. *Octane Fitness*, 572 U.S., at ___ (quoting *Fogerty*, 510 U.S., at 534).

Awards of enhanced damages under the Patent Act over the past 180 years establish that they are not to be meted out in a typical infringement case, but are instead designed as a "punitive" or "vindictive" sanction for egregious infringement behavior. The sort of conduct warranting enhanced damages has been variously described in our cases as willful, wanton, malicious, bad-faith, deliberate, consciously wrongful, flagrant, or—indeed—characteristic of a pirate. District courts enjoy discretion in deciding whether to award enhanced damages, and in what amount. But through nearly two centuries of discretionary awards and review by appellate tribunals, "the channel of discretion ha[s] narrowed," Friendly, *Indiscretion About Discretion*, 31 EMORY L.J. 747, 772 (1982), so that such damages are generally reserved for egregious cases of culpable behavior.

B

The *Seagate* test reflects, in many respects, a sound recognition that enhanced damages are generally appropriate under §284 only in egregious cases. That test, however, "is unduly rigid, and it impermissibly encumbers the statutory grant of discretion to district courts." *Octane Fitness,* 572 U.S., at ___ (construing §285 of the Patent Act). In particular, it can have the effect of insulating some of the worst patent infringers from any liability for enhanced damages.

1

The principal problem with *Seagate*'s two-part test is that it requires a finding of objective recklessness in every case before district courts may award enhanced damages. Such a threshold requirement excludes from discretionary punishment many of the most culpable offenders, such as the "wanton and malicious pirate" who intentionally infringes another's patent—with no doubts about its validity or any notion of a defense—for no purpose other than to steal the patentee's business. *Seymour*, 16 How. at 488. Under *Seagate*, a district court may not even consider enhanced damages for such a pirate, unless the court first determines that his infringement was "objectively" reckless. In the context of such deliberate wrongdoing, however, it is not clear why an independent showing of objective recklessness—by clear and convincing evidence, no less— should be a prerequisite to enhanced damages. Our recent decision in *Octane Fitness* arose in a different context but points in the same direction. In that case we considered §285 of the Patent Act, which allows district courts to award attorney's fees to prevailing parties in "exceptional" cases. 35 U.S.C. §285. The Federal Circuit had adopted a two-part test for determining when a case qualified as exceptional, requiring that the claim asserted be both objectively baseless and brought in subjective bad faith. We rejected that test on the ground that a case presenting "subjective bad faith" alone could "sufficiently set itself apart from mine-run cases to warrant a fee award." 572 U.S., at ___. So too here. The subjective willfulness of a patent infringer, intentional or knowing, may warrant enhanced damages, without regard to whether his infringement was objectively reckless.

The *Seagate* test aggravates the problem by making dispositive the ability of the infringer to muster a reasonable (even though unsuccessful) defense at the infringement trial. The existence of such a defense insulates the infringer from enhanced damages, even if he did not act on the basis of the defense or was even aware of it. Under that standard, someone who plunders a patent—infringing it without any reason to suppose his conduct is arguably defensible—can nevertheless escape any come-uppance under §284 solely on the strength of his attorney's ingenuity.

But culpability is generally measured against the knowledge of the actor at the time of the challenged conduct. *See generally* RESTATEMENT (SECOND) OF TORTS §8A (1965) ("intent" denotes state of mind in which "the actor desires to cause consequences of his act" or "believes" them to be "substantially certain to result from it"); W. KEETON, D. DOBBS, R. KEETON, & D. OWEN, PROSSER AND KEETON ON LAW OF TORTS §34, p. 212 (5th ed. 1984) (describing willful, wanton, and reckless as "look[ing] to the actor's real or supposed state of mind"); *see also Kolstad* v. *American Dental Assn.*, 527 U.S. 526, 538 (1999) ("Most often . . . eligibility for punitive awards is characterized in terms of a defendant's motive or intent"). In *Safeco Ins. Co. of America* v. *Burr*, 551 U.S. 47 (2007), we stated that a person is reckless if he acts "*knowing* or *having reason to know* of facts which would lead a reasonable man to realize" his actions are unreasonably risky. *Id.*, at 69 (emphasis added and internal quotation marks omitted). The Court found that the defendant had not recklessly violated the Fair Credit Reporting Act because the defendant's interpretation had "a foundation in the statutory text" and the defendant lacked "the benefit of guidance from the courts of appeals or the Federal Trade Commission" that "might have warned it away from the view it took." *Id.*, at 69–70. Nothing in *Safeco* suggests that we should look to facts that the defendant neither knew nor had reason to know at the time he acted.*

Section 284 allows district courts to punish the full range of culpable behavior. Yet none of this is to say that enhanced damages must follow a finding of egregious misconduct. As with any exercise of discretion, courts should continue to take into account the particular circumstances of each case in deciding whether to award damages, and in what amount. Section 284 permits district courts to exercise their discretion in a manner free from the inelastic constraints of the *Seagate* test. Consistent with nearly two centuries of enhanced damages under patent law, however, such punishment should generally be reserved for egregious cases typified by willful misconduct.

2

The *Seagate* test is also inconsistent with §284 because it requires clear and convincing evidence to prove recklessness. On this point *Octane Fitness* is again instructive. There too the Federal Circuit had adopted a clear and convincing standard of proof, for awards of attorney's fees under §285 of the Patent Act. Because that provision supplied no basis for imposing such a heightened standard of proof, we rejected it. See *Octane Fitness*, 572 U.S., at ___. We do so here as well. Like §285, §284 "imposes no specific evidentiary burden, much less such a high one." *Ibid.* And the fact that Congress expressly erected a higher standard of proof elsewhere in the Patent Act, *see* 35 U.S.C. §273(b), but not in §284, is telling. Furthermore, nothing in historical practice supports a heightened standard. As we explained in *Octane Fitness*,

---

* Respondents invoke a footnote in *Safeco* where we explained that in considering whether there had been a knowing or reckless violation of the Fair Credit Reporting Act, a showing of bad faith was not relevant absent a showing of objective recklessness. *See* 551 U.S., at 70, n. 20. But our precedents make clear that "bad-faith infringement" *is* an independent basis for enhancing patent damages. *Aro Mfg. Co.* v. *Convertible Top Replacement Co.*, 377 U.S. 476, 508 (1964); *see supra*, at 2–5, 9–10; *see also Safeco*, 551 U.S., at 57 (noting that "'willfully' is a word of many meanings whose construction is often dependent on the context in which it appears" (some internal quotation marks omitted)).

"patent-infringement litigation has always been governed by a preponderance of the evidence standard." 572 U.S., at ___. Enhanced damages are no exception.

3

Finally, because we eschew any rigid formula for awarding enhanced damages under §284, we likewise reject the Federal Circuit's tripartite framework for appellate review. In *Highmark Inc.* v. *Allcare Health Management System, Inc.*, 572 U.S. ___ (2014), we built on our *Octane Fitness* holding to reject a similar multipart standard of review. Because *Octane Fitness* confirmed district court discretion to award attorney fees, we concluded that such decisions should be reviewed for abuse of discretion. *Highmark*, 572 U.S., at ___.

The same conclusion follows naturally from our holding here. Section 284 gives district courts discretion in meting out enhanced damages. It "commits the determination" whether enhanced damages are appropriate "to the discretion of the district court" and "that decision is to be reviewed on appeal for abuse of discretion." *Id.*, at ___.

That standard allows for review of district court decisions informed by "the considerations we have identified." *Octane Fitness*, 572 U.S., at ___. The appellate review framework adopted by the Federal Circuit reflects a concern that district courts may award enhanced damages too readily, and distort the balance between the protection of patent rights and the interest in technological innovation. Nearly two centuries of exercising discretion in awarding enhanced damages in patent cases, however, has given substance to the notion that there are limits to that discretion. The Federal Circuit should review such exercises of discretion in light of the longstanding considerations we have identified as having guided both Congress and the courts.

III

. . . . [R]espondents' main argument for retaining the *Seagate* test comes down to a matter of policy. Respondents and their *amici* are concerned that allowing district courts unlimited discretion to award up to treble damages in infringement cases will impede innovation as companies steer well clear of any possible interference with patent rights. They also worry that the ready availability of such damages will embolden "trolls." Trolls, in the patois of the patent community, are entities that hold patents for the primary purpose of enforcing them against alleged infringers, often exacting outsized licensing fees on threat of litigation.

Respondents are correct that patent law reflects "a careful balance between the need to promote innovation" through patent protection, and the importance of facilitating the "imitation and refinement through imitation" that are "necessary to invention itself and the very lifeblood of a competitive economy." *Bonito Boats, Inc.* v. *Thunder Craft Boats, Inc.*, 489 U.S. 141, 146 (1989). That balance can indeed be disrupted if enhanced damages are awarded in garden-variety cases. As we have explained, however, they should not be. The seriousness of respondents' policy concerns cannot justify imposing an artificial construct such as the *Seagate* test on the discretion conferred under §284. . . .

COMMENTS AND QUESTIONS

1. What types of conduct fall within the enhanced damages ambit? Is willfulness still required? Could other conduct give rise to an enhancement? What kinds of conduct?

Justice Breyer, joined by Justices Alito and Kennedy, concurred in the unanimous *Halo* decision but wrote separately to emphasize that "willful misconduct" does "not mean that a court may award enhanced damages simply because the evidence shows that the infringer knew about the patent and nothing more." They expressed the view that the Court's opinion should be read to mean that enhanced damages are appropriate "only in egregious cases"—characterized by bad-faith infringement, malicious piracy, or objective recklessness. They note that the owner of a small firm, or a scientist, engineer, or technician working there, could, "without being 'wanton' or 'reckless,' reasonably determine that its product does not infringe a particular patent, or that that patent is probably invalid." They further highlight that the proliferation of demand letters by patent assertion entities ought not to impose undue investigative burdens on the many businesses, hospitals, and individuals targeted.

2. The *Seagate* two-part test reduced the need for companies to obtain opinion letters because they could rely instead on a plausible, although ultimately unsuccessful, legal defense. Does *Halo* make such letters more important? Justice Breyer sought to downplay the need for such letters, but is that a prudent approach?

3. The *Seagate* "objective reasonableness" prong afforded district judges greater leeway to reject enhanced damages at the summary judgment stage and to limit wide-ranging discovery into the defendant's intent. Will *Halo* re-open that discovery Pandora's Box and make it difficult to resolve willfulness prior to trial? Might a hasty or unduly cautious email create treble exposure?

4. Who decides the enhanced damages question—judge or jury? Before *Halo*, juries tended to decide the second part of the *Seagate* test–good faith belief–but district courts determined both the objective merit of the defense and whether willfulness, if proven, justified treble damages. The *Halo* Court speaks of the district court's discretion. Does that suggest that the court rather than the jury should decide willfulness?

5. A common critique of willfulness doctrine pre-*Seagate* was that it created a disincentive for research and development staff to read competitors' patents. (It was thought that this practice would establish a company's knowledge of a patented invention, leading to a finding of willful infringement and the attendant increased damages.) *See, e.g.*, Note, *The Disclosure Function of the Patent System (Or Lack Thereof)*, 118 HARV. L. REV. 2007 (2005). *Seagate* reduced that concern. Does *Halo* exacerbate it?

6. Do we need a doctrine of willful infringement? Is there a risk that without some sort of damages enhancement infringers will just copy patented inventions with impunity, secure in the knowledge that they will only have to pay a reasonable royalty? Or does the risk of being enjoined mid-production serve as an adequate deterrent? *See* generally ROGER D. BLAIR & THOMAS F. COTTER, INTELLECTUAL PROPERTY: ECONOMIC AND LEGAL DIMENSIONS OF RIGHTS AND REMEDIES 42-66 (2005) (modeling compensation and deterrence in patent cases, and discussing doctrinal implications).

4. Attorneys' Fees

Section 285 provides that the "court in exceptional cases may award reasonable attorney fees to the prevailing party." The Supreme Court has interpreted this standard to afford district judges discretion to award attorney fees where it finds that the case "simply . . . stands out from others with respect to the substantive strength of a party's litigating position . . . or the unreasonable manner in which the case was litigated." *Octane Fitness LLC v. Icon Health & Fitness Inc.*, 134 S.Ct. 1749, 1755-76 (2014) (rejecting the Federal Circuit's rule that a defendant may only be awarded fees where it demonstrates that the patentee litigated with subjective bad faith and that the suit was objectively baseless). The Court directed district courts to consider the totality of the circumstances. Such determinations are reviewable for abuse of discretion. *Highmark Inc. v. Allcare Health Mgmt. Sys., Inc.*, 134 S.Ct. 1744, 1749 (2014).

H. DESIGN PATENTS

In 1842, Congress extended patent protection to "new and original designs for articles of manufacture." The intent of the statute was to "give encouragement to the decorative arts." *Gorham Mfg. Co. v. White*, 81 U.S. (14 Wall.) 511, 524-25 (1871). Appearance, rather than utility, is the crucial factor for consideration in design patent protection. A design may consist of surface ornamentation, configuration, or a combination of both. The Design Patent Act, which was codified in 35 U.S.C. §§171-73, allows an applicant to obtain a design patent for "any new, original and ornamental design for an article of manufacture" and provides that most provisions relating to patents for inventions also apply to design patents. §171. Design patents now receive a 15-year patent term.[14]

1. Requirements for Patentability

A design is patentable if it meets the patent requirements of novelty, originality, and nonobviousness. Additionally, a design must be ornamental, and functional considerations must not dictate its form. The Patent and Trademark Office defines a design as "the visual characteristics or aspects displayed by the object. It is the

---

[14] Patents issued from design applications filed before May 13, 2015 have a 14 year term from the date of grant.

appearance presented by the object which creates a visual impact upon the mind of the observer." U.S. PATENT AND TRADEMARK OFFICE, MANUAL OF PATENT EXAMINING PROCEDURE, §1502 (5th ed. 1988).

An "article of manufacture" has been broadly defined to include silverware, *Gorham Mfg. Co. v. White*, 81 U.S. (14 Wall.) 511 (1871); cement mixers, *In re Koehring*, 37 F.2d 421 (C.C.P.A. 1930); furniture, *In re Rosen*, 673 F.2d 388 (C.C.P.A. 1982); and containers for liquids, *Unette Corp. v. Unit Pack Co.*, 785 F.2d 1026 (Fed. Cir. 1986). In *In re Hruby*, 373 F.2d 997, 1000 (C.C.P.A. 1967), the Court of Customs and Patent Appeals held that "a manufacture is anything 'made by the hands of man' from raw materials whether literally by hand or by machinery or by art" and found that a design created by the flow of water in a fountain was patentable. While the patented design must be embodied in an article of manufacture, a design patent may be obtained for only part of an article. *In re Zahn*, 617 F.2d 261 (C.C.P.A. 1980) (holding that the shank of a drill bit was patentable under §171). Thus the subject matter of a design patent is not limited to designs for discrete articles.

i. Claim Requirements

Like utility patents and unlike copyrights, design patents are examined and not merely registered. *See* USPTO, MANUAL OF PATENT EXAMINING PROCEDURE, part 1500 *et seq*. The examination is significantly less searching than for utility patents, however, and the overwhelming majority of design patent applications are approved. The §112 requirements of adequate disclosure and definite claiming also apply to design patents. *See In re Owens*, 710 F.3d 1362 (Fed. Cir. 2013). In the case of design patents, both disclosure and definiteness are accomplished through the drawings. Only one claim is permitted in design patent applications. This claim takes the form of "the ornamental design of the specified article as shown." Although only one claim is permitted, a design application may illustrate multiple embodiments of a design if they involve a single inventive concept. *See In re Rubenfield*, 270 F.2d 391 (C.C.P.A. 1959).

The USPTO requires an applicant to "designate the particular article" for which a design patent is sought, although the patent need not depict the article and can represent it generically (as in the case of surface ornamentation). The degree of specificity with which an applicant must describe and claim the article is not straightforward. For designs of "an ornament, impression, print or picture to be applied to an article of manufacture," an applicant may make a broad claim to the use of the ornament on more than one article. *See In re Schnell*, 46 F.2d 203 (C.C.P.A. 1931). In this case, the applicant must teach the manner of applying the design to show reduction to practice. For designs that consist of a shape or configuration for an article of manufacture, the claim and specification must be narrower. *Id.*

Drawings must contain a "sufficient number of views to constitute a complete disclosure of the appearance of the design." 37 C.F.R. §1.152(a) (2014). If the drawings are insufficient, a patent may be declared invalid under §112. The solid lines of a drawing define the scope of the claimed invention. The dotted or dashed lines merely provide context; they do not limit the scope of the claimed design. The illustration below reflects a typical design patent:

US Patent No. D517,789 S

ii. Novelty

Novelty is established if no prior art shows exactly the same design. *OddzOn Prod., Inc. v. Just Toys, Inc.*, 122 F.3d 1396, 1404 (Fed. Cir. 1997). A design is novel if the "ordinary observer," viewing the new design as a whole, would consider it to be distinct from, rather than a modification of, an already existing design. *See, e.g., Clark Equip. Co. v. Keller*, 570 F.2d 778, 799 (8th Cir. 1978).

The claim is compared to the design disclosed in the allegedly anticipatory prior art reference, assuming that reference has qualified as prior art under the applicable provisions of §102. If the claimed design and the alleged prior art design are substantially the same, the alleged prior art design anticipates the claimed design. Designs are "substantially the same" when their resemblance is deceptive to the extent that it would induce the ordinary observer to purchase an article, supposing it to be the other. *Door-Master Corp. v. Yorktowne, Inc.*, 256 F.3d 1308, 1313 (Fed. Cir. 2001). Once identity is established, a prior design will anticipate even though it is an article of different use or is in a non-analogous art. *See In re Glavas*, 230 F. 2d 447, 450 (C.C.P.A. 1956).

The experimental use exception to the §102(b) "public use" and "on sale" bars has limited application to design patents. An ornamental design alone for an article of manufacture cannot qualify under the experimental use exception. *In re Mann*, 861 F.2d 1581 (Fed. Cir. 1988) ("obtaining the reactions of people to a design, whether they like it or not, is not experimentation"). However, where experimentation is directed to the functional features of an article, the use may fall within the experimental use exception. *See Tone Bros., Inc. v. Sysco Corp.*, 28 F.3d 1192 (Fed. Cir. 1994).

iii.   Nonobviousness

Like utility patents, design patents must also meet the non-obviousness requirement of §103. *See Titan Tire Corp. v. Case New Holland, Inc.*, 566 F.3d 1372, 1380 (Fed. Cir. 2009). Challenges to a design patent under §103 may include evidence from one skilled in the art regarding prior art references and whether and how those references would be combined to form a design that compares to the claimed design. The test for obviousness is different from the test for infringement and anticipation. Whereas the comparison of the claimed design to an accused article or potentially anticipatory prior art is seen through the eyes of the "ordinary observer," the comparison of the claimed design to the prior art for obviousness purposes is seen through the eyes of the "ordinary designer." *High Point Design LLC v. Buyers Direct, Inc.*, 730 F. 3d 1301, 1311 (Fed. Cir. 2013); *Apple, Inc. v. Samsung Elecs. Co.*, 678 F.3d 1314, 1324 (Fed. Cir. 2012) ("In addressing a claim of obviousness in a design patent, the ultimate inquiry is whether the claimed design would have been obvious to a designer of ordinary skill who designs articles of the type involved.").

Federal Circuit decisions set forth a two-step process for the obviousness inquiry, which includes a "primary reference" requirement. In the first step, one must find a single prior art reference that has design characteristics "basically the same as the claimed design" (the "primary reference"). In the second step, "other references may be used to modify it to create a design that has the same overall visual appearance as the claimed design." *High Point*, 730 F. 3d at 1311 (quoting *Durling v. Spectrum Furniture Co.*, 101 F.3d 100, 103 (Fed. Cir. 1996)) (internal quotations omitted).

The pertinent references sought to be combined to show obviousness need not be analogous arts in the mechanical sense, but must be so related that the "appearance of certain ornamental features in one would suggest the application of those features to another." *In re Glavas*, 230 F.2d 447 (C.C.P.A. 1956).

iv.   Ornamentality/Non-functionality

A patentable design must be ornamental, creating a more pleasing appearance. To satisfy the requirement of ornamentality, a design "must be the product of aesthetic skill and artistic conception." *Blisscraft of Hollywood v. United Plastics Co.*, 294 F.2d 694, 696 (2d Cir. 1964). Articles outside the realm of traditional "art" have met this requirement. *See In re Koehring*, 37 F.2d 421, 422 (C.C.P.A. 1930) (determining a design for a cement mixer to be ornamental because it "possessed more grace and pleasing appearance" than prior art). Some cases have denied patentability to designs which are concealed during the normal use of an object because ornamentality requires the design is visible during the object's normal and intended use.

Design patents protect only ornamental or "non-functional" designs. The design of an article is deemed to be "functional" when the appearance is dictated by the use or purpose of the article. *See L.A. Gear, Inc. v. Thom McAn Shoe Co.*, 988 F.2d 1117, 1123 (Fed. Cir. 1993); *In re Carletti*, 328 F.2d 1020, 1022 (C.C.P.A. 1964) (when a configuration is the result of functional considerations only, the resulting design is not patentable as an ornamental design—even where the result is "pleasing to look upon"). A patent for a design that is primarily functional rather than ornamental is invalid. *See Richardson v. Stanley Works, Inc.*, 597 F.3d 1288, 1293-94 (Fed. Cir. 2010). But the test for functionality is different, and far narrower, than the corresponding tests in copyright and trademark law. A design may be protected even though it serves a function as long as it is not dictated by that function. *See* Michael Risch, *Functionality and Graphical User Interface Design Patents*, 17 STAN. TECH. L. REV. 53 (2013); Mark P. McKenna & Katherine J. Strandburg, *Progress and Competition in Design*, 17 STAN. TECH. L. REV. 1 (2013).

While a design may be part of an object or device that has a function (e.g., a hammer with specific design), the design aspect itself must be non-functional. The determination of whether the patented design is dictated by the function of the article ultimately rests on an analysis of its overall appearance. *See PHG Techs., LLC, v. St. John Cos.*, 469 F.3d 1361, 1366 (Fed. Cir. 2006). In determining whether a design feature is purely functional, courts consider factors such as: (i) whether there are alternate ways to design the article to achieve the same function, *see Seiko Epson Corp. v. Nu-Kote Int'l, Inc.*, 190 F.3d 1360, 1368 (Fed. Cir. 1999); (ii) the existence of any concomitant utility patents, *see Traffix Devices, Inc. v. Mktg. Displays, Inc.*, 532 U.S. 23, 29 (2001) ("A utility patent is strong evidence that the features therein claimed are functional."); (iii) whether the design is aesthetically pleasing and not dictated by function alone, *see Bonito Boats, Inc. v. Thunder Craft Boats, Inc.*, 489 U.S. 141, 148 (1989); (iv) whether alternative designs would adversely affect the utility of the article, *see PHG Techs.*, 469 F.3d at 1366; and (v) whether there are any elements in the design or an overall appearance clearly not dictated by function, *see id.*

2. Infringement

Egyptian Goddess, Inc. v. Swisa, Inc.
United States Court of Appeals for the Federal Circuit
542 F.3d 665 (Fed. Cir. 2008) (en banc)

BRYSON, Circuit Judge.

We granted rehearing en banc in this design patent case to address the appropriate legal standard to be used in assessing claims of design patent infringement.

Appellant Egyptian Goddess, Inc., ("EGI") brought this action . . . alleging that Swisa, Inc., had infringed EGI's U.S. Design Patent No. 467,389 ("the '389 patent"). The patent claimed a design for a nail buffer, consisting of a rectangular, hollow tube having a generally square cross-section and featuring buffer surfaces on three of its four sides. Swisa's accused product consists of a rectangular, hollow tube having a square cross-section, but featuring buffer surfaces on all four of its sides.

The district court first issued an order construing the claim of the '389 patent. In so doing, the district court sought to describe in words the design set forth in Figure 1 of the patent, which is depicted below:

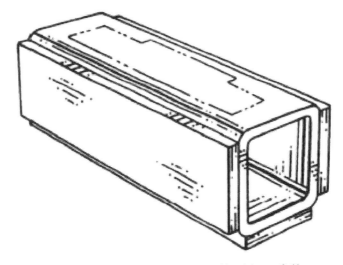

Upon study of the claimed design, the court described it as follows:

A hollow tubular frame of generally square cross section, where the square has sides of length S, the frame has a length of approximately 3S, and the frame has a thickness of approximately $T = 0.1S$; the corners of the cross section are rounded, with the outer corner of the cross section rounded on a 90 degree radius of approximately 1.25T, and the inner corner of the cross section rounded on a 90 degree radius of approximately 0.25T; and with rectangular abrasive pads of thickness T affixed to three of the sides of the frame, covering the flat portion of the sides while leaving the curved radius uncovered, with the fourth side of the frame bare.

In the same order, the district court ruled that "Swisa has not shown that the appearance of the Buffer Patent is dictated by its utilitarian purpose." The court therefore held that the patent is not invalid on the ground that the design was governed solely by function.

Swisa then moved for summary judgment of noninfringement. The district court granted the motion. Citing precedent of this court, the district court stated that the plaintiff in a design patent case must prove both (1) that the accused device is "substantially similar" to the claimed design under what is referred to as the "ordinary observer" test, and (2) that the accused device contains "substantially the same points of novelty that distinguished the patented design from the prior art. After comparing the claimed design and the accused product, the court held that Swisa's allegedly infringing product did not incorporate the "point of novelty" of the '389 patent, which the court identified as "a fourth, bare side to the buffer."

The district court noted that the parties disagreed as to the points of novelty in the '389 patent. EGI identified four elements in its design, and for each element it identified prior art that did not embody that element. EGI therefore contended that the point of novelty of the '389 patent is the combination of those four elements. The district court, however, declined to address the question whether the point of novelty could be found in the combination of elements not present in various prior art references, because the court found that a single prior art reference, United States Design Patent No. 416,648 ("the Nailco patent"), contained all but one of the elements of the '389 design. The court described the Nailco Patent as disclosing "a nail buffer with an open and hollow body, raised rectangular pads, and open corners." The only element of the '389 patent design that was not present in the Nailco patent, according to the district court, was "the addition of the fourth side without a pad, thereby transforming the equilateral triangular cross-section into a square." Because the Swisa product does not incorporate the point of novelty of the '389 patent—a fourth side without a pad—the court concluded that there was no infringement.

EGI appealed, and a panel of this court affirmed. . . .

This court granted rehearing en banc and asked the parties to address several questions, including whether the "point of novelty" test should continue to be used as a test for infringement of a design patent; whether the court should adopt the "non-trivial advance test" as a means of determining whether a particular design feature qualifies as a point of novelty; how the point of novelty test should be administered, particularly when numerous features of the design differ from certain prior art designs; and whether district courts should perform formal claim construction in design patent cases.

I

The starting point for any discussion of the law of design patents is the Supreme Court's decision in *Gorham Co. v. White*, 14 Wall. 511 (1871). That case involved a design patent for the handles of tablespoons and forks. In its analysis of claim infringement, the Court stated that the test of identity of design "must be sameness of appearance, and mere difference of lines in the drawing or sketch ... or slight variances in configuration ... will not destroy the substantial identity." *Id.* at 526–27. Identity of appearance, the Court explained, or "sameness of effect upon the eye, is the main test of substantial identity of design"; the two need not be the same "to the eye of an expert," because if that were the test, "[t]here never could be piracy of a patented design, for human ingenuity has never yet produced a design, in all its details, exactly like another, so like, that an expert could not distinguish them." *Id.* at 527.

The Gorham Court then set forth the test that has been cited in many subsequent cases: "[I]f, in the eye of an ordinary observer, giving such attention as a purchaser usually gives, two designs are substantially the same, if the resemblance is such as to deceive such an observer, inducing him to purchase one supposing it to be the other, the first one patented is infringed by the other." 81 U.S. at 528. In the case before it, the Court concluded that "whatever differences there may be between the plaintiffs' design and those of the defendant in details of ornament, they are still the same in general appearance and effect, so much alike that in the market and with purchasers they would pass for the same thing—so much alike that even persons in the trade would be in danger of being deceived." *Id.* at 531.

Since the decision in Gorham, the test articulated by the Court in that case has been referred to as the "ordinary observer" test and has been recognized by lower courts, including both of this court's predecessors, as the proper standard for determining design patent infringement. . . .

II

EGI argues that this court should no longer recognize the point of novelty test as a second part of the test for design patent infringement, distinct from the ordinary observer test established in Gorham. Instead of requiring the fact-finder to identify one or more points of novelty in the patented design and then determining whether the accused design has appropriated some or all of those points of novelty, EGI contends that the ordinary observer test can fulfill the purposes for which the point of novelty test was designed, but with less risk of confusion. As long as the ordinary observer test focuses on the "appearance that distinguishes the patented design from the prior art," EGI contends that it will enable the fact-finder to address the proper inquiry, i.e., whether an ordinary observer, familiar with the prior art, would be deceived into thinking that the accused design was the same as the patented design. Relatedly, EGI argues that if the ordinary observer test is performed from the perspective of an ordinary observer who is familiar with the prior art, there is no need for a separate "non-trivial advance" test, because the attention of an ordinary observer familiar with prior art designs will naturally be drawn to the features of the claimed and accused designs that render them distinct from the prior art.

Several of the amici make essentially the same point, referring to the proper approach as calling for a three-way visual comparison between the patented design, the accused design, and the closest prior art. . . .

Swisa counters that this court may not, and should not, abandon the point of novelty test. According to Swisa, the point of novelty test was adopted by the Supreme Court in *Smith v. Whitman Saddle Co.*, 148 U.S. 674 (1893). . . .

We disagree with Swisa's submission. A close reading of Whitman Saddle and subsequent authorities indicates that the Supreme Court did not adopt a separate point of novelty test for design patent infringement cases. In fact, a study of the development of design patent law in the years after Gorham shows that the point of novelty test, in its current form, is of quite recent vintage. After a review of those authorities, which we examine in some detail below, we conclude that the point of novelty test, as a second and free-standing requirement for proof of design patent infringement, is inconsistent with the ordinary observer test laid down in *Gorham*, is not mandated by *Whitman Saddle* or precedent from other courts, and is not needed to protect against unduly broad assertions of design patent rights. . . .

[T]his court has cited *Litton Systems* for the proposition that the point of novelty test is separate from the ordinary observer test and requires the patentee to point out the point of novelty in the claimed design that has been appropriated by the accused design. We think, however, that Litton and the predecessor cases on which it relied are more properly read as applying a version of the ordinary observer test in which the ordinary observer is deemed to view the differences between the patented design and the accused product in the context of the prior art. When the differences between the claimed and accused design are viewed in light of the prior art, the attention of the hypothetical ordinary observer will be drawn to those aspects of the claimed design that differ from the prior art. And when the claimed design is close to the prior art designs, small differences between the accused design and the claimed design are likely to be important to the eye of the hypothetical ordinary observer. It was for that reason that the Supreme Court in *Whitman Saddle* focused on the one feature of the patented saddle design that departed from the prior art—the sharp drop at the rear of the pommel. To an observer familiar with the multitude of prior art saddle designs, including the design incorporating the Granger pommel and the Jenifer cantle, "an addition frequently made," 148 U.S. at 682, the sharp drop at the rear of the pommel would be important to the overall appearance of the design and would serve to distinguish the accused design, which did not possess that feature, from the claimed design.. . .

Not only is this approach consistent with the precedents discussed above, but it makes sense as a matter of logic as well. Particularly in close cases, it can be difficult to answer the question whether one thing is like another without being given a frame of reference. The context in which the claimed and accused designs are compared, i.e., the background prior art, provides such a frame of reference and is therefore often useful in the process of comparison. Where the frame of reference consists of numerous similar prior art designs, those designs can highlight the distinctions between the claimed design and the accused design as viewed by the ordinary observer.

Applying the ordinary observer test with reference to prior art designs also avoids some of the problems created by the separate point of novelty test. One such problem is that the point of novelty test has proved difficult to apply in cases in which there are several different features that can be argued to be points of novelty in the claimed design. In such cases, the outcome of the case can turn on which of the several candidate points of novelty the court or fact-finder focuses on. The attention of the court may therefore be focused on whether the accused design has appropriated a single specified feature of the claimed design, rather than on the proper inquiry, i.e., whether the accused design has appropriated the claimed design as a whole.

In addition, the more novel the design, and the more points of novelty that are identified, the more opportunities there are for a defendant to argue that its design does not infringe because it does not copy all of the points of novelty, even though it may copy most of them and even though it may give the overall appearance of being identical to the claimed design. In such cases, a test that asks how an ordinary observer with knowledge of the prior art designs would view the differences between the claimed and accused designs is likely to produce results more in line with the purposes of design patent protection.

This court has characterized the purpose of the point of novelty test as being "to focus on those aspects of a design which render the design different from prior art designs." *Sun Hill Indus., Inc.*, 48 F.3d at 1197, quoting *Winner Int'l Corp. v. Wolo Mfg. Corp.*, 905 F.2d 375, 376 (Fed.Cir.1990). That purpose can be equally well served, however, by applying the ordinary observer test through the eyes of an observer familiar with the prior art. If the accused design has copied a particular feature of the claimed design that departs conspicuously from the prior art, the accused design is naturally more likely to be regarded as deceptively similar to the claimed design, and thus infringing. At the same time, unlike the point of novelty test, the ordinary observer test does not present the risk of assigning exaggerated importance to small differences between the claimed and accused designs relating to an insignificant feature simply because that feature can be characterized as a point of novelty.

This approach also has the advantage of avoiding the debate over the extent to which a combination of old design features can serve as a point of novelty under the point of novelty test. An ordinary observer, comparing the claimed and accused designs in light of the prior art, will attach importance to differences between the claimed design and the prior art depending on the overall effect of those differences on the design. If the claimed design consists of a combination of old features that creates an appearance deceptively similar to the accused design, even to an observer familiar with similar prior art designs, a finding of infringement would be justified. Otherwise, infringement would not be found.

One function that has been served by the point of novelty test, according to Swisa and its supporting amici, is to cabin unduly broad assertions of design patent scope by ensuring that a design that merely embodies or is substantially similar to prior art designs is not found to infringe. Again, however, we believe that the preferable way to achieve that purpose is to do so directly, by relying on the ordinary observer test, conducted in light of the prior art. Our rejection of the point of novelty test does not mean, of course, that the differences between the claimed design and prior art designs are irrelevant. To the contrary, examining the novel features of the claimed design can be an important component of the comparison of the claimed design with the accused design and the prior art. But the comparison of the designs, including the examination of any novel features, must be conducted as part of the ordinary observer test, not as part of a separate test focusing on particular points of novelty that are designated only in the course of litigation.

On the basis of the foregoing analysis, we hold that the "point of novelty" test should no longer be used in the analysis of a claim of design patent infringement. Because we reject the "point of novelty" test, we also do not adopt the "non-trivial advance" test, which is a refinement of the "point of novelty" test. Instead, in accordance with *Gorham* and subsequent decisions, we hold that the "ordinary observer" test should be the sole test for determining whether a design patent has been infringed. Under that test, as this court has sometimes described it, infringement will not be found unless the accused article "embod[ies] the patented design or any colorable imitation thereof." *Goodyear Tire & Rubber Co.*, 162 F.3d at 1116–17.

In some instances, the claimed design and the accused design will be sufficiently distinct that it will be clear without more that the patentee has not met its burden of proving the two designs would appear "substantially the same" to the ordinary observer, as required by Gorham. In other instances, when the claimed and accused designs are not plainly dissimilar, resolution of the question whether the ordinary observer would consider the two designs to be substantially the same will benefit from a comparison of the claimed and accused designs with the prior art, as in many of the cases discussed above and in the case at bar. Where there are many examples of similar prior art designs, as in a case such as *Whitman Saddle*, differences between the claimed and accused designs that might not be noticeable in the abstract can become significant to the hypothetical ordinary observer who is conversant with the prior art.

We emphasize that although the approach we adopt will frequently involve comparisons between the claimed design and the prior art, it is not a test for determining validity, but is designed solely as a test of infringement. Thus, as is always the case, the burden of proof as to infringement remains on the patentee. However, if the accused infringer elects to rely on the comparison prior art as part of its defense against the claim of infringement, the burden of production of that prior art is on the accused infringer. To be sure, we have stated that the burden to introduce prior art under the point of novelty test falls on the patentee. Under the ordinary observer test, however, it makes sense to impose the burden of production as to any comparison prior art on the accused infringer. The accused infringer is the party with the motivation to point out close prior art, and in particular to call to the court's attention the prior art that an ordinary observer is most likely to regard as highlighting the differences between the claimed and accused design. Regardless of whether the accused infringer elects to present prior art that it considers pertinent to the comparison between the claimed and accused design, however, the patentee bears the ultimate burden of proof to demonstrate infringement by a preponderance of the evidence. . . .

III

One of the issues raised by this court in its order granting en banc review was whether trial courts should conduct claim construction in design patent cases. While this court has held that trial courts have a duty to conduct claim construction in design patent cases, as in utility patent cases, the court has not prescribed any particular form that the claim construction must take. To the contrary, the court has recognized that design patents "typically are claimed as shown in drawings," and that claim construction "is adapted accordingly." *Arminak & Assocs., Inc.*, 501 F.3d at 1319. For that reason, this court has not required that the trial court attempt to provide a detailed verbal description of the claimed design, as is typically done in the case of utility patents. *See Contessa Food Prods., Inc.* [*v. Conagra, Inc.*, 282 F.3d 1370, 1377 (Fed.Cir.2002)] (approving district court's construction of the asserted claim as meaning "a tray of a certain design as shown in Figures 1–3").[1]

As the Supreme Court has recognized, a design is better represented by an illustration "than it could be by any description and a description would probably not be intelligible without the illustration." *Dobson v. Dornan*, 118 U.S. 10, 14 (1886). The Patent and Trademark Office has made the same observation. MANUAL OF PATENT EXAMINING PROCEDURE §1503.01 (8th ed. 2006) ("[A]s a rule the illustration in the drawing views is its own best description."). Given the recognized difficulties entailed in trying to describe a design in words, the preferable course ordinarily will be for a district court not to attempt to "construe" a design patent claim by providing a detailed verbal description of the claimed design.

With that said, it is important to emphasize that a district court's decision regarding the level of detail to be used in describing the claimed design is a matter within the court's discretion, and absent a showing of prejudice, the court's decision to issue a relatively detailed claim construction will not be reversible error. At the same time, it should be clear that the court is not obligated to issue a detailed verbal description of the design if it does not regard verbal elaboration as necessary or helpful. In addition, in deciding whether to attempt a verbal description of the claimed design, the court should recognize the risks entailed in such a description, such as the risk of placing undue emphasis on particular features of the design and the risk that a finder of fact will focus on each individual described feature in the verbal description rather than on the design as a whole. In this case, for example, the district court came up with a detailed verbal description of the claimed design. We see no inaccuracy in the court's description, and neither party has pointed to any prejudice resulting from the court's interpretation. Yet it is not clear that the considerable effort needed to fashion the verbal description contributed enough to the process of analyzing the case to justify the effort.

---

[1] This court has required that in determining obviousness, a district court must attempt to "translate [the] visual descriptions into words" in order to communicate the reasoning behind the court's decision and to enable "the parties and appellate courts TTT to discern the internal reasoning employed by the trial court." *Durling v. Spectrum Furniture Co.*, 101 F.3d 100, 102 (Fed.Cir.1996). Requiring such an explanation of a legal ruling as to invalidity is quite different from requiring an elaborate verbal claim construction to guide the finder of fact in conducting the infringement inquiry.

While it may be unwise to attempt a full description of the claimed design, a court may find it helpful to point out, either for a jury or in the case of a bench trial by way of describing the court's own analysis, various features of the claimed design as they relate to the accused design and the prior art. . . .

. . . We therefore leave the question of verbal characterization of the claimed designs to the discretion of trial judges, with the proviso that as a general matter, those courts should not treat the process of claim construction as requiring a detailed verbal description of the claimed design, as would typically be true in the case of utility patents.

IV

We now turn to the facts of this case. It is agreed that the general shape of the accused nail buffer at issue in this case is the same as that of the patented buffer design. The difference between the two is that the accused buffer has raised buffing pads on all four sides, while the patented buffer has buffing pads on only three sides. The two closest prior art nail buffers before the court were the Falley nail buffer, which has a solid, rectangular cross section with slightly raised buffers on all sides, and the Nailco patent, which shows a nail buffer design having a triangular shape and a hollow cross section, and in which raised buffing pads are located on all three sides. The four nail buffers are pictured below:

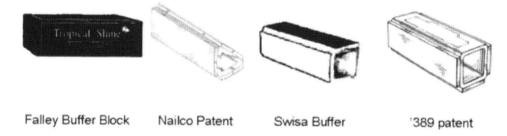

Falley Buffer Block   Nailco Patent   Swisa Buffer   '389 patent

The question before this court under the standard we have set forth above is whether an ordinary observer, familiar with the prior art Falley and Nailco designs, would be deceived into believing the Swisa buffer is the same as the patented buffer. EGI argues that such an observer would notice a difference between the prior art and the '389 patent, consisting of "the hollow tube that is square in cross section and that has raised pads with exposed gaps at the corners." To support that contention, EGI invokes the declaration of its expert witness, Kathleen Eaton. After viewing the patented, accused, and Nailco buffers, Ms. Eaton concluded that the patented and accused designs would "confuse an ordinary observer into purchasing the accused buffer thinking it to be the patented buffer design." She reached that conclusion, she explained, because "the substantially similar appearance [between the accused and patented designs] results from both designs having a hollow tube, square in cross section and rectangular in length, with multiple raised rectangular pads mounted on the sides, and that do not cover the corners of the tube." While recognizing that the accused buffer has pads on all four sides and that the claimed design has buffer pads on only three sides, she stated that "I do not believe that, to an ordinary observer and purchaser of nail buffers, the presence of one more buffer pad[s] greatly alters the ornamental effect and appearance of the whole design as compared to the whole patented design."

Swisa counters that the '389 patent closely tracks the design of the Nailco nail buffer, except that it "add[s] a fourth side without an abrasive pad, resulting in square ends." In light of the close prior art buffers, including a number having square cross-sections, Swisa argues that an ordinary observer would notice the difference between the claimed and accused designs. To support that contention, Swisa cites the declaration of its expert, Steve Falley. Mr. Falley addressed the differences among the prior art designs, the accused design, and patented design, and he concluded that

you could simply add to the Nailco Buffer a fourth side without an abrasive on it. This merely takes the Nailco Buffer to the block shape of the original Falley Buffer Block, while keeping the hollow aspect of the Nailco Buffer. As there had already been on the market for a long time 3–way buffer blocks that had no abrasive on one side, it was also obvious after the Nailco Buffer that you could have a three way hollow buffer that had four sides but with no abrasive on one side.

Mr. Falley added that "four-way" nail buffers having four different abrasive surfaces have been made since 1985, and that four-sided "buffer blocks" have been on the market since 1987. He pointed to catalogs showing three-sided and four-sided buffer blocks that have been offered for sale since at least 1994, and in light of his knowledge of the industry, he stated that the "number of sides with abrasive surface on them would be important to purchasers because it determines whether a buffer is a 'three way buffer' or a 'four way buffer.'" Accordingly, he concluded:

The difference between a buffer with abrasive on three sides—a "three-way buffer"—and a buffer with abrasive on four sides—a "four-way buffer"—is immediately apparent to any consumer used to buying nail buffers. Even if such a consumer did not have a preference for either three-way or four-way buffers (although they almost always do), they would at a glance be able to tell that a buffer with abrasive on only three sides had abrasive on three sides, and was a three-way buffer, while a buffer with abrasive on four sides had abrasive on all four sides, and was a four-way buffer. I cannot imagine consumers would buy buffers with abrasive on four sides thinking that they were buying buffers with abrasive on three sides.

The problem with Ms. Eaton's declaration is that she characterized the accused and patented designs as similar because they both have square cross sections and "multiple" raised buffer pads, without directly acknowledging that the patented design has three pads while the accused design has four, one on each side. She also failed to address the fact that the design of the Nailco patent is identical to the accused device except that the Nailco design has three sides rather than four. Thus, she could as easily have said that the Nailco buffer design "is like the accused design because both designs have a hollow tube, have multiple rectangular sides with raised rectangular pads mounted on each side that do not cover the corners of the tube," in which case the Nailco prior art buffer would be seen to closely resemble the accused design. Nothing about Ms. Eaton's declaration explains why an ordinary observer would regard the accused design as being closer to the claimed design than to the Nailco prior art patent. In fact, Ms. Eaton's reference to the prior art buffers is limited to the single, and conclusory, comment that an ordinary observer and purchaser of nail buffers would consider the patented design and the accused buffer to be substantially similar, "particularly in light of other nail buffers, such as a solid block buffer and the hollow triangular Nailco buffer."

In light of the similarity of the prior art buffers to the accused buffer, we conclude that no reasonable fact-finder could find that EGI met its burden of showing, by a preponderance of the evidence, that an ordinary observer, taking into account the prior art, would believe the accused design to be the same as the patented design. In concluding that a reasonable fact-finder could not find infringement in this case, we reach the same conclusion that the district court reached, and for many of the same reasons. Although we do so by using the ordinary observer test as informed by the prior art, rather than by applying the point of novelty test, our analysis largely tracks that of the district court. After analyzing the Nailco patent and the claimed design, as they related to the accused design, the district court concluded that "in the context of nail buffers, a fourth side without a pad is not substantially the same as a fourth side with a pad." While the district court focused on the differences in the particular feature at issue rather than the effect of those differences on the appearance of the design as a whole, we are satisfied that the difference on which the district court focused is important, viewed in the context of the prior art.. . .

AFFIRMED.

COMMENTS AND QUESTIONS

1. *Point of Novelty.* The court dismissed the point of novelty inquiry. Does that make sense to you? Consider the following objection to *Egyptian Goddess*:

[S]ubsequent Federal Circuit cases have used Egyptian Goddess as precedent in concluding that point of novelty is no longer the test for the invalidity of a design patent either.

Think about this for a minute. It is no longer the law that the defendant must incorporate the very thing that makes the patented invention patentable. As long as an ordinary observer would confuse the two products, the fact that that confusion arises from similarities that already exist in the prior art doesn't defeat a finding of infringement. It might or might not create a defense that the patent is invalid for anticipation, though again that seems to depend on what an ordinary observer would think when comparing the patented design and the prior art. Translated for a moment into terms of utility patents, it is as though we granted a patent on a car having an intermittent windshield wiper as the novel feature and then allowed the patentee to sue a car maker that didn't include that feature because the cars otherwise had the same elements. That can't possibly be the right rule.

. . . [O]ne reasonable reading of the case is that the court intended not to make the point of novelty irrelevant but simply to change the burden of proof on whether the defendant appropriated the novelty of the patentee's invention. . . . But if avoiding burden-shifting was the court's goal, it didn't do a very good job of achieving it. Whatever the legal standard, we don't want patentees suing defendants who do no more than practice the prior art. Such suits can't succeed in utility patent law because of the requirement that each element be present in the accused device. If the defendant is merely practicing the prior art and the patent is construed so broadly that it covers what the defendant is doing, the patent will be invalid. So to infringe a utility patent, the defendant must include the thing that makes the invention patentable. But after Egyptian Goddess, there is no longer such a requirement in design patent law. A design patent can now be infringed even by a product that lacks the new feature encompassed by the patent as long as an ordinary observer would think the two were substantially the same.

Mark A. Lemley, *Point of Novelty*, 105 Nw. U. L. Rev. 1253, 1271-72 (2012).

2. *Claim Construction.* How does claim construction of design patents compare with claim construction of utility patent claims? Does it make sense to try to compare three-dimensional objects via verbal descriptions of them?

3. *Interplay of Infringement, Nonobviousness, and Functionality Analysis.* Is it possible to conduct the infringement comparison without considering originality and functionality? To what extent does the "three-way" test incorporate these considerations? We will revisit these issues when we get to copyright and trademark infringement analysis. We note here that copyright law filters out the unprotectible elements before comparing the protected and allegedly infringing work. In addition, both copyright and trademark law carefully separate the functional features of the sculptural or functional work. Would such an approach make sense for design patent law?

3. Remedies

i. *Injunctive Relief*

A design patent plaintiff must satisfy the *eBay* test for preliminary or permanent injunctive relief, just as in a utility patent case. Because the analysis focuses on the *ornamental design* depicted in the patent, the patentee must make a slightly different factual showing with respect to the first *eBay* factor, irreparable injury: the design patentee must show "some causal nexus between" the defendant's *design* and the plaintiff's alleged injury. *Apple, Inc. v. Samsung Elecs. Co.*, 678 F.3d 1314, 1324 (Fed. Cir. 2012). It also is possible to demonstrate irreparable harm by showing "design dilution," meaning that the presence of similar substitutes diminishes the value of the patented design. *Id.* at 1325 (noting, however, that the lower court properly had not found design dilution in the case at bar).

ii. Damages

There is a special additional remedy available to design patentees:

> Whoever during the term of a patent for a design, without license of the owner, (1) applies the patented design, or any colorable imitation thereof, to any article of manufacture for the purpose of sale, or (2) sells or exposes for sale any article of manufacture to which such design or colorable imitation has been applied shall be liable to the owner to the extent of his *total* profit, but not less than $250, recoverable in any United States district court having jurisdiction of the parties.

> Nothing in this section shall prevent, lessen, or impeach any other remedy which an owner of an infringed patent has under the provisions of this title, but he shall not twice recover the profit made from the infringement.

§289 (emphasis added). Thus, a design patent owner can obtain the infringer's *total* profits for sale of an article to which the infringing design has been applied, but no less than $250. *See Apple Inc. v. Samsung Electronics Co., Ltd.*, 786 F.3d 983 (Fed. Cir. 2015) (rejecting contention that §289 incorporates an apportionment requirement under basic causation principles); *see also Schnadig Corp. v. Gaines Mfg. Co.*, 620 F.2d 1166, 1171 (6th Cir.1980).

To establish profits under §289, the patentee need only demonstrate the defendant's total sales. The defendant typically then demonstrates what portion of those sales is not attributable to the infringing design. Importantly, §289(2) applies to any entity that "sells or exposes for sale any article of manufacture to which such design or colorable imitation has been applied." This means that distributors and retailers can be liable for *their* total profit, which likely far exceeds the manufacturer's total profit. Thus, design patent cases often give rise to indemnity disputes between manufacturers and retailers, because the possible total exposure for accused items with significant retail markups can easily surpass the manufacturer's total revenue, to say nothing of its total profit.

While §289 is an additional remedy available to design patent holders, a design patentee cannot "twice recover" an infringer's profits. *See* §289 ("Nothing in this section shall prevent, lessen, or impeach any other remedy which an owner of an infringed patent has under the provisions of this title, but he shall not twice recover the profit made from the infringement."). For example, a patentee is not entitled to both a reasonable royalty *and* the infringer's profits. *See Catalina Lighting, Inc. v. Lamps*

Plus, Inc., 295 F.3d 1277, 1291 (Fed. Cir. 2002). Similarly, when a utility patent and a design patent are asserted against the same accused product, a patentee can only recover damages for the single infringing act. *See id.* at 1292.

COMMENTS AND QUESTIONS

1. *Apportioning Damages*. For most of the history of design patents, the articles of manufacture protected were generic products with decorative ornamentation. Many of the early design patterns covered area rugs and cast iron radiators and stoves. The ornamental design is what separated products in the marketplace. By contrast, some modern design patents cover complex, multi-component, technological goods, such as smartphones. Does it make sense to award the "total profit" for infringing articles? *See* Mark A. Lemley, *A Rational System of Design Patent Remedies*, 17 STAN. TECH. L. REV. 219 (2013) (arguing for reform of §289 to allow for apportionment). Note however that even though products such as mobile phones involve many components, and many design elements, the overall impression of the product is still largely a function of its design. Thus even if some form of apportionment is reinstated, the value of design elements may prove to be substantial. One trade group, for example, named Apple Computer the top design shop in the U.S. over the past 50 years. *See* http://www.dezeen.com/2012/09/20/apple-named-best-design-studio-of-past-50-years-at-one-off-dad-awards/. For this reason, some commentators believe that the traditional "total profits" rule of §289 might still make sense. *See* Jason J. Du Mont & Mark D. Janis, *The Origins of American Design Patent Protection*, 88 IND. L.J. 837 (2013).

The Supreme Court granted certiorari in 2016 to consider this issue.

PROBLEM

Problem III-19. Apple Corp. obtained US D504,889 S on March 17, 2004 on an "Electronic Device."

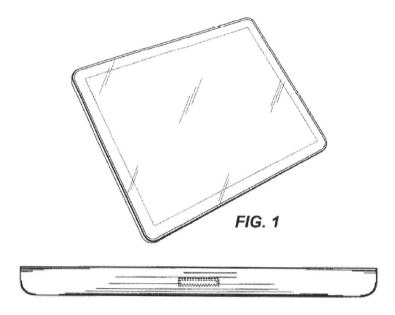

FIG. 1

FIG. 8

Samsung has entered the electronic tablet marketplace with a similar looking device.

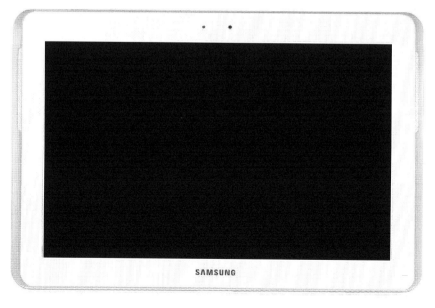

We have discovered the following prior art references. The 1994 Fidler tablet is a tablet newspaper reader.

In 2002, Compaq introduced the TC1000 tablet.

Can Apple could succeed in a design patent infringement against Samsung? If so, what remedies could it obtain?

I. INTERNATIONAL PATENT LAW

To obtain international protection for patented technology, lawyers and businesspeople must ultimately rely on the domestic patent law of each country. In two respects, however, international treaties do come into play. First, a number of international conventions streamline the procedures under which patents originating outside the host country are prosecuted. Second, certain international treaties provide a uniform substantive floor of protection, a minimum set of rights below which treaty signatories must not fall in conferring patents. Chief among these is the Trade-Related Aspects of Intellectual Property (TRIPs) Agreement, part of the 1994 Uruguay Round of GATT revisions, which are discussed later in this section.

1. Procedural Rules

The most important set of international procedural rules for patentees involve filing and priority dates. To understand them, however, one must first recognize that in practice they interact with elements of each country's domestic law. Recall, in this regard, the crucial divergence between U.S. and foreign priority rules. Until March 15, 2013, the U.S. judged novelty based on the complex 1952 Act first-to-invent regime. Although those rules still apply to applications files up until that date, the U.S. has moved to a first-to-file system, although it uses a unique grace period. All other countries, with trivial exceptions, establish priority based on a "first-to-file" system. If an inventor has an interest in securing patent protection overseas—whether in addition to U.S. protection or in place of it—he or she must file there *as soon after invention as possible.*

i. *Coordinating International Prosecution*

Patent lawyers face two problems in coordinating the prosecution of a series of national patents. First, a common priority date must be obtained to ensure that protection will be uniform and unaffected by prior art published (or otherwise having an effective date) before one or more of the national patent applications. Also, a common date will ensure that prosecution of a patent in country *A* does not somehow compromise the patentability of the invention in Country *B.* Second, the patent lawyer has to deal with the logistics of international protection; she must oversee multiple filings in diverse languages in numerous countries. The wide variations in national practices and the high cost of conducting a large-scale application barrage make multiple filings one of the more challenging professional tasks in patent law.

Fortunately, two international agreements make these tasks a bit more tolerable. First is the Paris Convention, a longstanding international organization created by treaty in 1886 whose primary function is to guarantee a uniform worldwide priority date across all member countries. An applicant may file in any member country of the Convention up to one year after an initial (typically home-country) filing, without losing the priority date of the initial filing. (This treatment is provided under United

States law in 35 U.S.C. §119.) The second international agreement is the Patent Cooperation Treaty (PCT), which streamlines the filing of multiple national patent applications. Each agreement in its own way is an indispensable tool of the patent trade. Although detailed discussion of the agreements would take up too much room for this volume, a few words about the essential features of each is in order.

ii.   The Paris Convention

The Paris Convention was signed in 1883, a product of the first true "internationalization" wave in the field of patent law. Paris Convention for the Protection of Industrial Property, as last revised, July 14, 1967, 21 U.S.T. 1583, T.I.A.S. No. 6295, 828 U.N.T.S. 305 (the last revision, sometimes referred to as the "Stockholm" revision, entered into force April 26, 1970). Its primary function is to define a common priority date so that one may file an application in one member state and have the benefit of that same filing date when filing later in another member state. One purpose of this is to prevent interlopers from copying patents applied for or issued in one state and claiming them as their own in another, before the legitimate owner has time to file in the other country.

The key provision in the Convention as regards priority is Article 4. The relevant portions read as follows:

Article 4

A(1) Any person who has duly filed an application for a patent, or for the registration of a utility model, or of an industrial design, or of a trademark, in one of the countries of the Union, or his successor in title, shall enjoy, for the purpose of filing in the other countries, a right of priority in the periods hereinafter fixed.

(2) Any filing that is equivalent to a regular national filing under the domestic legislation of any country of the Union or under bilateral or multilateral treaties concluded between countries of the Union shall be recognized as giving rise to the right of priority.

(3) By a regular national filing is meant any filing that is adequate to establish the date on which the application was filed in the country concerned, whatever may be the subsequent fate of the application.

B. Consequently, any subsequent filing in any of the other countries of the Union before the expiration of the periods referred to above shall not be invalidated by reason of any acts accomplished in the interval, in particular, another filing, the publication or exploitation of the invention, the putting on sale of copies of the design, or the use of the mark, and such acts cannot give rise to any third-party right or any right of personal possession. Rights acquired by third parties before the date of the first application that serves as the basis for the right of priority are reserved in accordance with the domestic legislation of each country of the Union.

    C(1) The periods of priority referred to above shall be twelve months for patents and utility models, and six months for industrial designs and trademarks.

Thus filing in one country that is a signatory to the Paris convention gives an applicant some "breathing room"—12 months in which to prepare to file in other signatory nations.

iii.   The Patent Cooperation Treaty (PCT)

    The PCT was signed in 1970. The Patent Cooperation Treaty, opened for signature June 19, 1970, 28 U.S.T. 7645, T.I.A.S. No. 8733 (entered into force Jan. 24, 1978). Its major purpose is to streamline the early prosecution stages of patent applications filed in numerous countries. It is often described as a clearinghouse for international patent applications. As a practical matter, its major advantage is that it gives an inventor (and her patent lawyer) more time, a precious commodity in the prosecution of an application destined for many countries. The signatories to the PCT have agreed to permit an applicant to wait for up to 30 months after the initial filing of a patent application in one country to begin the in-depth prosecution of the application in other countries. This allows the inventor more time, compared to non-PCT prosecution, in which to test the product, decide which countries' protection is worthwhile, and pay the patent office filing fees in the various countries.

    There are two main parts of the PCT. Chapter 1 provides that an applicant who files in a national patent office may elect within 12 months to add a PCT filing. The PCT filing is simply an additional filing in any national patent office designated in the PCT. In this case, the applicant has up to 20 months from the initial filing to request that the PCT preliminary prosecution procedure be initiated. At that time, the applicant must also select the PCT member nations in which the applicant wishes to prosecute the patent. Note that Chapter 1 preserves the applicant's priority date (in PCT member countries), without having to begin active prosecution, for eight months longer than the simple Paris Convention priority period.

    Chapter 2 of the PCT extends the election period to 30 months. To qualify under Chapter 2, the applicant must make her PCT filing at most five months after the first national filing. Chapter 2 gives an inventor 18 extra months, compared to the Paris Convention, to select countries for coverage and initiate multiple national prosecutions. In other words, so-called "Chapter Two" PCT filings give the inventor up to 30 months to make his or her "national elections."

    The extra time is a substantial advantage. Besides simply delaying the expenditure of filing and examination fees, the PCT allows an inventor a significant extra period to assess the technical merits and commercial potential of the invention. This extra time helps the inventor save wasted filing fees for inventions that fail to blossom; for those that show great promise, the various patent applications that grow out of the PCT filing can be tailored to reflect the commercially significant embodiments that have emerged from the extensive testing.

2. Substantive Harmonization and GATT-TRIPs

As noted earlier, the lasting impact of the Paris Convention was primarily procedural, especially with respect to the uniform, worldwide priority date it made possible. The Paris Convention did, however, contain some minimum substantive standards of protection, as described earlier. Even so, further efforts at harmonizing worldwide standards of patentability, patentees' rights, and infringement bore little fruit for most of the twentieth century.

Harmonization proceeded slowly because the international business community had little interest in parsing the detailed, esoteric issues that harmonization requires. Although it was cumbersome to deal with the divergent standards held by the world's many individual domestic patent jurisdictions, some level of effective protection was available in most of the commercially important countries. Furthermore, patent law harmonization was the domain of a highly specialized affiliate of the United Nations, the World Intellectual Property Organization (WIPO), a forum not thought to be particularly friendly to Western business interests.

Things were changing by the mid-1980s, however. For one thing, the perceived value of intellectual property was increasing; it was beginning to take on a more central role in business planning and strategy. Of special concern was the increasing importance to U.S. businesses of overseas markets in developing countries—countries that had traditionally opposed strong intellectual property protection. Businesses in the United States and Europe, aware both of the increasing importance of intellectual property and of WIPO's slow progress in harmonization, were thus on the lookout for an alternative forum in which to pursue harmonization. The search ended with the announcement of the Uruguay Round of negotiations to revise the main international trade agreement/organization, the General Agreement on Tariffs and Trade (GATT).

In addition to proposed reforms to the core function and structure of the GATT, the early Uruguay Round agenda soon grew to encompass negotiations on the "Trade-Related Aspects of Intellectual Property," or TRIPs, as it became known. The reference in the title to "Trade-Related" issues was a concession to those who doubted the relevance of intellectual property to the basic GATT mission; it soon became clear, however, that most of the basic elements of intellectual property protection would be up for discussion and potential harmonization in the TRIPs negotiations. By the time the GATT round ended in late 1993, TRIPs had become one of the principal components in the overall package of changes.

Although the post-TRIPs amendments to U.S. law are important, they pale in contrast to the revolutionary changes the agreement makes to the intellectual property regimes of many developing countries. To summarize the highlights, all signatories of the Uruguay Round treaty (who, under the agreement, become members of the World Trade Organization (WTO)) must now:

- Include virtually all important commercial fields within the ambit of patentable subject matter, a major change for countries that, for example, have traditionally refused to enforce pharmaceutical patents on public health/access grounds.

- Test patent applications for (a) the presence of an inventive step, which is defined as precisely synonymous with nonobviousness under §103 of the U.S. Patent Act, and for (b) "industrial application," similarly defined as coextensive with the U.S. utility requirement.

- Include in the patentees' bundle of exclusive rights the right to control the market for imports of the patented products.

- Eliminate or severely curtail the practice of granting compulsory licenses for patented technology.

See Final Act Embodying the Results of the Uruguay Round of Multilateral Trade Negotiations, Apr. 15, 1994 2-3 (GATT Secretariat 1994); Annex 1C: Agreement on Trade-Related Aspects of Intellectual Property Rights, *id.* at 6-19, 365-403. For implementation in the United States, Uruguay Round Agreements Act, Pub. L. No. 103-465 (H.R. 5110), Dec. 8, 1994. *See also* J.H. Reichman, *Universal Minimum Standards of Intellectual Property Protection Under the TRIPs Component of the WTO Agreement*, 29 INT'L LAW. 345 (1995) (able summary of provisions and open questions).

The most important GATT-related changes to U.S. law were:

- Changing the U.S. patent term to 20 years, measured from the date the patent application is filed, rather than 17 years from the date the patent was issued by the Patent Office. §154. (Under certain circumstances, such as interferences and appealed rejections, this term may be extended for up to five years. *Id.*).

- Opening up the U.S. "first-to-invent" system by allowing members of the WTO to introduce evidence of inventive acts in their home country for purposes of establishing priority. §104.

- Expanding the definition of infringement to include acts of unauthorized offering for sale and importing. §271.

- Adding a new procedure for filing "provisional applications," §111, which must satisfy §112 but need not include claims. Such an application does not begin the 20-year clock for the applicant's patent term.

- Requiring publication of U.S. patent applications covering inventions also claimed in foreign applications. §122(b).

These changes furthered the substantive harmonization of world patent law by bringing the United States into line with the rest of the world on a number of important issues. The AIA further harmonized U.S. patent law with patent law in many other nations. So long as patent applicants must file and prosecute (and pay fees) in each country in which they require protection, however, the impact of substantive harmonization will be limited.

In addition to worldwide harmonization, Europe has also taken significant steps to harmonize its patent law, with mixed results. European countries have for decades been able to file a single patent application at the European Patent Office instead of filing in member state patent offices. Beginning in 2016, European patents may also be enforced in a Europe-wide patent court. In both instances, however, the pan-European system supplements rather than replaces the national systems of prosecution and enforcement, leaving a hodgepodge of national and EU-level rights.

J.   FEDERAL PREEMPTION

The Supremacy Clause of the U.S. CONSTITUTION provides that

This Constitution, and the Laws of the United States which shall be made in Pursuance thereof; and all Treaties made, or which shall be made, under the Authority of the United States, shall be the supreme Law of the Land; and the Judges in every State shall be bound thereby, any Thing [sic] in the Constitution or Laws of any State to the Contrary notwithstanding

U.S. CONSTITUTION, ART. VI, CL. 2. Thus, the Supremacy Clause nullifies state law attempts to duplicate or interfere with federal intellectual property protection. More difficult cases involve state laws that do not directly conflict with federal authority but instead address interstitial gaps within the federal regime. Courts must grapple with whether Congress intended to leave such gaps unfilled, thereby precluding state protection, or simply allowed state law to fill these voids. This logical structure—which involves a search for the intent behind uncovered cases, sometimes in cases where technology has outpaced legislative foresight—makes preemption particularly challenging. The doctrinal distinctions are subtle and elusive.

Bonito Boats, Inc. v. Thunder Craft Boats, Inc.
Supreme Court of the United States
489 U.S. 141 (1989)

Justice O'CONNOR delivered the opinion of the Court. . . .

I.

In September 1976, petitioner Bonito Boats, Inc., a Florida corporation, developed a hull design for a fiberglass recreational boat which it marketed under the trade name Bonito Boat Model 5VBR. Designing the boat hull required substantial effort on the part of Bonito. A set of engineering drawings was prepared, from which a hardwood model was created. The hardwood model was then sprayed with fiberglass to create a mold, which then served to produce the finished fiberglass boats for sale. The 5VBR was placed on the market sometime in September 1976. There is no indication in the record that a patent application was ever filed for protection of the utilitarian or design aspects of the hull, or for the process by which the hull was manufactured. The 5VBR was favorably received by the boating public, and "a broad interstate market" developed for its sale.

In May 1983, after the Bonito 5VBR had been available to the public for over six years, the Florida Legislature enacted Fla. Stat. §559.94 (1987). The statute makes "it . . . unlawful for any person to use the direct molding process to duplicate for the purpose of sale any manufactured vessel hull or component part of a vessel made by another without the written permission of that other person." §559.94(2). The statute also makes it unlawful for a person to "knowingly sell a vessel hull or component part of a vessel duplicated in violation of subsection (2)." §559.94(3). Damages, injunctive relief, and attorney's fees are made available to "any person who suffers injury or damage as the result of a violation" of the statute. §559.94(4). The statute was made applicable to vessel hulls or component parts duplicated through the use of direct molding after July 1, 1983. §559.94(5).

On December 21, 1984, Bonito filed this action in the Circuit Court of Orange County, Florida. The complaint alleged that respondent here, Thunder Craft Boats, Inc., a Tennessee corporation, had violated the Florida statute by using the direct molding process to duplicate the Bonito 5VBR fiberglass hull, and had knowingly sold such duplicates in violation of the Florida statute. . . .

III.

We believe that the Florida statute at issue in this case so substantially impedes the public use of the otherwise unprotected design and utilitarian ideas embodied in unpatented boat hulls as to run afoul of the teaching of our decisions in *Sears* and *Compco*. It is readily apparent that the Florida statute does not operate to prohibit "unfair competition" in the usual sense that the term is understood. The law of unfair competition has its roots in the common-law tort of deceit: its general concern is with protecting *consumers* from confusion as to source. . . .

In contrast to the operation of unfair competition law, the Florida statute is aimed directly at preventing the exploitation of the design and utilitarian conceptions embodied in the product itself. The sparse legislative history surrounding its enactment indicates that it was intended to create an inducement for the improvement of boat hull designs. *See* Tr. of Meeting of Transportation Committee, Florida House of Representatives, May 3, 1983 ("There is no inducement for [a] quality boat manufacturer to improve these designs and secondly, if he does, it is immediately copied. This would prevent that and allow him recourse in circuit court"). To accomplish this goal, the Florida statute endows the original boat hull manufacturer with rights against the world, similar in scope and operation to the rights accorded a federal patentee. Like the patentee, the beneficiary of the Florida statute may prevent a competitor from "making" the product in what is evidently the most efficient manner available and from "selling" the product when it is produced in that fashion. Compare 35 U.S.C. §154. The Florida scheme offers this protection for an unlimited number of years to all boat hulls and their component parts, without regard to their ornamental or technological merit. Protection is available for subject matter for which patent protection has been denied or has expired, as well as for designs which have been freely revealed to the consuming public by their creators. That the Florida statute does not remove all means of reproduction and sale does not eliminate the conflict with the federal scheme. See *Kellogg*, 305 U.S., at 122. In essence, the Florida law prohibits the entire public from engaging in a form of reverse engineering of a product in the public domain. This is clearly one of the rights vested in the federal patent holder, but has never been a part of state protection under the law of unfair competition or trade secrets. . . .

Moreover, as we noted in *Kewanee*, the competitive reality of reverse engineering may act as a spur to the inventor, creating an incentive to develop inventions that meet the rigorous requirements of patentability. 416 U.S., at 489-490. The Florida statute substantially reduces this competitive incentive, thus eroding the general rule of free competition upon which the attractiveness of the federal patent bargain depends. . . . The Florida statute is aimed directly at the promotion of intellectual creation by substantially restricting the public's ability to exploit ideas that the patent system mandates shall be free for all to use. Like the interpretation of Illinois unfair competition law in *Sears* and *Compco*, the Florida statute represents a break with the tradition of peaceful coexistence between state market regulation and federal patent policy. The Florida law substantially restricts the public's ability to exploit an unpatented design in general circulation, raising the specter of state-created monopolies in a host of useful shapes and processes for which patent protection has been denied or is otherwise unobtainable. It thus enters a field of regulation which the patent laws have reserved to Congress. The patent statute's careful balance between public right and private monopoly to promote certain creative activity is a "scheme of federal regulation . . . so pervasive as to make reasonable the inference that Congress left no room for the States to supplement it." *Rice v. Santa Fe Elevator Corp.*, 331 U.S. 218, 230 (1947). . . .

COMMENTS AND QUESTIONS

1. Does this result make sense? Is it consistent with *Kewanee Oil Co. v. Bicron Corp.*, 416 U.S. 470 (1974) (excerpted in Chapter II(H))? *Bonito Boats* can be reconciled with trade secrets statutes if one accepts the reverse engineering rationale described above. Whatever one thinks of the *Bonito* result, the last sentence remains troubling. Characterizing patent law as "pervasive federal regulation" suggests that it

might preempt the field, automatically striking down all state laws that attempt to regulate intellectual property. If taken seriously, that approach would leave no room at all for state protection of inventions.

2. Note the similarity between the statutes struck down in *Sears* and *Bonito Boats*. In both cases, what was prohibited was the direct copying of a competitor's design. The *Bonito Boats* statute is more limited than that in *Sears*, since it prohibits only one particular method of copying. Nonetheless, the Court struck it down. Why should the courts be concerned about these comparatively narrow statutes when they allowed the far broader statute in *Kewanee* to pass muster?

3. The *Bonito Boats* decision has been criticized. *See* John S. Wiley, Jr., *Bonito Boats: Uninformed but Mandatory Federal Innovation Policy*, 1989 SUP. CT. REV. 283. *Cf.* Symposium, *Product Simulation: A Right or a Wrong?*, 64 COLUM. L. REV. 1178 (1964) (articles criticizing the analogous decisions in *Sears* and *Compco*). Does this criticism make sense? Or is *Bonito Boats* a needed barrier to the creation of state laws that would undo the balance struck by Congress?

As part of the Digital Millenium Copyright Act, Congress created a new federal intellectual property right protecting "original" boat hull designs. 17 U.S.C. §§1301 et seq., discussed in Chapter IV. Can Congress lawfully accomplish here what the states cannot? Does *Bonito Boats* suggest some sort of constitutional limitation on any form of protection (state or federal) in this area?

4. Some lawyers have tried to apply *Bonito Boats* in contexts beyond the patent-like legislation actually considered in the case. This has not met with much success, however; like other broad preemption decisions before it, *Bonito Boats* has been hemmed in by subsequent qualifications. In *Waits v. Frito-Lay, Inc.*, 978 F.2d 1093 (9th Cir. 1992), a right of publicity case based on an advertising campaign imitating Tom Waits' distinctive vocal qualities, the Ninth Circuit had the following to say about *Bonito Boats:*

> *Bonito Boats* involved a Florida statute giving perpetual patent-like protection to boat hull designs already on the market, a class of manufactured articles expressly excluded from federal patent protection. The Court ruled that the Florida statute was preempted by federal patent law because it directly conflicted with the comprehensive federal patent scheme. In reaching this conclusion, the Court cited its earlier decisions in *Sears Roebuck & Co. v. Stiffel Co.*, 376 U.S. 225 (1964), and *Compco Corp. v. Day-Brite Lighting*, 376 U.S. 234 (1964), for the proposition that "publicly known design and utilitarian ideas which were unprotected by patent occupied much the same position as the subject matter of an expired patent," i.e., they are expressly unprotected. *Bonito Boats*, 489 U.S. at 152.
>
> The defendants seize upon this citation to *Sears* and *Compco* as a reaffirmation of the sweeping preemption principles for which these cases were

once read to stand. They argue that *Midler* [*v. Ford Motor Co.*, 849 F.2d 460 (9th Cir. 1988) (another sound-alike right of publicity case that is reproduced in Chapter VI(D)] was wrongly decided because it ignores these two decisions, an omission that the defendants say indicates an erroneous assumption that *Sears* and *Compco* have been "relegated to the constitutional junkyard." Thus, the defendants go on to reason, earlier cases that rejected entertainers' challenges to imitations of their performances based on federal copyright preemption, were correctly decided because they relied on *Sears* and *Compco*. *See Sinatra v. Goodyear Tire & Rubber Co.*, 435 F.2d 711, 716-18 (9th Cir. 1970), *cert. denied*, 402 U.S. 906 (1971); *Booth v. Colgate-Palmolive Co.*, 362 F. Supp. 343, 348 (S.D.N.Y. 1973); *Davis v. Trans World Airlines*, 297 F. Supp. 1145, 1147 (C.D. Cal. 1969). This reasoning suffers from a number of flaws.

Bonito Boats itself cautions against reading *Sears* and *Compco* for a "broad pre-emptive principle" and cites subsequent Supreme Court decisions retreating from such a sweeping interpretation. "[T]he Patent and Copyright Clauses do not, by their own force or by negative implication, deprive the States of the power to adopt rules for the promotion of intellectual creation." *Bonito Boats*, 489 U.S. at 165 (citing, inter alia, *Goldstein v. California*, 412 U.S. 546, 552-61 (1973) and *Kewanee Oil Co. v. Bicron Corp.*, 416 U.S. 470, 478-79 (1974)). Instead, the Court reaffirmed the right of states to "place limited regulations on the use of unpatented designs in order to prevent consumer confusion as to source." *Id. Bonito Boats* thus cannot be read as endorsing or resurrecting the broad reading of *Compco* and *Sears* urged by the defendants, under which Waits' state tort claim arguably would be preempted.

Moreover, the Court itself recognized the authority of states to protect entertainers' "right of publicity" in *Zacchini v. Scripps-Howard Broadcasting Co.*, 433 U.S. 562 (1977). In *Zacchini*, the Court endorsed a state right-of-publicity law as in harmony with federal patent and copyright law, holding that an unconsented-to television news broadcast of a commercial entertainer's performance was not protected by the First Amendment. *Id.* at 573, 576-78. The cases *Frito* asserts were "rightly decided" all predate *Zacchini* and other Supreme Court precedent narrowing *Sears*' and *Compco*'s sweeping preemption principles. In sum, our holding in *Midler*, upon which Waits' voice misappropriation claim rests, has not been eroded by subsequent authority.

Waits v. Frito-Lay, Inc., 978 F.2d 1099-1100.

The Federal Circuit has allowed state claims that tread on patent law, particularly where the claims are made against patent owners rather than in an effort to create a new form of intellectual property protection. *See, e.g., Dow Chemical v. Exxon Corp.*, 139 F.3d 1470 (Fed. Cir. 1998) (unfair competition claims by accused infringer based on alleged inequitable conduct not preempted); *Univ. of Colorado Found. v. American Cyanamid, Inc.*, 196 F.3d 1366 (Fed. Cir. 1999) (state claims of fraud and unjust enrichment against patentee who stole invention from plaintiff not preempted). The court has, however, required that state claims that touch on areas of federal patent interest be judged by federal, not state, standards, so that they do not upset the balance struck by patent law. *See Univ. of Colorado, supra; Midwest Industries v. Karavan Trailers*, 175 F.3d 1356 (Fed. Cir. 1999). Is this a reasonable compromise?

5. In a number of cases, restrictions on the content of licensing contracts are said to raise preemption issues. One might question whether contracts are equivalent to state statutes for preemption purposes. On at least one occasion, the Supreme Court has suggested that protection of unpatentable goods (which would be prohibited under state misappropriation statutes) is permissible under contract law. *See, e.g., Aronson v. Quick Point Pencil*, 440 U.S. 257 (1979). On the other hand, there are a variety of circumstances in which federal patent policy precludes the parties from contracting to the contrary. *See, e.g., Brulotte v. Thys Co.*, 379 U.S. 29 (1964) (holding unenforceable patent licensed in agreement that extends beyond patent term); *Kimble v. Marvel Entertainment, LLC*, 135 S.Ct. 2401 (2015) (upholding *Brulotte*); *Lear, Inc. v. Adkins*, 395 U.S. 653 (1969) (contracts estopping licensee from challenging the validity of a patent are void); *Everex Systems Inc. v. Cadtrak Corp.*, 89 F.3d 673 (9th Cir. 1996) (federal policy precluding assignment of nonexclusive patent licenses prevailed over state doctrine permitting such assignments). Note that in some of these cases, such as *Everex*, federal preemption actually works to the benefit of the intellectual property owner.

Regardless of the particular limitations federal law imposes on licensing agreements, patent licensing in general is a question of state (not federal) law. *See Gjerlov v. Schuyler Labs. Inc.*, 131 F.3d 1016 (Fed. Cir. 1997).

6. A recent development has raised new preemption concerns: State laws providing a remedy when patentees send threatening "demand letters" without adequate research. The laws operate under fair trade or consumer protection statutes in various states. But they obviously have the potential to affect the enforcement powers of federal patentees. *See, e.g.*, Robin Feldman, *Federalism, First Amendment & Patents: The Fraud Fallacy*, 17 COLUM. SCI. & TECH. L. REV. 30, 32 (2015); Paul R. Gugliuzza, *Patent Trolls and Preemption*, 101 VA. L. REV. 1579, 1580 (2015).